Joining the Conversation

Writing in College and Beyond

Joining the Conversation

Writing in College and Beyond

Mike Palmquist

Colorado State University

Bedford/St. Martin's   Boston * New York

For Bedford/St. Martin's

Senior Executive Editor: Leasa Burton
Developmental Editor: Rachel Goldberg
Senior Production Editor: Bridget Leahy
Senior Production Supervisor: Dennis J. Conroy
Marketing Manager: Molly Parke
Editorial Assistant: Sarah Guariglia Macomber
Production Assistant: Lidia MacDonald Carr
Copyeditor: Linda McLatchie
Senior Art Director: Anna Palchik
Text Design: Lisa Garbutt
Cover Design: Donna Dennison
Composition: NK Graphics
Printing and Binding: RR Donnelley and Sons

President: Joan E. Feinberg
Editorial Director: Denise B. Wydra
Editor in Chief: Karen S. Henry
Director of Marketing: Karen R. Soeltz
Director of Editing, Design, and Production: Marcia Cohen
Assistant Director of Editing, Design, and Production: Elise S. Kaiser
Managing Editor: Elizabeth M. Schaaf

Library of Congress Control Number: 2009929005

Manufactured in the United States of America.

4 3 2

f e d

For information, write: Bedford/St. Martin's, 75 Arlington Street, Boston, MA 02116
(617-399-4000)

ISBN-10: 0–312–41215–0
ISBN-13: 978–0–312–41215–9

Preface for Instructors

More than two decades ago, as I was working on my dissertation, I spent a year observing a colleague teach two strikingly different writing courses. In one course, the instructor focused on writing as a form of information exchange, encouraging students to become experts on a subject and write confidently about it for a general audience. Students chose their own topics and shared what they had learned with their classmates. In the other course, the instructor, inspired by Kenneth Burke's parlor, presented writing as a form of scholarly exchange, asking students to make contributions to an ongoing conversation about a particular subject. All students wrote about a common class topic for an entire semester, reinforcing the notion of shared conversation.

The students in both courses produced solid written work and, in most cases, emerged well prepared for writing in other settings. I was intrigued, however, by the differences in how students in each course understood what it meant to write and to be a writer. The students in the course based on the conversation metaphor came to view writing as a means of shaping the attitudes, beliefs, and actions of their readers. Writing, for them, became more than just a means of sharing information. It became a tool for advancing ideas and arguments and connecting with readers. They could see their own roles as writers much more clearly, and as a result, they understood how writing—and particularly their own writing—had real purpose.

My reflections on that early study, in concert with subsequent studies of computer-supported writing classrooms and my own experiences as a teacher, have shaped the development of this book in important ways. Foremost is the book's premise that good writers make decisions shaped primarily by rhetorical concerns—the writer's purpose; the readers' needs, interests, and background; and the contexts within which a document is written and read. Recognizing that students need a concrete framework to help ground these concepts, *Joining the Conversation* lays out a clear process for inquiry-based writing that asks students to listen in on the conversations happening around them, to carefully consider their readers' expectations, especially about genre and design, and to focus on their roles as writers as they choose their topics, develop their ideas, and draft and design their documents. The result is a text that gives students the support they need as they learn to engage readers and compose meaningful contributions to conversations both in the academy and beyond.

Writing Is a Social Act

Students are reading, writing, and collaborating now more than ever through online social networking and blogging. So, online and face-to-face, they already know how to listen to what others have to say, how to acknowledge contributions made by others, and how to advance the discussion by adding something new. *Joining the Conversation* recognizes this and helps students connect these familiar everyday practices to the kinds of inquiry-based and collaborative work that they will be asked to do in writing for college and in their professional lives.

Of course, the conversation metaphor also clearly demonstrates the exchange of ideas at the core of source-based writing. The idea that writing is a social interaction makes academic contexts more concrete for students: all writers draw on sources as they listen in and develop their own contributions to the conversation. No writer speaks in isolation. Working with other writers—whether online, in print, or in person—is essential to making a new contribution to an ongoing conversation. By presenting writing as necessarily social, *Joining the Conversation* emphasizes the importance of considering the purposes of both writers and readers as well as the social and historical contexts in which written conversations take place. Part One of the book introduces students to the rhetorical concepts that make the book tick and includes a thorough chapter on working together through collaborative writing and peer review, with lots of activities that students can carry out with classmates, friends, or family. The Part Two assignment chapters continue this collaborative

Working Together and Peer Review boxes emphasize collaborative writing.

See page 143. ↱

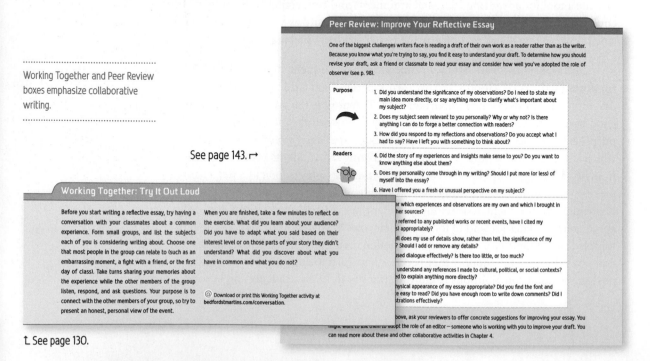

Peer Review: Improve Your Reflective Essay

One of the biggest challenges writers face is reading a draft of their own work as a reader rather than as the writer. Because you know what you're trying to say, you find it easy to understand your draft. To determine how you should revise your draft, ask a friend or classmate to read your essay and consider how well you've adopted the role of observer (see p. 98).

Purpose
1. Did you understand the significance of my observations? Do I need to state my main idea more directly, or say anything more to clarify what's important about my subject?
2. Does my subject seem relevant to you personally? Why or why not? Is there anything I can do to forge a better connection with readers?
3. How did you respond to my reflections and observations? Do you accept what I had to say? Have I left you with something to think about?

Readers
4. Did the story of my experiences and insights make sense to you? Do you want to know anything else about them?
5. Does my personality come through in my writing? Should I put more (or less) of myself into the essay?
6. Have I offered you a fresh or unusual perspective on my subject?

Working Together: Try It Out Loud

Before you start writing a reflective essay, try having a conversation with your classmates about a common experience. Form small groups, and list the subjects each of you is considering writing about. Choose one that most people in the group can relate to (such as an embarrassing moment, a fight with a friend, or the first day of class). Take turns sharing your memories about the experience while the other members of the group listen, respond, and ask questions. Your purpose is to connect with the other members of your group, so try to present an honest, personal view of the event.

When you are finished, take a few minutes to reflect on the exercise. What did you learn about your audience? Did you have to adapt what you said based on their interest level or on those parts of your story they didn't understand? What did you discover about what you have in common and what you do not?

@ Download or print this Working Together activity at bedfordstmartins.com/conversation.

↳ See page 130.

thread through **Working Together** boxes that offer more group activities and **Peer Review** boxes with guidelines and prompts for specific assignments. By emphasizing the importance of working with other writers on individual and collaborative projects, *Joining the Conversation* encourages students to become active participants in the exchange of ideas.

Technology Has Fundamentally Changed Writing

Technology has changed not only how we write but what writing looks like as well. For students, it's a given that composing, collaborating, and doing research all start online and constantly evolve. *Joining the Conversation* incorporates these new practices and genres to show students how designing documents, collaborating, and using sources are integral parts of the composing process. As writers listen in to conversations and explore their topics, they might need to track blog discussions, use search engines in a targeted way, or consult databases. As they choose visuals and design their documents, they'll want to consider the range of options available in word processors and multimedia presentation software. In the Part Two assignment chapters, such suggestions are carefully integrated into the writing process when and where writers need them in order to help guide and remind students about their choices without overwhelming them. If students need a fuller understanding, the text refers them to Parts Three and Four where they can find more detailed descriptions of word processing and research tools along with specific advice about working with sources and drafting and designing documents. Additional "how to" guides and tutorials can be found on the *Student Center for Joining the Conversation*.

And, because technology has also changed what writing looks like, readings and examples throughout the book reflect the range of online and visual genres that writers draw on for both sources of ideas and examples of design conventions to inspire and adapt. The *Joining the Conversation e-Book* even includes multimodal readings for each of the assignment chapters in lively genres such as video, audio, and multimedia web sites.

Writers Respond to All Kinds of Readings and Sources

Joining the Conversation recognizes that the volume and variety of information that students are likely to come across as they develop their ideas can be overwhelming. Writers need sharply honed critical reading skills in order to recognize and analyze the differences among conversations and readers' expectations. To this end, Chapter 3, Reading to Write, suggests specific strategies for reading actively and evaluating sources, and introduces the concept of "reading like a writer" with in-depth student examples and opportunities for practice.

To illustrate the variety of genre, tone, and style within each writing purpose, assignment chapters include a diverse selection of professional readings by authors such as Rick Bragg, Wangari Maathai, Stephen King, Virginia Postrel, Barbara Ehrenreich, and Richard H. Thaler and Cass R. Sunstein. Readings not only serve as examples of admirable writing but also demonstrate successful design choices, whether traditional print essays or real-world genres, such as brochures, blogs, and multimedia presentations. The layout of the textual readings has also been carefully designed to vary by genre in order to give students a realistic sense of the original source. Each selection is accompanied by questions for critical reading that ask students to consider both the piece's writing situation and genre.

↲ See page 213.

Diverse reading selections reflect a range of print, online, and visual genres.

See page 167. ↱

Purpose and Genre Are Critical to the Writing Situation

Joining the Conversation supports writers through the process of developing ideas, drafting, and revising. Its six assignment chapters introduce students to the most common purposes for writing: to reflect, to inform, to analyze, to evaluate, to solve problems, and to convince or persuade. *Joining the Conversation* also emphasizes that purpose and genre are inextricably linked, by showing how a variety of genres can serve the same purpose and consequently how genres change and respond to a writer's purpose or role. Given that students grasp this dynamic most easily—almost intuitively—through simple visual comparisons, each assignment chapter opens with **Genres in Conversation,** a two-page spread that juxtaposes three documents on the same topic and invites students to analyze how genre and writing situation influence design choices.

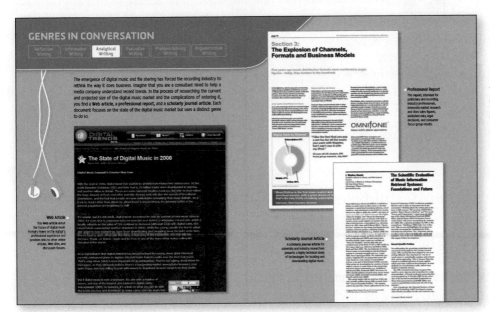

Genres in Conversation chapter openers help students analyze design choices.

↰ See pages 208–209.

To help make the concept of purpose even more tangible for students, each assignment chapter also identifies a related role that writers adopt in written conversations and personifies each role with an avatar—the Observer reflects, the Reporter informs, the Interpreter analyzes, the Evaluator evaluates, the Problem Solver solves problems, and the Advocate convinces or persuades. As students become familiar with the different writers' roles, they learn to recognize how specific writing situations affect both their choice of genre and the content of their documents.

To further draw connections among elements of the rhetorical situation, colorful concept maps introduce and illustrate the relationships among reader, writer, purpose, genre, sources, and context. Elements from the maps then act as visual cues throughout the book to reinforce the concepts that writers need to consider as they assess their rhetorical situations.

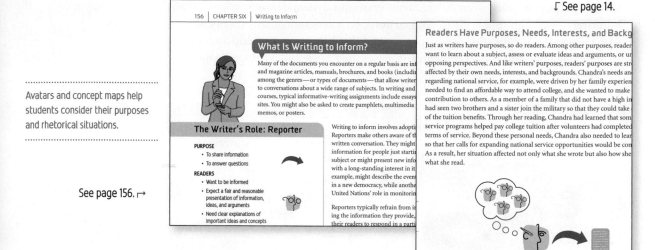

↳ See page 14.

Avatars and concept maps help students consider their purposes and rhetorical situations.

See page 156. ↦

Students Still Need Support as They Write

The true measure of a textbook should be how well it works for student writers. Just because students can type, search, and read the news at the same time doesn't mean they can juggle all the skills they need to engage readers with their ideas and make a contribution to a meaningful conversation. *Joining the Conversation* not only reflects a new kind of writing process for students, it also supports students as they work through their own writing processes, reminding them constantly to reflect on—and reconsider—their writing situation. **Practice** boxes offer specific, accessible strategies for finding a conversation to join, gathering information from sources, and preparing a draft—all tailored to each writing purpose.

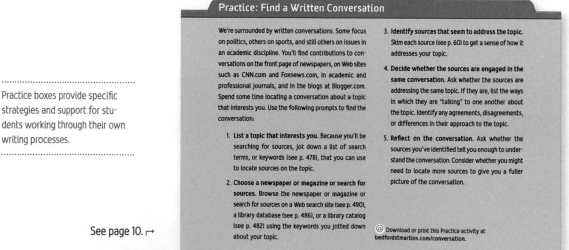

Practice boxes provide specific strategies and support for students working through their own writing processes.

See page 10. ↦

Because students learn from listening to each other, each assignment chapter includes an essay by a Featured Student Writer and follows that student's process throughout the chapter. **In Process** boxes highlight specific points in the featured writers' processes, showing the materials they used and created, including database searches, brainstorming notes, outlines, survey questions, and peer review materials. Examples throughout the book illustrate how real students solve problems as they work with sources, draft, and design their documents—all with the goal of putting students at the center of the writing process and helping them to apply concepts in the book to their own writing.

In Process

Supporting Reasons with Evidence

Ali Bizzul identified three major reasons to support her interpretive claim that gaining weight hurts football players more than it helps:

> Reason 1: Heat-related injuries associated with the use of diet supplements
>
> Reason 2: Long-term health problems associated with obesity
>
> Reason 3: Decrease in athletic performance

Ali used each of these reasons as the basis for a general statement in her draft. Here is her preliminary list of evidence to support her second reason, the long-term health problems associated with obesity:

> The extra weight gained for football can complicate the health of ex-athletes:
>
> — high blood pressure (Harp and Hecht)
>
> — sleep-disordered breathing (Harp and Hecht)
>
> — joint damage/arthritis (Groeschen)
>
> — heart disease (Korth, Longman)
>
> — diabetes (Korth, Longman)

As she drafted her essay, Ali used her lists of evidence to remind herself of sources she might turn to while making her points.

In Process boxes offer insight into the writing processes of featured student writers.

⌐ See page 253.

Joining the Conversation Works with the Council of Writing Program Administrators' (WPA) Outcomes

The Council of Writing Program Administrators established a set of desired outcomes for first-year composition courses across the country. As an inquiry-based rhetoric focusing on purpose and genre, *Joining the Conversation* helps instructors and students accomplish these teaching and learning goals. The following table provides detailed information on how *Joining the Conversation* supports each outcome.

Joining the Conversation and the Council of Writing Program Administrators' (WPA) Outcomes

DESIRED OUTCOMES	RELEVANT FEATURES IN *JOINING THE CONVERSATION*
Rhetorical Knowledge	
Focus on a purpose	**Chapter 1** introduces the concept of writing for particular purposes ("Writing Has a Purpose," p. 13). **Chapter 2** invites students to determine their purposes as they assess their writing situations ("Determine Your Purpose," p. 28).
	Chapters 5–10 present the most common purposes for writing—to reflect, to inform, to analyze, to evaluate, to solve problems, and to convince or persuade. **Avatars** in these chapters (see p. 210, for example) personify writers' roles to make the concept of purpose more concrete.
Respond to the needs of different audiences	**Chapter 1** explains that readers' needs affect how they read documents ("Readers Have Purposes, Needs, Interests, and Backgrounds," p. 14), while **Chapter 2** helps students identify their readers at the start of the writing process ("Determine Who Your Readers Are," p. 28).
	Chapters 16 and 18 continue to help students respond to readers' needs as they organize, draft, and design their documents.
Respond appropriately to different kinds of rhetorical situations	Each of the assignment chapters (**Chapters 5–10**) focuses on a different rhetorical situation that students are likely to encounter. **The Writer's Role boxes** in these chapters analyze the purpose, readers, sources, and context for each rhetorical situation (see p. 98, for example), and each chapter offers advice for reading, responding, drafting, and revising that is specific to the writer's situation, purpose, and audience.
Use conventions of format and structure appropriate to the rhetorical situation	**Chapter 1** introduces the concepts of genre and design and shows how they relate to the writer's purpose ("What Should I Know about Genre and Design?" p. 18).
	Advice about writing in **Chapters 5–10** helps students make effective genre and design choices for their documents.
	Chapter 18 provides practical advice and **Checklists** (see p. 606, for example) for following the design conventions of academic essays, multimodal essays, articles, and Web sites.
Adopt appropriate voice, tone, and level of formality	Readings in **Chapters 5–10** demonstrate how various audiences, genres, and rhetorical situations call for different levels of formality, and **essays by Featured Student Writers** (see p. 144, for example) model appropriate tone for academic work.
	Chapter 19 provides practical advice for writing with style and using appropriate voice, tone, language, and formality.
Understand how genres shape reading and writing	**Chapter 1** introduces the concept of genre as linked to purpose and design and provides a practice activity on analyzing genre ("What Should I Know about Genre and Design?" p. 18).
	Chapters 5–10 open with a **Genres in Conversation** feature that invites students to analyze how genre and writing situation influence design choices (see pp. 96–97, for example). Readings in those same chapters are designed to reflect the various genres in which they were originally published.
Write in several genres	Readings in **Chapters 5–10** cover thirty genres, including memoirs, short stories, literacy narratives, brochures, Web sites, magazine articles, news analyses, multimedia presentations, literary criticism, progress reports, speeches, and proposals.
	Each assignment chapter also ends with **Project Ideas** for essays and other genres suited to that chapter's purpose (see p. 150, for example).
	Chapter 18 features **Checklists** for creating documents in a range of genres (see p. 613, for example), and **Chapter 20** helps students consider genre during the revision process ("Consider Genre and Design," p. 634).

Critical Thinking, Reading, and Writing

Use writing and reading for inquiry, learning, thinking, and communicating	Throughout the text, the metaphor of writing as conversation emphasizes writing as a tool for inquiry and the exchange of ideas.
	Chapter 2 covers inquiry extensively, establishing reading and writing as part of written conversations that in turn inspire and inform further discourse.
	Chapter 3 provides advice and strategies for reading critically and actively, evaluating sources, and reading for a purpose.
	Starting a Conversation questions (see p. 112, for example) enable students to engage critically with each reading in **Chapters 5–10**.
Understand a writing assignment as a series of tasks, including finding, evaluating, analyzing, and synthesizing appropriate primary and secondary sources	**Chapter 2** breaks down the steps of analyzing an assignment and assessing the writing situation ("How Can I Analyze an Assignment?" pp. 28–32).
	Chapter 3 explains how to evaluate sources based on relevance, use of evidence, author, publisher, timeliness, comprehensiveness, and genre ("How Can I Evaluate Sources?" pp. 60–66).
	Chapters 5–10 discuss the kinds of sources best suited to each type of assignment, from print and electronic sources to interviews, observations, and surveys.
	Chapters 11–14 offer strategies for developing a search plan, locating print and electronic sources, conducting field research, taking notes on sources, and avoiding plagiarism.
Integrate their own ideas with those of others	By approaching writing as conversation, the book demonstrates the exchange of ideas at the core of source-based writing.
	Chapter 17 provides specific advice for integrating sources effectively; summarizing, paraphrasing, and quoting strategically; and avoiding plagiarism.
	Chapters 21 and 22 help students document sources in MLA and APA style correctly and provide models for dozens of source types.
Understand the relationships among language, knowledge, and power	**Chapter 1** introduces students to the idea of writing as a conversation that can help them share information, ideas, and arguments.
	Readings in **Chapters 5–10**, from a Nobel Prize acceptance speech to anti-drug advertisements, illustrate the profound effects of writing on readers. Furthermore, Chapter 10 provides detailed coverage of claims, evidence, and counterarguments.

Processes

Be aware that it usually takes multiple drafts to create and complete a successful text	Writing processes based on multiple drafts are demonstrated throughout **Chapters 5–10**.
	Chapter 20 emphasizes the importance of revising and editing and offers specific advice for working with multiple drafts ("What Should I Focus on When I Revise?" p. 632).
Develop flexible strategies for generating ideas, revising, editing, and proofreading	**Chapter 2** suggests different ways to generate ideas, including brainstorming, freewriting, looping, clustering, and mapping ("How Can I Find Interesting Conversations?" p. 33).
	Demonstrating that writing processes must vary with each writing situation, **Chapters 5–10** provide purpose-specific guidance for generating ideas, preparing drafts, and reviewing and improving drafts.
	Chapter 20 offers practical advice and **Checklists** for revising and editing.

(continued on next page)

Joining the Conversation and the Council of Writing Program Administrators' (WPA) Outcomes

Processes (cont.)	
Understand writing as an open process that permits writers to use later invention and re-thinking to revise their work	**Chapter 2** introduces the concept of writing as a process that requires revision ("Understand That Writing Is a Process," p. 44).
	In Process boxes in Chapters 5–10 (see p. 311, for example) follow Featured Student Writers through their writing processes from the early stages to the final draft. **"Review and Improve Your Draft" sections** in each of those chapters offer purpose-specific advice for revising different types of assignments (see p. 321, for example).
Understand the collaborative and social aspects of writing processes	By framing writing as conversation, the book underscores writing as a social act. **Chapter 4** explains the value of working with other writers and offers specific guidance for both individual and collaborative projects.
	Peer Review boxes in Chapters 5–10 help students work together to review and improve drafts (see p. 196, for example).
	Working Together boxes throughout Chapters 1–10 suggest group activities to help students work through different stages of individual assignments (see p. 72, for example).
Learn to critique their own and others' works	**Chapter 4** offers guidelines for giving and receiving feedback on written work ("Respond to Written Work," pp. 81–84).
	Peer Review boxes in Chapters 5–10 help students work together to review and improve drafts (see p. 196, for example).
Learn to balance the advantages of relying on others with the responsibility of doing their part	**Chapter 4** explains how working with others can benefit a writing project ("Why Should I Work with Other Writers?", p. 76).
	Working Together boxes in that chapter help students develop solutions to potential problems (p. 85), establish ground rules (p. 86), and create a project plan (p. 87).
Use a variety of technologies to address a range of audiences	Readings in **Chapters 5–10** model a variety of technologies and media, with examples drawn from photo essays, Web sites, multimedia presentations, and blogs.
	Chapters 12 and 17 provide advice for finding and integrating electronic sources, images, video, and audio. (See "How Can I Locate Sources Using Electronic Resources?", pp. 480–501 and "Use Images, Audio, and Video," pp. 586–589.)
	Chapter 18 covers design conventions for multimodal essays (pp. 608–611) and Web sites (pp. 613–615).
Knowledge of Conventions	
Learn common formats for different kinds of texts	The concept of genre-specific design and formatting is foregrounded in **Chapter 1** ("What Should I Know about Genre and Design?" p. 18).
	Readings in **Chapters 5–10** are designed to reflect the various genres in which they were originally published to familiarize students with common formats and design conventions.
	Genres in Conversation chapter openers (see pp. 272–273, for example) help students analyze the reasons for various design choices as they relate to purpose and the writing situation.
	Chapter 18 provides advice and **Checklists** for following appropriate conventions for academic essays, multimodal essays, articles, and Web sites ("What Design Conventions Should I Follow?" pp. 605–615).

Knowledge of Conventions

Develop knowledge of genre conventions ranging from structure and paragraphing to tone and mechanics	**Starting a Conversation questions** following each reading in Chapters 5–10 focus on genre to help students analyze the structure, style, tone, and conventions of various types of writing. (See p. 348, for example.)
Practice appropriate means of documenting their work	**Chapter 14** is devoted to questions of plagiarism and research ethics.
	Chapter 17 provides specific advice for integrating sources effectively and avoiding plagiarism.
	Chapters 21 and 22 help students correctly document sources in MLA and APA style.
Control such surface features as syntax, grammar, punctuation, and spelling	**Chapter 19** addresses syntax, effective transitions, and consistent point of view, and **Chapter 20** helps with the finer points of grammar, spelling, and punctuation as part of the process of editing a final draft.

Composing in Electronic Environments

Use electronic environments for drafting, reviewing, revising, editing, and sharing texts	**Chapter 4** explains how to use chat sessions, e-mail discussion lists, Web discussion forums, wikis, and blogs to generate and refine ideas; file-sharing Web sites to share documents; and word processing programs to conduct peer review ("Use Technological Tools," pp. 88–90).
Locate, evaluate, organize, and use research material collected from electronic sources, including scholarly library databases; other official databases (e.g., federal government databases); and informal electronic networks and internet sources	**Chapters 6, 7, 8, and 10** integrate examples of students' online research practices into advice about the writing process. **In Process boxes** in these chapters illustrate library catalog, database, and Web searches
	Chapter 11 offers detailed advice on managing digital source material ("How Can I Keep Track of My Sources?" pp. 466–478).
	Chapter 12 explains how to perform effective searches using electronic library catalogs, scholarly and other subject databases, the Web, and media search sites ("How Can I Locate Sources Using Electronic Resources?" pp. 480–501). It also demonstrates how to use Boolean terms and define search limits for more targeted results.
Understand and exploit the differences in the rhetorical strategies and in the affordances available for both print and electronic composing processes and texts	Readings in **Chapters 5–10** illustrate a variety of print and multimodal genres, from short stories, essays, and letters to advertisements, Web sites, and multimedia presentations.
	Chapter 18 addresses effective and appropriate design for academic essays, multimodal essays, articles, and Web sites ("What Design Conventions Should I Follow?" pp. 605–615).

You Get More Digital Choices for *Joining the Conversation*

Joining the Conversation doesn't stop with a book. Online, you'll find both free and affordable premium resources to help students get even more out of the book and your course. You'll also find convenient instructor resources, such as downloadable sample syllabi, classroom activities, and even a nationwide community of teachers. To learn more about or order any of the products below, contact your Bedford/St. Martin's sales representative, e-mail sales support (sales_support@bfwpub.com), or visit the Web site at bedfordstmartins.com/conversation/catalog.

Student Center for *Joining the Conversation*

bedfordstmartins.com/conversation

Send students to free and open resources, allow them to choose an affordable e-book option, or upgrade to an expanding collection of innovative digital content.

Free and open resources for *Joining the Conversation* provide students with easy-to-access reference materials, visual tutorials, and support for working with sources.

- **Featured Student Writers in Process** collects notes, outlines, rough drafts, and final essays completed by the six student writers in the assignment chapters.

- **"How-to" Guides** offer specific advice for using online library catalogs, databases, search engines and directories, and other electronic resources, along with up-to-date support for designing documents and creating Web sites.

- **Practice, Working Together, and Peer Review boxes** from the text can be downloaded or printed for individual or group work.

- ***Research and Documentation Online* by Diana Hacker** promises clear advice across the disciplines on how to integrate outside material into a paper, how to cite sources correctly, and how to format the paper in MLA, APA, *Chicago*, or CSE style. The site also includes links to specialized online resources for more than 30 disciplines.

- ***Exercise Central,*** the largest database of editing exercises on the Web, is now a comprehensive resource for skill development as well as skill assessment. In addition to over 8,000 exercises offering immediate feedback and reporting, *Exercise Central* can help identify students' strengths and weaknesses, recommend personalized study plans, and provide tutorials for common problems.

VideoCentral is a growing collection of videos for the writing class that captures real-world, academic, and student writers talking about how and why they write. Writer and teacher Peter Berkow interviewed hundreds of people—from Michael Moore to Cynthia Selfe—to produce 50 brief videos about topics such as revising and getting feedback. *VideoCentral* can be packaged with *Joining the Conversation* at a significant discount. An activation code is required. To order *VideoCentral* packaged with the print book, use ISBN-10: 0-312-64362-4 or ISBN-13: 978-0-312-64362-1.

Re:Writing Plus gathers all of Bedford/St. Martin's premium digital content for composition into one online collection. It includes hundreds of model documents, the first-ever peer-review game, and *VideoCentral*. *Re:Writing Plus* can be purchased separately or packaged with the print book at a significant discount. An activation code is required. To order *Re:Writing Plus* packaged with the print book, use ISBN-10: 0-312-62602-9 or ISBN-13: 978-0-312-62602-0.

E-book Options

Bedford/St. Martin's e-books let students do more and pay less. For about half the price of a print book, the e-book for *Joining the Conversation* offers the complete text of the print book combined with convenient digital tools such as highlighting, note-taking, and search. Both online and downloadable options are available. The online interactive e-book includes additional readings that provide multimodal examples of each writing purpose and introduce new genres, including video diaries and interactive Web sites—and it can be packaged with the print book for free. An activation code is required. To order *Joining the Conversation* packaged free with the online interactive e-book, use ISBN-10: 0-312-62566-9 or ISBN-13: 978-0-312-62566-5.

CompClass for *Joining the Conversation*

yourcompclass.com

An easy-to-use online course space designed for composition students and instructors, *CompClass for Joining the Conversation* comes preloaded with the *Joining the Conversation e-Book* as well as other Bedford/St. Martin's premium digital content, including *VideoCentral*. Powerful assignment and assessment tools make it easier to keep track of your students' progress. *CompClass for Joining the Conversation* can be purchased separately at yourcompclass.com or packaged with the print book at a significant discount. An activation code is required. To order *CompClass for Joining the Conversation* with the print book, use ISBN-10: 0-312-62565-0 or ISBN-13: 978-0-312-62565-8.

More Options for Students

Add more value to your text with one of the following resources, free when packaged with *Joining the Conversation*. To learn more about package options or any of the products below, contact your Bedford/St. Martin's sales representative or visit the Web site at bedfordstmartins.com/conversation/catalog.

i-series on CD-ROM This popular series presents multimedia tutorials in a flexible format—because there are things you can't do in a book.

- *ix visual exercises* helps students put into practice key rhetorical and visual concepts. To order *ix visual exercises* packaged with the print book, use ISBN-10: 0-312-62562-6 or ISBN-13: 978-0-312-62562-7.

- *i•claim visualizing argument* offers a new way to see argument—with 6 tutorials, an illustrated glossary, and over 70 multimedia arguments. To order *i•claim visualizing argument* packaged with the print book, use ISBN-10: 0-312-62561-8 or ISBN-13: 978-0-312-62561-0.

- *i•cite visualizing sources* brings research to life through an animated introduction, four tutorials, and hands-on source practice. To order *i•cite visualizing sources* packaged with the print book, use ISBN-10: 0-312-62560-X or ISBN-13: 978-0-312-62560-3.

***Portfolio Keeping,* Second Edition, by Nedra Reynolds and Rich Rice,** is the first guide that provides all the information students need to use the portfolio method successfully in a writing course. *Portfolio Teaching,* a companion guide for instructors, provides the practical information instructors and writing program administrators need to use the portfolio method successfully in a writing course. To order *Portfolio Keeping* packaged with the print book, use ISBN-10: 0-312-62564-2 or ISBN-13: 978-0-312-62564-1.

***Oral Presentations in the Composition Course: A Brief Guide* by Matthew Duncan and Gustav W. Friedrich** offers students the advice they need to plan, prepare, and present their work effectively. With sections on analyzing audiences, choosing effective language, using visual aids, collaborating on group presentations, and dealing with the fear of public speaking, this booklet offers help for students' most common challenges in developing oral presentations. To order *Oral Presentations in the Composition Course* packaged with the print book, use ISBN-10: 0-312-62563-4 or ISBN-13: 978-0-312-62563-4.

Instructor Resources

bedfordstmartins.com/conversation/catalog

You have a lot to do in your course. Bedford/St. Martin's wants to make it easy for you to find the support you need—and to get it quickly.

The *Instructor's Manual for Joining the Conversation* is available in PDF that can be downloaded from the Bedford/St. Martin's online catalog or the *Student Center*. In addition to chapter overviews and teaching tips, the *Instructor's Manual* includes sample syllabi, correlations to the Council of Writing Program Administrators' Outcomes Statement, and suggestions for classroom activities.

Teaching Central offers the entire list of Bedford/St. Martin's print and online professional resources in one place. You'll find landmark reference works, sourcebooks on pedagogical issues, award-winning collections, and practical advice for the classroom—all free for instructors.

Bits collects creative ideas for teaching a range of composition topics in an easily searchable blog. A community of teachers—leading scholars, authors, and editors—discuss revision, research, grammar and style, technology, peer review, and much more. Take, use, adapt, and pass the ideas around. Then, come back to the site to comment or share your own suggestion.

Content cartridges for the most common course management systems—Blackboard, WebCT, Angel, and Desire2Learn—allows to you easily download Bedford/St. Martin's digital materials for your course.

Acknowledgments

This project represents five years of weekends and evenings that might otherwise have been spent with my family. For their patience and support, I offer my deepest thanks to my family, Jessica, Ellen, and Reid.

I offer my thanks as well to the colleagues who have inspired me as I worked on this book. David Kaufer and Chris Neuwirth helped me understand the power of the conversation metaphor and provided valuable advice as I entered the discipline. Richard Young not only inspired me but provided me with the tools to think carefully and productively about the role of textbooks within the discipline. Will Hochman, Nick Carbone, Lynda Haas, Kate Kiefer, Sue Doe, Carole Clark Papper, and Jill Salahub have helped me test ideas and given me useful feedback.

A project like this necessarily involves the contributions of a wide range of colleagues who worked on key resources for the book. I am grateful to Jeff Osbourne, for creating the reading apparatus; to my colleagues Carrie Lamanna and David Bowen, for researching and writing the apparatus for the multimodal selections; to my colleague Sue Doe, for writing the instructor's manual; to Chandra Brown, for gathering sample documents; to Kate Mayhew, for researching potential reading selections; and to Mary Ellen Smith, for updating the citation models. I also thank Andy Flax, Jennifer D. Huggins, Liz Jackson, Kou Chieh Lin, James Redigan, Deborah Sattler, Jennifer M. Sevcik, and Jenna R. Tice for their work on materials that contributed to the early development of this book.

I am also indebted to the following reviewers who offered careful critiques of drafts of this book: Jeffrey T. Andelora, Mesa Community College; Anonymous, University of Delaware; Mark Browning, Johnson Community College; Deborah H. Burns, Merrimack College; Cherie Post Dargan, Hawkeye Community College; Sarah Duerden, Arizona State University; Brenda Mann Hammack, Fayetteville State University; Katherine Heenan, Arizona State University; Michael Hogan, Southeast Missouri State University; Randall McClure, Florida Gulf Coast University; Miles McCrimmon, J. Sargent Reynolds Community College; Bryan Moore, Arkansas State University; Carole Clark Papper, Hofstra University; Barbara Schneider, University of Toledo; Scott R. Weeden, Indiana University—Purdue University, Indianapolis. Their reactions and thoughtful suggestions helped me understand where my initial vision for the book was strong and where it needed to be corrected and I thank them for the time and care they took in their reviews.

I have been extraordinarily fortunate to find, in my colleagues at Bedford/St. Martin's, a group of editors and assistants who care deeply about producing the best possible textbooks. For their patience as I worked on this book, for their constant support and encouragement, and for their good hearted approach to editing, I thank my development editors, Rachel Goldberg, Ellen Kuhl Repetto, and Sara Eaton Gaunt. They unfailingly offered good advice and thoughtful commentary on drafts of the book. I am also grateful to editorial assistants, Sarah Guaraglia Macomber and Joanna Lee, for their many contributions to this project, from finding additional readings to tracking down sources to (always and ably) handling unexpected tasks as they arose. I am also deeply appreciative of the efforts of Nick Carbone and the New Media Group, and in particular Dan Schwartz, for their superb work on the companion Web site. I am indebted, as well, to Anna Palchik and Lisa Garbutt for the innovative and engaging design of this book; to my production editor, Bridget Leahy, for her attention to detail in directing its complex production; and to Linda McLatchie for her careful copy editing. I also offer my thanks to editor in chief

Karen Henry for her leadership throughout the years this book was in development, and to Michelle Clark for her early advice on this project.

Many years ago, Rory Baruth introduced me to the editors at Bedford/St. Martin's. I am grateful not only for the introduction but for the good advice he has offered since. Thanks as well to Joan Feinberg and Denise Wydra for their support of *Joining the Conversation* and for their good ideas during its development. I offer particular thanks to Leasa Burton for her tireless devotion to this project. From her comments on its initial conceptualization to her careful review of its final drafts, Leasa's investment of time and effort into this book has been a constant source of inspiration to me.

Finally, I offer my thanks to the six student writers whose work is featured in this book and on the companion Web site: Alison Bizzul, Caitlin Guariglia, Dwight Haynes, Donovan Mikrot, Jennie Tillson, and Hannah Steiner. I deeply appreciate their willingness to share their work and their insights about their writing processes with other student writers. I hope that their superb examples inspire the students who use this book to join and contribute to their own written conversations.

Mike Palmquist
Colorado State University

Brief Contents

Contents

3 READING TO WRITE   49

PART TWO: CONTRIBUTING TO A CONVERSATION 93

5 WRITING TO REFLECT 95

GENRES IN CONVERSATION: REFLECTIVE WRITING 96

6 WRITING TO INFORM   153

9 WRITING TO SOLVE PROBLEMS   335
GENRES IN CONVERSATION: PROBLEM-SOLVING WRITING   336

10 WRITING TO CONVINCE OR PERSUADE   **401**

GENRES IN CONVERSATION: ARGUMENTATIVE WRITING   402

What is writing to convince or persuade?   404

What kinds of documents are used to convince or persuade?   405

How can I write an argumentative essay?   424

PART THREE: WORKING WITH SOURCES 457

11 PREPARING TO USE SOURCES IN AN ACADEMIC ESSAY 459

LOCATING SOURCES   479

PART FIVE: DOCUMENTING SOURCES   643

21 USING MLA STYLE   645

22 USING APA STYLE   667

PART ONE

Thinking of Writing as Conversation

01 Making Connections

▶▶ Writing is often referred to as a mysterious process. Some people even consider the ability to write well a rare and special gift. Well . . . perhaps. But only if you're talking about the ability to write a prize-winning novel or a poem that will be celebrated for generations. If, on the other hand, you're talking about conveying information, ideas, and arguments clearly and convincingly, the writing process is anything but mysterious.

In fact, once you realize that writing shares a surprising number of similarities with participating in a conversation, you'll find that writing is an activity you can approach with confidence.

Why Think of Writing as Conversation?

Learning to write is similar to learning other complex processes, such as playing a musical instrument, taking up a new sport, or figuring out how to work with people.

- Learning to write takes time and effort.

- It helps if you can turn to others for guidance and advice.

- Most important, it helps if you can connect what you're learning to what you already know.

In this book, writing is treated as an activity similar to conversation. The documents you'll write are contributions that move a conversation forward. The designs you'll choose reflect your purposes and those of your readers. And the processes you'll use to write are similar to those used to participate in a discussion. By thinking of writing as conversation, you'll be able to use your already extensive understanding of how conversations work to become a confident, effective writer.

You Already Know How Conversations Work—Online and Off

Imagine yourself at a party. When you arrived, you said hello to friends and found something to eat or drink. Then you walked around, listening briefly to several conversations. Eventually, you joined a group that was talking about something you found interesting.

If you're like most people, you didn't jump right into the conversation. Instead, you listened for a few minutes and thought about what was being said. Perhaps you learned something new. Eventually, you added your voice to the conversation, other members of the group picked up on what you said, and the conversation moved along. The same thing happens when you join a new group online. Whether you join a discussion board or a Facebook group, more than likely you listen in (or read up) to learn a little about the group's interests before you make any posts.

Most writers understand how conversations work—more important, most good writers are good conversationalists. They understand that writing is about more than simply saying what they know. They view writing as a process of joining and contributing to an ongoing conversation about an issue.

If you want to write with confidence, build on what you already know about engaging in conversation. In practical terms, you should

- read about a topic before you write about it (just as you'd listen for a while before speaking),

Members of an online discussion forum about nonprofit organizations share their experiences of volunteering internationally.

- think carefully about what you've read (just as you'd think carefully about what you had just heard),

- acknowledge what other writers have added to the written conversation you've decided to join, and

- add something new to the conversation.

Thinking of writing as a form of conversation allows you to build on skills you already possess. In addition, because written conversations take place over much longer periods of time than spoken conversations do, you can use your conversational skills to far greater advantage. You can thoroughly consider your purposes and analyze your readers' needs, interests, and backgrounds. And you can explore the contexts—physical, social, and cultural—that will shape how your document is written and read.

Today, many of us are as likely to engage in conversations through writing as through speaking. Some of us prefer a text message to a phone call. Some of us spend more time using e-mail than talking with friends. Some of us spend entire evenings on Web discussion forums, sharing information or arguing about the best new games, music, or movies. Some of us post, read, and reply to blogs on a regular basis. And some of us spend more time keeping up with friends on Facebook or MySpace than we do hanging out together.

Interestingly, if you ask people who spend significant amounts of time online whether they do much writing, they'll often say they don't. They don't think of creating text messages, e-mail messages, status updates, comments, notes, forum posts, or blog entries as writing. Yet it is. And the writing you've done in these settings can help prepare you for the writing you'll be asked to do in class or at a job.

Of course, there are differences between the writing you do online and the writing you do in an academic essay. Using abbreviations such as FWIW, OMG, or LOL in an essay might go over just about as well as writing "In summary, the available evidence suggests" in a text message. Just as you will adapt your tone or level of formality in a spoken conversation to the people involved in the conversation—for example, treating new acquaintances differently than you treat old friends—you're likely to adapt your writing to the situation in which you find yourself.

You can build on your experiences as a writer in a wide range of settings. Just as you'll tailor your comments to friends when you write on their Facebook or MySpace pages, you can consider the interests and experiences of the people who will read your next academic essay. Similarly, as you consider how to learn about a current issue, you can draw on your experiences surfing the Web to learn about a product you were thinking of purchasing. And just as you've learned to be critical — even suspicious — of what you read online, you can apply the same concerns to your reading of the sources you encounter as you work on your class assignments.

Practice: Inventory Your Writing Life

We all have writing lives. Even if you think yours is on life support, you probably do much more writing than you think. Use this activity to conduct an inventory of your writing activities and to reflect on how you might use your experiences to enhance the writing you'll do for class assignments. To get started, use the following prompts:

1. **Create a list of everything you do that involves typing.** Be sure to include typing on phones, personal digital assistants such as iPaqs or Palms (if you have one), and computers.

2. **List everything you do that involves handwriting.** Include everything from grocery lists to notes passed in class to personal letters.

3. **Identify the purposes and audiences of each activity you've listed.** Take a look at your list. For each item, indicate why you do it or what you hope to accomplish by doing it (purpose). Then indicate who reads it (audience). In some cases, such as shopping lists, your audience might be yourself.

4. **Identify activities that involve locating information.** For each activity on your list, indicate whether you read sources (such as newspaper or magazine articles, Web sites, blogs, or books), search the Web, collect information through observation, or talk to others in the course of carrying out the activity.

5. **Review your list to identify writing activities that might prepare you for academic writing.** Look for activities that involve trying to accomplish a purpose. Look for activities that involve thinking about the needs, interests, and experiences of your readers. Look for activities that involve collecting information. Consider how carrying out these activities might help you succeed at academic writing assignments.

@ Download or print this Practice activity at bedfordstmartins.com/conversation.

Conversations Help You Share Information, Ideas, and Arguments

Much like a spoken conversation, a written conversation involves an exchange of information, ideas, and arguments among readers and writers. Instead of spoken words, however, the people engaged in the conversation communicate through written documents. Just as most people listen to what's being said before contributing to a conversation, most writers begin the process of writing about a topic by reading.

Consider the experiences of Chandra, a college student in south Florida who was interested in finding ways to fund her education. Chandra had heard about tuition support offered by national service agencies such as AmeriCorps and City Year and wanted to learn more. She started to listen in on the written conversation about the topic by searching for information and reading some of the Web sites, brochures, and articles she found.

Writers learn about a topic through reading.

Reading about a topic implies, of course, that someone has written the documents you read—most likely, people who share your interest in the topic. Chandra, for example, found material written by students involved in national service programs, by program directors, by public relations staff, by political analysts, and by people whose communities had been helped by national service programs, among others. Eventually, Chandra would write a document that responded to these people. First, however, she learned about what they thought by reading what they had written.

After they've read about a topic, most writers reflect on what they've learned. Then they contribute to the conversation by writing their own document. In turn, that document will be read by other participants in the conversation. If these participants are interested, concerned, or even offended by what another writer has added to the conversation, they might write their own documents in response. In this sense, a conversation among writers and readers becomes a cyclical process in which the information, ideas, and arguments shared through documents lead to the creation of new documents.

After reading about a topic, writers share information with readers, who may respond in writing themselves.

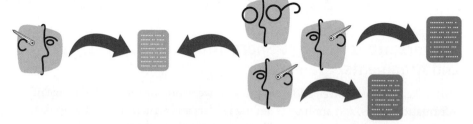

After reading widely about her topic, Chandra realized that she wanted to encourage others to learn about national service and the opportunities it provides to students. She decided to add an entry to her blog—a personal journal published on the Web— so that she could share her thinking with others who were interested in the topic. Some of Chandra's readers responded directly to her by posting replies to her blog entries. Some linked their blog entries to hers. And a few authors commented on her ideas in articles they published in newspapers and magazines.

Most of Chandra's readers knew little about her background and interests, aside from what she chose to share with them through her blog. This is not unusual. Many readers and writers never meet face-to-face—they might be separated by distance or time. You've probably read Web pages or blog entries written by people in other countries, for example, and you've almost certainly read work by authors who have long since passed away, such as William Shakespeare or Thomas Jefferson.

You can see the exchange between readers and writers in a number of contexts. Articles in scholarly and professional journals almost always refer to previously published work. Similarly, in the letters to the editor section of newspapers and magazines, you'll frequently see reference to earlier letters. You can even see this process in writing

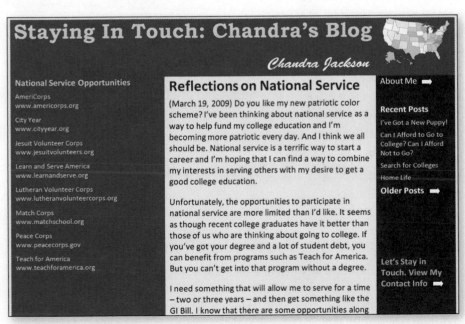

t Chandra's Blog Entry

classes. As writers share their work with classmates and instructors, they receive feedback that often leads to important changes in their final drafts. In turn, as writers read the work of their classmates, they often refine their thinking about their own writing projects.

Practice: Find a Written Conversation

We're surrounded by written conversations. Some focus on politics, others on sports, and still others on issues in an academic discipline. You'll find contributions to conversations on the front page of newspapers, on Web sites such as CNN.com and Foxnews.com, in academic and professional journals, and in the blogs at Blogger.com. Spend some time locating a conversation about a topic that interests you. Use the following prompts to find the conversation:

1. **List a topic that interests you.** Because you'll be searching for sources, jot down a list of search terms, or keywords (see p. 478), that you can use to locate sources on the topic.

2. **Choose a newspaper or magazine or search for sources.** Browse the newspaper or magazine or search for sources on a Web search site (see p. 490), a library database (see p. 486), or a library catalog (see p. 482) using the keywords you jotted down about your topic.

3. **Identify sources that seem to address the topic.** Skim each source (see p. 60) to get a sense of how it addresses your topic.

4. **Decide whether the sources are engaged in the same conversation.** Ask whether the sources are addressing the same topic. If they are, list the ways in which they are "talking" to one another about the topic. Identify any agreements, disagreements, or differences in their approach to the topic.

5. **Reflect on the conversation.** Ask whether the sources you've identified tell you enough to understand the conversation. Consider whether you might need to locate more sources to give you a fuller picture of the conversation.

@ Download or print this Practice activity at bedfordstmartins.com/conversation.

Conversation Allows You to Adopt Roles

In spoken conversations, we often take on roles. A speaker might explain something to someone else, in a sense becoming a guide through the conversation. Another speaker might advance an argument, taking on the role of an advocate for a particular position. These roles shift and change as the conversation moves along. Depending on the flow of the conversation, a person who explained something at one point in the conversation might make an argument later on.

A similar form of role-playing—and shifting—takes place in written conversation. The roles writers take on reflect their purpose, their understanding of their readers, and the type of document they plan to write. To help them achieve their purpose, writers typically adopt one or more of the roles you'll learn about in later chapters of this book.

OBSERVERS (Chapter 5) focus on learning about and exploring the implications of a person, an event, an object, an idea, or an issue. They typically reflect on their subject and often trace their thinking about it.

I wonder what my life would be like if I majored in advertising.

REPORTERS (Chapter 6) present themselves as experts and present detailed but neutral information. A reporter might also provide an overview of competing ideas about a topic, such as a guide to the positions of candidates for public office.

I'm focusing on the advertising dollars generated by sites like Facebook and MySpace.

INTERPRETERS (Chapter 7) analyze and explain the significance of ideas or events.

I have to wonder about the truthfulness of the ads aired during this year's Super Bowl. I think I'll check a few of them out.

EVALUATORS (Chapter 8) consider how well something meets a given set of criteria. Their judgments are usually balanced, and they offer evidence and reasoning to support their evaluation.

Who cares about the truth? I wonder which ads were most effective. Did sales actually go up as a result of the ads? Did people view the products more favorably?

PROBLEM SOLVERS (Chapter 9) identify and define a problem, discuss its impact, and offer solutions based on evidence and reasoning.

The problem I'm wrestling with is how smaller companies can benefit from events like the Super Bowl. How can they get their message out when the ads are so expensive?

ADVOCATES (Chapter 10) present evidence in favor of their side of an argument and, in many cases, offer evidence that undermines opposing views.

If anybody cares about the truth, it's me. And I'm sure I'm not alone. We need to do something about deceptive advertising. And I know just what that is.

As in spoken conversations, the roles writers play are not mutually exclusive. In an introduction to an argumentative essay, you might find yourself adopting the role of reporter, helping your readers understand an issue so that they will be better positioned to understand the argument you'll advance later. Similarly, you might find yourself adopting the role of advocate in a problem-solving essay as you shift from explaining a potential solution to arguing that it should be put into effect. To understand how this fluid shifting of roles can take place — and make sense — reflect on your experiences in spoken conversations. You'll find that thinking of writing as a conversation will make it easier to understand how, and when, to shift roles.

Working Together: Explore Roles

Work together with your classmates to explore roles during a conversation. In a group of five, ask three people to talk about a topic that has recently been in the news or that has been the focus of attention on campus. As the conversation unfolds, the other two members of the group should listen and write down the different roles that are adopted during the conversation, noting when and why the roles were adopted. After five minutes of conversation, respond to the following prompts:

1. **What roles were adopted?** The two observers should share their list of roles. Ask whether the observers saw the same roles. If there are differences, discuss them.

2. **When were different roles adopted?** Ask when each role was adopted. Which roles were adopted at the beginning of the conversation? Did the members of the conversation shift roles during the conversation? If so, when?

3. **Why were different roles adopted?** Explore the reasons for adopting each role. For example, ask whether people who knew more about the topic adopted different roles than did those who knew less. If you saw shifts in role, ask why those shifts occurred.

4. **Connect the activity to your work as a writer.** Consider how the idea of roles might play out in your own writing. As a group, discuss roles you've adopted in the past, and consider how you might use the idea of roles in your future writing.

@ Download or print this Working Together activity at bedfordstmartins.com/conversation.

What Should I Know about Writing Situations?

When people participate in a spoken conversation, they pay attention to a wide range of factors: why they've joined the conversation, who's involved in the conversation, and what's already been said. They also notice the mood of the people they're speaking with, their facial expressions and body language, and physical factors such as background noise. In short, they consider the situation as they listen and speak. Similarly, when writers engage in written conversation, they become part of a **writing situation** — the setting in which writers and readers communicate with one another. Writing situations are shaped by several factors, among them the purposes, needs, interests, and backgrounds of the writers and readers of a document; the contexts — physical, social, and cultural — in which the document is written and read; related documents that have already been written by other writers; and the type of document that is written.

Writing Has a Purpose

As is the case with spoken conversations, writers join written conversations for particular **purposes**, which in turn affect the roles they adopt (see pp. 10–12). Writers hoping to persuade or convince their readers, for example, take on the role of advocate, while those hoping to inform readers take on the role of reporter. You can read more about the roles writers adopt in Chapters 5 to 10.

Writers often have more than one purpose for writing a document. Writers of academic essays, for instance, might complete their essays not only to earn a grade and pass the course but also to learn about a particular topic or improve their composition skills. Similarly, writers of newspaper and magazine articles usually write because an editor has given them an assignment. But they often find themselves interested in their subjects and end up writing as much for themselves as for their readers.

Writers often have more than one purpose for writing a document.

Writers' purposes for joining a conversation are shaped by their **needs**, **interests**, and **backgrounds**. For example, a person who suffers from asthma might need to ensure that plans to build a coal-powered electrical generating plant near his neighborhood

 reader writer sources context documents purpose

will take health concerns into account. Another person with a strong interest in the use of clean coal technologies might want to support proposed legislation on reducing power-plant emissions. Still others, such as those employed by the power industry, might be concerned about how proposed legislation on power-plant emissions might affect their employment.

Your purposes will affect what you choose to write about and how you compose a document. Chandra, the student who wrote a blog about national service opportunities, wanted not only to explore her options for participating as a volunteer but also to call attention to a need to expand such opportunities for others. As she wrote in her blog, her purposes affected her choice of what to write about, which information to use as supporting evidence for her points, and how to address the information, ideas, and arguments she encountered in her reading.

Readers Have Purposes, Needs, Interests, and Backgrounds

Just as writers have purposes, so do readers. Among other purposes, readers often want to learn about a subject, assess or evaluate ideas and arguments, or understand opposing perspectives. And like writers' purposes, readers' purposes are strongly affected by their own needs, interests, and backgrounds. Chandra's needs and interests regarding national service, for example, were driven by her family experiences. She needed to find an affordable way to attend college, and she wanted to make a genuine contribution to others. As a member of a family that did not have a high income, she had seen two brothers and a sister join the military so that they could take advantage of the tuition benefits. Through her reading, Chandra had learned that some national service programs helped pay college tuition after volunteers had completed their terms of service. Beyond these personal needs, Chandra also needed to learn enough so that her calls for expanding national service opportunities would be convincing. As a result, her situation affected not only what she wrote but also how she evaluated what she read.

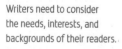

Writers need to consider the needs, interests, and backgrounds of their readers.

As writers craft their contribution to a written conversation, they ask who their readers are likely to be. They reflect on their readers' values and beliefs, determine what their readers are likely to know about a subject, and take into account their readers' likely experiences—if any—with the subject. They consider what readers need to know about a subject, and what readers might be interested in knowing. They ask why potential readers would want to read their document—and what might cause readers to stop reading. In short, writers try to understand and connect with their readers.

Writing Builds on the Work of Others

One of the most important ways in which writing situations resemble spoken conversations is their reliance on taking turns. In spoken conversations—at least in those that are productive—people take turns sharing their ideas. To move the conversation forward, speakers build on what has been said, often referring to specific ideas or arguments and identifying the speakers who raised them. Comments such as "As Ellen said . . ." and "Reid made a good point earlier when he pointed out that . . ." are frequently made in spoken conversations. They show respect for the contributions made by others and help speakers align themselves with or distance themselves from other members of the conversation.

Written conversations also build on earlier contributions. Writers refer to the work of other authors to support their arguments, provide a context for their own contributions, or differentiate their ideas from those advanced by other authors. For example, an opinion columnist might show how her ideas differ from those offered by other members of the conversation by quoting a statement made by another columnist. Later in the same column, she might use a statement made by yet another author to support her argument.

Writers also use sources to introduce new ideas, information, and arguments to a conversation. A blogger concerned with the challenges faced by young families wishing to purchase a home, for example, might share information from a congressional hearing on lending practices with readers. Similarly, a reporter might conduct research on market trends and use what she learns to compare the conditions home buyers faced twenty years ago with those of today. When writers use sources in this way, they provide citations to indicate that the information is provided by another author and to help readers locate the sources should they wish to review them.

Even when writers do not refer directly to other sources, the work of other writers is likely to influence their thinking about a subject. As you compose your contribution to a conversation, be aware that what you've read, heard, seen, and experienced will shape your thinking about the subject — and by doing so, these sources will affect the information, ideas, and arguments in your document.

Writing Takes Place in Context

Just as in spoken conversations, written conversations are affected by the contexts — or settings — in which they take place.

- **Physical context** affects how you read and write (on paper or on a computer screen) and how well you can concentrate (for example, consider the differences between trying to read in a noisy, crowded, jolting bus and in a quiet, well-lit room).

- **Social context** affects how easily writers and readers can understand one another. Readers familiar with topics such as violence in American secondary schools, for example, will not need to be educated about them — they will already know the key points. This reduces the amount of time and effort writers need to devote to providing background information.

- **Cultural context** refers to a larger set of similarities and differences among readers. For instance, readers from the American Midwest might find it easier to understand the allusions and metaphors used in a document written by someone from Oregon than those in a document written by someone from Peru or Sri Lanka. Similarly, today's teenagers might find it easier to follow what's being said in a document written one month ago by a high school senior in Milwaukee than a document written in 1897 by a retired railroad engineer from Saskatchewan.

Physical, social, and cultural contexts affect the writing and reading of documents.

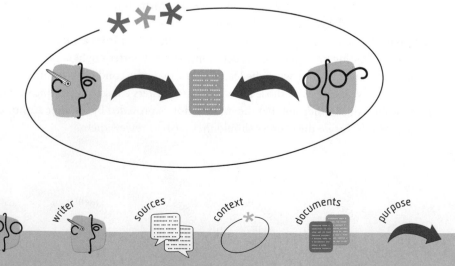

reader   writer   sources   context   documents   purpose

For students, one of the most important social and cultural contexts shaping their written work is academic life itself, that complex mix of instructors, fellow students, classes, tests, labs, and writing assignments that you negotiate on a daily basis. Academic culture—and U.S. and Canadian academic culture in particular—is the product of hundreds of years of arguments, decisions, revisions, and reinventions of a way of thinking and behaving. Academic culture affects far more than how you behave in class, although that's certainly an important element of it. It also shapes the writing you'll do during and after your time in college.

In nearly every instance, what you say and how you say it will reflect a combination of contexts. For instance, the fact that Chandra's blog was both written and read online allowed her to link directly to other digital documents, such as Web sites and other blogs. At the same time, because her work would be read on a computer monitor, she was cautious about readers having to scroll through multiple screens. As a result, her blog entries tended to be brief. Because she was writing to an audience that knew her well (friends and family), she didn't need to provide a great deal of background information about her educational and career goals. And because many of her friends and family shared her beliefs about the value of higher education and community involvement, she did not feel that she had to justify her beliefs as strongly as she might have were she writing to another group of readers.

Working Together: Analyze a Writing Situation

Work together with your classmates to analyze a writing situation. Generate a list of documents that members of the group have written recently. Then choose one and analyze its writing situation. To conduct your analysis, respond to the following prompts:

1. **What was written?** Describe the document in enough detail to allow other members of the class to understand its main point.

2. **What were the writer's purposes?** List the purpose or purposes that drove the writer's work on the document. Why did he or she write it? What did he or she hope to gain by writing it? How was the writer's purpose shaped by his or her needs, interests, values, beliefs, knowledge, and experience?

3. **Who were the intended readers?** Describe the people who might have been expected to read the document, and list their purpose or purposes for reading it. How would their reading of the document have been shaped by their needs, interests, values, beliefs, knowledge, and experience?

4. **What sources were used in the document?** Identify the sources of information, ideas, and arguments used in the document. Indicate how the sources were used (for example, to support a point or to differentiate the writer's ideas from those of another author).

5. **What contexts shaped the writing and reading of the document?** Identify the physical, social, and cultural contexts that shaped the writer's work on the document and the readers' reading of it.

@ Download or print this Working Together activity at **bedfordstmartins.com/conversation.**

What Should I Know about Genre and Design?

As you craft your contribution to a written conversation, you can draw on two powerful tools to create an effective document: genre and design. Genre and design are closely related. In fact, the characteristic design of a particular type of document—for example, the use of columns, headings, and photographs in a newspaper article—can help you distinguish one type of document from another.

Genres Are General Categories of Documents

You're probably familiar with generic drugs. If you have a headache, for example, you can take a pain reliever. You might choose a brand-name drug based on the chemical compound acetaminophen, such as Tylenol or Anacin III. Or you might choose a less expensive, generic equivalent based on the same compound. If you're allergic to acetaminophen, you might turn to pain relievers based on aspirin or ibuprofen. Again, you would have a choice between brand-name drugs, such as Bufferin or Motrin, and their generic equivalents.

The word *genre*, like *generic*, is based on the Latin word *genus*, which means "kind" or "type." In the same way that generic drugs refer to general categories of pharmaceuticals, genres refer to general categories of documents. When you use the word *novel*, for example, you're referring to a general category of long fiction. If you say that you like to read novels, you aren't talking about reading a particular book; instead, you're expressing a preference for a general type of document.

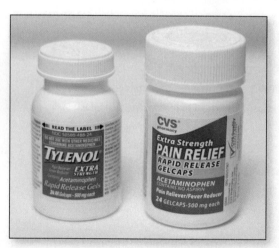

ⵏ Brand name or generic?

Opinion columns, academic essays, scholarly articles, and personal Web pages are all genres. So are personal journals, thank-you letters, and entries on personal blogs. In fact, there are a wide variety of genres, and the number seems to grow larger every few years. Until the 1990s, for example, personal home pages didn't exist. Nor did blogs. Nor, for that matter, did phone-based text-messaging. Yet all of these have become important genres.

Although the word *genre* is typically used to refer to general categories of documents, such as novels or Web pages, it can also be used to refer to more specific categories. For example, you might refer not simply to novels but also to romance novels, mystery novels, and historical novels. Or you might refer to different types of academic essays, such as reflective essays, argumentative essays, or analytical essays. The word *genre*, in this sense, is somewhat imprecise. Sometimes it's used in the largest possible sense, and sometimes it refers to highly specific categories of documents.

Design Is a Writing Tool

Document design is the use of visual elements—such as fonts, colors, page layout, and illustrations—to enhance the effectiveness of written documents. A well-designed chart, for example, can be far more effective at conveying complex information to a reader than even the most clearly written paragraph can. Similarly, the emotional impact of a well-chosen illustration, such as a photograph of a starving child or a video clip of aid workers rushing to help victims of a natural disaster, can do far more

Including a powerful photograph makes this document even more persuasive than text alone might have.

than words alone to persuade a reader to take action. By understanding and applying the principles of document design, you can increase the likelihood that you'll achieve your purposes as a writer and address the needs and interests of your readers. Throughout this book, you'll find design treated as a central writing strategy, and you'll find numerous examples of the design characteristics of the genres discussed in each chapter. You'll also find an in-depth discussion of design in Chapter 18.

Genre and Design Are Related

You can tell genres apart by focusing on why they are written, how they are written, and what they look like. When you read a document, you'll probably recognize it as a particular genre. The style in which it's written, its organization and use of sources, and its appearance work together to help you understand that a document is a scholarly journal article, a blog entry, a letter to the editor, or a brochure. On the basis of design alone, for example, it's usually quite easy to tell the difference between an academic essay and an article in a popular magazine. As you read a document, and without really thinking about it, you'll notice characteristic features of a genre, such as the use of boldface headlines or detailed footnotes. And once you've identified the genre, you'll find that it's easier to read the document. For example, understanding how a document is organized can make it easier to locate information. Similarly, if you recognize a document as an advertisement, you're less likely to be swayed by questionable reasoning.

A PowerPoint presentation uses bulleted lists, images, graphs, and charts to summarize large amounts of information.

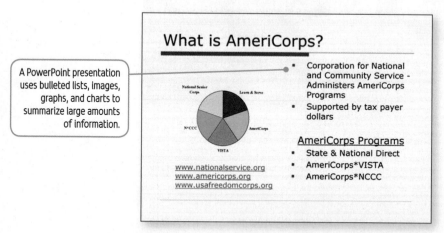

The following documents illustrate a wide range of genres that might be used to write about a topic. Each document addresses the topic of national service. The documents range from a brochure and a journal article to a PowerPoint presentation and a Web site. As you look at each document, think about the purpose for which it was written, the readers it addresses, the genre conventions it follows, and the design it uses.

CAMPUS COMPACT FOR NEW HAMPSHIRE AMERICORPS*VISTA PROGRAM

Campus Compact for New Hampshire

The spirit of The Old Man in the Mountain watches over the White Mountains and the beautiful natural landscape of New Hampshire. As a VISTA member with CCNH, you will have the opportunity to work toward making the goals of VISTA a reality. Depending on placement, a VISTA member may be supporting a partnership between a community based organization and a local college campus, coordinating community service programming on campus, assisting with service-learning programs, or any number of activities which support service on college campuses.

Founded in 1997, CCNH is a statewide consortium of college and university presidents in NH who are united in their commitment to the civic purposes of higher education. Member presidents believe that through sustained and creative student, faculty and institutional involvement in community service, higher education realizes its goals of educating citizens, preparing tomorrow's leaders and contributing to the life of America's communities.

Campus Compact *for New Hampshire*

If you would like to become a member of the CCNH VISTA Program, please send your resume, four references and a cover letter to:

**Stephanie Soule Lesperance
Campus Compact for NH
3 Barrell Court, Suite 200
Concord, NH 03301**

**AMERICORPS *VISTA
HELPING OTHERS HELP THEMSELVES.**

There's a way to make your mark on New Hampshire that's unlike any other—by giving yourself to

AmeriCorps*VISTA is a project of the Corporation for National and Community Service. Together with the USA Freedom Corps, the Corporation is working to build a culture of citizenship, service and responsibility in America.

Corporation for NATIONAL & COMMUNITY SERVICE ★★★

VOLUNTEERS

IN SERVICE

TO AMERICA

END POVERTY

ONE LIFE, ONE COMMUNITY AT A TIME.

Use your skills and experience to improve lives and serve your country.

> Brochures provide information by using large, descriptive titles and colorful images to draw the reader's eye to important information.

The Resource Center
Tools and Training for Volunteer and Service Programs

Corporation for NATIONAL & COMMUNITY SERVICE ★★★

Subscribe or unsubscribe here | **e**newsletter

Call for help >>> **800-860-2684**

>>>>>>> **SEARCH** this site for resources relating to community service and volunteering.

Enter a Search Term | go | Or more search options

Online Resources
Printed Publications
Frequently Searched Topics
Effective Practices
Conference & Training Calendar
Training Providers
Corporation Initiatives
Service-Related Links
Help

My Improvement Plan
Create a tailored set of resources based on your service program's specific needs

Effective Practices Collection
Find good ideas, successful strategies, and studied findings for your service program

Featured National Service Resource (view all)
EnCorps: Tried-and-True Resources for Member Development

Featured Effective Practice (view all)
Utilizing baby boomer volunteers as advisors to service-learning projects

Featured Lending Library Resource
Cultivating Community: Principles and Practices for Community Gardening as a Community-Building Tool

Featured Expert on Volunteer Leveraging
Lori Jean Mantooth, National Service Training Manager at Hands On Network

> Web sites provide information, links to other documents, and contact information.

Leslie Lenkowsky
Indiana University-Purdue University

James L. Perry
Indiana University

Reinventing Government: The Case of National Service

> An article published in a scholarly journal is directed to readers who are familiar with research on a topic. It offers an abstract and headings to help readers quickly identify key information and ideas.

When Bill Clinton embraced national service as one of his administration's priorities, he took a step forward on two of his key initiatives. Not only was national service a new initiative in its own right, but Clinton also held it up as a model of his efforts to reinvent government. It would be an exemplar of government that is catalytic, competitive, decentralized, and results oriented. This case study examines the theory and reality of reinvention. The Corporation for National Service and its programs have come under fire for being more political than catalytic, being simultaneously too centralized and too decentralized, and pursuing too many unclear goals. This article seeks to identify discontinuities between the rhetoric and the reality of reinvention in this instance and draw lessons for public-sector reform.

Bill Clinton is often referred to as a "new" Democrat. It is not surprising, therefore, that he brought to his presidency some unconventional ideas about government, among them reinventing government and national service. In fact, Clinton boldly joined these two sets of ideas in the National and Community Service Trust Act of 1993. The act simultaneously became an experiment in changing how government does its business (Osborne and Gaebler 1992) and in rekindling the spirit of public service.

This case study of national service addresses the relationship between reinvention and national service as it has played out since 1993. We are interested in examining how the reinvention model actually took shape in a particular political and historical context. We begin with a discussion of how reinvention principles were applied to national service programs. We then explore the realities of what transpired in the aftermath of the 1993 act. We conclude with some lessons about the reinvention movement from its application to national service programs.

Applying Reinvention to National Service

The phrase "reinventing government" came into popular usage with the publication of David Osborne and Ted Gaebler's book *Reinventing Government* (1992). The cen-

tral theme of the book is that government in America is restructuring in response to citizen dissatisfaction, competitive pressures of a global marketplace, and revolution in information technology. Reinvention achieved movement status with the Clinton–Gore National Performance Review (Gore 1993) and the National Commission on the State and Local Public Service (Thompson and Radin 1997; National Commission on the State and Local Public Service 1993).

Government reform initiatives are known for being short lived, owing in part to the attention spans of politicians (March and Olsen 1983), so the longevity of the reinvention movement is notable. After all, President Reagan's Grace Commission recommendations received only fleet-

Leslie Lenkowsky is professor of philanthropic studies and public policy at Indiana University–Purdue University at Indianapolis and a research associate of the Indiana University Center on Philanthropy. He was appointed to the board of directors of the Corporation on National Service by President Clinton and had previously been appointed by President Bush to the Commission on National and Community Service. The views expressed in this article are his own.

James L. Perry is Chancellors' Professor in the School of Public and Environmental Affairs, Indiana University–Bloomington. Among his honors are the Charles H. Levine Memorial Award for Excellence in Public Administration and the Distinguished Research Award, both given jointly by the American Society for Public Administration and the National Association of Schools of Public Affairs and Administration. He is a fellow of the National Academy of Public Administration.

298 Public Administration Review • July/August 2000, Vol. 60, No. 4

Genres Help Writers Achieve Their Goals

Typically, genres develop to help writers accomplish a general purpose. Informative essays, for example, help writers demonstrate their knowledge to an instructor, while informative articles in newspapers, magazines, and newsletters help writers share information and ideas with their readers. Opinion columns and letters to the editor, in contrast, are often used by writers to advance arguments.

Documents in a particular genre are usually written for the same general purpose. Documents that follow a particular genre also tend to use similar writing conventions, such as level of formality or the type of evidence used to support a point. For example, newspaper obituaries are usually formal and serious, while e-mail messages are often relaxed and informal. Scholarly articles almost always refer to the source of evidence offered to support their points, while letters to the editor sometimes offer no evidence at all. In addition, documents in a particular genre often use similar design elements. Academic essays, for example, are usually written with wide margins and double-spaced lines, while magazine articles often use columns and make extensive use of color and illustrations.

In most cases, genres are social inventions, shaped by the social and cultural contexts from which they emerge. When writers and readers form a community—such as an academic discipline, a professional association, or a group that shares an interest in a particular topic or activity—they begin to develop characteristic ways of communicating with one another. Over time, members of a community will come to agreement about the type of evidence that is generally accepted to support arguments, the style in which sources should be cited, and how documents should be designed and organized. Over time, the specific needs of a community will result in subtle but important changes to a genre. If you've ever read informative articles in magazines for automobile or motorcycle enthusiasts, for example, you'll notice that they differ in important ways from informative articles in magazines about contemporary music. Similarly, you'll find important differences in the organization and evidence used in scholarly articles written by diverse groups of scholars such as sociologists and chemists.

As the needs and interests of a community change genres will change to reflect those needs and interests. In some cases, a genre will change. Academic essays, for example, might begin to make greater use of color and illustrations. In other cases, a single genre might evolve into several distinct genres. For an example of this, take a look at the Web. As the number of readers on the Web has exploded over the past decade, Web sites have become far more specialized. In the mid-1990s, most Web sites looked alike. Today, you'll find characteristic differences among Web sites published by individuals, companies, government agencies, and special-interest groups.

To learn more about genre and design, pay attention to the wide range of documents you encounter in your reading. The most important part of this process is simply being aware that genres exist. By thinking about how writers use different types of documents, you'll take the first steps toward using genres to achieve your own purposes and consider your readers.

Practice: Analyze a Genre

For this exercise, analyze the Montana *Campus Corps Connections* newsletter and respond to the following prompts:

The Montana *Campus Corps Connections* newsletter informs readers of news and initiatives related to the program. You can view the complete newsletter at bedfordstmartins.com/ conversation

CAMPUS CORPS CONNECTIONS

A Montana Campus Corps publication

Volume 4, Issue 1   **November 2007**

Montana | **Campus Compact**

Building Engaged Citizens Conference 2007

Participating Campuses:

- Blackfeet Community College
- Carroll College
- Flathead Valley Community College
- Fort Belknap College
- Fort Peck Community College
- MSU-Billings
- MSU-Bozeman
- MSU-Northern
- Montana Tech
- Salish Kootenai College
- UM-Missoula

On September 21-23, Montana Campus Compact hosted the Building Engaged Citizens Conference (BEC) in Billings, MT. The conference was an opportunity for Campus Corps, Montana Campus Compact VISTA and Raise Your Voice members from across Montana to meet, network, and participate in exciting and relevant training and leadership development. BEC participants are comprised of individuals who are increasingly taking on meaningful roles as community volunteers, activists and citizens, and the conference is designed to support and strengthen their work.

Ron Tussing, the Mayor of Billings, led the '07-'08 Campus Corps swearing-in ceremony.

Our Mission:
Montana Campus Corps is an AmeriCorps program that engages college students in meeting community-identified needs.

Shining Moments of Benevolence

Approximately seventy Campus Corps members took the AmeriCorps pledge at an evening swearing-in ceremony at Riverfront Park in Billings. Following the ceremony, the new class of members enjoyed a hearty barbeque dinner. As the crowd began to disperse, the Carroll College Campus Corps team, including Heather Hass, Jaimie Hedrick, Chrystine Miller and Tyler Evilsizer, along with the Billings Team Leader, McKenzie Clapper, noticed that there was enough leftover food

to feed the entire crowd again. When they saw all the food that could potentially go to waste, the group thought about who could benefit from a warm meal. McKenzie, who recently moved to the Billings area, remembered the regular congregation of homeless people in the downtown area. This sparked the team into action; they took the food to people on the streets in downtown Billings. The recipients of the warm meal were very appreciative. Jaimie summed up the

experience by saying, "Our AmeriCorps positions are about direct service, and giving back to our communities, but there is something different about spontaneous interactions with those in need. The unplanned acts of service seem to mean so much more to me. I suppose that is because they truly come from the heart".

1. **Writing style.** Is the newsletter written in a formal or an informal style? Somewhere in between? How would you describe the relationship that the authors of the newsletter's articles attempt to establish with readers?

2. **Evidence.** What sort of evidence is used in the newsletter? Why do you think articles in the newsletter use this kind of evidence?

3. **Organization.** How is the newsletter organized? Did you find it easy to follow? Difficult? Somewhere in between? Why?

4. **Citation style.** Are sources cited in the newsletter? If so, how are the sources cited — in a works cited list, in footnotes, in the text itself? Why do you think the author cites (or doesn't cite) sources in this way?

5. **Design.** Briefly identify the design elements used in the document, such as columns, photographs, and text formatting. (For more information on design elements, see Chapter 18.) How does the design of the document set up expectations about its content? To what extent does the design help or hinder your ability to read and understand the document?

@ Download or print this Practice activity at bedfordstmartins.com/conversation.

In Summary: Reading to Write

○ Think of writing as a form of conversation (p. 4).

○ Understand writing situations (p. 13).

○ Learn about genre and design (p. 18).

02 Getting Started

In the most general sense, getting started on a writing project involves "listening in" on conversations and choosing one that interests you. To begin this process, analyze your assignment and generate ideas about potential topics. Then spend time learning about the conversations that interest you most.

How Can I Analyze an Assignment?

Writers in academic and professional settings usually work in response to an assignment. You might be given general guidelines; you might be asked to choose a topic within a general subject area; or you might be given complete freedom. However, no matter how much freedom you have, your assignment will provide important clues about what your instructor and your other readers will expect.

Analyzing an assignment involves assessing your writing situation, identifying requirements and limitations, and looking for opportunities. On page 29, you'll find a typical assignment for a writing course. As you'll discover in the pages that follow, a close reading of an assignment can reveal not only its basic requirements and goals but also useful information about your purpose, readers, sources, and context. Most important, a close reading can help you develop a successful response to the assignment.

Assess Your Writing Situation

What you write about depends on your writing situation—your purpose, readers, sources, and context. In many cases, your assignment will identify or suggest these elements for you. If it doesn't, take some time to think about why you're writing, who will read your document, what kinds of sources you might use, and what factors will influence you and your readers.

DETERMINE YOUR PURPOSE

Every writer has a purpose, or reason, for writing. In fact, most writers have multiple purposes (see p. 13). In Chapters 5 to 10, you'll explore a range of goals that you might be asked to pursue: to reflect, to inform, to analyze, to evaluate, to solve problems, and to convince or persuade. You will also bring your personal goals to a writing project. If you are working on an assignment for a class, for instance, your purposes might include learning something new, improving your writing skills, convincing others to adopt your point of view, and getting a good grade. If you are an employee working on a progress report, your purposes might include performing well enough to earn a promotion and gaining valuable experience in project management.

DETERMINE WHO YOUR READERS ARE AND WHY THEY WOULD READ YOUR DOCUMENT

Your assignment might identify your readers, or audience, for you. If you are working on a project for a class, one of your most important readers will be your instructor. You might also have other readers, such as your classmates, people who have a

Essay Assignment

For this assignment, you'll identify and describe a problem that affects the community in which you grew up. Your purpose will be to inform members of your community about how the problem affects them, the consequences of not addressing the problem, and the costs of addressing it effectively.

> The choice of topic is left to the writer, although some general guidelines are provided. The purpose is discussed here and in the requirements section.

Due Date: October 1, at the beginning of class

Your Readers: Your audience will be the members of your community. I will also be a reader, but my primary role will be to consider how well you've addressed the members of your community.

> The assignment specifies the readers and defines the role the instructor will play as a reader.

Essay Requirements: Your essay should be between 750 and 1,000 words in length. Your essay should

> The genre is identified as a standard academic essay.

- introduce the problem you are addressing

- describe the potential effects of the problem

- propose a solution to the problem

- estimate the costs of putting the solution into effect

- support your points with evidence (personal experience, information from sources)

- clearly document your sources following MLA style

> The repeated use of the words *problem* and *solution* indicates that the writer's purpose is to write a problem-solving essay.

Conclude your essay by doing more than simply summarizing what you've said so far. In general, try to leave your readers with something to think about after they've read your essay. Finally, revise to clarify and strengthen your argument, and edit to remove errors in spelling, grammar, and mechanics so that your writing is clear and readable.

> Aside from the due date, requirements are listed in a separate section. Key requirements include length, content, and documentation system.

Format: Please submit your essay in a folder clearly labeled with your name and e-mail address. Your folder should contain the following:

- the final draft of your essay, formatted with one-inch margins, double-spaced lines, and a readable (e.g., not italic or script) 12-point font

- rough drafts of your essay

- a list of additional sources you consulted as you created your essay

- the homework you completed as you worked on your essay

- the workshop comments you received from your classmates on drafts of your essay

- your workshop comments on your classmates' essays

> The assignment requires students to turn in not only the final essay but also rough drafts, home-work, and comments on classmates' drafts.

∟ Essay Assignment

professional or personal interest in your topic, or, if your project will be published, the readers of a particular newspaper, magazine, or Web site. If you are writing in a business or professional setting, your readers might include supervisors, customers, or other people associated with the organization. The assignment on the previous page identifies both the members of a specific community and the instructor as important readers. In some cases, you might be asked to define your own audience. As you consider possible topics, ask yourself which topics these readers would be most interested in learning about.

Regardless of who your readers are, remember that they aren't empty vessels waiting to be filled with information. They will have their own purposes for reading what you write, so try to figure out what they need and expect from your writing. If the topic you ultimately select doesn't meet your readers' purposes, they will probably stop reading.

CONSIDER THE ROLE OF SOURCES

Most documents are influenced by the work of other writers. In some cases, you'll refer to those sources directly and cite them in your document. In other cases, your understanding of a topic will be shaped by what you read or learn through interviews, observation, surveys, or other forms of field research (see p. 506).

As you analyze an assignment, consider the role sources will play in your writing project, and be sure to understand any requirements regarding sources. Determine whether you'll need to cite a minimum or a maximum number of sources and whether you're required to use a specific documentation system, such as the system created by the Modern Language Association (MLA) or the American Psychological Association (APA). The assignment on page 29, for instance, asks writers to draw on personal experience and published sources for evidence and requires MLA-style documentation. It does not, however, limit the number or types of sources writers may use.

Whether or not an assignment provides guidelines for sources, ask what you'll need to learn to complete your project, and then identify potential information resources. You can read more about finding and using sources in Part Three of this book.

IDENTIFY THE GENRE AND CONTEXT

Context refers to the physical, social, and cultural settings that shape the writing and reading of a document. As you identify the context for your writing project, consider how it will affect your decisions as a writer. Ask, for example, whether your document will be read in print or online. And ask whether it will need to take the form of a particular genre (or type of document). Many assignments in writing courses involve writing various types of essays, such as the problem-solving essay assignment on page 29. In addition, you might be asked to write reports, Web sites, articles, opinion columns, letters to the editor, multimedia presentations, brochures, or flyers. The genre of your document will affect not only the kinds of topics you choose but also how you design your document.

You should also consider the social and cultural context that will shape how your readers read your document. Like you, your readers will be aware of recent events and influenced by the cultural context in which they live. Ask how these contexts might shape their understanding of and attitudes toward a topic.

Note Requirements and Limitations

If you are working on a writing project for a class, examine the requirements of your assignment, including

- the required length or word count
- the project due date
- the number and type of sources you must use (electronic, print, and field)
- any suggested or required resources
- specific requirements about the organization of your document (a title page, introduction, body, conclusion, works cited list, and so on)
- expected documentation format (such as MLA, APA, *Chicago*, or CSE)
- any intermediate reports or activities due before you turn in the final document (such as thesis statements, notes, outlines, and rough drafts)

The assignment shown on page 29 lists its requirements in a separate section. In some cases, you'll need to read the assignment carefully to identify all of its requirements.

In addition to requirements, you might also face certain limitations, such as lack of access to sources or lack of time to work.

Considering your requirements and limitations will help you weigh the potential drawbacks of choosing a particular topic. In the face of a looming due date or a limited word length, you might find that you need to narrow the scope of a topic significantly.

Recognize Opportunities

Sometimes writers get so wrapped up in the requirements and limitations of an assignment that they overlook their opportunities. As you think about possible topics, ask yourself whether you can take advantage of opportunities such as

- access to a specialized or particularly good library
- personal experience with and knowledge about a topic
- access to experts on a topic

Recognizing your opportunities can help you take advantage of important resources and, in the long run, can save you a lot of time and effort.

Working Together: Analyze an Assignment

Work together with your classmates to analyze your assignment. Use the following prompts to guide your analysis:

1. **Determine whether a topic has been assigned.** If a topic has been assigned, look for indications of how you should address the topic. If you are allowed to choose your own topic, look for indications of what the instructor considers an appropriate topic.

2. **Examine the assignment for discussions of purpose.** What purposes might a writer pursue through this assignment? Identify your own purposes — personal, professional, academic — and those of your classmates for working on this assignment.

3. **Identify and describe potential readers.** Describe their likely needs, interests, backgrounds, and knowledge of the topic. Ask why readers would want to read your document.

4. **Determine the role of sources in your document.** Identify potential sources of information that will help you learn about your topic. Then determine whether you need to cite a minimum number of sources or use a specific documentation system, such as MLA or APA.

5. **Identify the context in which the document will be written and read.** For example, will your document be read in print or online? How have historic or recent events shaped your readers' understanding of and attitudes toward your topic?

6. **Identify the genre, if any, defined by the assignment.** If the assignment leaves the choice of genre open, identify genres that are well suited to the assignment.

7. **Understand requirements and limitations.** Look for specific requirements and limitations, such as document length and due date, that will affect your ability to address a particular topic. Identify other requirements, such as number of sources, document structure, documentation system, and intermediate assignments or rough drafts.

8. **List potential opportunities.** Identify opportunities that might save time or enhance the quality of the document.

@ Download or print this Working Together activity at bedfordstmartins.com/conversation.

How Can I Find Interesting Conversations?

Writers aren't mindless robots who create documents without emotion or conviction — or at least they shouldn't be. One of the most important things you can do as a writer is look for a conversation that interests you and will keep you motivated as you work on your writing project.

Analyzing an assignment will help you think of general topics that interest you and that fit your writing situation. Even if you are assigned a specific topic, you can almost always find an approach that will engage you and still accomplish the goals of the assignment. In fact, most successful writers have learned to deal with "boring" topics by creating personal connections to them. Essentially, they try to convince themselves that they actually care about a topic — and in many cases, they end up developing a genuine interest. You can do this by generating ideas and asking questions about potential topics, taking care not to rule out any topics until you've given them a chance.

Generate Ideas

You can generate ideas about possible topics of conversation by using prewriting activities such as brainstorming, freewriting, looping, clustering, and mapping. These activities are useful not only for deciding which topics interest you most but also for identifying a focus that is well suited to your writing situation.

BRAINSTORM

Brainstorming involves making a list of ideas as they occur to you. This list should not consist of complete sentences — in fact, brainstorming is most successful when you avoid censoring yourself. Although you'll end up using only a few of the ideas you generate during brainstorming, don't worry about weeding out the less promising ideas until later.

Brainstorming sessions usually respond to a specific question, such as "What interests me personally about this project?" or "Why would anyone care about _____?" For example, Lisa, a student taking a writing course in a small college in eastern Kentucky, had long been interested in efforts to restore land damaged by coal mining in the area where she'd grown up. As she considered this topic, she brainstormed the following list in response to the question, "What will happen if the land is not restored?"

continued erosion

streams won't get healthy

wildlife habitat won't be restored

tourist destination? forget it

no jobs after coal mining ends

This brainstorming list helped Lisa recognize that her topic might range from environmental concerns to impacts on tourism to job loss.

FREEWRITE

Freewriting involves writing full sentences quickly, without stopping and—most important—without editing what you write. You might want to start with one of the ideas you generated in your brainstorming activity, or you could begin your freewriting session with a prompt, such as "I am interested in _____ because . . ." Some writers set a timer and freewrite for five, ten, or fifteen minutes; others set a goal of a certain number of pages and keep writing until they meet that goal.

After brainstorming about the consequences of not restoring land damaged by coal mining, Lisa freewrote about her readers' purposes and interests.

> People at home are interested mostly in keeping their jobs. They're not real thrilled with environmentalists coming in and messing things up. The land's been messed up for a long time, and most people are used to it. So their real focus is on making enough money to get by, keeping schools funded, taking care of economic needs. I don't think they want to give up much to restore the land. But that might be because they don't see the real problem. If they could see that there are real benefits to restoring the land, they wouldn't mind doing it. The question is how to get them to see the benefits. Maybe the best thing is to let them know what might happen if things don't change — erosion, no animals to hunt, silted-up creeks and streams, and nothing left after the coal runs out.

To freewrite, write as much as you can, don't pause to consider whether your sentences are "good" or "bad," and don't pay attention to details such as spelling and grammar. (Hint: If you find it difficult to write without editing, try blindwriting— freewriting on a computer with the monitor turned off.) If all of this work results in a single good idea, your freewriting session will be a success.

LOOP

Looping is an alternative form of freewriting. During a looping session, you write for a set amount of time (five minutes works well) and then read what you've written. As you read, identify one key idea in what you've written, and then freewrite again with this new idea as your starting point. If you're using a word-processing program, you can copy the sentence and paste it below your freewriting; if you are writing by hand, highlight or draw a circle around the sentence. Repeat the looping process as needed to refine your ideas.

Lisa's looping session built on the last sentence of her freewriting exercise.

> Maybe the best thing is to let them know what might happen if things don't change — erosion, no animals to hunt, silted-up creeks and streams, and nothing left after the coal runs out. And the coal companies will be gone when the coal runs out, so they won't be able to help out with the cost of reclaiming the land. Best to work on the problem now, because we won't have the coal companies to help later. Maybe if people could see that the coal companies can be part of the solution, things will move forward.

CLUSTER

Clustering involves putting your ideas about a topic into graphic form. As you map out the relationships among your ideas, clustering can help you gain a different perspective on a topic. It can also help you generate new ideas.

Lisa created the cluster on page 36 to explore the topic of restoring lands damaged by coal mining.

To cluster ideas about a topic, place your main idea, or a general topic that interests you, at the center of a page. Jot down key ideas—such as subcategories, causes and effects, or reasons supporting an argument—around the main idea. Then create clusters of ideas that branch out from the key ideas. In these clusters, list groups of related ideas, evidence, effects, causes, consequences—in short, ideas that are related to your key ideas.

MAP

Mapping is similar to clustering in that it places related ideas about a topic in graphic form. Unlike clustering, however, mapping helps you define the relationships among those ideas. The practice is especially helpful if you are exploring a topic in terms of causes and effects, sequences of events, costs and benefits, or advantages and disadvantages. For example, you might create a map to predict what would happen if cigarette taxes were doubled. Or you might create a map to identify factors that led to an oil spill along the Oregon coast.

Lisa used her word-processing program to create a map that explored the effects of reclaiming lands damaged by coal mining (see p. 37).

To map a topic, place your main idea at the top of a page. If you are looking at more than one aspect of a topic, such as costs and benefits, list as many relationships as you can think of. If you are looking at causes and effects, start with a single effect. Then explore the topic by identifying related causes and effects, costs and benefits, advantages and disadvantages, and so on. For example, if you are mapping a topic

Lack of awareness of damage?
Lower profits for coal companies
Land will regenerate naturally?
Potential loss of jobs
Inadequate technology?

Mine closures
Potential job loss
Loss of taxes for schools
Loss of tax base

Reasons for not reclaiming

Costs of reclaiming

Lisa has listed a central idea and four key areas.

Land damaged by mining

Key areas are linked to clusters of related ideas.

Costs of not reclaiming

Benefits of reclaiming

Silted-up streams
Unsightly landscape
Unhealthy ecosystem
Lost tourism revenue
Erosion
Damage to groundwater?

New jobs
Improve habitat for wildlife
Potential tourist revenues
Better views
Healthier streams
Forests return
Agriculture returns

⌐ A cluster of ideas about the causes, costs, and benefits of reclaiming land damaged by mining

using causes and effects, treat each effect as a new cause by asking yourself, "If this happened, what would happen next?" Then use arrows to show the consequences. If you are mapping a topic using costs and benefits, show groups of costs and identify the relationships among them.

Main Idea: Costs and Benefits of Reclaiming Land Damaged by Mining

Costs

Mine closures
Potential job losses

Consequences: Loss of tax base

Results:

Lower funding for schools
Lower funding for town and country services

Benefits

Regrowth of forests
Healthier streams
Improved habitat for wildlife

Consequences:
Tourists begin visiting area
Vacation homes built
Agriculture returns

Result: New jobs

Result: Increased tax base

Result: Higher standard of living

> The writer listed a central idea and then mapped its costs and benefits. The map shows two sequences of effects and causes.

t. A map exploring the effects of reclaiming land damaged by mining

Ask Questions

When you have completed your brainstorming, freewriting, looping, clustering, and mapping activities, review what you've written. In all likelihood, these idea-generating techniques have provided you with a useful list of ideas for a topic. You can select the strongest candidate and generate additional ideas by asking questions. Writers often ask questions to

- define a topic
- evaluate a topic
- consider goals
- explore potential outcomes
- consider appropriate courses of action
- compare and contrast topics
- understand causes and effects
- solve problems

Each of the chapters in Part Two provides a series of questions that will help you narrow your focus and explore ideas for a particular kind of writing project. You can create your own exploratory questions by pairing question words—*what, why, when, where, who, how, would, could, should*—with words and phrases that focus on different aspects of a topic.

For example, Lisa generated the following questions to explore and focus her topic of reclaiming mine land:

Who would benefit from reclaiming mine lands?

What will happen if mine lands are reclaimed?

Where has mine land been reclaimed?

Why do opponents of reclaiming mine lands believe it is a bad choice?

When is it cost-effective to reclaim mine lands?

How can we minimize the costs of reclaiming mine lands?

Would it be possible to phase in the reclamation of mine lands?

Should the state fund the reclamation of mine lands?

Could mine lands return to a natural state without human intervention?

As you ask questions, be aware of the role you are adopting as a writer. If you are writing an informative essay, for example, the words *what*, *when*, and *where* are appropriate. If you are conducting an analysis, you might use the words *why* and *how*. If you are interested in goals and outcomes, try the words *would* and *could*. If you want to determine an appropriate course of action, ask questions using the word *should*.

The questions you ask will probably change as you learn more about a topic, so it's best to think of them as flexible and open-ended. By continuing to ask questions that reflect your growing understanding of a topic, you can build a solid foundation for your own contribution to the conversation.

Practice: Find a Topic That Interests You

Generate ideas for possible writing topics by conducting at least three of the prewriting activities described on pages 33–39: brainstorming, freewriting, looping, clustering, mapping, and asking questions. Then use your responses to the following prompts to decide which topic interests you most.

1. What are the three most important topics I have identified so far?

2. Of these topics, which one will best sustain my interest in this project?

3. Which one will best help me achieve my purposes as a writer?

4. Which one will best address my readers' needs, interests, and backgrounds?

5. Which one best fits the requirements of my assignment?

6. Which one is most appropriate for the type of document I plan to write?

7. Which one has the fewest limitations?

8. Which one allows me to best take advantage of opportunities?

9. Based on these answers, the topic I want to choose is _____.

@ Download or print this Practice activity at bedfordstmartins.com/conversation.

How Can I "Listen In" on Written Conversations?

If you've chosen a topic that appeals to more than a few individuals, it is almost certainly the subject of several ongoing conversations. Listening in on these conversations allows you to survey various aspects of the topic. Written conversations about the broad topic of federal regulation of new drugs, for example, might focus on issues such as childhood vaccination, prevention of birth defects, and the treatment of diseases such as AIDS and Alzheimer's. Each of these issues, in turn, might be addressed by different groups of people, often for quite different purposes. Childhood vaccination, for instance, might draw the attention of parents worried about potential side effects, health officials concerned about epidemics, and researchers interested in the growth of drug-resistant diseases. In other words, not only do conversations focus on different aspects of a topic, but the same aspect of a topic can also be discussed by different groups of people.

Listening in on these conversations allows you to determine which group you want to join. To make that decision, you don't have to engage in a full-blown research project. Instead, you only have to learn enough about a conversation to decide whether the topic and the people discussing it intrigue you. Think of listening in on a conversation as a preliminary exploration of a topic. You'll want to invest only enough time in the process to determine whether you want to learn more. At this early stage in your writing project, you are essentially eavesdropping in order to find the conversation you want to join.

By generating ideas about potential topics, you've already begun to identify conversations that might be well suited to your writing situation. To learn more about each conversation and to figure out what—or whether—you might contribute to it, "listen in" by discussing your ideas with others, observing a situation firsthand, and finding and reviewing published sources.

Discuss the Topic with Others

Discussing your writing project can provide valuable insights that you might not be able to gain on your own. Talking with an instructor, a supervisor, or a librarian can help you identify resources to learn about an ongoing conversation. You can find out what other people think about a topic by conducting interviews (see p. 186). You can gather information and insights by corresponding with experts in a subject area or with people who have been affected by a topic (see p. 508). You can even get a sense of how readers might respond to your ideas by visiting an Internet chat room devoted to discussion of serious topics (see p. 498).

Observe the Topic Firsthand

Observing something for yourself allows you to learn about a topic without filtering it through the interpretation of other writers. Lisa, for example, spent time walking through abandoned mine lands, writing her observations in a notebook and taking photos. Visiting the sites provided her with valuable firsthand impressions that allowed her to weigh her own understanding of the issue against the ideas advanced by other writers.

If you are considering a topic that focuses on a particular place, event, or activity, you might want to conduct one or more observations. If you're interested in a local issue, for example, you might attend a community meeting and listen to what people have to say. If you're interested in the impact of parental involvement in youth sports, you might spend time at a youth soccer game. If you're interested in connections between fast food and health issues, you might spend time watching people place their orders at a fast-food restaurant. For more on planning and conducting observations, see page 129.

Read What Others Have Written

Even if you are familiar with a topic, you need to learn as much about it as you can before you begin to write. Reading what others have written about a topic will help you gather new information and ideas; it is also an important step in identifying conversations and determining which ones interest you. You can locate relevant sources by searching online library catalogs, browsing library shelves, visiting the periodicals room, searching databases, searching and browsing the Web, and reviewing online discussion venues (see Chapter 12 for a detailed discussion of how to conduct searches).

- **Online library catalog.** Library catalogs allow you to search for sources by title, author, and subject words. Before you begin your search, generate a list of words and phrases that are related to the topic you want to explore.

- **Library shelves.** Once you've located a relevant book or periodical through your library's online catalog, you can usually find other relevant sources on the same or nearby shelves. If you locate a source that seems particularly useful, review its works cited list, footnotes, endnotes, or in-text citations for related sources. Then find and review these cited sources.

- **Periodicals room.** Most libraries have a dedicated space where you can find the latest magazines, newspapers, and scholarly journals. (Some libraries keep newspapers in a separate area.) Because it takes time to index and add new articles to databases, you can get a head start on the latest news and information about a topic by browsing periodicals.

- **Databases.** Databases organize information as records (or entries) on a particular topic. You can search these records just as you would search an online library catalog. If you have difficulty locating databases or aren't sure which databases are appropriate for a topic, ask a reference librarian for assistance.

- **The Web.** Search sites and directories allow you to locate a great deal of information about a topic—although not all of it will be reliable. Browsing the Web, in contrast, is similar to browsing the shelves in a library. That is, rather than searching with keywords, you can follow links from one site to related sites. Look for a page on the site with a name such as "Related Links."

- **Online discussion venues.** E-mail lists, newsgroups, and Web discussion forums can be excellent sources of information (as well as the source of some outrageous misinformation). Because most online discussion venues are unmoderated—that is, anything sent to them is published—you'll find everything from expert opinions to the musings of people who know little or nothing about a topic. If you read posted messages with a bit of skepticism, however, you can begin to learn about the issues surrounding a topic.

Focus Your Attention

As you learn about a topic, you'll begin the process of focusing on a specific issue—a point of disagreement, uncertainty, concern, or curiosity that is being discussed by a community of readers and writers. Look for patterns in the information, ideas, and arguments you encounter.

- **Notice central concepts.** When several sources refer to the same idea, you can assume that this information is central to the topic. Noticing this repetition can help familiarize you with some of the important issues being discussed about your topic.

- **Find broad themes.** Sources that discuss the same general theme are most likely involved in the same conversation. By recognizing these broad themes, you can identify some of the key conversations taking place about your topic.

- **Look for disagreements.** Some sources will explicitly indicate that they disagree with the arguments, ideas, or information in other sources. If you look for explicit statements of disagreement, you can identify a group of sources that are engaged in conversation with one another.

- **Recognize recurring voices.** As you read sources, you might find that some authors write frequently about your topic or that some authors are frequently cited by other writers. These authors might have significant experience or expertise related to the topic, or they might represent particular perspectives on the topic. Stay alert for these recurring voices.

As you review the conversations you've identified, ask what interests you most about each one. At a minimum, you'll want to choose a focus that interests you and is appropriate for your assignment. Ideally, this focus will also match up well with the purposes, needs, interests, and backgrounds of your readers.

Once you've selected an appropriate conversation, you'll be ready to learn more about it and determine what you want to say.

Practice: Choose a Conversation

Take the topic you selected at the end of the activity on page 39, and listen in on a few of the conversations taking place about it. You might discuss this topic with other people, conduct an observation, or read a few sources that address your topic. Identify the three most promising conversations you've found. To choose among the conversations, ask the following questions about each one:

1. Will joining this conversation help me accomplish my purpose?

2. Do my readers need to be exposed to this conversation?

3. Do my readers want to be exposed to this conversation?

4. How will my readers' backgrounds affect their reactions to this conversation?

@ Download or print this Practice activity at bedfordstmartins.com/conversation.

How Can I Prepare for a Successful Writing Project?

You can improve your chances of successfully completing a writing project by taking ownership of your writing project, familiarizing yourself with the writing process, and learning to manage your sources and your time.

Take Ownership

Successful writers have a strong personal investment in what they write. Sometimes this investment comes naturally. You might be interested in a topic, committed to achieving your purposes as a writer, intrigued by the demands of writing for a particular audience, or looking forward to the challenges of writing a new type of document, such as a Web site or a magazine article. At times, however, you need to create a sense of personal investment by looking for connections between your interests and your writing project. This can be a challenge, particularly when you've been assigned a project that normally wouldn't interest you.

The key to investing yourself in a project you wouldn't normally care about is to make it your own. Look for ways in which your project can help you pursue your personal, professional, and academic interests. Consider how it might help you meet new people or develop new skills. Or look for opportunities associated with the project, such as learning how to build arguments or how to design documents. Your goal is to find something that appeals to your interests and helps you grow as a writer.

To take ownership of a writing project, carry out the following activities:

- **Explore academic connections.** Is the writing project relevant to work you are doing in other classes or, more generally, in your major or minor? Look for ways that working on this project might help you develop useful academic skills or might expose you to information, ideas, or arguments that allow you to make progress as a student.

- **Consider personal connections.** Sometimes your personal interests—such as hobbies and other activities—can spark an interest in the writing project. Do any of your experiences relate to the project in some way? Will working on this project allow you to develop skills and abilities that might help you in your personal life?

- **Look for professional connections.** Does the writing project have any relevance to the job you currently have or one day hope to have? Will working on this project help you develop skills or expose you to information, ideas, or arguments that might be relevant to your professional goals?

Understand That Writing Is a Process

Few writers complete a major writing project in a single sitting. In fact, most writers spend more time learning about and reflecting on a topic than they do drafting, reviewing, and revising a document. You can avoid frustration and increase your chances of success by understanding the writing processes that experienced writers typically use: finding and listening in on a conversation, developing ideas, preparing a draft, and reviewing and rewriting.

You can also avoid frustration by recognizing that every writer approaches his or her writing situation in a manner that reflects the unique demands of that situation. In fact, writers seldom follow precisely the same process each time they write. As you work on your writing, you will no doubt find yourself moving from one process to another, and then back again. In a given composing session, you might move from reading to collecting sources to drafting to experimenting with a new idea. It's best, as a result, to think of the composing processes described here as a set of guidelines rather than a fixed sequence of steps.

FIND A CONVERSATION AND LISTEN IN

Settling on a topic is often the most challenging part of a writing project. If you are assigned a general topic, consider which aspect of that topic might help you accomplish your purposes and those of your readers. If you can choose your own topic, spend some time thinking about your writing situation before deciding what you'll write about. In either case, be sure to listen in on written conversations about potential topics. You'll almost certainly find that some conversations are better suited to your writing situation than others.

Narrowing your focus is a critical point in your writing process. Once you've chosen a general conversation and identified a specific aspect of it that intrigues you, you can begin to collect information in earnest, read with a purpose, and take notes. See pages 33–43 for tips on generating ideas and listening in on written conversations. In Chapter 3, you'll learn how to read actively and evaluate sources. Part Three discusses strategies for gathering information and working with your sources.

DEVELOP YOUR IDEAS

After you have listened in on a conversation, you'll begin the process of developing your own contribution to the conversation. Depending on your purposes and the role you've adopted as a writer (see pp. 11–12), you'll find that different kinds of activities come into play as you shape your ideas. Each of the chapters in Part Two helps you work through these activities: observing and reflecting on a subject (Chapter 5), determining how to inform your readers (Chapter 6), analyzing a subject (Chapter 7), evaluating a subject (Chapter 8), defining and solving problems (Chapter 9), or convincing or persuading your readers (Chapter 10).

PREPARE A DRAFT

Drafting involves expressing your thoughts in written form. That process begins with defining your main point and organizing the relationships among the information, ideas, and arguments you've located in sources and formed on your own. In general, writers use all of the initial work they've done — collecting sources, reading critically, and developing ideas — as the basis for a first rough draft. Each chapter in Part Two guides you through the process of preparing a draft for a given writing project, and Part Four offers strategies for specific elements of drafting — such as forming a thesis, crafting paragraphs, integrating sources, writing introductions and conclusions, outlining, and writing with style.

Preparing your draft also involves planning its design. By understanding and applying the principles of document design — the use of visual elements such as fonts, color, page layout, and illustrations — you can make your writing project more effective and easier to understand. You can also ensure that any document you create is consistent with the conventions of a particular genre. Chapter 18 offers strategies for using design elements in your writing.

REVIEW AND REWRITE

After you have completed a rough draft, you begin the process of revision. Revising involves rethinking and re-envisioning your document. It focuses on such big-picture issues as whether the document you've drafted is appropriate for your writing situation, whether your argument is sound and well supported, and whether you've organized and presented your information, ideas, and arguments clearly.

Polishing and editing, the final stages of a writing project, focus on improving your style and assessing the effectiveness, accuracy, and appropriateness of the words and sentences in your document. During these final stages, you'll also make sure that you've given credit to the writers whose ideas you've used in your work and that you have fully documented your sources. Chapter 20 offers strategies for revising and editing your writing. Chapters 21 and 22 provide information about documenting sources.

Revising your essay often relies on peer-review activities conducted in collaboration with other writers. Chapter 4 discusses peer review and other collaborative activities. You'll also find peer-review guidelines in Chapters 5 to 10, as well as a wide range of "Working Together" activities throughout this book.

Create a Writer's Notebook

A writer's notebook — where you can keep the sources you collect along the way and record your thoughts, observations, and progress — can help you keep track of what you find and think about as you work on your project. A writer's notebook can take many forms:

- a notebook
- a word-processing file or a folder on your computer
- a folder or binder
- a set of note cards

- notes taken on a smartphone or a personal digital assistant
- a tape recorder or voice recorder

Although it might seem like extra work now, creating a writer's notebook at the beginning of your project will save you time in the long run.

The *Student Center for Joining the Conversation* at **bedfordstmartins.com/ conversation** can help you create your writer's notebook. You'll find electronic versions of the activities throughout this book. You'll also find bibliography tools that allow you to save and manage the information you collect as you work on your project.

Manage Your Time

Time management should be a high priority as you begin your writing project. Without adequate time management, you might, for example, spend far too much time collecting information and far too little time working with it. As you begin to think about your writing project, consider creating a project timeline. A project timeline can help you identify important milestones in your project and determine when you need to meet them.

Practice: Create a Project Timeline

In your writer's notebook, create a project timeline like the one shown here. The steps in your process might be slightly different, but most writing projects involve these general stages. As you create your timeline, keep in mind any specific deadlines given in your assignment, such as the dates when you must hand in first drafts and revised drafts.

Project Timeline

Activity	Start date	Completion date
• Analyze your assignment		
• Generate ideas		
• Collect and read potential sources		
• Choose a focus		
• Develop your ideas		
• Write a first draft		
• Review and revise your first draft		
• Write and revise additional drafts		
• Polish your final draft		
• Edit for accuracy and correctness		
• Finalize in-text citations and works cited list		

@ Download or print this Practice activity at bedfordstmartins.com/conversation.

In Summary: Getting Started

○ Get started by analyzing your assignment and assessing your writing situation (p. 28)

○ Generate ideas for finding conversations about interesting topics (p. 33)

○ Ask questions about the conversations you've found (p. 38)

○ Listen in on promising conversations by discussing your topic with others, observing the topic firsthand, and reading what others have written (p. 39)

○ Choose a conversation to join (p. 43)

○ Lay the foundation for a successful writing project by taking ownership of your project, understanding writing processes, creating a writer's notebook, and managing your time (p. 43)

03 Reading to Write

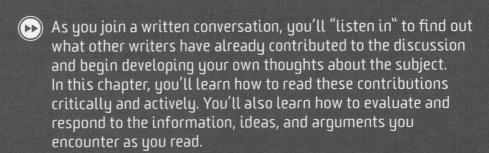 As you join a written conversation, you'll "listen in" to find out what other writers have already contributed to the discussion and begin developing your own thoughts about the subject. In this chapter, you'll learn how to read these contributions critically and actively. You'll also learn how to evaluate and respond to the information, ideas, and arguments you encounter as you read.

How Can I Read Critically?

Reading critically means reading with an attitude. It also means reading with your writing situation in mind. Through critical reading, you can quickly recognize the questions — points of disagreement, uncertainty, concern, or curiosity — that are under discussion in a written conversation as well as think about how you'll respond to one of these questions.

Read with an Attitude

As you learn about and prepare to contribute to a written conversation, both your point of view and your attitude are likely to change. Initially, your attitude might be one of curiosity. You'll note new information in your sources and mark key passages that provide insights. You'll adopt a more questioning attitude as you determine whether sources fit into the conversation or are reliable. Later, after you begin to draw conclusions about the conversation, you might take on a more skeptical attitude, becoming more aggressive in challenging the arguments made in sources than you were at first.

Growing familiarity with and understanding of an issue ———————→

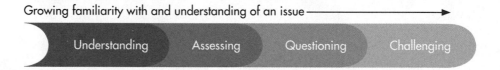

Understanding   Assessing   Questioning   Challenging

Regardless of where you are in your writing process, you should always adopt a critical attitude. Accept nothing at face value; ask questions; look for similarities and differences among the sources you read; examine the implications of what you read for your writing project; be on the alert for unusual information; and note relevant sources and information. Most important, be open to ideas and arguments, even if you don't agree with them. Give them a chance to affect how you think about the conversation you've decided to join.

Be Aware of Writing Situations

Reading critically involves approaching each source with an awareness not only of your own writing situation but also of the writing situation that shaped the source. Keep in mind that each document you read was written to accomplish a particular purpose and was intended for a particular group of readers. Realize that the physical, social, and cultural settings in which the document was produced affected how the writer presented information, ideas, and arguments. And remember that the writing situation that helped produce the source might differ significantly from your own writing situation.

As you read, remember what you are trying to accomplish. Your purpose will affect your assessment of the information, ideas, and arguments you encounter. Moreover, your readers' purposes, needs, interests, and backgrounds will affect your assessment of what you read.

Finally, and perhaps most important, remember that you are working on your writing project to make a contribution, to shape your readers' thinking about your subject. Avoid being overly deferential to the authors who have written before you. You should respect their work, but don't assume that their conclusions about the subject are the last word. Be prepared to challenge their ideas and arguments. If you don't do this, there's little point in writing, for you'll simply repeat the ideas of others instead of advancing your own.

What Strategies Can I Use to Read Actively?

Once you've thought about your writing situation and the writing situations that shaped your sources, you're ready to start reading actively. Reading actively means interacting with sources and considering them in light of the conversation you've decided to join. When you read actively, you might do one or more of the following:

- skim the source to get a general sense of what it's about
- write questions in the margins
- jot down your reactions
- identify key information, ideas, and arguments
- note how you might use information, ideas, and arguments in your document
- visually link one part of the source to another
- identify important passages for later rereading

To read actively, focus on three strategies: skimming, marking and annotating, and examining sources closely.

Identify the type of document to remind yourself of typical purposes, forms of evidence, and conventions of a genre. This page is part of an article from the professional journal *Adweek*.

Check the title (and table of contents, if one is provided) for cues about content.

Skim opening paragraphs to learn about the purpose and scope of the document.

Check headings and subheadings to learn about content and organization.

Case Study

The Marines And MySpace

How the 231-year-old institution got hip with CGC without losing control

BY WENDY MELILLO

Lt. Col. Mike Zeliff, a 21-year veteran of the U.S. Marines Corps, is seated in his office in Quantico, Va., surrounded by charts grouping potential recruits into categories like "rural heartlanders" or "disillusioned dreamers." His hair is closely cropped and his uniform neatly pressed to the point of crispness. In his hand is a copy of a *Wall Street Journal* article titled "MySpace, ByeSpace?"

Try reconciling the very buttoned-down Marines with social-networking site MySpace.com. Yet, that is exactly what Zeliff is doing. "On the Internet, you are always two clicks away from something bad," says Zeliff, assistant chief of staff for advertising at the USMC Recruiting Command. "We learned early on that if we advertise next to any unedited content, we could get caught up in an association that would not be appropriate for the Marine Corps."

Flirting with digital media may seem like the Wild West, where marketers must accept the influx of Web users into their territory and even hand over some of their hard-fought—and won—control. Not only have many advertisers come to accept the consumer as the new sheriff in town—witness Procter & Gamble CEO A.G. Lafley's speech at the annual meeting of the Association of National Advertisers in October—but some may forget there is room for negotiation, especially within the new consumer-generated environment. But, when the USMC began adopting new media for its recruiting campaigns, it did so cautiously—never willing to give up control of its brand—and along the way, the 231-year-old military institution convinced MySpace to work on its terms.

Just how the USMC keep a firm grip on its online profile on a popular site that solicits user comments and allows anyone to upload images is a story of risk, selectivity and a clear focus on the mission.

The USMC, which launched its MySpace profile in April, want the page to serve as a tool to drive interested 17- to 24-year-olds to the Marines.com Web site, where they can get more information and request to meet with a recruiter. It also knows what it doesn't want: to find itself entangled with content it can't control and that might tarnish its image.

The USMC is hardly alone in wanting to protect its brand—remember when Chevy ditched its contest after consumer-generated ads for the 2007 Tahoe showed how SUVs con-

IN CHARGE: Gunnery Sergeant Biggs appears as a drill leader in recent Marine Corps TV spots.

'We learned early on that ... we could get caught up in an association that would not be appropriate.' – LT. COL. MIKE ZELIFF

tributed to global warming? But Zeliff would be the first to admit the USMC is much more persnickety than many about it.

Passing the 'Blues Test'

When New York-based digital shop RMG Connect, which handles the Marines account, first suggested the idea of using MySpace in August 2005, the USMC subjected the site to what they call the "blues test." "Would I be proud to be in that context or at that event in my dress blues," Zeliff says. "We scrub any new advertising idea against whether we think it is an appropriate place to be."

MySpace certainly had the demographic the USMC was looking for. Of the 56 million

unique users in the U.S., 5.9 million are 15- to 24-year-olds who spend an average of 25 minutes on MySpace each day, according to comScore's Media Metrix.

But upon Zeliff's first look at the site, he was not inclined to don his dress blues. And at the time, MySpace was grappling with irate parents who were concerned the site wasn't doing enough to protect kids from sexual predators. So, although planning the profile began in '05, it wasn't until after the site hired a child-safety expert in April that Zeliff felt comfortable enough to launch the page.

"As aggressive as we will be when we know it's right, we are very slow to get to the point where we know it's right," he explains.

Skim captions of photos and figures, which often highlight important arguments, ideas, and information.

Look for pull quotes (quotations or passages called out into the margins or set in larger type) for a sense of the writer's main idea.

Read the first and last sentences of paragraphs to find key information

↑ **How to Skim a Print Document**

Skim for an Overview

Before investing too much time in a source, skim it. Skimming—reading just enough to get the general idea of what a source is about—can tell you a great deal in a short amount of time and is an important first step in reading a source critically. To skim sources, glance at surface elements without delving too deeply into the content.

Megan Martinez, a student working on an informative essay about social-networking sites such as Facebook and MySpace, used skimming to gain a quick overview of the information, ideas, and arguments that had been published on the subject. Using one of the databases available through her school's library, she found and skimmed an article in *Adweek* that explored the Marine Corps's use of MySpace for recruiting. She also skimmed a discussion of social networking and privacy on the University of Texas at Austin's Information Technology Services Web site.

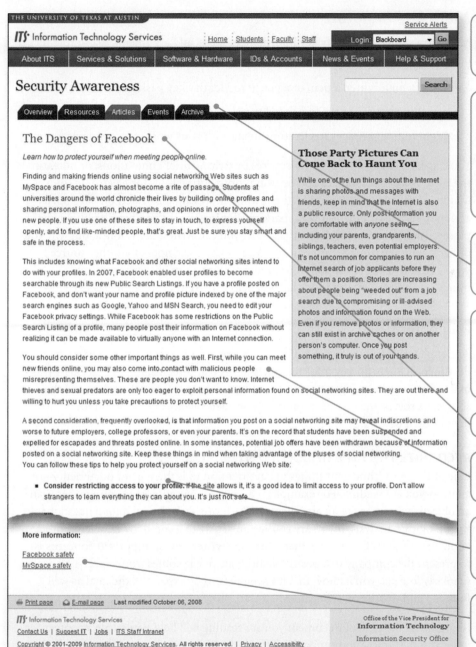

⌐ How to Skim a Web Page

Check the **page title** in the title bar of the browser for information about the purpose and content of the page.

Check the **URL** to learn about the purpose of a Web page — for instance, whether the page is part of a larger site. Extensions such as .com (for business), .edu (for education), and .gov (for government) can provide clues about the site's purpose.

Check the **navigation headers and menus** to learn about the site's content and organization.

Check for **information about the author** to learn about the author's background, interests, and purposes for writing the document.

Check the **title**.

Read the **first and last sentences of paragraphs** to find key information.

Scan for **boldface, colored, or italic text**, which might be used to emphasize important information.

Check for **links to other sites** to learn more about the issue.

Skim **captions of photos and figures**, which often highlight important arguments, ideas, and information.

Mark and Annotate

Marking a source to identify key information, ideas, and arguments is a simple yet powerful active-reading strategy. Common marking techniques include

- using a highlighter, a pen, or a pencil to identify key passages in a print source
- attaching notes or flags to printed pages
- highlighting passages in electronic texts with your word-processing program

You can further engage with your sources by writing brief annotations, or notes, in the margins of print sources and by using commenting tools for electronic sources. Many writers, such as Megan Martinez, whose notes are illustrated on page 55, use annotations in combination with marking. For instance, if you have highlighted a passage (marking) with which you disagree, you can write a brief note about why you disagree with the passage (annotating). You might make note of another source you've read that could support your argument, or you might write yourself a reminder to look for information that will help you argue against the passage.

Pay Attention

Although writing projects can differ greatly, you'll want to examine at least some documents closely for key information, ideas, and arguments. Noting various aspects of a written work during your active reading will help you better understand the source, its role in the conversation you've decided to join, and how you might use it in your own writing.

RECOGNIZE THE TYPE OF DOCUMENT

One of the most important things to pay attention to is the type of document—or genre—you are reading. For example, if a source is an opinion column rather than an objective summary of an argument, you're more likely to watch for a questionable use of logic or analysis. If you are reading an article in a company newsletter or an annual report, you'll recognize that one of the writer's most important concerns is to present the company in a positive light. If an article comes from a peer-reviewed scholarly journal, you'll know that it's been judged by experts in the field as well founded and worthy of publication.

Recognizing the type of document you are reading will help you create a context for understanding and questioning the information, ideas, and arguments presented in a source.

In America, we live in a paradoxical world of privacy. On one hand, teenagers reveal their intimate thoughts and behaviors online and, on the other hand, government agencies and marketers are collecting personal data about us. For instance, the government uses driver license databases to find "dead-beat dads" or fathers who are behind on their child support payments. Many government records have been turned into digital archives that can be searched through the Internet. Every time we use a shopping card, a retail store collects data about our consumer spending habits. Credit card companies can create even larger profiles of our shopping behaviors. Locked away on hundreds of servers is every minute detail of our daily lives from our individual buying preferences to personal thoughts. Galkin (1996) states: "Much of the information that people would like to keep secret is already lawfully in the possession of some company or government entity, and what we want is to stop further disclosure without authorization." [14] Many people may not be aware of the fact that their privacy has already been jeopardized and they are not taking steps to protect their personal information from being used by others.

In an age of digital media, do we really have any privacy?

In an age of digital media, do we really have any privacy? From Oscar Gandy's (1993) perspective, we probably do not. Using the metaphor of a Panopticon— an architectural design that allowed prisoners to be monitored by observers— Gandy argues that surveillance systems can exert the same type of control in contemporary culture. He states: "the panoptic sort is an antidemocratic system of control that cannot be transformed because it can serve no purpose other than that for which it is designed—the rationalization and control of human existence." [15] He calls for an agency that will be charged with ensuring the survival of privacy.

In post 9/11 America, government agencies appear to be doing the opposite. In 2005, the Department of Defense proposed to create a marketing and recruitment database to track students for military recruitment. According to the Electronic Frontier Foundation (2005), "Among the information kept on students were ethnicity, phone numbers, e-mail addresses, intended fields of study and extracurricular activities. The record system even included parents' attitudes about military recruitment." [16] But, the system was set up before notifying the public, a violation of the Privacy Act. Thus, establishing government agencies may not be a solution to the privacy dilemma. In a post 9/11 world, the U.S. government utilizes computer technology to exert some degree of control over its citizens, rather than protect their privacy.

Are we being tricked into thinking privacy is real?

Megan has highlighted key passages and has written notes in the margin.

Look this up.

Might be a good idea.

Check out the EFF.

Megan has identified a key point with highlighting and an annotation.

Can we trust the government?

⌐ Marking and Annotating a Source

IDENTIFY THE MAIN POINT

Most sources make a main point that you should pay attention to. An editorial in a local newspaper, for example, might urge voters to approve financing for a new school. An article might report a new advance in automobile emissions testing, or a Web page might emphasize the benefits of a new technique for treating a sports injury. Often the main point will be expressed in the form of a thesis statement. As you read critically, make sure you understand what the writer wants readers to accept, believe, or do as a result of reading the document.

FIND REASONS AND EVIDENCE THAT SUPPORT THE MAIN POINT

Once you've identified the main point, look for the reasons given to accept it. If an author is arguing, for instance, that English should be the only language used for official government business in the United States, that author might support his or her argument with the following reasons:

> The use of multiple languages erodes patriotism.
>
> The use of multiple languages keeps people apart — if they can't talk to one another, they won't learn to respect one another.
>
> The use of multiple languages in government business costs taxpayers money because so many alternative forms need to be printed.

Reasons can take a wide range of forms and are often presented in forms that appeal to emotions, logic, principles, values, or beliefs (see p. 439 in Chapter 10). As persuasive as these reasons might seem, they are only as good as the evidence offered to support them. In some cases, evidence is offered in the form of statements from experts on a subject or people in positions of authority. In other cases, evidence might include personal experience. In still other cases, evidence might include firsthand observations, excerpts from an interview, or statistical data.

In many cases, writers will present general conclusions based on evidence rather than a detailed discussion of the evidence. For example, a writer is much more likely to point out that more than half of the respondents to a survey agreed with a particular solution to a problem, rather than explain that 11 percent strongly disagreed, 22 percent disagreed, 7 percent had no opinion, 42 percent agreed, and 18 percent strongly agreed. When you use empirical evidence in a source, consider where the evidence comes from and how it is being used. If the information appears to be presented fairly, ask whether you might be able to use it to support your own ideas, and try to verify its accuracy by consulting additional sources.

A New Face for Schools

by Laura Lefkowits

Choice is ubiquitous in our lives. From on-demand TV programs to music downloads to "fast" gourmet restaurant chains that let customers build their ideal burrito, we like "having it our way."

This trend toward using technology to support individualization and customization has been immersing itself in our culture for the past decade, along with fears that such technologies would isolate us from one another, severely restricting face-to-face communications. Now, however, our fears are subsiding as another trend emerges—the rise of dozens of new voluntary communities, or social networks, that are bringing us together in unique, technology-driven ways.

Ask students about social networks, and they'll tell you that, whatever their geographic locale, they are a mere breath away from each other on Facebook. They regularly negotiate sales of everything from video games to car parts on eBay, prefer to share vacation memories and weekend photos on Flickr, and of course, create their alter-egos on MySpace.

The participation and active contribution of users is what makes these networks powerful, purposeful communities. My organization, the Denver-based Mid-continent Research for Education and Learning (McREL), believes these communities can have a powerful effect on student achievement in our 21st-century schools.

How "purposeful communities" work

In their work on school leadership, McREL researchers identify "purposeful community" as a critical component of successful education systems. In K–12 education, this community includes students, parents, teachers, school staff members, central office administrators and support personnel, the school board, other social agencies, and businesses.

A purposeful community has the collective ability to develop and use all available assets to accomplish purposes and produce outcomes that matter to all community members. Members come together to accomplish outcomes that individuals could not accomplish on their own, such as increasing graduation rates or reducing absenteeism.

Purposeful communities use both tangible assets (such as media centers and textbooks) and intangible assets (such as parent involvement and community support) to achieve their purposes. They also have agreed-upon processes for working together, which include both articulated and tacit operating principles governing their interactions.

These processes ensure the viability of the community and increase the likelihood of meeting shared goals. Finally, purposeful communities exhibit a sense of collective efficacy; they really do believe that together they can make a difference.

Compare the characteristics of a purposeful community to many social networking tools, and you find many similarities.

The power of social networks

Social networking sites are established for a specific purpose and depend on users adhering to agreed-upon processes to achieve common goals and to self-regulate on behalf of the community's interests. On Facebook (www.facebook.com), for example, you may only view another's profile if you have been "friended" by that person. This promotes a level of privacy with which all users are comfortable.

Most sites also have mechanisms that allow community members to flag posted items that they believe are inappropriate or outside the terms of use. For example, on the free classified advertising site Craig's List (www.craigslist.org), users looking for a new home can select a list of houses for sale by owner or a separate list for sale by agent. If an unscrupulous agent lists a house in the "for sale by owner" section, an observant user can flag the item, warning fellow users about the infraction. When an item receives a certain number of flags, it is pulled from the site.

Most "terms of use" statements do not specify each and every possible infraction warranting a flag. Rather, it is up to users themselves to set the standards, and over time, each virtual community develops its own set of tacit agreements and operating principles to guide its online behavior.

Perhaps the most powerful similarity between social networking and purposeful communities is the notion of collective efficacy. Writers such as Howard Rheingold and James Surowiecki have discussed the power inherent in online communities. Rheingold coined the term "smart mobs," and Surowiecki identified this phenomenon as the "wisdom of crowds." One only has to look at the impact of the Internet on the fundraising abilities of our presidential candidates to understand the strength inherent in a community of likeminded people joining together in a virtual world to support a shared goal.

And how can anyone deny the sense of collective efficacy at play this past March, when hundreds of California high school students, responding to text messages, walked out of school to protest budget cuts made by the school board that very morning? Students, particularly angered over the 50 percent cut to the sports programs, gathered at the high school and walked to the district offices carrying hastily prepared protest signs.

Ultimately, the students were invited to meet with school officials to discuss the possibility of initiating a ballot issue to raise funds for the sports program.

Social networking, school improvement

Could Facebook be a model for a 21st-century purposeful student community designed for school improvement? Possibly, but evidence suggests that education is not prepared to accept the dimension of purposeful communities offered by social networks.

In its 2007 report *Creating & Connecting*, the National School Boards Association revealed that 96 percent of students with online access spend nearly as much time using social networking technologies as watching television—nine hours and 10 hours respectively each week. Moreover, more than half of the respondents indicated that they use social networking tools to talk about education and collaborate on school projects, yet associated interviews with district leaders revealed that most K–12 school systems have strict rules against nearly all forms of online social networking while at school.

What's wrong with this picture?

Perhaps we should take a lesson from our students. They are, in fact, organically forming purposeful communities throughout cyberspace every day. Rather than restricting the most highly engaging form of communication and community-making available to students, what if schools embraced this technology and made use of its natural educational advantages?

True purposeful communities are composed of students, parents, teachers, and many others. Together, stakeholders' contributions to school improvement strategies could grow exponentially and virally in the same way one adds friends on Facebook. Imagine what the next generation of schools might look like when they are led by today's students, whose lives are filled with choice and whose communities are inherently purposeful.

Laura Lefkowits (llefkowits@mcrel.org) is vice president for policy and planning services at McREL. She served as an at-large member of the Denver Public Schools Board of Education from 1995 to 1999.

This article is adapted from one that originally appeared in the Winter 2008 issue of McREL's Changing Schools *(www.mcrel.org/topics/products/339).*

Reprinted with permission from American School Board Journal, *July 2008.*

Working Together: Identify Information in a Source

Working with a group of classmates, identify the main point, reasons, and evidence in Laura Lefkowits's article "A New Face for Schools."

1. **List the main point at the top of your page.** Determine what the author is asking you to know, believe, or do.

2. **Briefly list each reason to accept the main point** in the order in which it appears in the source. You might want to brainstorm lists individually based on your reading of the article and then share your ideas to create the group's list.

3. **Identify the most important evidence offered as proof for each reason.** Once you've agreed on the reasons, work together to identify the evidence used to support each reason.

@ Download or print this Working Together activity at **bedfordstmartins.com/conversation.**

CONSIDER ILLUSTRATIONS

A growing number of documents are using illustrations—photographs and other images, charts, graphs, tables, animations, audio clips, and video clips—in addition to text. Illustrations are typically used to demonstrate or emphasize a point, help readers better understand a point, clarify or simplify the presentation of a complex concept, or increase the visual appeal of a document. Illustrations can also serve as a form of argument by presenting a surprising or even shocking set of statistics or setting an emotional tone. As you read, be aware of the types of illustrations and the effects they produce. The types of illustrations you are likely to encounter include the following:

- **Photographs and images.** Photographs and other images, such as drawings, paintings, and sketches, are frequently used to set a mood, emphasize a point, or demonstrate a point more fully than is possible with text alone.

- **Charts and graphs.** Charts and graphs provide a visual representation of information. They are typically used to present numerical information more succinctly than is possible with text alone or to present complex information in a compact and more accessible form.

- **Tables.** Tables provide categorical lists of information. Like charts and graphs, they are typically used to make a point more succinctly than is possible with text alone or to present complex information in a compact form. Tables are frequently used to illustrate contrasts among groups, relationships among variables (such as income, educational attainment, and voting preferences), or change over time (such as growth in population during the past century).

- **Digital illustrations.** Digital publications, such as PowerPoint presentations and Web pages, can include a wider range of illustrations than print documents can. Illustrations such as audio, video, and animations differ from photographs, images, charts, graphs, and tables in that they don't just appear on the page—they do things.

You can read more about the uses of illustrations in Chapter 18.

RECORD NEW INFORMATION AND CHALLENGING IDEAS

As you read, mark and annotate passages that contain information that is new to you. In your writer's notebook, record new information in the form of a list or as a series of brief descriptions of what you've learned and where you learned it.

You might be tempted to ignore material that's hard to understand, but if you do, you could miss critical information. When you encounter something difficult, mark it and make a brief annotation reminding yourself to check it out later. Sometimes you'll learn enough from your continued reading that the passage won't seem as challenging when you come back to it. Sometimes, however, you won't be able to figure out a passage on your own. In that case, turn to someone else for help—your instructor, a librarian, members of an online forum or a newsgroup—or try searching a database, library catalog, or the Web using key words or phrases you didn't understand.

How Can I Evaluate Sources?

At the beginning of a writing project, you'll usually make quick judgments about the sources you come across. Skimming an article, a book, or a Web site (see p. 52) might be enough to tell you that spending more time with the document would be wasted effort. As you prepare to write, however, you should evaluate potential sources in light of your writing situation and your needs as a writer. Evaluating a source means examining its relevance, evidence, author, publisher, timeliness, comprehensiveness, and genre.

Determine Relevance

Relevance is the extent to which a source provides information you can use in your writing project. Remember your purpose when you evaluate potential sources. Even if a source provides a great deal of information, it might not meet your needs. For example, an analysis of the printing features in word-processing programs might contain a great deal of accurate and up-to-date information—but it won't be of much use if you're writing about color laser printers for college students.

Your readers will expect information that meets their needs as well. If they want to read about personal printers for college students, for instance, pass up sources that focus on high-capacity office printers.

Consider the Use of Evidence

Evidence is information offered to support a point. Statistics, facts, expert opinions, and firsthand accounts are among the many types of evidence you'll find. As a writer, you can evaluate not only the kinds of evidence in a source but also the quality, amount, and appropriateness of that evidence. Ask yourself the following questions:

- **Is enough evidence offered?** A lack of evidence might indicate fundamental flaws in the author's argument.

- **Is the right kind of evidence offered?** More evidence isn't always better evidence. Ask whether the evidence is appropriate for the reasons being offered and whether more than one type of evidence is being used. Many sources rely far too heavily on a single type of evidence, such as personal experience or quotations from experts.

- **Is the evidence used fairly?** Look for reasonable alternative interpretations, questionable or inappropriate use of evidence, and evidence that seems to contradict points made elsewhere in a source. If statistics are included, are they interpreted fairly or presented clearly? If a quotation is offered to support a point, is the quotation used appropriately?

- **Are sources identified?** Knowing the origins of evidence can make a significant difference in your evaluation of a source. For example, if a writer quotes a political poll but doesn't say which organization conducted the poll, you might reasonably question the reliability of the source.

Identify the Author

The significance of authorship is affected by context. For example, take two editorials that make similar arguments and offer similar evidence. Both are published in your local newspaper. One is written by a fourteen-year-old middle school student, the other by a U.S. senator. You would certainly favor the senator's editorial if the subject was U.S. foreign policy. If the subject was student perceptions about drug abuse prevention in schools, however, you might value the middle school student's opinion more highly.

Ask the following questions about the author of a source:

- **Is the author knowledgeable?** An author might be an acknowledged expert in a field, a reporter who has written extensively about an issue, or someone with firsthand experience. Then again, an author might have little or no experience with a subject beyond a desire to say something about it. How can you tell the difference? Look for a description of the author in the source. If none is provided, look for biographical information on the Web or in a reference such as *Who's Who*.

- **What are the author's biases?** We all have biases—a set of interests that shapes our perceptions. Try to learn about the author's affiliations so that you determine the extent to which his or her biases affect the presentation of arguments, ideas, and information in a source. For instance, you might infer a bias if you know that an author writes frequently about gun control and works as a regional director for the National Handgun Manufacturers Association.

Learn about the Publisher

Publishers are the groups that produce and provide access to sources, including books, newspapers, journals, Web sites, sound and video files, and databases. Like authors, publishers have biases. Unlike authors, they often advertise them. Many publishers have a mission statement on their Web sites, while others provide information that can help you figure out their priorities. You might already be familiar with a publisher, particularly in the case of major newspapers or magazines, such as the *New York Times* (regarded as liberal) or *U.S. News and World Report* (regarded as conservative). If the publisher is a scholarly or professional journal, you can often figure out its biases by looking over the contents of several issues or by reading a few of its editorials.

Establish Timeliness

The importance of a source's date of publication varies according to your writing situation. For example, if you're writing a feature article on the use of superconducting materials in new mass-transportation projects, you probably won't want to spend a lot of time with articles published in 1968. However, if you're writing about the 1968 presidential contest between Hubert Humphrey and Richard Nixon, then sources published during that time period will take on greater importance.

Print sources usually list a publication date. However, it can be difficult to tell when Web sources were created. When in doubt, back up undated information found on the Web with a dated source.

Assess Comprehensiveness

Comprehensiveness is the extent to which a source provides a complete and balanced view of a subject. Like timeliness, the importance of comprehensiveness varies according to the demands of your writing situation. If you are working on a narrowly focused project, such as the role played by shifts in Pacific Ocean currents on snowfall patterns in Colorado last winter, comprehensiveness in a source might not be important—or even possible. However, if you are considering a broader issue, such as the potential effects of global climate change on agricultural production in North America, or if you are still learning as much as you can about your subject, give preference to sources that provide full treatment.

Recognize Genre

Knowing the genre of a source can help you understand a great deal about its intended readers, the kind of evidence it is likely to use, and the kind of argument it is likely to make. An article in a professional journal, for example, will almost certainly rely on published sources or original research, and it will carefully document its sources so that readers can easily locate related documents. In contrast, a blog entry is more likely to rely on personal observation and reflection.

By understanding the conventions of a particular genre, you can understand whether the information, ideas, and arguments found in it might be of use to you as you work on your writing project. To evaluate a genre, carry out the following activities:

- **Analyze the writing style.** Determine how formally (or informally) the document is written. Check for the use of specialized terms that might be unfamiliar to general readers. Try to understand how the writer views himself or herself in relation to readers.

- **Consider how evidence is used.** Identify numerical information; quotations and paraphrases; summaries of other documents; charts, graphs, and tables; and images and other illustrations. Ask yourself why the writer chose the types of evidence you've found in the document.

- **Look at the organization.** Try to break the document into major sections. Ask whether you've seen this type of organization used in other documents, and think about the purposes of those documents. Documents within a genre often follow a similar structure.

- **Identify citation styles.** Determine whether the sources of information, ideas, and arguments are identified in the document.

- **Consider design.** A document's appearance can tell you a lot about its purpose, intended readers, and likely means of distribution. Is the document's medium print or digital? Does it use color, columns of text, and images or other illustrations? What types of readers might appreciate the use of these design elements? And what effect might these elements have on potential readers?

Examine Electronic Sources Closely

You can apply the general evaluative criteria discussed above to most types of sources. However, electronic sources can pose special challenges. Because anyone can create a Web site, start a blog, or post a message to a newsgroup, e-mail list, or Web discussion forum, approach these sources with more caution than you would reserve for print sources such as books and journal articles, which are typically published only after a lengthy editorial review process.

WEB SITES AND BLOGS

To assess the credibility of a Web site or a blog, consider its domain (.edu, .com, and so on), and look for information about the site (often available on the "About This Site" or "Site Information" page).

NEWSGROUPS, E-MAIL LISTS, AND DISCUSSION FORUMS

To assess the relevance and credibility of a message on a newsgroup, an e-mail list, or a Web discussion forum, check for a "signature" at the end of the message, and try to locate a Frequently Asked Questions (FAQ) list. A signature can provide information about the sender, such as a professional title, and the URL for a personal home page where you can learn more about the author. FAQs can tell you about the purpose of a newsgroup, an e-mail list, or a discussion forum; whether messages are moderated (reviewed before being posted); and whether membership is open or restricted to a particular group.

WIKIS

Wikis are Web sites that can be added to or edited by visitors to the site. Reference sites such as Wikipedia (en.wikipedia.org) have grown in importance on the Web, and many are highly ranked by search sites such as Ask, Yahoo!, and Google. Unfortunately, it can be difficult to evaluate the credibility of wiki pages because changes occur quickly and repeatedly, with no guarantee of accuracy or credibility. You might want to use wikis when you are beginning to learn about a topic, but avoid citing them as the "last word" on a topic. In fact, those "last words" might change before you submit your final draft.

Check the domain to learn about the site's purpose and publisher:

.biz, .com, .coop: business .mil: military
.edu: higher education .gov: government
.org: nonprofit organization .net: network organization

Check the title bar and page headers or titles to learn about the site's relevance and publisher.

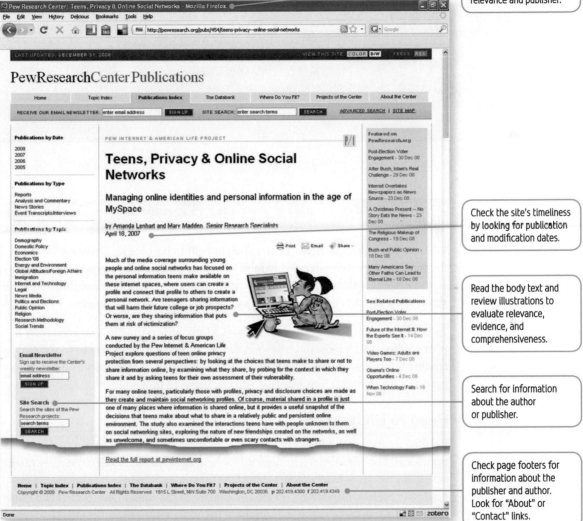

Check the site's timeliness by looking for publication and modification dates.

Read the body text and review illustrations to evaluate relevance, evidence, and comprehensiveness.

Search for information about the author or publisher.

Check page footers for information about the publisher and author. Look for "About" or "Contact" links.

↳ How to Evaluate a Web Site

Practice: Evaluate a Source

Select a source you have found as you've learned about a topic. In your writer's notebook, respond to the following questions:

1. Is the source relevant to your writing project?

2. Does the source present evidence and use it appropriately?

3. What can you learn about the author?

4. What can you learn about the publisher?

5. Is the source timely?

6. Is the source comprehensive enough?

7. What type of document is it?

@ Download or print this Practice activity at bedfordstmartins.com/conversation.

How Can I Read Like a Writer?

When you read like a writer, you prepare yourself to become an active member of the conversation you've decided to join. You learn where the conversation has been — and where it is at the moment. In short, reading like a writer helps you think critically about what you've read and prepares you to write your own document.

To engage more fully with the information, ideas, and arguments you encounter in your reading, you'll want to go beyond simply knowing what others have written. By reading to understand, reading to respond, and reading to make connections — and putting your thoughts into words — you can begin to find your voice.

Read to Understand

Reading to understand involves gaining an overview of the most important information, ideas, and arguments in a source. When writers read to understand, they often create summaries — brief descriptions of the main idea, reasons, and supporting evidence in a source. Depending on the complexity of the source, summaries can range from a brief statement about the argument found in a source to a detailed description of the key points and evidence it provides.

Many writers believe that a summary should be objective. It would be more accurate to say that a summary should be accurate and fair. That is, you should not misrepresent the information, ideas, or arguments in a source. Achieving accuracy and fairness, however, does not necessarily mean that your summary will be an objective presentation of the source. Instead, your summary will reflect your purpose, needs, and interests and — if you're writing for an audience — those of your readers. You'll focus on information, ideas, and arguments that are relevant to your writing situation. As a result, your summary is likely to differ from one written by another writer. Both summaries might be accurate and fair, but each one will reflect its writer's writing situation.

As you read to understand, highlight key points in the source, and note passages that include useful quotations or information you might use to add detail to your summary. If you are writing a summary for a class, it will typically take one of three forms: a main-point summary, a key-point summary, or an outline summary.

Megan Martinez found the article on page 68 during her search for information about social networking. Published by the Times Online, a Web site owned by leading British newspaper companies, the article suggested another way of looking at the benefits and drawbacks of social-networking sites.

MAIN-POINT SUMMARIES

A main-point summary reports the most important information, idea, or argument presented in a source. You can use main-point summaries to keep track of the overall claim made in a source, to introduce your readers to a source, and to place the main point of that source into the context of an argument or a discussion of a subject. Megan might have written the following main-point summary of Bernhard Warner's article:

> In his article "Is Social Networking a Waste of Time?" Bernhard Warner argues that the use of social-networking sites and other Web 2.0 media by students will ultimately benefit society — and the students themselves.

Main-point summaries are brief. They identify the source and its main point.

KEY-POINT SUMMARIES

Like a main-point summary, a key-point summary reports the most important information, idea, or argument presented in a source. However, it also includes the reasons (key points) and evidence the author uses to support his or her main point. Key-point summaries are useful when you want to keep track of a complex argument or understand an elaborate process.

> In his article "Is Social Networking a Waste of Time?" Bernhard Warner argues that the use of social-networking sites and other Web 2.0 tools by students will ultimately benefit society — and the students themselves. He notes that concerns expressed by members of the business community about lost productivity should not be extended to students' use of social-networking sites and tools. In fact, he points out that while adults tend to view the use of these sites and tools

The author, source, and main point are identified.

The concerns of people on the other side of the issue are briefly presented.

Is Social Networking a Waste of Time?

by Bernhard Warner

There has been much fuss of late over the loss of productivity brought on by employees multi-tasking between actual work and social networking. One estimate puts the cost to British industry at £6.5 billion per annum in lost productivity and questionable bandwidth usage. Another survey estimates that Britain's social media fanatics are spending as much as 12 hours per week on these sites, no doubt eating into valuable work time.

But what is the impact of this collective Facebook/MySpace/Bebo addiction on high school and university students, our bright future? A new survey this week by IT specialists Global Secure Systems (the ones who took a look at the impact on businesses and arrived at the £6.5 billion figure) says students are also guilty of sneaking in a fair bit of social networking during the school day.

In their survey of 500 English schoolchildren between the ages of 13 and 17, 51 percent confess to checking their social network profiles during lessons. Over a quarter admit their in-school daily social network fix exceeds over 30 minutes each day.

If this sounds surprising, you haven't been to school lately. Laptop-toting school kids are the norm these days, as are Wifi-enabled campuses. And when the laptop is in the locker, there are net-enabled smart phones at the ready. Add to the equation the rocket-fast texting ability of your typical 16-year-old and you get an explosion of social networking opportunities at the most unlikely points in the school day.

No educator would knowingly allow such a distraction in their classroom, and yet it appears to be happening right under their noses. It's hard enough getting the PlayStation generation to focus for even a half-hour on a lecture of, say, King John and the Magna Carta. Try competing with the latest lunchroom gossip being broadcasted to mobiles, Facebook, and Twitter. The significance of establishing modern-day democracy pales in comparison.

Before you shake your head and mutter something starting with the phrase "In my day . . . ," admit it—how many of you have shirked off work on an important business project to tend to a personal e-mail, text, or, these days, a Facebook query? How many of you have done it today? How many of you are doing it now?

We adults might regard tidying up our profile, sending messages to friends or contacts, joining the odd (or oddball) group, or participating in a movie knowledge quiz to be a harmless distraction, the kind of thing that keeps us sane during the workday. (While writing this column, I have been twice drawn to my Facebook profile to attend to small matters, but that's it. No more for me today. Okay, maybe after lunch.) But teens are deadly serious about social networks. For them, failing to attend to these duties could end friendships, sink reputations, and mean missed opportunities to climb the fickle and precarious social ladder of young adulthood. I say we ought to go easy on them if they are neglecting some of their responsibilities while they fuss around with their online persona.

As a university lecturer at John Cabot University in Rome I encourage my students, all in their early twenties, to embrace social media and every other Web 2.0 application out there. Yes, posting photos of you and your semi-clad friends boozing it up late at night could sink your chances with a prospective employer, who will no doubt be snooping around for this very type of incriminating evidence. But the good far outweighs the bad. I encourage the students to be creative, to promote our online student newspaper, which just over a year from launch is pulling in steadily rising traffic. No doubt all the blog, Facebook, and MySpace mentions are helping. I've had students who use social networking sites to build and promote projects on fighting poverty and eradicating hunger, organizing music gigs, art and photo exhibitions, plus coordinating meetups for political rallies.

I admire the growing number of young students who dedicate hours to designing complicated widgets and applications too. Yes, they're probably neglecting their history paper to complete it, but the end product is a far more valuable lesson learned in creativity, courage, and computer coding. When I look at all the creativity, the collaboration, and the activism being generated in these networks, I am hopeful for the future. Perhaps it is we educators who need to learn how to harness this power into our everyday classroom lessons.

Bernhard Warner, a freelance journalist and media consultant, writes about technology, the Internet, and media industries. He can be reached at techscribe@gmail.com.

as "a harmless distraction," many students fear that not using them "could end friendships, sink reputations, and mean missed opportunities to climb the fickle and precarious social ladder of young adulthood" (par. 7). Overall, Warner argues, the advantages of using social-networking sites and other Web 2.0 tools — in terms of "the creativity, the collaboration, and the activism being generated in these networks" — far outweigh the disadvantages (par. 9).

OUTLINE SUMMARIES

Sometimes called a plot summary, an outline summary reports the information, ideas, and arguments in a source in the same order used in the source. In a sense, an outline summary presents the overall "plot" of the source by reporting what was written in the order in which it was written. Outline summaries are useful when you need to keep track of the sequence of information, ideas, and arguments in a source.

In his article "Is Social Networking a Waste of Time?" Bernhard Warner argues that despite concerns expressed by members of the business community about lost productivity, we should not discourage students from using social-networking sites and tools. Warner reports that a recent survey of 500 English students between the ages of 13 and 17 indicates that more than half check social-networking sites during lessons and that more than a quarter spend more than 30 minutes each day on social-networking sites. Yet he points out that these behaviors are similar to those of adults, who tend to view the use of social-networking sites and other Web 2.0 tools as "a harmless distraction." Moreover, he notes that failing to use these tools can have significant consequences for students, many of whom fear that not using them "could end friendships, sink reputations, and mean missed opportunities to climb the fickle and precarious social ladder of young adulthood" (par. 7).

> The author, source, and main point are identified.

> The summary identifies each of the major points made in the article in the order in which they were made.

> The author's name is mentioned whenever information from the source is used.

> Terms such as "moreover" and "overall" provide a sense of movement through the source.

Warner, himself a teacher, argues that rather than trying to reduce students' use of social-networking sites and tools, we should instead channel them in productive ways. He reflects on his own successful use of social-networking tools and sites to support learning projects focused on "fighting poverty and eradicating hunger, organizing music gigs, art and photo exhibitions, plus coordinating meet-ups for political rallies" (para. 8). Overall, Warner argues, the advantages of using social-networking sites and other Web 2.0 tools — in terms of "the creativity, the collaboration, and the activism being generated in these networks" — far outweigh the disadvantages (para. 9).

Practice: Summarize a Source

Using the following guidelines, write an outline summary of Laura Lefkowits's article "A New Face for Schools" (p. 57):

1. Record the author and title of the source.

2. Identify the main point and key points made by the writer. Present the main point and key points in the order in which they appear in the source. For each point, briefly describe the evidence provided to back it up.

3. Clearly credit the author for any information, ideas, and arguments you include in your summary: use quotation marks for direct quotations, and identify the page from which you've drawn a paraphrase or quotation. (See Chapter 17 for guidelines on documenting sources.)

@ Download or print this Practice activity at bedfordstmartins.com/conversation.

Read to Respond

Reading to respond allows you to begin forming your own contribution to a conversation. Your response will help you focus your reactions to the information, ideas, and arguments you've encountered in a source. To prepare to write a response to a source, note passages with which you agree or disagree, reflect on interesting information and ideas, and record your thoughts about the effectiveness of the argument advanced in the source.

AGREE/DISAGREE RESPONSES

If you want to explore an idea or argument in a source, try freewriting about why you agree or disagree with it. In your response, clearly define the idea or argument to which you are responding. Then explain whether you agree or disagree with the idea or argument—or whether you find yourself in partial agreement with it—and why.

REFLECTIVE RESPONSES

A reflective response allows you to consider the meaning or implications of what you read. You might focus on a key passage or idea from a source, explaining or elaborating on it. Or you might reflect on your own experiences, attitudes, or observations in relation to a piece of information, an idea, or an argument. You can also use a reflective response to consider how an idea or argument might be interpreted by other readers, how it might be applied in a new context, or how it might be misunderstood.

ANALYTIC RESPONSES

An analytic response focuses on the important elements of a source, such as its purpose, ideas, argument, organization, focus, evidence, and style. For example, you might ask whether the main point is stated clearly, or whether appropriate types of evidence are used to support an argument. You might also analyze the logic of an argument or map its organization. Or you might offer suggestions about how an author could have made the source more effective.

Even when writers choose a particular type of response, they often draw on the other types to flesh out their ideas. For example, you might consider why you disagree with an argument by analyzing how effectively the source presents the argument. Or you might shift from agreeing with an idea to reflecting on its implications.

Practice: Respond to a Source

Putting your response into words can help you sort out your reactions to the ideas, information, and arguments in a source. Use the following guidelines to write an informal response to Bernhard Warner's essay (p. 68) or Laura Lefkowits's article (p. 57):

1. Identify a focus for your response. You might select important information, an intriguing idea, or the author's overall argument.

2. Decide what type of response you are going to write: agree/disagree, reflective, analytical, or some combination of the three types.

3. Write an introduction that identifies the information, idea, argument, or source to which you are responding, lays out your overall response (your main point), and identifies the source's author and title.

4. Provide reasons to support your main point and evidence to support your reasons.

5. Clearly credit the sources of any information, ideas, or arguments you use to support your response: use quotation marks for direct quotations, and identify the page or paragraph from which you've drawn a paraphrase or quotation. (See Chapter 17 for guidelines on documenting sources.)

@ Download or print this Practice activity at bedfordstmartins.com/conversation.

Read to Make Connections

You can learn a lot by looking for similarities and differences among the sources you read. For example, you might identify a group of authors with a similar approach to a subject, such as favoring increased government support for wind energy. You could then contrast this group with other groups of authors, such as those who believe that market forces should be the primary factor encouraging wind power, or those who believe we should focus on other forms of energy. Similarly, you can take note of information in one source that supports or contradicts information in another. These notes can help you build your own argument or identify information that will allow you (and your readers) to better understand a conversation.

As you read more and more about a subject, you'll start to notice common themes and shared ideas. Recognizing these connections among groups of authors can help you understand the scope of the conversation. For example, knowing that people involved in your conversation agree on the overall definition of a problem might

Working Together: Make Connections among Sources

Work together with a group of classmates to identify general approaches to the subject of social networking. To prepare for the group activity, each member should read, mark, and annotate the articles, Web pages, and reports on social networking in this chapter. During class, you should carry out the following activities:

1. Members of the group should take turns reporting what they've learned about one of the sources.

2. As each report is made, the other members of the group should take notes on the key ideas highlighted by the reporter.

3. When the reports have been completed, the group should create an overall list of the key ideas discussed in the individual reports.

4. Identify sources that seem to share similar approaches to the issue. Give each group of sources a name, and provide a brief description of the ideas its authors have in common.

5. Describe each group in detail. Explain what makes the authors part of the same group (their similarities) and how each group differs from the others you've defined.

Once you've completed the activity, consider how you would respond to each group of authors. Ask whether you agree or disagree with their approach, and describe the extent to which you agree or disagree. Consider whether you would want to join a group, whether you would want to refine a particular approach to better fit your understanding of the subject, or whether you would rather develop a new approach.

@ Download or print this Working Together activity at bedfordstmartins.com/conversation.

lead you to focus your efforts on either challenging that definition with an alternative one or suggesting a possible solution. If you find yourself agreeing with one group of authors, you might start to think of yourself as a member of that group—as someone who shares their approach to the subject. If you don't agree with any of the groups you've identified, perhaps you are ready to develop a new approach to the subject.

To make connections among authors, jot down notes in the margins of your sources or in your writer's notebook. Each time you read a new source, keep in mind what you've already read, and make note of similarities and differences among your sources. When you notice similar themes in some of your sources, review the sources you've already read to see whether they've addressed those themes.

Beyond a collection of notes and annotations, reading to make connections might also result in longer pieces of freewriting (see p. 34). In some cases, you might spend time creating a brief essay that defines each group, identifies which authors belong to each group, and reflects on the strengths, weaknesses, and appropriateness of the approach taken by each group.

In Summary: Reading to Write

○ Read with a purpose (p. 50).

○ Become an active reader (p. 51).

○ Evaluate potential sources in light of your writing situation (p.60).

○ Summarize useful ideas, information, and arguments (p. 66).

○ Respond to what you read (p. 70).

○ Explore connections among sources (p. 72).

04 Working Together

▶▶ Some of us would rather have a root canal than work with another writer on a writing project. The reasons for this attitude range from bad experiences on collaborative projects to an overwhelming confidence that we're better off on our own. However, the skills required for successful collaboration are among the most important a writer can have. In fact, they're strongly related to the skills you draw on when you engage in any written conversation—listening carefully, treating others with respect, and deciding how to contribute effectively to a project. In this chapter, you'll learn how to benefit from working together and how to do so effectively and efficiently.

Why Should I Work with Other Writers?

With rare exceptions, writing is a social act. You write to inform, to entertain, to bring about change. You write to share ideas. You write to make a difference. Most important, you write *to someone* and *for a purpose*. To write a more effective document, turn to other writers. Working with other writers can help you improve your own document, enhance your writing process, and increase the likelihood of successfully completing major writing projects. For these reasons, you'll find a number of Working Together activities throughout this book. These activities are designed to help you make progress on your current writing projects and to prepare you for work on other projects in your college courses and after graduation.

Work Together to Improve Your Document

Working with other writers gives you the benefit of multiple perspectives. To increase your chances of creating an effective document, you might ask for help generating ideas, identifying potential sources of information, planning, or revising. You might ask a friend, "What do you know about . . . ?" or "Do you think it would be effective if . . . ?" and "Does this seem convincing to you?" Once you write a draft, you can ask for feedback on your work. You might solicit general reactions to your document. You might ask a friend or classmate to pretend to be part of the intended audience for your document. You might ask for feedback on specific aspects of your document, such as its tone or style or use of evidence.

Work Together to Enhance Your Writing Process

In addition to the direct benefits you can gain through assistance and feedback from other writers, you can benefit from providing assistance or feedback *to* other writers. By helping another writer generate ideas, you can practice effective brainstorming strategies. By participating in a planning session, you can learn something new about planning your own documents. By reading and responding to documents written by other writers, you might pick up some new strategies for organizing an essay, crafting an introduction, incorporating illustrations, or using evidence effectively. Perhaps most important, learning how to analyze other people's work can help you assess your own writing more effectively.

Work Together to Succeed on a Major Project

Working on collaborative projects has become common in many writing and writing-intensive courses. In engineering courses, for example, teams of students often carry out a complex project and produce presentations and written reports. Web design courses frequently involve students in team projects. Similarly, first-year writing courses often include a collaborative writing project. Typically, these projects are far more ambitious than those assigned to individual students. It is only through the contributions of all the members of the group that they can be completed at all.

Working Together: Develop Guidelines for Collaborative Work

Most writers can look back at a group project and find something they didn't like about the experience. They might have been in a group dominated by an ineffective leader. They might have had to do far more than their fair share on a project. At the last minute, they might have been left in the lurch by someone who failed to deliver a critical part of the project. Whatever the reason, many writers often prefer to work alone. Yet group work can add a great deal to a writing project, and most experienced writers can point to a wide range of situations in which working with other writers significantly improved their work on a writing project.

To get ready to work with other writers, reflect on your experiences with group work. Then, working with the members of your group, develop a set of guidelines that would improve the quality of group work. To carry out this activity, follow these steps:

1. Individually, spend five minutes brainstorming (p. 33) or freewriting (p. 34) about your experiences with collaborative work. List both positive and negative experiences.

2. As a group, discuss your experiences. Each person should note the advantages and disadvantages of collaborative work.

3. As a group, identify the most significant challenges to working together effectively.

4. As a group, create a list of guidelines that would address these challenges.

Once you've completed the activity, share your guidelines with other groups in the class. As a class, create a list of guidelines for collaborative work in your course.

@ Download or print this Working Together activity at bedfordstmartins.com/conversation.

How Can I Work with Others on Individual Projects?

Writers frequently solicit support from other writers as they work on individual projects. In some cases, they seek this support independently, usually by asking for advice about the choice of a topic or by requesting feedback on a draft. In other cases, a writing instructor might direct students to work together to generate ideas, collect sources on a common topic, or engage in peer review.

Generate and Refine Ideas

You might be asked to help another writer generate ideas. Or you might ask for help yourself. Common strategies for generating ideas with other writers include group brainstorming and role-playing activities.

GROUP BRAINSTORMING

Group brainstorming is frequently used to generate ideas for a shared topic. For example, a group of students working on an essay about new advances in communication technologies could take turns suggesting ideas that might be addressed in an essay.

To engage in group brainstorming, follow these guidelines:

- **Take notes.** Ask someone to record ideas.

- **Encourage everyone in the group to participate.** Consider taking turns. If your group chooses to contribute ideas as they occur to members, establish a ground rule that no one should cut off other group members as they're speaking.

- **Be polite.** Avoid criticisms and compliments. Treat every idea, no matter how odd or useless it might seem, as worthy of consideration.

- **Build on one another's ideas.** Try to expand on ideas that have already been generated, and see where they take you.

- **Generate as many ideas as possible.** If you get stuck, try asking questions about ideas that have already been suggested.

- **Review the results.** Once you've stopped brainstorming, look over the list of ideas, and identify the most promising ones.

ROLE-PLAYING

Role-playing activities are frequently used to generate and refine ideas. By asking the members of a group to take on roles, you can apply a variety of perspectives to a subject. For example, you might ask one person to play the role of a "doubting Thomas," someone who demands evidence from a writer for every assertion, or a devil's advocate, who responds to a writer's arguments with counterarguments. Role-playing activities that are useful for generating and refining ideas include staging debates, conducting inquiries, and offering first-person explanations.

Staging a Debate In a debate, speakers who represent different perspectives argue politely with one another about an issue. You might try one or more of the following role-playing activities:

- **Adopt the role of the authors of readings used in a class.** Each "author" presents his or her perspective on the issue.

- **Adopt the role of a political commentator or celebrity who has taken a strong stand on an issue.** One member of a group might adopt the role of Rachel Maddow, for example, while another might adopt the role of Rush Limbaugh, and still others might adopt the role of Keith Olbermann, Joe Scarborough, or Bill O'Reilly. Each "commentator" or "celebrity" presents his or her perspective on the issue. To prepare for the debate, watch or listen to commentaries on a site such as YouTube.com to learn about the positions these commentators have taken in the past.

- **Adopt the role of an authority on an issue,** such as a scientific adviser to a local zoning commission, the manager of a small business, or the director of a nonprofit organization. To prepare for the debate, conduct research in your library's databases or on the Web about the person whose role you are adopting.

- **Adopt the role of someone affected by an issue or event.** For example, if you were generating ideas about a natural disaster, such as the effects of a flood in the Mississippi River valley, you might take on the roles of people who lost their homes and were forced to move, health care workers and police officers who stayed on duty, students who lost their schools, or small business owners who lost their livelihood, each of whom could discuss the impact of this natural disaster on their lives. To prepare for the debate, conduct research on how the community was affected by the event.

Conducting an Inquiry An inquiry is an attempt to understand a situation or an event. For example, a military tribunal might review soldiers' actions during a military operation, while a medical inquiry might focus on the causes of a problem that occurred during a medical procedure. To conduct an inquiry, try the following role-playing activities:

- **Defend a contemporary or historical figure.** The writer presents a case for this person, and the other group members ask questions about the person's actions or ideas.

- **Review a proposal.** The writer presents a proposal to address an issue or a problem. The other members of the group raise questions about the merits of the proposal and suggest alternatives.

Giving Testimony First-person explanations offer insights into the causes of, effects of, or solutions to a particular issue or problem. Role-playing activities that involve giving testimony include

- **Adopt the role of devil's advocate.** The writer offers an explanation, and one or more respondents offer reasonable objections. Each devil's advocate — the term is drawn from the process by which the Roman Catholic Church confers sainthood, in which an advocate of the devil argues that the candidate is not worthy of sainthood — asks for clarification of the points made by the writer and suggests alternative explanations.

- **Adopt the role of a person affected by an issue.** The writer takes on the role of someone who has been affected by the issue. After the writer explains the effects, the other members of the group ask questions about the writer's experiences with this issue.

Working Together: Role-Play

Work together with your classmates to generate and refine ideas for your writing project. Choose one of the categories of role-playing activities — staging a debate, conducting an inquiry, or giving testimony — and assign roles to the members of your group. Then do the following:

1. Appoint a member of your group — ideally, someone who is not involved in the role-playing activity — to record the ideas.

2. Create a framework for the role-playing. Decide who will speak first, how long that person will speak, and what sort of responses are appropriate.

3. As you conduct the role-playing, be polite (within bounds, of course — some political commentators are far from polite to their opponents).

4. If you are responding to a writer's ideas, ask for evidence to support his or her arguments or explanations.

5. If you are adopting a role that requires you to disagree, don't overdo it. Be willing to accept a reasonable argument or explanation.

Once you've completed the activity, review the notes taken by your recorder, and assess what you've learned.

@ Download or print this Working Together activity at **bedfordstmartins.com/conversation.**

Collect and Work with Information

You might be asked—by an instructor or by another writer—to work together to collect, critically read, evaluate, and take notes on information from sources. Common collaborative activities for collecting and working with information include the following:

- **Develop a search strategy for published sources.** Depending on the scope of a writing project, creating a plan for finding sources can be quite challenging. Working with other writers can improve the odds of developing an effective and appropriate plan. You can learn more about developing a search plan on page 464.

- **Assign responsibility for locating sources.** When a group is working on a shared topic, instructors often encourage the group to collaboratively compile a collection of sources. For example, one member of the group might search for sources through a library catalog, another through full-text databases, and still another through searches of the Web. Each person locates promising sources and makes copies for other members of the group. See Chapter 12 for more information about locating sources.

- **Assign responsibility for field research.** In writing projects that involve surveys, interviews, observation, or correspondence (see p. 506), a group might develop a plan to conduct a particular type of field research. After reviewing the plan, each member of the group carries out his or her assigned research task and shares it with the group.

- **Create shared annotated bibliographies.** Members of a group working on a shared topic can create citations and annotations (brief summaries) for each source they collect. You can learn more about creating annotated bibliographies on page 474.

- **Share evaluations of sources.** Writers working on a shared topic meet to discuss the merits of the sources they've collected and read. For more information on evaluating sources, see page 60.

- **Share notes on sources.** Writers working on a shared topic compile their notes on the sources they have read. You can learn more about taking notes in Chapter 13.

Respond to Written Work

Writers often ask for feedback on their drafts. Feedback can help a writer learn whether a main point is conveyed clearly, whether sufficient evidence is offered, whether a document is organized effectively, and whether readers are likely to react favorably to the information, ideas, and arguments in a draft. Feedback can also help a writer identify passages in a draft that might benefit from additional revision, polishing, or editing.

Chapters 5 to 10 provide structured peer-review activities that will help you get feedback on drafts for various kinds of writing projects.

GENERAL GUIDELINES FOR WRITERS

Whenever you ask for feedback—and as you prepare to give feedback to other writers—keep the following guidelines in mind.

When you ask for feedback on a draft:

- **Be clear.** Tell your reviewers where you'd like them to focus. For example, let them know that you need feedback only on the organization of your document or that you need help with grammar and punctuation. There's little point in receiving detailed suggestions for fixing mechanical errors when you know you'll be revising the argument and organization of the draft.

- **Be reasonable.** Your reviewers have more to do in life than review your draft. Don't expect—or ask—them to spend more time reviewing a draft than you spent writing it. For that matter, don't expect them to put more than half an hour into a review—if that.

- **Be prepared.** Provide a draft that is easy to review. If you are asking the writer to comment on a printed draft, format it with double-spaced lines and wide margins.

When you receive feedback on a draft:

- **Be open to criticism.** Don't dismiss constructive criticism as a problem with the reviewer's comprehension. A reviewer might make poor suggestions for revision, but it's more likely that he or she is reacting to a problem in the draft. Even when the suggested revision is inappropriate, it might point to an area that needs attention.

- **Be willing to ask questions.** If you aren't sure what a reviewer's comments mean, ask for clarification.

- **Be willing to change.** If a reviewer offers a critique of your argument or ideas, consider addressing it in your document. You will make a stronger argument if you tell readers about alternative ways of looking at an issue—particularly when you can dismiss the alternative effectively.

- **Be fair to yourself.** It's your draft. Don't feel obligated to incorporate every suggested change into your draft.

GENERAL GUIDELINES FOR REVIEWERS

When you provide feedback to another writer, consider the following guidelines.

To prepare for a peer-review session:

- **Be certain you understand the assignment.** Ask the writer to describe the draft's purpose and audience, and read the assignment sheet, if there is one.

- **Be certain you understand the writer's needs.** Ask the writer what type of response you should provide. If you are reviewing an early draft that will be revised before it's submitted for a grade, focus on larger writing concerns such as the overall argument, evidence, and organization. If the writer wants help with proofreading and editing, focus on accuracy, economy, consistency, sexist language, style, spelling, grammar, and punctuation (see pp. 638–639).

- **Be certain you understand any peer-review guides.** If you are using a feedback form, make sure you understand it. If you don't, ask the instructor or the writer for clarification.

- **Set aside sufficient time to review the draft.** Take your job seriously, and give the draft the time it deserves. You'll want the same courtesy when your draft is reviewed.

Before you make comments:

- **Be prepared.** Read the draft all the way through.

- **Be organized.** Take a few minutes to identify the areas most in need of work.

As you make comments:

- **Be positive.** Identify the strengths of the draft.

- **Be judicious.** Focus on the areas of the draft most in need of improvement. Avoid commenting on everything that might be improved.

- **Be clear.** If you are addressing an overall issue, define it. If you are addressing a specific passage, indicate where it can be found.

- **Be specific.** Avoid general comments, such as "This draft suffers from a lack of clarity." This kind of statement doesn't give the writer direction for improving the draft. Instead, offer specific comments, such as "I found it difficult to understand your explanation of the issue in the second paragraph."

- **Be constructive.** Offer concrete suggestions about how the draft might be improved, rather than just criticizing what you didn't like.

- **Be reasonable.** Keep the writing assignment in mind as you make suggestions for improvement. Don't hold the draft to a higher standard than the instructor's.

- **Be kind.** Be polite. Don't put down the writer simply because you find a draft inadequate, confusing, or annoying.

- **Be responsible.** Review your comments before you give them to the writer.

How Can I Work with Others on Collaborative Projects?

Collaborative writing has become a common feature not only in writing and writing-intensive classes but also in business, nonprofit, and government settings. The extent of collaboration can vary widely, from assigning sections of a report to different writers and editing them so that they share a common voice, to passing drafts of a document from one writer to another, to working together — electronically or in person — to plan, design, draft, polish, revise, and edit a document. To prepare to work with other writers on collaborative projects, become familiar with the purposes, processes, and potential pitfalls of working with a team. Learning how to work together while you are a student can help you succeed as a writer long after you've completed your degree.

Understand the Purposes of Writing Collaboratively

The wide range of collaborative writing activities you might encounter inside or outside the classroom reflect a variety of purposes. To increase your effectiveness as part of a team, identify the purpose of the document and the types of collaboration that will be involved in its creation. Take note as well of the length and intensity of the work. Collaborating on a letter to the editor (see p. 414), for example, requires far less planning than collaborating on a Web site or an annual report. Similarly, coauthoring an opinion column or a movie review involves far less time than drafting a 2,500-word analytical essay.

The decision to share a writing project reflects a set of beliefs about the value of collaboration. In corporate settings, for example, working together on a writing project might be a means not only of ensuring that a document is accurate and effective but also of building a sense of togetherness and commitment to a project among team members. In an academic setting, a group project allows students to create a document that a single student would find difficult to produce alone, helps them learn more about a subject, and familiarizes them with the collaborative processes they might encounter in their professional lives. In this sense, collaborating on a project might be as important as — or even more important than — producing a document.

Understand Potential Problems and Develop Solutions

Recognizing — and taking steps to avoid — potential pitfalls can increase the likelihood that a collaborative project will succeed. Common problems encountered during group work range from individual concerns about participating in a group to behaviors that undermine the group's effectiveness. If you want to collaborate successfully, be aware of these problems, and learn how solve them.

- **Some writers prefer to work alone,** and they make those feelings all too clear, often to the point of insulting their classmates. Remind them of the reasons the group is working together and the danger their attitude poses to the long-term success of the project.

- **Some writers worry about losing a sense of individual worth.** Assure them that their contributions not only are important but also will be recognized as such — if not formally, then by other members of the group.

- **Some people will try to dominate a group,** perhaps believing that the project will fail unless they take control. To avoid this problem, make sure at the outset of the project that everyone's ideas are heard and respected, and explain that developing a plan for the project is not a process of arguing for the superiority of a particular set of ideas so much as it is the synthesis of useful ideas.

- **Some members will find it difficult to schedule or attend group meetings.** Ensure that meeting times and locations accommodate everyone's needs. If you can't do so, have the group discuss the problem with the instructor.

- **Some members of a group will use meeting time unproductively** — at least in the eyes of other members of the group. This can cause problems, particularly when it is difficult to find time to meet or if meeting time is limited. To address this issue, be sure the group establishes and sticks to an agenda for each meeting.

- **Some group members will want to work only on what they feel capable of doing well.** In nonacademic settings, where a strong emphasis is often placed on the effectiveness of the final document, this is usually not a problem. In academic settings, however, where the goals of most collaborative projects include learning new skills and acquiring new knowledge, it is important that all members of a group take on new challenges.

- **Some members of a group won't contribute as much as others — and some won't contribute at all.** In collaborative writing projects for a class, you'll find that some members refuse to participate. Perhaps they assume that they can't make much of a contribution, or perhaps they're trying to save time by not participating. Regardless of their intentions, their lack of participation causes hurt feelings and might affect the overall quality of the project. To avoid these problems, establish ground rules about how to address unequal participation.

- **Some members of a group will resent the extra time required to coordinate work on a project.** Remind these people of the reasons for working together, and the benefits of doing so.

- **As the group works on a project, disagreements will arise.** As you develop ground rules for working together, consider how you'll address disagreements. Strategies include voting, discussing until consensus emerges, and seeking guidance from an instructor or a supervisor.

Establish Ground Rules

At the beginning of a project, spend time discussing potential difficulties and establishing ground rules. These can include guidelines for

- selecting meeting times and places
- conducting discussions

Working Together: Establish Ground Rules for a Collaborative Writing Project

In your writer's notebook, develop a set of ground rules for your writing group by responding to the following prompts. Share your responses with the members of your group, and agree on a formal set of rules.

1. Meetings will be held at [indicate location] on [dates and times].

2. Discussions will be [moderated by the same person at each meeting, moderated by a different person at each meeting, unmoderated], and notes will be taken by [the same person, different persons].

3. When disagreements arise, they will be resolved by _____.

4. The following members of the group will take the lead on the following activities: [list names and activities].

5. To ensure equitable contributions by each group member, we will _____.

6. Group members who do not contribute equitably will face the following consequences: [list consequences].

7. Group members who drop out of the project will face the following consequences: [list consequences].

@ Download or print this Working Together activity at bedfordstmartins.com/conversation.

- resolving disputes
- determining individual contributions to the project
- ensuring equitable contributions from group members
- defining the consequences for inadequate participation

Ground rules can take various forms, ranging from an informal agreement among group members to a detailed statement signed by each member.

Create a Project Plan

Once ground rules have been established, develop a plan for completing the project. Plans do not have to be highly detailed, particularly at the beginning stage of the project. However, they should define the overall goals of the project and identify key steps that must be taken to achieve those goals. An effective plan will define deadlines for the completion of each step, identify who is responsible for specific activities associated with completing a given step, and suggest strategies for carrying out those activities.

Working Together: Create a Plan for a Collaborative Writing Project

In your writer's notebook, develop a plan to complete your project. Then share your plan with the members of your group, and develop a group plan.

1. The overall goal of this project is _____.

2. This project will require completing the following steps: [Fill out this information for each step.]
_____

   Step:
_____

   Deadline:
_____

   Ideas for Completing the Step: Responsible Group Member:
_____
_____
_____
_____
_____

@ Download or print this Working Together activity at bedfordstmartins.com/conversation.

What Resources Can I Draw on as I Work with Other Writers?

Resources that support collaborative work include technological tools, as well as your instructor, classmates, family, and friends.

Use Technological Tools

For many writers, the phrase "working together" implies face-to-face meetings, often during class. In fact, many collaborative activities can be carried out without the need to meet in person.

- If you are working with other writers to generate and refine ideas, you might use chat programs to meet online. At the end of the chat session, you might want to save a transcript of the session for later review. If your class is supported by Web discussion forums, you can carry out your discussion in that format. Similarly, you can refine and generate ideas by using an e-mail distribution list (or by sending each message to all of the people in your group). You might also post ideas on a blog and then use the blog's Comments tool to generate responses to each idea.

Chat programs, such as Windows Messenger, can be used to contact members of your writing group.

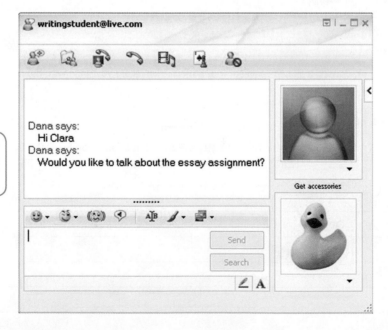

File-sharing sites, such as Google Docs (docs.google.com), allow writers to share documents.

- If you are collaborating with other writers to collect and work with sources for a shared topic, you can use discussion forums, wikis, Web file folders, and e-mail to distribute sources, source citations, source evaluations, and source notes.

- If you are conducting peer review, you can share your drafts by sending them as e-mail attachments. Reviewers can open the attachments in a word-processing program, comment on them using the program's Comment and Track Changes tools, save the file with a new name, and return them to you.

- If your class is supported by a course management system, you can ask your instructor to create discussion forums, wikis, and file-sharing folders to support your group work. You can take advantage of e-mail to share ideas, schedule meetings, and exchange files. You might also have access to electronic whiteboard programs that allow you to meet online and work on drafts of your document.

@ View a guide for using your word-processing program's Track Changes and Comments tools at **bedfordstmartins.com/ conversation**.

To learn more about blogs, see page 497. To learn more about discussion forums, see page 498. If you have questions about the technological tools that are available to support collaborative writing, ask your instructor.

Consult Instructors, Classmates, Friends, and Family

The most important resources for collaborative work are your instructor, your classmates, and your friends and family. Not only can family and friends provide honest feedback on the quality of your drafts, but they can also be resources for

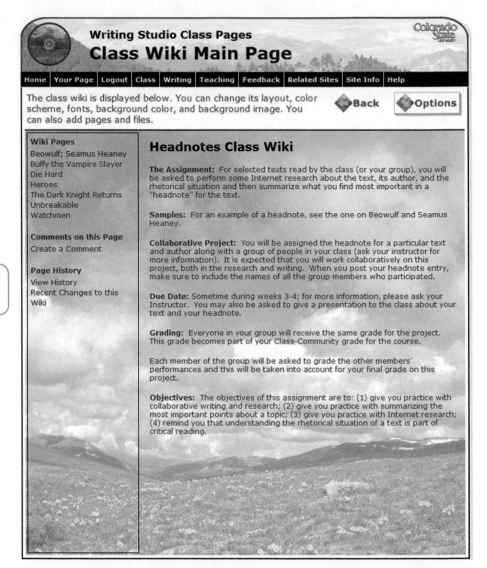

Wikis allow an entire class to work together on writing projects.

generating ideas about and planning a writing project. Simply discussing a writing project with sympathetic friends or family members can help you make progress on the project. They might remind you of something you'd forgotten about the topic; they might share new information with you; or they might respond in a way that sparks a new idea.

Similarly, classmates and instructors can help you fine-tune a draft by serving as a sounding board for your ideas and by responding to it. Instructors can also show you how to work with peer-review forms and can provide feedback on the quality of the comments you offer to your classmates. Finally, and perhaps most important, instructors can help you understand your assignment—but only if you ask them for advice.

In Summary: Working Together

○ Work with others to become a better writer (p. 76).

○ Generate and refine ideas collaboratively (p. 78).

○ Share responsibilities, sources, and notes (p. 81).

○ Conduct peer reviews to improve individual documents (p. 83).

○ Combine efforts on major projects (p. 84).

○ Take advantage of resources that support group work (p. 88).

PART TWO

Contributing to a
Conversation

05 Writing to Reflect

I write as an *observer* when I reflect on a topic.

GENRES IN CONVERSATION

| Reflective Writing | Informative Writing | Analytical Writing | Evaluative Writing | Problem-Solving Writing | Argumentative Writing |

The plight of children in war-torn nations gained a lot of attention after thousands of boys and young men escaped the conflicts in Sudan and Sierra Leone to settle in the United States. In the documents shown here—a **memoir,** an **opinion column,** and a **blog entry**—three writers use distinctly different genres to share reflections and engage in a conversation on the troubling phenomenon of child soldiers. Although all three authors focus on the same topic, they chose genres that employ distinct visual forms.

1

THERE WERE ALL KINDS of stories told about the war that made it sound as if it was happening in a faraway and different land. It wasn't until refugees started passing through our town that we began to see that it was actually taking place in our country. Families who had walked hundreds of miles told how relatives had been killed and their houses burned. Some people felt sorry for them and offered them places to stay, but most of the refugees refused, because they said the war would eventually reach our town. The children of these families wouldn't look at us, and they jumped at the sound of chopping wood or as stones landed on the tin roofs flung by children hunting birds with slingshots. The adults among these children from the war zones would be lost in their thoughts during conversations with the elders of my town. Apart from their fatigue and malnourishment, it was evident they had seen something that plagued their minds, something that we would refuse to accept if they told us all of it. At times I thought that some of the stories the passersby told were exaggerated. The only wars I knew of were those that I had read about in books or seen in movies such as *Rambo: First Blood*, and the one in neighboring Liberia that I

6   ISHMAEL BEAH

had heard about on the BBC news. My imagination at ten years old didn't have the capacity to grasp what had taken away the happiness of the refugees.

The first time that I was touched by war I was twelve. It was in January of 1993. I left home with Junior, my older brother, and our friend Talloi, both a year older than I, to go to the town of Mattru Jong, to participate in our friends' talent show. Mohamed, my best friend, couldn't come because he and his father were renovating their thatched-roof kitchen that day. The four of us had started a rap and dance group when I was eight. We were first introduced to rap music during one of our visits to Mobimbi, a quarter where the foreigners who worked for the same American company as my father lived. We often went to Mobimbi to swim in a pool and watch the huge color television and the white people who crowded the visitors' recreational area. One evening a music video that consisted of a bunch of young black fellows talking really fast came on the television. The four of us sat there mesmerized by the song, trying to understand what the black fellows were saying. At the end of the video, some letters came up at the bottom of the screen. They read "Sugarhill Gang, 'Rapper's Delight.'" Junior quickly wrote it down on a piece of paper. After that, we came to the quarters every other weekend to study that kind of music on television. We didn't [...] that t[...] beat.

La[...] some [...] ing ho[...] how t[...] and p[...] and it[...] while [...] Know[...] our cl[...]

Memoir ▶

This **memoir,** designed as a standard print book, recounts the experiences of Ishmael Beah, who at the age of twelve was forced to serve as a soldier in Sierra Leone's civil war.

#1 NATIONAL BESTSELLER

a long
way gone

Memoirs of a
Boy soldier

ishmael
beah

"Everyone in the world should read this book . . . We should read it to learn about the world and about what it means to be human." —Carolyn See, *The Washington Post*

Alissa Quart
WITNESS

The Child Soldiers of Staten Island

While Hollywood swoons over teen guerrillas, the real lost boys are hidden in plain sight.

THIS IS THE YEAR child soldiers went pop. They were the centerpiece of *Blood Diamond*, in which Leonardo DiCaprio played a child-soldier-rescuing diamond trader. African kids with guns made appearances in *The Last King of Scotland* and in the latest James Bond movie. *Lost* introduced a subplot in which the series' West African strongman was revealed to have been a child soldier. Indie actor Ryan Gosling is reportedly set to direct his own script about child soldiers, perhaps inspired by *War/Dance*, a Sundance award-winning documentary that *Variety* called "*Spellbound* with orphans."

In February, a handsome 26-year-old named Ishmael Beah published *A Long Way Home*, a bloody, moving memoir of how he went from being a guerrilla in Sierra Leone to getting adopted by an American woman and finally attending Oberlin College. The *New York Times Magazine* put him on its cover; Starbucks sponsored his 10-city book tour and prominently displayed his memoir in its outlets. *Time* sneered that we'd hit the "cultural sweet spot for the African child soldier."

This sudden fascination with photogenic survivors such as Beah seemingly assures us that Africa's young fighters can be redeemed if only they step forward to share their stories or win the heart of a kindly Westerner. But most former child soldiers remain in the shadows, whether they're

22 MOTHER JONES | JULY/AUGUST 2007

Sweet Sierra Leone

🔲 12 MARCH, 2007

Claiming Ishmeal Beah, Identification and national Allegory

Claiming Ishmael Beah, Identification and National Allegory

On March 5th 2007, I had the opportunity to sit in on a reading by author of a Long Way Gone; Ishmael Beah. I was a tad bit late so I missed the reading itself. The room was packed full with standing room only for me and my two salone friends who were unlucky enough to be late. The room was full of mostly white folks and my two friends and I accounted for 50% of the Sierra Leonean population in the room.

Ishmael stood at the podium while about twenty or so copies of his book piled on a table waiting for Ishmael's signature hungry fingers and eyes waiting to devour his memoir (a bit of exoticism for Otherness of his experience filled the room). A Long Way gone is a heart wrenching, painful read that reminds us all about the fragility of human lives and quickness with which things can change. But even more important than that it is a testimony of the resiliency of the human spirit. The images from this memoir will remain imprinted in my mind for a long time.

As I strained my neck to look at Ishmael those horrid images had faded from my mind. In fact it didn't even occur to me that the young brown skinned man talking at the podium was that orphan, victim and one time aggressor in the book. As we stood in the crowd I jokingly whispered to my friend that Ishmael should try to not too good "cause white people will take him". A joke I borrowed from Paul Mooney on Chappelle Show.

Yes there is universality about Ishmael Beah's story as there are children everywhere that have similar stories if not worse. These children don't just come from the developing world either cause 17, 18, 19 year olds are serving and dying in the US military in Iraq, Afghanistan, and elsewhere. However, as a Sierra Leonean, I don't want Ishmael to be a Universalist. I want very badly to claim him as Sierra Leonean and to own his experience as part of our collective Sierra Leonean experience and recent history. I understand the need to draw attention to the international plight of children used as carriers, sex slaves, and soldiers but Sierra Leone badly needs Ishmael Beah to represent us too. In a country where so few of us ordinary citizens ever get an opportunity to "talk truth to power" in the international community we need someone who has that opportunity to do so for sweet Sierra Leone.

WELCO
LEONE

Welcome to S
will find a dive
related topics/
Everything fron
other stuff in between. If you have any questions or topics you would like to see discussed or presented on Sierra Leone let me know and i will do my best to satisfy you. Enjoy. On the copyright tip, unless otherwise indicated most photos on this site were taken by me and belong to me. Share wisely :-)

Labels

- About Me (8)
- Arts and Culture (10)
- Books (6)
- Commentaries/Opinion articles (17)
- Ishmael Beah (1)
- SL Development (9)
- SL People (7)
- SL Photos (43)
- SL Politics (11)

1000 plus pictures perspectives of sweet sierra leone

www.flickr.com

What Is Writing to Reflect?

Writing to reflect is one of the most common activities writers undertake. At the beginning of almost every writing project, writers spend time exploring and deepening their understanding of their subject. In this sense, writing to reflect provides a foundation for documents that inform, analyze, evaluate, solve problems, and convey arguments.

Reflection can also be the primary purpose for writing a document. In journals and diaries, writers reflect on a subject for personal reasons, often with the expectation that no one else will read their words. Hoping their insights will benefit others, writers also use reflection to share their thoughts in more public documents—such as memoirs, letters, opinion columns, and blogs.

Reflective writing is carried out by writers who adopt the role of *observer*. These writers spend time learning about and considering a subject. Sometimes they explore the implications of putting a particular idea into practice. Sometimes they trace relationships among ideas and information. Sometimes they ask whether or how an author's words might help them better understand their own lives. Sometimes they ask whether their understanding of one situation can help them better understand another.

Readers of reflective documents usually share the writer's interest in a subject. They want to learn what another person thinks about the subject, and often they'll use what they've read as the basis for their own reflections. In general, readers of reflective documents expect writers to provide a personal treatment of a subject, and they are willing to accept—and are likely to welcome—an unusual perspective.

To gather details for their observations, writers of reflective documents use sources, including their personal experiences and expertise, reports of recent events, and cultural materials such as music, art, movies, plays, books, short stories, and poems. These sources can also provide the inspiration for a reflective document. For example, a writer might reflect on an experience, a book, a poem, or a song.

The Writer's Role: Observer

PURPOSE

- To share a writer's insights about a subject
- To connect with readers

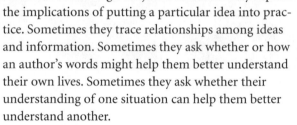

READERS

- Want to learn about other people's ideas and experiences
- Expect a personal treatment of the subject
- Welcome an unusual perspective

SOURCES

- Personal experiences and observations are often the major sources for reflective writing.
- Published sources might provide additional information to support a reflection.
- Cultural productions, such as music, art, movies, plays, and literature, can inspire reflection.

CONTEXT

- Reflections often draw on readers' knowledge of social events and their awareness of cultural context.
- Design choices anticipate the physical context in which the document is likely to be read.

Writers of reflective documents often connect their observations to the social, cultural, and historical contexts they share with their readers. For example, they might refer to events or people who have recently received considerable attention from the news media. In addition, they might refer to works of art, such as the *Mona Lisa*, or quotations from well-known works of literature, such as Hamlet's question "To be, or not to be?" Writers of reflective documents are also aware of the physical contexts in which their documents are likely to be read, and they design their documents to meet the needs of those contexts: for instance, a short essay for a writing class will typically feature double-spaced text with wide margins and few, if any, adornments, while a blog entry might include animated graphics, audio and video clips, or links to related Web sites.

Whether writing for themselves or others, writers use reflective writing to connect ideas and information, often in new and intriguing ways. Through reflection, writers can create new ways of understanding the world in which we live.

What Kinds of Documents Are Used to Share Reflections?

As a writer, you can use the reflections of other writers in many ways. Among other purposes, they can help you gain firsthand impressions from people who have been affected by an event. They can allow you to learn more about a particular historical period. They can help you understand the motivations and experiences of key figures in a political, cultural, or social movement. And they can help you develop a fuller understanding of your own experiences as you prepare your own reflective document.

You can begin to understand the contributions made by reflective documents by learning about the purposes, readers, sources, and contexts that have influenced other writers. In the following sections, you'll find discussions and examples of memoirs, photo essays, short stories, literacy narratives, and reflective essays.

View a multimedia example of reflective writing in the e-book at **bedfordstmartins.com/ conversation**.

Memoirs

A memoir is a narrative that presents and reflects on personal experience, usually from a writer's past. In some cases, memoirs draw extensively on information, ideas, and arguments from written sources, interviews, and observations. A memoir such as Ishmael Beah's book *A Long Way Gone* (see p. 96), for example, uses the work of other authors to shape his reflections on his experiences as a boy soldier in Sierra

Leone. By contrasting his personal memories with the observations and analyses published by reporters and historians, Beah is able not only to base his reflections on his own experiences but also to deepen his personal insights by drawing on ideas that have shaped international discussions about war and human rights.

Memoirs can vary greatly in length, from a few hundred words to multiple-volume books. Writers of shorter memoirs often focus on a specific moment and address readers of a particular publication, such as a newspaper, magazine, journal, or Web site. Writers of longer (book-length) memoirs usually address a more general audience of readers who share their interest in a certain aspect of their lives. Regardless of length, writers of memoirs usually employ the first-person point of view (*I*, *me*, *we*), emphasize text over visuals, and look for ways to make their personal stories relevant for readers.

 **Firoozeh Dumas**
Waterloo

"Waterloo" is a chapter from the best-selling book *Funny in Farsi: A Memoir of Growing Up Iranian in America* (2003). In this brief narrative, Firoozeh Dumas reflects on her father's failed attempts to teach her how to swim and considers what it finally took for her to overcome her fear of drowning. At the same time—and as Dumas has explained—she attempts to counter American fears of Middle Easterners by underscoring the universalities of human experience.

Waterloo

My father is a proud man. He was the first member of his family to study in America, the first to win a Fulbright scholarship, and, years later, the first to settle permanently in America. Because of him, his siblings and their families ended up in Southern California, where they all live within half an hour of one another. "I am the Christopher Columbus of the family," he always says.

Nothing, however, has made my father as proud as his role as the family swim instructor. In Iran, people learned to swim on their own, if they learned at all. My mother, like most women of her generation, never learned to swim. Neither did four of her five sisters, or her brother. This was the norm. My father, always the progressive man, decided that every one of his children and his nieces and nephews would learn to swim. Abadan, having been built by the British, contained many luxuries not readily found in other areas, including a clubhouse with a large pool. Every summer my relatives came from all over Iran to stay with us, and, sure enough, it was always some child's turn to learn to swim. Like a game-show host announcing the next contestant, my father would say, "This summer, it's *your* turn, Mahmood!"

My father had a perfect track record, a topic he loved to talk about. "I have a gift," he'd always say. We had all resigned ourselves to having to listen over and over again to his description of the exact moment at which each niece and nephew learned to swim and the spellbinding tension leading up to it. "Mahmood said, 'Uncle Kazem, I can't do this,' and I said, 'Yes, you can,' and he lifted his arm like this and I pushed him a little bit and he kicked like this and he started to swim like a fish, so I said, 'Hey, you never told me you knew how to swim!'" He'd always end these riveting tales by telling us, "You should've been there!" We were all glad we hadn't been. The stories were interesting the first fourteen times, but beyond that, they became the equivalent of the neighbor's vacation slides showing the cathedrals of France from all angles. Unfortunately, there just wasn't much anyone could do to put an end to these tales. Each new swimmer represented a victory, and talking about it made my father relive his moments of glory over and over again. The twinkle in his eye, the excitement in his voice, the pride in his face all made it clear that my father would never stop retelling his stories.

History, however, has shown us that even the greatest of generals must eventually face defeat in battle, and thus was carved my destiny. I was my father's Waterloo.

My father, an engineer, had an entirely logical approach to teaching his students to swim. In a methodical manner, he would explain all the necessary ingredients in swimming. "Your head goes like this, thus creating buoyancy; your feet go like this, thus propelling you forward; your arms go like this to steer you. You put it all together and you've got it!" Hearing him explain it made swimming seem as easy as baking a Betty Crocker cake from a mix. You just add water and there you go.

The cerebral approach worked on all of my father's swimming students, most of whom, not coincidentally, grew up to be engineers. I, however, needed something else. I've never been interested in why exactly an airplane can fly; I want to know if the pilot has had enough sleep. In learning to swim, I just wanted to know that I wasn't going to die. My father, however, never quite understood the role of anxiety in my fruitless swimming lessons. He eventually decided that perhaps if he yelled or hurled insults, I might learn more quickly. "You're like a rock! You're hopeless! What's wrong with you?" This method may work wonders in the army, but it didn't work with me. I now had two hurdles to overcome, fear of water and fear of being in the water with my father.

After a couple summers' worth of lessons, I had managed, by age six, to learn nothing, setting an all-time failure record for my father. In hindsight, I believe my ability to dodge all learning opportunities did reveal a certain inner strength, a persistent refusal to be like the others. But the British never appreciated Gandhi's persistence, and my family didn't appreciate mine.

My father eventually decided that we didn't actually have to be in a pool for him to get angry with me for not knowing how to swim. He started to have a somewhat Pavlovian reaction toward me. If anybody used the word "swim," my father would glare at me with a combination of shame and anger, a look that said, "I wish I had kept the receipt." To save face, he had come up with a theory of why I couldn't swim. "She's built like a rock," he'd always say. "She just sinks." This wasn't entirely true. I had never actually let go of my father in the pool, preferring instead to cling to him like a koala on a eucalyptus branch during an earthquake. His determination to peel me off himself matched, but did not exceed, my determination to hold on to him.

Sadly enough, my father stopped talking altogether about his glorious swimming lessons. He knew that no impressive tale could match his one big failure, *moi*. He finally announced to the world, which for us consisted of my aunts, uncles, and cousins, that some people are incapable of swimming. "Firoozeh is one of them," he concluded.

When I was eight years old, we went to Switzerland to visit my aunt Parvine, my mother's sister. Aunt Parvine has always been considered something of a deity in our family because she managed, despite being an Iranian woman of her generation, to become a doctor and to set up a successful practice in Geneva. The woman overcame so many hurdles to reach her dream that she deserves to have her likeness carved in marble. The fact that she actually lives in Switzerland further adds to her allure. Iranians have always considered Switzerland the apogee of civilization: a small, clean country where bus drivers don't have to check for tickets since everyone is so genetically honest. Besides, Switzerland has never particularly welcomed Iranians, thus accruing the magnetism that comes only with repeated rejection.

Aunt Parvine told my father that *she* was going to teach me how to swim. My parents decided to leave me with her one afternoon while she worked her medical magic. It didn't occur to them that perhaps they should stay and watch the swimming lesson. My aunt took me to the deep end of the pool and there, this highly educated woman, whom I had grown up worshiping from afar, let go of me. I sank. Perhaps because of her medical training, or perhaps because she couldn't face the prospect of having to explain to my parents that she had killed their child, Parvine eventually decided to intervene. Moments before I got to see the tunnel with the light at the end and the angels beckoning me to join them, she lifted me out of the water.

My aunt dragged me out of the pool and, doing her best imitation of General Patton in a bad mood, announced that I was hopeless. When my parents joined us, she announced, "Firoozeh is a rock."

News of my European failure soon reached the rest of my relatives, thus cementing my reputation as The One Incapable of Swimming. Oddly enough, no one questioned my aunt's method of instruction; she was, after all, a doctor in Switzerland.

My near-drowning experience brought with it an unexpected ray of hope, like a wildflower blooming in a battlefield: my family was now completely resigned to my inability to swim. My father no longer insulted me; instead, he treated me with pity, since he now assumed that I was missing the chromosome necessary for buoyancy. His pity often led to trips to the toy store, thus proving that I was far smarter than my cousins. I managed to acquire eight new tea sets, while my cousins had merely learned to swim.

Most fruits, if left alone on a tree, eventually do ripen, especially if they're not being yelled at. It was thus that I, at the age of ten, decided that I was finally ready to learn to swim. There was, however, one proviso: I wanted to learn to swim in the sea by myself. I proudly made this announcement to my father, who, once he stopped laughing, said: "You never learned to swim in the pool, so now you want to go drown in the ocean?"

That summer, we headed for our annual weeklong vacation by the Caspian Sea. Because of work commitments, my father was unable to join us. My two brothers, my mother, and my aunt Sedigeh and uncle Abdullah and their four sons, who knew how to swim courtesy of my father, headed north to the Caspian. Once we arrived, I went straight to the beach. I took a few steps into the water, where a gentle wave lifted me and I started to swim. Simple as that.

When we returned to Abadan, I proudly told my father the news. He did not believe me. He and I headed straight for the pool, where he watched in disbelief. "You, Firoozeh," he said, shaking his head, "are an odd child." "No," I said, "there was nobody yelling at me in the sea."

Years later, when we moved to Newport Beach, I discovered that one of the greatest joys in life is jumping from a boat into the deep, blue Pacific ocean. That was before I discovered snorkeling in the crystal-clear waters of the Bahamas with sea turtles and manta rays swimming around me. Later still, my husband introduced me to the cerulean waters of the Greek islands, where I spent hours swimming with the hot, Mediterranean sun burning on my back. But despite my dips in the many beautiful bodies of the water in the world, I have never forgotten that first gentle wave in the Caspian Sea, the one that lifted me and assured me that, yes, the pilot has had enough sleep.

Starting a Conversation: Respond to "Waterloo"

In your writer's notebook, consider how Dumas responds to her writing situation by answering the following questions:

1. On its surface, "Waterloo" gives an account of how the writer's father and aunt tried (and failed) to teach her how to swim. In what ways does this brief memoir also reflect on Dumas's identity, both within her family and beyond it? What do her struggles — and ultimate success — suggest about her character and sense of self?

2. In contrasting herself with her father and siblings, Dumas writes, "I've never been interested in why exactly an airplane can fly; I want to know if the pilot has had enough sleep" (par. 6). What distinction is she making here? Why does she close her reflections by referring back to this sentence?

3. Dumas quotes her father and other relatives several times in her memoir. What do their voices reveal about their personalities and attitudes? Does Dumas hear them differently than they hear themselves? How can you tell?

4. When *Funny in Farsi* was published in 2003, the United States was at war in Afghanistan and had just invaded Iraq; many Americans were suspicious of, even hostile toward, people from the Middle East. What strategies does Dumas use to connect with her readers? Do you see any parallels between her learning experience and her attempts to familiarize Americans with Iranian culture?

@ Download or print this Starting a Conversation activity at **bedfordstmartins.com/ conversation.**

Photo Essays

A photo essay combines text and photographs to create a dominant impression of a subject, often suggesting the author's main idea rather than stating it outright. As a visual document, a photo essay offers a powerful and refreshing opportunity to convey thoughts and emotions that might not easily be put into words and to present complex concepts in a way that readers can grasp almost intuitively.

Many reflective photo essays visually explore subjects that have spurred debate, seem misunderstood, or are relatively unknown to readers. Others are deeply personal, highlighting images and experiences intimately connected to the writer's life. Writers might rely on published images from historical and contemporary sources or present

Lost Memories

Kazuyoshi Ehara

Only loved ones remember what an Alzheimer's patient has lost. Yoshikazu Ehara is my grandfather. Eight years ago, when he was eighty, he was diagnosed with Alzheimer's disease. Daily life has become a struggle for Yoshikazu and his family as the disease has slowly erased his memories and abilities. This is the story of my grandfather's struggle with the disease and his changing relationship with my grandmother, his wife Sakae.

original photographs. In either case, the pictures serve a central role in the author's reflection because they contribute to the meaning of the document. Text and image play off each other to reinforce ideas and to clarify what the writer has to say. Readers are invited to draw their own conclusions from what they see, although the author typically uses the surrounding text to nudge them in a particular direction.

Kazuyoshi Ehara and Rhiana Ehara
Lost Memories

The award-winning photo essay reprinted here is from *Geist*, a Canadian literary magazine that includes fiction, nonfiction, poetry, and photography. With six short

Yoshikazu Ehara looks out the window of a senior daycare centre in Nanguo, Japan.

paragraphs and a handful of photographs, Kazuyoshi and Rhiana Ehara document the daily struggle of Kazuyoshi's grandparents as they deal with his grandfather's Alzheimer's disease. But "Lost Memories" also connects the intimate life of one specific family to a disease that affects people everywhere. In the process, the photo

Yoshikazu often stops near the front door to converse with a doll for long enough that a family member can catch up with him and accompany him when he goes outside. In the evenings, Sakae waits for Yoshikazu to fall asleep before she does so herself.

In the advanced stages of Alzheimer's, easy tasks can become difficult. Sometimes Yoshikazu tries to put on pants as though they were a shirt.

essay reflects on the mysteries of memory, identity, and love. A native of Japan, Kazuyoshi Ehara studied photojournalism in Canada; he has worked for the *Toronto Star*, and his photo essays have been featured in many international publications.

Yoshikazu has trouble sleeping at night and rests sporadically during the day. He takes a nap in the morning while Sakae waits for a caregiver to arrive from the nursing home.

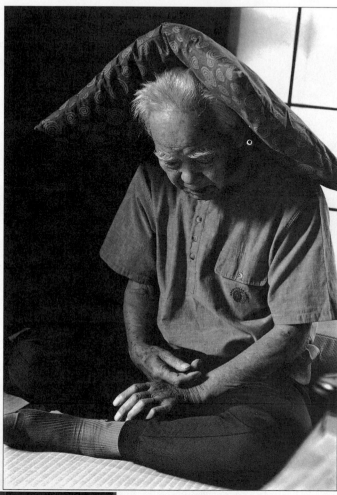

Yoshikazu falls asleep in his living room after putting a cushion on his head.

Yoshikazu claps his hands in bed after placing neckties around himself during the night.

"I have to go," says Yoshikazu when he wants to leave. Nobody knows why or where he wants to go.

Kazuyoshi Ehara lives in Toronto. His work can be seen at www.sakanaphotography.com. He is represented by Klixpix.

Starting a Conversation: Respond to "Lost Memories"

In your writer's notebook, reflect on the ideas presented in Ehara's photo essay by responding to the following questions:

1. A reflective photo essay such as this one might not have a strictly defined thesis statement. But how would you describe the main idea of Ehara's work? What is the dominant impression created by his mix of words and pictures?

2. In the opening sentence, Rhiana Ehara refers to "what an Alzheimer's patient has lost." How, specifically, do the photographs create a sense of loss?

3. In addition to contemporary photographs, Ehara includes images of his grandparents in their younger years. How does this choice connect to his purpose? What effect does it have on the reader?

4. Why do you suppose Ehara chose to use black-and-white images? Would color photographs have had more impact, or less impact? Why do you think so?

5. Besides appearing in *Geist*, "Lost Memories" was featured at an international conference on Alzheimer's disease in Tokyo, Japan. What might this intimate, personal photo essay contribute to the medical community's understanding of the disease?

@ Download or print this Starting a Conversation activity at **bedfordstmartins.com/ conversation**.

Short Stories

The painter Pablo Picasso said that "art is the lie that tells the truth," a definition that can also be applied to short stories. Unlike writers of memoirs or photo essays, fiction writers are free to present their own versions of "reality." They can invent their own characters, plots, and dramatic scenarios and can create and arrange details to suggest particular patterns, effects, and meanings. Most important, fiction writers are allowed to explore ideas and conflicts unfettered by the need to record things as they "really" happened.

Short stories can be as short as a single page or as long as a short novel, although they usually run somewhere between five and twenty-five pages. Short story writers tend to focus on a particular event or situation and are far less likely than novelists to address multiple subjects or story lines. Readers of short stories understand that short stories are not "true" in the way that a magazine or newspaper article is. However, readers do expect the characters and plot in a short story to seem real and credible. Readers also expect a short story to provide the kind of "truth" that Picasso referred to—an insight or a revelation that emerges from careful reflection.

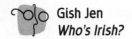
Gish Jen
Who's Irish?

"Who's Irish?" is a chapter from Gish Jen's short story collection *Who's Irish?: Stories* (1999), which explores the lives of Chinese-American immigrants as they deal with assimilation and difference in American culture. Through her characters, Jen also delves into issues of identity, race, and class; her stories frequently reflect the experiences of other ethnic and immigrant communities — in this case, Irish Americans. Jen is a second-generation Chinese American raised in Scarsdale, New York; she later earned a degree in English from Harvard University and married an Irish-American man, an experience which inspired her to write *Who's Irish?*. Many of her short stories and novels, including *Typical American* (1991) and its sequel, *Mona in the Promised Land* (1996), also portray families navigating cultural differences and new identities.

CHAPTER ONE

||||||||||||||||||||||||||||||||

Who's Irish?

In China, people say mixed children are supposed to be smart, and definitely my granddaughter Sophie is smart. But Sophie is wild, Sophie is not like my daughter Natalie, or like me. I am work hard my whole life, and fierce besides. My husband always used to say he is afraid of me, and in our restaurant, busboys and cooks all afraid of me too. Even the gang members come for protection money, they try to talk to my husband. When I am there, they stay away. If they come by mistake, they pretend they are come to eat. They hide behind the menu, they order a lot of food. They talk about their mothers. Oh, my mother have some arthritis, need to take herbal medicine, they say. Oh, my mother getting old, her hair all white now.

I say, Your mother's hair used to be white, but since she dye it, it become black again. Why don't you go home once in a while and take a look? I tell them, Confucius say a filial son knows what color his mother's hair is.

My daughter is fierce too, she is vice president in the bank now. Her new house is big enough for everybody to have their own room, including me. But Sophie take after Natalie's husband's family, their name is Shea. Irish. I always thought Irish people are like Chinese people, work so hard on the railroad, but now I know why the Chinese beat the Irish. Of course, not all Irish are like the Shea family, of course not. My daughter tell me I should not say Irish this, Irish that.

How do you like it when people say the Chinese this, the Chinese that? she say.

You know, the British call the Irish heathen, just like they call the Chinese, she say.

You think the Opium War was bad, how would you like to live right next door to the British? she say.

And that is that. My daughter have a funny habit when she win an argument, she take a sip of something and look away, so the other person is not embarrassed. So I am not embarrassed. I do not call anybody anything either. I just happen to mention about the Shea family, an interesting fact: four brothers in the family, and not one of them work. The mother, Bess, have a job before she got sick, she was executive secretary in a big company. She is handle everything for a big shot, you would be surprised how complicated her job is, not just type this, type that. Now she is a nice woman with a clean house. But her boys, every one of them is on welfare, or so-called severance pay, or so-called disability pay. Something. They say they cannot find work, this is not the economy of the fifties, but I say, Even the black people doing better these days, some of them live so fancy, you'd be surprised. Why the Shea family have so much trouble? They are white people, they speak English. When I come to this country, I have no money and do not speak English. But my husband and I own our restaurant before he die. Free and clear, no mortgage. Of course, I understand I am just lucky, come from a country where the food is popular all over the world. I understand it is not the Shea family's fault they come from a country where everything is boiled. Still, I say.

She's right, we should broaden our horizons, say one brother, Jim, at Thanksgiving. Forget about the car business. Think about egg rolls.

Pad thai, say another brother, Mike. I'm going to make my fortune in pad thai. It's going to be the new pizza.

I say, You people too picky about what you sell. Selling egg rolls not good enough for you, but at least my husband and I can say, We made it. What can you say? Tell me. What can you say?

Everybody chew their tough turkey.

I especially cannot understand my daughter's husband John, who has no job but cannot take care of Sophie either. Because he is a man, he say, and that's the end of the sentence.

Plain boiled food, plain boiled thinking. Even his name is plain boiled: John. Maybe because I grew up with black bean sauce and hoisin sauce and garlic sauce, I always feel something is missing when my son-in-law talk.

But, okay: so my son-in-law can be man, I am baby-sitter. Six hours a day, same as the old sitter, crazy Amy, who quit. This is not so easy, now that I am sixty-eight, Chinese age almost seventy. Still, I try. In China, daughter take care of mother. Here it is the other way around. Mother help daughter, mother ask, Anything else I can do? Otherwise daughter complain mother is not supportive. I tell daughter, We do not have this word in Chinese, *supportive*. But my daughter too busy to listen, she has to go to meeting, she has to write memo while her husband go to the gym to be a man. My daughter say otherwise he will be depressed. Seems like all his life he has this trouble, depression.

No one wants to hire someone who is depressed, she say. It is important for him to keep his spirits up.

Beautiful wife, beautiful daughter, beautiful house, oven can clean itself automatically. No money left over, because only one income, but lucky enough, got the baby-sitter for free. If John lived in China, he would be very happy. But he is not happy. Even at the gym things go wrong. One day, he pull a muscle. Another day, weight room too crowded. Always something.

Until finally, hooray, he has a job. Then he feel pressure.

I need to concentrate, he say. I need to focus.

He is going to work for insurance company. Salesman job. A paycheck, he say, and at least he will wear clothes instead of gym shorts. My daughter buy him some special candy bars from the health-food store. They say THINK! on them, and are supposed to help John think.

John is a good-looking boy, you have to say that, especially now that he shave so you can see his face.

I am an old man in a young man's game, say John.

I will need a new suit, say John.

This time I am not going to shoot myself in the foot, say John.

Good, I say.

She means to be supportive, my daughter say. Don't start the send her back to China thing, because we can't.

Sophie is three years old American age, but already I see her nice Chinese side swallowed up by her wild Shea side. She looks like mostly Chinese. Beautiful black hair, beautiful black eyes. Nose perfect size, not so flat looks like something fell down, not so large looks like some big deal got stuck in wrong face. Everything just right, only her skin is a brown surprise to John's family. So brown, they say. Even John say it. She never goes in the sun, still she is that color, he say. Brown. They say, Nothing the matter with brown. They are just surprised. So brown. Nattie is not that brown, they say. They say, It seems like Sophie should be a color in between Nattie and John. Seems funny, a girl named Sophie Shea be brown. But she is brown, maybe her name should be Sophie Brown. She never go in the sun, still she is that color, they say. Nothing the matter with brown. They are just surprised.

The Shea family talk is like this sometimes, going around and around like a Christmas-tree train.

Maybe John is not her father, I say one day, to stop the train. And sure enough, train wreck. None of the brothers ever say the word *brown* to me again.

Instead, John's mother, Bess, say, I hope you are not offended.

She say, I did my best on those boys. But raising four boys with no father is no picnic.

You have a beautiful family, I say.

I'm getting old, she say.

You deserve a rest, I say. Too many boys make you old.

I never had a daughter, she say. You have a daughter.

I have a daughter, I say. Chinese people don't think a daughter is so great, but you're right. I have a daughter.

I was never against the marriage, you know, she say. I never thought John was marrying down. I always thought Nattie was just as good as white.

I was never against the marriage either, I say. I just wonder if they look at the whole problem.

Of course you pointed out the problem, you are a mother, she say. And now we both have a granddaughter. A little brown granddaughter, she is so precious to me.

I laugh. A little brown granddaughter, I say. To tell you the truth, I don't know how she came out so brown.

We laugh some more. These days Bess need a walker to walk. She take so many pills, she need two glasses of water to get them all down. Her favorite TV show is about bloopers, and she love her bird feeder. All day long, she can watch that bird feeder, like a cat.

I can't wait for her to grow up, Bess say. I could use some female company.

Too many boys, I say.

Boys are fine, she say. But they do surround you after a while.

You should take a break, come live with us, I say. Lots of girls at our house.

Be careful what you offer, say Bess with a wink. Where I come from, people mean for you to move in when they say a thing like that.

Nothing the matter with Sophie's outside, that's the truth. It is inside that she is like not any Chinese girl I ever see. We go to the park, and this is what she does. She stand up in the stroller. She take off all her clothes and throw them in the fountain.

Sophie! I say. Stop!

But she just laugh like a crazy person. Before I take over as baby-sitter, Sophie has that crazy-person sitter, Amy the guitar player. My daughter thought this Amy very creative — another word we do not talk about in China. In China, we talk about whether we have difficulty or no difficulty. We talk about whether life is bitter or not bitter. In America, all day long, people talk about creative. Never mind that I cannot even look at this Amy, with her shirt so short that her belly button showing. This Amy think Sophie should love her body. So when Sophie take off her diaper, Amy laugh. When Sophie run around naked, Amy say she wouldn't want to wear a diaper either. When Sophie go *shu-shu* in her lap, Amy laugh and say there are no germs in pee. When Sophie take off her shoes, Amy say bare feet is best, even the pediatrician say so. That is why Sophie now walk around with no shoes like a beggar child. Also why Sophie love to take off her clothes.

Turn around! say the boys in the park. Let's see that ass!

Of course, Sophie does not understand. Sophie clap her hands, I am the only one to say, No! This is not a game.

It has nothing to do with John's family, my daughter say. Amy was too permissive, that's all.

But I think if Sophie was not wild inside, she would not take off her shoes and clothes to begin with.

You never take off your clothes when you were little, I say. All my Chinese friends had babies, I never saw one of them act wild like that.

Look, my daughter say. I have a big presentation tomorrow.

John and my daughter agree Sophie is a problem, but they don't know what to do.

You spank her, she'll stop, I say another day.

But they say, Oh no.

In America, parents not supposed to spank the child.

It gives them low self-esteem, my daughter say. And that leads to problems later, as I happen to know.

My daughter never have big presentation the next day when the subject of spanking come up.

I don't want you to touch Sophie, she say. No spanking, period.

Don't tell me what to do, I say.

I'm not telling you what to do, say my daughter. I'm telling you how I feel.

I am not your servant, I say. Don't you dare talk to me like that.

My daughter have another funny habit when she lose an argument. She spread out all her fingers and look at them, as if she like to make sure they are still there.

My daughter is fierce like me, but she and John think it is better to explain to Sophie that clothes are a good idea. This is not so hard in the cold weather. In the warm weather, it is very hard.

Use your words, my daughter say. That's what we tell Sophie. How about if you set a good example?

As if good example mean anything to Sophie. I am so fierce, the gang members who used to come to the restaurant all afraid of me, but Sophie is not afraid.

I say, Sophie, if you take off your clothes, no snack.

I say, Sophie, if you take off your clothes, no lunch.

I say, Sophie, if you take off your clothes, no park.

Pretty soon we are stay home all day, and by the end of six hours she still did not have one thing to eat. You never saw a child stubborn like that.

I'm hungry! she cry when my daughter come home.

What's the matter, doesn't your grandmother feed you? My daughter laugh.

No! Sophie say. She doesn't feed me anything!

My daughter laugh again. Here you go, she say.

She say to John, Sophie must be growing.

Growing like a weed, I say.

Still Sophie take off her clothes, until one day I spank her. Not too hard, but she cry and cry, and when I tell her if she doesn't put her clothes back on I'll spank her again, she put her clothes back on. Then I tell her she is good girl, and give her some food to eat. The next day we go to the park and, like a nice Chinese girl, she does not take off her clothes.

She stop taking off her clothes, I report. Finally!

How did you do it? my daughter ask.

After twenty-eight years experience with you, I guess I learn something, I say.

It must have been a phase, John say, and his voice is suddenly like an expert.

His voice is like an expert about everything these days, now that he carry a leather briefcase, and wear shiny shoes, and can go shopping for a new car. On the company, he say. The company will pay for it, but he will be able to drive it whenever he want.

A free car, he say. How do you like that?

It's good to see you in the saddle again, my daughter say. Some of your family patterns are scary.

At least I don't drink, he say. He say, And I'm not the only one with scary family patterns.

That's for sure, say my daughter.

Everyone is happy. Even I am happy, because there is more trouble with Sophie, but now I think I can help her Chinese side fight against her wild side. I teach her to eat food with fork or spoon or chopsticks, she cannot just grab into the middle of a bowl of noodles. I teach her not to play with garbage cans. Sometimes I spank her, but not too often, and not too hard.

Still, there are problems. Sophie like to climb everything. If there is a railing, she is never next to it. Always she is on top of it. Also, Sophie like to hit the mommies of her friends. She learn this from her playground best friend, Sinbad, who is four. Sinbad wear army clothes every day and like to ambush his mommy. He is the one who dug a big hole under the play structure, a foxhole he call it, all by himself. Very hardworking. Now he wait in the foxhole with a shovel full of wet sand. When his mommy come, he throw it right at her.

Oh, it's all right, his mommy say. You can't get rid of war games, it's part of their imaginative play. All the boys go through it.

Also, he like to kick his mommy, and one day he tell Sophie to kick his mommy too.

I wish this story is not true.

Kick her, kick her! Sinbad say.

Sophie kick her. A little kick, as if she just so happened was swinging her little leg and didn't realize that big mommy leg was in the way. Still I spank Sophie and make Sophie say sorry, and what does the mommy say?

Really, it's all right, she say. It didn't hurt.

After that, Sophie learn she can attack mommies in the playground, and some will say, Stop, but others will say, Oh, she didn't mean it, especially if they realize Sophie will be punished.

This is how, one day, bigger trouble come. The bigger trouble start when Sophie hide in the foxhole with that shovel full of sand. She wait, and when I come look for her, she throw it at me. All over my nice clean clothes.

Did you ever see a Chinese girl act this way?

Sophie! I say. Come out of there, say you're sorry.

But she does not come out. Instead, she laugh. Naaah, naah-na, naaa-naaa, she say.

I am not exaggerate: millions of children in China, not one act like this.

Sophie! I say. Now! Come out now!

But she know she is in big trouble. She know if she come out, what will happen next. So she does not come out. I am sixty-eight, Chinese age almost seventy, how can I crawl under there to catch her? Impossible. So I yell, yell, yell, and what happen? Nothing. A Chinese mother would help, but American mothers, they look at you, they shake their head, they go home. And, of course, a Chinese child would give up, but not Sophie.

I hate you! she yell. I hate you, Meanie!

Meanie is my new name these days.

Long time this goes on, long long time. The foxhole is deep, you cannot see too much, you don't know where is the bottom. You cannot hear too much either. If she does not yell, you cannot even know she is still there or not. After a while, getting cold out, getting dark out. No one left in the playground, only us.

Sophie, I say. How did you become stubborn like this? I am go home without you now.

I try to use a stick, chase her out of there, and once or twice I hit her, but still she does not come out. So finally I leave. I go outside the gate.

Bye-bye! I say. I'm go home now.

But still she does not come out and does not come out. Now it is dinnertime, the sky is black. I think I should maybe go get help, but how can I leave a little girl by herself in the playground? A bad man could come. A rat could come. I go back in to see what is happen to Sophie. What if she have a shovel and is making a tunnel to escape?

Sophie! I say.

No answer.

Sophie!

I don't know if she is alive. I don't know if she is fall asleep down there. If she is crying, I cannot hear her.

So I take the stick and poke.

Sophie! I say. I promise I no hit you. If you come out, I give you a lollipop.

No answer. By now I worried. What to do, what to do, what to do? I poke some more, even harder, so that I am poking and poking when my daughter and John suddenly appear.

What are you doing? What is going on? say my daughter.

Put down that stick! say my daughter.

You are crazy! say my daughter.

John wiggle under the structure, into the foxhole, to rescue Sophie.

She fell asleep, say John the expert. She's okay. That is one big hole.

Now Sophie is crying and crying.

Sophie, my daughter say, hugging her. Are you okay, peanut? Are you okay?

She's just scared, say John.

Are you okay? I say too. I don't know what happen, I say.

She's okay, say John. He is not like my daughter, full of questions. He is full of answers until we get home and can see by the lamplight.

Will you look at her? he yell then. What the hell happened?

Bruises all over her brown skin, and a swollen-up eye.

You are crazy! say my daughter. Look at what you did! You are crazy!

I try very hard, I say.

How could you use a stick? I told you to use your words!

She is hard to handle, I say.

She's three years old! You cannot use a stick! say my daughter.

She is not like any Chinese girl I ever saw, I say.

I brush some sand off my clothes. Sophie's clothes are dirty too, but at least she has her clothes on.

Has she done this before? ask my daughter. Has she hit you before?

She hits me all the time, Sophie say, eating ice cream.

Your family, say John.

Believe me, say my daughter.

A daughter I have, a beautiful daughter. I took care of her when she could not hold her head up. I took care of her before she could argue with me, when she was a little girl with two pigtails, one of them always crooked. I took care of her when we have to escape from China, I took care of her when suddenly we live in a country with cars everywhere, if you are not careful your little girl get run over. When my husband die, I promise him I will keep the family together, even though it was just two of us, hardly a family at all.

But now my daughter take me around to look at apartments. After all, I can cook, I can clean, there's no reason I cannot live by myself, all I need is a telephone. Of course, she is sorry. Sometimes she cry, I am the one to say everything will be okay. She say she have no choice, she doesn't want to end up divorced. I say divorce is terrible, I don't know who invented this terrible idea. Instead of live with a telephone, though, surprise, I come to live with Bess. Imagine that. Bess make an offer and, sure enough, where she come from, people mean for you to move in when they say things like that. A crazy idea, go to live with someone else's family, but she like to have some female company, not like my daughter, who does not believe in company. These days when my daughter visit, she does not bring Sophie. Bess say we should give Nattie time, we will see Sophie again soon. But seems like my daughter have more presentation than ever before, every time she come she have to leave.

I have a family to support, she say, and her voice is heavy, as if soaking wet. I have a young daughter and a depressed husband and no one to turn to.

When she say no one to turn to, she mean me.

These days my beautiful daughter is so tired she can just sit there in a chair and fall asleep. John lost his job again, already, but still they rather hire a baby-sitter than ask me to help, even they can't afford it. Of course, the new baby-sitter is much younger, can run around. I don't know if Sophie these days is wild or not wild. She call me Meanie, but she like to kiss me too, sometimes. I remember that every time I see a child on TV. Sophie like to grab my hair, a fistful in each hand, and then kiss me smack on the nose. I never see any other child kiss that way.

The satellite TV has so many channels, more channels than I can count, including a Chinese channel from the mainland and a Chinese channel from Taiwan, but most of the time I watch bloopers with Bess. Also, I watch the bird feeder — so many, many kinds of birds come. The Shea sons hang around all the time, asking when will I go home, but Bess tell them, Get lost.

She's a permanent resident, say Bess. She isn't going anywhere.

Then she wink at me, and switch the channel with the remote control.

Of course, I shouldn't say Irish this, Irish that, especially now I am become honorary Irish myself, according to Bess. Me! Who's Irish? I say, and she laugh. All the same, if I could mention one thing about some of the Irish, not all of them of course, I like to mention this: Their talk just stick. I don't know how Bess Shea learn to use her words, but sometimes I hear what she say a long time later. *Permanent resident. Not going anywhere.* Over and over I hear it, the voice of Bess.

Starting a Conversation: Respond to "Who's Irish?"

In your writer's notebook, examine the ideas and writing strategies in Jen's short story by answering the following questions:

1. What do you think are the most significant themes in this story? What insights did you gain from reading the narrative?

2. As a reflective document, "Who's Irish?" not only relates a series of events from the narrator's point of view but also explains and interprets her

experiences. At what specific points in the story can you see the narrator moving between — or blending — the roles of observer and interpreter? (For an overview of writers' roles, see p. 10.)

3. From evidence in the story (such as language, references, events, and images), how do you think Jen imagines her readers? What makes the story accessible to a larger audience?

4. The narrator is conscious of being different, not only from Americans but also from the Shea family and her own daughter. How does she illustrate and emphasize these contrasts?

5. The story hints at several social and political issues — including ethnicity, identity, and assimilation. Choose one such issue and explain what the narrator's experience might reveal about Jen's thinking on the subject. How does framing her thoughts as fiction allow the author to engage her readers in a contemporary debate without presenting a formal argument?

@ Download or print this Starting a Conversation activity at **bedfordstmartins.com/ conversation.**

Literacy Narratives

Literacy narratives allow writers to reflect on the people, ideas, and events that have shaped them as writers and readers. What distinguishes literacy narratives from other reflective documents is not their design — they are often indistinguishable in appearance from essays or brief memoirs — but their purpose. They exist solely to help writers share their reflections about their relationship with reading and writing. Some literacy narratives, such as the following one, focus on a critical event or series of events that influenced a person's identity as a writer. Others offer a comprehensive overview of the experiences that shaped the writer's relationship with words. Because of their focus on the writer's life, most literacy narratives use details drawn from personal experience to support points. In some cases, writers draw on information from published sources to provide a context for their narrative.

Literacy narratives are often assigned in college classes because they give students an opportunity to examine their past experiences with written expression and, in doing so, to overcome any assumptions or fears they might have. Experienced writers, too, frequently write literacy narratives, sometimes to share their joy of reading or their reasons for writing, but just as often to connect with their readers by exploring the challenges and rewards of learning to read and write.

Tayari Jones
Among the Believers

Tayari Jones is the author of two novels that explore life in the South: *Leaving Atlanta* (2002) and *The Untelling* (2005). In this literacy narrative, first published in the *New York Times* in 2005, she explores the relationship between spirituality and language by reflecting on a childhood shaped by her father's atheism and her grandmother's faith, her immersion in a society that takes Christian faith as a given, and her struggles to find the words that would help her fit in. Born and raised in Atlanta and currently living in the Northeast, Jones teaches creative writing at Rutgers University, Newark.

Among the Believers

In elementary school, I spent a great deal of energy trying to explain the difference between atheism and devil worship. Until second grade I answered the commonplace query: "Where do you go to church?" with this: "My father says that we don't believe in God." Adults took this information with shocked silence, but children lack restraint. "You're a devil worshiper?" they asked. I didn't think I was, but I asked Daddy, who assured me that we were not. "Atheists," he explained, "don't believe in the devil either."

Though most of the other children found this argument to be convincing, they still demonstrated the difference between chilly tolerance and the warmth that came from actually fitting in. But I remained true to my faithlessness for the same reasons most children are true to a faith: because it is what their parents tell them.

My father, a preacher's son, had not been so obedient. When I visited his hometown, Oakdale, Louisiana, I was constantly aware that I was the daughter of the son who strayed.

During my summers in Oakdale, I understood what an outsider I really was. Unable to sing hymns from memory, not knowing when to stand or sit during the sermon—all of these things marked me as an infidel among believers. The most humiliating moment came at meals, when we all bowed our heads and one-by-one recited a Bible verse before starting to eat. My cousin Shunda—three years older, supremely disdainful and thus intimidatingly sophisticated—possessed a vast repertoire of pre-meal utterances. When my turn came, I could say only, "Jesus wept," which is like the tricycle of verses.

The summer before I entered fifth grade, my visit to Oakdale happened to coincide with vacation Bible school. At last, I could receive the remedial religious instruction I'd been longing for!

I looked forward to discussions in which I could ask some of the questions that I had previously posed to my father, who gave the most unsatisfying responses:

Q. If God made the world, who made God?
A. God didn't make the world.
Q. Then why does it say so in the Bible?
A. Makes people feel better.

Q. How do the angels get their clothes on? Don't the wings get in the way?

A. The same way Santa gets down the chimney.

To my chagrin, there was little theological analysis in vacation Bible school. Mostly we used stumpy crayons to color bizarre pictures: line drawings of animals in pairs, dead giants, bread and fish. There weren't even captions saying who was who and what was what. We didn't learn any good hymns. By the third day of the five-day program, the only useful thing I had learned was that Job rhymed with "robe," not with "bob." On the fourth day, we used Popsicle sticks and yarn to make ornamental crucifixes called "God's Eyes." On the last day, the Bible school teacher pulled me aside and asked what was troubling me.

I blurted my most pressing question: "If God made the world, who made God?"

She squinted: "Are you trying to be funny?"

"No," I told her. I just wanted to understand religion and be like everyone else for a change. The teacher gave me a little smile and handed me a mimeographed sheet to read at home. It was the text of the 23rd Psalm. I read the opening line, "The Lord is my Shepherd; I shall not want." I knew this verse; it was Shunda's. Oh, the wonder of punctuation. When she quoted the verse, I thought it a bit rude, rejecting the Lord as one's shepherd, whatever that meant. But now I understood.

Feeling something akin to faith, I vowed to learn at least a verse or two. I imagined the adoring faces of my relatives as I surprised them at Sunday dinner. I smiled back at the teacher, and she probably imagined that she had converted me, the daughter of Oakdale's best-known nonbelieving son.

The 23rd Psalm is not terribly long; before I knew it, I'd memorized the whole thing. Had I not won a prize the previous school year for reciting both "Hiawatha" and "Annabel Lee"? In Bible school we'd been told that God gives each person a special gift, a ministry. Perhaps dramatic recitation was mine.

At Grandmother's house the next Sunday, we all gathered around the table with our heads bowed. Beside me, my cousin said demurely, "Peace, be still." It was now my turn. Although most people pray with their eyes closed, I opened mine, wanting to see their expressions as I let loose with my Psalm.

"The Lord is my shepherd; I shall not want." Working my way through the first stanza, carefully pronouncing the "th" on "maketh," I felt something real. I pictured myself lying down in green pastures. In my mind's eye, I saw myself eating at the table prepared by the Lord. I'll never forget that moment of connection between myself and the glorious words; the comfort they described, was the warmth of well-being that I felt. By the time I got to the good part, I'd whipped myself into a fine crescendo: "Yea, though I walk through the valley of the shadow of death . . ."

At this instant, Shunda released a disapproving gasp-sigh. "Shut up," she said without saying. "The food is getting cold, you boring, annoying, little freak."

Chastened, I closed my eyes, but I continued my recitation, oblivious to the reaction of the others at the table, and the food cooling on the platters, riding the buoyancy of the words, filling my mind and heart with the lyrics of this strange and powerful song.

Now people think it charming when they find out that I grew up black, Southern, and atheist. At a recent cocktail party, on hearing about my background, a woman said to me, "How idiosyncratic!" I suppose she is right. Left to find my own way in matters of religion, I have a quirky collection of experiences that have helped me sort out my relationship with the divine.

The 23rd Psalm mimeographed on cheap paper gave me my first glimpse into spirituality, but the moment was not marked by the speaking of tongues. That moment will be forever etched in my memory as the day that language revealed to me if not its full power, its awesome potential. Maybe this is the day it was decided that I would be a writer, when I saw in the beauty of a poem the true glory of God.

Starting a Conversation: Respond to "Among the Believers"

In your writer's notebook, analyze what Jones's writing strategies contribute to her reflection by responding to the following questions:

1. In the early sections of her narrative, Jones highlights her status as an outsider, "an infidel among believers" (par. 4). In what ways does that status change or remain by the end of the essay?

2. In her conclusion, Jones describes people who find her background "charming" and "idiosyncratic" (par. 23). What does her description suggest about her readers and their assumptions? What does it suggest about Jones's attitude toward them?

3. Jones uses personal experience throughout her literacy narrative, sometimes re-creating conversations she had with teachers and family members. Do you find the dialogue realistic and convincing? Does it matter if the quotations are perfectly accurate? Why or why not?

4. Jones says that she could not get satisfying answers to her theological questions as a child, either from her father or at Bible school. What was she searching for? What does she ultimately discover?

@ Download or print this Starting a Conversation activity at bedfordstmartins.com/ conversation.

5. Literacy narratives focus on moments or events that shape a person's relationship with words. How would you describe the change in Jones's understanding of language? Of faith? What, exactly, is the connection between the two for her? Why did learning a psalm affect her so deeply?

Reflective Essays

Reflective essays convey a writer's observations and thoughts on a subject to a group of writers and readers involved in a written conversation. Like memoirs and literacy narratives, reflective essays draw on personal experience and are often written from a first-person (*I, me, my*) point of view. However, writers of reflective essays generally move beyond themselves as the primary focus of their essays, typically by using personal experience as a foundation for exploring more abstract ideas. In so doing, they show the significance of their experiences in a broader context.

In academic settings, such as writing and writing-intensive classes, reflective essays are often written in response to the information, ideas, or arguments found in another document, such as an article, an opinion column, or a personal essay. (If writers refer to another source, they cite it in the body of the essay and in a works cited or references list using a documentation system such as MLA or APA; see Chapters 21 and 22.) Because instructors and classmates will review and comment on them, reflective essays written for college courses are usually designed with wide margins, readable fonts, and double-spaced lines. In some cases, writers use illustrations, such as photographs and drawings, to set a mood or illustrate a point.

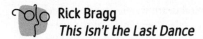 ### Rick Bragg
This Isn't the Last Dance

The following reflective essay was written in the immediate aftermath of Hurricane Katrina, when New Orleans was under water and the city's residents were struggling just to survive. In it, Rick Bragg evokes the elusive spirit of a city that has always both courted and mocked death. In the process, he reflects on the nature of places, the loving feelings we develop for them, and the need for hope in the face of disaster. Bragg is a Pulitzer Prize–winning journalist who has worked for several newspapers, including the *New York Times* and the *Washington Post*. He has also written memoirs and nonfiction books, focusing on life in the American South.

This Isn't the Last Dance

It has always had my heart in a box.

In the clip-joint souvenir shops in the gaudiest blocks of the Quarter, with canned Cajun music drilling rock-concert-loud into my ears, I could never resist opening the toy wooden coffins to see what was inside. I knew it would be just a cut-rate voodoo doll—a wad of rags, cheap plastic beads, and blind, button eyes. But every time, it made me smile. What a place, what a city, that can make you laugh at coffins and believe in magic—all the way to the cash register.

What a place, where old women sit beside you on outbound planes complaining about their diabetes while eating caramel-covered popcorn a fistful at a time. "It's hard, so hard, sweet baby," they will say of their disease, then go home and slick an iron skillet with bacon grease, because what good is there in a life without hot corn bread?

What a place, where in the poorest cemeteries the poorest men and women build tinfoil monuments to lost children in a potter's field, while just a few blocks over, the better-off lay out oyster po'boys and cold root beer and dine in the shade of the family crypt, doing lunch with their ancestors and the cement angels in cities of the dead.

What a place, so at ease here at the elbow of death, where I once marched and was almost compelled to dance in a jazz funeral for a street-corner conjurer named Chicken Man, who was carried to his resting place by a hot-stepping brass band and a procession of mourners who drank longneck beers and laughed out loud as his hearse rolled past doorways filled with men and women who clapped in time.

Now, for those of us who borrowed that spirit and used that love and then moved away, these past few awful days have seemed like a hospital death watch — and, in fact, for so many people it has been. And we stare deep into the television screen, at the water that had always seemed like just one more witch, one more story to scare ourselves into a warmer, deeper sleep, and we wonder if there is just too much water and too much death this time.

Ever since I was barely in my twenties, I have loved New Orleans the way some men love women, if that means unreasonably. I fell in love with the city and a Louisiana State University sophomore on the same night, eating shrimp cooked seven ways in the Quarter, riding the ferry across the black, black river where fireworks burned the air at Algiers Point. I drank so much rum I could sleep standing up against a wall. The sophomore left me, smiling, but the city never did.

There is no way to explain to someone who has never lived here why every day seemed like parole. Every time I would swing my legs from under the quilt and ease my toes onto the pine floors of my shotgun double, I would think, I am getting away with something here.

How long now before the streetcar rattles down St. Charles Avenue and beads swing into the two-hundred-year-old trees? How long before Dunbar's puts the chicken and stewed cabbage on the stove, or the overworked ladies at Domilisie's dress a po'boy on Annunciation Street, or the midday drinkers find their way back to Frankie and Johnny's on Arabella Street? Does my old house still stand on Joseph? It was high, high ground, on the lip of the bowl, and you could hit the Mississippi River with a silver dollar if you threw it twice.

I cannot stand the idea that it is broken, unfixable. I look at the men using axes to hack their way into hundred-year-old houses to save people trapped there by the suffocating water. I know there is life and death to be fought out for a long, long time. But I can't help but wonder what will come, later.

My wife, as wives do, voiced what most of us are afraid to say.

"I'm glad you took me there," she said. "Before."

We went there on our honeymoon.

Just a few weeks ago, I spent a week there, walking along Magazine, walking the Quarter, not minding the heat because that is what the devil sends, heat and water, to make you appreciate the smell of crushed cherries and whiskey on the balcony at the Columns Hotel, to make you savor the barbecued shrimp, to make your hear, really hear, the sound of a twelve-year-old boy blowing his heart out into a battered trumpet by a ragged cardboard box full of pocket change.

How long before that city reforms? Some people say it never will.
But I have seen these people dance, laughing, to the edge of a grave.
I believe that, now, they will dance back from it.

**Starting a
Conversation:
Respond to
"This Isn't the
Last Dance"**

In your writer's notebook, reflect on the meaning and implications of Bragg's essay by responding to the following questions:

1. Why does Bragg devote most of his introduction to celebrating the culture of death in New Orleans? What do his examples suggest about the overall significance of his observations?

2. Bragg claims, "Ever since I was barely in my twenties, I have loved New Orleans the way some men love women, if that means unreasonably" (par. 7). How does his relationship with the city affect his point of view—the perspective he takes when he describes and reflects on his subject? Does it make him more credible or less? Why?

3. According to Bragg, "There is no way to explain to someone who has never lived [in New Orleans] why every day seemed like parole" (par. 8). Moreover, he includes many local references and insider terms without explaining them. What does Bragg achieve by implying that some readers simply cannot understand his point? What does it suggest about his presumed audience? About his purpose?

4. Reflective essays often rely on observation and careful description to familiarize readers with a subject. How does Bragg take advantage of the five senses (sight, sound, touch, taste, and smell) to show what has happened to the city of New Orleans? Find examples of at least one of each among his descriptions. What do they contribute to the overall impression Bragg is trying to make?

5. Hurricane Katrina was an enormous national catastrophe with wide-ranging political, environmental, geographical, and racial consequences that are still being felt and discussed several years later. How does "This Isn't the Last Dance" connect to these larger conversations? For example, what is the essay's significance with regard to whether and how New Orleans is rebuilt?

@ Download or print this Starting a Conversation activity at **bedfordstmartins.com/ conversation**.

How Can I Write a Reflective Essay?

For some writers, the greatest challenge in writing a reflective essay is getting past the idea that no one would be interested in reading their reflections on a subject. In fact, readers show a great deal of interest in reflective writing. They buy memoirs and autobiographies, visit blogs, and read opinion columns. They read articles and essays in which writers share their thoughts about their experiences and ideas. Some readers even try to pick the locks on their sisters' diaries.

Reflective writing is popular not only among readers but also among writers. Reflective essays allow you to share your insights with instructors and classmates, people who are likely to have an interest in your perspective on a subject.

Writing a reflective essay involves choosing and reflecting on a subject, preparing a draft, and reviewing and improving what you've written. As you work on your essay, you'll follow the work of Caitlin Guariglia, an Italian American student who wrote a reflective essay about a family trip to Italy.

Find a Conversation and Listen In

Reflective essays allow you to share your thoughts about a subject with readers who might have a common interest in it. You might reflect on a personal experience, an idea you've encountered in a book or a blog, a photograph or other physical object that holds special meaning for you, a person you've met or read about, a troubling conversation with a friend, or a recent event. In fact, you can reflect on almost anything. To get started on your reflective essay, spend some time thinking about your purpose, your readers, and the context in which your writing will be read (see p. 98). Then generate some ideas about possible subjects for your reflection, choose one that seems promising, and learn more about it by observing it closely or discussing it with others.

EXPLORE YOUR EXPERIENCES

Brainstorming (see p. 33) provides a good way to generate ideas for the subject of a reflective essay. Start by asking questions about your past or recent experiences, such as the following:

- Why is my favorite childhood memory so special to me?
- Did I learn anything about myself this weekend?

In Process

A Reflective Essay about a Summer Vacation

Caitlin Guariglia wrote a reflective essay for her introductory composition course. Caitlin based her reflection on a family trip to Italy, using her observations of the people she met in Rome to reflect on how cultural influences affect her Italian American family's behavior. Follow her efforts to write the essay by visiting **bedfordstmartins.com/conversation.** You can read excerpts of interviews with Caitlin about her work on the essay and read drafts of her essay.

- What surprised me in my history class this week?
- What story that is currently in the news annoys me the most?
- What is the last thing that made me laugh?
- What do I worry about most?
- What in my life do I wish had gone differently?
- What am I most proud of, and why?

Use your imagination to come up with questions about your personal, academic, and professional experiences. Quickly jot down answers to your questions. Then review your answers to identify a subject that will meet your purpose, interest your readers, and be suitable for the context, requirements, and limitations of your writing assignment. If you're still not sure you've found the right inspiration for a topic, check the writing project ideas at the end of this chapter for additional suggestions (p. 150).

ASK QUESTIONS ABOUT PROMISING SUBJECTS

You can begin to focus on a subject by asking questions about it (see p. 38). If you were considering writing a reflective essay about online communities such as MySpace or Facebook, for example, you might use the following strategies to identify interesting aspects of the subject.

- **Ask *why, why not, when, where,* and *who*.** You might ask why so many parents react negatively to social-networking sites such as MySpace, or you might ask who is likely to cause difficulties for members of online communities.

- **Ask how your subject functions as a whole.** You might ask how Web sites such as MySpace are changing how people communicate, whether they represent a new kind of community, or why they're so popular with teenagers.

- **Ask about parts of a whole.** You might ask which aspects of online communities are more attractive than others or whether one subgroup in an online community is likely to behave differently than another subgroup.

- **Ask questions about degree and extent.** You can ask about the degree to which something affects something else or about the extent of a problem. For instance, you might ask how friendships formed at a school direct the formation of online communities or whether the dangers associated with social-networking sites are as widespread as reported.

CONDUCT AN OBSERVATION

If you've chosen a subject that lends itself to observation, you might find it useful to conduct one. Observing a subject firsthand can provide you with valuable insights that simply aren't possible when you're learning about the subject secondhand—for

Working Together: Try It Out Loud

Before you start writing a reflective essay, try having a conversation with your classmates about a common experience. Form small groups, and list the subjects each of you is considering writing about. Choose one that most people in the group can relate to (such as an embarrassing moment, a fight with a friend, or the first day of class). Take turns sharing your memories about the experience while the other members of the group listen, respond, and ask questions. Your purpose is to connect with the other members of your group, so try to present an honest, personal view of the event.

When you are finished, take a few minutes to reflect on the exercise. What did you learn about your audience? Did you have to adapt what you said based on their interest level or on those parts of your story they didn't understand? What did you discover about what you have in common and what you do not?

@ Download or print this Working Together activity at bedfordstmartins.com/conversation.

example, through discussion or through reading a book, magazine, or Web page. In addition, conducting an observation can increase your credibility as a writer. A reflective essay usually carries more weight if the writer has taken the time to observe the subject personally.

Although some observations can involve a significant amount of time and effort, an observation need not be complicated to be useful. Effective observations usually involve the following activities.

Want to know more about field research? See Chapter 12.

Decide whether to conduct an observation. Before you take the time to conduct an observation, ask yourself what kind of results you expect to gain, what those results will contribute to your writing project, and whether you could obtain comparable support for your ideas more effectively and efficiently in another way.

Some subjects are more suited for observation than others. For example, a reflective essay about how parents behave during soccer games would lend itself well to observation. On the other hand, a writer would be more likely to turn to interviews (see Chapter 6) or published sources for an essay on community resistance to No Child Left Behind legislation.

Decide what you should observe and how often to observe it. Your decision will depend largely on the role your observations will play in your essay. If you want to learn more about a subject but don't plan to include what you observe as part of your reflection, a fairly limited observation should suffice. The same holds true if you hope to gather a few details but will base your reflection on your own experience. However, if your subject is complex, or if you expect to use details from what you observe throughout your essay, you might need to conduct multiple observations, possibly in more than one setting.

Decide what to look for. The biggest limitation of observation is that you can see only one thing at a time. Experienced observers focus on activities that are most relevant to their writing projects. As a result, their observations are somewhat selective. Spreading yourself too thin will result in fairly "thin" results. Then again, narrowing in too quickly can cause you to miss important aspects of a setting or an event. Your reasons for conducting an observation and what you hope to gain from it are probably your best guide to what to focus on.

Find out whether you need permission to observe. Seeking permission to observe an individual or a group can be complicated. People have expectations about privacy even in public settings, but people can (and often do) change their behavior when they know they are being watched. As you consider whether to ask for permission, imagine yourself in the position of someone who is being observed. If you are still uncertain, ask your instructor for advice.

Conduct your observation. To conduct your observation, follow these steps:

1. Arrive early.

2. Review your planning notes.

3. If appropriate, introduce yourself.

4. If you are using recording equipment, set it up. Make sure you have a notepad and pens or pencils nearby.

5. Take notes, even if you are using recording equipment.

6. If you have asked for permission to observe, leave your contact information and send a thank-you note.

Reflect on Your Subject

Perhaps you've had the opportunity to listen to musicians jamming during a concert, or perhaps you're a musician yourself. If so, you know about the ebb and flow of the music, how one line of melody plays off another, how the music circles and builds. Reflection is similar to this process. As you reflect on a subject, your thinking moves from one aspect to another, flowing smoothly forward at some times and circling back at others. Reflection can involve seeking understanding, making connections, and exploring contrasts. In the same way that a jam session offers surprises not only to listeners but also to the musicians, reflection can lead you in unexpected directions. The key to reflecting productively is a willingness to be open to those directions.

Reflection is most effective when you record your thoughts. Writing them down as notes in a writer's notebook or as entries in a journal allows you to keep track of

In Process

Conducting an Observation

Caitlin Guariglia's reflective essay was based on a series of informal observations of strangers in Rome and family members at home. She recorded her observations in a journal.

> 5-24-07
>
> Saw the funniest thing today—Dad and I were waiting for Mom to come out of a shop by Piazza di Spagna, so we got to stand on a side street for a while and watch people go by. There was water in the street by this one restaurant, and the guy who owned the place was pacing around the sidewalk. Practically everyone walking by felt like they had to stop and put in their two cents about the problem! And they would all wind up gesturing and pointing. Dad and I just kept trying not to laugh. Dad said it was the same way where he grew up—if something went wrong, everyone tried to help, even though half the time they just ended up getting in the way.

Caitlin reviewed her notes as she planned and then began to draft her essay.

your thinking. As you make decisions about your writing project, you can turn to your notes to review your reflections.

Reflection begins with viewing your subject from a particular perspective. It also involves collecting details and finding significance. To prepare to reflect, place yourself in a relaxing situation that will allow you to think. Take a walk, ride a bike, go for a run, enjoy a good meal, listen to music, lie down — do whatever you think will free you from distractions.

EXAMINE YOUR SUBJECT

Begin to reflect on your subject by viewing it through a particular lens, such as how it compares to something else, what caused it or what effects it might have, or what challenges and difficulties you associate with it. Although some perspectives are likely to be better suited to your subject than others, try to look at your subject from more than one angle.

Explore processes. Thinking of something as a process can help you understand how it works as well as its contributions to the context in which it takes place. For example, instead of reflecting on text-messaging as a social phenomenon, reflect on the processes involved in text-messaging. Ask how it works, what steps are involved in composing and sending a message, and how people understand and respond to messages.

Consider implications. Considering the implications of a subject can help you understand its impact and importance. You can ask questions such as what is likely to happen, what if such-and-such happens, what will happen when, and so on. As you reflect on implications, stay grounded: don't get so carried away by speculation that you lose track of your reason for reflecting.

Examine similarities and differences. Use comparison and contrast to find points of connection for your subject. You might examine, for example, the similarities and differences between new communication technologies, such as e-mail and text-messaging, and older means of staying in touch, such as letter-writing and passing notes in class. Or you might compare and contrast the ways in which people get to know one another, such as hanging out together, joining organizations, and dating.

Trace causes and effects. Thinking about causes and effects can help you better understand a subject. For example, you might reflect on the origins of complaints—some dating back to the ancient Greeks—that the latest generation of young people is not only impolite and uncultured but also likely to undo the accomplishments of previous generations. You might also reflect on the effects that this attitude has for relationships between the old and the young.

Consider value. Reflection often involves considering factors such as strengths and weaknesses, costs and benefits, and limitations and opportunities. For example, you might reflect on the relative strengths and weaknesses of a candidate for political office. Or you might weigh the costs and benefits of a proposed law to make the Internet safer for children. Similarly, you might consider the limitations and opportunities associated with proposals to increase funding for higher education.

Identify challenges and difficulties. Getting to the heart of an issue or idea often involves determining how it challenges your assumptions or values or identifying the nature of the difficulties it poses for you. For example, ask yourself why an idea bothers you, or ask why it might bother someone else.

Reflect on your experiences. As you reflect on your subject, search for connections to your own life. Ask whether your personal experiences would lead you to act in a particular way. Ask how they are likely to influence your reactions and attitudes. Ask whether you've found yourself in situations that are relevant to your subject.

COLLECT DETAILS

People are fond of saying, "It's all in the details." Although this is true for nearly all types of writing, it's especially true for reflective essays. Without details, even the best essay can fall flat. You might get a laugh out of the following story, for example, but few people will find it truly satisfying:

> "Once upon a time, they all lived happily ever after."

To collect details for a reflective essay, use the following strategies.

Describe your subject. If you can, use observation to collect details about your subject (see p. 129). If you have firsthand experience with the subject, freewrite or brainstorm about it to refresh your memory: write down what you saw and heard, what you felt, even what you smelled. Provide as much detail as possible.

Compare your subject with something else. Many subjects are best understood in relation to others. Darkness, for example, is difficult to understand without comparing it to light. Success is best understood in the context of its alternatives. And for those who live in colder climates, spring is all the more welcome because it follows winter. To find useful points of comparison, create a two-column log: place your subject at the top of one column and a contrasting subject at the top of the other, and then record your reflections on the similarities and differences between the two subjects in each column. Use the results to provide details for your essay.

In Process

Making Comparisons

Caitlin Guariglia used comparison to reflect on her experiences with strangers in Rome and with her family. She used a two-column table to make direct comparisons.

Strangers in Rome	Family in America
get involved in other people's business if they feel like they know how to do it better and can help	get involved in your business, whether you like it or not!
cool, confident, witty, LOUD	not always so cool, but definitely loud, full of themselves, and usually really funny
passionate about their city, its history, and its food	love NY, but not all are passionate about it, definitely opinionated about Italian food
beautiful Italian accents	only speak a little Italian, NY accents
really big on family, and like to make you feel like part of theirs	exactly the same

Caitlin used her notes to shape a point in her final essay:

Our ancestors may have brought the food, the expressions, and the attitudes with them to the United States a few generations ago, but it is safe to say that over the years, we have lost some of the style and the musical language that Italians seem to possess from birth.

Discuss your ideas. If you talk about your subject with other people, you might be able to use their comments to add detail to your essay. You might want to set up a formal interview with someone who is an expert on the subject or with someone who has been affected by it (see Chapter 6), but you can also simply bring up your subject in casual conversations to learn what others think. If they tell a story about their experiences with your subject, ask whether you might add their anecdote to your reflection. Similarly, if you hear an interesting turn of phrase or a startling statement related to your subject, consider quoting it. (See Chapter 17 to learn more about integrating quotations into an essay.)

Learn more about your subject. As you gain a better idea of how you'll focus your essay, look for opportunities to add to your understanding of the subject. Browse newspapers and magazines in your library's periodical room to pick up bits of information that will add depth to your essay, or see what's been written recently about your subject on the Web and in blogs (see Chapter 12). As you read about your subject, take note of interesting details that might grab your readers' attention.

FIND SIGNIFICANCE

Every good story has a point. Every good joke has a punch line. Every good reflective essay leaves its readers with something to think about. As you reflect on your subject, consider why it's important to you, and think about how you can make it important for your readers. Then ask whether they'll care about what you've decided to share with them. The main idea of your reflective essay should hold some significance for your readers. Ideally, after reading your essay, they'll continue to think about what you've written.

By now, you'll have reflected a great deal on your subject, and you'll be in a good position to identify the most significant aspects of what you've learned. To find significance, freewrite or brainstorm about your subject for ten or fifteen minutes. Ask yourself what your readers will need or want to know about it. Ask what will spark their imaginations. Ask what will stir their emotions. Then ask whether the ideas you've come up with will help you accomplish your goals as a writer.

Prepare A Draft

As you prepare to draft your reflective essay, you'll think about how to convey your main idea, how to shape your reflection, which details to include, and what point of view to take. You'll also make decisions about how to design and craft your essay. You can read about other strategies related to drafting academic essays, such as writing strong paragraphs and integrating information from sources, in Part Four.

CONVEY YOUR MAIN IDEA

Reflective essays, like other kinds of academic essays, should have a point. Before you begin writing, try to express your main idea in the form of a tentative thesis statement, a single sentence that articulates the most significant aspect of your reflections on your subject. By framing your main idea in a particular way, you can focus your efforts and help your readers see why your reflection should matter to them.

Consider the differences among the following tentative thesis statements about pursuing a career as a writer:

> Without commitment and discipline, pursuing a career as a writer would be a waste of time.

> Without a genuine love of words and a desire to share your ideas with others, pursuing a career as a writer would be a waste of time.

> The paths that lead to a career in writing are as varied as the writers who follow them.

Each of these statements would lead to significantly different reflective essays. The first frames becoming a writer as a test of character. It implies that writers can't succeed unless they are prepared to dedicate themselves to the hard work of writing. The second thesis statement shifts the focus from discipline and commitment to the writer's relationship with words and readers. It paints a warmer, less intimidating picture of what it takes to become a writer. The third thesis statement shifts the focus completely away from the qualities shared by successful writers, suggesting instead that each writer has different reasons for pursuing a career in writing. You can read more about developing a thesis statement in Chapter 15.

Even though having a main idea is necessary, the final draft of a reflective essay doesn't always include a formal thesis statement. Depending on the nature of the reflection, writers sometimes choose to use their observations to create a dominant impression of a subject. That is, they tell a story or build up details to show—rather than state outright—why the subject is significant.

Need help with main ideas? See Chapter 15.

TELL A STORY

Almost every type of writing—at least, writing that's interesting—tells a story. An autobiography tells readers about events in the writer's life. An opinion column uses an anecdote—a brief description of an event or experience—to personalize an abstract issue. An article on ESPN.com describes what happened in a game—and speculates about what it means for the playoffs. In fact, some people have said that everything we do can be understood as a story.

If the subject of your reflection is an event in your past, shaping your essay as a story (that is, a chronological narrative with a beginning, a middle, and an end) is a natural way to proceed. But other kinds of subjects also lend themselves to storytelling. For example, because writers of reflective essays often share their thinking about a subject by explaining how they arrived at their conclusions, they essentially tell a story about their reflections.

As you draft, think about what kind of story you want to share. Will it be a tale of triumph against all odds? Will it lead to a surprising discovery? Will it have a happy ending? Will it be a tragedy? A comedy? A farce?

To create a story, consider the following elements:

- **Setting.** Where does your story take place? What are the characteristics of the setting? How does the setting affect the story?

- **Character.** Who is involved in your story? What motivates them? What do they want to accomplish? What are their hopes and dreams?

- **Plot.** What happens in your story? In what order do the events take place?

- **Conflict.** Do the characters in your story disagree about something? What do they disagree about? Why do they disagree?

- **Climax.** What is the defining event in the story? What does the story lead the reader toward?

- **Resolution.** How is the conflict resolved in your story?

- **Point of view.** Who is telling this story? How is it told?

Even if you don't present your reflection as a traditional story, the elements of story-telling can help you shape your observations in a more concrete manner. For example, by asking who is involved in your subject and how they have dealt with conflicts, you can decide whether you should focus on a character's actions or on the reasons leading to a conflict. By asking about the climax of your story, you can decide whether to focus your reflection on a single event or on the results of that event.

GO INTO DETAIL

Experienced writers are familiar with the advice "Show. Don't tell." This advice, more often applied to creative writing than to academic writing, is founded on the belief that characters' words and actions should be used to convey a story. Simply explaining what happened is far less satisfying for readers than viewing it through a series of unfolding events.

In the sense that a reflective essay conveys the story of your thinking about a subject, showing how you came to your main idea can be preferable to telling readers what it is. As you reflect, consider sharing what you've seen and heard about your subject that place others — the characters in your story — at the center of your essay. Use details to convey their actions. Use dialogue to convey their words.

Each point you present in your essay, each event you describe, and each observation you make should be illustrated with details. As you reflected on your subject, you collected details that helped you understand the subject. Now, return to those details and decide which ones to include in your essay. You can go over your notes, reread your brainstorming and freewriting, and review the events and experiences associated with your subject. As you do so, select those details that will best help your readers understand your subject and grasp its significance, and add new ones as they occur to you.

CHOOSE YOUR POINT OF VIEW

In academic writing, point of view refers to the perspective the writer takes. Sometimes a writer will choose to reflect on a subject as a *detached observer*. Rather than participating in the action, the writer stands outside it, making observations or showing what happened without becoming a part of the story. This detached point of view is characterized by the use of third-person pronouns (*he*, *she*, *they*) and a seemingly objective relationship with the subject. Kazuyoshi Ehara, for example, adopts a detached point of view for his photo essay "Lost Memories" (p. 104). Even though Ehara has a deeply personal connection to his subject, by distancing himself he enables readers to consider his observations in a broader context.

At other times, a writer will reflect on a subject as a *participant observer*, someone who is centrally involved in the story being told. In this case, the writer shares experiences and observations from a personal perspective. This participatory point of view is characterized by the use of first-person pronouns (*I*, *me*, *we*) and a more personally involved relationship with the subject. By adopting this perspective, writers become key players in their own stories and can connect with their readers on a more intimate level. Consider, for example, "This Isn't the Last Dance" (p. 125), in which Rick Bragg uses the first-person point of view to personalize his reflections on the future of New Orleans after Hurricane Katrina.

Your decision about point of view will depend on the subject of your reflection, your relationship to the subject, and the amount of information you want to reveal about yourself. If you are reflecting on a subject with which you have little or no personal experience, or if you want to downplay your involvement, it's usually more effective to adopt the role of a detached observer. If, on the other hand, you want to directly convey your experiences with and perceptions of an event, or if you want to make an abstract subject more personal for readers, writing as a participant observer is often the better choice.

CONSIDER GENRE AND DESIGN

Reflective essays, like other academic essays, use design elements to make it easier for instructors and classmates to read and comment on drafts. As you draft your essay, consider how decisions about fonts, line-spacing, margins, and illustrations will help your readers respond to your ideas.

- **Choose a readable font.** If you've ever read a document formatted with a decorative font, such as **MAVERICK** or **Felt Tip Woman**, you know how difficult it can be to read. Now imagine that you're an instructor reading twenty-five, fifty, or even a hundred essays over a weekend. Think about how you would feel if you found yet another essay printed in a decorative script, in a bright color, in CAPITAL LETTERS, or in an *italic* face. It's generally best to choose a simple font that's easy to read, such as Times New Roman or Helvetica.

- **Provide generous margins and double-spacing.** If you are asked to submit your essay on paper, your instructor will usually make comments in the margins. Leave plenty of room for handwritten comments. Your margins should be at least one inch wide, and lines should be double-spaced.

- **Consider using illustrations.** Depending on your subject, your reflective essay might benefit from illustrations. Photographs and other images can set a mood and help your readers understand the subject more completely. If you do decide to include illustrations, be sure that they contribute to your reflection; purely decorative images are usually more distracting than helpful.

You can learn more about these and other elements of document design in Chapter 18.

FRAME YOUR REFLECTIONS

Once you've made decisions about the content and design of your essay, consider how you'll frame it, or direct your readers' attention to particular aspects of your reflections, rather than to others. Framing your reflections allows you to influence your readers' understanding of, and attitudes toward, what's most important to you.

Organization. The organization of a reflective essay is typically determined by the nature of the subject. Most stories, for instance, are arranged chronologically so that readers can easily follow the sequence of events. Reflections on a place or an object, on the other hand, might be arranged spatially, tracing the way a reader's eyes would take in the subject in person: top to bottom, left to right, near to far, and so on. If your reflections consider similarities and differences between your subject and something else, ordering your ideas by points of comparison and contrast might be most effective. (For more on these and other organizational patterns, see Chapter 16.)

Introduction and conclusion. Your introduction and conclusion provide the framework within which your readers will understand and interpret your reflections, so spend some time experimenting with them until they feel right. (Because these elements of an essay often prove the most challenging to draft, you might want to put them off until you finish the rest of the essay.) Several strategies are available for writing introductions and conclusions, but a few are particularly useful for reflective essays. For instance, you might open with a surprising statement or an anecdote—

a brief, pointed story—that sets the stage for your main idea. As you close your essay, consider circling back to a detail from the beginning or reiterating the significance of your reflections. (For advice on drafting introductions and conclusions, see Chapter 16.)

Review and Improve Your Draft

Completing your first draft is a major milestone. However, further reflection on your subject and a careful review of your draft will no doubt provide numerous opportunities to improve your essay. As you review your draft, pay particular attention to how you've presented and framed your main idea, the order in which you've presented your reflections, any use of dialogue, and your inclusion of details that show rather than tell.

ENSURE THAT YOUR MAIN IDEA IS CLEAR

Readers should be able to identify the point of your essay, even if you haven't provided a thesis statement. As you review your essay, ask whether your reflections support the tentative thesis statement you drafted before writing (see p. 136), and ask if everything you wrote helps your readers understand your subject in the way you intended.

In Process

Adding Dialogue

As she reviewed her first draft, Caitlin worried that a particularly important passage felt less interesting than it should:

> Anytime our group slowed down or started to get tired, Marco would yell to us to keep going, and suddenly we were revived. He knew everything about Rome, and everywhere we went, he knew someone. He loved his city and loved sharing it with all of us.

By adding dialogue, she created a better sense of Marco's personality and helped readers imagine themselves on a tour with him:

> Anytime our group slowed down or started to get tired, Marco would yell, "Andiamo! (Let's go!)," and suddenly we were revived. He knew everything about Rome, and everywhere we went, he knew someone. All day he was calling out to friends, "Ciao bella!" or "Come stai?" He loved his city and loved sharing it with all of us.

You might find that you need to revise your thesis statement to reflect your draft, or that you need to adapt your draft to better support your main idea.

EXAMINE THE PRESENTATION OF YOUR OBSERVATIONS

Reflective essays frequently rely on narrative, or storytelling. Review your draft to find out whether the order in which you've told your story makes sense and whether the details you have included will lead readers to be sympathetic to your observations. Upon review, you might decide that you should change the order, add important ideas or observations, or remove details that seem unnecessary or irrelevant.

REVIEW DIALOGUE

Many reflective essays use dialogue—spoken exchanges between key figures in a story—to help readers better understand a subject. Dialogue can underscore the significance of your subject and help readers gain insight into how people are affected by or react to the subject. Dialogue can also add interest to a story or allow others to make a point that you might not want to state outright. If you've included dialogue, ask whether you've used it effectively. For example, have you relied too heavily on other people's words? Are the right people engaged in dialogue? Does what they say make sense in the context of your story? If you haven't used dialogue, ask yourself where you might include it to liven up your essay or engage readers with your subject.

SHOW, DON'T TELL

As you review your draft, think about how you can bring your observations to life by placing the people and events involved with your subject at the center of your essay. Have you done more than simply summarize your points? Will adding details help your readers better understand and connect to your subject? Can you make your points more effectively by quoting dialogue among the characters in your story? Can you illustrate key ideas by showing characters in action?

After reviewing your essay, ask yourself how you might polish and edit it so that your readers will find it easy to read. For a detailed discussion of polishing strategies, see Chapter 19. For a discussion of editing strategies, see Chapter 20.

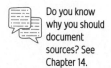 Do you know why you should document sources? See Chapter 14.

Finally, if you've drawn on ideas, information, or examples from written works such as essays or stories or cultural productions such as movies or concerts, make sure that you've documented those sources in the body of your essay and in a works cited or references list.

For guidelines on the MLA and APA documentation systems, see Chapters 21 and 22.

Peer Review: Improve Your Reflective Essay

One of the biggest challenges writers face is reading a draft of their own work as a reader rather than as the writer. Because you know what you're trying to say, you find it easy to understand your draft. To determine how you should revise your draft, ask a friend or classmate to read your essay and consider how well you've adopted the role of observer (see p. 98).

Purpose	1. Did you understand the significance of my observations? Do I need to state my main idea more directly, or say anything more to clarify what's important about my subject?
	2. Does my subject seem relevant to you personally? Why or why not? Is there anything I can do to forge a better connection with readers?
	3. How did you respond to my reflections and observations? Do you accept what I had to say? Have I left you with something to think about?
Readers	4. Did the story of my experiences and insights make sense to you? Do you want to know anything else about them?
	5. Does my personality come through in my writing? Should I put more (or less) of myself into the essay?
	6. Have I offered you a fresh or unusual perspective on my subject?
Sources	7. Is it clear which experiences and observations are my own and which I brought in from other sources?
	8. If I have referred to any published works or recent events, have I cited my source(s) appropriately?
	9. How well does my use of details show, rather than tell, the significance of my subject? Should I add or remove any details?
	10. Have I used dialogue effectively? Is there too little, or too much?
Context	11. Did you understand any references I made to cultural, political, or social contexts? Do I need to explain anything more directly?
	12. Is the physical appearance of my essay appropriate? Did you find the font and typeface easy to read? Did you have enough room to write down comments? Did I use illustrations effectively?

For each of the points listed above, ask your reviewers to offer concrete suggestions for improving your essay. You might want to ask them to adopt the role of an editor — someone who is working with you to improve your draft. You can read more about these and other collaborative activities in Chapter 4.

@ Download or print this Peer Review activity at bedfordstmartins.com/conversation.

Student Essay

 Caitlin Guariglia, "Mi Famiglia"

The following reflective essay was written by featured writer Caitlin Guariglia. You can follow Caitlin's efforts to write her essay by visiting **bedfordstmartins.com/conversation**. You can read excerpts of interviews in which she discusses her work on her essay, read the assignment, and read drafts of her essay.

Guariglia 1

> Information about the writer, class, and submission date is formatted according to MLA guidelines.

Caitlin Guariglia

Professor Edwards

ENG 1011.04

September 28, 2008

> Following MLA guidelines, the title is centered.

Mi Famiglia

> The opening paragraph grabs the reader's attention.

Crash! The sound of metal hitting a concrete wall is my first vivid memory of Rome. Our tour bus could not get any farther down the tiny road because cars were parked along both sides. This, our bus driver told us, was illegal. He did not tell us, exactly; he grumbled it as he stepped out of the bus. He stood there with his hands on his hips, pondering the situation. Soon, people in the cars behind us started wandering up to stand next to the bus driver and ponder along with him. That, or they honked a great deal.

> The writer begins to reflect on the experience.

> The writer returns to the image in the opening paragraph.

This is when I found out that Italians are resourceful people. They do not stand around waiting for someone else to fix a problem for them. They take initiative; they do what needs to be done to get things moving. Our bus driver and three other men started rocking the small cars parked crookedly along the sides of the narrow road, with every push moving them toward the concrete wall that lined the road. CRASH! The sound of the car hitting the wall was their signal that they were done pushing that car. And then they'd move to the next one in their way.

Guariglia 2

Angry people on Vespas sped by, making various hand gestures; some I knew and understood, but others I did not. The bus driver boarded the bus, his sleeves rolled up, sweat pouring down his face, and told us that these kind people on their Vespas were wishing us good luck. He moved the bus up about ten feet before he encountered another car he could not pass. The process repeated itself. CRASH! Another car moved. Soon a police officer walked up, talked to the bus driver, looked around, shrugged, and helped them shove the cars into the wall. People who had parked there began to come back and move their cars before it was done for them. When we finally made it the hundred feet down the rest of the road, everyone on our tour bus cheered. Our bus driver smiled sheepishly, as if to say, "Eh, it was nothing."

> Details help the reader visualize the writer's experience.

This was the sort of thing I hoped to see in Italy. I wanted to see how Italians live. My dad's side of the family is Italian, so I wanted to understand more about our heritage and our family traits, like why my family is so loud and concerned with everyone else's business. Was it a cultural thing? Or was it a family thing? Was it just something about the region of Italy where my family is from? I smiled when I read Elizabeth Gilbert's memoir *Eat, Pray, Love*. Gilbert writes, "The Neapolitan women in particular are such a gang of tough-voiced, loud-mouthed, generous, nosy dames, all bossy and annoyed and right up in your face just trying to friggin' *help* you for chrissake, you dope — *why they gotta do everything around here?*" (78). This sounds exactly like almost all of my great-aunts, and I was curious to find out if the women in Rome would have the same attitude.

> The writer explains what she hoped to gain from traveling to Italy.

> A quotation from another writer places the writer's questions about her heritage in a larger context.

> The page number for the quotation is provided, following MLA guidelines.

And the obsession with eating! My grandmother feeds us constantly. My dad and I always laugh at that scene in *Goodfellas* where the mobsters show up at two in the morning after killing someone, and one mobster's mother whips up a full pasta meal for them. We know that my grandmother would do the same thing: "Are you hungry? Here, sit, eat!" Grandma holds interventions

Guariglia 3

The writer connects questions about her heritage to her trip to Italy.

over pasta. If she is unhappy with something someone in the family is doing, she invites everyone over for pasta, and we hash it out together. Was this something all Italians do? Or was my idea of a typical Italian person all wrong? Our time in Rome clarified some of these questions for me.

When we finally got to our hotel, we met our tour guide Maresa. This small, stout, sweet Italian woman said we could call her Mama. Mama looked up our reservation, glanced at it, and said our last name. Normally, that would be nothing to celebrate. But she said our last name perfectly. Actually, not just

The writer uses text formatting (italics) to emphasize her point.

perfectly, she said it *beautifully*. After listening to Americans butcher my difficult Italian last name my entire life, hearing this Italian woman say it was music to my ears. My grandfather would have given her a standing ovation.

A transition indicates that time has passed.

The next morning we met our tour guide Marco. A large, sturdy man who looked like my grandmother cooked for him, he was confident and full of life. He took us to the main historical sites that day: the Vatican, the Colosseum, the Pantheon, the Roman Forum. While all of that was spectacular, I enjoyed listening to Marco more than anything we saw. He was a true Roman, big, proud, and loud. The Italian accent made it seem like he was singing every-thing he said, making it all seem that much more beautiful. Anytime our group slowed down or started to get tired, Marco would yell, "Andiamo! (Let's go!),"

The writer uses dialogue to make the scene more vivid.

and suddenly we were revived. He knew everything about Rome, and everywhere we went, he knew someone. All day he was calling out to friends, "Ciao bella!" or "Come stai?" He loved his city and loved sharing it with all of us. He had such a passion for Rome, and it made me passionate about it, too. He was also an entertainer; he enjoyed making us laugh. When our group reached a cross-walk near the Vatican, he knew all of us would not make it across in one light, so he told us to try to hurry up across the street. He told us if we did not make it before the light changed, it's okay, the cars won't hit us. "And if they beep at you," he added, "it's because they like-a the music."

Guariglia 4

Marco fit into what my family came to know as the image of the quintes-sential Roman man. All of the men have two-day stubble, enough to look chic and sophisticated, but not so much as to look scruffy or messy. They also have half-smoked cigarettes hanging from their mouths. It is never a freshly lit cig-arette, or a little butt, but right at that perfect halfway mark. There is a confi-dence, but not arrogance, in their walk. In essence, Roman men are eternally cool. In *Eat, Pray, Love*, Elizabeth Gilbert remembers watching a group of Roman men outside a bakery on their way home from a soccer game. They are "leaning up against their motorcycles, talking about the game, looking macho as anything, and eating *cream puffs*" (Gilbert 70). She is surprised at how cool they can look while eating something like cream puffs, but I have definitely seen what she means. Somehow they are manly without even having to try.

> The writer returns to her reflections about the connections between her family and her Italian heritage.

> The writer draws on a source to illustrate a point.

Romans, like many Italian Americans I've known, also have an opinion on everything and want you to know what that opinion is. Walking by the Spanish Steps on our second day in Rome, we saw a restaurant with a water leak that had spilled out into the street. It was a narrow street with mostly pedestrian traffic. As the water trickled between the cobblestones, the restaurant owner stood over the mess, looking a lot like our bus driver with his hands on his hips. Every Italian walking by had to stop and talk to this man, and then give him advice on how to go about fixing it. The two would wave their hands at each other, sometimes nodding in agreement, sometimes yelling and waving their hands harder. This reminded me of many of my own family. When any problem arises, all the men in the house stand around looking at it saying, "No! What you gotta do is . . ." None of them are listening to each other, but each of them wants their point to be heard. It felt like déjà vu watching the same thing happen on this street in Rome. It was funny that they were all being stubborn and acting like know-it-alls, but I saw underneath it that the people stopping by really thought they were helping. They were not being rude or bossy in their minds; they were just looking out for their fellow Roman.

Guariglia 5

The last morning, Mama herded our tour group onto a bus to take us to the train station. When she got to my family, she gave us all a kiss on the cheek and a hug. She told us, "You must come back again and visit!" Then she looked at my sister and me, winked, and said, "And bring some husbands!" She must have channeled my grandmother at that moment, telling us to settle down with a nice Italian boy. We laughed and thanked Mama for her kindness during our visit.

> The writer begins her conclusion by sharing her thoughts as her trip comes to a close.

As we pulled away from the station, I thought of all the wonderful people we met in Rome. I imagined them coming to our family reunion barbecue that takes place every summer. I think they'd fit right in. Mama would sit with Grandma and my father's aunts and talk about how beautiful their family is. Marco would sit with my dad and his cousins, drinking scotch and smoking cigars and cigarettes. Everyone would have a place.

> The conclusion offers reflections on differences between Italians and Italian Americans.

But then I thought of my cousin with two-day stubble, sitting on a Vespa, and I giggled. The image was ridiculous. Our ancestors may have brought the food, the expressions, and the attitudes with them to the United States a few generations ago, but it is safe to say that, over the years, we have lost some of the style and the musical language that Italians seem to possess from birth. Then why did so much of what I saw and heard in Italy feel strangely familiar? It seems that for Italians and Italian Americans, the traits we share are not just a cultural thing or just a family thing; they are both. It is impossible to separate the two. My time in Rome showed me that to Italians, a shared culture is a kind of family, one that extends even across the ocean.

Guariglia 6

Works Cited

Gilbert, Elizabeth. *Eat, Pray, Love: One Woman's Search for Everything Across Italy, India and Indonesia*. New York: Viking, 2006. Print.

Goodfellas. Dir. Martin Scorsese. Perf. Robert De Niro, Ray Liotta, Joe Pesci, and Lorraine Bracco. Warner Bros., 1990. DVD.

> Following MLA guidelines, the title of the Works Cited section is centered on its own line.

> Sources used in the essay are cited and formatted according to MLA guidelines.

⭐ Project Ideas

The following suggestions provide ways to focus your work on a reflective essay or another type of reflective document.

Suggestions for Essays

1. REFLECT ON A PERSONAL EXPERIENCE

Write a reflective essay about something you've done, or something that happened to you, within the last month or so. Support your reflections with personal observation and reasoning. You might also consider discussing the experience with friends or family members to gain their perspectives on it. If the experience was of a public nature or was related to a public event, consult news reports for background information and alternate perspectives.

2. REFLECT ON A PUBLIC EVENT

Reflect on a recent event covered in your local newspaper. In your essay, describe the event, and offer your reflections on its significance for you and your readers. Support your reflection with examples from personal experience, information published in the newspaper, or an interview with someone associated with the event (see Chapter 6). If you participated in the event yourself, be sure to include your observations of what happened.

3. REFLECT ON A POEM, SHORT STORY, OR NOVEL

Respond to a poem, short story, or novel that you've read recently. Support your reflection by describing your reactions to and understanding of the work. You might also read published reviews or analyses to get an idea of other readers' reactions. In your essay, briefly describe the work to which you're responding. Then offer your reflections on it: share with your readers why it affected you the way it did, and consider how it relates to your own experiences or beliefs.

4. REFLECT ON A PLAY OR MOVIE

Attend a play or movie and reflect on it. Support your reflection by drawing on your reactions to the play or movie, relevant personal experiences, and your own reasoning. You might also discuss the play or movie with a friend, a family member, a classmate, or an instructor who has seen it, or read other viewers' responses posted to online forums (see p. 498). In your essay, identify the subject of the play or movie, briefly summarize the plot and any key themes, and offer your reflections on the meaning or emotional impact of what you viewed.

5. REFLECT ON AN ISSUE OF INTEREST

Reflect on an issue in a discipline or profession in which you have an interest. For example, a writer interested in nuclear technology might reflect on the political or environmental implications of plans to store nuclear waste in Nevada. Support your reflection by drawing on your personal knowledge, experiences, and concerns, referring to information or arguments from published sources as necessary to inform your readers of the issue at hand. If appropriate, you might also interview an expert on the issue or conduct an observation to get a firsthand look at your subject. In your essay, introduce the issue and offer your reflections on it, but don't compose an argument. Instead, focus on how the issue affects you and your readers.

Suggestions for Other Genres

6. WRITE A MEMOIR

Write a brief memoir that reflects on a key event in your life. Carefully describe the event and offer your insights into its meaning and significance, keeping in mind the need to help readers understand, connect to, and benefit from your reflections. Your memoir should be based primarily on your memories. If you like, you might also discuss the event with a friend or family member and include some of their recollections and insights, or draw on published sources to give readers background information and context.

7. CREATE A PHOTO ESSAY

Take or gather several photographs that illustrate an important aspect of your life or a public issue that intrigues you. The pictures might be from your personal collection of photographs or from published sources such as history books, magazines, or Web sites. Select five to seven images that create a dominant impression of your subject. Then introduce them with a few paragraphs that reflect on what they show, or else write an introduction along with a sentence-length caption for each image. The final mix of images and words should lead your readers to think about the subject from a perspective they wouldn't have developed on their own.

8. WRITE A SHORT STORY

Choose a personal experience or a recent public event, and write a fictional story about it. You can use real-life episodes and examples, or you can make up elements (the characters, the specifics of what happened, the dialogue) as necessary to make the story lively and to draw readers in. Build your story around a central conflict and its resolution, and give readers a main idea to think about when they've finished reading the tale.

9. WRITE A COMPREHENSIVE LITERACY NARRATIVE

Write a literacy narrative that reflects on your overall attitudes toward literacy. Do you enjoy reading and writing, avoid them, struggle with them, find strength from engaging with them? Support your reflections by drawing on your personal experiences and insights into several events that have shaped your attitudes, as well as an assessment of your current relationship with writing and reading. To support your reflections, try to include a few telling comments made by family members or teachers about your experiences with literacy.

10. WRITE A LITERACY NARRATIVE ABOUT A KEY EXPERIENCE

Write a focused literacy narrative that identifies and reflects on a personal experience (or a series of closely related experiences) that strongly influenced you as a writer or reader. Shape your reflection as a story, building to a moment of insight to which your readers will relate. Conclude with a brief assessment of your current relationship with literacy.

In Summary: Writing a Reflective Essay

○ **Find a conversation and listen in.**
- Explore your experiences (p. 128).
- Ask questions about promising subjects (p. 129).
- Conduct an observation (p. 129).

○ **Reflect on your subject.**
- Examine your subject (p. 133).
- Collect details (p. 134).
- Find significance (p. 136).

○ **Prepare your draft.**
- Convey your main idea (p. 136).
- Tell a story (p. 137).

- Go into detail (p. 138).
- Choose your point of view (p. 139).
- Consider genre and design (p. 139).
- Frame your reflections (p. 140).

○ **Review and improve your draft.**
- Ensure that your main idea is clear (p. 141).
- Examine the presentation of your observations (p. 142).
- Review dialogue (p. 142).
- Show; don't tell (p. 142).

06 Writing to Inform

When I take on the role of a *reporter,* I focus on informing my readers about a topic.

GENRES IN CONVERSATION

| Reflective Writing | **Informative Writing** | Analytical Writing | Evaluative Writing | Problem-Solving Writing | Argumentative Writing |

Readers of informative documents often have a specific purpose or interest in the subject. Many diabetics need a regulated supply of insulin to control their blood glucose levels, so they have a personal interest in informative documents on this subject. A writer employed to provide information about a new insulin infusion device knows that readers will fall into two groups: those interested in learning how the device might help them, and those who have already decided to use the device and want to know how to use it.

The documents that follow—a **brochure**, a page from an **instruction manual**, and a company **Web site**—illustrate how informative documents can use different genres to meet the needs of their readers.

Brochure ▶

A **brochure** uses colorful, appealing photographs to present an overview of the features of a new insulin infusion pump and to put potential patients at ease.

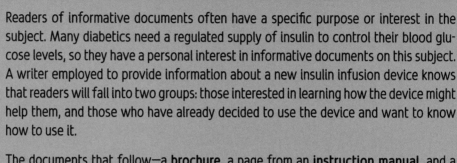

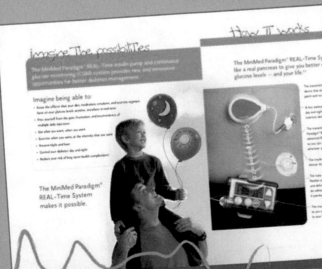

Install battery

CAUTION: Do not use a rechargeable or carbon zinc battery in your pump. For best results use a new Energizer AAA alkaline battery, size E92, type LR03.

Medtronic Diabetes designed the pump to only accept a new battery. As a safety measure, if you install a battery that does not have full power, the WEAK BATTERY or FAILED BATT TEST alarm may sound. If you receive a WEAK BATTERY alarm, respond to the alarm and continue. The pump will still operate normally, but with a decreased battery life. The pump uses one AAA alkaline battery.

1   Make sure all the following apply:
    - Clear (ESC, ACT) any alarms and/or alerts before removing and replacing the battery.
    - Make sure the pump is at the HOME (idle) screen when you remove the battery.
    - Do NOT remove the battery during a bolus or prime delivery.
2   Use the edge of a coin to remove the battery cap. Turn the cap in a counter-clockwise direction.

3   Remove the old battery and dispose of it per the disposable requirements of your state or country. Put the new battery in the pump with the negative end [(-) symbol] going in first. Check the label on the back of the pump to make sure the battery is inserted correctly.

NOTE: Do not use batteries that have been in cold storage, such as in the refrigerator or in your car during winter in cold climates.

4   Place the battery cap in the pump and tighten so the slot is aligned horizontally with the pump as shown here:

CAUTION: Do NOT over-tighten the battery cap. You should not turn the cap more than four half turns. If you over-tighten the cap you may not be able to remove it, and you can damage your pump.

Instruction Manual ▶

An **instruction manual** targets patients who have already decided to use the pump and provides detailed, easy-to-follow instructions with illustrations, captions, and callouts.

28   The basics

▲ Web Site

The company's **Web site** offers information and customer support for current or prospective users in a clear, navigable format.

What Is Writing to Inform?

Many of the documents you encounter on a regular basis are informative: newspaper and magazine articles, manuals, brochures, and books (including this textbook) are among the genres—or types of documents—that allow writers to add information to conversations about a wide range of subjects. In writing and writing-intensive courses, typical informative-writing assignments include essays, reports, and Web sites. You might also be asked to create pamphlets, multimedia presentations, memos, or posters.

The Writer's Role: Reporter

PURPOSE

- To share information
- To answer questions

READERS

- Want to be informed
- Expect a fair and reasonable presentation of information, ideas, and arguments
- Need clear explanations of important ideas and concepts

SOURCES

- Information can be drawn from published studies and reports, news media, and personal experience.
- Information can be obtained firsthand, through interviews, observation, surveys, correspondence, and attendance at public events.
- Reporters check that their sources are credible and accurate.

CONTEXT

- The level of detail is adjusted to anticipate what readers are likely to know already and to make new information easier to follow.

- Informative documents often use illustrations—such as charts, tables, graphs, and images—to help readers understand concepts and ideas.

Writing to inform involves adopting the role of *reporter*. Reporters make others aware of the facts central to a written conversation. They might provide background information for people just starting to learn about a subject or might present new information to those with a long-standing interest in it. One reporter, for example, might describe the events leading to elections in a new democracy, while another might explain the United Nations' role in monitoring those elections.

Reporters typically refrain from interpreting or analyzing the information they provide, and they seldom ask their readers to respond in a particular way. Instead, reporters allow readers to draw their own conclusions and to decide whether—and how—to act on what they've learned.

Readers of informative documents might be interested in a subject for personal or intellectual reasons, but typically they are looking for an answer to a question—whether it's a simple quest for a fact or a more general desire to understand an issue. They look for a focused treatment of a subject, and they find that visual elements—such as photos, images, charts, graphs, and tables—can help them understand key points. Readers want writers to be fair and reasonable, they appreciate clarity, and they expect that sources will be documented.

In most cases, reporters spend time learning about a subject to ensure that they have enough information to share. Whether they interview experts, collect information from published materials, or use data to create graphs and tables, reporters ensure that their sources are reliable and check that the evidence they provide is accurate.

Writers of informative documents often connect the information they provide to the social, cultural, and historical contexts they share with their readers. For example, they might refer to events or people who have recently been featured in the news media, and they might mention important sources that address the subject. At the same time, reporters take into consideration what their readers might already know, leaving out details and explanations that are unnecessary for their purposes and focusing instead on what they want readers to understand about their subject.

Writers of informative documents are concerned primarily with helping readers and other writers advance their understanding of a subject. They do this in a variety of ways. They might report original research or provide a broad summary of existing knowledge, or offer a detailed discussion of a narrow area of interest. Regardless of their focus on the subject or the originality of their research, their contributions to a written conversation are essential to moving the conversation forward.

What Kinds of Documents Are Used to Inform?

Whether you are writing for a course, for publication, or in the workplace, you'll find yourself turning to — and creating — informative documents on a regular basis. If you are new to a conversation, informative documents can help you learn about a subject. As you prepare to contribute to the conversation, they can help you understand what is generally agreed upon about the subject and what remains unknown or open to debate. And as you draft your contribution, you can use informative documents to introduce your subject, to support your points, or to illustrate alternative perspectives.

Good writers select a genre that allows them to best address their purpose, their readers, and the context of the conversation they want to join. In the following sections, you'll find examples and discussions of some of the most common types of documents used to inform readers: brochures, Web sites, articles, profiles, and essays.

Brochures

Companies, organizations, and community groups commonly produce brochures to provide essential information about products, goals, events, or issues. Brochures are designed as compact, easy-to-carry documents; their distinguishing features are the use of folded sheets of paper to create pages and the brevity of their content. Brochure writers present information in a condensed, readable form and aim to encourage readers to learn more about a subject—by directing them to a Web site, perhaps, or by inviting readers to call or write for more information.

 View a multimedia example of informative writing in the e-book at **bedfordstmartins.com/ conversation**.

A typical brochure emphasizes key points and frames information to help readers understand the subject in a particular way. Good design is critical to a brochure's success: headings, illustrations, color, fonts, pull quotes, and other design elements draw attention to particular areas of the brochure, highlighting important information and downplaying less significant details.

California Department of Fish and Game
Keep Me Wild

Published by the California Department of Fish and Game, the brochure shown here calls attention to the dangers of feeding coyotes and other wild animals. The text and images work together to reflect concerns about the increasing frequency of coyote-human contact at the boundaries of residential areas. The brochure also stresses how the most common solutions suggested when coyotes become comfortable living near humans can have disastrous consequences for wild animals. The writers' goals include educating the public about the issue and reducing behaviors that lead to problems.

Starting a Conversation: Respond to the "Keep Me Wild" Brochure

@ Download or print this Starting a Conversation activity at **bedfordstmartins.com/ conversation**.

In your writer's notebook, analyze this brochure's purpose and content by responding to the following questions:

1. Examine the brochure closely for clues about where it might have been distributed. Who might be expected to pick it up and read it? What elements of the brochure seem designed to appeal to those readers? Why do you think so?

2. What is the primary message of this brochure? What unstated question(s) does it attempt to answer? How can you tell?

3. What kinds of details do the writers provide to support the primary message of the brochure? Where does the information come from?

4. Which purpose do you think was more important to the writers of this brochure: reducing the danger to coyotes, or reducing the danger to humans and pets? Why do you think so?

Stash Your Food and Trash

Allowing coyotes access to human food and garbage is reckless and deadly.

Coyotes primarily hunt rodents and rabbits for food, but will take advantage of whatever is available, including garbage, pet food, and domestic animals.

- Put garbage in tightly closed containers that cannot be tipped over.
- Remove sources of water, especially in dry climates.
- Bring pets in at night, and do not leave pet food outside.
- Put away bird feeders at night to avoid attracting rodents and other coyote prey.
- Provide secure enclosures for rabbits, poultry, etc.
- Pick up fallen fruit and cover compost piles.
- Ask your neighbors to follow these tips.

Please respect and protect wild animals. Keep them wild.

www.keepmewild.org

For More Information
Contact the California Department of Fish and Game

Sacramento Headquarters, (916) 653-6420

Northern California, North Coast Region
Redding, (530) 225-2300

Sacramento Valley, Central Sierra Region
Rancho Cordova, (916) 358-2900

Central Coast Region
Napa, (707) 944-5500

San Joaquin Valley, Southern Sierra Region
Fresno, (559) 243-4005 ext. 151

South Coast Region
San Diego, (858) 467-4201

Eastern Sierra, Inland Deserts Region
Ontario, (909) 484-0167

Alternate communication formats are available upon request. If reasonable accommodation is needed contact the Department of Fish and Game, (916) 653-6420, lbernard@dfg.ca.gov or the California Relay Service for the deaf or hearing-impaired from TDD phones at (800) 735-2929.

A campaign for all wild animals.

KEEP ME WILD™

Feeding Wildlife is Dead Wrong.

California Department of Fish and Game

Wild Animals Ruined, Even Killed by People's Carelessness!

Wild animals are in trouble, and the problem is people who are careless with food and garbage.

Coyotes play an important role in the ecosystem, helping to keep rodent populations under control. They are by nature fearful of humans.

If coyotes are given access to human food and garbage, their behavior changes. They lose caution and fear. They may cause property damage. They might threaten human safety. They might be killed.

Relocating a problem coyote is not an option because it only moves the problem to someone else's neighborhood.

Help prevent deadly conflicts for these beautiful wild animals.

A campaign for all wild animals.

"Coyote country" precautions

- Never feed or attempt to tame coyotes. The result may be deadly conflicts with pets or livestock, or serious injuries to small children.
- Do not leave small children or pets outside unattended.
- Install motion-sensitive lighting around the house.
- Trim ground-level shrubbery to reduce hiding places.
- Be aware that coyotes are more active in the spring, when feeding and protecting their young.
- If followed by a coyote, make loud noises. If this fails, throw rocks in the animal's direction.
- If a coyote attacks a person, immediately contact the nearest Department of Fish and Game or law enforcement office.

Stash Your Food and Trash

Coyote-Proof Containers

Use garbage cans that have a locking mechanism on the lid. Use a rope or elastic cord to secure the can to a fence or other solid object so that it cannot be tipped over.

New Laws

Feeding coyotes is illegal in some communities. Many local ordinances make wildlife feeding punishable by fines and requirements to install wildlife-proof garbage containers.

The coyote's range covers the entire state of California. Most conflicts occur along borders between urban and wild areas.

Coyote Conflicts

You Can Help

Please visit www.keepmewild.org for downloadable posters, newspaper advertisements and other *Keep Me Wild™* materials.

Web Sites

Since its emergence in the mid-1990s, the World Wide Web has become a powerful tool for accessing information about products, services, entertainment, and political movements, among other subjects. Its rapid growth has resulted in the beginnings of what might be termed *Web genres*. Among the most important of these genres is the informative Web site. Typically, informative Web sites offer information and advice on a range of subjects, from politics to news and entertainment to activities such as how to build decks and patios, prepare zucchini, and choose a college or university.

Web sites engage readers in ways that print documents cannot—they can link directly to related sites, allow visitors to access video and audio files, and support communication between a site's readers and writers. Given the diverse characteristics of a Web site's potential audience, writers must anticipate the needs of a far wider range of readers than is the case with informative print documents. Informative Web sites typically provide broad overviews on their main pages and add detailed information on related pages, allowing readers to move around according to their own needs and interests. Because of this, site organization is a key concern for Web writers. The content and location of individual pages within the site, the navigational structure, the placement of visuals, and even links to other sites can strongly affect how readers move through and interpret the information on a Web site. (You can read more about designing Web sites in Chapter 18.)

CNN.com
Uncovering America: The Asian-American Journey

Take a look at how information is presented on the following Web page, selected from CNN.com's special report "Uncovering America: The Asian-American Journey." The report chronicles Asian immigration to the United States since the 1840s, highlights individuals and groups who are emblematic of the Asian immigrant experience, and calls attention to key issues facing Asian Americans. The opening page of the report summarizes the scope of the report, offers interactive tools such as timelines and maps, and provides links that function as a table of contents. Other pages in the report offer insights into immigrant experiences and allow readers to share their personal experiences.

CNN.com. Member Center: Sign In | Register   International Edition

SEARCH   ◉ THE WEB   ○ CNN.COM   [   ]   [Search]

CNN.com Home Page - U.S. - [More CNN.com sections: ▾] [-] Feedback   Special Reports

UNCOVERING AMERICA:
The Asian-American JOURNEY

Asian-Americans are more visible than ever before across society's many roles; from TV and journalism to cinema, academia, the business world and sports. Yet, many challenges remain.

i REPORT   Your stories

In a quest for understanding, CNN.com asked readers for their perspectives on the Asian-American experience. These are some responses.

Your video: On acceptance | A voice
Your photos | **Your e-mails**

[MAP]   [CHART]   [TIMELINE]

THE JOURNEY SO FAR

The experiences of the groups that define the term "Asian-American" are as diverse and unique as their languages and cultures.

- Diverse voices share similar stories
- Push to achieve tied to Asian-American suicide rate
- Immigrants became 'paper sons' to enter the U.S. ▣
- **Gallery:** Notable Asian-Americans
- A glance at some Asian-American pioneers
- CNN's Betty Nguyen on being Asian-American ▣
- CNN anchors recount their experiences ▣

ON CNN TV

Watch as CNN takes a look at some of the issues confronted by the Asian-American community.

- Are Asian students smarter? ▣
- The cost of diversity ▣
- An Asian glass ceiling? ▣
- Asian men want 'real' roles in Hollywood ▣
- The hopes of Asian mail order brides ▣
- What it's like growing up as a Hapa ▣
- Dr. Gupta: Spotlight on Asians' health ▣

QUICKVOTE

What do you think is the state of the Asian-American community today?

○ Fully integrated into American society

○ Progressing but challenges remain

○ Still a long way to go

[Vote] or View Results

YOUR E-MAIL ALERTS

○ Asian-American

○ Immigration

○ China

○ India

[Activate] or Create your own

Manage alerts | What is this?

Starting a Conversation: Respond to "Uncovering America: The Asian-American Journey" Web Site

@ Download or print this Starting a Conversation activity at **bedfordstmartins.com/ conversation**.

In your writer's notebook, consider how this Web site presents information by responding to the following questions:

1. This site was written for a general audience. Assess how well the writers present information on the site. Is the information clear and easy to understand? Does the site anticipate your questions about the Asian immigrant experience? Are the visuals and the language appropriate? Why or why not?

2. Look at the structure and design of the site's front page. Does the organization suggest that the site is easy to navigate? Where might the site's design confuse readers? How does the design make information stand out as important? What other information, if any, should have been similarly highlighted, and why?

3. In what ways does this site's use of multimedia materials, such as video clips and photo galleries, serve an informative purpose? What other purposes might these materials serve?

4. The site includes a section called "Your Stories," where readers can submit their own videos, photos, and e-mails. What informative purpose would the reader-submitted materials serve? How might these materials enhance or detract from the site as a whole?

Articles

Magazine and newspaper articles report information about a single event, issue, person, or group. Because most articles are written for a specific publication, writers typically have a clear picture of their readers (in terms of age, income, education, hobbies, and so forth) and can target information to the needs and interests of a narrowly defined group. An article about an election, for example, might report on turnout among younger voters, offer a profile of a recently elected senator from the Midwest, or describe the activities of an organization such as the League of Women Voters.

Articles rely heavily on information obtained by the author from sources such as books, Web sites, government reports, interviews, surveys, and observation. Writers often use illustrations to highlight key information or to explain complicated concepts; most also draw on quotations from interviews to present or expand on important points.

Matt Richtel
Devices Enforce Silence of Cellphones, Illegally

The following article, written by technology reporter Matt Richtel for the *New York Times*, is typical of many informative newspaper articles. As you read it, pay attention to how the writer uses information from interviews and written reports to inform readers about the growing use and potential consequences of cell phone jammers.

Devices Enforce Silence of Cellphones, Illegally

By Matt Richtel | November 4, 2007

SAN FRANCISCO, Nov. 2—One afternoon in early September, an architect boarded his commuter train and became a cellphone vigilante. He sat down next to a 20-something woman who he said was "blabbing away" into her phone.

"She was using the word *like* all the time. She sounded like a Valley Girl," said the architect, Andrew, who declined to give his last name because what he did next was illegal.

Andrew reached into his shirt pocket and pushed a button on a black device the size of a cigarette pack. It sent out a powerful radio signal that cut off the chatterer's cellphone transmission—and any others in a 30-foot radius.

"She kept talking into her phone for about 30 seconds before she realized there was no one listening on the other end," he said. His reaction when he first discovered he could wield such power? "Oh, holy moly! Deliverance."

As cellphone use has skyrocketed, making it hard to avoid hearing half a conversation in many public places, a small but growing band of rebels is turning to a blunt countermeasure: the cellphone jammer, a gadget that renders nearby mobile devices impotent.

The technology is not new, but overseas exporters of jammers say demand is rising and they are sending hundreds of them a month into the United States—prompting scrutiny from federal regulators and new concern last week from the cellphone industry. The buyers include owners of cafes and hair salons, hoteliers, public speakers, theater operators, bus drivers, and, increasingly, commuters on public transportation.

The development is creating a battle for control of the airspace within earshot. And the damage is collateral. Insensitive talkers impose their racket on the defenseless, while jammers punish not just the offender, but also more discreet chatterers.

"If anything characterizes the 21st century, it's our inability to restrain ourselves for the benefit of other people," said James Katz, director of the Center for Mobile Communication Studies at Rutgers University. "The cellphone talker thinks his rights go above that of people around him, and the jammer thinks his are the more important rights."

The jamming technology works by sending out a radio signal so powerful that phones are overwhelmed and cannot communicate with cell towers. The range varies from several feet to several yards, and the devices cost from $50 to several hundred dollars. Larger models can be left on to create a no-call zone.

Using the jammers is illegal in the United States. The radio frequencies used by cellphone carriers are protected, just like those used by television and radio broadcasters.

The Federal Communication Commission says people who use cellphone jammers could be fined up to $11,000 for a first offense. Its enforcement bureau has prosecuted a handful of American companies for distributing the gadgets—and it also pursues their users.

Investigators from the FCC and Verizon Wireless visited an upscale restaurant in Maryland over the last year, the restaurant owner said. The owner, who declined to be named, said he bought a powerful jammer for $1,000 because he was tired of his employees focusing on their phones rather than customers.

"I told them: put away your phones, put away your phones, put away your phones," he said. They ignored him.

The owner said the FCC investigator hung around for a week, using special equipment designed to detect jammers. But the owner had turned his off.

The Verizon investigator was similarly unsuccessful. "He went to everyone in town and gave them his number and said if they were having trouble, they should call him right away," the owner said. He said he has since stopped using the jammer.

Of course, it would be harder to detect the use of smaller battery-operated jammers like those used by disgruntled commuters.

An FCC spokesman, Clyde Ensslin, declined to comment on the issue or the case in Maryland.

Cellphone carriers pay tens of billions of dollars to lease frequencies from the government with an understanding that others will not interfere with their signals. And there are other costs on top of that. Verizon Wireless, for example, spends $6.5 billion a year to build and maintain its network.

"It's counterintuitive that when the demand is clear and strong from wireless consumers for improved cell coverage, that these kinds of devices are finding a market," said Jeffrey Nelson, a Verizon spokesman. The carriers also raise a public safety issue: jammers could be used by criminals to stop people from communicating in an emergency.

In evidence of the intensifying debate over the devices, CTIA, the main cellular phone industry association, asked the FCC on Friday to maintain the illegality of jamming and to continue to pursue violators. It said the move was a response to requests by two companies for permission to use jammers in specific situations, like in jails.

Individuals using jammers express some guilt about their sabotage, but some clearly have a prankster side, along with some mean-spirited cellphone schadenfreude [the enjoyment of others' troubles]. "Just watching those dumb teens at the mall get their calls dropped is worth it. Can you hear me now? NO! Good," the purchaser of a jammer wrote last month in a review on a Web site called DealExtreme.

Gary, a therapist in Ohio who also declined to give his last name, citing the illegality of the devices, says jamming is necessary to do his job effectively. He runs group therapy sessions for sufferers of eating disorders. In one session, a woman's confession was rudely interrupted.

"She was talking about sexual abuse," Gary said. "Someone's cellphone went off and they carried on a conversation."

"There's no etiquette," he said. "It's a pandemic."

Gary said phone calls interrupted therapy all the time, despite a no-phones policy. Four months ago, he paid $200 for a jammer, which he placed surreptitiously on one side of the room. He tells patients that if they are expecting an emergency call, they should give out the front desk's number. He has not told them about the jammer.

Gary bought his jammer from a Web site based in London called PhoneJammer.com. Victor McCormack, the site's operator, says he ships roughly 400 jammers a month into the United States, up from 300 a year ago. Orders for holiday gifts, he said, have exceeded 2,000.

Kumaar Thakkar, who lives in Mumbai, India, and sells jammers online, said he exported 20 a month to the United States, twice as many as a year ago. Clients, he said, include owners of cafes and hair salons, and a New York school bus driver named Dan.

"The kids think they are sneaky by hiding low in the seats and using their phones," Dan wrote in an e-mail message to Mr. Thakkar thanking him for selling the jammer. "Now the kids can't figure out why their phones don't work, but can't ask because they will get in trouble! It's fun to watch them try to get a signal."

Andrew, the San Francisco–area architect, said using his jammer was initially fun, and then became a practical way to get some quiet on the train. Now he uses it more judiciously.

"At this point, just knowing I have the power to cut somebody off is satisfaction enough," he said.

Starting a Conversation: Respond to "Devices Enforce Silence of Cellphones, Illegally"

In your writer's notebook, examine the strategies Richtel uses to inform his readers by responding to the following questions:

1. Reflect on how Richtel frames his topic. What is the effect of opening the article by using a brief story about the use of a jammer? Did you identify — or sympathize — more with the person using the cell phone or the person jamming the call? How do you think the writer imagines his audience?

2. How would you describe the overall purpose of "Devices Enforce Silence of Cellphones, Illegally"? What are the unstated questions that Richtel attempts to answer?

3. Reporters generally try to remain objective. Does Richtel seem impartial to you, or do you detect any evidence that he either supports or opposes the use of cell phone jammers? Point to examples from his article to support your conclusion.

4. List the people Richtel interviewed for the article. What makes them good sources for an informative article about cell phone jamming?

5. The article notes that jamming technology is not new but that demand for these devices is increasing. Why do you think that is? What larger social, cultural, or legal concerns might be raised by the growing use of this technology?

@ Download or print this Starting a Conversation activity at **bedfordstmartins.com/ conversation**.

Profiles

Profiles use information to describe a place, a group, or a person, often someone who has been in the news or who represents a number of people affected by an issue. Following the flooding of New Orleans, for example, Mayor C. Ray Nagin was the subject of several profiles; at the same time, a number of residents with no claim to fame were the subject of profiles that conveyed the experiences of people who had lost family, friends, homes, and businesses to the disaster.

Because they appear so often in popular periodicals, most profiles are relatively brief. They also tend to focus on a particular moment in time, rather than on a lifetime. Profiles typically draw on interviews and observations, and sometimes on published sources such as biographies or news reports, to give readers a thorough understanding of the subject. Photographs of the subject of a profile are another common feature of this genre—although such images are not always strictly factual.

 ### Chris Nashawaty and Art Streiber
Danger Is Their Middle Name

Written by senior staff writer Chris Nashawaty with photographs by Art Streiber, the profile shown here first appeared in a special photo issue of *Entertainment Weekly* (October 19, 2007). As you read it, notice the sources of information and the uses of staged photography. The genre overlaps somewhat with photo essays (see p. 104), but the article is also typical of profiles: Nashawaty introduces the Eppers, a multi-generational family of Hollywood stuntpeople, and establishes their role in Hollywood history, while Streiber creates an irreverent portrait of their talents. Considered as a whole, their profile gives readers a sense not only of what stuntpeople do but also of what's at stake for their craft as filmmaking technologies become ever more sophisticated.

Danger Is Their Middle Name

story by Chris Nashawaty
photographs by Art Streiber

The great ones will tell you that when the moment comes there is no fear. But Matt Epper is afraid. He didn't think he would be. Maybe a little, but not like this. Everyone said it would be easy: his sister, his uncle, even his grandmother. But as he stands on the edge of the roof looking down at the ground, he can't hear any of them screaming for him to jump. All he can hear is his own heartbeat racing so fast that he feels like his chest might explode.

The boy is 10 years old. His hair is as blond as Southern California. And he has thought about this moment since he was 5 or 6. But now that it's finally here, he isn't so sure anymore. Then, out of the corner of his eye, he sees his mother.

"Just jump, Matt! Come on! There's nothing to it! Just kick your legs out and fly!"

What the hell is going on? Why would a mother tell her own son to jump off a roof? What kind of sense does that make? But it's his mother, so he puts aside his fear, closes his eyes, and jumps. The crash pad lets out a loud wheeze as he lands on his back. There's a thousand-watt smile on his face. It's over. He's safe. And just like that, the 10-year-old boy has become an Epper.

Matt's mother, Eurlyne, is a stuntwoman. His uncles and aunts are stuntpeople too. Even his grandmother is a stuntwoman. And if Matt winds up jumping off roofs for a living when he grows up, he'll take his place in the fourth generation of Eppers in the family business.

It's no exaggeration to say that for nearly as long as there have been movies where cowboys fall off horses, or cars get flipped, or bad guys get set on fire, there have been Eppers. By the family's best reckoning there have been 15 Eppers who have risked their necks in the film industry since the 1930s. A couple dozen more if you count in-laws and cousins. In fact, Steven Spielberg calls them "the Flying Wallendas of film," after the famous German high-wire family. Like Daleys in Chicago politics, or Mannings in pro football, the stunt business is a dynastic one. They're simply born into it.

> Don't let the tranquil smiles fool you. You're looking at some of the world's most fearless daredevils. Meet the Eppers, Hollywood's reigning dynasty of stunt-people. Thrill-seeking is in their genes.

The Eppers may not be the most famous stuntpeople in Hollywood, or the flashiest, but their roots undoubtedly go the deepest. If you watch an old Western with Gary Cooper doing a fancy dismount from a horse, you're watching an Epper. When you see Janet Leigh being stabbed in the shower in *Psycho*, the killer's hand is an Epper's. Kathleen Turner being swept down a mudslide in *Romancing the Stone*? An Epper. That bus ripped apart in the *Transformers* movie? Take a wild guess who was behind the wheel. This paragraph could go on all day.

It takes a certain breed of lunatic to lay his or her life on the line for a few feet of film. Making a living by taking big risks, putting all of your chips on black, believing that each stunt will somehow work out, would seem to most people to be a form of insanity. But if you ask any of the Eppers about why they do it, they just shrug and laugh like it's the first time they even considered the question. They just don't scare. Never have. It's that simple. The Eppers are the most fearless family in Hollywood.

Ever since the early days of Buster Keaton and Charlie Chaplin, when films were silent and stunts were mostly pratfalls and slapstick, stuntmen have referred to what they do as "gags." There are horse gags, car gags, fire gags. Let's say, for example, that a director asked you to be shot out of a cannon in a film. That's a cannon gag (although it's probably not very funny to the person in the cannon). John Epper's first gag was jumping a horse over a car.

Born in Gossau, Switzerland, in 1906, the patriarch of the Epper stunt clan was a member of the Swiss mounted cavalry who spoke five languages. His great-grandfather was a colonel in Napoleon's army. Epper came to America in 1926 and eventually wound up in California, where he took a job at a horse-riding academy. As a side business, they rented horses to the movie studios.

One day, while making a delivery to the MGM lot, Epper ran into a frantic director who needed someone to jump a horse over a Packard. The stuntman who'd been hired had tried the stunt, but couldn't pull it off. Epper volunteered, and before he knew it, he was being dressed up in a cowboy outfit. He nailed the jump on the first take, and the studio gave him 25 dollars. He was hooked. It was the golden age of the Western, and there was plenty of work for a daredevil who was comfortable in the saddle. Eventually, Epper began

↳ **Eppers, left to right: Jeannie, Alexis, Matthew, Amber, Eurlyne, Taylor, Clayton, Christopher; Airborne: Kurtis**

doubling for stars like Gary Cooper, Ronald Reagan, and Errol Flynn.

John Epper, his wife Frances, and their growing family lived on a ranch in North Hollywood back when the area was connected by dirt roads and every backyard had stables and an orange grove. Will Rogers' horse, Trigger, was stabled at the end of their street. Epper had six children — three boys and three girls — and soon they were running roughshod over the neighborhood. "We were the terrors of Long Ridge Avenue," says Tony Epper, the oldest of the sons, now 70. "We were a wild group," adds his brother Andy, 63. "We all rode horses by the time we were 4 and 5. We were happy kids. And we'd fight anybody who came across us. That was our reputation."

After school, the six Epper kids would practice galloping their father's horses alongside moving trains and leaping onto them from their mounts. When they got older, they would rent cars from Hertz and teach themselves how to stunt-drive. "They got wise to us after a while," recalls Andy, laughing. "The tires were never quite the same after we got through with them. We'd practice doing 180s and 360s and high-speed drifts. We never got busted, but they wouldn't rent cars to any more Eppers after a while."

↳ **Left to right: Eurlyne, Clayton, Taylor (on banister), Alexis (on bike), Amber**

Tony was the first to follow his father into the business. But soon Andy and the middle daughter, Jeannie, were getting bit parts in films like *The Day the Earth Stood Still*; Stephanie, the youngest of the girls, was standing in for the star of the TV show *My Friend Flicka*; and Gary was doing stunts on *Rin Tin Tin*. As the years went on, there was hardly a movie that came out of Hollywood that didn't include an Epper in its end credits. If you squint hard enough, you'll see a second-generation Epper falling down an elevator shaft or hanging from a helicopter in such smash-and-burn classics as *The Wild Bunch*, *The Poseidon Adventure*, *The Towering Inferno*, *Die Hard*, and *Commando*. "Twenty years ago, you couldn't walk onto a movie set and not see one of us," says Jeannie, 66.

As the Epper kids grew up and established themselves as some of the most reliable and toughest hired hands in the industry, they began to have Epper kids of their own (seven of whom would go on to become stuntpeople). Which isn't to say that the original Epper kids, the terrors of Long Ridge Avenue, had settled down. Burt Reynolds, who began his Hollywood career doing stunts alongside industry legend Hal Needham, remembers going to a favorite stuntman bar in North Hollywood called the Palomino, where the Eppers were known to raise hell.

"Let me tell you a story," says Reynolds, cracking a frisky smile. "Needham and I are sitting in the Palomino and two Epper girls are sitting at the bar. And a guy walks over to them and Hal says, 'I'll bet you a hundred bucks that that guy will be flat on his back in 30 seconds.' And 25 seconds later, that guy was laid out cold on the floor. The Epper girls are tougher than most of the men in the business. And the guys will admit it! They're amazing."

No Epper has ever died doing a movie stunt. Their bodies may creak like old Shaker furniture when they get out of bed in the morning, but none have ever been killed in the line of duty. While fatalities in the business are fairly rare, you'd think that given just how many Eppers there are out there being set on fire and jackknifing cars at ridiculous speeds, there'd be a few close calls. And you'd be right.

Next to the front door of Jeannie Epper's home in Simi Valley, Calif., is a sign that reads "All men are idiots, and I married their king." Jeannie is a great-grandmother now and married to a man who's 21 years younger than she is. Her knees are nearly shot, but she's still tough as an anvil. Last week she got paid to jump through a plate-glass window.

A couple of years ago, Jeannie was the subject of a documentary called *Double Dare*. But one thing that wasn't mentioned in the film was the time Jeannie almost died. In the late '60s, Jeannie was working on a TV show called *Lancer*, a *Bonanza*-style Western. She was standing in for a young actress who was supposed to be clutching a doll while trapped in a burning cabin. Before the scene, the director told Jeannie, "Whatever you do, don't let go of the doll." Jeannie had a feeling before the house was set on fire that something wasn't right with the gag. But it was too late. As the cabin started to go up in flames, beams started falling all around her. Fire was everywhere. She was trapped. "When I woke up in the hospital, all my hair was burned off," she says, "but I still had that little doll in my hands. You should have seen that doll, too. It was all fried up. We both were."

Jeannie Epper did her first professional stunt at 9: She rode a horse bareback down a cliff. Now, 57 years later, she's considered by many to be the greatest stuntwoman who's ever lived. Earlier this year, she was the first woman to receive a Lifetime Achievement Award at the Oscars of the stunt world, the Taurus World Stunt Awards. Right before they began the tribute, a procession of nearly a hundred stuntwomen walked on stage. All of them owed their careers to Jeannie.

In the '70s, Jeannie was Lynda Carter's stunt double on TV's *Wonder Woman*. And during the '80s, whenever you saw Krystle throwing down in a catfight with Alexis on *Dynasty*, that was Jeannie under a blond Linda Evans wig. But there's no question that her most famous stunt — or pair of stunts — came while shooting 1984's *Romancing the Stone*.

In addition to standing in for Kathleen Turner during the film's famous rain-forest mudslide, Jeannie swung on a vine across a 350-foot gorge. Terry Leonard, one of the film's stunt coordinators, remembers the gag as a particularly unfunny one. "While we were rigging the cables, we tied off to a tree. And when we did a test, the tree pulled right out of the ground because it had rained so much in Mexico. It went crashing down into the canyon. Something like that will take away your confidence pretty quickly. But Jeannie, she just stepped up and did it when it was time."

Jeannie, like a lot of men and women who cheat death for a living, is deeply religious. As the old battlefield saying goes, "There are no atheists in a foxhole." When she gets ready to do a stunt, she takes a moment to pray. "As far as I'm concerned, whenever I do a stunt, it's 150 percent going

⌐ **Left to right: Eurlyne, Christopher, Kurtis, and Jeannie**

to work out. But I'm a born-again Christian and I have a tendency to pray about it, get focused, and then say, 'God, it belongs to you now.'"

You'd think that with all of the close calls and banged-up body parts she's had over the years, a woman like Jeannie wouldn't exactly be thrilled about having her kids follow her into the business. But all three of her children, Richard, Eurlyne, and Kurtis, are stuntpeople (as is Eurlyne's 23-year-old son, Christopher). "I'll probably keep doing it until I can't walk anymore — like my mom," says Kurtis, a boyish-looking blond whose résumé includes jumping off the deck of an aircraft carrier in *Pearl Harbor*. "She needs a knee replacement, but she won't do it because she doesn't want to stop working."

All of Jeannie's brothers and sisters have retired from stuntwork. But there's something inside of her that won't, or can't, give it up. "Some guys don't like to put me in a really dangerous position anymore," she says. "It hurts your pride to acknowledge that you're getting older. I've had to go through that the past few years. But I'm not emotionally ready to stop yet. My neighbors think I'm nuts."

Whether through prayer, preparation, or just sheer craziness, stuntpeople are wired differently than people like you and me — the people who pay 10 bucks to see them anonymously risk their lives on screen. Tony Epper once crashed a propeller plane into the Pacific Ocean for a film,

> "I'll probably keep doing it until I can't walk anymore — like my mom," says stuntman Kurtis Epper.

⌐ **Left to right: Amber, Alexis, Eurlyne, Kurtis, Jeannie, Christopher, Taylor, Matthew**

was a mistake. But when we do stunts, there's just no room for fear."

Actually, there is one thing that stuntpeople are afraid of, and that's CGI. To anyone in the business, it's a four-letter word. Stunts that used to be done in real time by real men and women risking real danger are now being done on computers by digital F/X geeks. As a result, there's less stuntwork to go around. Also, the business is becoming more and more like, well, a business. "There's no more fun," complains Needham. "All that digital stuff — we used to do that crap for real! I hate that stuff. Young kids who play videogames seem to like it, but I don't."

Some diehards like Jeannie believe there will always be a demand to see stuntpeople wager their lives for a pay-check. "I just think people would rather watch real stunts and real risk in a movie. I think we still have that thirst from the gladiator days. If you know it's all going to be safe, who's going to hold their breath watching a stunt?"

Certainly, the business will never be the same as it was 20, 30, or 40 years ago — the Wild West outlaw days of *Hooper* and *The Fall Guy*, or working hard, playing hard, and getting into barroom brawls at the Palomino. But to some degree, Jeannie's absolutely right. The movies will always need crazy men and women working in the shadows, doing the stuff that actors are afraid to do. Cars will still need to be flipped. People will still need to be set on fire. Roofs will need to be jumped from. There will always be stuntpeople. Which is to say, there will always be Eppers unafraid to put aside their fear, close their eyes, and jump.

flipping it end over end like a pinwheel. Gary once did a high fall from 114 feet. Eurlyne's had three neck surgeries and still wakes up every morning and goes to work. "Is there fear? No, there isn't," says Needham. "Now, I've made mistakes. I've broken 56 bones in my body, and each one

Starting a Conversation: Respond to "Danger Is Their Middle Name"

In your writer's notebook, respond to the information and ideas in Nashawaty and Streiber's profile of the Epper family by answering the following questions:

1. What reasons might Nashawaty and Streiber have had for profiling the Epper family? Does their story illustrate a broader issue? What is it?

2. Take a close look at the photographs in this essay. Do you notice anything unusual about them? What do they add to the story?

3. Create an outline of the profile, indicating the main point, the supporting points, and the evidence for each point. What do you think of the structure of the profile? Did you find it informative? Why or why not?

4. Nashawaty uses a wide range of evidence in his profile of the Eppers: firsthand observation, interviews, and comments from famous actors and directors they have worked with. Identify an example of each type of evidence, and comment on its effectiveness.

@ Download or print this Starting a Conversation activity at **bedfordstmartins.com/ conversation**.

Informative Essays

Informative essays share information about a subject in a well-organized, well-supported, readable form. Although instructors are usually the primary readers of academic essays, students are often asked to address a different audience, such as other students, parents, politicians, or members of a particular profession. For example, in courses that use service learning, the primary audience for informative essays might be the director of an organization, employees of a government agency, or the members of a community group. In some cases, the choice of audience is left to the writer.

In academic settings, such as writing and writing-intensive classes as well as scholarly publishing, informative essays draw on sources (articles, books, Web sites, interviews, and so on) to provide evidence for the information the writer presents. Those sources should always be cited using a documentation system, such as MLA or APA (see Chapters 21 and 22). Writers of informative essays typically attempt to present a subject fairly, although their experiences with and attitudes toward the subject are likely to influence their approach to the subject and their selection and presentation of information from sources.

George Chauncey
The Legacy of Antigay Discrimination

George Chauncey is a professor of history at Yale University and a gay rights activist. His books include *Gay New York: Gender, Urban Culture, and the Making of the Gay Male World, 1890–1940* (1995) and *Why Marriage? The History Shaping Today's Debate over Gay Equality* (2004), where "The Legacy of Antigay Discrimination" first appeared. In it, Chauncey recounts the history of laws and regulations aimed at American gays and lesbians during the first half of the twentieth century and shows how such practices existed in almost every aspect of social, legal, political, and private life. (Like most historians, he uses the *Chicago Manual of Style*, or CMS, documentation system to cite his sources.) The author suggests that we must recover and understand the past because it affects current debates around controversial issues like gay marriage.

The Legacy of Antigay Discrimination

The place of lesbians and gay men in American society has dramatically changed in the last half century. The change has been so profound that the harsh discrimination once faced by gay people has virtually disappeared from popular memory. That history bears repeating, since its legacy shapes today's debate over marriage.

Although most people recognize that gay life was difficult before the growth of the gay movement in the 1970s, they often have only the vaguest sense of why: that gay people were scorned and ridiculed, made to feel ashamed, afraid, and alone. But antigay discrimination was much more systematic and powerful than this.

Fifty years ago, there was no *Will & Grace* or *Ellen*, no *Queer Eye for the Straight Guy*, no *Philadelphia* or *The Hours*, no annual Lesbian, Gay, Bisexual, and Transgender (LGBT) film festival. In fact, Hollywood films were *prohibited* from including lesbian or gay characters, discussing gay themes, or even inferring the existence of homosexuality. The Hollywood studios established these rules (popularly known as the Hays Code) in the 1930s under pressure from a censorship movement led by Catholic and other religious leaders, who threatened them with mass boycotts and restrictive federal legislation. The absolute ban on gay representation, vigorously enforced by Hollywood's own censorship board, remained in effect for some thirty years and effectively prohibited the discussion of homosexuality in the most important medium of the mid-twentieth century, even though some filmmakers found subtle ways to subvert it.[1]

Censorship extended to the stage as well. In 1927, after a serious lesbian drama opened on Broadway to critical acclaim—and after Mae West announced that she planned to open a play called *The Drag*—New York state passed a "padlock law" that threatened to shut down for a year any theater that dared to stage a play with lesbian or gay characters. Given Broadway's national importance as a staging ground for new plays, this law had dramatic effects on American theater for a generation.[2]

Fifty years ago, no openly gay people worked for the federal government. In fact, shortly after he became president in 1953, Dwight Eisenhower issued an executive order that banned homosexuals from government employment, civilian as well as military, and required companies with government contracts to ferret out and fire their gay employees. At the height of the McCarthy witch-hunt, the U.S. State Department fired more homosexuals than communists. In the 1950s and 1960s literally thousands of men and women were discharged or forced to resign from civilian positions in the federal government because they were suspected of being gay or lesbian.[3] It was only in 1975 that the ban on gay federal employees was lifted, and it took until the late 1990s before such discrimination in federal hiring was prohibited.

Fifty years ago, countless teachers, hospital workers, and other state and municipal employees also lost their jobs as a result of official policy. Beginning in 1958, for instance, the Florida Legislative Investigation Committee, which had been established by the legislature in 1956 to investigate and discredit civil rights activists, turned its attention to homosexuals working in the state's universities and public schools. Its initial investigation of the University of Florida resulted in the dismissal of fourteen faculty and staff members, and in the next five years it interrogated some 320 suspected gay men and lesbians. Under pressure from the committee, numerous teachers gave up their jobs and countless students were forced to drop out of college.[4]

Fifty years ago, there were no gay business associations or gay bars advertising in newspapers. In fact, many gay-oriented businesses were illegal, and gay people had no right to public assembly. In many states, following the repeal of prohibition in 1933, it even became illegal for restaurants and bars to serve lesbians or gay men. The New York State Liquor Authority, for instance, issued regulations prohibiting bars, restaurants, cabarets, and other establishments with liquor licenses from employing or serving homosexuals or allowing homosexuals to congregate on their premises.[5] The Authority's rationale was that the mere presence of homosexuals made an establishment "disorderly," and when the courts rejected that argument, the Authority began using evidence gathered by plain-clothes investigators of one man trying to pick up another or of patrons' unconventional gender behavior to provide proof of a bar's disorderly character.[6] One bar in Times Square was closed in 1939, for instance, because the Liquor Authority alleged it "permitted the premises to become disorderly in permitting homosexuals, degenerates and other undesirable people to congregate on the premises." A Brooklyn bar was closed in 1960 because it became "a gathering place for homosexuals and degenerates who conducted themselves in an offensive and indecent manner" by, among other things, "wearing tight fitting trousers," walking "with a sway to their hips," and "gesturing with limp wrists." A bar in upstate New York was closed in 1963 after an investigator observed "two females, one mannish in appearance, [who was] holding the hands of the other female."[7]

Any restaurant or bar that gained a gay reputation faced constant harassment and police raids until the police shut it down for good. Some bars in New York and Los Angeles posted signs telling potential gay customers: *If You Are Gay, Please Stay Away*, or, more directly, *We Do Not Serve Homosexuals*. In the thirty-odd years between the enactment of such regulations by New York state in 1933 and their rejection by the New York state courts in the mid-1960s, the police closed *hundreds* of bars that had tolerated gay customers in New York City alone.[8]

Fifty years ago, elected officials did not court the gay vote and the nation's mayors did not proclaim LGBT Pride Week. Instead, many mayors periodically declared war on homosexuals—or sex deviates, as they were usually called. In many cities, gay residents knew that if the mayor needed to show he was tough on crime and vice just before an election, he would order a crackdown on gay bars. Hundreds of people would be arrested. Their names put in the paper. Their meeting places closed. This did not just happen once or twice, or just in smaller cities. Rather, it happened regularly in every major city, from New York and Miami to Chicago, San Francisco, and LA. After his administration's commitment to suppressing gay life became an issue in his 1959 re-election campaign, San Francisco's mayor launched a two-year-long crackdown on the city's gay bars and other meeting places. Forty to sixty men and women were arrested every week in bar sweeps, and within two years almost a third of the city's gay bars had been closed.[9] Miami's gay scene was relentlessly attacked by the police and press in 1954. New York launched major crackdowns on gay bars as part of its campaign to "clean up the city" before the 1939 and 1964 World's Fairs. During the course of a 1955 investigation of the gay scene in Boise, Idaho, 1,400 people were interrogated and coerced into identifying the names of other gay residents.[10] Across America, homosexuals were an easy target, with few allies.

Fifty years ago, there was no mass LGBT movement. In fact, the handful of early gay activists risked everything to speak up for their rights. When the police learned of the country's earliest known gay political group, which had been established by a postal worker in Chicago in 1924, they raided his home and seized his group's files and membership list. A quarter century later, when the first national gay rights group, the Mattachine Society, was founded, it repeatedly had to reassure its anxious members that the police would not seize its membership list. The U.S. Post Office banned its newspaper from the mails in 1954, and in some cities the police shut down newsstands that dared to carry it. In 1959, a few weeks after Mattachine held its first press conference during a national convention in Denver, the police raided the homes of three of its Denver organizers; one lost his job and spent sixty days in jail. Such harassment and censorship of free speech made it difficult for people to organize or speak on their own behalf and for all Americans to debate and learn about gay issues.[11]

Fifty years ago, no state had a gay rights law. Rather, every state had a sodomy law and other laws penalizing homosexual conduct. Beginning in the late nineteenth century, municipal police forces began using misdemeanor charges such as disorderly conduct, vagrancy, lewdness, and loitering to harass gay men.[12] In 1923, the New York state legislature tailored its statutes to specify for the first time that a man's "frequent[ing] or loiter[ing] about any public place soliciting men for the purpose of committing a crime against nature or other lewdness" was punishable as a form of disorderly conduct.[13] Many more men were arrested and prosecuted under this misdemeanor charge than for the felony charge of sodomy, since misdemeanor laws carried fewer procedural protections for defendants. Between 1923 and 1966, when Mayor John Lindsay ordered the police to stop using entrapment by plainclothes officers to secure arrests of gay men, more than 50,000 men had been arrested on this charge in New York City alone.[14] The number of arrests escalated dramatically after the Second World War. More than 3,000 New Yorkers were arrested every year on this charge in the late 1940s. By 1950, Philadelphia's six-man "morals squad" was arresting more gay men than the courts knew how to handle, some 200 a month. In the District of Columbia, there were more than a thousand arrests every year.[15]

Fifty years ago, more than half of the nation's states, including New York, Michigan, and California, enacted laws authorizing the police to force persons who were convicted of certain sexual offenses, including sodomy—or, in some states, merely suspected of being "sexual deviants"—to undergo psychiatric examinations. Many of these laws authorized the indefinite confinement of homosexuals in mental institutions, from which they were to be released only if they were cured of their homosexuality, something prison doctors soon began to complain was impossible. The medical director of a state hospital in California argued that "Whenever a doubt arises in the judge's mind" that a suspect "might be a sexual deviate, maybe by his mannerisms or his dress, something to attract the attention, I think he should immediately call for a psychiatric examination." Detroit's prosecuting attorney demanded the authority to arrest, examine, and possibly confine indefinitely "anyone who exhibited abnormal sexual behavior, whether or not dangerous."[16]

Fifty years ago, in other words, homosexuals were not just ridiculed and scorned. They were systematically denied their civil rights: their right to free assembly, to patronize public accommodations, to free speech, to a free press, to a form of intimacy of their own choosing. And they confronted a degree of policing and harassment that is almost unimaginable to us today.

Notes

1. This chapter is more extensively footnoted than others, but it seemed important to provide documentation of the discriminatory measures it describes. The chapter draws heavily on sections I drafted for the Historians' Amicus Brief submitted in *Lawrence v. Texas*, and following it, I cite the recent work of historians on these issues. There is also a large and useful literature produced by lawyers and legal scholars. On the history of film censorship, see Gregory Black, *Hollywood Censored: Morality Codes, Catholics, and the Movies* (Cambridge: Cambridge University Press, 1994); Vito Russo, *The Celluloid Closet: Homosexuality in the Movies* (New York: Harper and Row, 1981); and George Chauncey, *Gay New York: Gender, Urban Culture, and the Making of the Gay Male World, 1890–1940* (New York: Basic Books, 1994), 353 and n.57.

2. Kaier Curtin, *"We Can Always Call Them Bulgarians": The Emergence of Lesbians and Gay Men on the American Stage* (Boston: Alyson, 1987). Chauncey, *Gay New York*, 311–313.

3. David K. Johnson, *The Lavender Scare: The Cold War Persecution of Gays and Lesbians in the Federal Government* (Chicago: University of Chicago Press, 2004), 166 and passim; Robert D. Dean, *Imperial Brotherhood: Gender and the Making of Cold War Foreign Policy* (Amherst: University of Massachusetts Press, 2001).

4. Stacy Braukman, "'Nothing Else Matters But Sex': Cold War Narratives of Deviance and the Search for Lesbian Teachers in Florida, 1959–1963," *Feminist Studies 27* (2001): 553, 555; see also 553–557, 573, and n.3.

5. Chauncey, *Gay New York*, 173, 337.

6. Ibid., 337.

7. See Chauncey, *Gay New York*, chapter 12, quotes on pp. 338, 344. Similar restrictions were imposed by the California Liquor Authority in the 1950s; see Nan Alamilla Boyd, *Wide Open Town: A History of Queer San Francisco* (Berkeley: University of California Press, 2003), 108–147. For similar policing in Buffalo, New York, see Elizabeth Lapovsky Kennedy and Madeline D. Davis, *Boots of Leather, Slippers of Gold: The History of a Lesbian Community* (New York: Routledge, 1993), 145–146.

8. Chauncey, *Gay New York*, 339.

9. John D'Emilio, *Sexual Politics, Sexual Communities: The Making of a Homosexual Minority, 1940–1970* (Chicago: University of Chicago Press, 1981), 182–184.

10. D'Emilio, *Sexual Politics*, 51; Chauncey, *Gay New York*, 340; Chauncey, *The Strange Career of the Closet: Gay Culture, Consciousness, and Politics from the Second World War to the Gay Liberation Era* (New York: Basic Books, forthcoming); John Gerassi, *The Boys of Boise: Furor, Vice, and Folly in an American City* (New York: Macmillan, 1966); Fred Fejes, "Murder, Perversion, and Moral Panic: The 1954 Media Campaign

Against Miami's Homosexuals and the Discourse of Civic Betterment," *Journal of the History of Sexuality* 9 (2000): 305–347.

11. On the Chicago Group, see Jonathan Ned Katz, *Gay American History: Lesbians and Gay Men in the U.S.A.* (New York: Crowell, 1976), 385–389; Katz, *The Gay/Lesbian Almanac* (New York: Morrow, 1983), 554–561; on Mattachine, see D'Emilio, *Sexual Politics*, 115, 120–121.

12. See John D'Emilio and Estelle B. Freedman, *Intimate Matters: A History of Sexuality in America* (San Francisco/New York: Harper and Row, 1988), 150–156, 202–215; Chauncey, *Gay New York*, 137–141, 183–186, 197–198, 249–250; Paul Boyer, *Urban Masses and Moral Order in America, 1820–1920* (Cambridge: Harvard University Press, 1978), 191–219.

13. Chauncey, *Gay New York*, 172.

14. Chauncey, "A Gay World, Vibrant and Forgotten," *New York Times*, 26 June 1994, E17.

15. John D'Emilio, "The Homosexual Menace: The Politics of Sexuality in Cold War America," in *Passion and Power: Sexuality in History*, eds. Kathy Peiss and Christina Simmons, with Robert A. Padgug (Philadelphia: Temple University Press, 1989), 231; Chauncey, "The Postwar Sex Crime Panic," in *True Stories from the American Past*, ed. William Graebner (New York: McGraw-Hill, 1993), 160–178.

16. Estelle B. Freedman, "'Uncontrolled Desires': The Response to the Sexual Psychopath, 1920–1960," *Journal of American History* 74 (1987): 83–106; Chauncey, "Postwar Sex Crime Panic."

Starting a Conversation: Respond to "The Legacy of Antigay Discrimination"

In your writer's notebook, consider how Chauncey responds to his writing situation by answering the following questions:

1. Informative essays often begin with a question that readers might have about a subject. What question(s) does "The Legacy of Antigay Discrimination" attempt to answer?

2. Writing to inform involves adopting the role of reporter — a position that often requires a writer to refrain from interpreting, analyzing, or drawing specific responses from readers. How well does Chauncey adopt that role? In what ways does he seem impartial or partial in this essay?

3. Issues such as gay marriage and gay rights are contentious and controversial. What assumptions does Chauncey seem to make about his readers throughout the essay? Do you think he anticipates resistance to his points, or agreement? Why?

4. Chauncey's essay is dense with historical information, all carefully documented, and the writer mentions that "it seemed important to provide

documentation of the discriminatory measures" outlined in his essay (note 1). Besides a general obligation to cite sources in an academic essay, why would Chauncey feel a particular need to document his evidence in this essay? How do the extensive source notes fit with his overall purpose?

5. "The Legacy of Antigay Discrimination" focuses on intolerance of homosexuality half a century ago. How does this historical information connect to—and affect—contemporary debates about gay and lesbian rights, particularly gay marriage?

@ Download or print this Starting a Conversation activity at **bedfordstmartins.com/ conversation**.

How Can I Write an Informative Essay?

The first step in writing a successful informative essay is recognizing that you don't have to be an expert on something to write about it — you simply have to know how to learn enough about it to share your findings with your readers. The second step is understanding how to collect and work with information. This doesn't mean that an informative essay needs to look like a research paper. As you've seen throughout this chapter, the amount and type of information used in informative documents can vary widely. What it does mean, however, is that you should understand where you can find information — for example, through interviews, published documents, the Web, direct observation, or personal experience — and how to work with it once you've collected it.

This section helps you tune in to the conversations around you and take on the role of reporter as you choose a subject, gather information, prepare your draft, and review and improve your draft. As you work on your essay, you'll follow the work of Hannah Steiner, a first-year student who wrote an informative essay about using hydrogen as a fuel source for automobiles.

Find a Conversation and Listen In

Informative essays offer a good opportunity to learn more about something that intrigues you and to report what you've learned to readers who share your interest in the subject. To get started on your informative essay, prepare yourself to take on the role of reporter, and spend some time thinking about your purpose, your readers,

In Process

An Informative Essay about the Hydrogen Economy

Hannah Steiner wrote an informative essay for her introductory composition course. To learn about her topic, Hannah read articles about hydrogen fuel and interviewed an engineering professor. Follow Hannah's efforts to inform her readers by visiting **bedfordstmartins .com/conversation**. You can read excerpts of interviews about her work on her informative essay, read her assignment, and read drafts of her essay.

and the context in which your writing will be read (see p. 156). Look around for a topic of conversation that will interest both you and your readers—and that you can investigate in the time available to you.

EXPLORE YOUR INTERESTS

Nobody knows everything, but most of us know a little (or a lot) about a few things—especially if they involve us personally. As you search for ideas for an informative essay, examine your daily life for inspiration.

- **Personal interests and hobbies.** What do you like to do in your spare time? What magazines do you read? What television shows do you like to watch? What are your favorite Web sites? What makes you happy? Curious? Angry? What frightens you? Amuses you?

- **Academics.** Your major and your favorite classes are rich sources for essay ideas. Think about recent class discussions that interested you, questions that puzzled you, or information that surprised you when you first learned it.

- **Work.** Any past or current job, volunteer activity, or career you hope to enter involves specialized knowledge of some sort, from learning how to fill a soda machine to getting to know the U.S. tax code. Ask yourself whether you would be interested in informing others about this specialized knowledge.

- **Reading.** What have you read recently that interested or surprised you? What annoyed you or made you angry? What have you read that made you think?

Any of these areas can serve as a jumping-off point for generating ideas for an informative essay. Spend some time brainstorming or freewriting about these aspects of

Working Together: Try It Out Loud

Before you start writing to inform, start a conversation with your classmates about something that interests you. Form small groups and choose a familiar subject (such as sports, family, your hometown, or the work of a favorite artist or musician). Take turns speaking while the other members of the group listen, respond, and ask questions. Your purpose is to inform the rest of the group, so try to present a fair and accurate view of your subject.

When you are finished, take a few minutes to reflect on the exercise. What did you learn about your readers? Did

you have to adapt what you said based on their interest level and what they already knew? What kind of questions did they ask? What seemed to interest them the most about the subject?

@ Download or print this Working Together activity at bedfordstmartins.com/conversation.

your life (see p. 33), and then review your notes to identify the areas that seem most promising. (For additional suggestions, see the writing project ideas at the end of this chapter.) As you think about your ideas, remember that the best subjects are usually out of the ordinary. Instead of writing about the broad issue of capital punishment, for example, you would do better to consider a little-known but potentially important aspect of the subject, such as how inmates on death row spend their last day before execution or the role of DNA testing in overturning convictions. Once you've identified a few possible subjects, select one or two that interest you most, and jot down your thoughts about what you already know and what you need to learn before you start writing.

USE YOUR LIBRARY

Learn more about promising subjects by using your library. You can gain a preliminary understanding of a subject by searching the library catalog, browsing library shelves, searching library databases, and consulting librarians. Begin by generating a few keywords and phrases related to the subject, and then search the catalog with them. Your search results will give you an overview of the subject. The titles of books and journals on the subject will give you insights into what other writers think is important about it. You'll also be able to learn whether the subject is too broad to tackle on its own — or whether it's so specialized that you'll need to expand your focus.

If you are still interested in the subject after this preliminary research, spend a few minutes browsing the shelves in your library. Jot down or print out the call numbers for books and journals that appear promising, and locate them on the shelves. Browse them, and then look for nearby books and journals on the same subject. Spending as little as ten or fifteen minutes browsing the shelves can either confirm that a subject is worth pursuing or help you decide to look at others.

Some subjects are so recent that few books or journals focus on them. If so, try to gain an overview of your subject by searching news and article databases such as LexisNexis Academic or Academic Search Premier using the keywords and phrases you generated for your catalog search. Examine the titles and descriptions of the sources you find. In some cases, you might find links to full-text articles. If so, skim them to learn about the subject.

You can read more about searching libraries and databases in Chapter 12.

Finally, consider talking with a librarian about the subjects you've identified. Reference librarians or subject-area specialists can direct you to relevant sources, suggest related subjects, or help you narrow your focus.

In Process

Using the Library Catalog

To learn more about the issue of technological barriers to the widespread use of hydrogen fuel, Hannah searched her library's catalog for sources that addressed her subject.

Hannah searched for the phrase *hydrogen economy*. She placed quotation marks around the phrase.

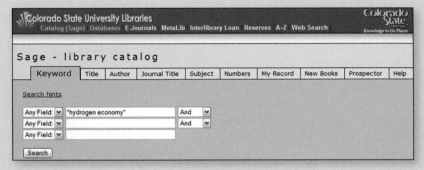

↰ **Hannah's Search of the Library Catalog**

Hannah's searches produced several promising sources, including the following.

Clicking on the title will show the complete record for the source.

The results show whether the source is available, its location, and (if available) a link to its Web site.

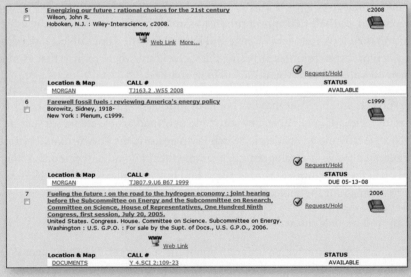

↰ **Results of Hannah's Library Catalog Search**

ASK QUESTIONS ABOUT PROMISING SUBJECTS

Writers who adopt the role of reporter often find themselves confronted with a seemingly endless amount of information on their subject. Before you begin examining sources closely, narrow your focus by determining which subjects interest you the most and which conversation you want to join. Each of the following questions focuses your attention on a general subject in a different way, and each provides a useful starting point for an informative essay. Depending on the subject, you'll find that some questions are more relevant than others.

- **Importance.** Why is this an important subject? Who believes that it is important? Why do they believe it is important?

- **Process.** How does _____ work? What steps are involved?

- **History.** What is the origin of _____? What recent events are related to it? What are the implications of those events?

- **Limitations.** What is limiting the use of _____? What has kept _____ from succeeding? What must happen before _____ is accepted?

- **Benefits.** Who benefits from _____? How do they benefit? Why do they benefit?

- **Advantages and disadvantages.** What are the advantages of _____? What are the disadvantages?

Gather Information

No matter how much you already know about a subject, you'll want to learn more about it before you begin planning and drafting your essay. Informative essays tend to draw extensively on information from other sources and, to a lesser extent, on personal knowledge and experience. To learn more about your subject, create a search plan, collect sources, evaluate those sources, take notes, and consider conducting interviews.

CREATE A SEARCH PLAN

Depending on your subject and the kinds of information you are seeking, you might search library catalogs, databases, or the Web (see Chapter 12); browse library shelves and visit periodicals rooms (see p. 502); or conduct interviews (see p. 186), observations (see p. 129), or surveys (see p. 372). Creating a research plan before you begin will save time and keep you focused.

To develop a search plan, think about what you need to know and how you plan to use what you find. Then try to identify the types of sources most likely to provide the information you are looking for. If you are writing about recent developments in

In Process

Asking Questions

After Hannah Steiner chose the general subject of "hydrogen cars" and searched her library catalog to get a feel for the kinds of information available on her subject, she considered which conversations she might join by clustering (see pp. 35–36). She placed the words *hydrogen cars* at the center of her cluster and then wrote questions about her subject. She used the questions to explore processes related to the production and storage of hydrogen fuel, factors limiting the adoption of hydrogen as a fuel source, the benefits of hydrogen fuel, and the advantages and disadvantages of hydrogen fuel. She represented her answers to these questions as words or phrases linked to each question.

After considering her assignment and writing situation, Hannah decided to focus on technological barriers to the widespread use of hydrogen fuel. She felt that this focus would allow her to accomplish her purpose of informing her readers about an important issue and believed that it would interest both her and her readers. She knew hydrogen cars had been getting a lot of hype in the media, and she wanted to present a balanced, informed assessment of the technology behind them.

Hannah placed her general topic — hydrogen cars — at the center of her cluster.

Hannah asked questions about her topic. Her questions focused on how hydrogen technologies worked, their benefits, their drawbacks, factors limiting their use, and so on.

Hannah wrote brief answers to her questions.

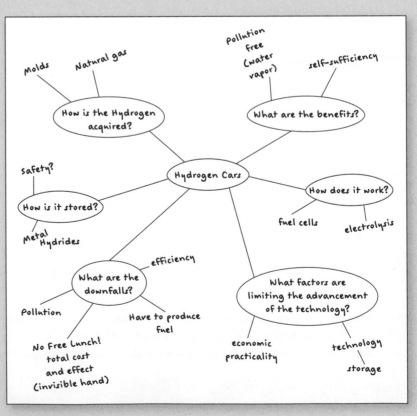

⌞ **Hannah's Cluster**

consumer robotics, for example, you want the most up-to-date information you can find. As a result, you should look in library databases focusing on the subject and search the Web. You might also want to interview an expert on the subject, such as a professor of engineering or computer science. In contrast, if you are writing about the influence of Greek culture on the Roman Empire, you would probably focus on books and scholarly journals that you find by searching your library catalog, browsing the shelves, and visiting periodicals rooms.

If you're not sure where to start, a reference librarian can suggest search strategies and relevant resources. You can learn more about creating a research plan and locating and using sources in Part Three.

Working Together: Plan Your Search for Sources

Before you visit the library, search a database, or browse the Web, sit down with a group of classmates to generate ideas for a search. To carry out this activity, follow these steps:

1. Explain your subject and discuss your purpose for informing readers. If your readers go beyond the instructor and your classmates, describe your readers and their needs, interests, knowledge, and backgrounds. Talk briefly about specific ideas you have for gathering information on your subject.

2. Once you've explained your subject, the other members of your group should brainstorm ideas about useful resources for locating sources, such as the library catalog, specific databases, useful Web sites and directories, and relevant field research methods.

3. For each resource that has been identified, the group should brainstorm suggestions for using it effectively. For example, the group might generate a list of specific keywords and phrases to use in your search, create a list of good candidates for an interview and useful interview questions, and make suggestions about what to look for in an observation.

4. At the end of the discussion, ask any questions you have about the resources and search strategies your classmates have suggested.

If you are working face-to-face, take notes on the discussion. If you are using a chat or instant-messaging program, record a transcript of the session. The goal of the session should be to generate as many useful search resources and strategies as possible. Don't rule out any ideas, no matter how trivial or ridiculous they might seem at first. When the exchange is completed, turn to the next writer and repeat the process.

@ Download or print this Working Together activity at bedfordstmartins.com/conversation.

COLLECT SOURCES

To collect sources, search for them in library catalogs, in databases, and on the Web. Visit your library to check out books and government reports, browse the shelves, and use the periodicals room. You can learn more about these activities in Part Three.

EVALUATE YOUR SOURCES

Depending on your subject, you might find yourself confronted with a dizzying array of promising sources, or you might find yourself gritting your teeth as one search after another comes up empty. In most cases, you'll collect at least a few useful sources, from books and scholarly articles to Web sites and blogs to video clips and news articles. Be aware, however, that not all information is created equal, and that some

In Process

Evaluating Sources

To learn more about challenges to the development of a hydrogen-based economy, Hannah Steiner read several articles she found through her library's periodical databases to get a thorough understanding of the technology and the issues surrounding it. She also searched the Web for up-to-date news and information. Not surprisingly, her searches of the Web pulled up several unreliable sources, such as this one.

Clip art and template design suggest an amateur Web author.

Page provides no indication of authorship or authority to write on the subject.

Assertions are not backed up with evidence.

Site has not been updated in several years.

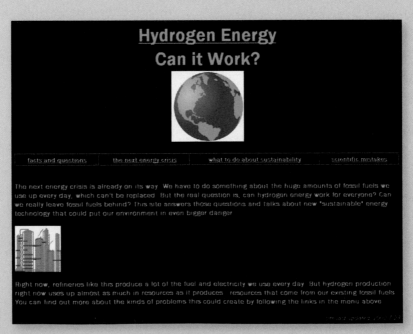

Hydrogen Energy
Can it Work?

facts and questions   the next energy crisis   what to do about sustainability   scientific mistakes

The next energy crisis is already on its way. We have to do something about the huge amounts of fossil fuels we use up every day, which can't be replaced. But the real question is, can hydrogen energy work for everyone? Can we really leave fossil fuels behind? This site answers those questions and talks about new "sustainable" energy technology that could put our environment in even bigger danger.

Right now, refineries like this produce a lot of the fuel and electricity we use every day. But hydrogen production right now uses up almost as much in resources as it produces—resources that come from our existing fossil fuels. You can find out more about the kinds of problems this could create by following the links in the menu above.

⌐ **An Unreliable Source**

sources will be more appropriate for an academic essay than others. Before you decide to use a source, assess its credibility and usefulness for your purposes. To evaluate print and electronic sources for an informative essay, focus in particular on the following:

- **Relevance.** Be sure the information in a source will help you accomplish your purposes as a writer. It should address your subject directly, and it should help you learn more about aspects of the subject that are important to you. Your readers will also want to find information that meets their needs. If they know little about your subject, you'll need to provide them with information that will help them understand it. If they are already familiar with the subject, you'll want to locate information that will allow them to learn more about it.

Hannah's searches of the Web also brought her to the home page of the U.S. Department of Energy's Hydrogen, Fuel Cells, and Infrastructure Technologies Program. On the site, she found several useful and easy-to-follow fact sheets explaining some of the challenges involved in building a hydrogen economy, including this one.

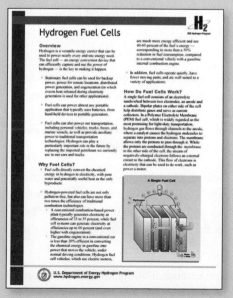
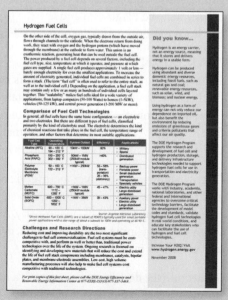

Layout and illustrations are carefully thought out and look professional.

Information in the table supports general statements made in the text.

Source information is provided.

Publication date is provided.

The footer clearly identifies the document as a government publication.

⌐ **A Reliable Source**

Hannah saved copies of the fact sheets, which were available as Portable Document Format (PDF) files, and printed them.

- **Evidence.** Reliable sources provide details and supporting information to back up a writer's statements and assertions. Be wary of any source that makes sweeping generalizations without providing evidence.

- **Authority.** Look for sources written by experts on your subject. Scholarly sources (such as peer-reviewed journal articles) are usually more reliable than popular ones (such as general-interest magazines) because they go through an extensive peer-review process before being published. On the Web, information found on government (.gov), educational (.edu), and nonprofit (.org) domains is likely to be more reliable than information provided on business (.com) sites and personal pages.

- **Timeliness.** In most cases, the more recently a source was published or updated, the more pertinent the information will be for your purpose.

Need a refresher on evaluating sources? See Chapter 3.

TAKE NOTES

Once you've located enough reliable and credible sources to inform your essay, spend time taking notes on them. Because note taking often involves putting information about a subject into your own words, it can help you learn more about your subject and the writers who have been contributing to the conversation you want to join. Taking notes can also help you identify the most important information in your sources.

By studying a source and noting important information, ideas, and arguments, you'll gain a clearer understanding of the source and your subject. Careful note taking also helps you avoid plagiarism and lays the foundation for drafting your document. You can learn more about taking notes in Chapter 13.

CONDUCT AN INTERVIEW

Interviews — in which one person seeks information from another — can provide firsthand accounts of an event, authoritative interpretations of an issue, and thoughts on a subject from the people who have been affected by it. You can conduct interviews face-to-face, over the telephone, via e-mail, and even through an instant-messaging program. Effective interviews usually involve the following activities.

Decide whether to conduct an interview. Before committing yourself to designing and conducting an interview, ask yourself what kind of results you expect and what role those results will play in your essay. Ask as well whether an interview is the best technique for gaining that information, or whether you might gain it more effectively and efficiently in another way.

Sometimes the decision to interview is a natural extension of the kind of work you're doing. A writer exploring the effects of caffeine on athletic performance, for example, might decide to interview an athlete, a coach, or a sports physiologist. Sometimes the decision to conduct an interview isn't so much the result of careful planning as it is the recognition of an available opportunity, such as knowing someone who has direct experience with your subject.

Decide whom to interview. Base your decisions about whom to interview on the kind of information you need for your essay.

- If you're trying to better understand a specific aspect of your subject, interview an expert in the field.

- If you want to learn what people in general think about your subject, interview a number of people who are affected by it.

- If you're hoping to collect quotations from authorities, interview someone who will be recognized as knowledgeable and credible.

When you contact someone to request an interview, be ready with a list of dates and times, as well as potential meeting locations, that are mutually convenient. Most people will be happy to answer questions for you, but be careful to respect their time. Provide an estimate of how long you expect the interview to take—and don't let it drag on longer than promised. Leave your phone number or e-mail address so that your interview candidate can contact you if a conflict arises.

Decide what to ask. Your questions should focus on the kinds of information you want to collect for your essay. Write them down ahead of time, keeping the following principles in mind:

- **Consider your purpose and the kind of information you want to collect.** Are you seeking background information, or do you want an opinion? An answer to the question "How did this situation come about?" will be quite different from an answer to the question "What do you think about this situation?"

- **Ask questions that require more than a yes/no answer.** You'll learn much more from an answer to a question such as "What factors will affect your vote on referendum X?" than from an answer to "Will you vote for referendum X?"

- **Prepare a limited number of main questions and several follow-up questions.** Good interviews seldom involve more than eight to ten main questions, but experienced interviewers know that each question can lead to several follow-up questions.

- **Be flexible.** Be ready for the interview to go in a different direction than you planned. Often the best information comes from questions and answers you didn't anticipate.

Carry out the interview. To increase the chances of a successful interview and leave the door open for additional questions following the interview, follow these guidelines:

1. Arrive early and review your questions.

2. Introduce yourself and ask for permission to record the interview.

3. Set up and test your recording equipment.

4. Ask your questions clearly, and be ready to respond with follow-up questions.

5. Take notes, even if you are using a video or audio recorder.

6. Be alert for related sources mentioned in the interview, and ask where you might find them.

7. Leave your contact information when the interview is over so that the interviewee can contact you in case new information comes up or clarifications need to be made.

8. Send a thank-you note.

Prepare a Draft

Writers of informative essays focus on reporting information to their readers. As you prepare a draft of your informative essay, you'll decide which information, ideas, and arguments to present and how you will share them with your readers.

Your decisions about what to focus on, which points to make, and which examples to use will influence what your readers learn about your subject and how they are likely to understand it. Although reporters strive for objectivity in their writing, experienced writers recognize the difficulty of presenting information in a completely unbiased manner. They understand that their choices can (and will) lead readers to think about a subject in a particular way. Consider a writer selecting details for an informative essay about the impact of a recent ban on smoking in bars and restaurants. Statistical information about register receipts would focus readers' attention on financial implications of the ban for small business owners; a photograph of an asthmatic bartender might encourage readers to consider the positive public health effects of such a ban; and an interview with a smokers' rights advocate could emphasize concerns about eroding personal freedoms. No matter how objectively the writer presents the information, the final mix of statistics, images, and quotations will affect the conclusions readers draw from the document.

It's best to begin by choosing a main point and expressing it as a thesis statement. Then you can decide what supporting points and details will most effectively support your main point. During the drafting process, you should also decide whether to include visual information, how to organize your ideas, and how to frame your introduction and conclusion.

PRESENT YOUR MAIN POINT

In an informative essay, the main point is usually presented in the form of a thesis statement. A thesis statement, typically no more than a single sentence, directs readers' attention to what you want them to learn about a subject. Consider how the following thesis statements about voter turnout among younger Americans directs readers' attention in a particular way:

> The high turnout among younger voters in the last presidential election underscores the growing importance of young Americans on the political scene.

> The growing political commitment of voters under the age of twenty-five has led to higher voter turnout, which, in turn, has reduced the historic imbalance in the relative political influence of younger and older Americans.

> Regardless of the causes, the overall pattern of increasing voter turnout among younger voters should be cause for celebration among voters — young and old alike.

Although each of these thesis statements would provide a sound foundation for an informative essay, the essays would have little in common. By focusing on distinctly different aspects of the subject, they require the writer to provide different supporting points and evidence.

Your thesis statement will be shaped by what you've learned about your subject; your purpose; your readers' purposes, needs, and interests; your readers' backgrounds; and the requirements and limitations of your writing project.

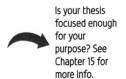

Is your thesis focused enough for your purpose? See Chapter 15 for more info.

DEVELOP SUPPORTING POINTS AND EVIDENCE

Most readers want more than a thesis statement—they want to know why they should accept it. If readers who are thinking about purchasing a car come across a thesis statement such as "For many drivers, renting a car on an occasional basis is a cost-effective alternative to owning one," they'll want to know why renting could be a better choice. If readers interested in financing a college education read a thesis statement such as "Today's college students have a wide range of options for reducing the overall cost of a college education," they'll want to know what those options are. To convince readers to accept your thesis statement, you'll need to provide supporting points and offer evidence for each point.

Choose your supporting points. Supporting points are the reasons you give readers to accept your main point. They are usually expressed as topic sentences in the form of general statements, such as "Renting a car means you can pay less in car insurance" or "If your family qualifies, Pell Grants can significantly reduce the cost of a college education." Consider, for instance, the way George Chauncey presents the supporting points for his essay about discrimination against gay and lesbian Americans (p. 171). Each paragraph opens with a clearly stated topic sentence ("Fifty years ago . . .") that identifies a form of discrimination from the past. As you choose your supporting points, keep in mind that they should not only serve as reasons to accept your main point, but also be consistent with how you've presented your thesis statement. In short, you should resist the urge to include every idea you've come across. You can find more advice on developing support for a thesis statement in Chapter 15.

Identify evidence for each supporting point. Without evidence to support them, even the most clearly expressed supporting points will not be enough to inform your readers fully. You need evidence to help them understand why they should accept the reasons you've used to support your thesis statement. In his profile of the Epper family (p. 166), for instance, Chris Nashawaty used evidence drawn from his interviews to illustrate a point about the family's extensive involvement in Hollywood films:

> As the years went on, there was hardly a movie that came out of Hollywood that didn't include an Epper in its end credits. If you squint hard enough, you'll see a second-generation Epper falling down an elevator shaft or hanging from a helicopter in such smash-and-burn classics as *The Wild Bunch, The Poseidon Adventure, The Towering Inferno, Die Hard,* and *Commando.* "Twenty years ago, you couldn't walk onto a movie set and not see one of us," says Jeannie, 66.

Writers of informative essays also use information from sources to present ideas and clarify statements. You might define a concept by quoting from an interview, paraphrasing an article, or summarizing a report. You might amplify a statement by providing examples from sources. Or you might qualify a statement by noting that it applies only to specific situations and then use a quotation or paraphrase from a source to back that up, as Matt Richtel does in his newspaper article (p. 163):

> Individuals using jammers express some guilt about their sabotage, but some clearly have a prankster side, along with some mean-spirited cellphone schadenfreude [the enjoyment of others' troubles]. "Just watching those dumb teens at the mall get their calls dropped is worth it. Can you hear me now? NO! Good," the purchaser of a jammer wrote last month in a review on a Web site called DealExtreme.

As you select information from sources for your essay, consider your writing situation (see p. 13). Be sure that the evidence you choose will help you accomplish your purpose; that you provide enough detail and explanation to help readers understand the information, ideas, or arguments you present to them; and that you can present the evidence in a way that won't conflict with your readers' values and beliefs.

To identify evidence to support your points, follow these guidelines:

1. List your supporting points.

2. Review your notes to identify evidence for each point.

3. If necessary, review your sources (or find new ones) for additional information.

4. Avoid relying too heavily on one type of information.

5. Avoid relying too heavily on information from a single source.

6. Consider how the evidence fits your writing situation.

In Process

Developing Support

For her informative essay on barriers to the widespread use of hydrogen power, Hannah Steiner identified the following supporting points:

Barrier 1: Technologies for producing hydrogen gas

Barrier 2: Cost of storing hydrogen gas

Barrier 3: Cost of distributing hydrogen gas

For her first draft, she expressed the second point as a general statement and offered evidence from two sources to support it.

Hydrogen fuels also cost far more to store. Storing hydrogen gas can be accomplished in three ways. It can be stored as a compressed gas in large and expensive pressure tanks. It can be stored as a metal hydride through chemical bonding to metals such as titanium, manganese, nickel, and chromium under conditions of extreme cold and high pressure (Crabtree, Dresselhause, and Buchanan 41). It can also — at least theoretically — be stored under conditions of extreme cold and high pressure in carbon nanotubes — extremely tiny crevices only one to two nanometers (1 nanometer is equal to 10^{-9} meters) in diameter (Research Review 12). Unfortunately, each of these storage approaches is either beyond the reach of current technology or far too expensive to allow hydrogen fuels to be economically competitive with fossil fuels.

Hannah's second supporting point

Hannah drew on information from two sources. She used MLA in-text citation style to acknowledge her sources.

Working Together: Brainstorm Supporting Points and Evidence

You can use group brainstorming sessions to help generate supporting points and evidence. You can work in person or online (using chat, instant messaging, or a threaded discussion forum). To carry out the activity, follow these steps:

1. The writer should describe his or her writing project, main point, and ideas for supporting points.

2. Each member of the group should make suggestions about the supporting points the writer mentions.

3. Each member of the group should suggest additional supporting points.

4. Each member of the group should make suggestions about potential sources of evidence to support each point.

If you are working face-to-face, ask one member of the group to take notes on the discussion. If you are using a chat or instant-messaging program, be sure to record a transcript of the session. The goal of the session is to generate as many potential supporting points as possible. Take care not to rule out any ideas, no matter how trivial or ridiculous they might seem at first. When the exchange is completed, turn to the next writer and repeat the process.

@ Download or print this Working Together activity at **bedfordstmartins.com/conversation.**

CONSIDER GENRE AND DESIGN

As is the case with other academic essays, the basic design of your informative essay will reflect the formatting requirements of your assignment and the expectations of your readers, particularly your instructor. Typically, those requirements specify the use of wide (one-inch) margins, double-spaced lines, page numbers, and a readable font. These design features make it easier for instructors and classmates to read and comment on the essay.

Other design elements can help you clarify information for your readers and add visual interest to your essay. As you think about how you will present information to your readers, consider the benefits of using visual evidence to support your points.

- **Illustrations** such as photographs and drawings allow you to clarify abstract concepts and demonstrate processes that might be difficult to follow were they presented in the main text of your essay.

- **Charts, graphs, and tables** let you convert dense numerical information or statistical data into more easily understood visual summaries.

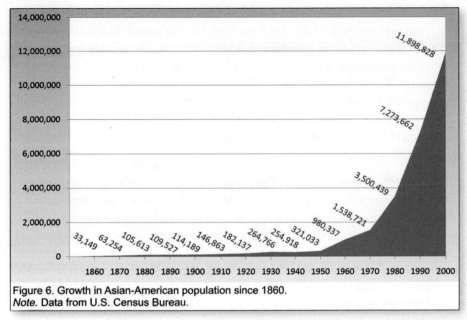

Figure 6. Growth in Asian-American population since 1860.
Note. Data from U.S. Census Bureau.

↑ A Chart Converting Data from a Source into Visual Evidence

You can draw on your sources for visual evidence in two ways. You might borrow an illustration from a print or online source to help readers understand a complex concept or process, such as the steps involved in cellular respiration. Or you might use data from one or more sources to create an original chart, graph, or table to clarify a point, such as the growth of the Asian American population.

As you draft your informative essay, carefully consider the use and placement of illustrations. You must acknowledge the source of any images or numerical information (see Chapter 14). Images, graphs, and tables should appear as close as possible to the point where they are mentioned in the text, and a title or caption should identify or explain the illustration.

You can read more about document design in Chapter 18.

FRAME YOUR INFORMATION
After you've settled on the supporting points you want to make and the evidence you'll use to develop your ideas, spend some time thinking about how you will put everything together for your readers.

Introduction. Your introduction sets the tone for your essay and influences how your readers understand and interpret the information that you give them. Most informative essays present the thesis statement in the introduction so that readers will grasp the writer's main idea from the start. Beyond stating your thesis, you can use a range of strategies to introduce your ideas. Two effective options are providing a historical account and asking a question. Historical accounts, such as the one George Chauncey offers at the beginning of "The Legacy of Antigay Discrimination" (p. 171), can help your readers understand the origins of a subject and how the situation has changed over time. Asking a question, as Chris Nashawaty and Art Streiber do at the beginning of their profile of the Epper family (p. 166), invites your readers to become participants in the conversation.

Organization. The organization of your essay also affects how readers respond to your points. Your organizing strategy should take into account your purposes and your readers' needs and interests, as well as the nature and amount of evidence you've assembled to support your points. To organize your essay, choose an organizational pattern and create an outline or a map. You can use a wide range of organizational patterns in an informative essay, but some are better suited to the genre than others. If you are informing your readers about an event or a series of events, for instance, you might want to use chronological order to structure your essay. If you are providing an overview of competing ideas about an issue, you might choose comparison and contrast. And if you are explaining the defining characteristics of a subject, such as the typical attitudes of college-age voters, description might be a useful pattern to follow.

Conclusion. You've probably read conclusions that simply summarize a document. These summaries can be effective, especially if your essay has presented complex concepts. A conclusion can do more, however, than simply restate your points. If you asked a question in your introduction, for instance, consider answering it in your conclusion. And if you want your readers to continue thinking about your subject after they've finished reading your essay, you might conclude by offering additional insights about what the information you've provided might mean for readers, as featured writer Hannah Steiner does in her finished essay (p. 197).

Chapter 16 provides additional strategies for writing introductions and conclusions, as well as information about organizational patterns, outlines, and maps.

Review and Improve Your Draft

Writing an informative essay involves juggling information, identifying main and supporting points, providing evidence for those points, and framing your ideas to accomplish your purposes. Any one of these activities can pose a significant challenge to a writer. Add them together and you've created a complex task that is sure to require additional work beyond a first draft. As you review your draft, pay particular attention to how well you've focused your discussion of the main point, the clarity of your discussion, your use of information from sources, and the effectiveness of your introduction and conclusion.

FOCUS YOUR DISCUSSION

Maintaining a clear focus is one of the most difficult challenges faced by writers of informative essays. Even when dealing with the most obscure subjects, the amount of information available to writers is still likely to be so large that it can be difficult to decide what to use and what to set aside. As you review your essay, make sure that your draft focuses on a single main point, your thesis statement clearly conveys that point, and every supporting point is relevant and well defined.

ENSURE CLARITY

Readers invest time reading an informative document because they want to learn about a subject. If the document is unclear or difficult to follow, they'll look elsewhere. Review your essay to ensure that you've discussed your subject as clearly as possible. To ensure clarity, make certain that you use information from sources accurately and that you refer to concepts and ideas consistently. Make your prose as economical as possible, and choose the right words for your purpose, readers, and subject. In addition, vary the structure of your sentences and paragraphs without making them overly complex. You can read more about strategies for ensuring a clear discussion in Chapters 19 and 20.

REVIEW YOUR USE OF SOURCES

The effectiveness of your informative essay depends heavily on your selection and use of information from sources. As you revise, ask yourself these questions: Have you chosen the right sources to support your points? Have you used enough sources to make your points effectively? Have you used the right amount of information from your sources? Have you clearly differentiated your own ideas from those of your sources? Have you clearly identified the sources from which you've drawn information? Have you provided appropriate citations in both the text and the works cited list? Have you paraphrased accurately and fairly? Have you quoted properly?

You can learn more about using information from sources in Chapter 17. For a fuller discussion of why you should document sources, see Chapter 14. For guidelines on the MLA and APA documentation systems, see Chapters 21 and 22.

ASSESS YOUR INTRODUCTION AND CONCLUSION

Your introduction and conclusion serve not only as the beginning and end of your essay but also as a means of framing your discussion. Your introduction calls your readers' attention to specific aspects of your subject — while turning their attention away from others—and your conclusion reinforces their understanding of the points you've made in the essay. If your introduction, conclusion, supporting points, and evidence are inconsistent with one another, your essay will be ineffective. To avoid inconsistencies, review your introduction and conclusion, keeping in mind your main point, supporting points, and use of information from sources. You can read more about framing your introduction and conclusion in Chapter 16.

Peer Review: Improve Your Informative Essay

One of the biggest challenges writers face is reading a draft of their own work as a reader rather than as the writer. Because you know what you're trying to say, you find it easy to understand your draft. To determine how you should revise your draft, ask a friend or classmate to read your essay and consider how well you've adopted the role of reporter (see p. 156).

Purpose	1. Did you find the essay informative? Did you learn anything new?
	2. What questions does the essay answer? Do I need to address any other questions?
Readers	3. Did you find the essay interesting? Why or why not?
	4. Does the information I've included in my essay address my readers' needs, interests, and backgrounds?
	5. Does the essay seem fair? Did you detect any bias or agenda in the way I presented information?
Sources	6. Does the information make sense? Can I add, clarify, or rearrange anything to help you understand the subject better? Do you think any of the details are unnecessary?
	7. Do my sources strike you as reliable and appropriate? Does any of the information seem questionable?
Context	8. Is my subject sufficiently narrow and focused? Is my thesis statement clear?
	9. Would any of the information be better presented in visual form?
	10. Is the physical appearance of my essay appropriate? Did you find the font easy to read? Did you have enough room to write down comments?

For each of the points listed above, ask your reviewers to provide concrete advice about what you should do to improve your draft. It can help if you ask them to adopt the role of an editor—someone who is working with you to improve your draft. You can read more about these and other collaborative activities in Chapter 4.

@ Download or print this Peer Review activity at **bedfordstmartins.com/conversation**.

Once you've revised your essay, ask yourself how you might polish and edit it so that your readers will find it easy to read—and ask a friend, relative, or classmate to proofread your final draft to make sure that it is free of distracting errors. For a detailed discussion of polishing strategies, see Chapter 19. For a discussion of editing and proofreading strategies, see Chapter 20.

Student Essay

 Hannah Steiner, "Barriers on the Road to a Hydrogen Economy"
The following informative essay was written by featured writer Hannah Steiner. You can follow Hannah's efforts to write her essay by visiting **bedfordstmartins.com/conversation**. You can read excerpts of interviews in which she discusses her work on her essay, read the assignment, and read drafts of her essay.

Steiner 1

Hannah Steiner

Professor Palmquist

COCC150 College Composition

12 February 2007

Barriers on the Road to a Hydrogen Economy

   In the early twentieth century, the products of Henry Ford's assembly lines introduced Americans to the joys of the open road. Large, powerful automobiles quickly became a symbol of wealth and success. With gas prices sky-high, Americans today are being forced to take a good, long look at their choices. The SUVs, trucks, and minivans popular until recently are largely viewed as symbols of excess and environmental irresponsibility, and many consumers now prefer fuel-efficient or hybrid vehicles, like the successful Toyota Prius. In fact, some drivers have become so determined to escape their pricey

> Information about the writer, class, and submission date is formatted according to MLA guidelines.

> Following MLA guidelines, the title is centered.

> The writer frames the subject by contrasting the beginning of the age of the automobile with current concerns about fuel prices and damage to the environment.

Steiner 2

dependence on fossil fuels that they've begun to seek out alternative energy sources. One of the most promising alternatives in development is hydrogen — an abundant fuel that is environmentally safe, is far more versatile than gasoline or diesel, can be used to create electricity and fuel internal combustion engines, and produces no waste. Because of these attributes, some experts have argued that a hydrogen economy — an energy system that uses only a hydrogen-oxygen reaction to create energy and electricity — could solve many fuel-related problems, from global warming to America's dependence on foreign oil (Crabtree, Dresselhause, and Buchanan 39). At first glance, hydrogen appears to be the perfect choice. However, three barriers stand in the way of widespread hydrogen usage: as a fuel, it is expensive to produce, difficult to store, and complicated to distribute.

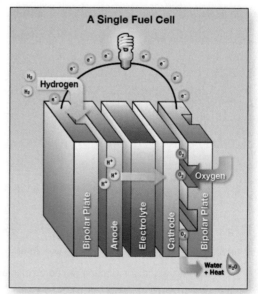

The key to a hydrogen economy is the fuel cell, which uses hydrogen gas and oxygen to produce electricity. In a way, a fuel cell is like a battery, but it never requires charging and it produces only electricity, heat, and water vapor (see Fig. 1). The U.S. Department of Energy (DOE) explains that hydrogen fuel cells use electrode plates to separate hydrogen's protons and electrons, diverting the stream of electrons to create electricity. A "stack" of fuel cells is scalable, so

Fig. 1. Simplified model of a fuel cell. United States Department of Energy, "Hydrogen Fuel Cells."

Margin annotations:

The writer lists the authors of the sources she cites and includes page numbers where the cited information can be found.

The final sentence of the paragraph presents the thesis statement and previews the three supporting points.

A figure reference calls the reader's attention to an illustration.

The figure title describes the figure and identifies its source.

Steiner 3

the same basic structure has many different uses ("Hydrogen Fuel"). In theory, stacks of hydrogen fuel cells could be made to run cars and heat homes of any size, saving energy, money, and the environment.

Refining pure hydrogen gas in the first place, though, is currently too costly and environmentally inefficient to be effective. Although hydrogen is the most abundant element in the universe, it is usually bonded to other elements. For example, two hydrogen atoms and an oxygen atom form water (H_2O), and hydrogen and chloride form hydrochloric acid (HCl). Hydrogen is a fairly faithful substance, and once bonded, it does not like to let go. For hydrogen to be used as an independent fuel, however, those bonds must be broken. The separation process requires a lot of energy — and a lot of money. Strangely, research done by scientists at the DOE found that one of the most cost-effective means of obtaining hydrogen is to separate it from natural gas, which explains why the vast majority of the U.S. hydrogen supply currently comes from reforming the methane in natural gas ("Production"). This approach is not environmentally friendly and does little to reduce our dependence on fossil fuels. Nor is it cost-effective: separating hydrogen from its bonded elements ultimately costs far more to the average consumer than fossil fuels do.

In addition to being expensive to produce, hydrogen fuels are also far more difficult and expensive to store than are fossil fuels. As the DOE points out, while gas tanks in cars and trucks are designed to maximize energy output in minimal space, current hydrogen compressed gas tanks are far larger, heavier, and more expensive, rendering them less than ideal options in light-duty vehicles. Hydrogen can also be stored as a cryogenic liquid at extremely low temperatures. While liquid tanks could store more hydrogen, additional energy is required to liquefy the gas, and tank insulation becomes necessary to prevent hydrogen loss ("Hydrogen Storage"). Thus, liquid hydrogen tanks

First supporting point

Following MLA guidelines, a title is used to distinguish one source from other sources written by the same author used elsewhere in the essay.

A transitional phrase — "In addition to" — connects ideas in the previous paragraph to those in this paragraph.

Second supporting point

Steiner 4

tend to be bulkier and heavier than the typical gas tank. Researchers George Crabtree, Mildred Dresselhause, and Michelle Buchanan suggest that hydrogen could be stored as a metal hydride through chemical bonding to metals such as titanium or manganese under conditions of extreme cold and high pressure — an example of materials-based storage. They note, however, that this process requires assuming control over the bonding properties and kinetics of multiple hydrogen layers (41). Scientists continue to explore the possibilities of materials-based hydrogen storage, but making the technology useful in everyday applications is still a major challenge that must be met before a reliable hydrogen fuel system can be utilized in cars and trucks.

> A page number identifies the location of cited information in the source.

> Third supporting point

Another major challenge is the need to build an infrastructure for distributing hydrogen fuel to consumers. Unlike the oil and gas pipelines already in place, hydrogen has no dedicated delivery system. Current hydrogen pipelines cover only a fraction of the area that natural gas pipelines serve, and hydrogen's small molecule size and its ability to damage pipe metals almost guarantee higher costs and more potential problems (DOE, "Hydrogen Distribution"). Putting liquefied hydrogen in tanker trucks is currently the most cost-effective way to carry the fuel long distances, but the energy required to make hydrogen gas into a liquid offsets a lot of the savings (DOE, "Hydrogen Distribution"). Plus, this method requires fossil fuels to power the trucks that carry the hydrogen. The process of building local hydrogen production plants and creating the equivalent of our current gas stations is likely to be long, tedious, and costly. The United States spent nearly a century wiring the countryside to an electrical grid in order to bring electricity to its citizens. It may take almost that long to make the shift from fossil fuels to hydrogen.

Because each of the production, delivery, and storage approaches currently in use are either beyond the reach of current technology or far too expensive to be practical, America will probably continue to rely on fossil fuels — and, in

Steiner 5

particular, on foreign fossil fuels—for the foreseeable future. In a 2007 interview, Dr. Wade Troxell, a professor of mechanical engineering at Colorado State University, discussed the realities of energy use in a free-market economy. He said that it is neither logical nor practical for a company or individual to pay more for hydrogen fuel if fossil fuels are available at a lower cost. What is most likely to happen in the short term, he theorized, is that America will move toward using a mix of hydrogen and fossil fuels. In the longer term, Troxell may be wrong—we might yet achieve a hydrogen economy. Crabtree, Dresselhause, and Buchanan point to promising developments in the generation of hydrogen gas based on processes used by plants and microbes (40). They also suggest that continuing advances in nanotechnology may decrease the cost of storing and distributing hydrogen gas. By using the reactivity and bonding properties of materials specially structured for the best storage and release of hydrogen, scientists are trying to engineer a more efficient system (41).

It is certain, though, that at some point, the fossil fuels that have sustained our society's electricity and run our motor vehicles for over a century will run out—or become so expensive that they'll no longer provide an economically viable source of energy. Whether that day comes in five years or fifty, we need to shift to a new energy source—one that is practical, economical, and environmentally friendly. Hydrogen has demonstrated great promise as a new candidate for fuel. To realize that promise, however, we must work to remove the barriers that currently prevent hydrogen's emergence as a mainstay of our future economy.

> Information from an interview is presented, and the person interviewed is identified.

> The writer offers an analysis of conflicting claims made by sources used in the essay.

> In the conclusion, the writer speculates on the future, extending the historical perspective adopted in the introduction.

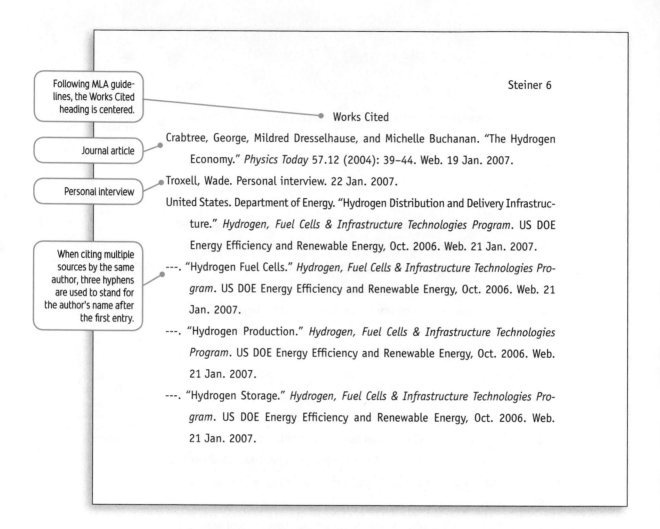

Following MLA guidelines, the Works Cited heading is centered.

Journal article

Personal interview

When citing multiple sources by the same author, three hyphens are used to stand for the author's name after the first entry.

Steiner 6

Works Cited

Crabtree, George, Mildred Dresselhause, and Michelle Buchanan. "The Hydrogen Economy." *Physics Today* 57.12 (2004): 39–44. Web. 19 Jan. 2007.

Troxell, Wade. Personal interview. 22 Jan. 2007.

United States. Department of Energy. "Hydrogen Distribution and Delivery Infrastructure." *Hydrogen, Fuel Cells & Infrastructure Technologies Program*. US DOE Energy Efficiency and Renewable Energy, Oct. 2006. Web. 21 Jan. 2007.

---. "Hydrogen Fuel Cells." *Hydrogen, Fuel Cells & Infrastructure Technologies Program*. US DOE Energy Efficiency and Renewable Energy, Oct. 2006. Web. 21 Jan. 2007.

---. "Hydrogen Production." *Hydrogen, Fuel Cells & Infrastructure Technologies Program*. US DOE Energy Efficiency and Renewable Energy, Oct. 2006. Web. 21 Jan. 2007.

---. "Hydrogen Storage." *Hydrogen, Fuel Cells & Infrastructure Technologies Program*. US DOE Energy Efficiency and Renewable Energy, Oct. 2006. Web. 21 Jan. 2007.

✱ Project Ideas

The following suggestions offer ideas for writing an informative essay or another type of informative document.

Suggestions for Essays

1. DESCRIBE A SITUATION TO YOUR CLASSMATES

Inform your classmates about a situation that is likely to affect them. For example, you might report on changes to your school's course registration system, or you might let them know about a proposed student fee increase. In your essay, describe the situation clearly, drawing on personal observation, an interview with someone who is familiar with the situation, or written sources.

2. EXPLAIN HOW SOMETHING WORKS

Explain how something works to an audience of your choice, such as your classmates, other college students, your instructor, your parents, or members of the community. For example, you might explain how a new technology improves the performance of a digital music player, or how a new diet supplement affects the health of those who use it. In your essay, identify the key features or processes that allow the subject of your essay to accomplish its purpose.

3. CHRONICLE A SEQUENCE OF EVENTS

Write an informative essay that describes a series of events. You might choose a historical event, such as the first Gulf War or the decision to send manned missions to the moon, or a more recent event, such as the decision to fire the coach of a local professional sports team, a major layoff at a national high-technology firm, or a recently passed law that has caused some controversy. In your essay, identify the event you will chronicle and lay out the sequence of events that led up to it.

4. DEFINE A PROBLEM

Write an essay that clearly defines a problem. Address your essay to your instructor, to people affected by the problem, or to those in a position to solve the problem. In your essay, describe the situation that you view as problematic. For example, you might call attention to a potential funding shortfall for your college or university or for a local school system. Or you might identify the lack of natural resources needed for a particular purpose, such as farming, manufacturing, power generation, or transportation. Then describe the potential consequences of the situation, indicate who or what will be affected by those consequences, and describe the severity of the effects.

5. REPORT THE NEWS

Share news of a recent event, discovery, revelation, or disaster with an audience of your choice. You might direct your essay to your instructor, your classmates, other college students, your friends, or people from your hometown. Choose a subject that would interest your readers but that they are unlikely to know about. For example, if you are writing to people from your hometown, you might choose to write about something that has occurred at your college or university. If you are writing to your instructor or classmates, you might choose something that recently occurred in your hometown.

Suggestions for Other Genres

6. CREATE AN INFORMATIVE BROCHURE

Begin working on your brochure by considering your purpose and your readers. Identify the single most important message you want to convey to your readers, and determine how you would like them to react to your message. Then brainstorm the organizational and design strategies you might use to convey that message. Once you've decided on the content, organization, and design of your brochure, create a mockup and ask for feedback from a friend, a classmate, a relative, or an instructor. Keep their feedback in mind as you revise and edit your brochure. (For information on brochure design, see Chapter 18.)

7. DEVELOP AN INFORMATIVE WEB SITE

Begin working on your Web site by considering your purpose and your readers. Once you've identified the information you want to provide, consider how best to present it. Give some thought to the overall structure of your site—that is, the number of and relations among the pages on your site. Then determine which information you will present on each page, and choose the type of navigation tools you'll provide so that your readers can easily move from page to page.

Once you've worked out the overall structure of the site, spend time developing a consistent look and feel for your pages. Your pages should have a similar design (such as a standard color scheme, consistent placement of navigation tools, consistent fonts for headers and body text, and so on). Finally, decide on the type of illustrations and the nature of communication tools, if any, that you'll use on the site. (For tips on designing Web sites, see Chapter 18.)

8. DRAFT AND DESIGN AN INFORMATIVE ARTICLE FOR A PRINT PUBLICATION

First, decide whether you want to write about a particular subject or to publish in a particular magazine, journal, or newspaper. If you want to write about a particular subject, search your library's databases and the Web for pertinent articles. This search can also help you identify publications that might be interested in your article. If you want to publish your article in a particular publication, read it carefully to determine the kinds of subjects it normally addresses. Once you've selected a target publication, analyze it to determine its writing conventions (such as level of formality and the manner in which sources are acknowledged) and design conventions.

As you learn about your subject and plan, organize, and design your article, keep in mind what you've learned about the articles you've read. Your article should reflect those writing and design conventions.

9. WRITE A PROFILE OF A FRIEND OR FAMILY MEMBER

Select a friend or family member and write a profile for a newspaper, magazine, journal, blog, or Web site. Interview the person you plan to profile and, if possible, interview friends or family members who might offer insights about the subject of your profile. Your profile should offer insights into the person's character and contributions to your life. Support your reflections about him or her with personal experience, information from interviews, and your own reasoning.

10. WRITE A PROFILE OF A PUBLIC FIGURE

Select a public figure who interests you on a personal, professional, or academic level and write a profile for a newspaper, magazine, journal, blog, or Web site. If you can, interview the person. If you cannot conduct an interview, locate sources that offer information about the person. Your profile should offer insights into his or her accomplishments, interests, and plans. You should reflect on the person's impact on society and the implications of his or her work for the future. Support your reflections with personal experience, information from a published source or an interview with someone who is aware of or acquainted with the person, and your own reasoning.

In Summary: Writing an Informative Essay

○ **Find a conversation and listen in.**
- Explore your interests (p. 178).
- Use your library (p. 179).
- Ask questions about promising subjects (p. 181).

○ **Gather information.**
- Create a search plan (p. 181).
- Collect sources (p. 184).
- Evaluate your sources (p. 184).
- Take notes (p. 186).
- Conduct an interview (p. 186).

○ **Prepare a draft.**
- Present your main point (p. 189).
- Develop supporting points and evidence (p. 189).
- Consider genre and design (p. 192).
- Frame your information (p. 193).

○ **Review and improve your draft.**
- Focus your discussion (p. 195).
- Ensure clarity (p. 195).
- Review your use of sources (p. 195).
- Assess your introduction and conclusion (p. 195).

07 Writing to Analyze

When I analyze
a topic, I take
on the role of
interpreter.

GENRES IN CONVERSATION

| Reflective Writing | Informative Writing | **Analytical Writing** | Evaluative Writing | Problem-Solving Writing | Argumentative Writing |

The emergence of digital music and file sharing has forced the recording industry to rethink the way it does business. Imagine that you are a consultant hired to help a media company understand recent trends. In the process of researching the current and projected size of the digital music market and the complications of entering it, you find a **Web article,** a **professional report,** and a **scholarly journal article**. Each document focuses on the state of the digital music market but uses a distinct genre to do so.

dt DIGITAL TRENDS BETA

Reviews | News | Videos | Downloads

Home | Guides | Features | First Looks | Podcasts | Forums | Shop

Digital Trends → News → Features → The State of Digital Music in 2006

The State of Digital Music in 2006

March 29th, 2006 | by Chris Nickson

Digital Music Demand is Greater than Ever

With the start of 2006, digital music has started its growth from infancy into adolescence. In the week between Christmas 2005 and New Year's, 20 million tracks were downloaded in America, and another million in Britain. Those are some seriously healthy numbers. Not only do they reflect the huge amount of iPods and other portable devices sold, but also the spread of broadband connections, and the fact that people are now comfortable consuming their music digitally, on a track-by-track rather than album-by-album basis. Long predicted, the listening habits of the general population are beginning to shift.

It's seismic, but it's still small—digital music accounted for only six percent of total music sales in 2005. Yet even that is a massive increase over the year before, a whopping 194 percent, which is fiscally valuable as the sales of CDs continue to decrease (although even with digital sales, the record labels experienced another downturn in 2005). While the young, usually the first to adopt and adapt to new technology, have been downloading and swapping music for quite some time, there's been a ripple effect into the older, warier area of the population, one that will only increase. Thank—or blame—Apple and its iPod, or any of the many other makes selling like hotcakes in the stores.

As a real indicator that digital demand has moved beyond the young, music giant Universal recently announced plans to digitize 100,000 tracks from its vaults over the next four years. That's a big move, but it's more important for its implications. They're not talking about music for teenagers, so they obviously believe there's a burgeoning market among baby boomers, now quite happy and very willing to part with money to download obscure songs from their youth.

But if digital music is now a teenager, it's one with a number of issues, and one of the biggest and trickiest is digital rights management (DRM). In essence, it's a limit on what you can do with the tracks you buy and download. In some cases, you can share the

Web Article ▶

This **Web article** about the future of digital music formats draws on the author's professional experience and provides links to other online articles, Web sites, and discussion forums.

Section 3:
The Explosion of Channels, Formats and Business Models

Five years ago music distribution formats were numbered in single figures – today, they number in the hundreds

In the digital era, record companies are licensing music across a multitude of platforms, in scores of different formats and with hundreds of different partners. New revenue streams are evolving as labels work with social networks, direct-to-consumer sites and brand partnerships

A-la-carte download services

A-la-carte downloads remain the dominant digital business model, with iTunes leading in the online sector. In the US, iTunes surpassed Amazon and Target in 2007 to become the third largest music retailer (NPD MusicWatch).

Other big brand names also came into the download market in 2007, notably Amazon, with its online music download store in partnership with all majors and many independent labels, and the announcement of Nokia's new 'Comes With Music' service.

Subscription services

Subscription services have grown steadily, particularly in the US. Revenues from subscription services, such as Napster and Rhapsody, grew by 63 per cent in the US between the first half of 2005 and the same period of 2007. Napster has a subscriber base of 750,000.

However, these services remain niche in other markets, held back by various factors, including their lack of interoperability with the dominant music player, the iPod, and under-investment in marketing and promotion. If these problems can be addressed, the potential for subscription models is enormous.

New initiatives emerged in the end of 2007. Advocates of these services point to their high level of "stickiness" once consumers first try them. A mass market channel combined with a compelling consumer proposition could potentially change the outlook on the subscriptions market.

> "I like the fact that you pay a set fee for all the music you want with Napster, but I can't use it with my iPod."
>
> **20 year old UK student, IFPI focus group research, July 2007**

Omnifone launched MusicStation, a new mobile subscription service designed to work on a wide variety of mobile handsets worldwide. It is already running in the UK, Hong Kong, Sweden and South Africa and there are plans to roll it out in many more countries in 2008.

MusicStation offers consumers access to a library of over 1.4 million tracks from all majors and many independent labels for a small weekly fee, with no extra data transfer charges. It backs up a users' library so that if a consumer mislays their handset they do not lose their music collection. In the UK, the service comes bundled into a range of existing price plans or is available on a Pay As You Go basis at £1.99 per week.

OMNIFONE™
Global mobile phone applications

At the end of 2007 there emerged a new subscription model based on the concept of 'bundling' music with other services or devices – be it an ISP subscription, a mobile phone or a portable player. While the music comes virtually 'free' to consumers under this model, record companies and artists get paid out of the sale of services or devices. These partnerships also create opportunities for more marketing and promotion of music services in the bundled offer.

Digital Sales by Channel

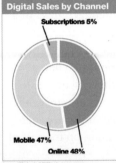

Subscriptions 5%
Mobile 47%
Online 48%

Source: IFPI, first half 2007 industry revenues

> " MusicStation is the first mass-market and download service, with a great choice of re that's the holy trinity of making subscriptio
>
> **Rob Lewis, Chief Executive, Omnifone**

J. Stephen Downie
Graduate School of Library and Information Science
University of Illinois at Urbana-Champaign
501 East Daniel Street
Champaign, Illinois 61820 USA
jdownie@uiuc.edu

The Scientific Evaluation of Music Information Retrieval Systems: Foundations and Future

Music Information Retrieval (MIR) is a multidisciplinary research endeavor that strives to develop innovative content-based searching schemes, novel interfaces, and evolving networked delivery mechanisms in an effort to make the world's vast store of music accessible to all. Some teams are developing "Query-by-Singing" and "Query-by-Humming" systems that allow users to interact with their respective music search engines via queries that are sung or hummed into a microphone (e.g., Birmingham et al. 2001; Haus and Pollastri 2001). "Query-by-Note" systems are also being developed wherein searchers construct queries consisting of pitch and/or rhythm information (e.g., Pickens 2000; Doraisamy and Rüger 2002). Input methods for Query-by-Note systems include symbolic interfaces as well as both physical (MIDI) and virtual (Java-based) keyboards. Some teams are working on "Query-by-Example" systems that take pre-recorded music in the form of CD or MP3 tracks as their query input (e.g., Haitsma and Kalker 2002; Harb and Chen 2003). The development of comprehensive music recommendation and distribution systems is a growing research area (e.g., Logan 2002; Pauws and Eggen 2002). The automatic generation of playlists for use in personal music systems, based on a wide variety of user-defined criteria, is the goal of this branch of MIR research. Other groups are investigating the creation of music analysis systems to assist those in the musicology and music theory communities (e.g., Barthélemy and Bonardi 2001; Kornstädt 2001). Overviews of MIR's interdisciplinary research areas can be found in Downie (2003), Byrd and Crawford (2002), and Futrelle and Downie (2002).

This article begins with an overview of the current scientific problem facing MIR research. Entitled "Current Scientific Problem," the opening section also provides a brief explication of the Text Retrieval Conference (TREC) evaluation paradigm that has come to play an important role in the community's thinking about the testing and evaluation of MIR systems. The sections which follow, entitled "Data Collection Method" and "Emergent Themes and Commentary," report upon the findings of the Music Information Retrieval (MIR)/Music Digital Library (MDL) Evaluation Frameworks Project with issues surrounding the creation of a TREC-like evaluation paradigm for MIR as the central focus. "Building a TREC-Like Test Collection" follows next and highlights the progress being made concerning the establishment of the necessary test collections. The "Summary and Future Research" section concludes this article and highlights some of the key challenges uncovered that require further investigation.

Current Scientific Problem

Notwithstanding the promising technological advancements being made by the various research teams, MIR research has been plagued by one overarching difficulty: there has been no way for research teams to scientifically compare and contrast their various approaches. This is because there has existed no standard collection of music against which each team could test its techniques, no standardized sets of performance tasks, and no standardized evaluation metrics.

The MIR community has long recognized the need for a more rigorous and comprehensive evaluation paradigm. A formal resolution expressing this need was passed on 16 October 2001 by the attendees of the Second International Symposium on Music Information Retrieval (ISMIR 2001). (See music-ir.org/mirbib2/resolution for the list of signatories.)

Over a decade ago, the National Institute of Standards and Technology (NIST) developed a testing and evaluation paradigm for the text-retrieval com-

Computer Music Journal, 28:2, pp. 12–23, Summer 2004
© 2004 Massachusetts Institute of Technology.

What Is Writing to Analyze?

Analytical writing begins with a question: To what extent does government surveillance of suspected terrorists impinge on civil liberties? How will new environmental laws affect a proposed housing development near a state park? Why do animated films from Pixar Studios appeal to so many adults? The types of documents—or genres (see p. 208)—writers create to share their answers are as varied as the questions they ask. And each document, in turn, reflects aspects of the writing situations in which writers find themselves: their purposes for analyzing a subject, the interests and expectations of their intended readers, the sources used to support the analysis, and the context in which the document will be read.

Analysis involves adopting the role of *interpreter*. Writers who adopt this role help readers understand the origins, qualities, significance, or potential impact of a subject. An interpreter might address the causes of a recent economic downturn, for example, while another might explore the cultural implications of a new album by Kanye West. Another writer might present a historical analysis of U.S. involvement in foreign wars, while yet another might try to help college students understand the impact of proposed legislation on the cost of attending college.

In many cases, interpreters are already knowledgeable about their subjects. More often, however, they spend time learning about a subject to ensure that they can offer a well-grounded interpretation. Whether they draw on the subject itself, interview experts, collect information from published sources, or use statistical evidence, effective interpreters provide even knowledgeable readers with enough information about a subject to explain the focus of their analyses and to ensure that their interpretations will make sense in the context in which they're read.

Readers of analytical documents usually share the writer's interest in the subject and want to understand

The Writer's Role: Interpreter

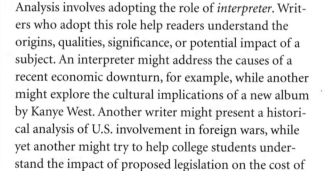

PURPOSE

- To find patterns of meaning
- To trace causes and effects
- To determine significance

READERS

- Want to understand the subject
- Expect a careful and appropriate use of analytical techniques
- Expect coherent, focused reasons and evidence for the writer's interpretation

SOURCES

- Especially in the case of textual analysis, the subject itself is often the main source.
- Data, background information, and other writers' interpretations are often obtained from published material.
- Field research (interviews, observation, surveys, correspondence) and personal experience can add details and support.

CONTEXT

- Analytical questions, interpretive frameworks, and genres are shaped by reader expectations and disciplinary standards and expectations.
- Interpreters usually need to frame a subject for readers before analyzing it.

it in greater depth, either because it affects them in some way or because they are curious about it. They expect a clear introduction to the subject, focused interpretation, thorough explanations of how the writer arrived at his or her conclusions, and reasonable support for those conclusions. Readers also tend to expect that an analytical document will use an interpretive framework that is appropriate to the subject and similar to those typically used by other writers in the field. For example, readers with a literary background would be surprised if an analysis of a major novel was based on the book's sales history, rather than on some form of textual interpretation. Similarly, readers with a background in political science might find an article that focused on the aesthetic qualities of a speech by a presidential candidate less interesting than one that analyzed the political implications of the candidate's arguments.

Interpreters' choices about interpretive framework, sources, and perspective can and do lead to different—sometimes extremely different—conclusions about a subject. As a result, analytical documents not only serve as significant contributions to a conversation but also provide a foundation for further contributions to the conversation.

What Kinds of Documents Are Used to Present an Analysis?

Writers share their interpretations of subjects through a strikingly large array of genres. Soldiers and aid workers in Iraq and Afghanistan, for example, have interpreted the events in which they are involved through books, blogs, and social-networking sites. Commentators analyze the political landscape through columns, editorials, and data analyses. Scholars examine subjects as diverse as Shakespeare's sonnets, the possibility of life on Mars, and the potential for electoral college reform through journal articles and conference presentations. And students are frequently asked to share their interpretations through Web-based articles, news analyses, multimedia presentations, literary criticism, and analytical essays.

Regardless of the genre a writer decides to use, most analytical writing begins with an attempt to understand how other writers have approached the challenges of analyzing a particular subject. Examining analytical documents can spark ideas about how to focus an analysis, offer insights into the kinds of interpretive frameworks that have been used to direct past analyses, and provide an understanding of the conclusions other writers have drawn.

Web-Based Articles

Most major magazines, such as *Newsweek*, *Atlantic Monthly*, and *Runner's World*, offer online versions of their publications, providing electronic copies of print articles along with material written specifically for the Web edition. Many newer magazines, however, publish exclusively on the Web. Some of these online publications, such as *Slate* and *Salon*, appeal to a general audience. Others, such as *Pedal Pushers Online* (pedalpushersonline.com) or *Vegetarian Women Online Magazine* (vegetarianwomen .com), cater to readers with specific interests. In either case, Web-based magazines typically offer a mix of traditional articles and essays, blogs, video entries, news feeds, and reader-response forums.

Analytical Web-based articles often begin with a question, or a problematic fact or puzzling situation that leads to a question. Writers of such articles must be knowledgeable and need to understand the history and significance of their subjects. Depending on the specific publication and writing situation, they might rely on statistical evidence, personal experience, or direct observation. In many cases, they must clearly explain unfamiliar background material to more general readers or interpret complex data.

Articles in online magazines can draw on a range of sources, ranging from interviews, surveys, published studies, and scholarly works to popular culture and personal observation. Writers of online articles often embed links to their sources within the text of their documents instead of listing them at the end, allowing readers to jump directly to cited works as they read. Commenting functions encourage readers to respond to writers in a public forum, creating an ongoing written conversation that anybody can join. In these and other ways, analytical discussions usually move forward more quickly and more unpredictably online than they do in print journals.

View a multimedia example of analytical writing in the e-book at **bedfordstmartins.com/ conversation**.

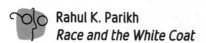

Rahul K. Parikh
Race and the White Coat

This Web-based article first appeared in *Salon*, a widely read online magazine sponsored by Salon Media Group. As you read it, notice how the author provides instant access to the scientific studies he used to develop his analysis of doctors' subconscious racial biases and their effects on medical care for minority patients. Rahul K. Parikh is a pediatrician and a regular contributor to *Salon*. A frequent host of the National Public Radio program *Perspectives*, he has also published articles in the *San Francisco Chronicle* and the *New York Times*.

salon.com

print   share   discuss   RSS

Race and the White Coat

Racial bias in doctors and health care workers is doing great harm. Is enough being done to stop it?

By Rahul K. Parikh, M.D.

Apr. 22, 2008 | Here's something the medical community has known for a long time: Minorities in this country, particularly African Americans, are not as healthy as whites. They suffer from high rates of cardiovascular disease, diabetes, HIV, cancer, asthma, and other chronic illnesses.

There are many reasons for the disparities. Blacks have less access to health care. Many lack health insurance altogether. A study in the New England Journal of Medicine showed that black communities have fewer primary care doctors, and that those doctors reported a harder time getting their patients quality services due to insurance restrictions.

When minorities get sick, they're likely to show up in an emergency room because they don't have anywhere else to go. When they get there, they're usually sicker because of the delay in seeking care. As the New England Journal study showed, minorities are more likely to get a doctor who isn't board certified and is of lower quality.

In 2002, the Institute of Medicine issued a sobering report about health disparities in America. In that report, the IOM challenged assumptions by asking one very hard question: Do doctors treat minority patients differently? Its answer, after reviewing more than 100 studies, was yes, "evidence suggests that bias, prejudice, and stereotyping on the part of health care providers may contribute to differences in care."

Most of these studies adjusted for differences in incomes, age, insurance status, and disease severity. In other words, the only factor that contributed to the disparity in treatment was the color of a patient's skin. Studies show that African Americans in general harbor suspicion toward the medical community, a feeling that may lead some blacks to decline or refuse recommended treatments. But the IOM determined that this couldn't account for the severity of black-white disparities.

Over the past decade, there's been a growing body of evidence to support the IOM's conclusion. A 2000 study demonstrated that doctors rated black patients as less intelligent, less educated, more likely to abuse drugs and alcohol, more likely to fail to comply with medical advice, more likely to lack social support, and less likely to participate in cardiac rehabilitation than whites, even after income, education, and personality characteristics were taken into account.

Researchers have also found that African Americans with chronic renal failure are less likely than whites to be offered information and a referral for a kidney transplant. They've learned that blacks are regularly undertreated for pain from fractures and cancer and are less likely to be prescribed appropriate medications for certain psychiatric problems.

Doctors are sworn by their oath and bound by law to treat patients equally. Most of us got into this business because we wanted to do right by people. Race, class, and gender aren't supposed to influence us. But it would seem something is amiss when we treat black patients.

To figure out why, a group of Harvard Medical School researchers turned the spotlight on doctors. The researchers took a group of 287 doctors and administered a computerized test. Called the Implicit Association Test (IAT), it has been around for a decade and has been used over 5 million times as a tool to measure implicit biases, as opposed to outright prejudice. In this case, the test subjects were shown pictures of black or white patients. They were asked about the person's attitude ("good" vs. "bad"), as well as their impressions of the person's general cooperativeness and medical cooperativeness.

Along with the photos, they were given a scenario in which the patient exhibited symptoms and a test result suggesting they were having a heart attack. Doctors were asked whether they thought the patient was having a heart attack and whether they would treat him with a thrombolytic drug, a medicine meant to break up a blood clot in the coronary arteries, which is a standard treatment for heart attack victims. Finally, physicians were asked questions that measured whether they harbored any explicit biases toward blacks.

It turns out the doctors didn't harbor any overt bias or prejudice. But the results of the IAT and the outcome of the heart attack scenario told us something quite different: More doctors subconsciously attributed negative traits to blacks (thinking them "uncooperative" or "bad") than whites. Worse was the way these biases translated into clinical decisions. While doctors diagnosed more blacks with a heart attack, they ended up prescribing treatment for blacks and whites in essentially equal numbers, meaning that black patients having heart attacks were going untreated. Further, as the degree of bias toward blacks increased, so did their likelihood of not getting treated.

This study, published last summer in the Journal of General Internal Medicine, was the first hard evidence that doctors' clinical decision making is influenced by race, and that those decisions stand to do harm.

Does this mean that doctors are racist? No. In fact, the discrepancy between explicit and implicit biases in the Harvard study suggests the opposite. But it's clear deeper biases exist, and for several reasons.

First, and most important, doctors are people. There's plenty of evidence that well-intentioned people, whatever their background, possess and demonstrate unconscious negative racial attitudes and stereotypes. Doctors are no different. We share many common conceptions about race in America. We bring those influences, right or wrong, with us to the office.

The second reason lies in the roots of the medical thought process. Every day, doctors and other health professionals make a lot of serious and complex decisions, usually without all the information we need to be certain about them. Many of these decisions are made under intense time pressure. To cope, we rely on intellectual and emotional shortcuts—ones that help to clarify things. We learn to think in terms of stereotypes; for example, in pediatrics, a child with a fever and an earache is likely to have an ear infection. It's likely that an adult with chest pain radiating to the left arm is having heart attack. In our library of shortcuts, we include "data" on stereotypical patients as well—an overweight person is at risk for high cholesterol and diabetes; Asians are at higher risk for stomach cancer; African Americans are at higher risk for asthma. We know these things to be true based on studies of disease patterns.

The paradox here is that: race, age, gender. Are we putting those factors too far in front of other factors in how we treat or don't treat our patients? Have culture and how we think led us to apply stereotypes detrimentally? This would seem to be the case.

The environment in which a doctor trains may also lead to biases. Many teaching hospitals are in tough urban areas where patients may be poorer, less educated minorities. Here's how that might play out in a resident's experience. Every day, he may see patient after patient who can't or won't take his advice on how to take care of asthma. Reasons for that may include anything from a lack of money, a lack of understanding, or suspicion about medicine. Seeing those patients get sicker and sicker, and show up again and again in the emergency room, is bound to be frustrating. So after the 100th patient, he may conclude "these types of people just won't take my advice." He's then a lot less likely to bother or care about offering that advice to the 101st patient.

All of this is another example of why race in America is so hard for this country to face. Whether we're talking about your doctor, your congressperson, or your neighbor, racial bias is hard to beat because so many times it's hard to even feel. In medicine, these biases clearly exist, they are clearly doing harm, and they need to stop.

It's certainly a good thing that we in the medical profession have checked ourselves on this issue. Training in cross-cultural competence is under way, although many emphasize that the training needs to be conducted carefully to help physicians understand and respect diversity rather than simply reinforce cultural stereotypes. Diversifying the workforce—not just doctors, but in all of health care—is something that many see as a long-term solution. A study funded by the W.H. Kellogg Foundation, chaired by former Health and Human Services Secretary Louis Sullivan, concluded that while blacks, Hispanics, and American Indians make up more than 25 percent of the U.S. population, they constitute only 9 percent of the nation's nurses, 6 percent of the doctors, and 5 percent of the dentists. Medical schools continue to recruit minority students; although, according to the report, progress has been slow for African Americans over the past decade.

In its 2002 report, the Institute of Medicine pointed to regulatory and policy changes that enforce the use of clinical practice guidelines to ensure doctors treat all patients in a standardized manner. In fact, there has been a proliferation of standardized guidelines in all fields of medicine. For example, those of us who are pediatricians have a clear idea, based on the best available evidence, as to how to treat a child with either chronic or acute asthma, regardless of anything—like a child's age or the severity of disease—other than clinical data.

At the same time, despite plenty of research in the past decade about health disparities, there's been precious little political or policy headway in making sure that doctors and health care workers address them. Maybe that's because we in the profession are trying hard to solve these issues on our own. Or maybe it's because nobody's watching.

Regardless, the first step to change has been in recognizing that racial biases exist and are affecting the quality of health care. As the Harvard study showed, health care workers, before completing the test on racial bias, were asked whether or not they agreed with the following statement: "Subconscious biases about patients based on their race may affect the way I make decisions about their care without my realizing it." Before the test, 60 percent of doctors said they agreed. Afterward, 72 percent agreed, and 75 percent said that taking the test would improve their care. Too bad the results weren't 100 percent. But it's a start.

Starting a Conversation: Respond to "Race and the White Coat"

In your writer's notebook, record your reactions to Parikh's analysis by responding to the following questions:

1. The first half of Parikh's analysis is devoted to establishing the existence of a troubling trend. What, exactly, is the trend that concerns him? What evidence does he offer to prove that it's a problem?

2. Parikh makes reference to both "implicit" and "explicit" bias (pars. 9–11). What is the difference between the two? Why does the distinction matter?

3. Parikh is a practicing physician; he is also of Indian descent. In what ways does he draw on his professional and personal background to establish his credibility to write on the subject of medical bias?

4. Toward the middle of his analysis, Parikh suggests that stereotypes are a necessary, and often positive, element of medical diagnosis (par. 15). What does he mean? Why must doctors rely on "shortcuts," and what effect does this have on their treatment of minority patients?

5. In paragraph 18, Parikh writes, "All of this is another example of why race in America is so hard for this country to face. Whether we're talking about your doctor, your congressperson, or your neighbor, racial bias is hard to beat because so many times it's hard to even feel." Why should it matter that many people don't recognize their own biases? What implications does this observation suggest for racial issues beyond medical care?

@ Download or print this Starting a Conversation activity at **bedfordstmartins.com/ conversation**.

News Analyses

A news analysis offers an interpretation of a recent event, such as a natural disaster, a change in government policy, or a business merger. For example, questions about the rapid rise in the price of fuel in recent years have been the subject of numerous news analyses. Other news analyses have focused on topics such as campaign finance reform, government efforts to deter terrorism, and proposed changes in immigration law.

News analyses are written for readers who seek a fuller understanding of the origins or implications of an event. Style and design tend to reflect the standards of the publication in which the news analysis appears—usually, but not always, a newspaper, a magazine, or a Web site. Most writers adopt a balanced tone, even when their analysis strongly reflects a particular set of values or beliefs, and they often include illustrations, such as photographs and charts, to persuade readers that their interpretations are reasonable and well founded. Writers of news analyses usually acknowledge their sources of information, although they don't necessarily use a formal citation system.

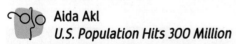

Aida Akl
U.S. Population Hits 300 Million

The following news analysis, written by Aida Akl and published by the Voice of America (VOA) on its Web site, calls attention to a milestone in U.S. population growth and explores the implications of specific growth trends. Like writers of other news analyses, Akl presents enough information to provide a basis for analysis. Her focus, however, is on the question of how current growth trends will shape the United States. Aida Akl is a broadcaster and journalist who has worked for the Voice of America in the Middle East and in Washington, D.C., for more than two decades. She is currently a correspondent for the daily VOA news analysis program *Focus*.

U.S. Population Hits 300 Million

By Aida Akl
Washington, D.C.
22 August 2006

America's population is projected to hit 300 million in October, making it the world's largest after China and India. But some analysts say America's population growth, largely fueled by immigration, could change the face of the nation.

The population gain reported by the U.S. Census Bureau—up 20 million in the past six years—is the result of both natural growth and an influx of immigrants. An annual birth rate of about 1 percent accounts for 60 percent of the population increase, while the remaining 40 percent is due to immigration.

Demographer William Frey of the Brookings Institution here in Washington says the population increase is a milestone for America.

"Not only is it the large number that establishes us as one of the most populous countries in the world, but it [i.e., the population increase] also means that people who are coming here to help make this 300 million situation are people from other parts of the world—from Latin America, from Asia. We would not have reached this goal as fast as we have were it not for all of these immigrants coming to the United States," says Frey.

About two-thirds of the nation's population is white, down from 70 percent at the start of the decade. Demographer Frey and many other experts say the percentage of non-Hispanic whites will fall further as more immigrants arrive and America's post–World War II Baby Boom generation continues to age.

A Major Demographic Shift

The average birth rate for the non-Hispanic white population is around two births per woman, compared to nearly three per woman among Hispanic whites. These trends, says demographer Mark Mather of the Washington-based Population Reference Bureau, will lead to major demographic shifts.

"I don't know of any other countries that have experienced changes in their racial ethnic composition to the extent that we are. So lots of demographers think that by 2050, racial and ethnic categories won't even be that meaningful anymore because we're going to be such a melting pot society that these categories may not even appear on the census form anymore," says Mather.

Many analysts are skeptical about the benefits of current population trends. They question whether the U.S. economy can produce enough jobs and argue that unchecked immigration will cause urban sprawl and strain natural resources. Others say far too many immigrants are entering the U.S. to be assimilated into mainstream society.

Demographer William Johnson of the Population Institute, an international educational group in Washington, says immigration strengthens America—if kept within manageable limits.

"America has evolved throughout its history, and migration has been a good thing

because of assimilation. We all come together to redefine ourselves every generation, and that's been the strength of our country. However," says Johnson, "if you don't have assimilation, if you have a cultural separation, if people who are migrants still first ally themselves and identify themselves with their countries of origin, then the value of that decreases. To what extent it would be a good thing or a divisive thing in the future is difficult to predict."

Ethnic Minorities and the Cultural Gap

Recent projections released by the Census Bureau show that ethnic minorities now account for one-third of America's population and will make up 40 percent of the U.S. population in the next decade. Non-Hispanic whites are now a minority in Hawaii, New Mexico, Texas, California, and the District of Columbia.

Demographer Joseph D'Agostino of the Population Research Institute in Virginia says concerns over the nation's changing demographic and cultural makeup are legitimate.

"A lot of people feel that immigrants are coming in too fast, or maybe they are not being assimilated fast enough. So many Americans have experienced large areas of cities where people cannot speak English," says D'Agostino. "And if we can't all communicate together with one language as Americans, it's very difficult to see how we are going to have a cohesive society in the long term. That's a major problem that can result in the 'Balkanization' of the United States over the long term."

Based on current trends, D'Agostino says one of two scenarios is possible. "If by the year 2050 you have one-third of the population with Spanish as their first language, if you have people who have not assimilated the American ideals of rule of law and democracy, etc., America could face some really huge prob-

lems," says D'Agostino. "If on the other hand we restrict immigration severely but the birth rate doesn't go up, then we'll have an even worse problem with [an] aging population and not enough workers. So we've got to figure out what the right balance is. One great step forward would be to eliminate multi-culturalism and then again put a great emphasis on the assimilation of immigrants."

But many analysts say such concerns are unjustified. They argue that America has successfully assimilated immigrants in the past and can do so again.

Planning for the Future

A key element to success, says demographer William Frey of the Brookings Institution, is careful planning to ensure immigrants get the services they need and to prevent them from becoming a permanent underclass.

"One of the things we do have to worry about is maybe the social inequality that may occur. We want to make sure that when we do bring people into the United States, they have a fair chance to get a job and live a nice lifestyle here. We need to then make sure they get a good education. It's a big challenge for us," says Frey.

Today, the United States receives largely two types of immigrants: the well educated who typically end up in high-tech jobs, and those with minimal education, who largely work in low-wage, manual labor or service industries.

Demographic projections put the U.S. population at 400 million people by 2050. If current population trends continue, most analysts agree that America will be an ethnically different nation.

This story was first broadcast on the English news program VOA News Now.

Starting a Conversation: Respond to "U.S. Population Hits 300 Million"

In your writer's notebook, respond to Akl's news analysis by answering the following questions:

1. What is the main point of Akl's news analysis? How would you summarize it in a sentence or two? What specific interpretive question(s) does Akl attempt to answer?

2. Throughout her article, Akl summarizes reports from the U.S. Census Bureau and presents the results of interviews with experts. Find specific instances where she cites authorities and published documents to support assertions, generalities, or predictions. What makes these sources reliable? What do they contribute to the effectiveness of Akl's analysis?

3. The authorities Akl cites disagree with one another. Identify and briefly summarize at least two conflicting opinions about the long-term implications of current population trends. What does Akl accomplish by presenting these competing points of view? Does she seem to favor one position over the others, or is she trying to be impartial? Why do you think so?

4. How do the subheadings (in bold type) contribute to your understanding of the article? How might a writer use subheadings to direct a reader's attention?

@ Download or print this Starting a Conversation activity at **bedfordstmartins.com/ conversation**.

Multimedia Presentations

Multimedia presentations, sometimes referred to as PowerPoint presentations because they are frequently created using Microsoft PowerPoint, consist of a series of slides that typically contain text and illustrations. Most multimedia presentations are designed to accompany and enhance the words of a speaker. The slides provide a foundation on which the presenter builds with additional spoken comments or notes. Some slides might contain highly detailed information in the form of lists, tables, charts, graphs, images, animation, video, or audio.

Many presentations have two audiences: a primary audience who attends the presentation and a secondary audience who might read the presentation slides and notes online or in print. In general, creators of multimedia presentations consider the expectations of the sponsoring organization and the characteristics of the target audience (primary and secondary) as they draft and polish their analyses. When multimedia presentations are distributed as stand-alone documents, as is the case when they are presented on a Web site or distributed via CD or DVD, summaries of the speaker's words are sometimes provided through notes attached to each slide. In a growing number of cases, video recordings of presentations can be viewed in a Web browser as well.

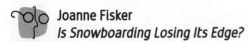

Joanne Fisker
Is Snowboarding Losing Its Edge?

How have attitudes toward snowboarders changed since the sport was first introduced? In this multimedia presentation, Joanne Fisker attempts to answer this question as she offers an analysis of the causes underlying a shift in public perception. Once seen as reckless and impolite, snowboarders are now viewed as similar to skiers in their values and behavior. The slides that follow are only part of the overall presentation. Although they provide important information, they serve primarily as a backdrop for the more detailed analysis presented during the speaker's spoken observations about the subject.

Is Snowboarding Losing Its Edge?

An Analysis of Changing Public
Perceptions of the Sport

Joanne Fisker

National Snowriding Association

A Brief History of Boarding

1965 Originates with the Snurfer, a snow toy for children

1980 Commercial boards in production. Burton boards use P-Tex base, like skis.

1985 39 of 600 ski areas allow boarding.

1998 Snowboarding competition at the Olympics. Giant slalom gold medalist tests positive for marijuana.

2006 Only 4 ski areas in the U.S. ban boarding.

Early Comments on Boarding

- "young and reckless"
- "&*/$! Kids!
- "It ruins the moguls."

Recent Comments on Boarding

"Snowboarding saved skiing. Skiing was dead. The snowboard made skiers think about things. Skiers were going to have to do something."

-- Norm Sayler, owner
Donner Ski Ranch

quoted in Evans, par. 10

Why the Change?

	2004	1997	1990
Participation (millions)	6.3	2.8	1.5
Average Age	22.6	17.1	16.2
Average Days Per Year	8.8	7.5	6.6

Source: National Ski & Snowboard Retailers Association

Conclusions

Perceptions of snowboarders as reckless and boorish have changed because:

- Boarders are older – and perhaps more polite.
- Boarders ride frequently. Because ski areas recognize them as a significant source of revenue, they are making strong efforts to welcome them.
- Many skiers also snowboard.
- Boarding is no longer seen as unusual and threatening.

Works Cited

Evans, Jeremy. "Does the feud between skiers and snowboarders still exist?" *Tahoe.com*. Tahoe.com, November 27, 2006. Web. January 9, 2007.

National Ski & Snowboard Retailers Association. "Snowboarding Participation". National Ski & Snowboard Retailers Association, n.d. Web. January 9, 2007.

Voje, Julian. *The History of Snowboarding*. Julian Voje, May 22, 2005. Web. January 5, 2007.

Links:

http://www.tahoe.com/article/20061127/SKITAHOE/61127006

http://www.nsaa.org/nsaa/press/0506/nsga-snbd-part-2004.pdf

http://www.sbhistory.de/

Starting a Conversation: Respond to "Is Snowboarding Losing Its Edge?"

In your writer's notebook, reflect on the ways in which this presentation supports Fisker's analysis by responding to the following questions:

1. Fisker's presentation refers to perceptions and misperceptions about snowboarders. Who is her intended audience, and how can you tell? How might the people attending the presentation in person interpret it differently than those who view the slides on the Web?

2. What sources does Fisker choose, and how do they support her claims? If you were to investigate this subject further, where would you look for more information?

3. In what ways does the PowerPoint format affect how the writer presents her ideas and evidence? Notice, for instance, Fisker's choice of photographs and her use of bulleted points and tables instead of paragraphs of text. How do these choices help get her main idea across?

4. Fisker's presentation serves as the foundation for a more thorough analysis, which is not included here. Choose one slide, and in a paragraph or two, try to reconstruct what her spoken comments might have been.

@ Download or print this Starting a Conversation activity at **bedfordstmartins.com/ conversation**.

Literary Criticism

Literary criticism is the analysis of literature, broadly defined as works of fiction, poetry, drama, and creative nonfiction. Literary critics typically ask questions about the origins, goals, effects, influences, methods, meaning, or importance of a literary work. Scholarly writers usually base their interpretations on critical theories such as feminism, cultural materialism, and deconstruction, although they might also use specialized interpretive frameworks such as discourse analysis, semiotic analysis, or Freudian analysis. Regardless of their interpretive framework, however, most literary critics examine a work closely, looking for themes, patterns, meaning, and implications while considering the author's techniques.

Literary criticism is most often shared in the form of an essay or article, but it can also take the form of a book, a blog, or a book review. Readers range widely in their knowledge of a subject. Readers of scholarly books, essays, and articles are frequently literary scholars who are experts in a particular literary period or form. Readers of literary criticism appearing in blogs or in publications such as the *New York Review of Books* range from those who have little or no knowledge of the subject to those who might easily have conducted the analysis themselves. Expert and novice readers alike expect writers to focus their analyses on literary issues, to make careful claims about their subject, and to support their analyses with evidence from the subject itself or from the work of others who have written about it.

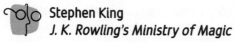

Stephen King
J. K. Rowling's Ministry of Magic

In this example of literary criticism for a popular audience, novelist Stephen King analyzes the literary merit of J. K. Rowling's wildly successful Harry Potter series. While he carefully interprets and evaluates the novels on their own merit, King also contemplates "what Ms. Rowling has wrought." In doing so, he provides insight into broader cultural questions, even as his analysis remains grounded in particular aspects of — and specific passages from — Rowling's novels. Stephen King is an American author best known for his horror fiction stories and novels, which have sold hundreds of millions of copies; he also writes a regular column for *Entertainment Weekly* magazine, where this selection first appeared. In 2003, King won the National Book Foundation's Medal for Distinguished Contribution to American Letters.

J. K. Rowling's Ministry of Magic

by Stephen King

And so now the hurly-burly's done, the battle's lost and won—the Battle of Hogwarts, that is—and all the secrets are out of the Sorting Hat. Those who bet Harry Potter would die lost their money; the boy who lived turned out to be exactly that. And if you think that's a spoiler at this late date, you were never much of a Potter fan to begin with. The outrage over the early reviews (Mary Carole McCauley of *The Baltimore Sun*, Michiko Kakutani of *The New York Times*) has faded . . . although the sour taste lingers for many fans.

It lingers for me, too, although it doesn't have anything to do with the ultimately silly concept of "spoilers," or the ethics of jumping the book's pub date. The prepublication vow of omertà was, after all, always a thing concocted by publishers Bloomsbury and Scholastic, and not — so far as I know — a part of either the British Magna Carta or the U.S. Constitution. Nor does Jo Rowling's impassioned protest ("I am staggered that some American newspapers have decided to publish . . . reviews in complete disregard of the wishes of literally millions of readers, particularly children . . .") cut much ice with me. These books ceased to be specifically

for children halfway through the series; by *Goblet of Fire*, Rowling was writing for everyone, and knew it.

The clearest sign of how adult the books had become by the conclusion arrives—and splendidly—in *Deathly Hallows*, when Mrs. Weasley sees the odious Bellatrix Lestrange trying to finish off Ginny with a Killing Curse. "NOT MY DAUGHTER, YOU BITCH!" she cries. It's the most shocking *bitch* in recent fiction; since there's virtually no cursing (of the linguistic kind, anyway) in the Potter books, this one hits home with almost fatal force. It is totally correct in its context — perfect, really — but it is also a quintessentially adult response to a child's peril.

The problem with the advance reviews — and those that followed in the first post-publication days — is one that has dogged Rowling's magnum opus ever since book 4 (*Goblet of Fire*), after the series had become a worldwide phenomenon. Due to the Kremlin-like secrecy surrounding the books, all reviews since 2000 or so have been strictly shoot-from-the-lip. The reviewers themselves were often great — Ms. Kakutani ain't exactly chopped liver — but the very popularity of the books has often undone even the best intentions of the best critical writers. In their hurry to churn out column inches, and thus remain members of good standing in the Church of What's Happening Now, very few of the Potter reviewers have said anything worth remembering. Most of this microwaved critical mush sees Harry — not to mention his friends and his adventures — in only two ways: sociologically ("Harry Potter: Boon or Childhood Disease?") or economically ("Harry Potter and the Chamber of Discount Pricing"). They take a perfunctory wave at things like plot and language, but do little more . . . and really, how can they? When you have only four days to read a 750-page book, then write an 1,100-word review on it, how much time do you have to really enjoy the book? To think about the book? Jo Rowling set out a sumptuous seven-course meal, carefully prepared, beautifully cooked, and lovingly served out. The kids and adults who fell in love with the series (I among them) savored every mouthful, from the appetizer (*Sorcerer's Stone*) to the dessert (the gorgeous epilogue of *Deathly Hallows*). Most reviewers, on the other hand, bolted everything down, then obligingly puked it back up half-digested on the book pages of their respective newspapers.

And because of that, very few mainstream writers, from *Salon* to *The New York Times*, have really stopped to consider what Ms. Rowling has wrought, where it came from, or what it may mean for the future. The blogs, by and large, haven't been much better. They seem to care about who lives, who dies, and who's tattling. Beyond that, it's all pretty much duh.

So what did happen? Where did this Ministry of Magic come from?

Well, there were straws in the wind. While the academics and bighead education critics were moaning that reading was dead and kids cared about nothing but their Xboxes, iPods, Avril Lavigne, and *High School Musical*, the kids they were worried about were quietly turning on to the novels of one Robert Lawrence Stine. Known in college as "Jovial Bob" Stine, this fellow gained another nickname later in life, as — ahem — "the *Stephen King* of children's literature." He wrote his first teen horror novel (*Blind Date*) in 1986, years before the advent of Pottermania . . . but soon you couldn't glance at a *USA Today* best-seller list without seeing three or four of his paperbacks bobbing around in the top 50.

These books drew almost no critical attention — to the best of my knowledge, Michiko Kakutani never reviewed *Who Killed the Homecoming Queen?* — but the kids gave them plenty of attention, and R. L. Stine rode a wave of kid popularity, partly fueled by the fledgling Internet, to become perhaps the best-selling children's author of the 20th century. Like Rowling, he was a Scholastic author, and I have no doubt that Stine's success was one of the reasons Scholastic took a chance on a young and unknown British writer in the first place. He's largely unknown and uncredited . . . but of course John the Baptist never got the same press as Jesus either.

Rowling has been far more successful, critically as well as financially, because the Potter books grew as they went along. That, I think, is their great secret (and not so secret at that; to understand the point visually, buy a ticket to *Order of the Phoenix* and check out former cutie Ron Weasley towering over Harry and Hermione). R. L. Stine's kids are kids forever, and the kids who enjoyed their adventures grew out of them, as inevitably as they outgrew their childhood Nikes. Jo Rowling's kids grew up . . . and the audience grew up with them.

This wouldn't have mattered so much if she'd been a lousy writer, but she wasn't — she was and is an incredibly gifted novelist. While some of the blogs and the mainstream media have mentioned that Rowling's ambition kept pace with the skyrocketing popularity of her books, they have largely overlooked the fact that her talent also grew. Talent is never static, it's always growing or dying, and the short form on Rowling is this: She was far better than R. L. Stine (an adequate but flavorless writer) when she started, but by the time she penned the final line of *Deathly Hallows* ("All was well."), she had become one of the finer stylists in her native country — not as good as Ian McEwan or Ruth Rendell (at least not yet), but easily the peer of Beryl Bainbridge or Martin Amis.

And, of course, there was the magic. It's what kids want more than anything; it's what they crave. That goes back to the Brothers Grimm, Hans Christian Andersen, and good old Alice, chasing after that wascally wabbit. Kids are always looking for the Ministry of Magic, and they usually find it.

It was children whom Ms. Rowling captivated first, demonstrating with the irrefutable logic of something like 10 bazillion books sold that kids are still perfectly willing to put aside their iPods and Game Boys and pick up a book . . . if the magic is there. That reading itself is magical is a thing I never doubted. I'd give a lot to know how many teenagers (and preteens) texted this message in the days following the last book's release: DON'T CALL ME TODAY I'M READING.

The same thing probably happened with R. L. Stine's Goosebumps books, but unlike Stine, Rowling brought adults into the reading circle, making it much larger. This is hardly a unique phenomenon, although it seems to be one associated mainly with British authors (there was *Huckleberry Finn*, of course, a sequel to its YA little brother *Tom Sawyer*). *Alice in Wonderland* began as a story told to 10-year-old Alice Liddell by Charles Dodgson (a.k.a. Lewis Carroll); it is now taught in college lit courses. And *Watership Down*, Richard Adams's version of *The Odyssey* (featuring rabbits instead of humans), began as a story told to amuse the author's preteen daughters, Juliet and Rosamond, on a long car drive. As a book, though, it was marketed as an "adult fantasy" and became an international best-seller.

Maybe it's the British prose. It's hard to resist the hypnotism of those calm and sensible voices, especially when they turn to make-believe. Rowling was always part of that straightforward storytelling tradition (*Peter Pan*, originally a play by the Scot J. M. Barrie, is another case in point). She never loses sight of her main theme—the power of love to turn bewildered, often frightened, children into decent and responsible adults—but her writing is all about story. She's lucid rather than luminous, but that's okay; when she does express strong feelings, she remains their mistress without denying their truth or power. The sweetest example in *Deathly Hallows* comes early, with Harry remembering his childhood years in the Dursley house. "It gave him an odd, empty feeling to remember those times," Rowling writes. "[I]t was like remembering a younger brother whom he had lost." Honest; nostalgic; not sloppy. It's a small example of the style that enabled Jo Rowling to bridge the generation gap without breaking a sweat or losing the cheerful dignity that is one of the series' great charms.

Her characters are lively and well-drawn, her pace is impeccable, and although there are occasional continuity drops, the story as a whole hangs together almost perfectly over its 4,000-plus page length.

And she's in full possession of that famously dry British wit, as when Ron, trying to tune in an outlaw news broadcast on his wizard radio, catches a snatch of a pop song called "A Cauldron Full of Hot Strong Love." Must have been some witchy version of Donna Summer doing that one. There's also her wry send-up of the British tabloids—about which I'm sure she knows plenty—in the person of

> Mostly Rowling is just having fun, knocking herself out, and when a good writer is having fun, the audience is almost always having fun too.

Rita Skeeter, perhaps the best name to be hung on a fictional character since those of Jonathan Swift. When Elphias Doge, the perfect magical English gentleman, calls Rita "an interfering trout," I felt like standing up and giving a cheer. Take that, Page Six! There's a lot of meat on the bones of these books—good writing, honest feeling, a sweet but uncompromising view of human nature . . . and hard reality: NOT MY DAUGHTER, YOU BITCH! The fact that Harry attracted adults as well as children has never surprised me.

Are the books perfect? Indeed not. Some sections are too long. In *Deathly Hallows*, for instance, there's an awful lot of wandering around and camping in that tent; it starts to feel like Ms. Rowling running out the clock on the school year to fit the format of the previous six books.

And sometimes she falls prey to the *Robinson Crusoe* syndrome. In *Crusoe*, whenever the marooned hero requires something, he ventures out to his ship—which has conveniently run aground on the reef surrounding his desert island—and takes what he needs from stores (in one of the most amusing continuity flubs in the history of English literature, Robinson once swims out naked . . . then fills his pockets). In much the same manner, whenever Harry and his friends get into a tight corner, they produce some new spell—fire, water to douse the fire, stairs that conveniently turn into a slide—and squiggle free. I accepted most of these, partly because there's enough child in me to react gleefully rather than doubtfully (in a way, the Potter books are *The Joy of Magic* rather than *The Joy of Cooking*) but also because I understand that magic is its own thing, and probably boundless. Still, by the time the Battle of Hogwarts was reaching its climax of clumping giants, cheering portraits, and flying wizards, I almost longed for someone to pull out a good old MAC-10 and start blasting away like Rambo.

If all those creative spells—produced at the right moment like the stuff from Crusoe's ship—were a sign of creative exhaustion, it's the only one I saw, and that's pretty amazing. Mostly Rowling is just having fun, knocking herself out, and when a good writer is having fun, the audience is almost always having fun too. You can take that one to the bank (and, Reader, she did).

One last thing: The bighead academics seem to think that Harry's magic will not be strong enough to make a generation of nonreaders (especially the male half) into bookworms . . . but they wouldn't be the first to underestimate Harry's magic; just look at what happened to Lord Voldemort. And, of course, the bigheads would never have credited Harry's influence in the first place, if the evidence hadn't come in the form of best-seller lists. A literary hero as big as the Beatles? "Never happen!" the bigheads would have cried. "The traditional novel is as dead as Jacob Marley! Ask anyone who knows! Ask us, in other words!"

But reading was never dead with the kids. Au contraire, right now it's probably healthier than the adult version, which has to cope with what seems like at least 400 boring and pretentious "literary novels" each year. While the bigheads have been predicting (and bemoaning) the post-literate society, the kids have been supplementing their Potter with the narratives of Lemony Snicket, the adventures of teenage mastermind Artemis Fowl, Philip Pullman's chal-

lenging *His Dark Materials* trilogy, the Alex Rider adventures, Peter Abrahams's superb Ingrid Levin-Hill mysteries, the stories of those amazing traveling blue jeans. And of course we must not forget the unsinkable (if sometimes smelly) Captain Underpants. Also, how about a tip of the old tiara to R. L. Stine, Jo Rowling's jovial John the Baptist?

I began by quoting Shakespeare; I'll close with the Who: The kids are alright. Just how long they stay that way sort of depends on writers like J. K. Rowling, who know how to tell a good story (important) and do it without talking down (more important) or resorting to a lot of high-flown gibberish (vital). Because if the field is left to a bunch of intellectual Muggles who believe the traditional novel is dead, they'll kill the damn thing.

It's good make-believe I'm talking about. Known in more formal circles as the Ministry of Magic. J. K. Rowling has set the standard: It's a high one, and God bless her for it.

Starting a Conversation: Respond to "J. K. Rowling's Ministry of Magic"

In your writer's notebook, consider how King responds to his writing situation by answering the following questions:

1. King discusses J. K. Rowling's readership as well as other critics' responses to the Harry Potter books. Who are King's intended readers? How is this audience related to (in King's words) "bighead academics" and "intellectual Muggles"?

2. King spends part of the essay discussing Rowling's prose style. How would you characterize King's own prose, in terms of its voice and tone?

3. At several points in the essay, King cites specific passages from the Harry Potter novels. What points does he make and support by using these textual examples?

4. Although King is analyzing Rowling's books in a broad context, he also uses personal experience and references to classic and popular literature to support his points. In what ways does his use of sources make him more credible — or less so?

5. Ever since King's own writings began to be taught in college courses (in the mid-1980s), some scholars and critics have argued that popular culture — and King's work in particular — does not merit academic study. In what ways might "J. K. Rowling's Ministry of Magic" represent King's response to these criticisms, on both a personal and an intellectual level?

@ Download or print this Starting a Conversation activity at **bedfordstmartins.com/ conversation**.

Analytical Essays

Analytical essays offer a thorough, well-considered interpretation of a subject for readers who share the writer's interest in the subject. Because just about anything is open to interpretation, analytical essays can address subjects as wide-ranging as political and social issues, sports, lifestyle, music and the arts, history, and science, to name only a few.

Because of the breadth of the subjects they consider, writers of analytical essays address a broad range of readers. When analytical essays are written for purposes such as publication in a magazine or on the Web, writers need to consider the readers who typically subscribe to the magazine or visit the Web site. When such essays are written for academic courses, writers are quite aware that their instructors are a primary audience, but they are aware as well of the importance of considering the needs, interests, knowledge, and backgrounds of other possible readers, such as classmates, friends, family, or members of a particular profession.

 **Tamara Draut**
Generation Debt

Tamara Draut is director of the economic opportunity program at the public policy and advocacy organization Demos. Her work has also appeared in the *New York Times*, the *Wall Street Journal*, and *Newsweek*. "Generation Debt," taken from her book *Strapped: Why America's 20- and 30-Somethings Can't Get Ahead*, considers the impact of college loans and credit card debt on younger Americans. The essay draws on evidence from sources to debunk stereotypes of debt-strapped college graduates as spendthrifts and offers a thoughtful, well-supported analysis of the subject.

CHAPTER THREE

⁃⁃⁃⁃⁃⁃⁃⁃⁃⁃⁃⁃⁃⁃⁃⁃⁃⁃⁃⁃⁃⁃⁃

Generation Debt

First job. First house. First child. These "firsts," when strung together, traditionally signal the arrival of adulthood. Today, we can add dodging debt-collection calls and filing bankruptcy to the list. Between college debt and the spillover effects of paycheck paralysis, piling up debt has become a new rite of passage into adulthood. It's not exactly the kind of generation-defining characteristic we wished for, but debt is perhaps the one shared experience of our diverse generation. If our generation had its own branding campaign, it would be "Debt—you can't leave home without it."

While young people have more debt than previous generations had at the same age, the explosion in credit card debt is a pan-generational phenomenon. Over the last decade, seniors have racked up credit card debt in record amounts. Middle-class families are also sinking into credit card debt. Those little pieces of plastic have become the monkey on the back of our moms and dads, aunts and uncles, and even our grandmas and grandpas.

People struggling to pay back credit card bills get very little sympathy for their plight. This is especially true for young adults, who, conventional wisdom holds, are wildly decadent about their spending. When people think of a young woman in debt, they probably envision a closet full of shoes, Manolo Blahniks, no doubt, and a wardrobe rich with designer brands, splurges courtesy of a generous credit line. And, of course, empty kitchen cupboards because she's out with friends most nights. If it's a young man sinking in credit card debt, the stereotype that springs to mind is a hall closet full of the latest sports equipment, like Calloway Big Bertha golf clubs. The guy's living room is furnished with a flat-screen television, replete with theater-surround sound. Bose speakers, naturally. His refrigerator is stocked with premium beers and not much else because he, too, always eats out.

These "kids" just need to learn some self-control.

Older adults, particularly parents, tend to be censorious about the endemic credit card debt facing this generation. Seventy percent of young adults with credit cards regularly carry balances on their cards that they don't pay off each month, compared to just over half of all households (Draut and Silva 3). Journalists love to churn out articles about how young people are profligate spenders and have poor budgeting skills. According to Margaret Webb Pressler of the *Washington Post*, "The growth in credit card debt is about instant gratification and the inability to live within one's means." She has lots of company. In fact, when it comes to credit card debt, America is full of finger-waggers. A survey that asked card holders about credit card usage found that most individuals think that other people don't know how to use credit wisely—but that they themselves do (Durkin 628). Typical finger-wagging logic.

In reality, there is very little extravagance behind the under-34ers' credit card debt. Most young adults have several grand in credit card debt with nothing to show for it. So, what exactly then are young adults charging? In interview after interview with young people all over the country, a few explanations emerged. The most common reason was the debt trap parked out front: car repairs. If the car is going to the shop, you might as well kiss a couple of hundred dollars good-bye, which most young adults don't have in their bank accounts.

Another big budget buster for young adults is travel, particularly for college-educated young professionals, who often live far from family and have friends sprinkled throughout the country. These friends inevitably get married. An out-of-town wedding is a huge expense for young adults, one that contributes to the steady accumulation of credit card debt among twenty-somethings. To beg off is to lose a friend.

Aside from using credit cards to keep the car running, and maintain good relationships with friends and family, many young adults get into debt from charging up the requisite goods that come with leaving the nest. For young people who can't or won't turn to parents for help, credit cards become their high-interest version of a trust fund. It's the money pot that allows them to put a down payment on an apartment and buy a bed, sheets, towels, and a toilet brush. This plastic trust fund also helps them buy the basics of a professional wardrobe: two suits, one good pair of shoes, and a couple of nice shirts — all carefully chosen so the pieces can be mixed and matched, giving the illusion of a much bigger wardrobe. Before a year of postcollege life has passed, most grads are easily in for two to three thousand to the plastic behemoths. Then, if they get their first pink slip, they sink even deeper into debt.

In fact, in her most recent book, *The Money Book for the Young, Fabulous and Broke*, the best-selling financial guru Suze Orman changes her usual antidebt stance when it comes to young adults. Recognizing the weight of student loans and the abysmal condition of the economy, she says it's okay for young adults to rely on credit cards to help meet monthly expenses, offering advice on how to best use credit cards during this fragile start-up period in a young person's life (Orman 83–84). When one of America's leading personal finance experts acknowledges that establishing an adult life now requires going into credit card debt, we're seriously in trouble.

Her acknowledgment that young people often must and should rely on credit to get through the rough-and-tumble twenties reflects the upside-down reality of our lives. The need to rely on credit cards after college stems in large part from the enormous student loan shackles that define young adults' entry into the real world. With the average college grad having to commit $200 or more every month to student loan payments, there's a lot less wiggle room in the budget. If we took away some of that burden, it's very likely credit card debt among young people would decline.

Works Cited

Draut, Tamara, and Javier Silva. *Generation Broke: The Growth of Debt Among Young Americans*. New York: Demos, 2004. Web.

Durkin, Thomas A. "Credit Cards: Use and Consumer Attitudes: 1970–2000." *Federal Reserve Bulletin* Sept. 2000: 623–34. Print.

Orman, Suze. *The Money Book for the Young, Fabulous and Broke*. New York: Penguin, 2005. Print.

Pressler, Margaret Webb. "Swimming in a Sea of Debt." *Washington Post*. Washington Post, 14 Dec. 2003. Web.

Starting a Conversation: Respond to "Generation Debt"

In your writer's notebook, examine the strategies Draut uses to present her analysis by responding to the following questions:

1. Draut refers to the "conventional wisdom" and "finger-wagging logic" around debt (pars. 3 and 5). What do these and other examples tell you about Draut's intended readers?

2. Draut asserts that "the explosion in credit card debt is a pan-generational phenomenon" (par. 2). What does this mean? What does her statement reveal about her purpose and the broad implications of her analysis?

3. Draut identifies a number of groups affected by credit card debt. How does she characterize each group? How do they differ from one another, and what do they have in common?

4. Draut uses quotations, paraphrases, and brief summaries of several sources, both to characterize the conversation surrounding her topic and to provide evidence to support her points. In what ways do her sources disagree about the causes of credit card debt among young Americans? Which side does Draut ultimately take? What does she add to the conversation?

5. "Generation Debt" seems to conclude that credit card debt has become an unavoidable — perhaps even a necessary — fact of young adult life. Do you agree? To what extent, if any, is Draut's conclusion predetermined by the information she chooses to present? If you were to dispute Draut's findings, what kinds of evidence would you look for?

@ Download or print this Starting a Conversation activity at **bedfordstmartins.com/ conversation**.

How Can I Write an Analytical Essay?

Got questions? Got an inquiring mind? Got the discipline to follow up on a question carefully and thoroughly? If you answered "yes" to these questions, you've got what it takes to start writing an analytical essay.

That's not all it takes, of course. Writing an analytical essay also involves refining your question, gaining a fuller understanding of your subject, applying an appropriate interpretive framework, and drafting your response to your analytical question. But the foundation of an analytical essay — and of all analytical documents, for that matter — is developing and responding to a question about a subject.

As you work on your analytical essay, you'll follow the work of Ali Bizzul, a first-year student who wrote an analytical essay about the health risks football players face when they put on extra weight.

Find a Conversation and Listen In

Analytical essays allow you to share your interpretation of a subject with your readers. Your analysis will reflect not only your analytical question and interpretive framework but also what other writers involved in the conversation about your subject have written and the types of analyses they've conducted. It will also reflect the demands

In Process

An Analytical Essay about Football & Health

Ali Bizzul wrote an analytical essay for her introductory composition course. Ali learned about her topic by reading articles about the short-term and long-term health risks football players face when they put on extra weight. Follow Ali's efforts to write her analytical essay by visiting **bedfordstmartins.com/ conversation**. You can read excerpts of interviews about her work on her analytical essay, read her assignment, and read drafts of her essay.

of your writing assignment. To get started on your analytical essay, review your assignment and spend some time thinking about your writing situation: your purposes for writing; your readers' needs, interests, knowledge, and background; potential sources of evidence; and the contexts that might affect your analysis (see p. 13). Then start generating ideas about the kinds of questions you could ask, find a conversation worth joining, and learn more about it.

EXPLORE YOUR SURROUNDINGS

Analysis is largely a search for patterns—and searching for patterns is something we do on a daily basis. As we learn to drive, for example, we start noticing the typical behaviors of other drivers as they approach an intersection. It doesn't take long to learn that we can reliably predict whether other drivers are planning to go through the intersection, stop, turn left, or turn right—even when they fail to use turn signals. When we see behaviors that are unusual or unexpected, we go on alert, making sure that we aren't hit by a driver who isn't paying attention. Similarly, we look for patterns in everything from playing tennis (noticing, for instance, how a player grips the racket before returning a shot) to reading the newspaper (learning where we can find stories that interest us or how to distinguish news from advertisements).

Humans are quite good at identifying and responding to patterns. But it takes time to notice them and even more time to figure out how they work. Before choosing a specific focus for your analytical essay, identify general topics that might interest you enough to explore in depth. One good way to begin is to brainstorm (see p. 33), freewrite (see p. 34), or loop (see p. 34) about the objects and events that surround you.

- **Your shelves.** Scan your collection of music, books, and movies, and think about anything you've listened to, read, or watched that grabbed your attention. You might be rewarded by looking beneath the surface for meaning or themes, or you might find yourself intrigued by a plot line or a style that appears to be part of a larger trend.

- **The daily news.** Whether you follow current events in newspapers, on television, or on the Web, recent and ongoing news stories offer rich opportunities for analysis: Why were some groups offended by a magazine cover? Is third-party health insurance to blame for the high cost of medical care? How do "bad girl" celebrities influence children's behavior? Be alert to the questions that occur to you as you read, to reactions (other people's and your own) that surprise you, and to themes that seem to pop up from one day to the next. You're likely to notice something you want to investigate further.

- **Your leisure activities.** No matter what you do for fun—participate in a sport, play video games, take photographs—you can probably find some aspects of your lifestyle that raise questions or suggest a trend. For instance, perhaps you've wondered whether the X Games will become more popular than the Olympics, or noticed that interactive group games seem to be gaining popularity over first-person shooters.

- **Your physical environment.** Take a look around you. A favorite poster in your bedroom, for instance, might be a good candidate for interpretation. A new bank in town might inspire questions about interest rates, community service, or architectural style. An overflowing trash bin might suggest an analytical essay on recycling or municipal waste management.

As you consider possible topics for your writing project, look for new or surprising ideas that interest you and your readers and lend themselves to analysis. If you come across a subject or a question that makes a good candidate for your essay, add it to your writer's notebook.

You'll find additional writing project ideas at the end of this chapter (p. 266).

ASK INTERPRETIVE QUESTIONS

The foundation for analysis is a question that is open to interpretation. For example, asking whether you have enough money to purchase a ticket to the latest Will Smith movie would not require an interpretive response. Either you have enough money or you don't. Asking whether Smith's performance breaks new ground, however, would require an analysis of his work in the film. Similarly, while a driver wouldn't need to conduct an analysis to determine whether a car has a full tank of fuel, a city planner might find it necessary to carry out an analysis to anticipate how high the cost of fuel must rise before commuters leave their cars at home and take public transportation.

You can generate potential interpretive questions about promising topics by brainstorming, freewriting, or clustering in response to the following prompts. Each prompt focuses your attention on a general topic in a different way, and each provides a useful starting point for an analytical essay. Depending on your topic, you'll find that some prompts are more productive than others.

- **Elements.** Think about the subject in terms of its parts. How does it break down into smaller pieces, or how can it be divided in different ways? Which parts are most important, and which are less significant?

- **Categories.** What groups does the subject belong to? How is it similar to or different from other subjects in a particular group? How can comparing the subject to related subjects help you and your readers understand it in a new way?

- **History.** Look into the origins of the subject. What recent events are related to the subject, and what are the implications of those events? Does your subject build on previous events? Will it continue to have influences in the future, and if so, how will it do so?

- **Causes and effects.** What caused the subject, and why is it the way it is? What are the subject's influences on people, events, and objects? Who or what affects the subject? What effects is the subject likely (or unlikely) to cause in the future?

- **Relationships.** How is the subject connected to other ideas, events, or objects? For example, are changes in the subject related to changes in related ideas, events, or objects?

- **Meaning.** What is the subject's significance and implications? Can different people find different meanings in the subject, and if so, why? Does a close examination of the subject reveal a new way of looking at it?

As you ponder ways to turn a general topic area into the subject of your analytical essay, spend time learning about other people's answers to the most promising questions you've generated. You can discuss the subject with people you know, skim sources published on the subject, or even observe the subject firsthand. You can learn more about gathering information in Chapter 2 and in Part Three.

Working Together: Try It Out Loud

Working in a small group, choose a popular song that everyone in your group likes, or choose one of the top songs of the week on Billboard or iTunes. Then use one set of the interpretive question prompts in the previous section to analyze the song. If you are doing this activity during class, the class might choose a single song, and each group might choose a different set of prompts. Take turns asking questions about the song while the other members of the group try to answer them. Record your answers, noting both agreements and disagreements. Your purpose is to interpret, so don't get distracted by whether the song is good or bad; instead, focus on its significance and implications. If you are doing this activ-

ity during class, each group should report its results to the class.

When you are finished, take a few minutes to reflect on the activity. What did you learn about different ways of approaching an analysis? Did some interpretive question prompts produce more useful or interesting results than the others? How did examining the song from multiple perspectives affect your interpretation of it?

@ Download or print this Working Together activity at **bedfordstmartins.com/conversation.**

SEARCH DATABASES

Once you've identified a promising question, learn whether—and how—other writers have attempted to answer it. Analytical essays tend to draw on information and analyses from other sources in addition to the writer's personal knowledge and interpretation, so even if you already know a great deal about a subject, be sure to review other writers' contributions to the conversation and to look for sources you can use to support your analysis.

Databases can give you an in-depth understanding of your subject, as well as a sense of useful interpretive frameworks, existing interpretations, and unanswered questions. They allow you to search for analyses that have been published on a particular subject or in a particular discipline. Although some databases, such as ERIC (eric.ed.gov), can be accessed publicly through the Web, most are available only through a library's computers or Web site.

To identify databases that might be relevant to the subject you are analyzing, review your library's list of databases or consult a reference librarian. The following questions can get you started.

- **Has the subject been addressed in recent news coverage?** If so, consider searching databases that focus on newspapers and weekly magazines, such as LexisNexis Academic, ProQuest Newspapers, or Alternative Press Index.

- **Is the subject related to a broad area of interest, such as business, education, or government?** If so, search databases that focus on general publications, such as Academic Search Premier, Articles First, or Catalog of U.S. Government Publications.

- **Is the subject related to a particular profession or academic discipline?** If so, consult databases that focus on that area. Many libraries provide guidance on which databases are relevant to a particular profession or discipline.

- **Have I already identified any promising sources?** By searching citation indexes (databases that identify sources that cite a particular source), you can identify additional sources that refer to the sources you already have. Depending on your subject, you might search the Science Citation Index, Social Sciences Citation Index, or Arts & Humanities Citation Index.

- **Is the full text of the source available?** Full-text databases offer the complete source for viewing or downloading. They cut out the middle step of searching for the physical periodical that published the article. If you don't know whether your library owns the sources provided by a database, or if you would simply like to locate them more quickly, consider using full-text databases. Databases such as Academic Search Premier, ERIC, and LexisNexis Academic offer some or all of their sources in full text.

Generate keywords and phrases that are related to your interpretive question, and search a few different databases for potential resources. Using the citation information provided by the database, check your library's online catalog for the title of the publication in which the article appears. Your library might own many of the sources you'll identify through a database search, but if it doesn't, you can usually request promising materials through interlibrary loan.

You can read more about searching databases in Chapter 12.

Conduct Your Analysis

An analytical essay helps readers understand the origins, qualities, significance, or potential effects of a subject. A successful essay builds on a carefully crafted analytical question, a thorough understanding of the subject, and a rigorous and fair application

In Process

Searching Databases

Ali Bizzul used her interpretive question — *Why do so many football players risk their health by adding extra weight?* — to develop search terms for searches of her library's databases. She knew from exploring her subject that it had been addressed in newspapers and magazines, so she searched databases such as LexisNexis Academic and Newspaper Source. Because she also wondered whether scientific studies had been conducted on the subject, she also searched the MedLine and PubMed databases.

Ali used the search terms *football, health,* and *weight.* She searched all fields in the database and used the Boolean operator AND to require that all three words be present (see Chapter 12).

⌐ **Ali's Search of the MedLine Database**

of an appropriate interpretive framework. It also builds on a clear understanding of your writing situation.

REFINE YOUR QUESTION

Begin your analysis by reviewing the interpretive questions you generated about your subject (see p. 235). Choose one that interests you and will allow you to carry out your assignment. Then review and refine your question. Ask yourself:

- How might I respond to this question? Will my response be complex enough to justify writing an essay about it? Will it be too complex for my assignment?

- Is the question appropriate for the conversation that I'm planning to join?

- Will the question help me accomplish my purposes?

- Will my response interest my readers or address their needs?

A good analytical question is open to interpretation. Questions that focus on factual or yes/no answers seldom provide a strong foundation for an analytical essay. In contrast,

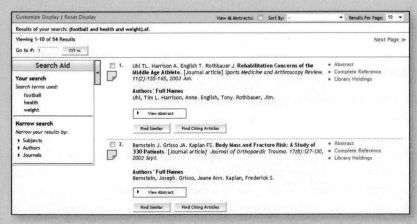

The search produced 54 results. The database allowed her to view abstracts (summaries of the source) and complete reference information.

The database allowed Ali to narrow her search.

⌐ **Ali's Search Results**

Ali's database searches produced sources in newspapers, magazines, and academic journals. She located one of the articles, a brief "letter" written by Joyce Harp and Lindsay Hecht, and printed it.

questions that lead you to investigate the origins or potential impacts of a subject, consider its qualities, weigh its significance, or explore its meaning are more likely to lead to success. Consider the differences between the following sets of questions.

Questions Leading to Factual and Yes/No Answers	Questions Open to Interpretation
When did the Iraq War begin?	What caused the Iraq War?
Has NASA's annual budget kept pace with inflation?	How can NASA pursue its mission on a reduced annual budget?
Who were the villains in the latest Indiana Jones movie?	In what ways do the key themes of the latest Indiana Jones movie reflect changes in American foreign relations?
Who won the last World Series?	What contributed to the success of the last World Series champions?

You should also consider how a question will direct your thinking about your subject. For example, you might want to understand the potential effects of a proposal to reduce the cost of attending your state's public colleges and universities by increasing class size and laying off faculty and staff. Asking a question about the plan's impact on education might direct your attention toward students and the trade-offs between lower costs and the quality of instruction. In contrast, asking a question about the plan's impact on the state budget might lead you to view the subject through the lens of business concerns and economic forecasts. Although the questions are related, they would lead to significantly different analyses.

SEEK A FULLER UNDERSTANDING OF YOUR SUBJECT

If you've ever talked with people who don't know what they're talking about but nonetheless are certain of their opinions, you'll recognize the dangers of applying an interpretive framework before you thoroughly understand your subject. To enhance your understanding of your subject, use division and classification. Division allows you to identify the elements that make up a subject. Classification allows you to explore a subject in relation to other subjects and to consider the similarities, differences, and relationships among its elements.

Division. Division breaks a subject into its parts and considers what each contributes to the whole. A financial analyst, for example, might examine the various groups within a company to understand what each group does and how it contributes to the overall value of the company. Similarly, a literary critic might consider how each scene in a play relates to other scenes and how it contributes to the play's major theme.

As you use division to examine a subject, keep in mind the following guidelines:

- **Pick a focus.** Division can take place on many levels. Just as you can divide numbers in different ways (100, for example, can be seen as ten 10s, five 20s, four 25s, and so on), you can divide subjects differently. A government agency, for instance, might be considered in terms of its responsibilities, its departments, or its employees. Trying to understand all of these aspects at once, however, would be difficult and unproductive. Use your analytical question as a guide to determine how best to divide your subject.

- **Examine the parts.** Most subjects can be thought of as a system of interrelated parts. As you divide your subject, determine what role each part plays, individually and in relation to other parts.

- **Assess contributions to the whole.** As you divide a subject, be sure to consider the contributions that each part makes to the larger whole. In some cases, you'll find that a part is essential. In other cases, you'll find that it makes little or no contribution to the whole.

Even though you can divide and reassemble a subject in a variety of ways, always take into account your purpose and your readers' needs, interests, and expectations. It might be easier to focus on a government agency's departments than on its functions, but if your question focuses on how the agency works or what it does, you'll be more successful if you examine its functions.

Classification. Classification places your subject — or each part of your subject — into a category. By categorizing a subject or its parts, you can discover how and to what extent your subject or a part of your subject is similar to others in the same category and how it differs from those in other categories. Identifying those similarities and differences, in turn, allows you to consider the subject, or its parts, in relation to the other items in your categories. As you use classification to gain a better understanding of your subject, consider the following guidelines:

- **Choose a classification scheme.** The categories you work with might be established already, or you might create them specifically to support your analysis. For example, if you are analyzing state representatives, you might place them into standard categories: Democrat, Republican, Libertarian, Green, and so on. Or you might create categories especially for your analysis, such as who voted for and against particular types of legislation.

- **Look at both similarities and differences.** When you place an item in a category, you decide that it is more similar to the other items in the category than to those in other categories. However, even though the items in a broad category will share many similarities, they will also differ in important ways.

Botanists, for example, have developed a complex system of categories and subcategories to help them understand general types of plants (such as algae, roses, and corn) as well as consider subtle differences among similar plants (such as corn bred for animal feed, for human consumption, and for biofuels).

- **Justify your choices.** Your decisions about what to place in a given category will be based on your definition of the category, if you've created it yourself, or your understanding of categories that have been established by someone else. In most cases, you'll need to explain why a particular category is the best fit for your subject. If you wanted readers to accept your classification of Wal-Mart as a mom-and-pop retailer, for instance, you would have to explain that your category is defined by origin (not current size) and then inform readers that the chain started as a single discount store in Arkansas.

Classification and division are often used in combination, particularly when you want to consider similarities and differences among different parts of your subject. For example, if you are examining a complex organization, you might use division to analyze each department; in addition, you might use classification so that you can analyze groups of departments that have similar functions, such as customer service and technical support, and contrast those departments with departments in other categories, such as sales, marketing, and research and development.

APPLY AN INTERPRETIVE FRAMEWORK

An interpretive framework is a set of strategies for identifying patterns that has been used successfully and refined over time by writers interested in a given subject area or working in a particular field. Writers can choose from hundreds (perhaps thousands) of specialized frameworks used in disciplines across the arts, sciences, social sciences, humanities, engineering, and business. A historian, for example, might apply a feminist, social, political, or cultural analysis to interpret diaries written by women who worked in defense plants during World War II, while a sociologist might conduct correlational tests to interpret the results of a survey. In a writing course, you'll most likely use one of the broad interpretive frameworks discussed here: trend analysis, causal analysis, data analysis, and text analysis.

By definition, analysis is subjective. Your interpretation will be shaped by the question you ask, the sources you consult, and your personal experience and perspective. But analysis is also conducted within the context of a written conversation. As you consider your choice of interpretive framework, reflect on the interpretive frameworks you encounter in your sources and those you've used in the past. Keep in mind that different interpretive frameworks will lead to different ways of seeing and understanding a subject. The key to success is choosing one that can guide you as you try to answer your question.

Trend analysis. Trends are patterns that hold up over time. Trend analysis, as a result, focuses on sequences of events and the relationships among them. It is based on the assumption that understanding what has happened in the past allows us to make sense of what is happening in the present and to draw inferences about what is likely to happen in the future.

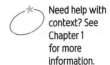

Need help with context? See Chapter 1 for more information.

Trends can be identified and analyzed in nearly every field, from politics to consumer affairs to the arts. For example, many economists have analyzed historical accounts of fuel crises in the 1970s to understand the recent surge in fuel prices. Sports and entertainment analysts also use trend analysis — to forecast the next NBA champion, for instance, or to explain the reemergence of superheroes in popular culture during the last decade.

To conduct a trend analysis, follow these guidelines:

- **Gather information.** Trend analysis is most useful when it relies on an extensive set of long-term observations. By examining news reports about NASA since the mid-1960s, for example, you can determine whether the coverage of

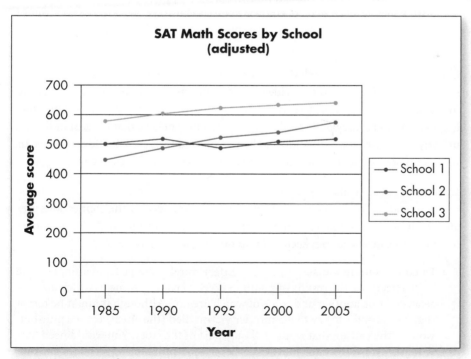

t. Trend analysis looks for patterns that hold up over time.

the U.S. space program has changed over time. By examining these changes, you can decide whether a trend exists. You might find, for instance, that the press has become progressively less positive in its treatment of the U.S. space program. However, if you don't gather enough information to thoroughly establish the trend, your readers might lack confidence in your conclusions.

- **Establish that a trend exists.** Some analysts seem willing to declare a trend on the flimsiest set of observations: when a team wins an NFL championship for the second year in a row, for instance, fans are quick to announce the start of a dynasty. As you look for trends, cast a wide net. Learn as much as you can about the history of your subject, and carefully assess it to determine how often events related to your subject have moved in one direction or another. By understanding the variations that have occurred over time, you can better judge whether you've actually found a trend.

- **Draw conclusions.** Trend analysis allows you to understand the historical context that shapes a subject and, in some cases, to make predictions about the subject. The conclusions you draw should be grounded strongly in the evidence you've collected. They should also reflect your writing situation — your purposes, readers, and context. As you draw your conclusions, exercise caution. Ask whether you have enough information to support your conclusions. Search for evidence that contradicts your conclusions. Most important, on the basis of the information you've collected so far, ask whether your conclusions make sense.

Causal analysis. Causal analysis focuses on the factors that bring about a particular situation. It can be applied to a wide range of subjects, such as the dot-com collapse in the late 1990s, the rise of terrorist groups, or the impact of calorie restriction on longevity. Writers carry out causal analysis when they believe that understanding the underlying reasons for a situation will help people address the situation, increase the likelihood of its happening again, or appreciate its potential consequences.

In many ways, causal analysis is a form of detective work. It involves tracing a sequence of events and exploring the connections among them. Because the connections are almost always more complex than they appear, it pays to be thorough. If you choose to conduct a causal analysis, keep in mind the following guidelines:

- **Uncover as many causes as you can.** Effects rarely emerge from a single cause. Most effects are the results of a complex web of causes, some of which are related to one another and some of which are not. Although it might be tempting, for example, to say that a murder victim died (the effect) from a gunshot wound (the cause), that would tell only part of the story. You would need to work backward from the murderer's decision to pull the trigger to the factors

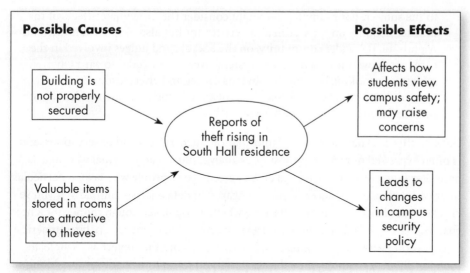

t. Causal analysis involves tracing connections among events.

that led to that decision, and then further back to the causes underlying those factors.

Effects can also become causes. While investigating the murder, for instance, you might find that the murderer had long been envious of the victim's success, that he was jumpy from the steroids he'd been taking in an ill-advised attempt to qualify for the Olympic trials in weight lifting, and that he had just found his girlfriend in the victim's arms. Exploring how these factors might be related—and determining when they are not—will help you understand the web of causes leading to the effect.

- **Determine which causes are significant.** Not all causes contribute equally to an effect. Perhaps our murderer was cut off on the freeway on his way to meet his girlfriend. Lingering anger at the other driver might have been enough to push him over the edge, but it probably wouldn't have caused the shooting by itself.

- **Distinguish between correlation and cause.** Too often, we assume that because one event occurred just before another, the first event caused the second. We might conclude that finding his girlfriend with another man drove the murderer to shoot in a fit of passion—only to discover that he had begun planning the murder months before, when the victim threatened to reveal his use of steroids to the press just prior to the Olympic trials.

- **Look beyond the obvious.** A thorough causal analysis considers not only the primary causes and effects but also those that might appear only slightly related to the subject. For example, you might consider the immediate effects of the murder not only on the victim and perpetrator but also on their families and friends, on the wider community, on the lawyers and judges involved in the case, on an overburdened judicial system, even on attitudes toward Olympic athletes. By looking beyond the obvious causes and effects, you can deepen your understanding of the subject and begin to explore a much wider set of implications than you might have initially expected.

Data analysis. Data is any type of information, such as facts and observations, and is often expressed numerically. Most of us analyze data in an informal way on a daily basis. For example, if you've looked at the percentage of people who favor a particular political candidate over another, you've engaged in data analysis. Similarly, if you've checked your bank account to determine whether you have enough money for a new coat, you've carried out a form of data analysis. As a writer, you can analyze numerical information related to your subject to better understand the subject as a whole, to look for differences among the subject's parts, and to explore relationships among the parts.

Use of social networking sites:

	# surveyed	% who use social networking regularly
Gender:		
Male	48	56%
Female	42	65%
Age:		
16–20	20	85%
21–30	31	71%
31–45	28	46%
45+	11	27%
Education:		
Some high school	12	35%
High school graduate	25	56%
Some college	34	65%
College graduate	16	64%
Graduate school	7	62%

⌐ Data analysis can involve assessing information from a variety of sources.

In Process

Applying Interpretive Frameworks

Ali Bizzul used a combination of trend analysis and causal analysis in her essay about the health risks football players face as they put on weight. After reading several reports of a rise in heat-related injuries among larger players (the effects), she tried to identify the factors contributing to this trend (the causes). Drawing on information from an article about obesity among players in the National Football League, she used freewriting to explore her ideas.

The study shows that football players, especially the guards, are becoming increasingly larger. 97% overweight and many of those class 2 and 3 obese. This is crazy. It causes health problems, such as high blood pressure and heart failure. It was also shown that it didn't really help rankings, so why would they do it? It is all in the minds of people. It is common sense that a bigger guy running into you is going to stop you better than a smaller guy. Even though it doesn't help scores, it can help in the defensive area. These men, the guards, are meant to be a sort of battering ram and are not hired for their speed and agility. The high school kids are seeing this on TV and thinking that they have to be just as large as the guys in the NFL. So they think that all they need to do is bulk up, but find that they can't carry the weight as well and it hurts more than it helps. Coaches are doing their part to help these guys stay healthy, but they don't really seem to try to educate their students about the implications of being overweight. They are just telling them to lose some weight, and that is just on a case-to-case basis. It really is just in these kids' minds. They think that the only way they will be noticed by recruiters is to be big and able to throw their weight around. Don't present a solution, just explain why it is happening. . . . Everyone believes that bigger is better. But it isn't. It is going to kill these guys, and it is setting a bad example for the younger generation.

> Ali doesn't worry about writing in complete sentences. She gets her ideas and reactions down as quickly as possible.

> Ali reminds herself about the purpose of her analytical essay.

To begin a data analysis, gather your data and enter the numbers into a spreadsheet or statistics program. You can use the program's tools to sort the data and conduct tests. If your set of data is small, you can use a piece of paper and a calculator. As you carry out your analysis, keep the following guidelines in mind:

- **Do the math.** Let's say you conducted a survey of student and faculty attitudes about a proposed change to the graduation requirements at your school. Tabulating the results might reveal that 52 percent of your respondents were female, 83 percent were between the ages of eighteen and twenty-two, 38 percent were juniors or seniors, and 76 percent were majoring in the biological sciences. You might also find that, of the faculty who responded, 75 percent were tenured. Based on these numbers, you could draw conclusions about whether the responses are representative of your school's overall population. If they are not, you might decide to ask more people to take your survey. Once you're certain that you've collected enough data, you can draw conclusions about the overall results and determine, for example, the percentage of respondents who favored, opposed, or were undecided about the proposed change.

- **Categorize your data.** Difference tests can help you make distinctions among groups. To classify the results of your survey, for example, you might compare male and female student responses. Similarly, you might examine differences in the responses between other groups—such as faculty and students; tenured and untenured faculty; and freshmen, sophomore, juniors, and seniors. To carry out your analysis, you might look at each group's average level of agreement with the proposed changes. Or you might use statistical techniques such as T-Tests, which offer more sensitive assessments of difference than comparisons of averages. You can conduct these kinds of tests using spreadsheet programs, such as Microsoft Excel, or statistical programs, such as SAS and SPSS.

- **Explore relationships.** Correlation tests allow you to draw conclusions about your subject. For example, you might want to know whether support for proposed changes to graduation requirements increases or decreases according to GPA. A correlation test might indicate that a positive relationship exists—that support goes up as GPA increases. Be cautious, however, as you examine relationships. In particular, be wary of confusing causation with correlation. Tests will show, for example, that as shoe size increases, so do scores on reading tests. Does this mean that large feet improve reading? Not really. The cause of higher reading scores appears to be attending school longer. High school students tend to score better on reading tests than do students in elementary school—and, on average, high school students tend to have much larger feet. As is the case with difference tests, you can use many spreadsheet and statistical programs to explore relationships. If your set of data is small enough, you can also use a piece of paper to examine it.

- **Be thorough.** Take great care to ensure the integrity of your analysis. You will run into problems if you collect too little data, if the data is not representative, or if the data is collected sloppily. Similarly, you should base your conclusions on a thoughtful and careful examination of the results of your tests. Picking and choosing evidence that supports your conclusion might be tempting, but you'll do a disservice to yourself and your readers if you fail to consider all the results of your analysis.

Text analysis. Today, the word *text* can refer to a wide range of printed or digital works—and even some forms of artistic expression that we might not think of as documents. Texts open to interpretation include novels, poems, plays, essays, articles, movies, speeches, blogs, songs, paintings, photographs, sculptures, performances, Web pages, videos, television shows, and computer games.

Students enrolled in writing classes often use the elements of literary analysis to analyze texts. In this form of analysis, interpreters focus on theme, plot, setting, characterization, imagery, style, and structure, as well as the contexts—social, cultural, political, and historical—that shape a work. Writers who use this form of analysis focus both on what is actually presented in the text and what is implied or conveyed "between the lines." They rely heavily on close reading of the text to discern meaning, critique an author's technique, and search for patterns that help them understand the

In the song "What is New Orleans, Part 2," recorded by Kermit Ruffins and the Rebirth Brass Band, a call-and-response pattern structures both the lyrics ("What is New Orleans? New Orleans is . . .") and also the interaction between Ruffins and the musicians. Frequently, after Ruffins sings a pattern of syllables, the musicians echo or answer him, as though the music itself is to be considered a sufficient response. Meanwhile, the song's lyrics highlight the importance of food in the city's culture by beginning with a list of meals. Each meal is associated with a specific time and day of the week, giving the impression that the rest of the week's events are scheduled around these meals. Ruffins then lists musicians and locations, moving from the specific to the general, from individual lounges to entire neighborhoods.

⌐ Text analysis can focus on a wide range of artistic expression.

text as fully as possible. They also tend to consider other elements of the wider writing situation in which the text was produced—in particular, the author's purpose, intended audience, use of sources, and choice of genre.

If you carry out a text analysis, keep the following guidelines in mind:

- **Focus on the text itself.** In any form of text analysis, the text should take center stage. Although you will typically reflect on the issues raised by your interpretation, maintain a clear focus on the text in front of you, and keep your analysis grounded firmly in what you can locate within it. Background information and related sources, such as scholarly articles and essays, can support and enhance your analysis, but they can't do the work of interpretation for you.

- **Consider the text in its entirety.** Particularly in the early stages of learning about a text, it is easy to be distracted by a startling idea or an intriguing concept. Try not to focus on a particular aspect of the text, however, until you've fully reviewed all of it. You might well decide to narrow your analysis to a particular aspect of the text, but lay the foundation for a fair, well-informed interpretation by first considering the text as a whole.

- **Avoid "cherry-picking."** Cherry-picking refers to the process of using only those materials from a text that support your overall interpretation and ignoring aspects that might weaken or contradict your interpretation. As you carry out your analysis, factor in *all* the evidence. If the text doesn't support your interpretation, rethink your conclusions.

Prepare a Draft

As you prepare to draft your analytical essay, you'll decide how to present the results of your analysis to your readers. Your draft will reflect not only your conclusions and your interpretive framework but also what others involved in the conversation have written about your subject and the types of analyses they've conducted. As you write, you'll focus on making an interpretive claim, explaining your interpretation, designing your essay, and framing your analysis.

MAKE AN INTERPRETIVE CLAIM

Your interpretive claim is a brief statement—usually in the form of a thesis statement (see Chapter 15)—that helps readers understand the overall results of your analysis. Essentially, it's a one- or two-sentence answer to your interpretive question. Just as your question should be open to interpretation, your claim should be open to debate. If it simply repeats the obvious—either because it is factually true or because it has long been agreed to by those involved in your written conversation—it will do little to advance the conversation.

Your claim will frame your readers' understanding of your subject in a particular way. It will also reflect the interpretive framework you've decided to use. Consider the differences among the following claims about distance running:

> Evidence collected since the mid-1990s suggests that distance running can enhance self-image among college students.

> Although a carefully monitored exercise program built around distance running appears to have positive effects for most cardiac patients, heart attack survivors who engage in at least two hours of running each week have a 30 percent higher survival rate than coronary artery bypass surgery patients who engage in the same amount of distance running.

> Since 2000, distance running has undergone a resurgence in the United States, allowing the country to regain its standing as a leader in the international running community.

> Distance running, when it is addressed at all in contemporary novels, is usually used to represent a desire to escape from the pressures of modern life.

Each of these interpretive claims would lead a writer to focus on different aspects of the subject, and each would reflect a different interpretive framework. The first calls readers' attention to a causal relationship between distance running and mental health. The second explores differences in the effect of distance running on two groups of cardiac patients. The third directs attention to a trend analysis of increasing competitiveness among elite distance runners. And the fourth makes a claim about how distance running is treated in literature.

EXPLAIN YOUR INTERPRETATION

People who read analyses are intelligent, curious people. They want to know more than just what you think of a subject; they want to know how you arrived at your interpretation and why your analysis is reasonable. Your readers won't always agree with your interpretation, and that's fine—but even if you can't persuade them to accept your analysis, you do want to convince readers that your take on the subject is insightful and well considered.

Provide relevant reasons for your interpretation. Build on your interpretive claim by presenting reasons for your readers to accept your analysis. The overall results of your analysis form your main point, and the reasons to accept your analysis become your supporting points.

Look over the results of your analysis, and ask yourself why readers should agree with your interpretation. You might come up with more reasons than you can possibly use—or you might find yourself struggling to find enough reasons to support your claim. Either way, try to generate as many potential reasons as possible, taking care not to rule out any at first, no matter how trivial or ridiculous they might seem.

Working Together: Generate Reasons for Your Interpretation

The goal of this collaborative activity is to generate potential reasons supporting your interpretation of your subject. You can work in person or online (using chat, instant messaging, or a threaded discussion forum). If you are working face-to-face, one member of the group should take notes on the discussion. If you are using a chat or instant-messaging program, be sure to record a transcript of the session.

To carry out the activity, follow these steps:

1. One writer should describe his or her writing project, the overall results of the analysis, and the reasons that will be offered to support the analysis.

2. Each member of the group should help evaluate the reasons identified by the writer. Are the reasons sound, appropriate, and credible?

3. Each member of the group should also suggest additional reasons the writer might consider.

When the exchange is completed, turn to the next writer and repeat the process.

@ Download or print this Working Together activity at **bedfordstmartins.com/conversation.**

Once you have generated a substantial list of potential reasons, select the ones that seem most likely to convince your readers that your analysis is sound. Some reasons will be more relevant than others. Rather than list every possible reason to accept your analysis, identify those reasons that are most directly related to your interpretive claim. The reasons you choose should also be consistent with the interpretive framework you've decided to follow. For example, you might find several reasons to support your analysis of a new novel's significance, among them comments published in literary journals such as *Proceedings of the Modern Language Association* and endorsements by celebrities such as Oprah Winfrey and Madonna. If you are using text analysis as your interpretive framework, you might find commentary offered by authorities in the field of literary studies more useful than celebrity endorsements.

Support your reasons with evidence. No matter which reasons you choose, each of them must be supported by evidence. Analytical essays tend to rely on a mix of evidence from the subject itself (particularly in the case of text analyses), from the writer's reflections and personal experience, and from published or field sources. Evidence can include the following:

- language or images from a text that is being analyzed
- quotations, paraphrases, and summaries from published sources such as reports and journal articles

- illustrations in the form of images, charts, graphs, and tables
- statements from personal interviews
- notes from an observation
- numerical information

You can use evidence to provide examples and illustrations, to define ideas and concepts, to illustrate processes, and to associate particular ideas and concepts with authorities, such as political leaders, subject-matter experts, or people who have been affected by the subject.

To organize your evidence, list all the reasons you will use to support your overall analysis, review your notes to find evidence that supports each reason, and then list the evidence below each reason. You might need to review your sources to locate additional evidence, or even obtain additional sources. If you are conducting a text analysis, be careful to avoid cherry-picking your evidence (see p. 250). If you are conducting another type of analysis, make sure that you haven't relied too heavily on a single source of evidence.

You can read more about how to use evidence to support your analysis in Chapter 15.

In Process

Supporting Reasons with Evidence

Ali Bizzul identified three major reasons to support her interpretive claim that gaining weight hurts football players more than it helps:

Reason 1: Heat-related injuries associated with the use of diet supplements

Reason 2: Long-term health problems associated with obesity

Reason 3: Decrease in athletic performance

Ali used each of these reasons as the basis for a general statement in her draft. Here is her preliminary list of evidence to support her second reason, the long-term health problems associated with obesity:

The extra weight gained for football can complicate the health of ex-athletes:
— high blood pressure (Harp and Hecht)
— sleep-disordered breathing (Harp and Hecht)
— joint damage/arthritis (Groeschen)
— heart disease (Korth, Longman)
— diabetes (Korth, Longman)

As she drafted her essay, Ali used her lists of evidence to remind herself of sources she might turn to while making her points.

Establish the context. It's quite possible — even likely — that others involved in a conversation will have conducted their own analyses of your subject. Be sure to check for those analyses so that you can place your analysis in a larger context. Ideally, you'll be able to present your interpretation as a contribution to a growing understanding of the subject, rather than simply as an isolated set of observations.

As you draft your analytical essay, keep in mind the other interpretations you've encountered. Review the sources you consulted as you learned about your subject and conducted your analysis. If you find reasonable interpretations that support — or contradict — yours, consider how to address them in your essay. You might offer similar interpretations to back up one or more of your reasons, or you might explain why another writer's analysis is less adequate than your own. In either case, you should briefly define significant existing analyses for your readers and explain how your interpretation complicates or improves upon what's been said before. You might also need to draw on evidence from other sources or from the subject itself.

CONSIDER GENRE AND DESIGN

A well-written analytical essay uses design for three primary reasons: to improve readability, to simplify the presentation of complex concepts and information, and to enhance the writer's ability to achieve his or her goals.

As you contemplate design options for your essay, make note of any formatting requirements specified in your assignment (such as margins, spacing, font, and the like). Consider as well the expectations of your readers, particularly your instructor. You might also think about including visual evidence such as figures and images.

- **Figures**, such as charts and graphs, can help readers better understand complex concepts or see trends that would be difficult to discern through textual descriptions alone. A chart, for example, can clearly show comparative cost figures for a state plan to subsidize public transportation. A graph could show changes over time in ridership of those who use trains, buses, subways, or private automobiles.

- **Images**, particularly when you are analyzing a visual text such as a photograph, video, or painting, can help readers better understand the subject and increase the likelihood that they'll accept your interpretation as valid and well founded.

- **Captions** are a necessary complement to figures and images. Be sure to include a caption for each figure or image in your essay. At a minimum, a caption should provide a figure number cross-referenced in the text, a descriptive label, and source information. You can also use the caption to briefly describe what is shown and to explain what it contributes to your analysis.

If you use figures and images in your essay, place them near their first mention in the text. You can learn more about figures, illustrations, captions, and other aspects of document design in Chapter 18.

In Process

Using a Figure to Support a Point

Ali Bizzul found a chart in a research study published in the *Journal of the American Medical Association*. She included it in her essay as evidence to support a point in her analysis of the health risks associated with weight gain among football players.

Heatstroke is not the only danger associated with increased size. Excess weight can cause serious health problems, even if some of the pounds are due to high muscle mass. According to Harp and Hecht (2005), two researchers at the University of North Carolina who conducted a study of 2,168 professional football players competing in the 2003–2004 season, 97% of NFL players would be considered "overweight" and 56% "obese" under the Body Mass Index (BMI) guidelines published by the National Institutes of Health for men in their twenties (see Fig. 1).

> Text is "wrapped" around the figure.

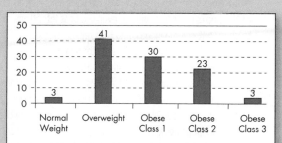

Fig. 1. Percentage of NFL players in National Institutes of Health Body Mass Index categories.

Note. Data from "Research Letter: Obesity in the National Football League," by Joyce B. Harp and Lindsay Hecht, 2005, *Journal of the American Medical Association 293*(9), pp. 1061–1062.

ㄴ **A Chart Used as Evidence**

> The illustration has a caption. The source of the illustration is identified in a note below the caption.

> Ali refers to the figure in parentheses. She places the figure close to the point where she mentions it.

The researchers noted that the group of football players with the highest rates of obesity — the linemen — also had higher blood pressure readings and higher incidences of sleep-disordered breathing than any other group of football players. It appears that athletes are not immune to the effects of obesity, in spite of their active lifestyles.

FRAME YOUR ANALYSIS

The results of your analysis will be strongly influenced by your interpretive question, interpretive framework, and sources of evidence. You can increase the odds that your readers will accept your conclusions if you help them understand your choices.

Introduction. Rather than launching immediately into your interpretation, begin by introducing readers to your subject and explaining its significance. Provide enough information about your subject—in the form of a summary or description of a text, an overview of a trend, or a report of a recent event—to help readers understand your focus and follow your line of thinking. Another useful strategy is to start by offering some context about the conversation you've decided to join. Consider, for example, how Stephen King begins his analysis of the Harry Potter series.

> The problem with the advance reviews — and those that followed in the first post-publication days — is one that has dogged Rowling's magnum opus ever since book 4 (*Goblet of Fire*), after the series had become a worldwide phenomenon. Due to the Kremlin-like secrecy surrounding the books, all reviews since 2000 or so have been strictly shoot-from-the-lip. The reviewers themselves were often great — Ms. Kakutani ain't exactly chopped liver — but the very popularity of the books has often undone even the best intentions of the best critical writers. In their hurry to churn out column inches, and thus remain members of good standing in the Church of What's Happening Now, very few of the Potter reviewers have said anything worth remembering. Most of this microwaved critical mush sees Harry — not to mention his friends and his adventures — in only two ways: sociologically ("Harry Potter: Boon or Childhood Disease?") or economically ("Harry Potter and the Chamber of Discount Pricing"). They take a perfunctory wave at things like plot and language, but do little more . . . and really, how can they? When you have only four days to read a 750-page book, then write an 1,100-word review on it, how much time do you have to really enjoy the book? To think about the book? Jo Rowling set out a sumptuous seven-course meal, carefully prepared, beautifully cooked, and lovingly served out. The kids and adults who fell in love with the series (I among them) savored every mouthful, from the appetizer (*Sorcerer's Stone*) to the dessert (the gorgeous epilogue of *Deathly Hallows*). Most reviewers, on the other hand, bolted everything down, then obligingly puked it back up half-digested on the book pages of their respective newspapers.
>
> And because of that, very few mainstream writers, from *Salon* to *The New York Times*, have really stopped to consider what Ms. Rowling has wrought, where it came from, or what it may mean for the future. . . .

Conclusion. Because analytical essays so often begin with a question, interpreters frequently withhold the thesis statement (the answer) until the end—after they've given readers sufficient reasons to accept their conclusions as reasonable. You might also wrap up your analysis by contemplating the implications of your interpretation, raising a related question for readers to ponder (as Ali Bizzul does in her final draft; see p. 259), or speculating about the future, as Aida Akl does in her news analysis.

Demographic projections put the U.S. population at 400 million people by 2050. If current population trends continue, most analysts agree that America will be an ethnically different nation.

You can learn more about using your introduction and conclusion to frame the
results of your analysis in Chapter 16.

Organization. The organization of your essay can also help frame your analysis,
because it will affect the order in which you present your reasons and evidence. Your
choice of organizing pattern should take into account your purposes and your readers'
needs and interests. For instance, if you are reporting the results of a trend analysis,
you might want to use chronological order as your organizing pattern. If, in contrast,
you are conducting a causal analysis, you might use the cause-and-effect organizing
pattern. Creating an outline or a map (see p. 550) can also help you organize your
thoughts, especially if your assignment calls for a relatively long essay, if you are
combining interpretive frameworks, or if you expect to present a lot of reasons or
evidence to support your interpretive claim. You can read more about organizing
patterns and outlines in Chapter 16.

Review and Improve Your Draft

Creating the first draft of an analytical essay is a complex and rewarding process. In
the course of learning about a subject, you've developed an interpretive question,
chosen an interpretive framework, and conducted an analysis; you've made and supported an interpretive claim; and you've organized your reasons and evidence and
framed your essay. Once you complete your first draft, you should step back and assess
its strengths and weaknesses. A careful review—done individually and with the help of
others—can help you pinpoint where you should invest time in improving your essay.

ENSURE THAT YOUR CLAIM IS DEBATABLE

If your interpretive claim is not debatable (see p. 250), it will do little to advance the
conversation about your subject. As you review your essay, focus on your interpretive claim, and ask how your readers will react to it. For example, will your interpretive claim lead readers to disagree with you, or will it surprise or shock them? Will it
make them think about the subject in a new way? Will it force them to reconsider
their assumptions? If you think that your readers might respond by asking "so
what?" you should take another look at your claim.

CHALLENGE YOUR CONCLUSIONS

As you review your essay, challenge your findings by considering alternative explanations and asking your own "so what?" questions. Your initial impressions of a subject
will often benefit from additional reflection. Those impressions might be refined, or
perhaps even changed substantially, through additional analysis. Or they might be
reinforced, typically by locating additional evidence.

EXAMINE THE APPLICATION OF YOUR INTERPRETIVE FRAMEWORK

Ask whether you've applied your interpretive framework fairly and rigorously to your subject. If you are carrying out a causal analysis, for example, ask whether you've ruled out the possibility that the causal relationships you are exploring are simply correlations. If you're conducting a text analysis, ask whether you've fully and fairly represented the text and whether you have considered alternative interpretations. Review how you've used your interpretive framework to make sure that you've applied it carefully and evenhandedly to your subject.

ASSESS YOUR ORGANIZATION

When readers can anticipate the sequence of reasoning and evidence that appears in your analytical essay, they'll conclude that the essay is well organized. If an essay is

Peer Review: Improve Your Analytical Essay

One of the biggest challenges writers face is reading a draft of their own work as a reader rather than as the writer. Because you know what you're trying to say, you find it easy to understand your draft. To determine how you should revise your draft, ask a friend or classmate to read your essay and consider how well you've adopted the role of interpreter (see p. 210).

Purpose	1. Is my interpretive claim clear and easy to understand? Is it debatable?
	2. Have I offered a careful and thorough analysis to support my claim?
Readers	3. Did the essay help you understand my subject in a new way? Why or why not?
	4. Does the analysis seem fair to you? Did you notice any cherry-picking? Can you think of any aspects of my subject that I neglected to consider?
Sources	5. Are the reasons I've offered for my interpretation coherent? Have I provided enough evidence to support each reason? Should I add or drop anything?
	6. Do my sources strike you as reliable and appropriate? Does any of the evidence I've used seem questionable?
Context	7. Did I provide enough (or too much) information about my subject to ground the analysis?
	8. Does the interpretive framework I've chosen seem like an appropriate choice for analyzing my subject? Would a different framework have been more effective?

For each of the points listed above, ask your reviewers to provide concrete advice about what you could do to improve your draft. It can help if you ask them to adopt the role of an editor — someone who is working with you to improve your draft. You can read more about working collaboratively in Chapter 4.

@ Download or print this Peer Review activity at bedfordstmartins.com/conversation.

confusing or difficult to follow, however, they'll conclude that it is poorly written or, worse, that the analysis is flawed. As you review your essay, ask whether your reasons and evidence seem easy to follow. If you find yourself growing puzzled as you try to read your essay, take another look at your choice of organizational pattern. Check, as well, whether your reasons are presented in an order that allows them to build on one another. If you have difficulty figuring out how you've organized your essay, consider creating a backward outline, an outline based on an already written draft. You can read more about organizing your essay and outlining in Chapter 16.

Once you've revised your essay, ask yourself how you might polish and edit your writing so that your readers will find your analysis easy to read. For a detailed discussion of polishing strategies, see Chapter 19. For an overview of editing strategies, see Chapter 20.

 ## Student Essay

Ali Bizzul, "Living (and Dying) Large"

The following analytical essay was written by featured writer Ali Bizzul. You can follow Ali's efforts to write her analytical essay by visiting **bedfordstmartins.com/conversation**. You can read excerpts of interviews in which she discusses her work on her analytical essay, read the assignment, and read drafts of her essay. Ali's essay follows the requirements of the sixth edition of the *APA Publication Manual*. However, this edition does not include specific instructions for formatting student essays, so Ali's essay has been formatted to fit typical requirements for undergraduate student writing. To see Ali's essay formatted for an APA publication, please visit **bedfordstmartins.com/conversation**.

Living (and Dying) Large 1

Information about the writer, class, and submission date is provided on the cover page.

Living (and Dying) Large

Ali Bizzul

COCC150 College Composition

Professor Palmquist

September 20, 2009

Living (and Dying) Large 2

Living (and Dying) Large

Bigger is better — or so says the adage that seems to drive much of American culture. From fast food to television sets to the "average" house, everything seems to be getting bigger. This is especially true for the athletes who play America's favorite fall sport — football. Twelve- and thirteen-year-olds are bulking up so they can make their junior-high football teams. High school players are adding weight to earn college scholarships. And the best college players are pulling out all the stops in hopes of making an NFL team. All of this is occurring despite the belief of many football coaches that extra weight does little to enhance a football player's performance — and might even derail it. Even worse, the drive to put on the pounds carries significant health risks for football players, both now and later in life. Despite what they believe, overweight players are less effective than their lighter peers — and at far greater risk of devastating harm.

While football requires both strength and speed, the media image of pro football players focuses mostly on their weight. NFL offensive linemen who weigh less than 300 pounds are often described as "undersized," so it's no surprise that young football players are getting the message that bigger is better — and bulking up. A recent study of high school linemen in Iowa showed that 45% were overweight and 9% were severely obese, while only 18% of other young males were overweight; even more troubling, a study in Michigan revealed that among football players from ages 9 to 14, 45% could be considered overweight or obese (as cited in Longman, 2007). Even those players who recognize that their size is unhealthy are reluctant to trim down. Consider Jeffery Espadron, a high school player who weighs 332 pounds: He is willing to lose some weight, but he refuses to go below 300 pounds because he sees NFL linemen weighing in at 290 to 300 pounds and believes he must do the same (Longman, 2007). As younger players like Espadron follow the footsteps of ever-bigger college and professional line-

---

The title is centered.

The writer frames the subject by calling attention to a common saying and then arguing that it does not apply to this case.

The essay's main point

First reason supporting the analysis: a connection between the behavior of NFL players and players as young as 9 years of age

Following APA style, information cited in a source is identified using the phrase "as cited in."

APA style uses author names and publication dates to identify sources.

Living (and Dying) Large 3

men, they appear to believe that simply packing on the pounds will get them recognized by colleges and maybe even the NFL.

In order to add weight and muscle mass quickly, however, some football players go to dangerous extremes. Many have even turned to legal but unproven dietary supplements as a way of increasing muscle mass, and in some cases, the consequences have been fatal. Minnesota Viking Korey Stringer, a 335-pound offensive lineman who was believed to be taking a dietary supplement, died of heatstroke during a July 2001 training camp; four years later, San Francisco offensive tackle Thomas Herrion died of heart disease after a preseason game (Korth, 2006). Although such fatalities are unusual, a growing number of doctors believe that use of dietary supplements increases the risk of heatstroke among football players. In an editorial in the medical journal *Neurosurgery*, three sports-medicine specialists noted that after a 1994 federal law exempted dietary supplements from regulation by the Food and Drug Administration, heat-related injuries among football players began to rise (Bailes, Cantu, & Day, 2002). They further argued that the increase appears to be related to the use of supplements such as ephedrine and creatine monohydrate (Bailes et al., 2002). Marketed as an energy booster and body builder, ephedrine has an effect similar to amphetamine: It can increase core body temperatures and decrease the body's ability to cool itself. Creatine monohydrate, which is marketed as a muscle builder, can shift body water from the bloodstream into muscle cells, increasing the likelihood of heatstroke. Bailes et al. (2002) noted that, despite such health risks, "the use of nutritional supplements [among football players] seems to be the rule rather than the exception" (p. 287). Many young football players today seem willing to overlook the potential harm in these supplements in the hope of gaining a small advantage on the field.

Heatstroke is not the only danger associated with increased size. Excess weight can cause serious health problems, even if some of the pounds are due to high muscle mass. According to Harp and Hecht (2005), two researchers at

Second reason supporting the analysis: impact of dietary supplements on health

Brackets are used in a quotation to provide missing information.

The page number for the quotation is provided.

Third reason supporting the analysis: effect of excess weight on health

Living (and Dying) Large 4

the University of North Carolina who conducted a study of 2,168 professional football players competing in the 2003–2004 season, 97% of NFL players would be considered "overweight" and 56% "obese" under the Body Mass Index (BMI) guidelines published by the National Institutes of Health for men in their twenties (see Fig. 1). The researchers noted that the group of football players with the highest rates of obesity—the linemen—also had higher blood pressure readings and higher incidences of sleep-disordered breathing than any other group of football players. It appears that athletes are not immune to the effects of obesity, in spite of their active lifestyles.

In addition, a player's large body mass may cause other serious health problems that aren't clear until years later. Added weight can be difficult to lose, and later in life, it can complicate the health of ex-athletes. Sports reporters Korth (2006) and Longman (2007) described studies establishing that diabetes, high blood pressure, heart disease, high cholesterol, joint damage, and sleep apnea are common among those who are overweight, even current or former athletes. As Dr. Tim Kremchek, a team physician for several high schools in the Cincinnati area, has warned, for overweight players,

> the issue is [that] they're not only hurting themselves for the short term, but [that] the long term effects are horrible. They're going to have arthritic problems in their joints. They'll need operations for their cartilage. They'll have herniated discs in their lower backs, they'll have more

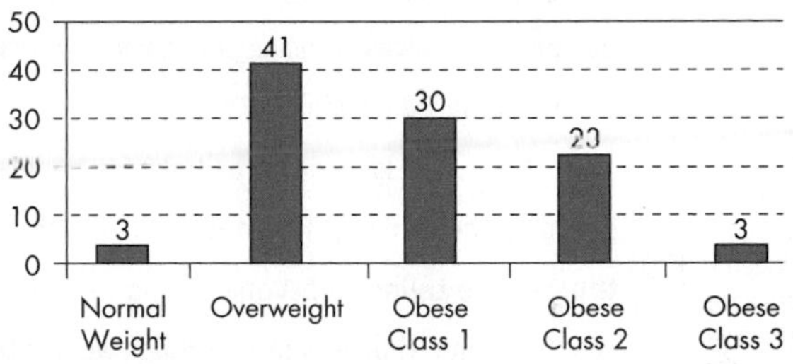

Fig. 1. Percentage of NFL players in National Institutes of Health Body Mass Index categories.

Note. Data from "Research Letter: Obesity in the National Football League," by Joyce B. Harp and Lindsay Hecht, 2005, *Journal of the American Medical Association 293*(9), pp. 1061–1062.

Marginal annotations:

- Summary of a relevant study
- Reference to a figure is provided in the text.
- The figure is wrapped by text and located near its reference in the text. A caption describes the figure, and information about the source of the data for the figure is provided in a note.
- The credentials of an expert cited in a source are provided.
- A block quotation is used to present a longer quotation.

Living (and Dying) Large 5

knee injuries, ankle injuries, hamstrings. . . . (as cited in Groeschen, 2008, para 8)

As dire as Kremchek's warnings sound, such effects are already evident in recently retired NFL players. Barry Pettyjohn, a high school coach and former NFL offensive lineman, increased his weight from 250 pounds to 280 for college, and again to 300 at the beginning of his NFL career; after he stopped playing, his weight ballooned to 375 pounds, and he has had 14 operations on his shoulders, knees, and elbows (Groeschen, 2008). While injuries on the field are often unavoidable, these kinds of self-inflicted injuries are not. It's up to the players themselves to make sure they don't cause their bodies any unnecessary, lasting harm by packing on weight.

Fourth reason supporting the analysis: bigger isn't better when it comes to performance on the field

When professional football players believe that bigger is better despite evidence to the contrary, it is not surprising that athletes as young as twelve and thirteen are trying to become as big as they can as quickly as they can. Most coaches agree that it is skill and not weight that impresses the scouts, but their message is ignored. Their advice to slim down and focus on technique doesn't seem to change the minds of young players, nor do reports of the deaths of college and professional athletes. Instead, the desire to outweigh opponents overshadows everything else. Former Buccaneers lineman Brad Culpepper, for instance, described what went through his mind during routine stops for fast food late at night:

It was gross, but [packing in calories] was the way to keep the weight on. In the back of my mind I thought, "I shouldn't be doing this; it's not healthy." But then the other side says, "Hey, you have to do what you have to do." (as cited in Korth, 2006)

In some sense, comments like these may be an example of players thinking that they are invincible. However, for many young players dreaming of a pro football career, this kind of thinking is both harmful and counterproductive.

Living (and Dying) Large 6

Health issues aside, many football players might be surprised to learn that bigger players aren't necessarily better. The widespread assumption is that larger football players—particularly those playing the line—are more effective than smaller players. Jeffery Espadron, for example, has noticed that college recruiters value bigger players, and he believes that "they're going to notice me because of my size" (as cited in Longman, 2007). Most coaches, however, disagree with that assumption and insist that bulk is a liability. As high school football coach Mickey Joseph commented, "The bigger they are, the worse they are. They can't move. They can't get out of their stance. They're out of breath" (as cited in Longman, 2007). Perhaps this observation should be shared with more professional players as well. In their study of NFL players, Harp and Hecht (2005) found no correlation between higher BMIs and the ranking of NFL teams. In fact, the team with the highest average BMI, the Arizona Cardinals, finished last in the National Football Conference in the 2003–2004 season. Players who deliberately bulk up often sacrifice speed and agility for sheer size, a strategy that does not always pay off when they're on the field.

> A partial quotation is used to support a point.

Given the potential dangers to their health and the fact that being large does little to make them effective players, why do athletes work so hard to get bigger? Perhaps they think the statistics won't apply to them personally—that adding pounds will improve their individual performance. Athletes also know that gaining weight is much easier than gaining muscle, and if weight gives players the slightest advantage, they may think the risks are worth it. Do these players love their sport so much that they will continue to sacrifice their health—or even their lives—for it? They may, if they remain unaware of the consequences, and if they push themselves to their limits without fully understanding the risks.

> In the conclusion, the writer speculates about why athletes are willing to endanger their health.

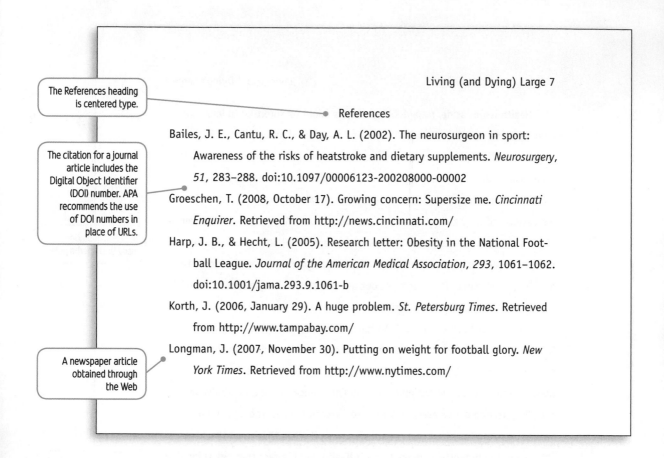

The References heading is centered type.

The citation for a journal article includes the Digital Object Identifier (DOI) number. APA recommends the use of DOI numbers in place of URLs.

A newspaper article obtained through the Web

Living (and Dying) Large 7

References

Bailes, J. E., Cantu, R. C., & Day, A. L. (2002). The neurosurgeon in sport: Awareness of the risks of heatstroke and dietary supplements. *Neurosurgery*, *51*, 283–288. doi:10.1097/00006123-200208000-00002

Groeschen, T. (2008, October 17). Growing concern: Supersize me. *Cincinnati Enquirer*. Retrieved from http://news.cincinnati.com/

Harp, J. B., & Hecht, L. (2005). Research letter: Obesity in the National Football League. *Journal of the American Medical Association*, *293*, 1061–1062. doi:10.1001/jama.293.9.1061-b

Korth, J. (2006, January 29). A huge problem. *St. Petersburg Times*. Retrieved from http://www.tampabay.com/

Longman, J. (2007, November 30). Putting on weight for football glory. *New York Times*. Retrieved from http://www.nytimes.com/

✳ Project Ideas

The following suggestions can help you focus your work on an analytical essay or another type of analytical document.

Suggestions for Essays

1. ANALYZE AN ACADEMIC TREND

Identify a trend in a field of study that interests you. For instance, you might have noticed the increasing use of statistical methods and advanced mathematics in biology courses, a decreasing emphasis on politics and great leaders in history courses, or a new focus on ethics in business courses. Confirm that the trend exists, and then analyze its implications for students in the discipline. To support your analysis, consult scholarly journals, survey instructors in the field, or interview students who are majoring in the field.

2. SPECULATE ABOUT A POPULAR TREND

Write an essay that explores a popular trend, such as the rise in popularity of a particular kind of music or growing interest in a particular area of study. Address your essay to your instructor. In your essay, describe the trend and provide evidence that shows how it has developed over time. To support your analysis, draw on written sources, or conduct field research using interviews, observations, or surveys.

3. TRACE THE CAUSES OF A RECENT EVENT

Interpret a recent event for an audience of your choice, such as your classmates, other college students, your instructor, your parents, or members of the community. The event might be a local ballot initiative, a natural disaster affecting your region, an incident involving law enforcement officers and college students, or anything you've read about in the news that intrigues or worries you. In your essay, describe the event and provide an analysis of its possible causes. Draw on written sources, interviews, or observations to support your analysis.

4. ASSESS THE EFFECTS OF A HISTORICAL EVENT

Analyze the long-term consequences of a historical event for an audience of your choice. You might direct your essay to your instructor, your classmates, other college students, your friends, or people working in a particular profession. Choose a historical event that has implications for your audience. For example, if you are writing for people from your hometown, you might choose to write about something that occurred when the town was founded. If you are writing for your instructor or classmates, you might choose something related to education, such as the passage of Title IX, which banned discrimination on the basis of sex in educational programs that receive federal funding, or the Morrill Act, which established public land-grant universities. In your essay, describe the event clearly, identify the sources you used to learn about it, and discuss the implications of the event for your readers.

5. ANALYZE AN ADVERTISEMENT

Write an essay that uses text analysis to interpret an advertisement. Address your essay to your instructor. Choose an ad that interests you, and develop an interpretive question to guide your analysis. For example, you might ask how ads for a credit card company attempt to elicit a positive response from readers, or you might ask how an ad for a popular brand of beer distinguishes the beer from its competitors. If possible, include part or all of the ad as an illustration in your essay. To support your analysis, draw on written sources, or conduct field research using interviews, observations, or surveys.

Suggestions for Other Genres

6. DRAFT AND DESIGN A COLUMN FOR A MAGAZINE

First decide whether you want to write about a particular subject or submit your column to a particular magazine. If you have a specific subject in mind, search your library's databases and the Web for articles that address it. This can help you identify magazines that might be interested in your column. If you want to publish your column in a particular magazine, read two or three issues cover-to-cover to determine the kinds of subjects it normally addresses. Once you've selected a target magazine, analyze it to determine its writing conventions (such as the level of formality and the manner in which sources are acknowledged) and design conventions. As you learn about your subject and plan, organize, and design your column, keep in mind what you've learned about the columns you've read. Your column should reflect those writing and design conventions.

7. CREATE A NEWS ANALYSIS

Begin working on your news analysis by identifying an event to analyze. Consider whether analyzing this event will help you accomplish your purposes as a writer. Then reflect on whether your readers will want or need to know about the event. Finally, identify the newspaper, magazine, or Web site where you'd like to publish your news analysis. Once you've made these preliminary decisions, learn more about the event by consulting your library's databases. Use what you learn about the event to plan, organize, and design your news analysis. Be sure to seek feedback on your drafts from other writers (friends, classmates, relatives) and from your instructor.

8. DEVELOP A MULTIMEDIA PRESENTATION

Begin working on your presentation by considering your purpose and your audience. After you've chosen a subject and conducted your analysis, identify the overall point you want to convey; choose the reasons you'll use to convince your readers to accept your analysis; and identify the evidence you'll use to support your reasons. Then consider the setting in which your audience will view your presentation, choose an organization for your points, and select an appealing and consistent design for your slides. Remember that an effective slide usually focuses on a single point and provides a limited amount of information to support that point. As you develop your presentation, ask for feedback from friends, classmates, instructors, or relatives.

9. ANALYZE A POEM, SHORT STORY, OR NOVEL

Analyze a poem, short story, or novel that you've read recently. Address your analysis to your instructor and other readers who share your interest in this work of literature. Focus on a clearly stated interpretive question and use text analysis as your interpretive framework. Support your analysis by drawing on the work of literature and published reviews or journal articles. In your essay, identify and briefly describe the work you're analyzing. Then offer your interpretation of the work.

10. POST A BLOG ENTRY

Identify a subject that is suitable for analysis and likely to interest a general group of readers. Then create a blog entry that analyzes the subject. As you write your entry, consider the possibilities and limitations associated with writing for the Web, and in particular for a blog. In your blog entry, provide enough background information on your subject to ground your analysis, introduce your interpretive question, and present your analysis. You should support your analysis by drawing on the subject and linking to other documents on the Web.

In Summary: Writing an Analytical Essay

○ **Find a conversation and listen in**
- Explore your surroundings (p. 234).
- Ask interpretive questions (p. 235).
- Search databases (p. 237).

○ **Conduct your analysis.**
- Refine your question (p. 239).
- Seek a fuller understanding of your subject (p. 240).
- Apply an interpretive framework (p. 242).

○ **Prepare a draft.**
- Make an interpretive claim (p. 250).
- Explain your interpretation (p. 251).
- Consider genre and design (p. 254).
- Frame your analysis (p. 256).

○ **Review and improve your draft.**
- Ensure that your claim is debatable (p. 257).
- Challenge your conclusions (p. 257).
- Examine the application of your interpretive framework (p. 258).
- Assess your organization (p. 258).

08 Writing to Evaluate

As an *evaluator,*
I write with
certain criteria
in mind.

GENRES IN CONVERSATION

| Reflective Writing | Informative Writing | Analytical Writing | **Evaluative Writing** | Problem-Solving Writing | Argumentative Writing |

Rising rates of childhood obesity have sparked interest in extracurricular programs that encourage physical activity. But what works best? A nonprofit organization focused on youth fitness sought to identify various outreach programs and to gauge their effectiveness. The organization's staff found a large number of documents about the subject. Three—a **newsletter article,** a **bibliography,** and an **article from a scholarly journal**—illustrate how different genres can be used to address distinct audiences.

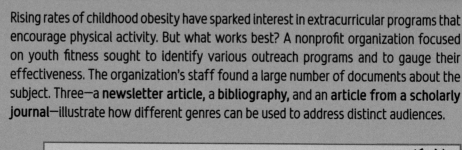

SFHP Funds Ten Access Improvement Projects

We know that providing health insurance isn't enough to improve the health of our members. We need to make sure members can see providers quickly when they have a problem. **One of our strategic goals, therefore, is to improve access to services.** But how?

"We could have spent a lot of time and money studying the problem," said Ellen Kaiser, SFHP's Director of Planning and Evaluation. "But in my 20 years of experience in large and small health care organizations, such studies never give you answers that you can act upon. So I suggested to our Governing Board that we **ask our providers to tell us what the problems are and give them the money to solve them."**

Based on this innovative approach, SFHP created the Access Enhancement Fund. The Governing Board **used $800,000 that SFHP won in a one-time settlement of a lawsuit with the State Department of Health Services** to fund it.

Access Enhancement Fund Award Recipients

- UCSF/SFGH Children's Health Center for weekend & evening appointments
- SFGH Dept. of Opthalmology for equipment for a mobile program to provide eye services at community health centers
- Los Portales Family Medical Center for a Spanish-speaking physician assistant to increase appointments for monolingual Spanish speakers
- North East Medical Services (NEMS) for a new telephone system that will make it easier for members to reach their physicians, and will include a nurse advice line
- Sunset Health Services for a nurse to provide telephone advice and same-day appointments
- San Francisco Hearing & Speech Center for a bi-lingual speech therapist to assist Spanish-speaking children
- San Francisco General Hospital for equipment to expand their urgent care center
- Valencia Health Services for a nurse to provide telephone advice triage demand for urgent and same-day appointments
- UCSF/SFGH Children's Health Center for hiring a nurse practitioner to improve access to patients with asthma
- Ocean-Park Health Center for a program to improve access to care for diabetics by using group visits and non-physician specialists

Through this fund, SFHP is granting $800,000 for ten projects in seven organizations.

"Non-profit health care systems cannot readily access the newest technologies that make health care more efficient," said Linda Bien, CEO of NEMS. "After years of insufficient funding, we've all fallen behind in using technology to make our services more efficient and effective. Our grant will go a long way toward allowing us to catch up."

Nearly 800 Children Receive Well-Checks Through New Program

(in just two months!)

Our latest program is a birthday card **offering a $15 Toys R Us gift certificate to parents who take their 3 to 6-year-old in for a well-visit.** And are SFHP parents interested? Absolutely!

Since its December 2003 implementation - less than two months ago - 800 birthday card claim tickets have been returned to SFHP, indicating that a child has received a well-check.

In the past, we noted that parents who had taken their infants and toddlers in regularly were not scheduling check-ups when their children got older. We found that the barrier was not the doctors, who wanted to see the children, but the busy parents who couldn't remember that their kids needed annual check-ups. So we decided to see if we could encourage our parents to make appointments with a reminder and an incentive.

"The initial response from parents has been overwhelming," said Dr. Michael van Duren, SFHP Medical Director. "Doctors like it too because they get to check in with parents on all sorts of developmental issues that they don't have time to address during a visit with a sick kid."

With this second successful member-oriented incentive, **we are looking at other areas that may be ripe for similar programs.** If you have any ideas, please email them to mvanduren@sfhp.org.

Gateway to Fitness Proves a *Greatway to Fitness* for Teens!

Last season we told you about San Francisco Health Plan's Gateway to Fitness program: a six-week program exposing teens to physical activities to which they wouldn't ordinarily have access.

Over 50 teens participated in the six-week pilot program, and some participants clearly were motivated: One member is now promoting an empowerment fitness program exclusively for teen girls!

"Our participants responded to two very important program aspects," said Lucy Smiles, Gateway to Fitness Program Coordinator. "Variety and choice. They decided for themselves which activities they wanted to continue with. It's an empowering part of growth that many found attractive."

We are now trying to decide how to broaden the program so we can reach the hundreds of SFHP members who need more physical activity. (Jean Fraser, our CEO and an avid bike commuter, would like to get all the kids on bikes, but the rest of the SFHP staff hold her back!)

One idea we are exploring is to encourage providers to give prescriptions for exercise to SFHP members along with temporary Boys & Girls Clubs membership cards. When a teen member presents the card at a Boys & Girls Club, SFHP would pay for a one-year membership.

"Due to public policy and lifestyle decisions, it will take years to reverse bad health habits in teens," commented Rowena Tarantino, SFHP Health Education Manager. "But that's the very reason why SFHP is involved. **We simply will not pass the buck as everyone else** does by saying 'It's not a covered service.'"

If you have an idea or comment about Gateway to Fitness, please email lsmiles@sfhp.org.

To subscribe to SFHP's Here for You, email info@sfhp.org, or call (415) 547-7818 ext. 261

Newsletter ▶

This **newsletter** uses color, bold fonts, and columns to publicize and introduce the San Francisco Health Plan's Gateway to Fitness program to a general audience.

Bibliography

This online **bibliography** provides health professionals and policy makers with links to the Harvard Family Research Project's evaluations of youth sports programs.

The Evaluation Exchange | FINE Network | OST Database | My Order

Harvard Family Research Project

Advanced Search — Go

| Home | Research Areas | Publications & Resources | HFRP News | About HFRP |

HFRP > Publications & Resources > Browse Our Publications > Health and Sports/Recreation Program Evaluations

PUBLICATIONS & RESOURCES

> Search Publications
> **Browse Our Publications**
> Publications Series
> How to Order Publications
> Order Form

Sign up to receive our latest News & Publications at our Subscription Center →

🖶 Print this page
✉ Send to a friend
+A Large text size
A Normal text size
-A Small text size
RSS

March 2005

Health and Sports/Recreation Program Evaluations

Erin Harris

The Harvard Family Research Project (HFRP) Out-of-School Time Program Evaluation Bibliography and Out-of-School Time Program Research and Evaluation Database both provide information on evaluations that have been conducted on sports/recreation and health-related out-of-school time (OST) programs, among other categories.

Out-of-School Time Program Research and Evaluation Bibliography

Our Out-of-School Time Program Research and Evaluation Bibliography contains citations for all the OST program evaluations that we are currently tracking. In our bibliography we provide basic program information as well as links to relevant evaluation reports. The bibliography is categorized by program type and includes both the category "Health" and the category "Sports/Recreation." The following programs are included in our bibliography in these two categories.

Health Programs

- Be Proud! Be Responsible!
- EarthFriends
- Hip Hop to Health
- Kids on the Move Program* (also in the Sports/Recreation category)
- NikeGO After School Program* (also in the Sports/Recreation category)
- Project 4-Health
- Rural Massachusetts Residential Summer Weight Loss Camp (also in the Sports/Recreation category)
- Workers of Wonder (also in the Sports/Recreation category)

Sports/Recreation Programs

- 4-H Youth Development Program—Project Castlerock
- After-School Express
- Austin City Council After School Programs
- Baltimore's After School Strategy—A-Teams*
- Career Horizons Program
- Chicago Lighthouse Program
- Cooke Middle School After School Recreation Program*
- Fairfax County Youth-Directed Teen Centers
- Girlfriends for KEEPS (Keys to Eating, Exercising, Playing, and Sharing)
- Grand Slam Program

Article Information

- Full Text (HTML)
- Request reprint permission
- How to cite
- Download Acrobat

Related Resources

- Aiming for Accountability: Minnesota
- The Guide to Results-Based Accountability: Annotated Bibliography of Publications, Websites, and Other Resources
- The Quality of School-Age Child Care in After-School Settings

---

Scholarly Article ▶

This **scholarly article** in a peer-reviewed journal reports the results of a scientific study of an extracurricular fitness program in Georgia schools to university faculty and researchers.

AN AFTER-SCHOOL PHYSICAL ACTIVITY PROGRAM FOR OBESITY PREVENTION IN CHILDREN
The Medical College of Georgia FitKid Project

ZENONG YIN
Medical College of Georgia

JOHN HANES, JR.
Regent University

JUSTIN B. MOORE
University of Louisville

PATRICIA HUMBLES
PAULE BARBEAU
BERNARD GUTIN
Medical College of Georgia

This article describes the process of setting up a 3-year, school-based after-school physical activity intervention in elementary schools. The primary aim of the study is to determine whether adiposity and fitness will improve in children who are exposed to a fitogenic versus an obesogenic environment. Eighteen schools were randomized to the control (obesogenic) or intervention (fitogenic) group. The study design, program components, and evaluation of the intervention are described in detail. The intervention consists of (a) academic enrichment, (b) a healthy snack, and (c) physical activity in a mastery-oriented environment. Successful implementation would show the feasibility of schools' being able to provide a fitogenic environment. Significant differences between the groups would provide evidence that a fitogenic environment after school has positive health benefits. If feasibility and efficacy are demonstrated, implementing an after-school program like this one in elementary schools could play a major role in preventing and reducing childhood obesity.

Keywords: prevention; children; physical activity; obesity; after-school program

AUTHORS' NOTE: The MCG FitKid Project is funded by the National Institute of Diabetes and Digestive and Kidney Diseases (RO1 DK93361). The authors would like to thank the FitKid students, their parents, and the Richmond County Board of Education for their cooperation and participation in this study. They also want to thank Janet Thornburg, Marlo Cavnar, and FitKid Instructors for their assistance in the implementation of the study. Correspondence concerning this article can be sent to Zenong Yin, University of Texas at San Antonio, Department of Health and Kinesiology, 6900 North Loop 1604 West, San Antonio, TX 78249; e-mail: zenong.yin@utsa.edu.

EVALUATION & THE HEALTH PROFESSIONS, Vol. 28 No. 1, March 2005 67-89
DOI: 10.1177/0163278704273079
© 2005 Sage Publications

What Is Writing to Evaluate?

Evaluative writing isn't just common—it's something readers are likely to seek out. We search for reviews of new movies and restaurants; we surf the Web to learn about the strengths and weaknesses of products ranging from treadmills to GPS devices to insect repellents; and we read editorials, letters to the editor, and columns in online magazines in the hope that they will help us develop an informed opinion about recent issues and events.

Writing to evaluate involves adopting the role of *evaluator*. Writers who adopt this role focus on reaching an informed, well-reasoned conclusion about a subject's worth or effectiveness and clearly conveying their judgment to readers. Their writing is usually balanced, and they generally offer clear reasoning and ample evidence to support their judgments.

Writers typically evaluate a subject with one of two general goals: to determine whether something has succeeded or failed, or to help readers understand how something might be improved or refined. They form their conclusions by learning about their subject and considering how well it meets a given set of *criteria*—the standards or principles on which judgments are based.

Readers of evaluations typically share the writer's interest in a subject and hope to learn more about it. They often share the writer's assumptions about which criteria are appropriate—few readers, for example, expect movie reviewers to justify their choice of criteria. Readers expect the writer to provide evidence and reasoning to support his or her judgments, and readers usually want the writer to acknowledge and address alternative opinions about the subject. In fact, not only are readers likely to know that alternative opinions exist (usually through reading other evaluations), but they might also hold those opinions themselves. As a result, readers are likely to dismiss an evaluation that seems unfair or unaware of different points of view.

The Writer's Role: Evaluator

PURPOSE

- To determine whether something has succeeded or failed
- To improve or refine something

READERS

- Want another person's opinion
- Expect judgments to be based on appropriate criteria and supported with evidence and analysis

SOURCES

- The subject itself is often an important source of evidence.
- Published documents, personal experiences, and, in some cases, interviews and observations provide additional support.
- Reviewing other sources alerts evaluators to alternative opinions and perspectives.

CONTEXT

- Decisions about criteria and evidence reflect a writer's knowledge of readers, of the subject, and of its background and setting.
- Effective evaluations balance positive and negative assessments and acknowledge alternative perspectives.

Writers' decisions about criteria and evidence are shaped by the contexts in which they find themselves. Writers who address a general audience, for example, might need to define their criteria carefully, while those who write to professionals in a particular field might reasonably expect their readers to be familiar with the criteria they've selected. Similarly, a writer's choice of evidence reflects the nature of the subject and readers' knowledge, expertise, and social and cultural backgrounds. For instance, an evaluation of a creative production such as a movie or a television documentary will usually draw most heavily on the subject itself for evidence, citing examples from the work and referring to expectations about the genre to support the writer's judgments. An evaluation of a building restoration project, on the other hand, is likely to bring in evidence from outside sources — such as budget reports, building codes, and interviews with community members and architects — to support the writer's assessment of the project's relative success or failure and recommendations for improving it.

Evaluative documents make important contributions not only to our personal lives but also to written conversations. On an individual level, evaluations help us make decisions that can affect everything from the brand of car we drive to how we vote in the next election to where we attend college. Within a written conversation, evaluations provide the basis for making collective judgments about how to move the conversation forward.

What Kinds of Documents Are Used to Share Evaluations?

Writers can draw on a wide range of documents to share their judgments. Their evaluations might appear in print, as is often the case with articles and editorials, or on the Web, which is increasingly home to reviews, many of them posted to discussion boards and electronic mailing lists. In writing and writing-intensive courses, the most frequently assigned evaluative projects include essays, reports, blog entries, and source evaluations.

Evaluative documents make important contributions to conversations that focus on the relative merits of products, media, policies, proposals, and artistic works, and they often stand on their own as assessments, opinions, or advice that readers seek out as they try to form their own judgments. Evaluations can also contribute to broader conversations that focus less on judgment alone and more on problem solving

View a multimedia example of evaluative writing in the e-book at **bedfordstmartins.com/ conversation**.

or argument. For example, an evaluative report on a U.S. government program might help a writer support a proposal to change foreign policy. The following sections offer discussions and examples of some of the most common evaluative genres: product reviews, media reviews, place evaluations, progress reports, and evaluative essays.

Product Reviews

A product review offers a writer's assessment of something readers might purchase, such as a cell phone, frozen dinner, or running shoe. The review considers how well a product measures up to the writer's expectations, with criteria usually centered around some combination of the manufacturer's claims and the product's benefits, drawbacks, and value. Evidence for product reviews typically comes from the reviewer's experiences with the products as well as from information in published sources. A writer evaluating a new line of running shoes, for example, might focus on comfort, weight, cushioning, cost, and durability. To gain insights into subjective issues such as comfort and cushioning, the reviewer would probably run a few miles in each pair of shoes. To compare more objective considerations such as weight and cost, the reviewer would most likely rely on the manufacturer's specifications. If the writer was conducting a long-term evaluation, criteria such as durability could also be assessed through personal experience.

Product reviews vary widely in length and appearance. Depending on where they are published (for example, in a magazine or newspaper, on a Web site, or in a blog), writers might use headings and subheadings, lists, or tables to help readers find and compare information quickly and easily. Similarly, the style and voice used in product reviews reflect the writer's purpose as well as an understanding of readers' expectations. Some reviews, particularly those published in popular media such as fan magazines, blogs, and Web sites, might deliberately show a great deal of bias or use highly informal language to engage readers' interest. In most cases, however, reviewers adopt an impartial, balanced tone to assure readers that the judgments are fair.

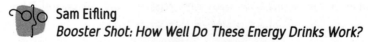

Sam Eifling
Booster Shot: How Well Do These Energy Drinks Work?

The following review of energy drinks, written by Sam Eifling for the online magazine *Slate*, relies heavily on the author's personal reactions to consuming the drinks. Despite his informal style, Eifling specifies his criteria clearly and applies them evenly. His choice of details and his tone reflect his awareness of his readers and the context in which he is writing. He is aware, for example, that many readers will be generally familiar with energy drinks but might lack specific knowledge about how they work and affect the people who drink them. He is also aware of the expanded possibilities for design offered by an online magazine such as *Slate*, which allows him to make extensive use of links and to provide readers with tools for tagging, discussing, and responding to the review. Eifling's work has also appeared in the *Chicago Tribune*, the *Miami Herald*, *Florida Today*, *New York*, and ESPN.com.

Slate

print | share | discuss | RSS

Booster Shot: How well do those energy drinks work?

By Sam Eifling

In spring of last year, some dudes in the park began passing out samples of Red Bull, the omnipresent energy drink, while I was playing football. I chugged a can. Immediately, I felt giddy and off-kilter. I started running around. Some guy with John Elway's arm and Kordell Stewart's aim passed the ball my way. I turned, reached for it, and felt my pinky dislocate at the middle joint. My finger did its impression of a clock face at 2:30 until an ER doctor wrangled it back into place. It took six weeks of physical therapy before I could make a proper fist.

I've had about two-thirds of a Red Bull since. That is, until about half an hour ago, when I cracked open a can. My feet have begun wiggling, unbidden. The TV seems too loud. But, whoa, do my fingers scamper along this keyboard! Red Bull, like most of its energy-drink ilk, claims to perk you up and keep you there — "gives you wings," its ads intone. It must provide something: The company reports that people worldwide consumed almost 2 billion cans of Red Bull in 2004.

Red Bull claims nearly half of the swiftly expanding U.S. energy-drink racket — the industry grew 74 percent last year. John Sicher, editor and publisher of *Beverage Digest*, attributes the drinks' tremendous growth to "consumers' growing interest in functional foods." A can of Coke keeps you awake, gives that sugar rush, rots your teeth, weakens your bones, softens your love handles. Black coffee has so little measurable nutritional value that the FDA doesn't require it to carry a label.

Most energy drinks, on the other hand, provide some combination of B vitamins (which help convert sugar to energy and help regulate red blood cells, which deliver oxygen), amino acids (e.g., taurine), antioxidants (milk thistle, vitamin C), and stimulants, ranging from the reliable (caffeine, guarana) to the alleged (horny goat weed). Unfortunately, they also deliver rafts of sugar in the form of maltodextrin, fructose, and glucose. And the citric acid that pervades the drinks isn't a friend of your teeth. Taste is hit or miss (it ranges from fruity to mediciney)—yet hardly critical. You almost want it to taste crappy, because that could mean it's good for you.

But can these energy drinks live up to their pronouncements? Do they improve "performance" and "reaction speed"? To determine this, I bought a slew and evaluated them over several weeks on three factors. First, do they taste like something a person would want to consume, or like chewable aspirin? Second, how do they affect my mental state, including focus, alertness, mood, and ability to play an electronic version of the board game Boggle? Third, how do they affect the way my body feels, both in terms of physical harmony and strenuous activities such as swimming, running, pickup basketball, push-ups, and coin-op arcade basketball? In other words, are these truly "performance" drinks?

The cashier at Food Store gasped when I approached the counter with three separate arm-loads of cans. "Goddamn," she said. "Can't you buy those cheaper at the grocery store?" Not really, unless you buy in bulk, and after imbibing about four gallons of energy drinks over the last month, I declare that prospect unlikely. But I was pleased to find that not all fizzy, fortified syrups are lousy. Herewith, the results, from worst to first.

Mountain Dew Amp Energy Drink

8.4 oz./120 calories
Touts: Vitamins B-6 and B-12, ginseng, taurine, guarana, caffeine.
Warns: "Not recommended for children."
Tastes: Like orangey Mountain Dew with a bitter, toned-down edge.
Effects: I drink a can to keep from nodding off while reading a novel. Immediately I perk up, start tapping my fingers on the book cover, bouncing my foot. No jitters, but a slight head-ache develops above my left ear. It's hard to focus. Boggle's not much better: In the final game, I find only three words on the board. Twenty minutes later, I'm physically and mentally wrung-out, and my stomach aches as though I might vomit unless I eat or drink something. A later sampling does not produce such a nasty reaction, but the flavor does not improve.

Verdict: The warning should be abbreviated to "Not recommended." Definitely the worst of the lot.

Full Throttle Energy Drink by Coca-Cola

16 oz./220 calories

Touts: Vitamins B-3, B-6, and B-12, taurine, ginseng, carnitine, guarana, caffeine.

Warns: Of nothing.

Tastes: Tart and vaguely fruity. Like Alka-Seltzer in Kool-Aid.

Effects: I guzzle a can on the way to take an 8-year-old boy to play in the park. I quickly realize that 16 ounces of anything fizzy is a lot to ask a moving stomach to digest. Other than bloat, I discern no effect, as I'm run ragged in no time. I do play Hoop Fever at the nearest arcade and score a ridiculous 74 points, besting the day's previous mark by 29 points.

Verdict: My concentration and shooting groove were great. As for energy, well, there wasn't much. Sicher predicts that in a few years, only drinks from the larger beverage companies (Pepsi, Coca-Cola, Red Bull, Hansen's) will emerge from the current glut. It'll be a shame if that's the case, considering the mediocre offerings from Pepsi and Coke.

Red Bull

8.3 oz./110 calories

Touts: Vitamins B-3, B 5, B-6, and B-12, taurine.

Claims: The farm. "Improves performance, especially during times of increased stress or strain, increases concentration and improves reaction time, stimulates the metabolism."

Warns: "Avoid while playing potentially harmful contact sports." No, I made that up.

Tastes: Sweet, fizzy, acrid. "Like corn syrup that burns" is one friend's accurate assessment.

Effects: Endows me with some verve that, per usual, dissipates when I start the push-ups. There's no endurance in these cans. To test the claim of "increased stress" I play Boggle while watching *Family Guy* and emerge with wildly varying scores. My stomach feels sour and a headache brews.

Verdict: Beats a trip to the emergency room, but I'm surprised this little can holds half the domestic market, considering how blah it is. The taste, while distinct, isn't exactly pleasant, and the energy it provides is fleeting.

Monster

16 oz./200 calories

Touts: Vitamins B-3, B-6, B-12, and C, taurine, ginseng, inositol, caffeine, L-carnitine.

Warns: "Consume responsibly—limit 3 cans per day. Not recommended for children, pregnant women or people sensitive to caffeine."

Tastes: Like subdued Mountain Dew, with a now-familiar vitaminy edge.

Effects: I see this everywhere, so I assume it's popular—but it has almost no noticeable effect on me. When I do push-ups, my body protests early, as when it's asked to run on too much sugar. In playing pickup basketball, I melt quickly. The thought hits me that perhaps I've acquired a resistance to vitamins and sugar water. On the other hand, the Boggle scores are among the best of any drink tested.

Verdict: A moderate disappointment, considering the bitchin' claw marks on the can. I can't figure out why I seem immune to this, and two other drinks called Energy Pro and Hansen's—all the spawn of Hansen's, the second-largest U.S. energy-drink manufacturer. I recently met an Iraq war veteran (who knows from stimulants) who buys this stuff by the case. Me, I can't see it, although a fair flavor and a lack of ill effects make it a borderline drink.

SoBe No Fear

16 oz./260 calories
Touts: Vitamins B-6, B-12, and C, folic acid, selenium, zinc, taurine, inositol, ginseng, guarana, creatine, grape seed extract, L-carnitine, L-arginine, caffeine.
Claims: "Super energy supplement."
Warns: "Not recommended for children, pregnant women or people sensitive to caffeine."
Tastes: Sweet, mildly fizzy, with a hint of grapefruit.
Effects: It does offer some extra kick first thing in the morning: My arms move faster even when drying myself off after a shower. When I type, my fingers move quickly and with precision. My heart seems to pound too hard during push-ups. I feel alert but distractible. Boggle scores are high; Hoop Fever scores disappointingly mediocre.

Verdict: What I'd reach for if falling asleep at the wheel. Not ideal if you need focus or fine motor skills.

Arizona Tea Caution Energy

8.3 oz./130 calories
Touts: Vitamins B-5, B-6, and B-12, taurine, caffeine, D-ribose, L-carnitine, ginseng, inositol, milk thistle, guarana.
Warns: "Not recommended for children, pregnant women or persons sensitive to caffeine."
Tastes: Like sweet tea with a dash of cough syrup. The only drink aside from Rock Star Cola that isn't completely overwhelmed with the strong citric acid.
Effects: No ill effects. I have strong Boggle scores and two bang-up games of Hoop Fever on this bad baby, scoring 63 and 64 points. Importantly, when I drink a can on an empty stomach, I get neither a headache nor tummy ache.

Verdict: Decent flavor, and the small dose kept me from feeling like I had the attention span of a terrier. One of the better finds. What I'd recommend for people who dislike energy drinks.

Everlast Nutrition Citrus Blast Energy Drink

8.3 oz./140 calories

Touts: Vitamins A, B-3, B-5, B-6, and B-12, caffeine, inositol, taurine.

Claims: "Improves performance, increases concentration, improves reaction speed, increases metabolism."

Warns: "One serving contains about as much caffeine as a cup of coffee. Not intended for young children and persons sensitive to stimulants such as caffeine, or for use with products that may contain stimulants such as medications for allergy, asthma, cough/cold, decongestants, or certain pain relief products. Do not use if pregnant or lactating."

Tastes: Like fizzy, sweet grapefruit juice. Pleasant.

Effects: Boggle scores are mediocre, and after a few minutes, I notice my handwriting deteriorate. But it does sit well when called into duty: I drink it just before playing basketball but after I've imbibed a pint of beer and a happy-hour whiskey. My stomach feels hot with the drink as soon as I start running, and I experience a moment of wooziness. But I recover and hit clutch shots in a game of three-on-three, with enough stamina to hustle on defense at the end.

Verdict: A nice flavor, and it earns plaudits for its slim size; 16 ounces of anything carbonated is too much before a run. Given the apparent boost it gave me in basketball, this drink is what I'd reach for if feeling sluggish before a jog.

Rockstar Energy Cola

16 oz./240 calories

Touts: Vitamins B-2, B-3, B-5, B-6, B-12, and C, caffeine, taurine, guarana, inositol, milk thistle.

Claims: "Party like a rockstar."

Warns: "Not recommended for children or those sensitive to caffeine."

Tastes: Pleasantly metallic. Like a cross between Coke and pennies.

Effects: I drink a can while on deadline. I'm keenly focused, and I'm typing sentences almost too quickly, spitting them out before I finish evaluating them in my head. Meanwhile, my foot bounces on the floor. With a little more verve than usual, I drop to the floor and pound out 15 push-ups in the time usually required to do five. The Boggle scores are on the low side, but no vitamin or caffeine headache accompany this beverage. In fact, it's kind of fun.

Verdict: Better for you than a can of Coke, and it doesn't leave that squeaky residue on your teeth. Out of the dozens of cans I mowed through, Rockstar Cola is the only drink that offers that feeling of physical exuberance you expect from an energy drink. And it's the only one I'd actually want to consume again anytime soon. To me, coffee remains king for a pick-me-up, but among this group, Rockstar rolls.

Starting a Conversation: Respond to "Booster Shot"

In your writer's notebook, record your reaction to Eifling's review by responding to the following questions:

1. "Booster Shot" is an evaluation of energy drinks. But Eifling uses a tone that is far removed from that of an objective product reviewer. How does Eifling come across as a writer? What does his manner reveal about his purpose?

2. Eifling begins his introduction by recounting his physical reaction to consuming a can of Red Bull. He then goes on to test similar products on himself and reports the results to support his conclusions. How does this approach affect the usefulness of his evaluation for readers?

3. Eifling refers to the "swiftly expanding" market for energy drinks and "consumers' growing interest in functional foods" (par. 3). He also cites the advertising language and claims for each of these products. What do these references imply about his understanding of the social and cultural contexts surrounding his review?

4. What are Eifling's criteria for evaluating these products, and where are they presented in the review? What do they suggest about the needs, interests, knowledge, and background of his readers?

5. Reviewers often choose to be balanced in their assessments. What evidence can you find of Eifling's balance and fairness in the essay? Similarly, what biases or assumptions does he seem to bring to the article, and where are they evident?

@ Download or print this Starting a Conversation activity at bedfordstmartins.com/conversation.

Media Reviews

Media reviews present an evaluation of a work of art, a song or music album, a television program, a book, a movie or play, a computer game, a DVD, a Web site, or any of a number of other cultural productions. The subject of the review reflects the shared interests of the group of writers and readers involved in a written conversation. For example, a group of horror fans might be interested in a new film based on one of Dean Koontz's novels, while people who play a particular video game will probably be interested in the latest version of the game.

Because media reviewers expect their readers to understand what's necessary for success in a particular medium, they often do not define their criteria. For example, a movie critic will assume that readers are familiar with the importance of acting, plot, and cinematography. The evidence used to determine whether the subject of a review has met the criteria for success is most often drawn from the subject itself and from the reviewer's personal interpretation, although writers sometimes include evidence from interviews, surveys, or published sources to support their evaluation.

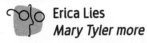

Erica Lies
Mary Tyler more

"Mary Tyler more" is a media review from *Bitch* magazine, a publication focused on feminist interpretations of popular culture. In it, Texas-based writer and performer Erica Lies evaluates the television show *30 Rock* and focuses on its star and creator, Tina Fey. Lies offers insight into the program's commercial and critical success but also discusses Fey's place in the larger context of women and television comedy. For the writer, both Fey and the character she plays represent a significant development in the role of women in American media and culture. In making her case, Lies depends not only on her own broad knowledge of gender and television but also on her readers' breadth of reference and sensitivity to feminist issues.

Mary Tyler more

Why Tina Fey is the best thing to happen to women in TV comedy

by Erica Lies

In a memorable episode of *30 Rock*, an awkward Liz Lemon stands with a lingerie-clad Jenna Maroney at a photo shoot, exclaiming unconvincingly, "Wow, this is . . . an honor. I'm friends with No. 4 on *Maxim*'s list of the sexiest women in comedy!" Maroney, the star performer in *The Girlie Show*, the TV sketch-comedy program for which Lemon is the chief writer, clutches a rubber chicken and just as unconvincingly insists that posing for *Maxim* will be a smart career move — even as she comically fails to achieve "sexy" when her grease-slathered legs slide off a leather chaise in the shoot.

It's a funny scene, and not just because it takes the just-out-of-the-pool imitation sex appeal of *Maxim*'s buxom babes to its laughable extreme. In fact, the scene's humor is hilariously meta, considering that Jenna's fictional appearance in *Maxim* was no coincidence, but part of a product-placement deal among Verizon, *Maxim*, and *30 Rock*. And

it's rooted in offscreen history, too: Fey herself was number 80 on *Maxim*'s "Hot 100 of 2002," taking her place on the list alongside usual suspects Tara Reid and Elisha Cuthbert — although Fey didn't pose for the list. When asked about her selection as a lad-mag hottie, Fey told *Believer* in 2004, "The *Maxim* thing was a little weird. It's probably a career move, but not one I care to be a part of."

The career moves Fey has chosen have been much smarter — creating and starring in the self-referential *30 Rock* has provided ample opportunity to influence the culture she loves to mock. The first season of *30 Rock* introduced us to Lemon, whose primary problems take the form of her insecure, egotistical staff of writers and performers, a nonexistent personal life, and a slimy corporate boss, Jack Donaghy, who is forever offering her advice. A comedy about making a comedy, *30 Rock* borrows material from Fey's own experiences as *Saturday Night Live* head writer, forming a metacommentary that gestures outside the show to satirize gender relations as well as politics, race, and the increasingly corporate media. While awkwardness in a lead character is nothing new in prime-time comedy, it's generally reserved for a universally relatable male character. Lemon stands out because she's a woman—and, specifically, a nerdy one. To top it off, she's played by an actual comedy writer, not a starlet.

Like Fey herself, Lemon is a professional comedy geek who wears glasses and makes crass jokes. Lemon pairs blazers with jeans and Converse shoes, and though she's successful in the cutthroat comedy world, she gets lettuce stuck in her hair. Her name suggests imminent disaster—the sour fruit, the letdown car, the Liz Lemon. A self-described square ("I don't drink. Don't do any drugs—except for my allergy medication"), Lemon is a bumbling manager with a history of awkwardly truncated romantic relationships and a boundless knack for *Star Wars* references. But in Lemon—the supposedly unfeminine, socially awkward, lonely-though-successful woman—Fey has created a brainy female character rarely seen at the center of a comedy.

While few are interested in challenging Fey's critical acclaim and comic chops, some folks have balked at *30 Rock*'s self-deprecating humor. Writing in the pages of this very publication, Sarah Seltzer lamented that Lemon's character perpetuates stereotypes attached to powerful women, citing the punch lines aimed at Lemon that highlight her status as "woefully single" and "allegedly unattractive" ("Sour Lemon," no. 36). Of course, half of the joke is that Fey is attractive, but Seltzer raises an important question: How exactly do audiences interpret humor that mocks a female character? And how does that self-deprecating humor function? The series aims many a punch line at Lemon's perceived lack of femininity ("She thought you looked like Jennifer Jason Leigh. I made her repeat it. I was sure she meant Jason Lee."), but who exactly is the butt of the joke? Is it Lemon, for falling short of society's feminine ideal, or is it the society that emphasizes that ideal? Recent male television characters have had the luxury of being aggressively antisocial (*Curb Your Enthusiasm*'s Larry David), or unhappily single (*Arrested Development*'s Michael Bluth). Yet their unflattering qualities aren't attributed to their gen-

der. Fey herself suggests it's unfair to ask individual female characters to represent their entire sex. In a 2004 *New Yorker* profile on Fey, Virginia Heffernan quoted Fey's response to a male colleague who asked if she thought her *SNL* sketches were antiwoman. Fey asserted that *SNL*'s job is "to make fun of people," adding, "If we don't make fun of women, the female performers don't have any parts."

Few successful recent sitcoms have revolved around a smart, independent woman, so it's no surprise that television critics relate *30 Rock*'s premise to venerable 1970s TV touchstone *The Mary Tyler Moore Show*. The comparison is not off the mark; Fey told the *New York Times* that she and her writers used *MTM* as a structural model when writing *30 Rock*'s early episodes. But in critics' nostalgia for the smart and independent Mary Richards, they forget that the show revealed its own set of anxieties surrounding independent women.

Alternately asserting her power and then retreating immediately, Mary could live alone at age 30, but her overaccommodating nature and inability to say no to both superiors and colleagues continually reassured viewers that she hadn't abandoned traditional femininity. Mary was portrayed as consistently smart and consistently pleasant. She never raised her voice, and for six seasons she called her boss "Mr. Grant" when everyone else simply called him "Lou." As the smartest character in the room, Mary had punch lines, but she was never the object of a joke, and she never had so much as a hair out of place. Mary Richards turned the world on with her smile, and—save for a stumble here and there—remained on her pedestal of perfection for the span of the show.

Liz Lemon, on the other hand, has Mary's central position but Rhoda Morgenstern's personality. Like Rhoda, Liz can say no—and be mean and inflexible when she does. *30 Rock*'s pilot episode opens with Lemon at a New York hot-dog stand, angrily protesting when a man cuts in front of her in line. To punish him, she buys all the vendor's hot dogs and refuses to give one to the line-cutter. A parody of the *MTM* theme song begins to play as Lemon walks away, teetering under the oversized box of hot dogs; she hands one to a homeless man, who responds by throwing it back at her in the next shot. When questioned by a coworker about the

> *30 Rock* aims many a punch line at Lemon's perceived lack of femininity, but who exactly is the butt of the joke? Is it Lemon, for falling short of the feminine ideal, or the society that emphasizes that ideal?

box, Lemon's grouchy response—"You know how I hate it when people cheat or break rules?"—busts through the *MTM* illusion: New York is not Minneapolis, and Liz Lemon is no Mary Richards.

In the years between *MTM* and *30 Rock*, several other workplace comedies have centered on a single professional woman, and each has played on the gender anxieties of its decade. In the late '80s, the title character of *Murphy Brown* did Mary Richards one better: A brilliant, hard-talking, self-centered TV journalist, Murphy was over 40 and utterly uninterested in the institution of marriage. (She's now best remembered for incurring Dan Quayle's public criticism when she became a single mother.) Murphy came very close to assuming the privileges of being a man at the time, but the show's plotlines often served to tame her fierce ego by the conclusion—in one episode, her much younger male boss ordered her out of work for two weeks for walking out on an interview. If working women like Murphy frightened the status quo with their dangerous financial independence, the late-'90s debut of young, insecure, and kittenish Ally McBeal tamed the working-woman shrew by conveniently co-opting the fearsome F-word. Ally was a Harvard-educated lawyer who critics also likened to Mary Richards (single, white, non-blond professionals seem to call up the comparison). She brazenly wore short skirts, dared to sue a sexual harasser, and was determined to find the right man. Like Mary, men precipitated Ally's professional and geographic moves—even her career was the result of following a boyfriend's dreams. Ally scolded herself for displaying wit on a date ("I hate myself when funny"), and her dancing-baby hallucinations are firmly implanted in public memory. Ally bemoaned inequality, but though she talked revolution, she was never a real threat: "If women want to change society, they could do it. I plan to do it. I just want to get married first."

Breakout female characters of the Mary Richards variety seem to come along at the rate of about once a decade (and are most often middle-class and white), but *30 Rock*'s Lemon debuted in the same season as another single brunet—Betty Suarez of ABC's *telenovela* sendup *Ugly Betty*. A young, up-for-any-challenge striver from working-class Queens, Betty lucks into a job at *Mode*, a fashion magazine where her coworkers mock her geeky, unsophisticated clothes, her untweezed eyebrows, and her mouth full of metal. But her competence makes her indispensable

to her playboy boss, who can barely get dressed without Betty's input, much less keep his job. Collectively, *30 Rock* and *Ugly Betty* have dominated comedy-award categories since their premieres in 2006, and *30 Rock* simultaneously acknowledges and distinguishes itself from its counterpart: In a meta moment when Lemon is caught literally crawling out of Jack Donaghy's office, she addresses the camera directly, sighing, "This would have worked on *Ugly Betty*." And therein lies the difference—while *30 Rock* traffics in gender satire, *Ugly Betty* primarily intersects with class. Situated comfortably within the white managerial rungs, Lemon alone has the privilege of screwing up. Betty is smart and honest, with rock-solid moral character and a personality that outshines her overplucked foils, but as an underling at her job, she is robbed of the opportunity to be mean. Betty has to ignore her shallow coworkers when they crack the wit whips, but Lemon can crack back.

Apparently prime-time television can now handle two lady-geek stars in the same decade, but it seems that two in the same show is still a no-go. Despite *30 Rock*'s onscreen criticisms of gender relations, the show itself is not exempt from the gender politicking that it lampoons. Rachel Dratch, Fey's fellow Second City and *SNL* alumna, was originally slated to play the lead actress on *30 Rock*'s fictional sketch show. Though a pilot had been shot with Dratch as Jenna, she was pulled at the last minute; separate interviews with Dratch and Fey in *New York* magazine and *Entertainment Weekly* claimed that *30 Rock*'s producers felt Dratch was better suited to sketch-style character roles. Was it Donaghy's favorite market-research tool, the focus group, that precipitated the change? Jane Krakowski (of *Ally McBeal* fame) stepped into the role of Jenna; the character was rewritten and the pilot reshot. Though Dratch has recurring cameos (most memorably as a lesbian cat wrangler with a crush on Liz), one wonders how the surely unavoidable tension filtered into the show—a common theme in Lemon's interactions with Donaghy has Fey repeating some version of the line, "But these are my friends; you can't just fire them!"

Of course, without Fey in a primary power role behind the scenes, it's hard to imagine that a character like Liz Lemon would even get written. Where Mary Richards laughed at jokes, Lemon writes them for a living—and makes them at other people's expense. After Liz takes a crack at a male junior writer in "The C-word," she overhears him call her that special derogatory word reserved for

C-Word" exemplifies the inconsistent messages bubbling beneath *30 Rock*, when Jenna consoles Liz in her characteristically vapid manner: "The difficult part of being a modern woman, Liz, is learning to protect your strength while maintaining your femininity." Jenna then reveals the back of her dress, which plunges southward in parodic excess, and adds, "Is this too much butt cleavage?"

As a performer who wrote her way to the screen, Fey's ordinary-girl persona chips away at a toweringly unrealistic physical expectation for female performers. In another episode, when Liz admits she secretly wanted part of her friend's spotlight, Jenna's shocked response is strategically inappropriate: "Liz, you couldn't have been serious about acting for a living — you have brown hair!" The joke lands on Lemon, but audiences can't look at her without seeing Fey, whose very career disproves the statement. The April 2008 issue of *Vanity Fair* featured Fey on its cover, while Alessandra Stanley's accompanying story on self-scripting female comedians (titled "Who Says Women Aren't Funny?" — a direct retort to pundit Christopher Hitchens' now-infamous January 2007 *VF* essay that said just that) praised Fey as a leader. Unfortunately, Stanley focused more on female comedians' desirability than on their material; while Fey is attractive, her primary goal is to be funny. (Dratch was excluded from the piece entirely, which didn't help unpack the story's equation of hot + funny = truly funny.)

Perhaps audiences love Fey-as-Lemon because of Fey's embrace of her brain and her relative disinterest in her sex appeal. Of course, *30 Rock* is aware of its male viewership (Fey's neckline seems to drop with every episode), but Lemon isn't simply eye candy in service of male titillation. Where *The Mary Tyler Moore Show* and *Murphy Brown* drew on societal concerns surrounding single, working women, Lemon taps into women's apprehensions directly. She's ambivalent about marriage ("Slow down. I'm not ready to move my humidifiers yet.") and slings feminist barbs that manage to be funny ("How come men can be heavy and still be respected, like James Gandolfini — or Fat Albert?"). On *30 Rock*, Fey has the confidence to make fun of herself while delivering potshots at the crusty Hitchens-esque status quo. As Lemon says to Jenna in the *Maxim* scene, "What does [being sexy] have to do with comedy?"

Apparently, I'm not the only one who's noticed her disinterest in being a pleaser — in the fall of 2007, Liz Lemon graced *Maxim*'s list of "TV's Least Attractive Ladies," alongside Betty Suarez and Jerri Blank. Guess the boys at *Maxim* just can't take a joke.

women in power, and spends the rest of the episode struggling between her desire to be liked and her need to be an effective — if not always popular — manager. Because the audience is aware of Fey's offscreen status as *30 Rock*'s showrunner, the episode delivers a satiric punch. Fey similarly drew on this double consciousness when she hosted the first post-strike episode of *SNL*, mocking the gendered criticisms of Hillary Clinton's campaign in a now-notorious statement — "People say Hillary is a bitch. Let me say something about that: Yeah, she is. So am I. . . . Bitches get stuff done."

Significantly, *30 Rock* uses Fey's experiences (and those of the female writers on her staff) to ridicule the contradictory expectations placed on single American women: Be professionally successful and independent, but also sexy, contained, and accommodating. A deleted scene from "The

Starting a Conversation: Respond to "Mary Tyler more"

In your writer's notebook, contemplate the ideas presented in Lies's evaluation by responding to the following questions:

1. Lies is evaluating the quality of *30 Rock* and the portrayal of its lead character, Liz Lemon. But the writer's purpose seems both deeper and broader than simply reviewing a television show. In your own words, what is her purpose?

2. Although Lies clearly approves of *30 Rock* and Fey's character, she also includes alternative opinions. Where in her review does she do this, and what important questions do these dissenting views raise? Do these questions undercut Lies's points, or do they help strengthen them? Why do you think so?

3. Evaluative writing commonly includes elements of comparison and contrast, as when a film critic weighs the qualities of one movie against another. What comparisons and contrasts does Lies include in her evaluation? How do they support her argument?

4. In her introduction, Lies refers to "metacommentary," as well as the "self-referential" and "hilariously meta" qualities of *30 Rock* (pars. 2, 3). What are the meanings of "metacommentary" and "self-referential," and what does Lies's use of the terms suggest about her understanding of her readers?

5. According to Lies, television shows such as *30 Rock* or *The Mary Tyler Moore Show* can reflect larger issues in our culture and society. What are some examples of these connections?

@ Download or print this Starting a Conversation activity at **bedfordstmartins.com/ conversation**.

Place Evaluations

Place evaluations consider and assess our surroundings, from suburban subdivisions and revived small town centers to skyscrapers and city parks. These documents help us understand not only places but also our own place within them by exploring the role of architecture, design, and development in our lives. Writers of place evaluations must take into account both the fine details of a location or building and the larger themes of its shape and form. They must also consider factors that affect how a place or building is understood, such as its history, its geography, and the social, cultural, and economic factors that shape it. Writers of place evaluations frequently use comparison and contrast to provide a context for readers. For example, a writer might compare a waterfront retail complex in one city with a similar complex in another city.

Place evaluations, which are often accompanied by photographs or drawings of the place under consideration, can vary in length, tone, and sources. An architectural review in a general-interest magazine or newspaper, for instance, will probably be less formal than one in a professional publication or scholarly journal. In either case, however, the writers can presume that their readers share their interest in the subject.

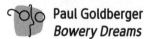 **Paul Goldberger**
Bowery Dreams

Paul Goldberger is a professor of architecture at the New School, as well as the author of books such as *Up from Zero: Politics, Architecture, and the Rebuilding of New York* (2004). The *New Yorker* magazine regularly features Goldberger's "Sky Line" column, in which this piece originally appeared. In "Bowery Dreams," Goldberger evaluates the New Museum of Contemporary Art in New York City, focusing not only on the building itself but also on its larger context.

Bowery Dreams
A new home for the New Museum of Contemporary Art
The Sky Line, by Paul Goldberger
November 19, 2007

In the past few decades, American museums have discovered an easy way to get themselves noticed: put up a building by an international architect who hasn't built much in this country before. Too often, though, these exciting débuts go nowhere. Mario Botta's San Francisco Museum of Modern Art, Josef Paul Kleihues's Chicago Museum of Contemporary Art, and James Stirling's Sackler Museum, in Cambridge, all failed to earn their creators any more American museum commissions.

In 2002, when the New Museum of Contemporary Art in New York began to plan for a new building on the Bowery, east of its previous location, in SoHo, it decided to limit the search to younger architects who had not built anything in New York. "We thought we should be consistent with our mission of supporting new art," Lisa Phillips, the director, told me. The search led the museum to SANAA, a twelve-

year-old firm in Tokyo, whose principals, Kazuyo Sejima and Ryue Nishizawa, are known for buildings of almost diaphanous lightness. When the museum hired them, Sejima and Nishizawa had just one American commission, the Glass Pavilion, at the Toledo Museum of Art, an eye-catching structure of curving glass walls, which opened last year. Their best-known work includes a low-slung circular art gallery with no clear front or back, in Kanazawa, Japan, and a design school in Essen, Germany, that is a concrete cube a hundred feet high, punctuated, seemingly at random, with windows of assorted sizes.

SANAA's refined style might seem odd on the Bowery, one of the grittiest streets in New York. The site, a former parking lot at the intersection with Prince Street, was framed by blocks of restaurant-supply stores, whose owners seemed to be the only property holders on the Lower East Side who showed no interest in selling out to condominium developers. But after two decades in SoHo the New Museum had seen both the upside and the downside of gentrification. Marcia Tucker established the museum in 1977 — the day after she was fired from the Whitney for curating shows that it found too controversial — in order to focus on cutting-edge art. Yet as the museum grew larger it drifted from its radical beginnings, just as the Museum of Modern Art had done two generations before. The decision to move to the Bowery was perhaps a clever way of assuring its supporters that its agenda remains radical.

But things have changed since the New Museum purchased the lot, in 2002. There is now a Whole Foods nearby, several luxury condominiums within view of the museum's front door, and expensive shops, including a Ralph Lauren, amid the former tenements around the corner. The area

hovers between a grungy past and an overpriced future. The New Museum may have left SoHo, but it is powerless to prevent SoHo from following it to the Bowery.

Sejima and Nishizawa have designed a building that is just right for this moment of the Bowery's existence. It is a pile of six boxes, stacked unevenly, like a child's blocks. Sometimes the blocks mount up in a pattern of setbacks like that of a traditional New York building; sometimes they jut out over open space in a way that suggests the architects had something more radical in mind. The building is original, but doesn't strain to reinvent the idea of a museum. Sejima and Nishizawa have a way of combining intensity with understatement.

What makes the museum unlike any other building in New York is its surface — corrugated-aluminum panels painted silvery gray, with an aluminum mesh suspended an inch and a half in front of them. The mesh is a standard industrial material but it gives the building the lightness of glass and the porosity of fabric. The visual signals this building sends — it is at once crisp and pliable, solid and permeable — seem deliberately ambiguous. When you look from a block or so away, the façade seems semitransparent — less like a wall than a scrim.

The depth and shadow and texture of the façade can be almost magical in the changing light. When you get near, however, the mystery is lost. You see that Sejima and Nishizawa have performed their magic with routine elements, and when you stand right in front of the building its metal mesh looks harsh, even abrasive. Once the museum opens, next month, the effect may be more welcoming: the ground floor is sheathed entirely in glass, and a gallery and bookstore will be visible from the street. At the moment, the museum is enticing from afar but off-putting up close.

Things get good again when you go through the door. SANAA's ability to design places that look simple but actually have a lot going on has resulted in galleries that combine the clear, flexible quality of loft spaces with some shrewd architectural intervention. The second, third, and fourth floors have large, white-walled exhibition spaces, with ceiling heights of as much as twenty-four feet. The galleries, illuminated in part by natural light (through skylights), have some of the virtues of neutrality but are more inviting than plain white boxes. The main gallery spaces are almost, but not precisely, rectangular. One wall is angled just a bit, reflecting the diagonal of the Bowery, but the shift is so subtle that you don't notice it until you look up and see that the front wall is not quite parallel to the steel beams that run across the ceiling. This gives the room a slight frisson, without making it any less flexible or hospitable to art. The floors are all finished in a richly toned polished concrete that has been poured without the usual expansion joints, allowing it to develop small cracks as it sets. It looks both ancient and modern, and has a stunning resonance against the stark walls. ("It almost looks like an Anselm Kiefer," Lisa Phillips said as we walked through, and she was exaggerating only slightly.)

There are more flourishes once you get away from the main exhibition area: aluminum-lined elevators painted a kind of electric chartreuse; shelves that snake through the lobby in a sensuous curve, the one counterpoint to the building's straight lines. The most exciting space in the building is only four feet wide and some fifty feet high, and is tucked behind the elevators: it contains a stairway connecting the third- and fourth-floor galleries. I have never been anywhere at once so eerily narrow and so gloriously monumental. The stair hall, if you can call it that, has a large window with a view to the north, and a landing that opens onto a tiny exhibit area, barely more than a balcony.

In keeping their architectural tricks away from most of the art, Sejima and Nishizawa establish a certain kinship with the original building of the Museum of Modern Art, by Philip Goodwin and Edward Durell Stone. When that building burst onto West Fifty-third Street, in 1939, you could create excitement simply by sticking a modern building into a row of brownstones. The New Museum, similarly, derives its drama from the way it breaks with its surroundings. The original Modern lost much of its architectural power from the nineteen-fifties onward, as the brownstones gave way to a series of additions extending the museum up and down the block, and modernism became the new architecture lingua franca. Right now, the New Museum looks, as the Modern once did, like a thunderbolt from another world, but, as the spread of condos and boutique hotels across the Lower East Side continues, it is at risk of becoming a victim of its own success.

Starting a Conversation: Respond to "Bowery Dreams"

In your writer's notebook, record your analysis of Goldberger's place evaluation by responding to the following questions:

1. Goldberger views the New Museum of Contemporary Art as inseparable from its particular location in the Bowery. Why do you think Goldberger thinks that the museum's surroundings are so important? How does his place evaluation take into account the museum's location?

2. What is Goldberger's overall assessment of the building's success or failure? On what criteria does he base his judgment?

3. Goldberger refers to "both the upside and the downside of gentrification" (par. 3). What does "gentrification" mean? How well does the author help you understand these "upsides" and "downsides"? How does his attention to gentrification make the place evaluation part of a larger conversation?

4. In the opening paragraph, Goldberger refers to three architects who have designed art museums in the past few decades. What sense of his readers do you get from these — and other — architectural and geographic references?

5. Goldberger is writing an evaluation, yet he is also playing the role of a reporter and an interpreter (see p. 11 for an overview of writers' roles). How does his selection and use of sources reflect these different roles?

@ Download or print this Starting a Conversation activity at **bedfordstmartins.com/ conversation**.

Progress Reports

Progress reports provide an assessment of a project or an initiative. For example, a state environmental agency might issue a report on its efforts to reduce pesticide and fertilizer runoff from farmland into state watersheds. Similarly, an account team at an advertising agency might report on its efforts to increase sales of a product through a national advertising campaign, while the development manager at a charitable organization might report on her efforts to increase donations through corporate subscriptions. Because most reports focus narrowly on a subject, they often use criteria that might be unfamiliar to readers, particularly those, such as supervisors and managers, who might not be as well versed in the subject as the specialists who write the report. As a result, the criteria used in the evaluation are often defined in detail and, when applied in the report, discussed at length. Longer reports, particularly those that assess the effectiveness of a project or an initiative, often rely on information gathered by researchers associated with the project. The source of this kind of evidence might include surveys, interviews, testing, observation, and reviews of published sources.

The formats in which reports are written and read vary widely. Government reports, for example, are often distributed as bound documents that resemble books, as well as in downloadable formats. In contrast, reports written for a company or a political group might be distributed to only a small group of readers, and great care might be taken to ensure that the document does not receive wide distribution. Regardless of the number of readers, however, the writers of these documents often put a great deal of effort into the report's design.

UNESCO
Education for All Global Monitoring Report

The 2008 report excerpted here evaluates progress on a worldwide effort to expand educational opportunities for children, youth, and adults by 2015. The project, initiated at the World Education Forum in Dakar, Senegal, in 2000, reflects a commitment by 164 nations to pursue "a comprehensive vision of education, anchored in human rights, affirming the importance of learning at all ages and emphasizing the need for special measures to reach the poorest, most vulnerable and most disadvantaged groups in society." The report is updated annually and serves as a reminder to participating nations that their progress is being monitored. It also provides information that can be used by various groups and agencies to judge their own progress. The authors are careful not only to provide a balanced assessment of progress but also to avoid singling out nations that support the project but have made limited progress in enacting its goals.

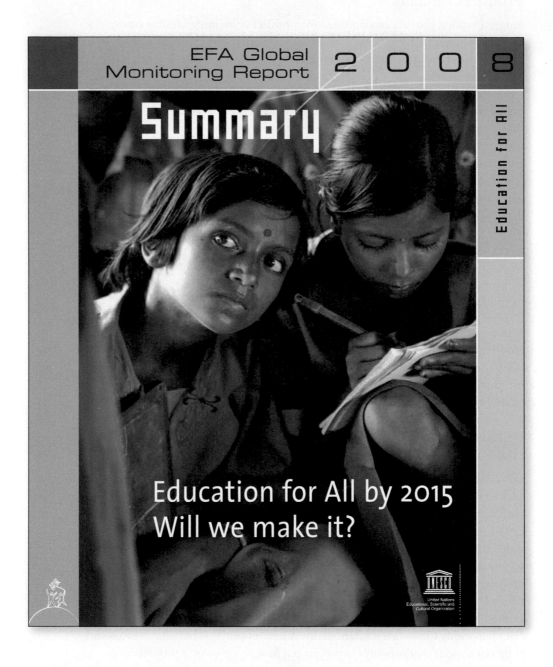

Pre-primary education: uneven progress, minimal access for disadvantaged children

Primary education: faster progress since 2000 in regions with low enrolments

Poor education quality: a global issue, especially where systems have expanded rapidly

Out-of-school children: rapid decline since 2002

▌▌▌▌ Chapter 2. The six goals: how far have we come?

Global literacy: small gains, with notable progress in China

Geographic disparities: often persisting despite increasing primary enrolment

Gender disparities: no significant decline, still acute in secondary and higher education

Teacher recruitment: not keeping pace with primary enrolment increases

Midway between 2000 and the 2015 target date for achieving EFA, this chapter assesses progress towards the six EFA goals, using data for the school year ending in 2005. The world has made significant but uneven progress towards EFA since Dakar. Education disparities within countries are widespread and poor education quality is emerging as a major concern.

Goal 1. Early childhood care and education: large gaps between regions

'Expanding and improving comprehensive early childhood care and education, especially for the most vulnerable and disadvantaged children.'

The case for well-designed ECCE programmes is compelling, especially for the most disadvantaged.[1] Holistic programmes improve children's health, nutrition, well-being and cognitive development, and leave them better prepared for entering and staying in primary school. Investing in such programmes yields high economic returns, offsetting disadvantage and inequality – especially for children from poor families.

Although the global under-5 mortality rate has declined since 1995 (down from 92 in every 1,000 children to 78), the rate remains high in sub-Saharan Africa. Nearly 10 million children under age 5 died in 2005, the majority

1. For details see the 2007 Report, *Strong foundations: early childhood care and education.*

in developing countries. Most of these deaths could have been prevented with basic health services and child nutrition programmes. Undernutrition and malnutrition affect one in four children under age 5 in developing countries. This situation has a direct impact on education, making children vulnerable to illness, less likely to enrol in school and more likely to drop out.

Programmes for under-3s that include nutrition, health and cognitive components have a positive impact on child well-being. Yet, only 53% of the world's countries have an official ECCE programme targeting this age group. These programmes are most prevalent in North America and Western Europe, Central Asia, and Latin America and the Caribbean. Their emergence partly reflects women's massive entry into the labour market. In other parts of the world, governments often view the care and education of very young children as the responsibility of families and/or private providers. As a result, there are few national frameworks for financing, coordinating and supervising ECCE programmes.

Uneven advances in pre-primary education

Governments are more active in providing for children between age 3 and the beginning of primary school. The number of children enrolled in pre-primary schools worldwide rose by 20 million to 132 million between 1999 and 2005. South and West Asia, and sub-Saharan Africa registered the largest increases (by 67% and 61%, respectively), while in East Asia the number of pupils fell largely because the relevant age group in China decreased.

Programmes for under-3s that include nutrition, health and cognitive components have a positive impact on child well-being

Participation in pre-primary education also increased, with the global gross enrolment ratio (GER) rising from 33% in 1999 to 40% in 2005 (see Figure 2.1). Regionally the ratio ranges widely, from 14% in sub-Saharan Africa to 83% in the Caribbean. The Pacific, and South and West Asia registered the highest gains, with fifteen percentage points each, followed by the Caribbean (twelve percentage points), and Central and Eastern Europe (ten percentage points), confirming the latter region's recovery from the 1990s. Participation is highest in developed and transition countries, in Latin America and the Caribbean, and in the Pacific.

Figure 2.1: GERs in pre-primary education, weighted average by region, 1999 and 2005

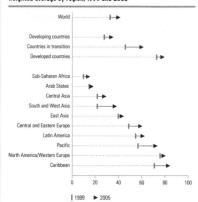

Source: See Chapter 2 in the full EFA Report.

Sub-Saharan Africa and the Arab States account for almost three-quarters of the fifty countries with participation rates under 30%. Nevertheless, several of these countries registered rapid change: GERs doubled or tripled from a very low base in Burundi, the Congo, Eritrea, Madagascar and Senegal. In some cases, the number of schools increased by over 100% (Senegal, the Congo); in others, governments introduced free kindergarten (Ghana) or supported the opening of new child care centres (Eritrea).

Although children from poorer and rural backgrounds are the most likely to benefit from ECCE programmes, they have the least access to them. Gender disparities in pre-primary, on the other hand, are less marked than at other levels of education, possibly because children enrolled are generally from more affluent backgrounds. The

gender parity index (GPI) was near or over 0.90 in all regions in 2005. High disparities against girls prevail in several countries, including Chad (0.48) and Morocco (0.65), but high disparities against boys are equally common.

Shortages of pre-primary teachers

The single most important determinant of quality in ECCE programmes is the interaction between the children and the carer or teacher. Adequate teacher training and relatively small classes are particularly crucial in maximizing the benefits children receive. Worldwide there were about twenty-two pupils per pre-primary teacher in 2005, slightly higher than in 1999. The pupil/teacher ratio (PTR) increased in 40% of the 121 countries with data. South and West Asia, and sub-Saharan Africa registered the sharpest increases, with the PTR reaching 40:1 in the former region. The number of pupils per trained teacher, an additional indicator of children's exposure to quality learning, can be much higher than the PTR: in Ghana, it reached 155:1, reflecting the country's difficulty in coping with the surge in kindergarten enrolment.

Goal 2. Universal primary education: moving but not yet close

'Ensuring that by 2015 all children, particularly girls, children in difficult circumstances and those belonging to ethnic minorities, have access to and complete, free and compulsory primary education of good quality.'

The world is making rapid strides towards UPE, partly due to the abolition of school tuition fees in several countries. The number of children entering primary school grew by 4%, from 130 million to 135 million, between 1999 and 2005. The most impressive gains were registered in sub-Saharan Africa (40%), the Arab States (11.6%), and South and West Asia (9.4%). Decreases in other regions are the result of declining fertility rates.

To reach UPE by 2015, all children of the relevant age group should be enrolled in school by 2009. Trends are positive, with the number of new entrants increasing in countries that have lagged in terms of access. But several countries, mostly in sub-Saharan Africa and the Arab States, will find it very difficult to approach UPE in the coming decade.

Participation in primary education is increasing but is still far from universal (see Figure 2.2). Worldwide 688 million children were enrolled in primary school in 2005, up 6.4% since 1999. Enrolment speeded up after Dakar in sub-Saharan Africa (growing by 29 million, or 36%), and South and West Asia (35 million, 22%), while in the Arab States

Although children from poorer and rural backgrounds are the most likely to benefit from ECCE programmes, they have the least access to them

Figure 2.2: NER in primary education, weighted average by region, 1999 and 2005

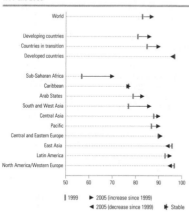

| 1999 | ▶ 2005 (increase since 1999) |
| ◀ 2005 (decrease since 1999) | ▐ Stable |

Source: See Chapter 2 in the full EFA Report.

parts of the eastern and central regions they are below 60%. In Guinea almost all children in the capital region of Conakry are enrolled, but ratios fall below 50% in outlying districts.

As education systems expand, are disparities decreasing within countries? There is no clear association between increasing NER levels and geographic disparities. Improvement in NERs has been associated with reduced geographic disparities in Brazil, Burkina Faso, Cambodia, Indonesia, Mali, Morocco, Mozambique, the Niger and the United Republic of Tanzania, but greater ones in Bangladesh, Benin, Ethiopia, the Gambia, Guinea, India, Kenya, Mauritania and Zambia. Stark contrasts can exist between countries with similar NERs, varying from high disparity in Ethiopia and Nigeria to very low in Ghana.

Households in rural or remote communities tend to be poorer and more socially marginalized, with less access to quality basic education. Household survey data from forty countries show that, in thirty-two of them, net attendance rates in urban areas are higher than those in rural ones. However, the 'urban advantage' does not work for all children, particularly those growing up in urban slums. In several countries, including Brazil, Guatemala, the United Republic of Tanzania, Zambia and Zimbabwe, enrolment ratios have decreased in slum areas.

> Demographic growth will continue to place education systems under pressure in the next decade

it continued at almost the same pace as before Dakar. Demographic growth will continue to place education systems under pressure in the next decade: primary school-age populations are expected to increase by 22% in sub-Saharan Africa and by 13% in the Arab States. In many other regions enrolment has been stable or decreased, a trend linked to smaller school-age populations.

In the Arab States, Central Asia, and South and West Asia, average net enrolment ratios (NERs) are below 90%, with lows in Djibouti (33%) and Pakistan (68%). The situation is most critical in sub-Saharan Africa, where more than 60% of the countries have values below 80% and more than one-third are below 70%. Most countries that had NERs below 95% in either 1999 or 2005 registered increases over the period, and in some the pace of progress has clearly accelerated since Dakar. In several cases this reflects the impact of public policies designed to facilitate enrolment of the most disadvantaged, such as the abolition of school tuition fees. Most of the countries that had the lowest values in 1999 registered improvement.

The opportunity gap: inequities in education

Progress in enrolment since Dakar has rarely been uniform across regions, provinces or states within a country. In Nepal, for example, NERs in the western and far-western regions are high (above 95%), whereas in

At school in the Syrian Arab Republic.

Household surveys conducted in several sub-Saharan African countries indicate that poor households suffer reduced attendance rates, regardless of whether they are in an urban or rural region.

A sharp drop in the number of out-of-school children

Just over 72 million primary school aged children were not in primary or secondary school in 2005, a sharp drop from 96 million in 1999. The decline was marked in South and West Asia (from 31 million to 17 million), and sub-Saharan Africa (from 42 million to 33 million). These two regions nevertheless account for 24% and 45%, respectively, of all out-of-school children. The decline has been particularly rapid since 2002 (by 19.2 million,

compared with 5.2 million between 1999 and 2002). This encouraging trend in the face of growing population numbers reflects the worldwide increase in primary school access and participation.

A global momentum has developed, with much now depending on a few countries. India, Nigeria and Pakistan together account for 27% of the world's out-of-school children. Including the other seven countries with more than 1 million out-of-school children (Burkina Faso, Côte d'Ivoire, Ethiopia, Kenya, Mali, the Niger and Viet Nam) raises the proportion to 40%. The thirty-five countries identified as fragile states were home to 37% of the world's out-of-school children in 2005. Providing places in primary schools for all these children will be particularly difficult. (Map 2.1)

> A global momentum has developed, with much now depending on a few countries

Map 2.1: Challenge of out-of-school children relative to NER, 2005

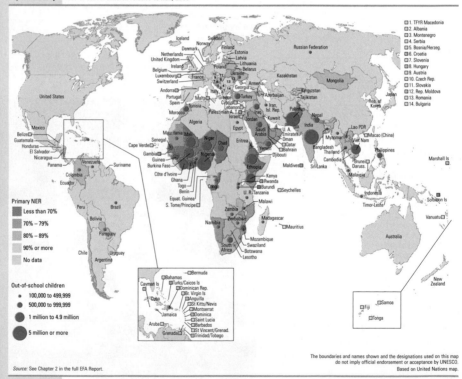

Source: See Chapter 2 in the full EFA Report.

The boundaries and names shown and the designations used on this map do not imply official endorsement or acceptance by UNESCO.
Based on United Nations map.

Around 16% of children counted as being out of school had initially enrolled but left before reaching the official age of completion. A further 32% may eventually enrol as late entrants. Overall, children are more likely to be out of school if they are from poor households, live in rural areas and/or have a mother with no schooling. Being a girl heightens the probability of not being in school. The share of girls among out-of-school children fell slightly between 1999 and 2005, from 59% to 57%. Girls remain most disadvantaged in these terms in South and West Asia (66%), and the Arab States (60%). Finally, disability is strongly associated with being out of school: on average across seven developing countries, case studies show that a disabled child was half as likely to be in primary school as one without a disability.

Advancing through primary school

Where repetition rates are high, so is dropout. Sub-Saharan Africa has the highest incidence of repetition (median of 15%), followed by South and West Asia, and Latin America and the Caribbean (5% each). In most regions, the rate peaks in grade 1 (e.g. 37% in Nepal, 34% in the Lao People's Democratic Republic, above 30% in Burundi, Comoros, Equatorial Guinea and Gabon, 27% in Brazil and 24% in Guatemala), partly because children enter school unprepared, having rarely participated in ECCE programmes, especially in the poorest countries or areas. Nonetheless, between 1999 and 2005, repetition decreased in two-thirds of the countries with data for both years. Some countries are adopting automatic promotion policies (Ethiopia) while others witnessed a decline with the introduction of a new curriculum (Mozambique).

Pupils dropping out before the end of primary school is cause for concern. In half the countries with available data for 2004, less than 87% of pupils who started grade 1 reached the last grade, a measure called the survival rate. In South and West Asia, the median survival rate to the last grade drops to 79%, and the measure is lowest in sub-Saharan Africa (63%), where in several countries fewer than half of pupils reach the last grade. At the other end of the spectrum, median values are 94% in the Arab States, 97% in Central Asia and above 98% in Central and Eastern Europe, and in North America and Western Europe.

The percentage of children reaching the last grade of primary education improved between 1999 and 2004 in most countries with data. In some, net enrolment increased while the number of children reaching grade 5 dropped, pointing to the difficulty of expanding access to education while also retaining pupils to the end of the primary cycle. Not all children who reach the last grade complete it, with gaps above twenty percentage points in Brunei Darussalam, Burundi, Grenada, Nepal, the Niger, Pakistan and Senegal.

Secondary education and beyond

Taking stock of secondary education is important for monitoring EFA progress. As increasing numbers of students finish primary education, demand for secondary education grows. Most governments view the extension of compulsory education to primary and lower secondary as an important policy objective. Worldwide three out of four countries include the lower secondary level in compulsory education. The gender parity goal also calls on countries to assure parity in both primary and secondary school.

In 2005, some 512 million students were enrolled in secondary schools worldwide, an increase of more than 73 million (17%) since 1999. The growth was driven by rises in sub-Saharan Africa (55%), South and West Asia, and the Arab States (25% each), and East Asia (21%).

Worldwide participation rates in secondary education have increased sharply since the early 1990s: the average secondary GER was 52% in 1991, 60% in 1999 and 66% in 2005. Two-thirds or more of secondary school-age students are enrolled in Latin America and in East Asia and the Pacific, with lower averages in sub-Saharan Africa (25%), South and West Asia (53%), and the Arab States (66%). Most countries in North America and Western Europe have almost achieved universal secondary education, and relatively high secondary NERs are found in Central and Eastern Europe, and Central Asia.

Tertiary education is also relevant to EFA goals as a component of the gender equality goal and as an important provider of teachers and administrators. Worldwide some 138 million students were enrolled in tertiary education in 2005, about 45 million more than in 1999. The vast majority of new places in tertiary institutions were created in developing countries (e.g. Brazil, China, India and Nigeria). However, only a relatively small share of the relevant age group has access to this level. The world tertiary GER was around 24% in 2005, with participation varying substantially by region, from 5% in sub-Saharan Africa and 11% in South and West Asia to 70% in North America and Western Europe.

Goal 3. Meeting the learning needs of young people and adults

'Ensuring that the learning needs of all young people and adults are met through equitable access to appropriate learning and life-skills programmes.'

Governments have mainly responded to the learning needs of young people and adults by expanding formal secondary and tertiary education. However, people also acquire skills through informal means and in non-formal

> The percentage of children reaching the last grade of primary education improved between 1999 and 2004 in most countries with data

settings. From an equity perspective these learning activities deserve attention because they often reach disadvantaged youth and adults, and because too many children do not go to school or leave school without acquiring basic skills. Non-formal education programmes are highly diverse and tend to be overseen by multiple ministries or other government bodies. In many countries, small-scale initiatives run by NGOs dominate the provision. Improved monitoring of supply and demand for non-formal education is urgently needed at national levels. While many types of learning activities take place outside formal education systems, the extent to which supply matches demand is largely unknown.

The 2008 Report draws on work from thirty countries regarding the provision of non-formal education. Household survey data show that non-formal education is the main route to learning for many disadvantaged youth and adults in some of the world's poorest countries.

> **Household survey data show that non-formal education is the main route to learning for many disadvantaged youth and adults in some of the world's poorest countries**

Large-scale literacy programmes, often encompassing life skills (health, civic rights) and livelihoods (income generation, farming), are common, especially in poor countries including Afghanistan, Ethiopia, Nepal and Senegal, where they benefit from substantial external support. Equivalency or 'second chance' services, sometimes linked to literacy programmes, are a common means of providing learning opportunities for young people (e.g. in Brazil, Cambodia, Egypt, India, Indonesia, Mexico, the Philippines, Thailand and Viet Nam). Other national programmes focus on skills development in the informal economy, including in China, Egypt, Ghana, South Africa and Viet Nam. Programmes focusing on rural development are run in cooperation with agriculture ministries in Brazil, Burkina Faso, China, Ethiopia, India, Nepal, the Philippines and Thailand.

Non-formal education programmes are often linked with community development. In many Asian countries community learning centres (Thailand, for instance, has over 8,000) provide a wide range of structured learning activities, driven by local needs and encompassing literacy, continuing education and skills training.

Goal 4. Literacy and literate environments: essential yet elusive

'Achieving a 50 per cent improvement in levels of adult literacy by 2015, especially for women, and equitable access to basic and continuing education for all adults.'

Literacy is a fundamental human right, a foundation not only for achieving EFA but, more broadly, for reducing poverty and broadening participation in society. Yet, about 774 million adults worldwide, 64% of them women, remain illiterate. This figure, moreover, is drawn from

censuses or household surveys that rely on indirect assessments; evidence from direct testing suggests that the full scale of the literacy challenge is actually much greater, as a recent survey in Kenya illustrates (Box 2.1).

Box 2.1: Kenya's national adult literacy survey

In 2006 Kenya conducted a national adult literacy survey using direct assessment of 15,000 households. It estimated the adult literacy rate at 62%, much lower than the self-estimated rate of 74% from the 2000 Multiple Indicator Cluster Surveys. Literacy and numeracy rates varied significantly by district, age and level of education completed, with a turning point between grades 4 and 5. Literacy rates were under 20% among adults who completed four grades or fewer, and over 65% for those who completed five grades or more. Many survey respondents said they did not attend literacy classes or had dropped out due to distance from a learning centre and a lack of teachers. This type of direct assessment improves the quality of literacy data and provides more accurate information with which to assess existing programmes and design appropriate policies.

Between the 1985–1994 and 1995–2004 periods the global adult literacy rate rose from 76% to 82%. The increase was more marked among developing countries (68% to 77%). The Arab States, and South and West Asia experienced the most sustained progress, each up twelve percentage points. The number of illiterate adults in the former region as well as in sub-Saharan Africa did not drop systematically, partly due to continuing high population growth. Adult literacy rates remain below the world average in South and West Asia, and in sub-Saharan Africa (59% in each) as well as in the Arab States and the Caribbean (about 71% each).

More than three-quarters of the world's illiterates live in only fifteen countries, including eight of the nine high-population countries (E-9): Bangladesh, Brazil, China, Egypt, India, Indonesia, Nigeria and Pakistan. In most of the fifteen countries, adult literacy rates have improved since 1985–1994, although continuing population growth translates into increases in absolute numbers of illiterates in several countries (e.g. Bangladesh, Ethiopia, Morocco). Adult literacy rates below 50% persist in several countries of South and West Asia, and sub-Saharan Africa. (Map 2.2)

The number of adult illiterates in China dropped sharply, by 98 million, which largely accounts for the rise in the average adult literacy rate for developing countries. China's achievement stemmed from sustained increases in primary school participation, highly targeted literacy programmes and the development of literate

Map 2.2: Adult literacy and number of illiterates, 1995–2004

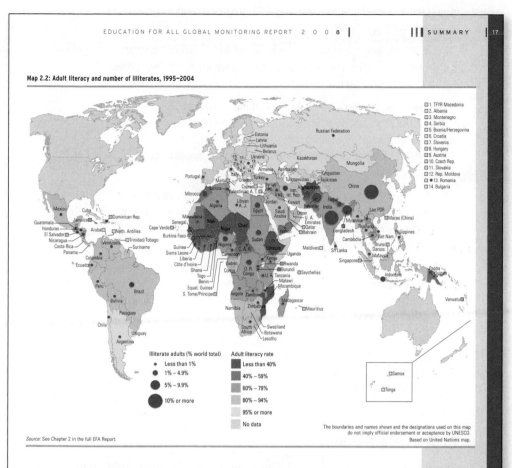

Illiterate adults (% world total)
- Less than 1%
- 1% – 4.9%
- 5% – 9.9%
- 10% or more

Adult literacy rate
- Less than 40%
- 40% – 59%
- 60% – 79%
- 80% – 94%
- 95% or more
- No data

1. TFYR Macedonia
2. Albania
3. Montenegro
4. Serbia
5. Bosnia/Herzegovina
6. Croatia
7. Slovenia
8. Hungary
9. Austria
10. Czech Rep.
11. Slovakia
12. Rep. Moldova
13. Romania
14. Bulgaria

Source: See Chapter 2 in the full EFA Report.

The boundaries and names shown and the designations used on this map do not imply official endorsement or acceptance by UNESCO. Based on United Nations map.

environments. Such environments, found in the public and private spheres and typically including written materials (newspapers, books, posters), broadcast media and information and communication technology (ICT), encourage the acquisition and use of literacy skills.

Youth literacy rates (among those aged 15 to 24) improved more rapidly in all regions, especially in the Arab States and East Asia, reflecting better access and participation in formal schooling among younger generations. In nearly all regions, the increase was accompanied by a reduction in the number of illiterates. Although youth literacy rates increased in sub-Saharan Africa by 9%, the region counted 5 million additional young illiterates, due to persisting high population growth and low school completion rates.

Literacy and equity

Globally, there are 89 literate women for every 100 literate men. Despite improvement over the 1985–1994 period, disparities are still marked in South and West Asia (67 literate women per 100 literate men), the Arab States (74) and sub-Saharan Africa (76).

Overall, illiteracy rates are highest in the countries with the greatest poverty, a link observed right down to the household level. More generally, for various social, cultural or political reasons, certain populations – such as migrants, indigenous groups and people with disabilities – suffer reduced access to formal education and literacy programmes.

Illiteracy rates are highest in the countries with the greatest poverty, a link observed right down to the household level

Starting a Conversation: Respond to "Education for All Global Monitoring Report"

In your writer's notebook, examine UNESCO's progress report by responding to the following questions:

1. What is the purpose of the opening paragraph of this excerpt? In what ways does it reflect the overall purpose of the report? In what ways does it help advance that purpose?

2. How do the structure and organization of the excerpt support the writers' purpose of evaluating progress on the expansion of educational opportunities? For example, in what ways do the numbered section headings support UNESCO's evaluation? How is the report's structure related to its evaluation criteria?

3. Although this report is about global education, it also discusses other issues such as malnutrition and poverty. Find and identify specific examples of this in the excerpt. How are these other issues related to the overall purpose of the document?

4. In the section discussing "Goal 4," why do the authors qualify the evidence they are using? What other kinds of evidence do the authors use, and what does their decision to use these kinds of evidence suggest about the report's intended readers?

5. Evaluative documents typically attempt to determine whether something has succeeded or failed, or to help readers understand how something might be improved or refined. How, specifically, does this report attempt to achieve these goals?

@ Download or print this Starting a Conversation activity at **bedfordstmartins.com/ conversation**.

Evaluative Essays

Evaluative essays convey a writer's judgments to readers who share an interest in a subject. The criteria that direct the writer's evaluation are usually identified early and are influenced by several factors, including the subject itself, the writer's purpose and perspective, prevailing opinions, and readers' knowledge of the subject. Unlike reviews, which usually focus on a single place or thing, or reports, which typically assess a particular project or initiative for a narrowly defined audience, evaluative essays often examine broader questions or issues for a more general group of readers.

In most cases, evidence from sources (such as published articles, personal interviews, direct observation, Web sites, and government documents) provides the basis for determining whether the subject of an evaluative essay measures up to the criteria. For example, details about the cost of an inner-city summer jobs program might be obtained from an interview with the program director or from published government reports.

Readers of evaluative essays—whether instructors, other students, politicians, or members of a particular profession—expect the writer's ideas to be well organized, well supported, and easy to read. Readers also expect the evaluation to be presented fairly and honestly, although they usually realize that writers will be influenced by their purposes, personal beliefs, and experiences.

 Christina Hoff Sommers and Sally Satel, MD
Emotional Correctness

In this essay, drawn from the book *One Nation under Therapy: How the Helping Culture Is Eroding Self-Reliance* (2005), Christina Hoff Sommers and Sally Satel evaluate the effectiveness of talk therapy for psychological health. The authors question the conventional wisdom that the most "well-adjusted" people are those who "focus attention on and talk about their feelings." Drawing on a wide range of sources, Sommers and Satel suggest that this dominant view comes up short and lacks empirical support. Christina Hoff Sommers is a philosopher and critic whose books include *Who Stole Feminism?* (1995) and *The War against Boys* (2001). Sally Satel is a psychiatrist and author whose work has appeared in the *New Republic*, the *Wall Street Journal*, and the *New York Times*.

Emotional Correctness

When the columnist Molly Ivins learned in 1999 that she had stage III inflammatory breast cancer, friends urged her to confront her feelings. Ivins tried it and found the experience "awful." As she wrote in *Time* magazine: "I am one of those people who are out of touch with their emotions. I tend to treat my emotions like unpleasant relatives—a long-distance call once or twice a year is more than enough. If I got in touch with them, they might come to stay."[1]

In an age when talking about one's feelings has become a mark of personal authenticity, Ivins's spirited refusal to open up is a breath of fresh air. Over the past thirty years or so, emotive outpouring has become routine on television and radio and in our leading news magazines. So powerful is this trend that Ivins's reluctance to dwell on her feelings about her cancer seems almost an affront. Merely suggesting to someone that she is talking too much about herself can be taken as "a form of abuse," observed Wendy Kaminer in her 1992 bestseller *I'm Dysfunctional, You're Dysfunctional*.[2] "What might have once been called whining is now exalted as a process of exerting selfhood," Kaminer continued, and "self-absorption is regarded as a form of self-expression."[3]

More than a decade after Kaminer's incisive exposé of confessional culture, the *New York Times Magazine* carried an article with the improbable title "Repress Yourself."[4] The author, psychologist Lauren Slater, sought to show that science was bearing out the value of self-restraint. "New research," she wrote, "shows that some traumatized people may be better off repressing the experience."[5] Slater cited recent studies showing that heart attack victims and bereaved spouses who "minimize, distract, and deny" felt far less anxious about their illness or loss months later.

Slater wasn't talking about everyone, of course. But she wanted to show that recounting one's anxieties (again and again) or pondering them (over and over) is not required for psychological health. It soon became clear that Slater had tapped a rich vein of rebellion against the still-pervasive idea that the well adjusted are those who focus attention on and talk about their feelings. Wrote one appreciative reader, "Maybe the talking cure would be helpful if you talked once, but most shrinks want the patient to go on and on, reducing you to only your horror story."[6] Another recalled Don Imus's remark "that in at least one of the early 'sessions' at the New Mexico ranch [for children with cancer], the children said, 'Send those psychologists home.'"[7]

By some definitions of "emotional intelligence" Slater and these readers are to be pitied. They are emotionally obtuse. Their reticence is supposed to put them at a disadvantage. But is this true?

About thirty years ago, a psychiatrist at the University of Wisconsin named John R. Marshall sought to confirm the already dominant view that openness was critical to mental health. In his essay "The Expression of Feelings," published in the *Archives of General Psychiatry*, Marshall noted that most mental health experts as well as the general public held the belief "that if a person can be convinced, allowed, or helped to express his feelings, he will in some way benefit from it."[8]

"Surely," Marshall postulated, "a concept so ubiquitous should be relatively easy to validate." But when he reviewed the literature for evidence of the benefits of sharing one's feelings, he found a confusing muddle of "ambiguous and contradictory studies."[9] The intervening years have produced a sizable and compelling body of research demonstrating that the expression of feelings is not a sure pathway to fulfillment. On the contrary, it often leads to unhappiness.

Consider anger. Charles Darwin was one of the first to observe that the verbal and physical expression of anger often begets anger. In *The Expression of the Emotions in Man and Animals*, published in 1872, he wrote that "the free expression by outward signs of an emotion intensifies it" and that "he who gives way to violent gestures will increase his rage."[10] A century later, experimental studies were confirming Darwin's observations.[11] By 1973 the president of the American Psychological Association, Albert Bandura, was calling for a moratorium on the use of "venting" in therapy.[12] That same year the psychologist Leonard Berkowitz, renowned for his work on aggression, wrote an article in *Psychology Today* called "The Case for Bottling Up Rage" in which he criticized "ventilationist" therapists.[13]

Following these pronouncements, data have continued to spill out of journals confirming, with few exceptions, that physical and verbal expression of anger is usually self-reinforcing.[14] Nor does talking about negative experiences necessarily ameliorate the anxiety accompanying them. Despite the claims of Jon G. Allen, a psychologist and author of *Treatment Approaches to Coping with Trauma*, who states that "the universal prescription for trauma [is to] talk about it with any trusted person who will listen," a number of studies show that talking per se has little effect on emotional recovery.[15] For example, Yale psychiatrists found no relationship between the degree to which Gulf War veterans talked with family about their experiences and their ratings of residual war-related anxiety.[16] After the 1989 Loma Prieta earthquake in Northern California, a Stanford University psychologist found no difference in distress between college students who talked about their experiences and those who did not.[17] Other researchers found a similar lack of protective effect of so-called social sharing on symptoms of distress.[18]

What about self-absorption? Intense contemplation of one's inner landscape, especially during times of distress, has long been considered necessary for deeper self-knowledge and, ultimately, for mental well-being. But this, too, turns out to be psychological lore. An incident from the life of John Stuart Mill, the nineteenth-century philosopher and one of the founders of utilitarianism, is exemplary.

Happiness was a state that Mill deemed the greatest good and believed it came from the pleasurable fulfillment of human desire. Now one might think this philosophy favors therapism since it seems to demand that we all pay a great deal of attention to our feelings and desires. But Mill found otherwise. A section in his autobiography called "A Crisis In My Mental History" describes his painful discovery that self-preoccupation can be disastrous.

In the fall of 1826, at age twenty, Mill suffered a debilitating, long-lasting depression. Antidepressants were not available to him. Nor was talk therapy; it was thirty years before Freud was even born. Mill's depression persisted and deepened. Relief came only by accident. Mill happened to read a very moving story that caused him to forget about his own psyche for a brief spell—and the depression lifted. This experience had a profound effect on him, leading the philosopher to adopt what he called an "anti-self-consciousness" theory. Here is how Mill describes the lesson he learned:

> The experience of this period had [a] very marked effect on my opinions and character. . . . Those only are happy who have their minds fixed on some object other than their own happiness; on the happiness of others, on the improvement of mankind, even on some art or pursuit. . . . Aiming thus at something else, they find happiness by the way. . . . The only chance is to treat, not happiness, but some end external to it, as the purpose of life. Let your self-consciousness, your scrutiny, your self-interrogation, exhaust themselves on [some external end].[19]

It is possible that Mill's depression was starting to fade before he found relief through literary distraction. In fact, an improvement in mood may be what gave him the capacity to be distracted in the first place; after all, a prominent symptom of major depression is the inability to focus on a task. In Mill's case, even if his depression were starting to melt as part of the natural cycle of remission, his ability to distract himself surely accelerated his recovery.[20] Ample research demonstrates that purposeful distraction can lift one's mood when depressed, just as ruminating about problems and the meaning of negative feelings can amplify them.

Now, two centuries after Mill and three decades after Marshall, despite a large body of research challenging the virtue of dwelling on and expressing one's emotions, those bedrock principles of therapism remain alive and well. We do not suggest that naturally passionate or voluble people should suppress their emotions or their desire to talk. But we caution against pressing, shaming, or subtly coercing anyone into trying to feel more deeply or be more expressive than befits his natural style.

Works Cited

1. Molly Ivins, "Who Needs Breasts, Anyway?" *Time*, February 18, 2002, p. 58.
2. Wendy Kaminer, *I'm Dysfunctional, You're Dysfunctional: The Recovery Movement and Other Self-Help Fashions* (New York: Vintage Books, 1993), p. 30.
3. Ibid., p. 31.
4. Lauren Slater, "Repress Yourself," *New York Times Magazine*, February 23, 2003.
5. Slater uses the term "repression" to refer to the conscious tamping down of particular thoughts and feelings rather than to a defensive process that operates outside of awareness. Freud used the term interchangeably. Slater might have used the word suppression (which refers to a conscious process only), but the article made her meaning clear.
6. *New York Times Magazine* discussion forum, entry 38 of 135, dated February 23, 2003.
7. Ibid., entry 30 of 135.
8. J. R. Marshall, "The Expression of Feelings," *Archives of General Psychiatry* 27, no. 6 (1972), pp. 786–90.
9. Ibid., p. 786.
10. Charles Darwin, *The Expression of the Emotions in Man and Animals*, 3rd ed. (New York: Oxford University Press, 1998), pp. 359–60.
11. Almost fifty years ago psychologist Seymour Feshbach encouraged a group of normal little boys to kick furniture and play with toy guns and generally run wild. Subsequently, they behaved much more aggressively during their free play times than they did before permission to run amok; see S. Feshbach, "The Catharsis Hypothesis and Some Consequences of Interaction with Aggression and Neutral Play Objects," *Journal of Personality and Social Psychology* 24 (1956), pp. 449–62; Shahbaz Khan Mallick and Boyd R. McCandless, "A Study of Catharsis Aggression," *Journal of Personality and Social Psychology* 4 (1966), pp. 591–96. A few years later psychologist R. Hornberger examined anger in adults. His subjects were insulted by a designated provoker and half of them instructed to pound nails into an object for about ten minutes. The other subjects did nothing. Next, all participants were given a chance to criticize the person who taunted them. Unexpectedly, the pounders, presumably having "released" their anger, were more hostile toward the person who insulted them than the nonpounders; see R. Hornberger, "The Differential Reduction of Aggressive Responses as a Function of Interpolated Activities," *American Psychology* 14 (1959), p. 354, abstract.
12. Albert Bandura in B. J. Bushman, "Does Venting Anger Feed or Extinguish the Flame? Catharsis, Rumination, Distraction, Anger, and Aggressive Responding," *Personality and Social Psychology Bulletin* 28 (2002), pp. 724–31.
13. Leonard Berkowitz, "The Case for Bottling Up Rage," *Psychology Today*, July 1973, p. 31; Leonard Berkowitz, "Experimental Investigations of Hostility Catharsis," *Journal of Consulting and Clinical Psychology* 35 (1970), pp. 1–7.

14. Carol Tavris, *Anger: The Misunderstood Emotion* (New York: Touchstone Books, 1989).

15. Jon G. Allen, *Coping with Trauma: A Guide to Self-Understanding* (Washington, D.C.: American Psychiatric Press, 1995), p. 237.

16. S. M. Southwick, C. A. Morgan III, and R. Rosenberg, "Social Sharing of Gulf War Experiences. Association with Trauma-Related Psychological Symptoms," *Journal of Nervous and Mental Disease* 188 (2000), pp. 695–700.

17. S. Nolen-Hoeksema and J. Morrow, "A Prospective Study of Depression and Posttraumatic Stress Symptoms After a Natural Disaster: The 1989 Loma Prieta Earthquake," *Journal of Personality and Social Psychology* 61, no. 1 (1991), pp. 115–21.

18. T. D. Borkovec and E. Costello, "Efficacy of Applied Relaxation and Cognitive Behavioral Therapy in the Treatment of Generalized Anxiety Disorder," *Journal of Consulting and Clinical Psychology* 61 (1993), pp. 611–19; Bernard Rime, "Mental Rumination, Social Sharing, and the Recovery From Emotional Exposure," in *Emotion, Disclosure, and Health*, ed. James W. Pennebaker (Washington, D.C.: American Psychological Association, 1995), pp. 271–92; P. P. Schnurr, J. D. Ford, M. J. Friedman et al., "PTSD in World War II Mustard Gas Test Participants: A Preliminary Report," *Annals of the New York Academy of Science* 821 (1997), pp. 425–29; R. Tait and R. C. Silver, "Coming to Terms with Major Negative Life Events," in *Unintended Thought*, ed. John A. Bargh and James S. Uleman (New York: Guilford Press, 1989), pp. 351–82.

19. John Stuart Mill, *Autobiography* (New York: Penguin, 1989), pp. 117–18.

20. Notably, Mill biographers believe that his encounter with depression created a need to reconcile the intellectual, rational self with the feeling self and thus led to a broader definition of liberalism. See Bruce Mazlish, *James and John Stuart Mill* (New York: Basic Books, 1975); J. Geller, "A Crisis in My Mental History," *Psychiatric Services* 54, no. 10 (2003), pp. 1347–49.

Starting a Conversation: Respond to "Emotional Correctness"

In your writer's notebook, consider how Sommers and Satel respond to their writing situation by answering the following questions:

1. Sommers and Satel question a "still-pervasive idea" (par. 4) that is broadly accepted throughout American culture. What is this idea, and how do they characterize it? What does their characterization reveal about their own attitude toward the subject?

2. The authors use the phrase "emotional intelligence" (par. 5) but do not define it explicitly. What do you think the term means? Why is it relevant to their evaluation?

3. What criteria do Sommers and Satel rely on to evaluate the effectiveness of emotional openness and the "talking cure"? What is their overall judgment, and how do they translate that judgment into a recommendation for their readers?

4. Sommers and Satel draw on several different kinds of sources to support their evaluation. Locate examples of anecdotal evidence, psychological studies, self-help literature, and historical perspective. To what end do the authors use each type of evidence? How does the mix of sources contribute to their overall purpose?

5. In paragraph 9, Sommers and Satel quote an author with whom they disagree. Why do they do this? How does it support their point?

@ Download or print this Starting a Conversation activity at **bedfordstmartins.com/ conversation**.

How Can I Write an Evaluative Essay?

In Process

An Evaluative Essay about Programs to Reduce College Drinking

Dwight Haynes wrote an evaluative essay for his introductory composition course. Dwight learned about his topic by reading articles about approaches to reducing alcohol consumption by college students. Follow Dwight's efforts to write his evaluative essay by visiting **bedfordstmartins.com/conversation**. You can read excerpts of interviews with Dwight and read drafts of his essay.

If you regularly make purchases online, you've almost certainly run into reviews on sites such as Amazon or NexTag. Chances are also good that you've turned to your local newspaper or searched the Web for help deciding which movie to watch or which new restaurant to try. It turns out that product and media reviews are both plentiful and easy to locate. That's not the case, however, for other types of evaluations. For instance, if you're hoping to learn whether it would be better to work an extra ten hours per week or to take out a college loan, or if you're trying to determine whether your community should invest in renewable energy credits or start its own wind farm, you're likely to find that the best place to look for answers is in the mirror.

Evaluative essays allow you to address subjects—some as complex as genetic engineering in agriculture and others as seemingly straightforward as deciding how to travel between home and school—that connect to your personal, academic, or professional life. Like other academic essays, they also present some intriguing challenges for writers. In addition to choosing an appropriate subject for evaluation, you must identify criteria on which to base your judgment, learn enough about your subject to make an informed judgment about how well it measures up to your criteria, and convey your judgments in a well-written, well-organized, readable manner.

This section helps you tune in to the conversations around you and take on the role of evaluator as you choose a subject, conduct your evaluation, prepare your draft, and review and improve your draft. As you work on your essay, you'll follow Dwight Haynes, a first-year student who wrote an evaluative essay about approaches to reducing alcohol consumption by college students.

Find a Conversation and Listen In

Evaluative essays allow you to share your judgments with readers who will consider your conclusions seriously and, in many cases, act on your recommendations. Your decision about which conversation to join should reflect your interests and your writing assignment. For example, were you surprised by a government plan to regulate the banking industry? Are you wondering whether a promising new television show has a future? Are you skeptical about claims that a new battery technology will usher in the age of the electric car? If so, ask yourself what interests you most about the subject, and then start listening to what others have had to say about it.

EXPLORE YOUR NEEDS, INTERESTS, AND CONCERNS

Evaluative documents are most successful when their subject matches up with readers' needs, interests, or concerns. Readers of *Skiing* magazine, for instance, typically view the sport as an important part of their lives and are interested in new developments in equipment and techniques. An evaluation of the latest skis from Rossignol is likely to address the needs and interests of these readers, many of whom might be in the market for new equipment. Similarly, readers of the magazine might be interested in an evaluation of the effectiveness of conditioning techniques or energy bars.

Readers are also likely to read evaluative documents that address their concerns. Subscribers to *Skiing*, for example, might be concerned about the impact of climate change on skiing or about plans to allow oil shale excavation in areas near ski resorts.

Engaging and effective evaluative essays deal with subjects that address not only your readers' needs, interests, and concerns but also your own. As you consider potential subjects for your essay, ask yourself what has caught your attention lately — or better yet, what has long been a matter of interest or concern to you. And be sure to consider your current needs. If you can write about a subject that will help you address your needs, you'll be more invested in conducting the evaluation. To explore your needs, interests, and concerns, cast a wide net. Use idea-generating strategies such as brainstorming, freewriting, or clustering (see pp. 33–37) to respond to questions like these:

- **Products.** Take an inventory of your personal interests, such as hobbies, outdoor activities, or sports. What new products have been introduced lately? Are you thinking of buying (or have you bought) any of them? Are they truly useful, or has the manufacturer overhyped them? Would you recommend them to others?

- **Media.** What's new and interesting in books, movies, television, music, video games, or the Web? What have you read, watched, or listened to that made you think? Have you noticed any developments that trouble you? Have you heard or read criticisms that you think are unfair?

- **Campus life.** Are you thinking about joining a club, team, or group but can't decide if it's worth your time? Do your peers engage in any behaviors that seem dangerous or unhealthy to you? Have you attended a guest lecture or student performance that you felt was overrated or underappreciated? Has a new building or work of public art sparked controversy?

- **Ideas.** Have you been worried or intrigued by a new development you read about in a professional or trade journal? Have you heard an unusual proposal for a new public policy or business incentive? How have you responded to the different teaching methods you've encountered in your high school and college classes? What do you make of conflicting arguments in your course readings?

You'll find additional ideas for evaluative writing projects at the end of this chapter (p. 331).

Working Together: Try It Out Loud

Before you start conducting an evaluation, start a conversation with your classmates about the advantages and disadvantages of majoring in a particular subject. Form small groups and choose a subject area to evaluate, such as English, history, business, psychology, chemistry, math, art, or sociology. As a group, identify the kinds of criteria you will use to evaluate each major, such as personal rewards, academic challenges, skill development, or future employment opportunities. Then take turns applying the criteria to your major (or the major that currently interests you most) while the other members of the group listen, respond, and ask questions. After everyone has had a chance to speak, revisit your criteria. Were they useful in helping you evaluate the majors? Would you consider changing these criteria?

If you are doing this activity during class, share your conclusions about your criteria with other groups. Then, as a class, take a few minutes to reflect on the exercise. Did every group use the same criteria? If not, what might account for the differences?

@ Download or print this Working Together activity at bedfordstmartins.com/conversation.

SEARCH THE WEB
The World Wide Web is a rich source of information and ideas for writers conducting evaluations. Product and media reviews are among the most popular items on the Web, and online editions of newspapers and magazines offer a seemingly endless

collection of commentary and critique on everything from the latest diets to current affairs to new techniques for studying and taking exams. If you're interested in whether professional soccer has a future in the United States, for example, you could find data and opinions on Web sites such as SoccerTimes.com and USSoccer.com, check out developments reported in the sports sections of newspapers that have a Web presence, and read the online versions of magazines such as *SoccerAmerica* and *90:00*. To search for information and evaluations for just about any subject that intrigues you, consult the following Web search resources.

General Web search. The easiest way to learn about a subject through the Web is to visit an established search site, such as Google (www.google.com), Ask (www.ask.com), Bing (www.Bing.com), Yahoo! (www.yahoo.com), or AllTheWeb (www.alltheweb.com). In response to your key words and phrases, these sites present ranked lists of sites they judge relevant to your search terms. These sites also provide advanced search forms that allow you to specify which keywords and phrases must, might, or should not appear on a page; to limit search results to particular domains such as .gov or .org; and to limit your search to Web sites updated within a specific time period, such as the last week or month.

Web directories. You can also search the Web using Web directories, such as Open Directory Project (www.dmoz.org) and WWW Virtual Library (http://vlib.org). Directories allow you to browse lists of prescreened sites by clicking on general topics, such as Arts or Business, and then successively narrow your search by clicking on sub-topics. The lists are created and maintained by people — rather than by computer programs — so they provide more selective results than a broad search can; however, these lists also reflect the biases and assumptions of their creators, so you might miss out on other sites that are relevant to your topic.

Meta search. Meta search sites, such as Dogpile (www.dogpile.com) and Metacrawler (www.metacrawler.com), allow you to conduct a single search and return results from several Web search engines or Web directories at the same time. These sites typically search leading general search sites and directories and then present a limited number of results on a single page.

News search. To conduct focused searches for current and archived news reports, try sites such as Google News (http://news.google.com) and World News (www.wn.com).

Reference search. Sites such as Encyclopedia.com (www.encyclopedia.com) and Information Please (www.infoplease.com) allow you search for information that has been collected in encyclopedias, almanacs, atlases, dictionaries, and other reference resources.

Media search. The Web is home not only to textual information but also to a growing collection of other types of media, such as photographs, podcasts, and streaming video. You can locate useful information about your subject by searching for recordings of radio broadcasts, television shows, documentaries, podcasts, and other media using established search sites, such as Ask, Google, and Yahoo!, as well as specialized sites such as YouTube (www.youtube.com) for video, Picsearch (www.picsearch.com) for images, and Song Fiend (www.songfiend.com) for music.

Deep Web search. If your search comes up empty, try sites such as AcademicInfo.net (www.academicinfo.net) and Complete Planet (http://aip.completeplanet.com), which provide access to thousands of searchable, public-access databases and can locate information that is not available through other types of Web searches.

You can learn more about searching the Web in Chapter 12.

In Process

Searching the Web

Dwight Haynes learned about promising subjects by searching for information on the Web.

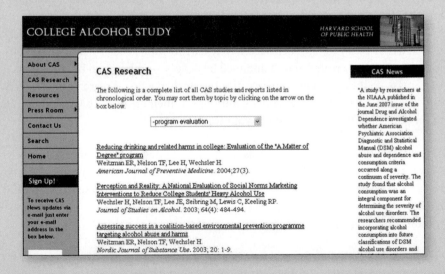

Dwight used the search terms *alcohol* and *college*. He found several journal articles on the Harvard School of Public Health's College Alcohol Study Web site.

Dwight used a search engine to look for Web sites with keywords such as *alcohol, higher education, drinking, college, students,* and *awareness.* His searches allowed him to identify and locate enough sources that he was able to get a good initial understanding of the subject. Because he was particularly interested in how colleges respond to student drinking, he decided to download a study written by E. R. Weitzman and her colleagues at the Harvard School of Public Health, who had found correlations between a particular type of alcohol prevention campaign — the environmental approach — and reduced alcohol consumption among students.

NARROW YOUR FOCUS BY ASKING QUESTIONS

As you learn about possible subjects for your evaluation, use the following questions to identify which ones capture your interest and best meet the needs of your assignment. Each question focuses your attention on a subject in a different way, and each provides a useful starting point for an evaluative essay. Depending on the subject, you'll find that some questions are more relevant than others.

- **Importance.** Do you think this is an important subject? If so, why? Who else believes that it's important? Why do they believe that it's important? What would readers do with an evaluation of this subject?

- **Appropriateness.** What aspects of this topic lend themselves to evaluation? Do you have the resources and the time to learn about it and examine it closely?

- **Effectiveness.** Is _____ an effective response to _____? Is it designed well? Is it likely to produce the intended results?

- **Costs/benefits.** What are the benefits of _____? What are the costs? Are the benefits worth the costs?

- **Prevailing opinion.** How have others responded to this subject? How did they reach their conclusions? What have they neglected to consider?

In Process

Focusing on a Subject

Dwight Haynes brainstormed in response to the questions above about a subject he was considering for his evaluative essay: binge drinking among college students. As he asked and answered questions, two promising focuses emerged: the costs and benefits that college students associate with drinking and the effectiveness of different approaches to reducing drinking on college campuses.

Costs: delayed graduation, failure to graduate, health problems, social problems (losing friends), poorer academic performance/lower GPA, less learning (just getting by)

Benefits: fun, relaxation, less difficult to talk with people, being part of the group, looking cool

Effectiveness of approaches for stopping or reducing drinking:
— education (might work)
— punishment/prevention (hasn't worked very well)
— alternative activities (might work for some)

> Dwight used two sets of questions to guide his brainstorming. He generated lists of ideas in response to each approach.

After reviewing the results of his brainstorming, Dwight decided that it would be difficult to evaluate the costs and benefits of drinking. Instead, he chose to focus on the effectiveness of approaches to reducing drinking on campus.

Conduct Your Evaluation

Far too many evaluators tell readers little more than "this is good (or bad or ineffective or the best choice) because I say so." It's as if these writers believe that readers will accept their conclusions without question or doubt.

As a reader, when was the last time you did that?

If you're like most readers, you probably expect evaluators to provide sound reasoning and appropriate evidence to back up their judgments. As a writer, you should strive to offer the same things to your readers. The judgments you reach in your evaluation should move beyond knee-jerk reactions or general pronouncements. For example, rather than saying a baseball manager should be fired merely because the team failed to win the division, you should also consider the quality of players available throughout the season, the strength of the competition, and the decisions made during key games.

An effective evaluative essay is based on a clear understanding of your subject, a carefully chosen set of criteria, and well-supported judgments — first, about how well the subject of your evaluation meets each criterion and, second, about the overall results of your evaluation. As you conduct your evaluation, start by choosing a set of criteria that are relevant and clearly defined. Then review what you've learned about your subject, and consider whether you've collected enough evidence to make an informed judgment. Finally, use your criteria and evidence to make your judgments, making an effort to ensure that your evaluation is balanced and fair.

DEFINE YOUR CRITERIA

Criteria are the factors on which your judgments about a subject are based. In many written conversations, criteria are well established. Movie reviewers, for example, typically base their judgments on plot, characterization, cinematography, editing, and directing, while restaurant reviewers tend to use criteria such as the taste and presentation of the food, the attentiveness and courteousness of the waitstaff, the cleanliness and attractiveness of the restaurant, and the cost of a meal. Similarly, writers of progress reports tend to focus on a fairly consistent set of criteria, most often results, responses to unexpected challenges, and cost-effectiveness.

Even when evaluating well-established subjects, however, writers often depart from the norm. A movie reviewer might focus on the use of product placement in a film, while a music reviewer might draw criteria from poetry or drama to evaluate a new rap album.

Often, you will have the option of choosing among a wide range of evaluative criteria. Consider, for example, the criteria you might use to evaluate competing health plans for employees at a small company:

- overall cost to the company
- cost per employee to participate in the plan
- deductibles
- coverage
- choice of health care providers
- ease of access to plan information
- access to plan administrators
- required paperwork
- speed of reimbursement to employees

If you chose all of these criteria, your evaluation would be quite lengthy. To keep the evaluation brief and to the point—and, of course, useful for readers—you would focus on only a few criteria. If you were creating a brief overview of competing health care plans for managers, you might focus on overall cost to the company, employee costs, coverage, required paperwork, and access to plan administrators. If you were creating a report for employees, on the other hand, criteria might include employee costs, deductibles, coverage, choice of health care providers, ease of access to plan information, and speed of reimbursement. The key is to choose those criteria most relevant to your subject, your purpose, and the needs, interests, and backgrounds of your readers.

IDENTIFY EVIDENCE

Evidence provides evaluators with a basis for making their judgments. Evaluative essays tend to rely on a mix of evidence from published sources, observations, and personal experience.

Some evidence is quantitative—that is, it can be measured. For instance, the rate of inflation over the past decade or the number of people participating in a noontime activity program can be found through sources such as public documents or direct observation. Other evidence is qualitative—that is, it is based on the writer's experiences with and reactions to the subject. Music reviewers, for example, usually base their evaluations on the originality of the music, the quality of the performance, and the quality of the recording and production. Some criteria, such as cost, can be judged on both quantitative and qualitative evidence. For instance, you can calculate the amount of money that would be required to pay for a particular program or solution, but you can also view cost in terms of its impact on quality of life or on the environment.

To identify evidence for your evaluation, list the criteria you'll use to conduct your evaluation. Determine whether each criterion will rely on quantitative or qualitative evidence. Then pinpoint potential sources of evidence for your evaluation by reviewing your initial research and any notes you've taken. Next to each criterion, list the evidence on which you'll base your judgments. If you find that you don't have enough evidence to support a thorough evaluation, look for more information.

MAKE YOUR JUDGMENTS

Once you've identified and organized your evidence, you're ready to determine how well your subject measures up to the criteria you've selected. The quality of your judgments depends not only on the number and kinds of criteria you've defined and the amount and types of evidence you've collected but also on your commitment to being fair and reasonable. If you are applying quantitative evidence to a small number of criteria, making your judgments might be a fairly straightforward process. However, if you are making multiple judgments on the basis of qualitative evidence, it might take significantly more time and effort to complete your evaluation. The challenge you face in making your judgments will also depend on how much impact your decision has on your life or the lives of others. For example, weighing which of three job offers to accept is of far greater consequence than comparing the features and costs of two video game systems.

To make judgments about your subject, list your criteria and examine the evidence you've assembled. Write down your judgments in as much detail as possible so that you can draw on them as you draft your essay.

Prepare a Draft

Writers of evaluative essays focus on conveying the results of their evaluation process to their readers. As you prepare your draft, you'll decide how to convey the overall result of your evaluation, present and define your criteria, share the evidence on which you've based your judgments, design your essay, and frame your evaluation for your readers.

Your draft will be strongly influenced by the purpose of your evaluation. If your intention is to help readers understand whether something has succeeded or failed, for example, consider how your readers will react to your judgments. If you are arguing that a project has failed, you might want to discuss whether the project should be carried out with specific changes or whether it should be abandoned altogether. If you are offering your judgments about which of several options is best, you might want to discuss the trade-offs associated with accepting your judgment. And if you are trying to help readers understand how your subject might be improved or refined,

In Process

Making Judgments

For his evaluation of approaches to reducing college drinking, Dwight Haynes selected two criteria: the overall effectiveness of programs that used a particular approach and the effort required to create programs based on an approach. To sort through his notes and decide what information would best support his evaluation, he created a table that identified possible evidence for his criteria as they applied to two competing approaches and then made preliminary judgments about each approach.

Approach	Criterion	Evidence	Judgment
Social norms	Effort	Relatively low effort. Turner says it focuses on marketing and education, using ads on Facebook, campus posters, etc.	Easy to start and maintain without tons of work.
	Effectiveness	Some research raises concerns about effectiveness (Wechsler et al.), but DeJong et al. found it associated with lower perceptions of student drinking levels and lower alcohol consumption.	Effective. Good choice for smaller schools or those without the resources for another approach.
Environmental	Effort	Larger and more ambitious than social norms programs. Includes collaborations with local law enforcement agencies, the local business community, and local health care providers (Weitzman et al.).	Complex, but justified by effectiveness.
	Effectiveness	Effective because it addresses more of the factors involved in student drinking (Weitzman et al. and Dowdall interview).	Most effective.

you might want to include guidance about how to put those improvements or refinements into practice.

STATE YOUR OVERALL JUDGMENT

The goal of an evaluative essay is to share your judgment about a subject, often with the intention of helping readers make a decision. It's usually a good idea, then, to give readers a summary of your overall judgment—your verdict—in the form of a thesis statement. In some cases, you'll want to mention the criteria on which your judgment is based so that readers understand the thinking behind your evaluation. Your thesis statement can also frame your subject in a way that helps achieve your purpose and address the needs and interests of your readers. Consider, for example, how the following thesis statements about locally grown produce set up different expectations among readers.

> **Thesis statement 1:** Buying your fruits and vegetables at a farmer's market might be a little less convenient and a little more expensive than going to the supermarket, but you'll be rewarded with healthier, tastier food.

> **Thesis statement 2:** Importing fruits and vegetables carries hidden environmental costs that outweigh the benefits of having year-round access to seasonable produce.

> **Thesis statement 3:** By insisting on produce that has been grown nearby, consumers can support family farms and have a positive impact on their local economies.

Each of these thesis statements focuses on different aspects of the same subject. The first one emphasizes consumer concerns about price, convenience, and quality. The second thesis statement directs attention to the environmental consequences of shipping food long distances. The third one points to the economic benefits of supporting local businesses. Each thesis statement would lead to quite different evaluative essays.

Where you place your thesis statement depends largely on your understanding of your readers' needs and interests. Sharing your overall judgment at the beginning of the essay allows readers to follow the logic of your evaluation process and better understand how the criteria and evidence relate to the evaluation's overall result. However, if your overall judgment is likely to be seen as unusual or controversial, it might be best to share it later in the essay, after allowing evidence to unfold in a way that helps readers understand the reasons underlying your conclusions.

Is your thesis statement focused enough? See Chapter 15 for help.

PRESENT YOUR EVALUATION

To be effective, your evaluative essay must do more than present a straightforward report of criteria, evidence, and judgments. It should help readers understand your subject in a particular way and show them that you've chosen appropriate criteria and evidence. Equally important, it should prove to your readers that you've based your judgments on sound and thorough reasoning and that you've conducted a balanced evaluation.

Explain your criteria. Criteria are an essential part of any evaluation (see p. 312). Your readers should understand not only what your criteria are but also why you've selected them. In some cases, you can rely on general knowledge to supply the rationale for your choice of one or more of your criteria. If you were evaluating an advertising campaign for a new soft drink, for example, you could probably rely on a widespread understanding that sales figures are an important factor in the evaluation. Similarly, you wouldn't need to justify your use of nutrition and weight loss in an evaluation of diet programs.

In most cases, however, you should define your criteria explicitly. For example, if you were evaluating a new state program that encourages high school students to take additional driver education courses after receiving their licenses, you might use criteria such as teenagers' willingness to sign up for the courses and the effectiveness of the program. But how would you define a criterion such as *effectiveness*? In the context of continuing education courses for newly licensed drivers, it might mean lowering the number of accidents attributable to inexperience, or preventing injuries or deaths associated with teenage drivers, or increasing drivers' awareness of the problems caused by distraction or impatience, or some combination of these factors. Your readers should understand how you've defined your criteria so that they can follow — and, ideally, accept — your evaluation.

Support your judgments with evidence. Providing evidence to explain the reasoning behind your judgments helps readers accept your evaluation as valid and carefully thought out. Evidence can also help deepen your discussion of the overall results of your evaluation. In general, you'll want to apply evidence to each of your criteria to show readers how your subject measures up. You can also use evidence to

- introduce your subject
- define your criteria
- provide examples and illustrations
- associate particular ideas and concepts with authorities, such as political leaders, subject-matter experts, or people who have been affected by your subject

Whether you draw your evidence from print, broadcast, or electronic sources, or from field research, be sure to identify your sources. Evaluative essays typically rely on citation systems such as those provided by the Modern Language Association and

In Process

Using Evidence to Support Judgments

Dwight Haynes drew on information and opinions from his sources to support his judgment that the social norms marketing approach to reducing alcohol consumption among college students is not as effective as it might seem.

> Dwight cites information from a journal article, identified by the authors' names. He includes the page on which the quotation can be found.

> An expert is identified in an attribution.

> Using APA style, Dwight notes that one source is cited in another.

The environmental approach involves a mix of strategies designed to reduce or eliminate alcohol consumption, using the resources of both the campus community and the surrounding town or city. According to Weitzman et al. (2004), "Drinking-related norms and behaviors result from interactions over time and space between individuals and their environments" (p. 188). By changing the "contextual forces," like availability of alcohol, that encourage students to drink, this approach more strongly emphasizes policies that directly put a stop to excessive drinking—unlike the social norms marketing approach, which relies on influencing individual behavior (p. 187). As George W. Dowdall, author of *College Drinking: Reframing a Social Problem*, has argued, "Informational approaches used alone simply don't work. Trying to deal with college drinking as only an individual's choice doesn't work either. Instead, colleges should try to shape the entire environment that shapes college drinking" (as cited in Jaschik, 2009). By cracking down on when and how alcohol is available on campus, and by taking steps to keep underage students from accessing alcohol off campus, colleges that adopt the environmental approach tend to be more successful in decreasing the overall rate of student drinking and the negative consequences that can come from excessive alcohol use.

the American Psychological Association to identify sources. If you are unsure about which citation system to use, consult your instructor. (You can read more about how to use evidence to support your evaluation in Chapter 17.)

Be fair. To be effective, your evaluation must be fair. The notion of fairness is sometimes confused with objectivity. In fact, being truly objective is difficult—and perhaps impossible. Each writer approaches an evaluation with a particular set of experiences, values, and beliefs that lead to a particular outlook on a subject. These differences among writers—even the most disciplined and rigorous—lead to minor and sometimes major differences in their judgments, even when they work with the same criteria and evidence. Being fair and reasonable, as a result, does not necessarily mean coming to the same conclusion as another writer. Instead, it means taking the time to consider different points of view, weighing evidence carefully, and being as consistent in your judgments as possible.

One way to ensure fairness is to provide a context for your evaluation. By making it clear to your readers what you've evaluated, what you've considered during the evaluation process, and how you've approached the evaluation process, you can help them understand how and why you've come to your conclusions. By providing this context, you'll increase the likelihood that your readers will view your evaluation as sound and well supported.

Working Together: Ask Whether Your Judgments Are Fair

Use feedback from other writers to assess the fairness of your judgments. Describe your subject, briefly define your criteria, present your evidence, and discuss your judgments. The other members of the group should pose reasonable questions about your choice of criteria, selection of evidence, and judgments, paying particular attention to the reasonableness of your judgments. Whenever possible, they should also suggest alternative judgments. Take notes on the doubts expressed by other members of the group so that you can consider them during revision.

@ Download or print this Working Together activity at bedfordstmartins.com/conversation.

CONSIDER GENRE AND DESIGN

Like other academic essays, evaluative essays can benefit from thoughtful consideration of design. Bear in mind your readers' expectations about design elements such as wide margins, double-spaced lines, page numbers, and a readable body font. In addition, consider the benefits of using headings and subheadings and bulleted and numbered lists.

- **Headings and subheadings** can help readers understand the organization of the essay, serve as transitional devices between sections and subsections, and add visual interest to what would otherwise be pages of unbroken text.

- **Numbered and bulleted lists** display brief passages of related information using numbers or symbols (usually round "bullets"). The surrounding white space draws the eye to the list, highlighting the information for your readers, while the brief content in each entry can make concepts or processes easier to understand.

These design elements can make significant contributions to the readability and overall effectiveness of your essay. Headings and subheadings identify and briefly summarize the sections of your essay, helping readers to compare the judgments you've made in different sections of your essay. Numbered and bulleted lists allow you to present evidence or a series of judgments about a subject in a compact form. If you use similar lists—for example, of strengths and weaknesses or of costs and benefits—in different sections of your essay, readers will find it easier to locate and compare the lists.

You can find a detailed discussion of document design in Chapter 18.

FRAME YOUR EVALUATION

The choices you make as you structure your essay will affect how your readers understand and interpret your evaluation. Your strategies for organizing, introducing, and concluding your essay should take into account your purposes—for example, whether you are assessing success and failure or making a recommendation, and what you hope readers will do after they've read your essay—as well as your readers' needs and interests. They should also take into account your criteria and the nature and amount of evidence you've assembled to support your judgments.

Organization. To decide how to organize your criteria, evidence, and judgments, create an outline or a map (see p. 550). Most evaluative essays are organized either according to the items that are being evaluated or by the criteria used to evaluate them. If you are evaluating a single item, such as a proposed change to class registration procedures or the performance of a musical group on a recently released album, you are likely to present your evaluation as a series of judgments, applying one criterion after another to your subject. Paul Goldberger takes this approach in his place evaluation, "Bowery Dreams" (see p. 287). If you are evaluating more than one item, you can use your criteria to organize your discussion, or, as Sam Eifling does in his review of energy drinks (p. 276), you can discuss each item in turn. Evaluative essays can also employ several of the organizational patterns discussed in Chapter 16, such as comparison and contrast, costs and benefits, or strengths and weaknesses.

Introduction. Most evaluative essays begin with some explanation of the context and a description of the subject. In some cases, your readers will be unfamiliar with particular aspects of the subject—or even with the subject as a whole. For example, if you are evaluating a new technology for distributing movies online, your readers will probably appreciate a brief discussion of how it works. Similarly, if you are reviewing a movie, it can help to provide some details about its plot, characters, and setting—although not, of course, its ending or surprising plot twists. Once you've established the parameters of your evaluation and decided how to frame your introduction, you can use a range of strategies to put it into words, including asking questions, leading with a quotation, or telling a story. You can read more about strategies for introducing your essay in Chapter 16.

Conclusion. Your conclusion offers an opportunity to highlight or even, as Paul Goldberger did in his place evaluation, to present the overall results of your evaluation. If you've already presented your overall results in the form of a thesis statement earlier in the essay, you might use your conclusion to reiterate your main judgment or to make a recommendation for your readers. You can also turn to other strategies to conclude your essay, such as linking to your introduction, asking a question, or speculating about the future. Chapter 16 provides more strategies for using your conclusion to frame the results of your evaluation.

Review and Improve Your Draft

Writing a successful evaluative essay depends on choosing an appropriate subject, considering your writing situation, selecting appropriate criteria and evidence, making fair judgments, and deciding how to frame and organize your evaluation. Don't be surprised if your first draft doesn't successfully address all of these challenges: few first drafts do. Instead, take advantage of the opportunity to revise. As you review your draft, pay particular attention to your choice of criteria, your selection of evidence, and the fairness of your judgments.

REVIEW YOUR CRITERIA

Once you've written a first draft, read it carefully. Then step back and ask questions about your criteria. Ask whether you've used enough—or too many—criteria (generally, evaluative essays include between two and five). Most important, ask whether you've considered the most significant criteria. For example, an evaluation of competing approaches to funding intercollegiate athletic programs that doesn't consider the impact of those approaches on tuition and fees is missing an important criterion.

RECONSIDER YOUR EVIDENCE

Good criteria and reasonable judgments are the heart of an effective evaluative essay, but they are seldom sufficient to convince readers to accept your point of view. Presenting an evaluation—even a careful one—that lacks well-chosen evidence is like telling your readers, "Look. I'm really smart, and I'm making good judgments. Trust me." Few readers, of course, give their trust so easily. As you review your essay, ask whether you've provided enough evidence to support your judgments. Then ask whether you've chosen the right evidence. As you conduct your review, make sure that you haven't relied so heavily on a single source of evidence that it appears as

Peer Review: Improve Your Evaluative Essay

One of the biggest challenges writers face is reading a draft of their own work as a reader rather than as the writer. Because you know what you're trying to say, you find it easy to understand your draft. To determine how you should revise your draft, ask a friend or classmate to read your essay and consider how well you've adopted the role of evaluator (see p. 274).

Purpose	1. What subject does the essay address? Is it a subject that readers will need or want to know about?
	2. Does the thesis statement clearly convey an overall judgment?
	3. What role does this essay take on? Is it recommending improvements or making a final judgment?
Readers	4. Did you find the essay interesting? Why or why not?
	5. Does the evaluation address my readers' needs, interests, and backgrounds?
	6. Do the criteria seem appropriate for the subject? Did I use too many criteria? Too few? Should I add or remove any criteria?
Sources	7. Have I provided enough evidence to support my judgments? Too much?
	8. Have I relied on a particular source — or a particular type of source — too heavily?
	9. Do my sources strike you as reliable and appropriate? Does any of the evidence I've used seem questionable?
Context	10. Have I provided enough information about the subject? About my reasons for evaluating it?
	11. Do the judgments made in the essay seem fair? Did you detect any bias or agenda in the way I presented my evaluation? Do you know of any alternative points of view that I should take into consideration?
	12. Is the physical appearance of my essay appropriate? Should I consider adding headings or lists?

For each of the points listed above, ask your reviewers to provide concrete advice about what you should do to improve your draft. It can help if you ask them to adopt the role of an editor — someone who is working with you to improve your draft. You can read more about these and other collaborative activities in Chapter 4.

@ Download or print this Peer Review activity at bedfordstmartins.com/conversation.

though you're simply borrowing someone else's evaluation. Try to draw evidence from multiple sources, such as published documents and personal experience.

ENSURE THAT YOUR JUDGMENTS ARE FAIR AND REASONABLE

The most important question you can ask about your evaluative essay is whether your judgments are well grounded and convincing. Individual judgments should reflect the criteria and evidence you've presented to your readers. And your overall conclusion should reflect your judgments as a whole. If your judgments do not line up with your criteria and evidence, your readers will question your conclusions. Similarly, if your judgments are based on poorly chosen criteria or inadequate evidence, your readers will also question your conclusions. On the other hand, if your readers see your criteria as appropriate and your judgments as reasonable and well supported, they'll be far more likely to act on your evaluation.

 ## Student Essay

 Dwight Haynes, "Making Better Choices: Two Approaches to Reducing College Drinking"

The following evaluative essay was written by featured writer Dwight Haynes. Follow Dwight's efforts to write his essay by visiting **bedfordstmartins.com/conversation**. You can read excerpts of interviews in which he discusses his work on his essay and also read drafts of his essay. Dwight's essay follows the requirements of the sixth edition of the *APA Publication Manual*. However, this edition does not include specific instructions for formatting student essays, so Dwight's essay has been formatted to fit typical requirements for undergraduate student writing. To see Dwight's essay formatted for an APA publication, please visit **bedfordstmartins.com/conversation**.

Making Better Choices 1

A cover page provides the essay title and information about the writer, class, and submission date.

Making Better Choices: Two Approaches to Reducing College Drinking

Dwight Haynes

CO150 College Composition

Professor Palmquist

March 20, 2009

Making Better Choices 2

Making Better Choices: Two Approaches to Reducing College Drinking

Over the past few decades, alcohol consumption among college students has
received a great deal of attention. Despite humorous portrayals of college parties
and the drunken antics depicted in movies and on television, serious concerns
have been raised about health, safety, and academic issues associated with
heavy drinking on campus. Most alarming, excessive levels of drinking are thought
to cause between 1,400 and 1,700 student deaths each year (Jaschik, 2009).
Also significant are the physical harm and violent behavior that tend to arise
from heavy drinking: 500,000 students each year sustain injuries as a result of
alcohol use, and another 600,000 per year report being victims of alcohol-
fueled assaults, including rape (Wechsler et al., 2003). Heavy drinking has been
blamed for a host of other problems as well, including vandalism, alcohol poi-
soning, and academic failure. Rather than waiting until after students suffer
the consequences of alcohol abuse to intervene, colleges have found that pre-
ventative programs can teach better habits and help students avoid the problems caused by underage or irresponsible drinking. What kinds of approaches
are colleges using to reduce student drinking, and how well do they work?

Two current strategies being tried on college campuses are the social norms
marketing approach and the environmental approach. The *social norms marketing*
approach assumes that college students drink heavily because they think
everyone else does it. Supporters of this approach argue that telling students
about normal drinking behaviors, typically through mass marketing campaigns,
will lead them to drink less (Turner, Perkins, & Bauerle, 2008). The *environmental* approach focuses on changing the factors within the campus and
community — like discount drink specials at local bars and inconsistent enforcement of underage drinking laws — that may encourage college students to drink
(Weitzman, Nelson, Lee, & Wechsler, 2004). Supporters of the environmental
approach believe that students are unlikely to change their behavior in an

The writer contrasts
humorous depictions of
college drinking with
sobering statistics about
drinking-related deaths,
injuries, and crimes.

Following APA style,
source information is
cited in parentheses.

The writer identifies
and defines the two
leading approaches that
he will evaluate.

environment that supports harmful levels of drinking. This essay will look at each of these approaches in turn, examining their effectiveness by comparing the reported rates of student drinking and harmful consequences after each approach is used, and by considering how easily their strategies can be implemented.

The Social Norms Marketing Approach

The social norms marketing approach is based on the theory that correcting a person's misperceptions will lead to a change in behavior (Turner et al., 2008). This approach is popular and relatively easy to implement, since it focuses largely on standard education and marketing techniques — something colleges and universities are well equipped to provide (Turner et al., 2008). DeJong et al. (2006) found that, when done with pervasive and consistent marketing messages, social norms campaigns were associated not only with lower perceptions of student drinking levels but also with lower alcohol consumption. Turner et al. (2008) used posters, Facebook ads, student newspaper articles, and e-mails over the course of six years to inform students at one college how often their fellow students consumed alcohol (and how much), as well as how often they showed "protective behaviors" like helping friends avoid driving while drunk (p. 86). Between 2001 and 2005, the percentage of students who reported experiencing negative consequences of drinking, like performing poorly in class or being the victim of assault, dropped significantly (Turner et al., 2008). Likewise, DeJong et al. (2006) found that social norms marketing campaigns at 18 colleges and universities across the country provided a "meaningful . . . effect," with students consuming fewer drinks per week and at parties than before the campaign (p. 878). These results indicate that students absorbed the social norms messages put forth by their schools, and although they didn't stop drinking entirely, they did change their behavior to match their perceptions of other students' drinking habits.

An overview of the essay is provided.

The evaluation criteria — effectiveness and ease of implementation — are introduced and defined.

A heading is set off from body text using bold formatting.

A source is cited using APA style.

A partial quotation indicates that the phrase is taken from the source named in the attribution. The page number of the quotation is provided.

An evaluation of the effectiveness of the approach is provided.

Making Better Choices 4

However, Wechsler et al. (2003) analyzed trends at schools using social norms marketing and revealed that the campaigns did not necessarily decrease student drinking; in some cases, schools even reported higher alcohol consumption, according to seven criteria that measured whether students drank, how much, and how often. The team, of the Harvard School of Public Health's College Alcohol Study, suggested that because social norms marketing was first developed at a small school that wasn't very diverse, it might not be as suitable for schools with many different kinds of people. As the researchers explained, "Individual students' drinking behaviors align more closely to the drinking behaviors of their immediate social group rather than to the overall student population at a given school" (p. 492). Students at larger schools, then, might not be as receptive to the social norms marketing approach as other studies indicated, especially if their personal experience contradicts the messages distributed in a campaign.

Unexpected factors may also complicate the perceived success of social norms marketing campaigns. One study noted that campaigns at several schools resulted in only "relatively small changes in [heavy] drinking behavior, from a 1.1% decrease to a 10.6% increase" over three years, while a control group of schools not using any kind of alcohol prevention experienced surprising increases in heavy drinking — between 17.5% and 24.7% (DeJong et al., 2006, p. 877). Although social norms marketing in this case did not appear to reduce consumption, the fact that alcohol use increased so much in the control group indicates that the social norms marketing may have served to keep drinking levels steady at schools that might have otherwise experienced a similar jump in alcohol use.

Given this evidence, it seems clear that social norms marketing is not a one-size-fits-all solution. Students might ignore statistics and facts in social norms advertisements because they don't believe the ads represent the peers whose opinions they care about most. But for smaller schools looking to curb

A summary of contrasting evidence is provided, indicating that the approach might not be effective at all schools.

A quotation conveys conclusions offered by the researchers who conducted the study. The page number is provided.

The writer offers his interpretation of the results of the study.

Additional information is offered regarding the potential positive effects of the approach.

An overall judgment on the approach is provided.

heavy drinking and its consequences, social norms marketing might be a good strategy, especially where colleges want to change student behavior without making significant changes to school or community alcohol policies.

The Environmental Approach

The environmental approach involves a mix of strategies designed to reduce or eliminate alcohol consumption, using the resources of both the campus community and the surrounding town or city. According to Weitzman et al. (2004), "Drinking-related norms and behaviors result from interactions over time and space between individuals and their environments" (p. 188). By changing the "contextual forces," like availability of alcohol, that encourage students to drink, this approach more strongly emphasizes policies that directly put a stop to excessive drinking — unlike the social norms marketing approach, which relies on influencing individual behavior (p. 187). As George W. Dowdall, author of *College Drinking: Reframing a Social Problem*, has argued, "Informational approaches used alone simply don't work. Trying to deal with college drinking as only an individual's choice doesn't work either. Instead, colleges should try to shape the entire environment that shapes college drinking" (as cited in Jaschik, 2009). By cracking down on when and how alcohol is available on campus, and by taking steps to keep underage students from accessing alcohol off campus, colleges that adopt the environmental approach tend to be more successful in decreasing the overall rate of student drinking and the negative consequences that can come from excessive alcohol use.

One drawback of the environmental approach is that it can be more time-consuming and difficult to implement than social norms marketing, as it relies on the cooperation of campus administrators, faculty, community members, law enforcement, and business owners in enforcing sometimes unpopular changes in alcohol policies. However, Dowdall pointed out that harmful levels of drinking among students already result in arrests and disciplinary actions, which involve

---

Annotations:

A detailed definition of the second approach is provided.

Following APA style, information cited in a source is identified using the phrase "as cited in."

A weakness of the approach is considered in light of the implementation criterion.

Making Better Choices 6

community and campus resources after the fact (as cited in Jaschik, 2009).
Instead of using these resources in reaction to drinking-related problems,
schools and towns that adopt an environmental approach can use them pro-
actively to prevent problems from happening in the first place.

> A summary of a source provides evidence about the effectiveness of the approach.

In fact, research suggests that environmental changes are needed for consistent and lasting change in student drinking levels. Weitzman et al. (2004)
looked at an environmental approach program that decreased the availability
and appeal of alcohol at several colleges through many different, simultaneous
methods like police enforcement of party regulations, substance-free residence
halls, and parental notification for alcohol-related violations. The team found
that significantly fewer students experienced drinking-related problems, like
missed classes and alcohol-fueled fights, after the program was implemented.
Just as important, and in contrast with the results of some social norms marketing programs, students across the sample also reported lower amounts of
drinking overall. The study looked at public and private colleges of different
sizes across the nation, showing that the environmental approach works for a
range of different student populations (Weitzman et al., 2004). Environmental
changes reach beyond the individual student to shape the community as a
whole, making sure that the campus and its surroundings are not contributing
to the problem of student drinking but helping to solve it.

Conclusions

> The conclusion focuses on the higher level of overall effectiveness of the environmental approach, despite the complexities involved with its implementation.

While social norms marketing appears to offer a strong combination of positive outcomes and ease of implementation, the environmental approach is more
effective overall. Despite being more complicated and demanding more school
and community resources, it delivers stronger results by involving students'
entire college community. The environmental approach has a much greater scope
than that of the social norms marketing approach and is suitable for schools of
all sizes and types. Therefore, it has the potential to affect not only students

who drink heavily because they think that's the normal thing to do but also students who are either unaware of the dangers of using alcohol or who will moderate their drinking only in the face of severe consequences for not doing so. Given appropriate resources, a program based on the environmental approach to curb heavy drinking is likely to be the best choice.

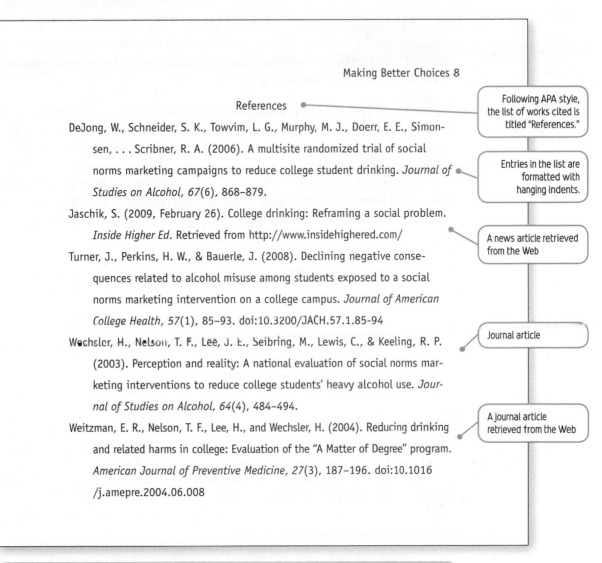

Making Better Choices 8

References

DeJong, W., Schneider, S. K., Towvim, L. G., Murphy, M. J., Doerr, E. E., Simonsen, . . . Scribner, R. A. (2006). A multisite randomized trial of social norms marketing campaigns to reduce college student drinking. *Journal of Studies on Alcohol, 67*(6), 868–879.

Jaschik, S. (2009, February 26). College drinking: Reframing a social problem. *Inside Higher Ed*. Retrieved from http://www.insidehighered.com/

Turner, J., Perkins, H. W., & Bauerle, J. (2008). Declining negative consequences related to alcohol misuse among students exposed to a social norms marketing intervention on a college campus. *Journal of American College Health, 57*(1), 85–93. doi:10.3200/JACH.57.1.85-94

Wechsler, H., Nelson, T. F., Lee, J. E., Seibring, M., Lewis, C., & Keeling, R. P. (2003). Perception and reality: A national evaluation of social norms marketing interventions to reduce college students' heavy alcohol use. *Journal of Studies on Alcohol, 64*(4), 484–494.

Weitzman, E. R., Nelson, T. F., Lee, H., and Wechsler, H. (2004). Reducing drinking and related harms in college: Evaluation of the "A Matter of Degree" program. *American Journal of Preventive Medicine, 27*(3), 187–196. doi:10.1016/j.amepre.2004.06.008

Following APA style, the list of works cited is titled "References."

Entries in the list are formatted with hanging indents.

A news article retrieved from the Web

Journal article

A journal article retrieved from the Web

✳ Project Ideas

The following suggestions provide means of focusing your work on an evaluative essay or another type of evaluative document.

Suggestions for Essays

1. EVALUATE A PROPOSED SOLUTION TO A PROBLEM

Evaluate a proposed solution to a problem. You might focus on proposed legislation for addressing problems with public schools in your state, or on a proposal for addressing a foreign policy problem. Or you might evaluate a new means of dealing with copyright on digital media such as music or videos. You should define the problem, outline the proposed solution, identify and define a set of criteria on which to base your evaluation, and collect information about the problem and its proposed solution by collecting sources or interviewing an expert.

2. EVALUATE THE EFFECTIVENESS OF A PUBLIC OFFICIAL OR GROUP

Write an essay that evaluates the effectiveness of an elected official or group, such as a mayor, a state legislator, or a city council. Your evaluation might focus on overall performance, or on performance related to a specific issue, such as addressing urban growth. Identify and define the criteria you'll use to conduct your evaluation. Collect information from published sources. If you can, interview or correspond with the official or a representative of the group.

3. EVALUATE A PERFORMANCE

Review a public performance, such as a concert, a play, or a poetry reading, for your classmates. To prepare, read reviews that have appeared in print and online publications, and familiarize yourself with the criteria that other reviewers have used. In your review, describe the performance and evaluate it, keeping in mind the characteristics of your readers. Take notes and, if possible, interview others who attended the performance. If you can, interview one of the performers. Your review should focus primarily on your personal assessment of the performance. You should draw on your notes and interviews to introduce ideas, illustrate a point, or support your conclusions.

4. EVALUATE A PRODUCT

Select a product you are thinking about purchasing, such as a kitchen gadget, a surround sound system, a laser printer, a cosmetic, or a piece of athletic equipment. Evaluate it using the criteria of effectiveness, cost, and quality. Provide clear definitions of each criterion in terms of the product you've chosen to evaluate. Your evaluation should draw on written sources, interviews with people who have used the product, and, if possible, your own use of the product.

5. EVALUATE AN ATHLETE OR A COACH

Evaluate the performance of a professional athlete, such as a basketball or baseball player, or evaluate the effectiveness of a coach. Select criteria such as the contributions made to the team's success, leadership qualities, entertainment provided to fans, contributions to the community, and so on. In your essay, identify the athlete or coach, explain the contributions that person has made to his or her team or sport, identify and define the criteria you are using to evaluate his or her performance, and present your evaluation to your readers. To support your evaluation, draw on your observations of the athlete or coach, interviews or surveys of other sports fans familiar with the athlete or coach, and published sources that discuss the athlete or coach. If possible, you might also interview the athlete or coach.

Suggestions for Other Genres

6. POST A MOVIE REVIEW

Review a recently released movie for the readers of a specific blog or Web site. To prepare, read movie reviews that have appeared on the site you have selected, and familiarize yourself with its conventions. In your review, describe the movie and evaluate it, keeping in mind the interests of your readers. Take notes and, if possible, interview others who have seen the movie. Visit the movie's Web site to learn about the movie, its director, and its cast. Your review should focus primarily on your personal assessment of the movie. Draw on your notes, interviews, and materials from the movie's Web site to introduce ideas, illustrate a point, or support your conclusions.

7. POST A RESTAURANT REVIEW

Review a restaurant for the readers of a specific blog or Web site. To prepare, read restaurant reviews that have appeared in the blog or on the Web site you have selected, and familiarize yourself with its conventions. To conduct the review, have a meal at the restaurant with one or more friends. Order a variety of items, examine the decor, and keep track of the quality of the service provided by the waitstaff. After you leave the restaurant, take notes to remind yourself of your impressions of the food, decor, and service. Ask your friends for their reactions, and take note of them as well. In your review, describe the restaurant and evaluate it, keeping in mind the interests of readers who read the blog or visit the site. Your review should focus primarily on your personal assessment of the restaurant. Draw on your notes to introduce ideas, illustrate a point, or support your conclusions.

8. EVALUATE A SOURCE

Choose a source that you might use in another assignment (if possible, a group assignment) for your writing class. Evaluate the source for your instructor and your classmates. Select criteria such as the source's relevance to the project, use of evidence, clarity and organization, timeliness, comprehensiveness, author, and publisher. Using these criteria, evaluate the contribution the source might make to your writing project. To support your evaluation, draw on the requirements of the assignment and your reading of the source.

9. EVALUATE AN ASSIGNMENT

Choose an assignment you've been given in one of your classes, and evaluate it for your instructor and your classmates. Select criteria such as the assignment's contribution to your understanding of the subject, the amount of work required to obtain an educational benefit from the assignment, the clarity of the assignment, its relevance to the course, and so on. Describe the course and the assignment, identify and define the criteria you are using to evaluate the assignment, and present your evaluation to your readers. To support your evaluation, draw on your experiences with the assignment, interviews or surveys of other students who have completed the assignment, and related course materials. You can also interview the instructor who gave the assignment.

10. WRITE A PROGRESS REPORT

Write a report that evaluates the progress that a group you belong to or an organization in which you are a member has made during a particular period of time, such as the last six months or the last year. To develop the criteria for your progress report, interview key members of the group or organization, or locate any written documents that define its goals. Draw on your personal experience with the group, interviews, and documents (such as funding proposals or a Web site) as sources of evidence for your evaluation. Your report should define the group or organization's goals and assess its progress in meeting them. The report might also include recommendations about strategies for enhancing the group's or organization's efforts to meet its goals.

In Summary: Writing an Evaluative Essay

○ **Find a conversation and listen in.**

- Explore your needs, interests, and concerns (p. 307).
- Search the Web (p. 308).
- Narrow your focus by asking questions (p. 311).

○ **Conduct your evaluation.**

- Define your criteria (p. 312).
- Identify evidence (p. 313).
- Make your judgments (p. 314).

○ **Prepare a draft.**

- State your overall judgment (p. 316).
- Present your evaluation (p. 316).
- Consider genre and design (p. 319).
- Frame your evaluation (p. 320).

○ **Review and improve your draft.**

- Review your criteria (p. 321).
- Reconsider your evidence (p. 321).
- Ensure that your judgments are fair and reasonable (p. 323).

09 Writing to Solve Problems

> *Problem solvers* like me define a problem and offer possible solutions.

GENRES IN CONVERSATION

| Reflective Writing | Informative Writing | Analytical Writing | Evaluative Writing | **Problem-Solving Writing** | Argumentative Writing |

The growing problem of identity theft has sparked a large number of conversations devoted to understanding it and finding solutions. Some of these conversations focus on penalties for people who steal identities. Others focus on technological solutions. Still others focus on the impact of identity theft on victims and communities. The documents shown here—a **magazine article,** an **advertisement,** and a **government Web site**—share a common purpose of helping people avoid identity theft. Notice how each genre accomplishes that purpose through the careful use of visual design.

SECURITY WATCH

Defending Your Identity

Hardly a week goes by without companies and universities losing digital identities. What can be done?

BY ROBERT LEMOS

IDENTITY THEFT IS A BOOMING business, and not just for the criminals. We frequently hear news of companies and universities losing digital information for large numbers of consumers. In April, for example, the University of Texas at Austin warned that a hacker had breached a system at the UT business school, downloading personal data—in many cases including Social Security numbers—on 197,000 students, alumni, and employees. And the state of Ohio recalled CDs containing information on 7.7 million voters from more than 20 political campaign offices after it discovered that the discs included the voters' Social Security numbers, the key to consumers' financial accounts.

When such institutions are so careless with personal information, it's no wonder that identity theft is a relatively common occurrence. By far the greatest share—about 37 percent—of the fraud complaints that the Federal Trade Commission received in 2005 was due to identity theft. A 2005 study from Javelin Research pegged the total loss to U.S. businesses and consumers at $52.6 billion. Not all indicators are bad, however. Between 2004 and 2005, the estimated number of victims of identity theft in the U.S. decreased from 10.1 million to 9.3 million. The average time to resolve identity theft also dropped 15 percent, to 28 hours.

Despite threats of phishing, stolen databases, and other online fraud, most people become victims via off-line methods. According to the Javelin study, only 11.6 percent of identity theft occurred online. Users who monitored their accounts online suffered an average of $451 in losses, far less than the average of $4,543 for cases detected by paper statements.

Unfortunately, the law does not give consumers much control. Correcting mistakes in a credit report can take days, if not weeks or months. And though in 2003 Congress passed the Fair and Accurate Credit Transactions Act (FACTA), which allows consumers annual access to their credit reports, the law bars states from adopting stronger consumer protections and requires a police report before a long-term fraud alert may be placed on a credit account.

Credit-card companies and credit bureaus have created a variety of Internet solutions to help con-

SCORING YOUR CREDIT *Identity-protection sites generally show a credit score, its factors, and data on open accounts.*

sumers. But some of these companies are responsible for the poor security of people's financial records in the first place.

Other services have popped up to add security to the credit-approval process. LifeLock puts fraud alerts on accounts to block credit offers and unsolicited access to credit information. And a startup, Debix, is testing a service that attempts to lock access to a person's account, requiring a one-time key for any company or person to open a new credit account in the owner's name.

For you, one of these services may be overkill. So a good place to start is to get a free credit report and check it over carefully. From there you can decide whether you need one of the monitoring or credit-security services in the sidebar on this page.

Since the majority of identity theft still takes place outside cyberspace, don't just toss old bills, bank statements, and financial records. Invest in a paper shredder and use it. Don't carry your Social Security card in your wallet, and when registering for Web sites don't enter personal information that can be traced to financial records. And you should never give any information to telemarketers or respond to phishing e-mails that spoof sites such as PayPal asking you to update your account information. Consumers and businesses must work in tandem to prevent identity theft.

Robert Lemos is a freelance technology journalist and the editor-at-large for SecurityFocus.

SECURITY BLANKETS

AnnualCreditReport.com
www.annualcreditreport.com
Industry-created site that helps consumers get annual credit reports from the three major credit bureaus. Free.

IdentityGuard
identityguard.com
Quarterly access to reports; daily notification of changes by e-mail; monitoring credit card accounts; $20,000 in insurance. $12.99 per month.

LifeLock
www.lifelock.com
Annual access to four different credit reports; removes consumers from junk-mail lists and preapproved credit-card lists; monitors checking accounts; $1 million in insurance. $10 per month, $110 per year.

MyFICO Identity Theft Security (Fairlsaac)
www.myfico.com/ Products/IDF/ Description.aspx
Quarterly credit reports from TransUnion; weekly notifications of changes; $25,000 in insurance. $4.95 per month, $49.95 per year.

»» KEEP YOURSELF SAFE!
Subscribe to our Security Watch newsletter and get up-to-date info on the latest threats delivered to your inbox automatically: *go.pcmag.com/ securitywatchletter*

JULY 2006 **PC MAGAZINE** 143

Magazine Article ▶

This **article** in *PC Magazine,* formatted in a typical magazine layout using columns and graphics, is aimed at computer-literate readers and draws on interviews with industry leaders, published reports, and the writer's personal experience and expertise.

Advertisement ▶

This advertisement, designed to capture attention quickly through a striking visual image, promotes a particular product as a solution to identity theft.

WITH VISA, YOU'RE PROTECTED. Whether it's a Visa credit or check card, Visa's multiple layers of security protect you from fraud, online and off. And if fraudulent charges do occur, rest assured that you won't be liable: No matter what you want to do in life, life takes Visa.

LIFE TAKES VISA

*Visa's Zero Liability Policy covers U.S.-issued cards only and does not apply to commercial credit cards, ATM transactions, or PIN transactions not processed by Visa. Cardholder must notify card issuer promptly of any unauthorized use. Consult issuer for additional details or visit visa.com/security. ©2007 Visa U.S.A. Inc.

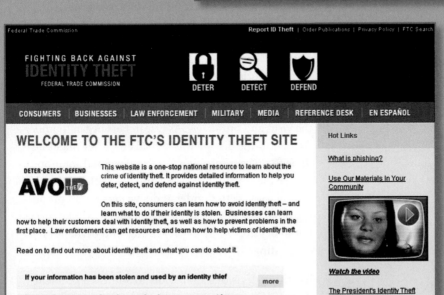

◀ Government Web Site

A government Web site offers resources for addressing identity theft and links to government documents, instructional videos, related Web sites, and published sources.

What Is Writing to Solve Problems?

The word *problem* is slippery. When a problem affects us directly, it might take on the dimensions of a crisis: we want to know how to solve it—and the sooner the better. When a problem affects someone else, it might seem, to us, more like an interesting challenge than an imminent disaster. And sometimes a problem is nothing of the sort. It's simply a label for lack of knowledge. For example, when a research scientist says that she's working on an interesting problem, she usually means that she's investigating an intriguing puzzle, which, when solved, will advance our knowledge in a specific area.

Writers who adopt the role of *problem solver* carry out activities such as calling readers' attention to problems, discussing the nature and extent of those problems, or proposing solutions. Whether a writer focuses on defining, discussing, or proposing a solution to a problem depends on how much is known about it. Consider, for example, the evolution of our understanding of the HIV/AIDS epidemic. In the early 1980s, when little was known about HIV—the virus that causes AIDS—it wasn't clear that the growing number of illnesses caused by HIV were related to one another. As a result, the first writers who addressed the problem focused largely on defining the symptoms and arguing that a problem existed. Later, as more information became available about the origin and effects of the disease, medical researchers began writing reports and scholarly articles that discussed its potential impact on people who carried the virus and on society. As researchers began to understand how the disease was spread and what might be done to prevent infection, writers proposed solutions to reduce the spread of HIV. Eventually, as the nature of HIV became better understood, writers began proposing programs of medical research that might be carried out to develop a way of preventing, and perhaps even eradicating, the spread of the virus.

A writer's decisions about how to address a problem depend largely on context. Until the nature and significance of a problem are understood, it does little good

The Writer's Role: Problem Solver

PURPOSE

- To identify a problem
- To explain the significance of a problem
- To propose solutions

READERS

- Expect information, ideas, and insights to be presented fairly
- Expect a clear explanation of a proposed solution

SOURCES

- Published information (such as studies, reports, blogs, the Web, and news media), personal experience, and field research (including interviews, observation, surveys, and correspondence) help writers define and learn about previous attempts to solve problems.

CONTEXT

- Writers consider what readers are likely to know, assume, and value, and they focus on what readers want or need to understand about the problem.

- Illustrations — such as charts, tables, graphs, and images — can improve readers' understanding.

to propose a solution. Because of the critical role played by writers who help define and understand problems, they are actively involved in solving these problems—even when they don't propose a fully developed solution.

No matter how aware readers are of a problem, however, more often than not they are seeking a solution. Readers expect a clear definition of the problem and a thorough discussion of options for addressing it. And although readers might not be surprised when a writer uses emotionally charged language, they usually prefer that problem-solving documents discuss the problem in a straightforward, balanced manner.

Most readers also expect writers not only to explain and discuss the benefits of their proposed solution but also to address its advantages over other solutions. They expect a fair and reasonable presentation of a subject, clear explanations of important ideas and concepts, and thorough documentation of sources. Readers usually react favorably to the use of visual elements—such as photos, images, charts, graphs, and tables—that help them understand the problem and its solution.

Writers of problem-solving documents are concerned primarily with helping readers understand the nature of and potential solutions to a problem. Sometimes they define and discuss the origins or impact of a problem. Sometimes they reflect on the strengths and weaknesses of potential solutions to a problem. In most cases, however, they analyze a problem and offer readers a thoroughly considered, well-supported solution. In doing so, they play a critical role in advancing our understanding of and response to problems.

What Kinds of Documents Are Used to Solve Problems?

It's rare to spend a day without running across documents that promise to solve a problem: advertisements alert us to solutions for problems (with our health, our love lives, our breath) that we might not know we have; e-mail messages ask us for our help with problems ranging from hunger to funding for the arts; and entire Web sites, such as Project Vote Smart and FightGlobalWarming.com, promote solutions to problems. Unfortunately, the number of unsolved problems far exceeds those with solutions. As a result, writing to solve problems is a common occurrence.

In your work writing a problem-solving essay, you might turn to sources as varied as books, reports, pamphlets, posters, memos, opinion columns, and blog entries—

View a multimedia example of problem-solving writing in the e-book at **bedfordstmartins.com/ conversation**.

any of which might define a problem or advance solutions to a problem. The following examples illustrate some of the problem-solving documents you're likely to encounter: correspondence, professional articles, speeches, proposals, and problem-solving essays.

Correspondence

Correspondence is written communication between two or more people, usually in the form of letters, memos, or e-mail messages. Correspondence can be used to alert a reader to a problem and offer a solution tailored to the interests and abilities of the recipient. An e-mail message, for example, can be used to communicate a writer's concern about a problem to someone who has the resources to support a solution or the authority to put it into action. Letters and memos can be used to the same effect.

Because of the brevity of most correspondence, sources of information usually are not identified. The style and level of formality of correspondence depend on the relationship between the writer and the recipient, as well as the genre used. When the writer of an e-mail message or a personal letter knows and is comfortable with a recipient, the style is often relaxed and informal. Memos and business letters, on the other hand, tend to have a more formal style. Most correspondence consists of a greeting, a few paragraphs of text, and a closing. Letters and memos typically include addressing information and a corporate or organizational logo, while e-mail messages might include the writer's *signature*—brief lines of contact information and, if relevant, a job title.

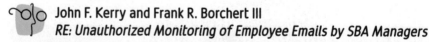

John F. Kerry and Frank R. Borchert III
RE: Unauthorized Monitoring of Employee Emails by SBA Managers

In the following exchange of letters, Senator John Kerry (D-Mass.) writes to the head of the U.S. Small Business Administration (SBA), urging him to take specific action to address a concern about a managerial practice that "discourages potential whistleblowers from reporting misconduct to Congress." In response, the SBA's general counsel, Frank R. Borchert, provides a counter perspective—and places the problem in a different context.

United States Senate
COMMITTEE ON SMALL BUSINESS & ENTREPRENEURSHIP
WASHINGTON, DC 20510–6350

January 11, 2008

The Honorable Steven C. Preston
Administrator
U.S. Small Business Administration
409 Third Street, S.W.
Washington, D.C. 20416

Re: Unauthorized Monitoring of Employee Emails by SBA Managers (OIG Report
No. 08-02)

Dear Administrator Preston:

The purpose of this correspondence is to address the troubling findings set forth in
a recent report issued by the SBA's Office of Inspector General (OIG). The OIG
report indicates that SBA managers in the Office of Disaster Assistance (ODA)
accessed the emails of an SBA employee who served as a confidential source to the
Senate Committee on Small Business and Entrepreneurship. According to the OIG's
report, the monitoring took place after the ODA employee submitted hearing
testimony to the Committee on an anonymous basis. I am extremely concerned
that this practice discourages potential whistleblowers from reporting misconduct
to Congress.

In its oversight capacity, the Committee often relies upon information received
from SBA employees who ask that their communications remain confidential. When
the SBA permits managers to arbitrarily access employee emails, confidentiality
cannot be assured, and SBA employees are less likely to communicate with the
Committee. As a result, the Committee's ability to properly carry out its oversight
function is undermined.

In addition, the practice could have a chilling effect on an SBA employee's right to
provide information to the Committee. The Civil Service Reform Act of 1978
(CSRA) provides that an agency employee's right to furnish information to a Congressional committee "may not be interfered with or denied" (15 U.S.C. §7211).
Granting SBA managers the power to monitor employee emails may interfere with
that right by diminishing an employee's ability to effectively report misconduct to
the Committee.

The Honorable Steven C. Preston
January 11, 2008
Page 2

Furthermore, under federal whistleblower statutes like the CSRA, an agency employee has the right to report allegations of misconduct on a confidential basis. The whistleblower statutes provide important protections to those employees who are courageous enough to report waste and abuse despite the obvious risks. Last month I joined Senators from both sides of the aisle in approving the Federal Employee Protection of Disclosures Act (S. 274), a bill that will further enhance agency employees' whistleblower protections. Ironically, the bill would specifically prohibit the SBA from instituting "retaliatory investigations" against whistleblowers like the SBA employee in question.

Notwithstanding this pending legislation, I urge the SBA to take preemptive, independent action to avoid future encroachments on the whistleblower rights of its valued employees. My staff informs me that the SBA, in conjunction with the OIG, is in the process of revising its email access authorization guidelines, which are currently set forth in SBA Standard Operating Procedure (SOP) 90 49. I ask that you include appropriate members of the Committee's staff in those discussions to ensure that the new SOP includes proper safeguards for whistleblowers who contact Congress via email. In the meantime, please provide the Committee with the most recent version of the draft SOP that has been circulated between the SBA's Office of General Counsel and the OIG.

If you have any questions, or if we can be of assistance in achieving the objectives set forth in this letter, please contact me or have a member of your staff contact Nick Coutsos of my staff at 202-224-5175. Thank you for your prompt attention to this matter.

Sincerely,

John F. Kerry
Chairman

U.S. SMALL BUSINESS ADMINISTRATION
WASHINGTON, D.C. 20416

January 24, 2008

The Honorable John F. Kerry
Chairman
Committee on Small Business & Entrepreneurship
Washington, DC 10510-6350

Re: Monitoring of Employee E-mails by SBA Managers

Dear Chairman Kerry:

Thank you for your recent inquiry to Administrator Steven Preston regarding the Small Business Administration's (Agency) Office of Inspector General (OIG) Report No. 08-02, which addresses monitoring of employee e-mails and the Agency's response to the OIG's findings. The Administrator has asked that I respond directly to your inquiry. While we share your concerns regarding unauthorized access to employee e-mail, senior Agency supervisory personnel may at times have a legitimate need to have access to material contained in Agency files including an employee's e-mails. If an employee uses his/her governmental computer to communicate with Congress, these e-mails are maintained within the government's information systems. Employees are made aware of this through FOIA/Privacy Act training and computer awareness training that employees are required to take on at least a yearly basis. Presently, protections are in place to protect individual employees' e-mail communications with Congress. This includes recently adopted measures to limit the circumstances under which a senior manager may access employees' e-mail. These protections, in addition to limiting who may access an employee's e-mail, further limit when that can occur and for what purpose. We feel that these guidelines appropriately protect employees' rights and hopefully address your concerns.

While it is established Agency policy in SOP 90 49 that employees do not have a right to or an expectation of privacy when using SBA's computer systems, including e-mail, SBA determined that it was necessary to establish written procedures governing the Agency's rights and accountabilities and to insure compliance with those policies.

Examples of when access to an employee's e-mail might be necessary include: (1) an employee's unexpected and/or prolonged absence from work; (2) conducting a fact finding or investigation; (3) preserving e-mails due to an employee's departure from the Agency; (4) normal management of litigation matters and (5) other legitimate management reasons.

These policies seek to balance the need to protect sensitive and confidential communications of employees with the legitimate Agency need for access to information in appropriate situations. As a result, on December 21, 2007 the Agency issued SBA Procedural Notice 9000-1720 which specifies the procedures necessary for obtaining authorization to access and/or monitor an employee's e-mails. Access can only be granted with the specific approval of a manager, senior official, OCIO Chief Information Security Officer, the General Counsel and the Chief Human Capital Officer. Chief Human Capital Officer approval is not necessary for litigation matters. These procedures will ensure that a senior manager has a legitimate need for reviewing an employee's e-mail and that access is provided in a very limited and appropriate manner.

As your letter correctly and appropriately points out, the Civil Service Reform Act recognizes an employee's right to furnish information to a Congressional committee and that right "may not be interfered with or denied." 5 U.S.C. 7221. This provides a measure of protection to an employee who feels that his/her right to communicate has been denied or compromised. To further protect employee rights, the Agency has now set limits on who may access an employee's e-mail and under what circumstances.

Similarly, whistleblower statutes support the Agency's position that employees have adequate legal remedies available to them should managers act in an illegal manner. We support the rights of employees and desire to protect those who report waste, fraud and abuse. As such, SBA's Policy Notice provides guidance and direction to all managers and employees on when, where and how employee e-mails may legally be accessed and explaining what actions must be taken prior to any such review.

With respect to Senate bill S. 274, Federal Employee Protection for Disclosures Act, cited in your letter, the Department of Justice has set forth the Administration's position regarding the specifics of the bill in its December 17, 2007 letter. The Department stated that the remedies set forth in the Bill are unnecessary and legally problematic. In particular, they note that the expanded definition of what would be considered a "protected disclosure" would greatly upset the balance of whistleblower protection and the ability of federal managers to manage the workplace.

Finally, pursuant to your request, we are herewith providing a copy of SBA Procedural Notice 900-1720, which was effective December 21, 2007. As described above, we feel that this Notice properly strikes a balance between employee rights, whistleblower protections and the legitimate business needs of the Agency. While we appreciate your suggestion to have appropriate members of your committee staff participate in the revision of the new operating procedures, since the policy has already been adopted (prior to receipt of your letter) we are unable to accommodate your request to include them in revision discussions. In this regard, it should be noted that we did have discussions with Mr. Coutsos of your staff prior to the implementation of the present policy.

Thank you for your continued support of small business. Should you wish to discuss this further, I may be reached at (202) 205-6634.

Sincerely,

Frank R. Borchert III
General Counsel

Starting a Conversation: Respond to "RE: Unauthorized Monitoring of Employee Emails by SBA Managers"

In your writer's notebook, analyze Kerry's and Borchert's problem-solving efforts by responding to the following questions:

1. Kerry's stated purpose is to "address the troubling findings" in a report showing that SBA managers had accessed the e-mails of SBA employees without authorization. How does Kerry define the nature, significance, and implications of this problem?

2. What measures does Kerry propose to solve the problem, and in what part of the letter are his solutions located?

3. In defining the broader implications of the problem as well as in posing a solution, what sources or evidence does Kerry use to make his case?

4. Although Kerry's letter has an explicitly stated purpose, Borchert's response does not. How would you define the purpose of Borchert's letter? How does his understanding of the problem differ from Kerry's? How do his assumptions, evidence, and point of view contrast with Kerry's?

5. Readers generally prefer that problem-solving documents approach problems in a straightforward, balanced manner. Which of these two documents seems more straightforward or balanced? Why do you think so? Which document seems to propose a more fully-developed solution? Why do you think so?

@ Download or print this Starting a Conversation activity at **bedfordstmartins.com/ conversation**.

Professional Articles

Professional articles appear in trade or professional magazines and journals, such as *Advertising Age*, *The Real Estate Professional*, and *Professional Pilot*. These articles typically define a problem or propose a solution to a problem that would interest the professionals who subscribe to the publication. For example, an article for an information technology (IT) journal might discuss the problem of malicious popup ads that have been appearing on legitimate Web sites and might offer suggestions for how IT professionals can stop the attacks. An article for *Civil Engineering* magazine might examine ways that seismic engineers working in the Northeast can respond to builders' resistance to adhering to earthquake safety requirements in building codes.

Sources of information used in professional articles are usually identified in the text, although formal works cited lists typically are not provided. In this sense, professional articles more closely resemble the articles that appear in popular magazines. And like magazine articles, they usually make use of design elements such as columns, headings and subheadings, and illustrations.

Professional articles are usually written in a straightforward, seemingly objective voice. Because they are written for readers who are knowledgeable about their profession, their authors assume that readers understand key concepts and issues relevant to the field. For example, the author of an article appearing in *Publishers Weekly* on electronic copyright protection is unlikely to provide a detailed description of the issue because readers of the magazine will almost certainly be familiar with it. As a result, professional articles might seem obscure and challenging to readers who are not members of the profession.

 ### Jami Jones
Drug Testing Needs Improvement, Not Clearinghouse

In a special report published in *Land Line*, the official magazine of the Owner-Operator Independent Drivers Association, senior editor Jami Jones addresses problems associated with the establishment of a national database to track truckers who have failed drug and alcohol tests. She reports the reaction of the association's director of regulatory affairs, Rick Craig, who points out that although the problem being addressed is a serious one, industry concerns in the areas of privacy, security, and oversight indicate that the proposed solution is not yet ready to be put into practice. Craig has an alternative solution to the problem, as Jones explains.

SPECIAL REPORT: Drug testing needs improvement, not clearinghouse

Friday, November 2, 2007 — When it comes to supporting the goal of making the trucking industry free of drug and alcohol abuse, the Owner-Operator Independent Drivers Association is all for it — if it's done right.

That's the stance OOIDA took at a November 1 hearing of the U.S. House of Representatives Subcommittee on Highways and Transit on drug and alcohol testing of commercial motor vehicle drivers.

The hearing was the culmination of several months of investigations by the Transportation and Infrastructure Committee and Government Accountability Office staff. The GAO released a report on the day of the hearing that did not give a glowing report on the industry's drug testing procedures and regulatory compliance.

The GAO's comments didn't come as any big surprise to OOIDA. However, in his testimony to the subcommittee, OOIDA Director of Regulatory Affairs Rick Craig pointed out that many of the proposed solutions to fixing the problems with the drug testing won't do anything to reduce drug use in the industry and may very well just create more problems.

Clearinghouse concerns

One of the options discussed at the hearing was a national clearinghouse of positive drug and alcohol testing results, proposed by the American Trucking Association.

"OOIDA fully supports the goal of striving to make the trucking industry free of drug and alcohol abuse," Craig said in his testimony. "However, OOIDA remains unconvinced of the need for a national clearinghouse for positive drug and alcohol testing results."

Collecting positive test results in a single database presents a variety of potential problems, according to Craig.

For starters, simply collecting the results will not guarantee that a motor carrier actually removes a driver with a positive drug or alcohol test from performing safety functions.

The proposed clearinghouse also raises considerable privacy, operational, security, and oversight concerns. The Constitution protects against unreasonable searches and seizure, including those inside the human body.

How the data collected by either the federal government or a contract third-party provider would be used, who has access to it, its security, and its accuracy were just a few of the numerous concerns Craig raised.

"The ATA proposal casts a wide net without any assurances that necessary privacy precautions can be accomplished," Craig said.

It's not inconceivable that there could be drivers who would be victims of such a system, he added.

Craig pointed out that in OOIDA's view, all that ATA's proposed clearinghouse appears to accomplish is to "lift a burden from motor carriers' shoulders and reduce carriers' liability with regard to their often inadequate hiring practices."

Off the mark in Oregon

One drug testing program receiving national attention and purported as a success was "Operation Trucker Check" conducted by the Oregon Highway Patrol in April and September of this year.

During Operation Trucker Check, voluntary and anonymous urine specimens were collected. The OHP reported that one out of every 10 samples collected tested positive for certain types of drugs. That 10 percent rate is much higher than the national average of 2 percent reported by the Federal Motor Carrier Safety Administration.

That alone raises concerns about the procedures used in Operation Trucker Check, according to Craig. He explained to the subcommittee that there are simple, viable explanations as to why Oregon's results came back so high.

"There are numerous safeguards built into the DOT testing criteria. One such safeguard provides for specific cutoff concentrations. . . . The cutoff levels are employed to minimize the incidence of false positive tests that may result from 'innocent' activities such as the ingestion of certain legal substances," Craig explained.

"It's OOIDA's understanding that [the Oregon Highway Patrol] used no cutoff concentration criteria to guard against false positives."

In addition to setting cutoff points, the DOT testing procedures outline what happens when a sample comes back positive. It's not a "one strike and you're out" scenario. Anyone with a positive result in a DOT test will be contacted by a Medical Review Officer.

"An important part of the Medical Review Officer's duties involves making contact with a driver for which a positive test result is confirmed to inquire about any medications the driver may have used, or determine whether there is any other legitimate medical explanation," Craig said.

There's plenty of legitimate reasons for a false positive, Craig explained to the subcommittee, including legally prescribed medications that have no impact on a trucker's ability to drive.

"Under an anonymous collection and testing regime such as Oregon describes there can be no such follow-up to determine whether the result is a false positive," Craig said.

A simple solution

The core of the problem with the drug-testing program is that there isn't a real incentive for drug-free truckers.

"The current system subjects the vast majority of drivers, who are not drug users, to a costly and burdensome testing program that does not offer them any direct reward for their continued drug-free status," Craig told the subcommittee. "Nor is there any reward for employers whose exemplary driver hiring and training programs result in a drug-free group of drivers."

Craig proposed a simple solution that focuses more directly on detecting the small group of drug users while at the same time rewarding drug-free drivers and their employers.

He said a system could be set up that allows drivers who have repeatedly tested negative on random drug tests and have never had a positive DOT drug test result of any kind to be removed from the pool of drivers subject to the annual 50 percent random drug testing requirement. They would then be placed in a separate pool subject to an annual 25 percent random testing rate.

All other drivers—those who have not proven themselves to be drug free—should still be subject to the 50 percent testing requirement, according to Craig.

By Jami Jones, senior editor
jami_jones@landlinemag.com

Starting a Conversation: Respond to "Drug Testing Needs Improvement, Not Clearinghouse"

In your writer's notebook, consider how Jones responds to her writing situation by answering the following questions:

1. Jones is writing about drug testing and drug-testing policies. What problem or problems does her article seek to address and solve? What aspects of these problems does the article seem to ignore?

2. Professional articles generally strive for a straightforward, objective voice and tone. In what ways does this article achieve that goal, and in what ways does it fall short of that goal?

3. What roles does Jones adopt in this article? In what ways is she a reporter, an advocate, an observer, or a problem solver? (See p. 10 for an overview of writers' roles.)

4. This article originally appeared in *Land Line*, the official publication of the Owner-Operator Independent Drivers Association. What aspects of its language and style indicate that it's written for a specialized audience? How might this group of readers — and the article's publication in a professional journal — determine the writer's choice of sources and point of view?

Download or print this Starting a Conversation activity at **bedfordstmartins.com/ conversation**.

Speeches

Problem-solving speeches typically define a problem and propose a solution. The subject of the speech reflects the needs, interests, and backgrounds of the people in the audience as well as the occasion for which the speech is given. For example, a speech before a local school board is likely to focus on a problem associated with educational practices in the school district.

Speakers have the advantage of directly appealing to their listeners in a human voice, and speechwriters usually write with an awareness that their speech will be heard, rather than read. Their choice of words and style, as well as their decisions about the order in which to present ideas and information, will be strongly influenced by their awareness that listeners cannot stop and reread a passage that is difficult to understand. As a result, speechwriters are more willing to repeat points than are writers of other types of documents. Similarly, they often try to capture their listeners' attention — and imagination — with memorable anecdotes or images that illustrate the meaning or purpose of their speeches. Speechwriters might provide evidence in the form of brief mentions of statistics or relevant quotations, but they usually do so less extensively than if they were writing a document intended primarily for readers.

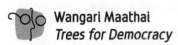

Wangari Maathai
Trees for Democracy

Dr. Wangari Muta Maathai is an environmental and political activist. She was also an elected member of Kenya's parliament. In 2004, she became the first African woman to receive the Nobel Peace Prize. In her acceptance speech, she addresses serious and persistent problems and makes direct calls to action, yet her language is neither angry nor self-righteous. She looks at the history of an interrelated set of problems, measures the progress made in three decades, and suggests prospects for addressing — and perhaps even resolving — those problems in the future.

Trees for Democracy

By Wangari Maathai

City Hall, Oslo, Norway

December 10, 2004

Your Majesties

Your Royal Highnesses

Honorable Members of the Norwegian Nobel Committee

Excellencies

Ladies and Gentlemen,

I stand before you and the world humbled by this recognition and uplifted by the honor of being the 2004 Nobel Peace Laureate.

As the first African woman to receive this prize, I accept it on behalf of the people of Kenya and Africa, and indeed the world. I am especially mindful of women and the girl child. I hope it will encourage them to raise their voices and take more space for leadership. I know the honor also gives a deep sense of pride to our men, both old and young. As a mother, I appreciate the inspiration this brings to the youth and urge them to use it to pursue their dreams.

Although this prize comes to me, it acknowledges the work of countless individuals and groups across the globe. They work quietly and often without recognition to protect the environment, promote democracy, defend human rights, and ensure equality between women and men. By so doing, they plant seeds of peace. I know they, too, are proud today. To all who feel represented by this prize I say use it to advance your mission and meet the high expectations the world will place on us.

This honor is also for my family, friends, partners, and supporters throughout the world. All of them helped shape the vision and sustain our work, which was often accomplished under hostile conditions. I am also grateful to the people of Kenya — who remained stubbornly hopeful that democracy could be realized and their environment managed sustainably. Because of this support, I am here today to accept this great honor.

I am immensely privileged to join my fellow African Peace laureates, Presidents Nelson Mandela and F. W. de Klerk, Archbishop Desmond Tutu, the late Chief Albert Luthuli, the late Anwar el-Sadat, and the UN Secretary General, Kofi Annan.

I know that African people everywhere are encouraged by this news. My fellow Africans, as we embrace this recognition, let us use it to intensify our commitment to our people, to reduce conflicts and poverty, and thereby improve their quality of life. Let us embrace democratic governance, protect human rights, and protect our environment. I am confident that we shall rise to the occasion. I have always believed that solutions to most of our problems must come from us.

In this year's prize, the Norwegian Nobel Committee has placed the critical issue of environment and its linkage to democracy and peace before the world. For their visionary action, I am profoundly grateful. Recognizing that sustainable development, democracy, and peace are indivisible is an idea whose time has come. Our work over the past 30 years has always appreciated and engaged these linkages.

My inspiration partly comes from my childhood experiences and observations of Nature in rural Kenya. It has been influenced and nurtured by the formal education I was privileged to receive in Kenya, the United States, and Germany. As I was growing up, I witnessed forests being cleared and replaced by commercial plantations, which destroyed local biodiversity and the capacity of the forests to conserve water.

Excellencies, ladies, and gentlemen: In 1977, when we started the Green Belt Movement, I was partly responding to needs identified by rural women, namely lack of firewood, clean drinking water, balanced diets, shelter, and income.

Throughout Africa, women are the primary caretakers, holding significant responsibility for tilling the land and feeding their families. As a result, they are often the first to become aware of environmental damage as resources become scarce and incapable of sustaining their families.

The women we worked with recounted that unlike in the past, they were unable to meet their basic needs. This was due to the degradation of their immediate environment as well as the introduction of commercial farming, which replaced the growing of household food crops. But international trade controlled the price of the exports from these small-scale farmers, and a reasonable and just income could not be guaranteed. I came to understand that when the environment is destroyed, plundered, or mismanaged, we undermine our quality of life and that of future generations.

Tree planting became a natural choice to address some of the initial basic needs identified by women. Also, tree planting is simple, attainable, and guarantees quick, successful results within a reasonable amount of time. This sustains interest and commitment.

So, together, we have planted over 30 million trees that provide fuel, food, shelter, and income to support their children's education and household needs. The activity also creates employment and improves soils and watersheds. Through their involvement, women gain some degree of power over their lives, especially their social and economic position and relevance in the family. This work continues.

Initially, the work was difficult because historically our people have been persuaded to believe that because they are poor, they lack not only capital, but also knowledge and skills to address their challenges. Instead they are conditioned to believe that solutions to their problems must come from "outside." Further, women did not realize that meeting their needs depended on their environment being healthy and well managed. They were also unaware that a degraded environment leads to a scramble for scarce resources and may culminate in poverty and even conflict. They were also unaware of the injustices of international economic arrangements.

In order to assist communities to understand these linkages, we developed a citizen education program, during which people identify their problems, the causes, and possible solutions. They then make connections between their own personal actions and the problems they witness in the environment and in society. They learn that our world is confronted with a litany of woes: corruption, violence against women and children, disruption and breakdown of families, and disintegration of cultures and communities. They also identify the abuse of drugs and chemical substances, especially among young people. There are also devastating diseases that are defying cures or occurring in epidemic proportions. Of particular concern are HIV/AIDS, malaria, and diseases associated with malnutrition.

On the environment front, they are exposed to many human activities that are devastating to the environment and societies. These include widespread destruction of ecosystems, especially through deforestation, climatic instability, and contamination in the soils and waters that all contribute to excruciating poverty.

In the process, the participants discover that they must be part of the solutions. They realize their hidden potential and are empowered to overcome inertia and take action. They come to recognize that they are the primary custodians and beneficiaries of the environment that sustains them.

Entire communities also come to understand that while it is necessary to hold their governments accountable, it is equally important that in their own relationships with each other, they exemplify the leadership values they wish to see in their own leaders, namely justice, integrity, and trust.

Although initially the Green Belt Movement's tree planting activities did not address issues of democracy and peace, it soon became clear that responsible governance of the environment was impossible without democratic space. Therefore, the tree became a symbol for the democratic struggle in Kenya. Citizens were mobilized to challenge widespread abuses of power, corruption, and environmental mismanagement. In Nairobi's Uhuru Park, at Freedom Corner, and in many parts of the country, trees of peace were planted to demand the release of prisoners of conscience and a peaceful transition to democracy.

Through the Green Belt Movement, thousands of ordinary citizens were mobilized and empowered to take action and effect change. They learned to overcome fear and a sense of helplessness and moved to defend democratic rights.

In time, the tree also became a symbol for peace and conflict resolution, especially during ethnic conflicts in Kenya when the Green Belt Movement used peace trees to reconcile disputing communities. During the ongoing re-writing of the Kenyan constitution, similar trees of peace were planted in many parts of the country to promote a culture of peace. Using trees as a symbol of peace is in keeping with a widespread African tradition. For example, the elders of the Kikuyu carried a staff from the thigi tree that, when placed between two disputing sides, caused them to stop fighting and seek reconciliation. Many communities in Africa have these traditions.

Such practices are part of an extensive cultural heritage, which contributes both to the conservation of habitats and to cultures of peace. With the destruction of these cultures and the introduction of new values, local biodi-versity is no longer valued or protected, and as a result, it is quickly degraded and disappears. For this reason, the Green Belt Movement explores the con-cept of cultural biodiversity, especially with respect to indigenous seeds and medicinal plants.

As we progressively understood the causes of environmental degradation, we saw the need for good governance. Indeed, the state of any country's envi-ronment is a reflection of the kind of governance in place, and without good governance there can be no peace. Many countries, which have poor gover-nance systems, are also likely to have conflicts and poor laws protecting the environment.

In 2002, the courage, resilience, patience, and commitment of members of the Green Belt Movement, other civil society organizations, and the Kenyan public culminated in the peaceful transition to a democratic government and laid the foundation for a more stable society.

Excellencies, friends, ladies, and gentlemen: It is 30 years since we started this work. Activities that devastate the environment and societies continue unabated. Today we are faced with a challenge that calls for a shift in our think-ing, so that humanity stops threatening its life-support system. We are called to assist the Earth to heal her wounds and in the process heal our own—indeed, to embrace the whole creation in all its diversity, beauty, and wonder. This will happen if we see the need to revive our sense of belonging to a larger family of life, with which we have shared our evolutionary process.

In the course of history, there comes a time when humanity is called to shift to a new level of consciousness, to reach a higher moral ground. A time when we have to shed our fear and give hope to each other.

That time is now.

The Norwegian Nobel Committee has challenged the world to broaden the understanding of peace: there can be no peace without equitable development; and there can be no development without sustainable management of the environment in a democratic and peaceful space. This shift is an idea whose time has come.

I call on leaders, especially from Africa, to expand democratic space and build fair and just societies that allow the creativity and energy of their citizens to flourish.

Those of us who have been privileged to receive education, skills, and experiences and even power must be role models for the next generation of leadership. In this regard, I would also like to appeal for the freedom of my fellow laureate Aun San Suu Kyi so that she can continue her work for peace and democracy for the people of Burma and the world at large.

Culture plays a central role in the political, economic, and social life of communities. Indeed, culture may be the missing link in the development of Africa. Culture is dynamic and evolves over time, consciously discarding retrogressive traditions, like female genital mutilation (FGM), and embracing aspects that are good and useful.

Africans, especially, should re-discover positive aspects of their culture. In accepting them, they would give themselves a sense of belonging, identity, and self-confidence.

Ladies and gentlemen: There is also need to galvanize civil society and grassroots movements to catalyze change. I call upon governments to recognize the role of these social movements in building a critical mass of responsible citizens, who help maintain checks and balances in society. On their part, civil society should embrace not only their rights but also their responsibilities.

Further, industry and global institutions must appreciate that ensuring economic justice, equity, and ecological integrity are of greater value than profits at any cost.

The extreme global inequities and prevailing consumption patterns continue at the expense of the environment and peaceful coexistence. The choice is ours.

I would like to call on young people to commit themselves to activities that contribute toward achieving their long-term dreams. They have the energy and creativity to shape a sustainable future. To the young people I say, you are a gift to your communities and indeed the world. You are our hope and our future.

The holistic approach to development, as exemplified by the Green Belt Movement, could be embraced and replicated in more parts of Africa and beyond. It is for this reason that I have established the Wangari Maathai Foundation to ensure the continuation and expansion of these activities. Although a lot has been achieved, much remains to be done.

Excellencies, ladies, and gentlemen: As I conclude, I reflect on my childhood experience when I would visit a stream next to our home to fetch water for my mother. I would drink water straight from the stream. Playing among the arrowroot leaves, I tried in vain to pick up the strands of frogs' eggs, believing they were beads. But every time I put my little fingers under them, they would break. Later, I saw thousands of tadpoles: black, energetic, and wriggling through the clear water against the background of the brown earth. This is the world I inherited from my parents.

Today, over 50 years later, the stream has dried up, women walk long distances for water, which is not always clean, and children will never know what they have lost. The challenge is to restore the home of the tadpoles and give back to our children a world of beauty and wonder.

Thank you very much.

Starting a Conversation: Respond to "Trees for Democracy"

@ Download or print this Starting a Conversation activity at **bedfordstmartins.com/ conversation**.

In your writer's notebook, reflect on Maathai's strategies as a writer, speaker, and problem solver by responding to the following questions:

1. What specific aspects of this text mark it as a speech, rather than an essay or some other kind of document? How do its content and style reflect the specific occasion on which the speech was delivered?

2. In her speech, Maathai appeals directly and explicitly to different groups of people. Who are these groups? What techniques does she use to make her appeals?

3. What are the primary problems that Maathai is trying to identify, explain, and help solve three decades after the Green Belt Movement began its work? In what ways are these problems interrelated? How does her speech advance the audience's understanding of potential solutions?

4. Maathai's organization has proposed—and enacted—a specific solution to the problems she addresses. What is it? How is the solution both practical and symbolic? In what ways does the solution link to environmental, social, political, and economic issues?

5. What relationship does Maathai's conclusion have to the rest of her speech? What effect might she have intended it to have on her listeners?

Proposals

Proposals offer a plan for solving a specific problem. They are usually presented to groups or individuals who have resources that might be used to address the problem, or who can grant permission for putting a plan into effect. For example, a nonprofit organization might propose that a charitable foundation fund an after-school tutoring program for children of one-parent families. Or a research center at a university might request approval from a city council for a pilot program to improve wheelchair access in local parks.

Proposals typically define a problem, describe a plan for addressing the problem, and argue that the person or group making the proposal has the capacity to carry out the plan. They might also include budgets, plans for evaluating outcomes, and information about the person or group making the proposal.

The structure and general appearance of proposals vary widely and tend to reflect the interests of the intended audience; often, proposals must follow strict guidelines outlined in grant application instructions or a call for proposals. Some proposals resemble academic essays, with wide margins, double-spaced lines, headings and subheadings, and limited use of color and illustrations. Others more closely resemble magazine articles or brochures, with heavy use of color, illustrations, columns, and other design elements.

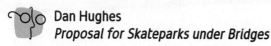

Dan Hughes
Proposal for Skateparks under Bridges

Skateboarding enthusiast Dan Hughes submitted the following proposal to the City of Seattle. The proposal offers background on the benefits of skateboarding for young people and identifies a problem in the lack of appropriate venues for young skateboarders in the city. The proposal then offers a detailed plan for solving the problem by creating skateparks under bridges and highway overpasses. In structure, style, and tone, the proposal anticipates potential objections from city officials and offers persuasive details to support the plan as a viable solution.

PROPOSAL FOR SKATEPARKS UNDER BRIDGES

BACKGROUND

Skateboarding is a high-energy activity that builds both physical and mental strength, as it requires an individual to be self-reliant while sharing space with other individuals.

Part of what makes skateboarding a positive activity is that it allows people to focus on their personal abilities and skills. As a sport, skateboarding has no prescribed rules, no governing body, and no restrictions that require a team effort. Kids who are not served by team sports are attracted to skateboarding because it doesn't require them to join a team and compete until a winner and a loser are declared. It is an activity in which there are no losers, only winners. Anyone can simply grab a board and skate anytime to improve his or her skills.

Skateboarding has other positive attributes, as older skaters can attest. It builds confidence, and often it's this confidence in oneself that allows one to make the right choices in life. It also teaches kids that they can do things they never thought possible. For parents and kids alike, skating also provides opportunities for learning and acting as positive role models. One only has to look at champion skater Tony Hawk to see how skateboarding has become a way for him to connect with his kids.

It is well known that social problems occur in cities when adequate facilities and challenging activities for young people are not available. Skateboarding offers one solution, but skateboarding cannot occur in the rain, or when it's excessively hot, or in the dark winter months. Ultimately, a well-designed and well-built skatepark is necessary to provide a challenging and safe environment for young skaters. Older skaters would also use and enjoy such a park, and this mix of age groups would give younger skaters the opportunity to learn and grow, not only as skaters but also as people.

PROPOSAL

This proposal puts forth a plan for building skateparks in underutilized spaces under bridges and overpasses in Seattle. Skateparks can take organic, asymmetrical forms; they need not be bound in squares like other sports fields. This key feature allows for more efficient use of space that otherwise may be rendered useless (such as land under bridges or freeways).

Using land under a bridge has two main advantages compared to other skatepark locations. First, it largely eliminates the "N.I.M.B.Y." (Not In My Back Yard) problem, which happens when local residents do not want loud or disruptive activities near their houses. Because these areas already accommodate a freeway or a noisy bridge, skatepark-generated noise is no longer an issue. Second, skateparks discourage illegal activities that often occur under bridges of this sort. A good example is the area under the Burnside Bridge in Portland. This location was home to all kinds of criminal activity (drug deals, prostitution, abandoned cars, and so on) before Mark Scott and other skaters started building a skatepark there in 1990. The skaters cleaned up the area and kept the criminals out, to the point that the surrounding businesses took notice and volunteered their time and money toward expanding the skatepark. Even the local police chief donated money towards the effort. (This information was taken from a personal interview with Joanne Ferrero, who is owner and operator of Ferrero Equity Inc., a company right next to the Burnside Skatepark.)

In addition to these advantages for cities, using land under bridges and overpasses also provides an advantage for skaters. The bridge provides protection from rain in the winter and excessive heat in the summer. With the addition of lights, the skatepark can be used after dark as well.

OBJECTIVES

1. Give skaters a good, covered place to skate that can be used rain or shine, day or night, throughout the year.

2. Effectively use space that most wouldn't think to use as park land. Effective use of this space fulfills the goals of the City by providing a designated area for skateboarders and serves the community by freeing up more land to be used for other types of parks.

3. Provide kids with a healthy and intense activity. At skateparks, kids learn how to skateboard and are given a positive kinesthetic and creative outlet for their energy.

PROJECT DETAILS

Suggested Locations

1. <u>Under I-90 along Royal Brougham</u>. This area is centrally located with access to public transportation. It features a large covered space that is largely unused.

2. <u>Under I-5 between NE 40th Street, and NE 42nd St</u>. This area is close to the University District, where there are lots of students who skateboard. It, too, features access to public transportation and a very large covered area that is largely unused.

Clientele

Two different groups would be likely to use skateparks in the suggested locations. The first and most important group is made up of young people who live nearby and who frequently skate in the area already. The second group is made up of skaters of all ages who live in various parts of the city and who would travel to this park (either by car or bus) because it is usable even in the rain, unlike most other outdoor skate parks.

Both clientele groups are essential components of this project, and it is expected that both would make significant use of the skatepark. Skateboarding is currently one of the fastest growing sports, and facilities such as these are used more heavily than basketball courts or baseball fields in similar locations.

Methods

The primary methods for achieving these objectives:

- The design and construction of a skatepark using concrete as its surface material.
- The use of experienced design and contracting companies comprised of skateboarders.
- The development of the area under a bridge as a full-fledged city park, complete with restrooms, trash cans, and lights.

Potential Objections and Responses

Skateparks under bridges are hidden, allowing for illegal activities. As the Burnside skatepark has proven, skateparks under bridges actually discourage crime in these areas. Skateboarders concentrate on their skateboarding, not on illegal activities. Lights, restrooms, picnic tables, a play area for toddlers, and vending machines will attract parents of the kids who are skateboarding. In Newberg, Oregon, this adult-friendly approach has been very successful at promoting self-policing of the skatepark.

Seismic safety. Traffic safety engineers design such bridges specifically to withstand the weight and stress of consistent car travel. If the bridge is safe for auto travel, one can reasonably assume it is safe for skateboarders beneath the bridge.

The land is not the property of the city. Currently there is a skatepark under I-90 in Spokane, Washington, which sets a precedent that Seattle can follow.

A park that attracts people from surrounding cities doesn't serve Seattle. In fact, it does. A good example is the skate bowl in Ballard Commons Park. Skaters come from all around to skate there, and the surrounding businesses, such as the QFC and Texaco, benefit—as does the city. The bottom line is that skaters spend money when they travel, and if they travel to Seattle, they will spend money in Seattle.

Lights are expensive. Darkness arrives early during Seattle's winter, just after the school day ends. This causes skaters to look for lighted places to skate, such as the streets or parking garages, both of which are illegal. It's far better to have the kids in one place like a skatepark, where their parents and the authorities can keep track of them. If lights can be used at a tennis court, then they can be used in the same way for a skatepark. Lights need not stay on all night. They can shut off automatically at a designated time or have a coin-operated switch to turn them on (to help offset the cost).

Needed Resources

- **Site Acquisition/Lease from Washington State Department of Transportation or the City of Seattle**
- **Personnel:** No personnel will be needed to staff the park.
- **Facilities Maintenance:** Emptying trash, cleaning restrooms, changing lights, and so on.
- **Design and Construction Costs:** Central Contractors Association estimates approx. $15/sq ft.
- **Infrastructure Maintenance Costs:**
  - Skate-only and concrete with steel coping: $0
  - Skate-only with pool coping: about $3000 the first year and $2000 a year thereafter
  - BMX: about $5000 a year

Additional Possibilities for Sites in Seattle

1. Under the Ballard Bridge
2. Under Interstate 5 in Seattle along Airport Way
3. Under the 12th Street Bridge and Dearborn Ave.
4. Under 45th St. next to University Village
5. Under Highway 509 at the intersection of Highway 99 and 509 and W. Marginal Way
6. Under Highway 99 at South Hanford St.
7. Under Hwy 99 at South Atlantic St.
8. Under I-5 and Spokane St.
9. Under I-5 at Shelby St.
10. I-90 next to Rainer Ave. and Goodwill
11. Under West Seattle Bridge at Duwammish St.

Dan Hughes
NorthwestSkater.com

Starting a Conversation: Respond to "Proposal for Skateparks under Bridges"

In your writer's notebook, evaluate Hughes's proposal by responding to the following questions:

1. What elements of Hughes's proposal demonstrate his sensitivity to the concerns of skateboarders? What elements demonstrate his awareness of the concerns of city officials?

2. How would you characterize the structure of this proposal? In what ways does the form — background, problem definition, proposed solution, and so on — help the writer achieve his purpose?

3. Hughes addresses possible objections to his proposed solution in the section "Potential Objections and Responses." Where else in the proposal does he address potential objections and how does he refute them? Can you think of additional possible objections? What questions might remain in readers' minds?

4. At several points in his proposal, Hughes refers to examples such as the Ballard Skatepark and the Burnside Skatepark. How do these sources support his claims? What important details, if any, are missing?

5. Do you think Hughes's proposal is likely to be accepted or rejected? Why?

Download or print this Starting a Conversation activity at **bedfordstmartins.com/ conversation**.

Problem-Solving Essays

Like other types of problem-solving documents, essays define problems and offer solutions for readers who share a writer's interest in an issue. What distinguishes essays from other problem-solving genres, however, is their tendency to offer a more reflective and comprehensive treatment of a problem. In addition to explaining a problem and offering a concrete solution, they are also likely to offer the writer's personal insights into the problem, the situation out of which it emerges, and the reasons why the proposed solution is preferable to competing solutions. While writers of problem-solving essays typically do their best to define a problem and propose a solution as fairly as possible, they frequently allow their experiences with and attitudes toward the problem to influence both their presentation of the problem and their selection and presentation of information from sources, such as articles, Web sites, and interviews.

Readers of problem-solving essays might be part of a broad audience, such as subscribers to a general-interest magazine such as *Time* or *Atlantic Monthly*, or they might comprise a more narrowly defined group, such as community college administrators, parents of autistic children, small-town mayors, or members of a particular church.

In academic settings, instructors are usually the primary readers, although students are often asked to *address* a different audience, such as fellow students, politicians, or the members of a particular community.

 Richard H. Thaler and Cass R. Sunstein
Easy Does It

The following problem-solving essay first appeared in *The New Republic*, a magazine that covers American politics and culture. In "Easy Does It," economist Richard H. Thaler and legal scholar Cass R. Sunstein suggest that business and government should use "choice architecture" to "nudge" people into making better decisions, while at the same time preserving individual freedom. Thaler teaches at the University of Chicago; Sunstein is a professor at Harvard School of Law and was picked by the Obama administration to lead the Federal Office of Information and Regulatory Affairs. They collaborated on the book *Nudge: Improving Decisions about Wealth, Health, and Happiness* (2008).

Easy Does It:
How to Make Lazy People
Do the Right Thing

by Richard H. Thaler and Cass R. Sunstein, The New Republic

As everyone knows, many guys are slobs. And, yes, we plead guilty to being guys. It is not that we set out to be sloppy. We have a lot of important stuff on our minds. Whom can we find for a tennis game tomorrow? How is our team going to defend against their three excellent wide receivers? You can see the problem. With these burdens distracting us, how can we be expected to keep a neat desk?

As all women who have ever shared a toilet with a man can attest, men can be especially spacey when it comes to their, er, aim. In the privacy of a home, that may be a mere annoyance. But, in a busy airport restroom used by throngs of travelers each day, the unpleasant effects of bad aim can add up rather quickly. Enter an ingenious economist who worked for Schiphol International Airport in Amsterdam. His idea was to etch an image of a black house fly onto the bowls of the airport's urinals, just to the left of the drain. The result: Spillage declined 80 percent. It turns out that, if you give men a target, they can't help but aim at it.

In the grand sweep of global affairs, dirty bathrooms may be a relatively minor problem. But, by placing fly images on its urinals, the Amsterdam airport was using a technique with broad applications in the world of business and even politics. We call that technique "choice architecture." A choice architect is anyone who influences the context in which people choose — say, by deciding what order to put menu items in, or what path to encourage shoppers to take through a supermarket, or what information to give investors about their retirement savings options, or what to tell patients deciding how to deal with a medical problem. Because seemingly tiny changes in the environment can influence behavior, choice architects wield immense power. Theirs is a gentle power, since they merely nudge rather than coerce. But their nudges can have major effects.

To see why choice architects wield so much power, consider several aspects of human nature. For one thing, there are limits on the number of items to which we can pay attention at one time. We are surrounded by stimuli, and, to survive, we have to direct our attention to what seems most important (such as the road in front of us while we are driving). As a result, we may miss things that are also significant but not currently in focus. When men use an airport urinal, chances are they have things on their mind other than making sure their aim is precise. Placing a fly image in a urinal upends this state of affairs: It causes men to focus on something they would normally ignore — nudging them toward behavior that produces a socially desirable outcome.

Choice architecture derives additional power from two other human fallibilities: inertia and limited self-control. When in doubt, humans tend to do nothing, even when the costs of making a change are trivial and the benefits are significant. We can even be too lazy to pick up the remote and change the channel, which is why networks spend so much time thinking about which show should follow another. We also often have trouble managing ourselves. To take an obvious example, an alarming percentage of Americans are overweight. Most of them would like to be thinner but can't get themselves to diet or exercise. Ever since Adam took a bite of that apple, human beings have tended to show a weakness of will.

In light of these human traits, one important tool at the choice architect's disposal is the designation of a default option. The default option determines what happens if the decision-maker takes no action. Because of limited attention,

> **Because seemingly tiny changes in the environment can influence behavior, choice architects wield immense power.**

inertia, and lack of will, the selection of the default can have pronounced effects. Defaults are ubiquitous and powerful. They are also unavoidable, because, for any system of choice architecture, there must be a rule that determines what happens if you do nothing. Of course, the usual answer is that, if you do nothing, nothing changes; whatever is happening continues to happen. But not always. Some dangerous machines, such as chain saws and lawn mowers, are designed with "dead man's switches," so that, once you are no longer gripping the machine, it stops. When you leave your computer alone to answer a phone call, nothing will happen — for a time. But, if you talk long enough, the screen saver will come on; and, if you neglect the computer for longer still, it may lock itself. Of course, you can choose how long it takes before your screen saver appears, but that, in and of itself, takes some action. Your computer probably came with a default time lag for the screen saver. Chances are, that is the one you still have.

Many businesses have discovered the power of default options. When people subscribe to a magazine or website these days, they are typically enrolled in an automatic renewal program. When their subscription runs out, it is automatically renewed unless the subscriber takes some action; and, in many cases, the action requires quite a bit of patience and persistence. One of us (not to mention names, but the lawyer) still has subscriptions to several magazines that he never reads and actually hates, because he has not gotten around to canceling them.

Businesses can manipulate default options toward good ends too, not just selfish ones. Take the issue of employee savings. Economists have long argued that Americans do not save enough for retirement. How might they be nudged to do so? Are tax incentives necessary? New government programs? Actually, there is a much easier way.

Traditionally, when employees first become eligible to join their company's 401(k) plan, they receive a notification from the human resources department along with a bunch of forms. Essentially they are told, if you want to join the plan, fill in these forms, choose a savings rate, decide how you want your money invested, and send the forms back. When it comes to filling in forms, many of us have a tendency to procrastinate, especially if those forms seem to require making important decisions. The tendency is to think, "Oh, I better do some research on which funds to pick before I sign up." The problem is that, once put off, signing up for the plan gets in line with everything else on the "to do" list, right after cleaning the garage.

To solve this problem, some companies have adopted what has come to be called automatic enrollment. Under this regime, when employees become eligible, they get the same package in the mail but are told that, unless they fill out some forms, they will be automatically enrolled with a prespecified savings rate and investment plan. Studies have shown that automatic enrollment greatly increases participation in 401(k) plans. (Workers are more likely to join, and they join sooner.) Since joining the plan is almost always an excellent idea, especially when the firm is making some matching contributions, automatic enrollment successfully nudges workers toward better choices.

Companies have also nudged employees to save more by giving them a chance to commit to gradually increasing their savings rates. One system, devised by one of us (Thaler) and collaborator Shlomo Benartzi, is called "Save More Tomorrow." The idea is that workers are offered the opportunity to sign up for a plan under which their savings rates automatically increase every time they get a pay raise, until they reach some savings cap. In the first firm that adopted this plan, those who joined more than tripled their savings rates. Of course, workers can switch out of this plan at any time. The point is to have a default option going forward that calls for their savings rates to increase along with their wages. Research is now underway on an extension of this idea known as "Give More Tomorrow," by which workers commit themselves to donating part of their future wage increases to charity. It seems possible that Give More Tomorrow, if offered widely, could produce dramatic increases in charitable contributions.

The government is inevitably involved in choice architecture and nudging as well. Some of these nudges involve default options, while others — much like placing fly images in urinals — simply create an incentive where none had previously existed. The 2006 Pension Protection Act, for instance, gently nudges firms to adopt automatic enrollment and a primitive form of Save More Tomorrow. If firms adopt those features and match employee contributions at a specified rate, then they are exempted from the somewhat onerous process of showing they were in compliance with certain federal regulations. No firm is required to adopt these policies — just given a small incentive to do so.

Of course, some government nudging makes people nervous, and rightly so. We would not want public officials to nudge people toward certain religious convictions. We would not want the government (meaning incumbents) manipulating the order in which candidates are displayed on ballots, since the candidate listed first gets a 2 to 5 percent bump in votes. In this domain, the proper thing for government to do is to insist that ballot order be settled randomly — or, better yet, varied across voting places, so the benefit of being listed first is shared by all candidates.

But, sometimes, government can do much better than pick things at random. An infuriating example of inept government choice architecture is the Medicare Part D prescription drug program. Although this program is heavily subsidized and mostly a good deal for seniors, it is much reviled, not only by seniors but by their grown children who get roped into helping them deal with the intricacies of the plan. Those who designed the plan thought that the most important thing to offer seniors was choices; so, in most states, seniors are asked to choose from about 50 different insurance plans. "The more choices you have, the more likely it is you'll be able to find a program that suits your specific needs," President Bush told a clubhouse of Florida seniors in 2006. "In other words, one-size-fits-all is not a consumer-friendly program. And I believe in consumers. I believe in trusting people."

It is great to believe in trusting people, but, sometimes, it is also a good idea to offer them a helping hand. We wanted to see what exactly seniors face in making this decision, so we asked a friend of ours to give us a list of the drugs that her mother takes. Then we went to the Medicare Part D website and tried to figure out which insurance plan would work best for her. The first step is to type in a list of all the drugs you take. What a nightmare! The site does not have a spell checker; if you type "Zanax" instead of Xanax, you don't get one of those helpful "Did you mean" Google suggestions. This is a problem because drug names often resemble strings of random letters, so typing errors are to be expected. Other difficulties related to using the site — such as needing to select the correct dosages for all your medications — probably couldn't have been avoided. But the fact is, most senior citizens are bound to find the process arduous. After a couple of hours on the Part D website, we felt that we would soon need some Xanax ourselves.

Given how difficult this process is, you might think that the government would offer a default option for those who did not want to choose for themselves. The Bush administration decided not to do this — that trust thing again. But there was one group of participants for whom the government did have to create a default option: Medicare users who had previously been covered by Medicaid. Non-Medicaid users who didn't sign up for Medicare Part D simply would not be enrolled. But Medicaid users were required to switch to Medicare for their prescription drug coverage. Of course, some did not get around to choosing a plan, so the government had to make a choice for them. What do you think that choice was? We will let you pause to consider how you would do it.

Amazingly, the method the government picked was to choose a plan at random! This makes no sense. For many people, and especially for the elderly, it is actually pretty easy to predict what drugs you will take next year — namely, the same drugs you are taking this year. A fact of life is that, the longer you live, the more drugs you take routinely. And, for many of these drugs, once you start, you take them as long as you live. Since the government knows what drugs a patient is taking (from last year's claims) and knows what prices the insurance companies are charging, it is a straightforward matter to make a decent guess about which plan would be best. In fact, the state of Maine, alert to the importance of good choice architecture, has adopted such a plan. It is called "Intelligent Assignment." But the Bush administration has not encouraged other states to adopt the idea. Perhaps, if Maine had called its plan "Intelligent Design," it would have gone further.

Private and public institutions have unlimited opportunities to use good choice architecture to improve people's lives — in domains as varied as protecting the environment, increasing organ donations, and promoting fair divorces. If we want to cut greenhouse gas emissions, for example, we can nudge people simply by giving them vivid information about their current energy uses. Southern California Edison has encouraged consumers to conserve energy by giving them an Ambient Orb, a little ball that glows red when they are using lots of energy but green when their use is modest. Users of the Orb reduced their energy consumption in peak periods by 40 percent. If we want to increase the supply of organs to people whose lives depend on them, we can presume that people want their organs, at the time of death, to be available for use by others. The general American practice is to treat non-donation as the default, but many European countries have adopted the opposite system, called "presumed consent." A study by Eric Johnson and Dan Goldstein showed that changing the default could save thousands of lives annually. And, if we want to protect women, who are especially vulnerable during divorce, we can rely on suitable default rules, which would ensure, as many states do not, that women's income does not fall dramatically in the period after divorce. In all kinds of situations, governments and employers can nudge people toward making better decisions simply by making the better choice easier to adopt.

During the second half of the twentieth century, there was a lot of talk about the possibility of developing some kind of Third Way between capitalism and socialism. Now that socialism is dead, many Americans have come to think that the real decision is between two visions of capitalism — laissez-faire capitalism, which relies on unrestricted free markets, and progressive capitalism, which relies on government mandates and bans to ensure good outcomes. But this is frequently a false dichotomy. In countless domains, good choice architecture can allow governments to preserve freedom while encouraging people to make wise decisions. Sometimes, of course, governments do need to rely on mandates and bans to advance legitimate goals. But often a freedom-preserving nudge is the simplest and most effective tool of all.

Starting a Conversation: Respond to "Easy Does It"

In your writer's notebook, reflect on the problems and solutions presented in Thaler and Sunstein's essay by answering the following questions:

1. Thaler and Sunstein touch on a broad range of subjects in this essay, from dirty public restrooms to the difficulties seniors have with Medicare Part D. What do these problems have in common? To what extent are the authors more interested in promoting a particular solution than in addressing individual problems? How can you tell?

2. What, exactly, is choice architecture? According to the authors, why do choice architects wield so much power?

3. In paragraph 13, Thaler and Sunstein acknowledge that "some government nudging makes people nervous, and rightly so." Why do they admit that this objection is reasonable? How do they respond to it?

4. At several points in the essay, the authors use generalizations and stereotypes. Identify at least three instances of this. How do these examples support — or undermine — their claims?

5. Although their focus is not explicitly political, Thaler and Sunstein do refer to former president George W. Bush and policies associated with his administration. What can you tell about their political views from these references? What can you tell about the views of their presumed readers?

@ Download or print this Starting a Conversation activity at **bedfordstmartins.com/ conversation**.

How Can I Write a Problem-Solving Essay?

We all have problems. Some of us have more than others. You've probably heard someone say, "I've got a problem. My taxes are due." Or, "I'm about to be evicted from my apartment." Or, "My hard drive crashed." When people make statements like these, they are assuming that you share their understanding of the problem. Unfortunately, that's not always the case. You might assume that the person who has a problem paying taxes lacks the money to do so and that the best solution is to get a loan or pick up a part-time job. In fact, the problem might be based on a moral objection to how the government uses funds raised through taxes.

Until people share an understanding of a problem, it can be difficult to develop a solution and put it into effect. A successful problem-solving essay begins with the recognition that explaining a problem to others involves far more than saying, "I've got a problem with that. You know what I mean?" In this chapter, we'll work from the assumption that a problem is best understood as a situation that has negative consequences for an individual or a group. To address such a situation in writing, you need to carefully define your problem, consider its significance for readers, review past efforts to address it, and either develop your own solution or argue for the adoption of one that's been proposed by someone else.

In Process

A Problem-Solving Essay about College Tuition

Jennie Tillson wrote a problem-solving essay for her introductory composition course. Jennie learned about her topic by reading articles about the cost of higher education. Follow her efforts to write her problem-solving essay by visiting **bedfordstmartins.com/conversation**. You can read excerpts of interviews with Jennie and read drafts of her essay.

As you work on your own problem-solving essay, you'll follow the work of Jennie Tillson, a first-year student who wrote a problem-solving essay about the high cost of college tuition.

Find a Conversation and Listen In

Taking on the role of problem solver requires you to understand the nature of problems — an understanding that a surprisingly large number of writers appear to lack. By learning about problems, you can begin to identify and understand them, and even to address them in meaningful ways. Once you gain an understanding of what constitutes a problem, you can begin to look for and learn about problems that intrigue you. In the process, you'll position yourself to choose a problem to address in your essay.

EXPLORE DIFFICULTIES

A good problem-solving essay begins with what educational philosopher John Dewey called a "felt difficulty" — the recognition that something isn't right. As you learn about an issue, you might find yourself wondering why something is the way it is, or perhaps you'll say to yourself, "That's not right." Treasure these early moments of recognizing a problem. If you feel that something isn't right, there's a good chance that a problem is near at hand.

As you search for felt difficulties in the world around you, keep in mind the idea that a problem is a situation with negative consequences for an individual or a group. Your responses to the following sets of questions can help you identify subjects that might serve as the focus for a problem-solving essay. (For additional suggestions, see the writing project ideas on p. 396.)

- **Community.** What kind of difficulties have you encountered or noticed in your neighborhood? Have you been stuck in long lines at a bank or post office? Have you volunteered at a food pantry that has been overwhelmed by an influx of new clients? Run across a pothole so deep that it ruined one of your tires? Been bothered by the recent actions of local politicians or law enforcement officials?

- **Economy.** Are any of your friends or relatives having financial difficulties? Have you worried about what the future holds for you? For your parents? For your children?

- **Work.** Do any issues at your workplace need to be addressed? Is the industry in which you work facing any challenges? Have you grown aware, through your course work or general reading, of difficulties facing people in your field of study?

- **News.** What have you read recently that surprised or worried you? What annoyed you or made you angry? What have you read that made you think? What controversies have you noticed on the evening news or on the Web sites you visit?

To begin turning a felt difficulty into a defined problem, jot down what doesn't feel right and then brainstorm or freewrite about it (see pp. 33–37). As you list ideas or write about your felt difficulty, the problem will begin to come into focus.

It can take time to sketch the outlines of a problem. You might find it helpful to think about the problem over a period of a few days or a week. During that time, you might read more about the problem or talk with others about it. As you reflect on the problem, keep track of your ideas by recording them in your writer's notebook or in a word-processing file.

Working Together: Try It Out Loud

Before you start working on your problem-solving essay, start a conversation with a small group of your class-mates about a minor problem that affects you. Explain the problem as clearly as you can and tell the members of your group about how you think you might solve it. Ask them whether your preliminary solution seems likely to work and why. Then ask them to suggest additional solutions you should consider trying. Take turns speaking while the members of the group listen, respond, and ask questions.

When you are finished, take a few minutes to reflect on the exercise. What did you learn about your audience?

Did they understand the problem right away, or did you have to adapt your initial explanation to overcome their assumptions? How much detail did you have to give them before your solution made sense? Did they think your solution was reasonable? What kinds of solutions did they suggest as alternatives? Did their questions and suggestions help you develop a better understanding of your problem or give you new ideas about how to solve it?

@ Download or print this Working Together activity at **bedfordstmartins.com/conversation.**

ASK QUESTIONS ABOUT PROMISING SUBJECTS

Even if you think you know a great deal about each of the problems you've identified as potential subjects for your essay, check them out thoroughly before you begin trying to solve one. To learn more about a promising problem, reflect on your own experiences with it, discuss it with others, and find and review relevant published sources through your library or the Web. (You can learn more about locating, collecting, and managing information in Part Three.)

Once you've learned about the most promising problems, select those that continue to hold your interest, and spend a few minutes responding to the following questions. Each set of questions focuses your attention on a problem in a different way, allowing you to think not only about the problem but also about its potential as the focus of your problem-solving essay. Depending on the problem you work with, you'll find that some questions are more useful than others.

- **Relevance.** Is this problem widespread, or does it involve only a small group of people? Who is affected by it, and how are they affected? Will my readers think it's important? Can I address it within the limits of my assignment?

- **Definition.** What, exactly, is the problem? How can I explain it? What kinds of information will readers need to understand it?

- **Context.** When and where did this problem begin? How much is known about it? What solutions have been tried? Why haven't they worked?

- **Causes and effects.** What caused this problem? What must happen before it can be solved? What is likely to happen if it isn't solved?

As you think about your ideas, remember that the best problems to tackle in an essay are usually highly specific. For example, instead of writing about the general problem of encouraging college students to become teachers, you might focus on how to encourage students in a particular discipline, such as math or biology, to become high school teachers in rural school districts.

CONDUCT A SURVEY

A survey can help you learn about the beliefs, attitudes, or behaviors of people associated with a problem. For example, you might use a survey to discover whether the attitudes and beliefs about education differ among students who stay in school and those who drop out. Or you might use a survey to explore whether students who put a high value on community involvement are highly engaged in volunteer activities.

Typically, surveys help you answer *what*, *who*, or *how* questions—such as "What kinds of exercise do you engage in at least once a week?" "Who will you vote for in the next election?" or "How likely are you to use public transportation?" Surveys are less useful in obtaining the answers to *why* questions. In an interview, for instance, you can ask "Why did you vote the way you did in the last election?" and expect to get a reasonably well-thought-out response (see p. 186 to learn about interviews). In contrast, survey respondents seldom write lengthy answers to questions.

Conducting an effective survey usually involves the following activities.

Decide whether to conduct a survey. Your decision about whether to conduct a survey should be based on the role it will play in your essay, the amount of work required to do a good job, and the kind of information you are seeking. Surveys are useful if you want to collect evidence to support your assertion that a problem exists, or if you want to learn about the attitudes and behaviors of a large group of people (more than five or ten). If you simply want opinions from a handful of people, you can gain that information more efficiently by interviewing or corresponding with them.

Decide whom to survey. Most surveys collect information from selected members of a particular group to estimate the beliefs, attitudes, or behaviors of the group as a whole. For example, surveys completed by a hundred students might be used as evidence about the beliefs, attitudes, and behaviors of all students at a school. Similarly, "national" polls seldom survey more than a thousand people, yet they are used to provide an indication of the opinions of everyone in the country.

To select participants, you can choose people from your target group at random. For example, if you are interested in surveying students at your college or university, you could open your school's telephone directory and pick every twentieth name. Or you can stratify your sample. For example, you could randomly select a specific number of first-year, second-year, third-year, and fourth-year students—and then make sure that the number of men and women in each group is proportional to enrollment.

Decide what to ask and how to ask it. Designing effective surveys can be challenging. A survey item, such as a multiple-choice question or a true/false statement, that seems perfectly clear to you might confuse someone else. To identify confusing items, ask a few classmates, friends, or family members to try out your survey. Ask them what they think about each survey item. Then rewrite any items that caused confusion and test the survey again. Doing so will help you improve the clarity of your survey.

Understanding the strengths and weaknesses of the kinds of items that are frequently used in surveys is a good way to get started.

- **Yes/no items** divide respondents into two groups.

    Example: Do you have a Facebook account?   ○ Yes   ○ No

- **True/false items** more often deal with attitudes or beliefs than with behaviors or events.

    Example: People who have a Facebook account receive more spam e-mail than people who don't have Facebook accounts.   ○ True   ○ False

- **Ranking items** forces respondents to place items along a continuum.

  Example: Rank the following social-networking sites from best to worst using the numbers 1 (best) through 5 (worst):

  ___ Facebook

  ___ Gather

  ___ MySpace

  ___ Ning

  ___ Xanga

- **Likert-scale items** measure respondents' level of agreement with a statement, their assessment of the importance of something, or how frequently they engage in a behavior.

  Example: If you have a Facebook account, how often do you check it?

Never	Once a month	Once a week	Every day	Several times each day
○	○	○	○	○

- **Multiple-choice items** indicate whether a respondent knows something or engages in specific behaviors. Because they seldom include every possible answer, be careful when including them.

  Example: I use the following tools on social-networking sites:

  ___ Blogs

  ___ Messaging

  ___ Friends

  ___ "Walls"

  ___ Organization pages

  ___ Applications

- **Short-answer items** allow greater freedom of response, but they can be difficult to tabulate.

  Example: What do you like best about social-networking sites?

In Process

Developing a Survey

Jennie Tillson created a brief survey to learn what students at her university had considered when they were applying for college. She kept it brief so that more students would respond. She collected eighty-seven responses to the survey.

1. Which do you personally consider the most important factor when choosing a college? (Please check one.)

    ___ Academic ranking

    ___ Athletic programs

    ___ Tuition cost

    ___ Geographic location

    Comment:

> A multiple-choice question asks respondents to pick one answer.

> Room is provided for brief comments.

2. When you applied to college, which kinds of schools did you consider attending? (Check all that apply.)

    ___ Four-year private university

    ___ Four-year public university

    ___ Community college

    ___ Trade school

    ___ Other: _____

    Comment:

> A multiple-choice question asks respondents to pick multiple answers.

3. If you knew that a sibling or friend was concerned about being able to afford college, how likely would you be to recommend that they think about community college? (Please check one.)

    ___ Very likely

    ___ Somewhat likely

    ___ Neither likely nor unlikely

    ___ Somewhat unlikely

    ___ Not at all likely

    Comment:

> A Likert-scale question asks students to indicate the likelihood that they would recommend community college.

Conduct your survey. The large number of surveys people are asked to complete has reduced the public's willingness to respond to them. In fact, a "good" response rate for a survey is 60 percent. The following guidelines can help increase your response rate:

- Keep your survey short, preferably no longer than a single page.

- Make sure your survey is easy to read. Don't crowd the questions onto the page or jam questions into an e-mail message.

- Explain the purpose of your survey in a brief statement. If you are handing out your survey in person or during a class, provide a brief statement on the first page. If you are distributing the survey via e-mail or the Web, include a brief statement in the message or at the top of the Web page. A clear explanation can increase a respondent's willingness to complete the survey.

- Treat survey respondents with respect. If you are mailing your survey, address the envelopes by hand and use a cover letter to explain the survey.

- Make the survey easy to return. If you mail the survey, include a stamped, self-addressed envelope. If you are conducting your survey on the Web or via e-mail, provide directions for returning completed surveys.

Analyze your results. It's usually best to tabulate survey responses using a spreadsheet or statistics program. These kinds of programs provide flexibility when you want to analyze your results. For example, they offer statistical tests that allow you to look for differences between groups of respondents in the average rating given to a survey item. (You can learn about these tests through the program's online help.) If you prefer, you can also organize the results in a table in a word-processing program.

If you conduct a survey and use its results in your essay, include a copy of your survey questions in an appendix.

Develop a Solution

Once you've identified a promising problem and learned about it, you can begin to develop a solution to the problem. If your problem has already attracted the attention of other writers, the solution you choose might be one that another writer has already advanced, or it might be an improved version of someone else's proposed solution. If the problem has remained unresolved for some time, however, you might find it best to develop a new solution. If your problem is relatively new or is one that has not yet attracted the attention of other writers, you might develop your own solution to the problem, or you might look at how similar problems have been addressed and then adapt one of those solutions.

Whatever approach you take, remember that a clear problem definition is the single most important element in a problem-solving essay. Without it, even the most elegant solution won't be convincing. A problem definition enables you to take a problem apart, examine its causes and effects, and understand whom or what it affects. It also influences how your readers understand the problem and how they are likely to react to your solution.

In addition, remember that a solution must be practical. Few readers will be impressed by a solution that costs too much or takes too long to put into effect or that causes even more problems than it solves. As you consider potential solutions to your problem, carefully assess their feasibility and potential consequences.

DEFINE THE PROBLEM

Some people define a problem with a particular solution in mind. As a result, their solution usually looks good in theory. But a solution based on a weak problem definition seldom works well in practice, and it is unlikely to convince your readers. For this and other reasons, you should define your problem as clearly and accurately as possible.

You can define your problem by exploring situation and effects, focusing on actions, examining severity and duration, and considering goals and barriers.

Situation/effects. Explore the effects a problematic situation has on people or things. Ask yourself:

- What is the situation?

- What are its effects?

- Who or what is affected?

Agent/goals/actions/results. Focus on actions that have unwanted results. Ask yourself:

- Who or what is the *agent* (the person, group, or thing that acts in a manner that causes a problem)?

- What are the agent's *goals*?

- What *actions* does the agent carry out to accomplish the goals?

- What are the *results* of the agent's actions?

Severity and duration. Analyze the severity and duration of the effects of a problematic situation. Ask yourself:

- What is the situation?

- What effects are associated with the situation?

- How severe are the effects?

- What is the duration of the effects?

In Process

Defining a Problem

Jennie Tillson used the situation/effects questions (p. 378) to develop her problem definition by identifying the problematic situation and examining its effects on specific groups of people.

What is the situation? Over the last ten years, tuition at two-year colleges has risen by 53% and at four-year colleges by 85% (see Quinn). This increase has been paralleled by a comparable increase in family earning for middle- and upper-income Americans, but the cost has risen sharply for poor families (Quinn). Although the availability of financial aid has increased (College Board, cited in Quinn), more aid is coming as loans rather than as grants. And more aid is being given for merit rather than for financial need (College Board, cited in Quinn).

What are the effects? Some students have delayed or given up on a college education. Some have not been able to enroll at their first- or second-choice college or university, a problem that can affect the quality of education they receive. Some are working full-time as they take classes. Some students are graduating with a higher level of debt than classmates from wealthier families. Some colleges and universities have kept tuition lower by increasing class size, offering fewer classes, and hiring adjunct faculty rather than full-time faculty.

Who is affected? Poorer students and their families are affected directly. Indirectly, all Americans are affected because, as it gets harder to attend college, the gap between rich and poor will grow, and higher education will become segregated by income class (see Nyhan).

Because Jennie was trying to approach the problem of increasing tuition as a situation that affected all Americans, the situation/effects questions worked well for her. If she had been trying to identify the causes of the problem, she might have used the agent/goals/actions/results questions. If she had been interested in assessing how serious the problem is and its long-term impact, she might have used the questions that address severity and duration.

Goals and barriers. Identify goals, and ask what obstacles stand in the way of accomplishing them. Ask yourself:

- What are the goals?
- What barriers stand in the way of accomplishing the goals?

Most of these methods of defining a problem focus on cause/effect relationships, and many involve unintended consequences. However, each one allows you to view a problem from a different perspective. Because your problem definition has powerful effects on the development of a solution to your problem, it can be useful to experiment with different ways of defining the problem.

CONSIDER POTENTIAL SOLUTIONS

Use your problem definition to weigh potential solutions. If your problem definition focuses on the causes of the problem or barriers to achieving a goal, for example, consider solutions that address those causes or barriers. If your problem definition focuses on actions that have had unexpected or undesired effects, explore solutions that might address those effects. If your problem definition focuses on the duration and severity of a problem, ask yourself how the duration and severity of the problem might be reduced, or perhaps even eliminated.

As you generate ideas for possible solutions, keep in mind what you've learned about your problem. If you're dealing with a problem that other writers have addressed, pay attention to the solutions they've proposed. Even if those solutions have failed to solve the problem — which is likely given the continuing existence of the problem — they might have helped address at least some of its effects. Consider the impact of these earlier solutions, weigh their negative consequences, and ask whether you might adapt them — or parts of them — for your own use.

In your writer's notebook, create a list of potential solutions — both your own and those of other writers — and briefly describe them. Evaluate each solution by answering the following questions:

- How well does this solution address the causes of the problem?
- How well does this solution address the effects of the problem?
- To what extent does this solution address the needs of the people or things affected by the problem?
- What costs would be associated with this solution?
- What advantages does this solution have over other solutions?
- What disadvantages does this solution have?

Review your responses to the questions, and identify your most promising solutions. If you've identified more than one solution, ask whether the best features of each might be combined into a single solution. As you consider each solution, you'll gain a better understanding of the problem itself. Your problem-solving essay will be most effective if you clearly connect your solution to your problem definition, so you might find it useful to revise your definition to reflect the additional thinking you've put into the problem. Remember that your problem definition isn't set in stone. It can be revised and improved throughout the process of writing your essay.

In Process

Developing a Solution

To begin solving the problem she had defined, Jennie Tillson created a cluster map. Jennie used the situation/effects questions on page 378 to explore causes, effects, and potential solutions to the problem of rising college tuition.

Jennie placed her issue — increasing college tuition — in a bubble at the center of her cluster.

Each cause, effect, and solution generated more specific ideas.

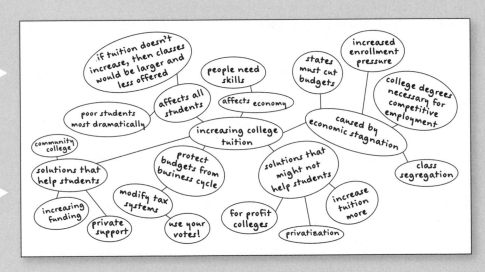

Jennie's cluster map helped her lay out potential solutions for students from poor and working-class families. With that in mind, she used freewriting to generate ideas that might solve that aspect of the problem.

The most viable option might be voting. People can vote for tax reform to make it easier for kids from poor families to attend college. People can vote to increase funding for higher ed. They can vote to set up rainy-day funds for colleges. They can make colleges set aside money for hard times. These things can help lower the real cost of college tuition, even if tuition still continues to rise.

ASSESS THE PRACTICALITY OF YOUR SOLUTION

Most problems can be solved given unlimited time, vast sums of money, revisions to the laws of physics, or changes in human nature. If your solution requires any or all of these, however, your readers are likely to question its practicality. Before you start drafting your essay, ensure that your solution is feasible by asking whether your solution can be implemented

- in a reasonable amount of time
- with available funding
- with available resources
- given current knowledge and technology
- without causing additional problems

Consider as well how your readers' needs, interests, and backgrounds will affect their response to your solution. For example, if your readers have strong religious beliefs about the use of birth control, they probably won't react favorably to a proposal to reduce teenage pregnancies by requiring public schools to dispense contraceptives.

Finally, consider potential objections to your solution. If your solution requires funding or resources that might be used for other purposes, for example, ask whether readers will object to reducing funding for those purposes. If you think that your readers will not accept the trade-offs associated with your solution, take another look at it. You might be able to modify your solution to account for likely objections, or you might want to prepare an argument about why the trade-offs are better than just leaving things as they are.

Prepare a Draft

As you get ready to draft your essay, review your problem definition, the solutions you've examined, and your notes on your proposed solution. You'll need to decide how to explain the problem, present your solution, and convince readers that your solution is worth pursuing. You'll also want to consider the role of document design in your essay, how you'll organize your ideas, and how you'll frame your introduction and conclusion.

EXPLAIN THE PROBLEM

Your problem definition is the single most important element of your problem-solving essay. It sets up your solution and shapes your thesis statement. It also affects your choice of sources and evidence to support the points you make in your essay.

As is the case with so many aspects of writing, however, you should pay attention not only to the content of your problem definition but also to how you present it to readers.

For example, consider how a reader might react to the statement "Teachers are the reason education is in trouble." Which of the following thoughts flashed through your mind?

- Teachers are lazy.

- Teachers are poorly prepared.

- Teachers are spreading left-wing propaganda and infecting the minds of our youth.

- Teachers are extraordinarily boring.

- Good teachers are quitting to become stockbrokers or advertising executives.

All of the above? None of the above? Now substitute "students" or "parents" or "politicians" or "television" or "video games" in the same statement. What flashes through your mind?

Statements like these are unclear because they don't define the problem. They don't explain, for example, what it is about teachers that causes education to be in trouble.

Consider the differences between "Teachers are the reason education is in trouble" and the following problem definitions.

> **Problem Definition 1:** The lack of certified science teachers in public schools has limited the development of a general understanding of key scientific concepts among Americans. Without that understanding, it will be difficult to carry out informed debates about policies that rely on an understanding of scientific concepts, such as the development of a hydrogen economy or decisions about how we deal with the causes of global climate change.

> **Problem Definition 2:** The relatively low salaries offered to beginning teachers, combined with the growing cost of higher education and the high debt burden incurred by many college graduates, have reduced the attractiveness of pursuing a career as an educator. The result is a growing shortage of qualified teachers in key areas, such as the sciences, mathematics, and the arts. Because of this shortage, students are not receiving the education they deserve.

Each of these problem definitions calls attention to the effects of a particular situation on specific groups or individuals. In the first example, the situation—a lack of certified science teachers—affects Americans' ability to understand and participate in debates about scientific issues. In the second example, the economic situation faced by beginning teachers affects college students' willingness to pursue careers as teachers, which in turn affects the education of students. Through their clarity and detail, both of these problem definitions offer significant advantages over "Teachers are the reason education is in trouble."

As you consider how best to explain your problem definition to your readers, reflect on what they already know about it. If they are already familiar with the problem, you might be able to convey your problem definition in a sentence or two that frames the solution that will follow. If they are unfamiliar with the problem, however, you might need to devote a significant portion of your essay to establishing the existence of the problem and explaining its consequences.

PROPOSE YOUR SOLUTION

Most problem-solving essays frame the problem in a way that prepares readers to accept the proposed solution. The problem of skyrocketing fuel prices, for example, might be framed so that the best solution would seem to involve the development of new technologies, while the problem of a growing national debt might be framed so that the best solution would appear to rely on changes in tax laws.

After you introduce a problem to your readers, you can present a thesis statement that summarizes your proposed solution. Your thesis statement should be closely tied to your problem definition, and it should suggest a logical and reasonable means of addressing the problem. Because your thesis statement will frame readers' understanding of your solution in a certain way, it serves as a powerful tool for influencing your readers. Consider the differences among the following thesis statements addressing the problem of low salaries for teachers who leave college with high levels of debt.

> **Thesis statement 1:** If we are to ensure an adequate supply of qualified teachers, we must increase their starting salaries.

> **Thesis statement 2:** The most promising approach to ensuring an adequate supply of qualified teachers is paying the tuition and fees for college students who promise to spend at least five years teaching in our public schools.

> **Thesis statement 3:** A public-private partnership designed to identify and support promising new teachers is the key to ensuring an adequate supply of qualified teachers in our public schools.

Each of these thesis statements calls attention to a different solution to the problem. The first focuses on salaries, suggesting that the promise of higher salaries will lead

Is your thesis statement focused enough? See Chapter 15 for help.

more students to consider a career in teaching and perhaps will encourage those who do become teachers to stay in the profession. The second thesis statement focuses on the cost of attending college, borrowing an approach used successfully to attract new doctors to rural parts of the country. The third focuses on recruiting students into the teaching profession. Each thesis statement offers a reasonable solution to the problem as it has been defined, yet each would also lead the writer to produce a significantly different essay.

EXPLAIN YOUR SOLUTION

Your solution is what most readers will remember about your essay. Once you've defined the problem and proposed your solution, explain your solution by going into detail, offering support for your ideas, and considering your solution in light of promising alternatives.

Go into detail. A surprising number of problem-solving essays spend several pages defining and discussing the consequences of a problem, only to offer a skimpy discussion of a proposed solution. However, readers are rarely satisfied by such an approach, so be sure to spend some time identifying the key aspects of your solution. Help your readers understand, in detail, how you would implement the solution, how much it would cost to put into effect, what kinds of effects the solution would have on the problem, and how you would judge its effectiveness in addressing the problem.

Provide support for your points. Most problem-solving essays rely heavily on evidence to establish the existence of a problem, support a proposed solution, and dismiss alternative solutions. Your solution should offer a reasonable and thoughtful response to the problem, and it should be clear that your proposed solution is superior to alternatives.

You can use evidence to

- identify and frame your solution

- provide examples and illustrations

- illustrate processes that might be required to put the solution into place

- associate particular ideas and concepts with authorities, such as political leaders, subject-matter experts, or people who have been affected by the problem

To develop support, list the key points you are making about your proposed solution. For each point, review your sources and notes to identify relevant evidence, and then list the evidence below each point. If your sources support your solution, draw on evidence from them to show your readers why your solution is likely to be effective. If your sources do not directly address your solution, consider using personal experience. You can read more about how to use evidence to support your points in Chapter 17.

In Process

Providing Support for Key Points

Jennie Tillson identified support for her key points by listing each point, reviewing her notes to locate sources that would support her points, and listing the relevant sources next to each point.

Key Points	Support
College tuition is increasing	Quinn
Tuition costs are hitting low-income students and families hardest, discouraging talented students from attending college.	Quinn, Lewin
We're all affected by this. It will cause a greater gap between rich and poor.	Nyhan
Change must begin with colleges and universities.	Clark, Lewin
Government must also play a role.	Quinn, Clark, Lewin
Students and their families must also play a role.	Young, my survey

Address promising alternative solutions. As you draft your problem-solving essay, be sure to consider alternative solutions that are likely to occur to your readers. In proposing a solution to a problem, you are essentially making an argument that your solution is preferable to others. If your readers can think of alternatives, especially alternatives that might be less expensive or more effective than yours, they might wonder why you haven't mentioned them.

To address (and dismiss) alternative solutions, you can do the following:

- Identify the strongest solution, explain why it's the best of several alternatives, and then explain why your solution is better.

- Identify a group of solutions that share the same weakness, such as high cost or impracticality, and explain why this group of solutions is weaker than yours.

- Identify a group of promising alternatives, and dismiss each solution one after the other.

You can gain insights into effective strategies for organizing your response to alternative solutions by reading about the organizational patterns discussed in Chapter 16.

CONSIDER GENRE AND DESIGN

Depending on the complexity of the problem you're addressing and the nature of the solution you propose, design can contribute greatly to the overall effectiveness of your essay. As is the case with other academic essays, you'll need to consider the expectations of your readers about design elements such as wide margins, double-spaced lines, page numbers, and a readable body font. But you can also use page layout elements as well as color, shading, borders, and rules to enhance the effectiveness of your essay.

- **Page layout elements,** such as marginal glosses, pull quotes, and headings and subheadings, can draw readers' attention to key points in your essay. For example, a pull quote—a passage of text set off from the body of your essay using borders or white space — can highlight an important idea. Similarly, headings and subheadings can help readers understand at a glance the main idea of a section in your essay.

- **Color, shading, borders, and rules** can be used to call attention to key information and ideas in your essay. For instance, you might use a shaded box to present a dramatic example or related information that doesn't fit well within the body of your essay, or use a contrasting color to draw the reader's eye to an important passage.

Other design elements—such as illustrations and captions, tables and figures, and bulleted and numbered lists—can also contribute to the effectiveness of your essay. As you consider how best to connect with your readers, reflect on which design strategies will help you accomplish your purpose. Chapter 18 provides a detailed discussion of document design principles and elements.

FRAME YOUR ESSAY

Once you've worked out how to define the problem and present your proposed solution, decide how you'll organize, introduce, and conclude your essay.

Organization. Most problem-solving essays start with an introduction, then define the problem and explain the proposed solution, and finish with a conclusion. Longer problem-solving essays often make use of the organizational patterns discussed in Chapter 16. For instance, process explanation can offer a helpful outline for explaining the steps involved in implementing a solution. The costs/benefits and strengths/weaknesses patterns both provide a practical structure for analyzing a problem and examining a solution's potential. And problem-solving essays that address several alternative solutions often take advantage of the comparison/contrast pattern.

Introduction. Your introduction creates a framework within which you can present your thesis statement and prepare your readers to understand how you've defined your problem. You can draw on a number of strategies to draw your readers in:

- Use an anecdote (a brief story) to personalize the problem.

- Use dramatic statistics, as Jennie Tillson does in her essay, to illustrate the scope of the problem.

- Use quotations from experts, or from people who have been affected by a problem, to make the problem hit home with your readers.

- Draw comparisons between this problem and other, more widely understood problems.

You can read more about strategies for introducing your essay in Chapter 16.

Conclusion. In much the same way that you can use your introduction to direct readers toward a particular understanding of a problem, you can use your conclusion to encourage them to accept your ideas for solving it. Most problem-solving essays end with a call to action, in which the writer urges readers to do something specific to help put the solution into effect. Other strategies you can employ to conclude your essay include summarizing your problem definition and proposed solution, circling back to the introduction, and speculating about the future. You can learn more about framing your conclusion in Chapter 16.

Review and Improve Your Draft

The success of your problem-solving essay rests heavily on how well you can define your problem, present your solution, convince readers that your solution is feasible, and consider alternatives and potential objections to your solution. Few writers can manage all of these tasks in a first draft, so keep them in mind as you assess your draft and revise your essay.

REASSESS YOUR PROBLEM DEFINITION

Now that your essay is in draft form, consider how well you present your problem definition and how effectively it leads to your proposed solution. Your problem definition should direct your readers' attention to the problem in a particular way. If not, they'll find it difficult to understand how your definition of the problem is related to your proposed solution. As you draft your essay—and spend additional time thinking about the problem—you will almost certainly deepen your understanding of the problem. Take a few moments now to ask whether your problem definition fully reflects that understanding.

Then ask some harder questions: Have you defined your problem in the best way (with "best" defined in light of the solution you've proposed and the needs, interests, and backgrounds of your readers)? Will your readers accept the problem definition you've developed? If you suspect that they'll object to it or find it inadequate, how can you change it to address their likely concerns?

REVIEW THE PRESENTATION OF YOUR SOLUTION

When you're in the midst of drafting, it's normal to spend more time on some aspects of your solution than others or to overlook key steps that will be required to put the solution into effect. As you review your draft, take a careful look at how you've presented your solution. Have you explained it logically and clearly? Have you provided your readers with a sufficiently detailed understanding of what the solution involves and how it could work? Have you presented sufficient evidence to support your points?

CHECK THE FEASIBILITY OF YOUR SOLUTION

When you're caught up in the details of presenting a solution, it's easy to lose sight of whether the solution will actually work. During your review, ask whether the solution you've proposed can be put into practice given the time, funding, and resources that are available. If you suspect that you've proposed a solution that might not be cost-effective—such as solving the problem of rising tuition costs by giving everyone who wants to attend college a $100,000 scholarship, a solution that would cost taxpayers roughly $1.8 trillion—reconsider your solution. Similarly, if the time and resources necessary to achieve a solution are simply not available, take another look at your options.

CONSIDER OBJECTIONS AND ALTERNATIVE SOLUTIONS

Put yourself in the position of your readers, and ask some hard questions. Why is this solution better than another? What are the major drawbacks of your proposed solution? Under what conditions would your solution be likely to fail? Identify the objections your readers might have to your solution, and address them in your essay.

Look as well for challenges to your solution that your readers might not consider but that you've become aware of in the course of your reading. Then address each challenge, explaining clearly why your solution is preferable to the alternatives you've identified.

Peer Review: Improve Your Problem-Solving Essay

One of the biggest challenges writers face is reading a draft of their own work as a reader rather than as the writer. Because you know what you're trying to say, you find it easy to understand your draft. To determine what you should do to revise your draft, ask a friend or classmate to read your essay and to assess how well you have adopted the role of problem solver (see p. 338) by answering the following questions.

Purpose	1. Is my problem definition sufficiently narrow and focused? Is it clear and easy to understand?
	2. Do you believe the problem is significant? Why or why not?
	3. Is my solution clearly presented? Does it seem like a reasonable response to the problem I've defined?
Readers	4. Were you aware of the problem before you read the essay? Are other readers likely to be familiar with it? Do I need to say more about it to help readers understand?
	5. Are you convinced that my solution can work? Does it seem feasible? Why or why not?
	6. Have I presented ideas fairly? Are you aware of any potential objections or alternative solutions that I should have addressed?
Sources	7. Does the evidence I've offered to define the problem and support my proposed solution make sense? Can I add or clarify anything to help you understand the problem and solution better? Do you think any of the evidence is unnecessary?
	8. Do my sources strike you as reliable and appropriate? Does any of the evidence I've used seem questionable?
Context	9. Have I taken my readers' knowledge, assumptions, and values into consideration?
	10. Would any of the information I've drawn on in this essay be better presented in visual form? Could I make changes in page layout, color, shading, or rules to improve the essay's appearance?

For each of the points listed above, ask your reviewers to provide concrete advice about what you should do to improve your draft. It can help if you ask them to adopt the role of an editor — someone who is working with you to improve your draft. You can read more about these and other collaborative activities in Chapter 4.

@ Download or print this Peer Review activity at bedfordstmartins.com/conversation.

✳ Student Essay

Jennie Tillson, "Death, Taxes, and College Tuition"
The following problem-solving essay was written by featured writer Jennie Tillson. Follow Jennie's efforts to write her essay by visiting **bedfordstmartins.com/conversation**. You can read excerpts of interviews in which she discusses her work on her essay, read the assignment, and read drafts of her essay.

Tillson 1

> **Information about the writer, class, and submission date is formatted according to MLA guidelines.**

Jennie Tillson

Professor Palmquist

March 3, 2009

COCC150 College Composition

> **Following MLA guidelines, the title is centered.**

Death, Taxes, and College Tuition

> **The writer provides a quotation to frame the issue.**

"In this world nothing can be said to be certain, except death and taxes."

— *Benjamin Franklin, in a letter to Jean-Baptiste Leroy,*

November 13, 1789

> **The writer plays off the opening quotation, explaining its relevance to readers.**

Please add one more item to that list, Mr. Franklin: higher college tuition. Each year, college tuition increases as surely as winter follows fall and spring follows winter. According to noted economic adviser Jane Bryant Quinn, over the past decade, tuition at two-year colleges has increased by 53% and at four-year colleges by 85%, more than double the rate of inflation. For the millions of Americans attempting to survive in an intensely competitive job market, a college degree can be a necessity. However, few students can ignore rising college tuition,

> **The writer uses a situation/effects problem definition to help readers understand the issue.**

and fewer still can afford to pay for college without draining family income or taking on enormous debt. Especially for students from low-income families, attending college may become an unreachable goal — not for academic reasons, but for financial ones. College administrations, government agencies, and stu-

Tillson 2

dents and their families all need to take action to address the rising costs of college tuition. No one group can solve this problem alone; the crisis has grown to the point where all involved must contribute and sacrifice in order to make college more accessible for tomorrow's students.

> The writer provides an overview of the solution she'll present in detail later in the essay.

During today's recession, many families are dealing with tight budgets and lost jobs, which can make paying for college difficult — if not impossible. This crisis affects students from lower-income families the most. While the cost of college as a percentage of family income remained fairly stable for students from upper-income and middle-income families over the course of a decade, the cost has risen sharply for lower-income families (Quinn). In 1999, the cost of sending a child to a public university was about 39% of a poor family's income. By 2008, that cost had increased to 55% (Lewin). While more and more middle-class college applicants are turning to loans to finance their education, going into debt is not always an option for low-income families (Lewin). More importantly, those students who receive federally funded Pell grants (which cover roughly 39% of a public four-year education for low-income students) are facing lower admission rates when compared to more well-off and out-of-state students who pay higher tuition (Quinn). Added together, these factors can discourage or even prevent many talented students from attending college just because they and their families can't afford it.

> The writer makes a key point about the impact on families of a difficult financial situation.

> An online source without page or paragraph numbers is cited by author only.

> The writer offers an overall assessment of the situation, based on information drawn from sources.

This situation affects all of us. As it becomes increasingly difficult for poor and working-class Americans to attend college, the gap between rich and poor will continue to grow, and American higher education will once again become segregated — this time by income class (Nyhan). As *Seattle Post-Intelligencer* reporter Paul Nyhan explains, "The divide between the wealthy and poor in educational opportunity threatens to perpetuate the cycle of poverty for thousands of working poor families." He points out that a college education offers the clearest path out of poverty, adding an average of $20,000 a year to graduates'

> The writer makes a second key point.

> Since the source of a quotation is named in an attribution and there is no page or paragraph number, no parenthetical citation is given.

> Information from a source is paraphrased.

Tillson 3

expected income. As a smaller and smaller proportion of students from low-income families enroll in colleges and universities, however, fewer will be able to take that path. For the nation as a whole, this means that fewer bright and capable citizens will reach their full potential, and the contributions they would otherwise have made to society will be lost.

The solution is introduced. The writer focuses first on the role that will be played by colleges and universities.

Change must begin with the colleges and universities. A recent report by the Delta Project on Postsecondary Education Costs, Productivity, and Accountability concluded that, today, the increased tuition students are paying is going to make up for funds cut by state budgets (Clark). Some of the biggest increases in college spending are surprisingly not in the area of classroom education, but instead in administration, support services, and maintenance. College presidents also argue that, since the tragedy at Virginia Tech in 2007, new security and counseling needs have become a new priority (Clark). While this is true, colleges must find ways to fund these new programs without affecting the quality of classroom education that students receive, or enrollment may suffer. In order to keep quality education in place, colleges will need to spend money strategically in ways that are most effective for the success of all students, regardless of family income.

The writer argues that financial aid systems must be revamped.

One way colleges should use tuition money to benefit students is by redesigning their financial aid systems. Although colleges have reportedly increased their need-based financial aid, most of these precious funds go to boost tuition aid for middle-class students. Tamar Lewin from the *New York Times* writes, "Student borrowing has more than doubled in the last decade, and students from lower-income families, on average, get smaller grants from the colleges they attend than students from more affluent families." Basing more award decisions on financial need instead of merit would allow more students from lower-income families to attend college. As hard economic times continue to affect family finances, some colleges are even offering emergency aid and loans, particularly in cases where parents have lost jobs (Young). More colleges must take

Tillson 4

similar steps to ensure that students from all economic backgrounds have a fighting chance at affording an education.

However, many state colleges and universities cannot begin to make significant changes to help the student population without support and funding from the government. State and federal governments must play a large role in ensuring college affordability, especially during the economic downturn. Solutions to the problem of increasing tuition costs are likely to be effective only if they address its root economic causes. Quinn, among others, has recognized that tuition is rising at public institutions, which educate roughly 80% of all American college students. This is in large part because state and federal funding for higher education has not kept pace with costs (Quinn). In the last ten years, a majority of states have actually cut funding for higher education, while most of the remaining states have either held funding steady (which amounts to a cut, given inflation) or raised funding only by modest amounts (Quinn). Over the past five years, after accounting for inflation and financial aid, students faced a 15% increase in costs to attend a public university (Clark). And in the coming year alone, some states anticipate budgets that require tuition increases as high as 20% in a single year (Lewin). Unless this trend changes, which appears unlikely in the current economic climate, public higher education institutions will continue to cover their costs by raising tuition and fees.

Instead of cutting education funding, states should provide more money for schools, especially now when jobs are scarce and even trained workers are eager to return to school. Patrick Callan, president of the National Center for Public Policy and Higher Education, said:

> When the economy is good, and state universities are somewhat better funded, we raise tuition as little as possible. When the economy is bad, we raise tuition and sock it to families, when people can least afford it. That's exactly the opposite of what we need. (qtd. in Lewin)

The writer argues that government must also play a role in the solution.

The writer speculates about what will happen if the government does not get involved in solving the problem.

The writer argues that states should add to their higher education funding.

A block quotation is used for a longer quotation.

Tillson 5

Only by investing in educating their citizens during hard economic times will states see the benefits of having educated workers and business owners — and higher-earning taxpayers — in the state during better times. For this reason, higher education should be a top priority in even trimmed-down state budgets so that students and their families won't face drastic increases in tuition.

> The writer presents the third part of the solution: the role of students and their families.

At the same time, students still ultimately bear the responsibility for finding the best path to an affordable college education. Students and their families are a necessary part of the solution. They should be willing to apply to a variety of schools, including those they can afford more easily without financial aid. Many students and their families are now considering less expensive routes to a college degree, such as enrolling in public universities or community colleges in their home states (Young). Out of eighty-seven college freshmen surveyed at Colorado State University, 80% were likely to recommend community college to a sibling or friend concerned about tuition costs (Tillson). When asked about the benefits of attending community college, students responded that they saw it as "easier to afford" and appreciated that it "makes it easier to work and attend school at the same time" (see fig. 1). The survey shows that students today are giving community colleges serious thought as an alternative to a four-year university.

> The writer presents findings from a survey that she conducted on her campus.

> Statistics and partial quotations are drawn from the survey.

> A pie chart provides an effective visual presentation of information. The chart is captioned, and the source is identified.

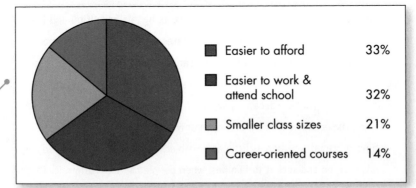

Easier to afford	33%
Easier to work & attend school	32%
Smaller class sizes	21%
Career-oriented courses	14%

Fig. 1: The perceived benefits of choosing a community college. Based on survey data from Tillson.

Tillson 6

Although community colleges are in no way immune to the funding problems that four-year public institutions face, they are still much less expensive. While private universities average $33,000 per year in tuition and fees, community colleges average around $3,200 (Lewin). Students can pay for just the classes they take, rather than paying a lump sum for a semester, making it much less expensive to earn a college degree. In many cases, students can also transfer credits to a four-year college and continue on the path to a bachelor's degree — for much less money and less debt. Students hoping to minimize college expenses can also take advantage of Advanced Placement courses during high school and summer courses during college, cutting down on the number of semesters they pay full tuition (Young). Using a combination of strategies will help students get the college education they want without the expense and debt they can't handle.

The rising price of higher education affects not only students and their families but the larger American society and economy as well. If we do not address the lack of access to higher education for the least affluent members of our society, we run the risk of creating a permanent gap between the poor and the wealthy, where even the best and brightest from poor and working-class families can't pursue the American dream. Our colleges, our students, and our government all must commit themselves to solving the problem of college tuition so that we protect the opportunities of all students to earn a college degree and a more financially secure life. Our future depends on it.

> The writer speculates about the future if steps are not taken to address the problem and argues that colleges, students, and government must all contribute to the solution she has proposed.

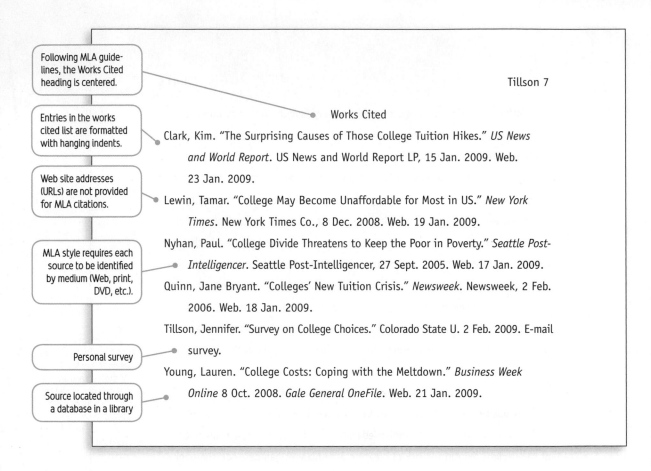

Following MLA guidelines, the Works Cited heading is centered.

Entries in the works cited list are formatted with hanging indents.

Web site addresses (URLs) are not provided for MLA citations.

MLA style requires each source to be identified by medium (Web, print, DVD, etc.).

Personal survey

Source located through a database in a library

Tillson 7

Works Cited

Clark, Kim. "The Surprising Causes of Those College Tuition Hikes." *US News and World Report*. US News and World Report LP, 15 Jan. 2009. Web. 23 Jan. 2009.

Lewin, Tamar. "College May Become Unaffordable for Most in US." *New York Times*. New York Times Co., 8 Dec. 2008. Web. 19 Jan. 2009.

Nyhan, Paul. "College Divide Threatens to Keep the Poor in Poverty." *Seattle Post-Intelligencer*. Seattle Post-Intelligencer, 27 Sept. 2005. Web. 17 Jan. 2009.

Quinn, Jane Bryant. "Colleges' New Tuition Crisis." *Newsweek*. Newsweek, 2 Feb. 2006. Web. 18 Jan. 2009.

Tillson, Jennifer. "Survey on College Choices." Colorado State U. 2 Feb. 2009. E-mail survey.

Young, Lauren. "College Costs: Coping with the Meltdown." *Business Week Online* 8 Oct. 2008. *Gale General OneFile*. Web. 21 Jan. 2009.

To see Jennie Tillson's survey questions, see page 375.

 ## Project Ideas

The following suggestions provide a means of focusing your work on a problem-solving essay or another type of problem-solving document.

Suggestions for Essays

1. DEFINE A PROBLEM AT YOUR SCHOOL

In a brief essay, define a problem at your college or university. Using one of the sets of problem-definition questions provided on page 377, describe the problem in as much detail as possible, and define its consequences if left unaddressed. Use a survey of affected students to collect information about the problem.

2. PROPOSE A SOLUTION TO A LOCAL PROBLEM

Identify and define a problem at your school or in your community, and then propose a solution. Collect information about the problem from published sources, such as a community newspaper, an alumni magazine, or local-area Web sites. Conduct research to locate other communities with a similar problem and find out how they've addressed it. If possible, interview or correspond with someone who knows about or has been affected by the problem. In your essay, discuss the potential consequences of the problem if left unaddressed, identify potential solutions to the problem, and argue for a particular solution.

3. IDENTIFY A CRITICAL PROBLEM IN YOUR MAJOR AREA OF STUDY

Define and discuss the potential consequences of a problem within your major area of study. Use one of the problem-definition question sets provided on page 377 to define the problem. To support your discussion of the potential consequences of the problem, locate sources in scholarly journals and on Web sites sponsored by one or more of the discipline's professional organizations. If time permits, conduct a survey of professors who teach in the field. You can find lists of names through scholarly associations; ask your instructor or a librarian for help identifying them.

4. TRACE THE DEVELOPMENT OF A PROBLEM

Identify a problem that has not yet been solved, and trace its development. Discuss its causes, factors that contribute to its ongoing status as a problem, and factors that have worked against the creation of a successful solution. To support your discussion, locate published sources that have considered the problem. If you can, collect evidence firsthand through observation, surveys, or interviews. Although you are not required to offer a solution, consider using your conclusion to suggest directions that might be pursued to solve the problem.

5. EVALUATE PROPOSED SOLUTIONS TO A PROBLEM

Evaluate solutions that have been proposed to solve a problem. In your essay, briefly define the problem, and discuss the long-term consequences of the problem if left unsolved. Then identify general approaches that have been proposed to solve the problem. Choose at least two and no more than four proposed solutions to evaluate. Define your evaluation criteria (see p. 312), and discuss how well each of the proposed solutions measures up. In your conclusion, offer your assessment of whether the solution you've judged to be most likely to succeed will actually be implemented. To support your discussion, locate published sources that have addressed the problem.

Suggestions for Other Genres

6. DRAFT AND DESIGN A PROBLEM-SOLVING ARTICLE FOR A NEWSPAPER OR MAGAZINE

Begin working on your article by deciding whether you want to write about a particular problem or publish in a particular newspaper or magazine. If you want to write about a particular problem, search your library's databases for articles about the problem. This can help you identify newspapers and magazines that have published articles dealing with the problem. If you want to publish your article in a particular newspaper or magazine, read it carefully to determine the kinds of problems it normally addresses. Once you've selected a target publication, analyze it to determine its writing conventions (such as level of formality and the manner in which sources are acknowledged) and design conventions.

As you learn about your problem and plan, organize, and design your article, keep in mind what you've learned about the articles you've read. Your article should reflect those writing and design conventions. In your article, define the problem you are addressing, argue for the importance of solving the problem, propose your solution, and consider and dismiss alternative solutions. You should support your argument with evidence from other sources, such as journal and magazine articles, newspaper articles, blogs, and Web sites. You can also interview an expert, such as a professor, or correspond with someone who has been affected by the problem.

7. WRITE A PROPOSAL TO SOLVE A PROBLEM

Locate a call for proposals (sometimes called a request for proposals) on an issue of interest to you, and write a proposal to solve a problem related to that issue. Your proposal should conform as much as possible to the formatting and content guidelines provided in the call for proposals. In your proposal, identify, define, and propose a solution for a specific problem. You should draw on published sources and interviews with experts to support your proposal. You should also provide a budget and an assessment plan. If you have questions about how best to complete the proposal, discuss them with your instructor.

8. PROPOSE A SOLUTION BY MAIL

Write a letter, a memo, or an e-mail message that proposes a solution to a problem. Your correspondence should be addressed to a person, group, or agency that has the capacity to solve the problem. To prepare your proposal, conduct research on the problem and on the person, group, or agency. Your letter, memo, or e-mail message should be no longer than 750 words. It should briefly define the problem, propose a solution, and explain why the person, group, or agency should take action to put the proposal into effect. If you have questions about how best to compose the letter, memo, or e-mail message, discuss them with your instructor.

9. WRITE A LETTER OF COMPLAINT

Write a letter that identifies and complains about a problem you've experienced with a product or service. Your letter should be addressed to a person, group, or agency that has the capacity to address the problem. To prepare your letter of complaint, conduct research on the problem and on the person, group, or agency. Your letter should be no longer than 1,000 words. It should clearly define the problem, explain why the recipient of the letter is in a position to address the problem, and explain how the complaint should be addressed. If you have questions about how best to compose the letter, discuss them with your instructor.

10. POST A PROBLEM-SOLVING ENTRY ON A BLOG

Identify a blog that is relevant to the problem you want to address and that allows contributions from readers, in the form of either a new entry or a response to an existing entry. Write an entry or a response that proposes a solution to the problem. To prepare your entry or response, conduct research on the problem and on the authors and readers of the blog. Your post should be no longer than 1,250 words. If you have questions about how best to compose your entry or response, discuss them with your instructor.

In Summary: Writing a Problem-Solving Essay

○ **Find a conversation and listen in.**
- Explore difficulties (p. 370).
- Ask questions about promising subjects (p. 371).
- Conduct a survey (p. 372).

○ **Develop a solution.**
- Define the problem (p. 377).
- Consider potential solutions (p. 379).
- Assess the practicality of your solution (p. 381).

○ **Prepare a draft.**
- Explain the problem (p. 381).
- Propose your solution (p. 383).

- Explain your solution (p. 384).
- Consider genre and design (p. 386).
- Frame your essay (p. 386).

○ **Review and improve your draft.**
- Reassess your problem definition (p. 388).
- Review the presentation of your solution (p. 388).
- Check the feasibility of your solution (p. 388).
- Consider objections and alternative solutions (p. 388).

Writing to Convince or Persuade

As an *advocate,* I write to convince or persuade my readers to see my perspective on a subject.

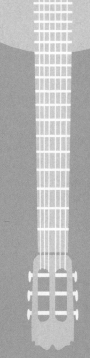

GENRES IN CONVERSATION

Faced with shrinking budgets, administrators in many school districts feel they must sacrifice the arts to ensure adequate funding for core educational programs. However, four high school juniors decided to push back after their school announced cuts to its music program. They hoped to persuade the school board that removing music from the curriculum would do more harm than good. With the assistance of their school librarian, the students found a wide range of argumentative documents to help build their case, including those shown here—a **professional article**, a **case history**, and a **brochure**. Notice how each genre makes a valuable contribution to this conversation.

ASBJ SPECIAL REPORT: A RICH PICTURE

Arts at the Core

How six school districts integrate arts education into the curriculum

RUTH E. STERNBERG

The performing and visual arts challenge students to use reasoning skills—both concrete and abstract—to draw conclusions and formulate ideas. They encourage creativity and imagination, from concept to process to completion. And in districts both large and small across the United States, they enhance learning for students and adults alike, as these six programs demonstrate.

BEAUFORT COUNTY SCHOOL DISTRICT
WWW.BEAUFORT.K12.SC.US

Students at South Carolina's Beaufort Middle School are learning about cell structure from an artist who draws for scientific journals. The artist, Melba Cooper, is also their classroom teacher.

"She takes the lab notebooks and coaches [students] to employ artistic principles to make their drawings more accurate," says Kristy Smith, arts coordinator for the Beaufort County School District. "A cell or a riverbed or the texture of a flower—the kids love it. Some kids get the science concepts, but they are not excited about doing a lab. Yet they love drawing the lab."

Another class prepares for a complicated project by taking a drumming break, guided by Dianne Hemmings, a teacher who learned the art form in Nigeria. "It's not written; it's observation and responding," Smith says of Hemmings' project. "It's important to note eye contact and body lan-

guage, so you know when to come in and pull out. It teaches students how to follow directions."

Approaching subjects from various viewpoints is the mission of the district, which serves the fastest growing county in South Carolina. This affluent coastal community spends $5 million annually to support more than 100 specialists in art, music, dance, drama, band, and voice and in such high school specialties as ceramics, photography, painting, and welding.

Some activities are supported through partnerships with the South Carolina Arts Commission, state and National Endowments for the Humanities, and the federal Title V program, but the rest are paid for with local tax dollars. Visiting artists from the local community also donate their time, bringing with them expertise and real-world perspectives.

By integrating the arts throughout the curriculum, teachers have found new ways to assess student gains and losses beyond

the state's traditional testing system. Visiting artist/educators train teachers to use the arts as a measure of success in all core subjects. Each teacher has a "statistical studio"—also known as a data wall—that displays student progress along with visual art, writing, photographs, or videos.

"Teachers might give a pre- and posttest, and since they used the arts to teach the unit, the evidence might be the arts interaction activities on display," says Smith. "It could be about Shakespeare. Do they know the story lines and what Elizabethan language is? What do they know before I go too far?"

Beaufort County's success, Smith says, proves that the arts can be a valuable tool for all school districts.

"You're preparing them for the world," she says. "The core subjects are a given. We shouldn't even be having that conversation anymore. We should be talking about the next couple of centuries and how our students are going to be creative problem solvers. It's no longer about one set of skills."

CLEVELAND MUNICIPAL SCHOOL DISTRICT
WWW.CMSDNET.NET

Gloria Doering might have been embarrassed. Her fourth-graders entered the galleries at the Cleveland Museum of Art and headed straight for a Vincent Van Gogh

Professional Article ▶

This **professional article** from *American School Board Journal* aims to convince educators that the arts can—and should—be integrated into the core curriculum.

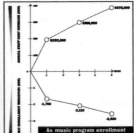

This table illustrates the relative value of a music performance teacher to a regular classroom teacher. In this case, the average student load of a 1.0 FTE teacher is 150 students, and the average student load of a music performance teacher is 200 – a common comparison. Numbers will, of course vary greatly from district to district. It is also important to realize that only part of a music performance teacher's load may be in band, choir and/or orchestra; and therefore, they may not actually be a 1.0 FTE in their area. Each teacher load must be carefully calculated or your figures will be inaccurate, potentially undermining the credibility of your analysis. (See the Music Participation Survey on the CD-ROM, file name: MuPartSurvey).

A Case History

The significance of this disparity is seen in this chart of a real-world case in FTE miscalculation.

Reverse Economics?

District "X" planned to save **$156,000** by cutting 5.2 FTE music teachers.

Instead, annual staffing costs would actually **increase by $378,000** after 5 years ...

... Resulting in an annual budget miscalculation of **$534,000!**

As music program enrollment decrease, staffing costs increase.

In this district case study, the administration proposed the elimination of 5.2 FTE band and orchestra instructors to "save" $156,000.

There were 2529 students (grades 4-12) involved in those two programs. Cuts would have necessitated the elimination of nearly 1800 students the first year, requiring the addition of 6.4 FTE classroom teachers to replace the 5.2 FTE music performance teachers proposed for elimination.

In other words, instead of saving $156,000, they would have been required to spend $192,000 the first year on replacement teachers with lesser FTE value.

The problem gets worse.

Extensive national case studies indicate that the elimination of an elementary feeder system will cause a minimum 65% loss in student participation at the secondary level within two to four years. This is in part because no new elementary students will be started (in this case) until year three, and a similar amount of students will have been graduated. So by year five, the annual budget miscalculation would exceed $500,000.

Short-sighted thinking on the part of administrators and boards, as well as a failure to realize the high FTE value of music teachers, have led many districts into an unpleasant budget shock.

Music study is valuable and essential in educating well-rounded citizens, both for its intrinsic value and as a building-block of intelligence. It is also a financially efficient way to provide for our children's education. When a music program is threatened, the entire community is in danger of suffering a loss. Music advocates are our first line of defense.

WANT MORE INFO?

Dr. John L. Benham has been involved in school district crisis intervention since 1981. His diverse background includes roles as parent, music teacher, administrator, businessman and two-term member of a local school board. He, and those under his mentorship, have saved and restored over $63,000,000 in music programs that were targeted for cuts.

He is the author of two excellent books on music advocacy and is available as a consultant to school districts and advocacy groups. His books can be ordered through the address below.

How To Save Your School Music and Arts Programs - A Handbook for the Arts Advocate . . . $18.00 US*

The Georgia Project: A Status Profile on Arts Education in the State of Georgia . . . $18.00 US* (*Plus shipping and handling . . . $5.00 US)

Dr. John L. Benham
Music In World Cultures, Inc.
3000 Bethel Drive
St. Paul, MN (USA) 55112
Tel: (651) 635-8015
Fax: (651) 635-6039
j-benham@bethel.edu

⑬

Case History ▶

This **case history** from the American Music Conference cites numerical data and real-world examples to counter claims that cutting music education saves money.

▲ **Brochure**

A **brochure** intended for parents uses large, appealing photographs, a colorful design, and a quotation from a student to highlight the academic benefits of music lessons.

What Is Writing to Convince or Persuade?

Some people love a good argument. Others go out of their way to avoid conflict. Regardless of where you stand, it's hard to deny the important role that debate and discussion play in our daily lives. Unfortunately, few of the arguments we encounter on a daily basis are well grounded and fully thought out. Whether you're listening to a talk show, reading the lunatic ravings of a misinformed blogger, or streaming a clever clip on YouTube about the issue of the day, it can be almost comically easy to pick out the flaws in a weak argument.

The Writer's Role: Advocate

PURPOSE

- To stake a position on an issue
- To persuade readers to take action

READERS

- Want thoughtful consideration of an issue that is important to them
- Look for a clearly stated claim supported by ample reasons and reliable evidence
- Expect a fair and reasonable presentation of information, ideas, and competing arguments

SOURCES

- Advocates appeal to readers' reason, emotion, and trust as they present arguments.
- Evidence can come from personal observation, print and electronic documents, or field research.
- Supporting information is often presented in visual form.

CONTEXT

- Effective writers consider opposing points of view and choose argumentative strategies that establish common ground with readers.
- Advocates might use color and illustration to set a mood and often present supporting information in visual forms — such as charts, tables, and graphs — to help readers understand an issue.

An effective argument, on the other hand, makes a well-supported, well-considered point about an issue in an attempt to convince or persuade readers. *Convincing* involves gaining readers' agreement that a position on an issue is reasonable and well founded. *Persuading* involves getting them to take action. One writer, for example, might seek to convince readers that the drinking age should be lowered to eighteen, while another might attempt to persuade teenagers to take a vow of sobriety.

Whether they attempt to convince or persuade, writers who make arguments adopt the role of *advocate*. An effective advocate considers not only the argument he or she will advance but also how best to formulate and express that argument for a particular audience. Although readers of arguments typically share the writer's assumption that an issue is important and are willing to consider new ideas, they bring their own values, beliefs, and experiences to the conversation. A writer who wants to change readers' minds or persuade them to act must give careful thought to who readers are and where they come from, what they value, how resistant or receptive they might be to an argument, and what strategies — such as logic, emotion, or authority — are most likely to sway them.

Sources of evidence used in argumentative documents include numerical data, reports of a writer's direct observation, and statements by experts, to name just a few. Advocates sometimes use charged language, but more often than not they adopt a straightforward, reasonable tone. They typically offer evidence and reasoning to align their arguments with authorities and with other writers, to provide background information, support their claims and reasoning, and refute opposing arguments. Advocates might also offer evidence in the form of illustrations, such as images, video and audio clips, or tables and charts, to set a mood or call attention to specific points. Their decisions about the type of evidence they use are shaped by both the type of document they choose to write and the context in which they find themselves.

Argumentative documents are the means through which many written conversations make progress on an issue. By stating a claim and providing evidence to support it, advocates help readers understand options for addressing an issue. By pointing out the drawbacks of competing arguments, they help participants in the conversation weigh alternatives. More than any other type of document, written arguments help us decide—individually and as a group—what we should believe and how we should act. In doing so, they have a profound effect on how we live our lives.

What Kinds of Documents Are Used to Convince or Persuade?

Argumentation involves making a claim, supporting it with reasons and evidence, addressing reasonable alternatives, and urging readers to accept or act on the writer's main point. Virtually any type of writing, then, can contain an argument—and even documents that serve primarily to reflect, inform, analyze, evaluate, or solve problems often contain some elements of argumentation.

Understanding the genres that can be used to convince or persuade can help you prepare to write your own argument. In this section, you'll find examples of common argumentative documents: advertisements, opinion columns, letters to the editor, blogs, and argumentative essays. As you read the following documents, reflect on the contexts in which the writers found themselves. Ask, for example, what readers need to know about an issue to be convinced or persuaded. Ask about the kinds of evidence that readers interested in a particular issue might accept—or reject. And ask about the design elements that might influence readers—positively or negatively—as they consider an argument.

View a multimedia example of argumentative writing in the e-book at **bedfordstmartins.com/ conversation**.

Advertisements

Advertisements seek to persuade the people who see or hear them to take a specific action—whether it's purchasing a product, supporting a cause, applying for a job, donating to a nonprofit organization, or voting for a political candidate. The argument usually takes the form of a simple claim, which might be conveyed through a brief slogan, such as "The Best Food in Texas"; through an image, such as a photo of people having a good time while they use a particular product (an adult beverage, for example, or a new sports car); or through an endorsement in which a celebrity extols the virtues of a particular product. The argument might even take the form of a detailed list of features and benefits, such as you might see in a brochure for a digital video recorder or a new prescription drug. In some cases, such as political campaigns or the battle between cable and satellite television providers, advertisements can also make negative claims.

Few readers seek out advertisements. They usually encounter them as they flip through a magazine, browse the Web, watch television, listen to the radio, or drive along a highway studded with billboards. Because most readers don't devote a great deal of time to considering an advertisement, most ads are designed to capture the reader's or viewer's attention and convey their claim as quickly as possible. As a result, they typically rely on images and limit the amount of written text. For example, the long-running advertising campaign originated by the California Milk Processors Board asks the simple question "Got Milk?" Another, developed by the U.S. Marines, urges enlistment with the slogan "The few. The proud. The Marines." Yet another ad, used so heavily in the 1980s and 1990s that it has become part of our cultural landscape, urges youth to "Just say no to drugs."

 ### White House Office of National Drug Control Policy
The Anti-Drug

The following public service advertisements, developed by the White House Office of National Drug Control Policy for its National Youth Anti-Drug Media Campaign, expands on the long-running "just say no" message with typical mixes of imagery and brief passages of text. Representing an effort to encourage youths from nine to eighteen years old to stay drug-free, the ads are designed to appear in magazines and are part of an extensive multimedia campaign that includes television and radio spots, informational brochures, and interactive Web sites in several languages.

You got high before shop class.
You thought you could handle the saw. You were wrong.
Weed can make you do stupid things like that.

freevibe.com

regret
THE ANTI-DRUG

Office of National Drug Control Policy/Partnership for a Drug-Free America®

You smoked weed. You got behind the wheel.
And you hit a six-year-old girl on her bike.
Weed can make you do stupid things like that.

freevibe.com

regret
THE ANTI-DRUG

Starting a Conversation: Respond to "The Anti-Drug" Advertisements

In your writer's notebook, analyze the argument put forth in "The Anti-Drug" advertising campaign by responding to the following questions:

1. Although the four advertisements are part of the same White House campaign, their specific messages are different. What particular actions does each advocate? What characteristics are shared by the four examples?

2. How would you describe the relationship between text and image in these examples from "The Anti-Drug" campaign? Which of the two elements seems more important, and why? What effect does the small or difficult-to-read text along the sides of the ads have on their overall message?

3. This campaign was aimed at people between the ages of nine and eighteen. How are these ads meant to appeal to that audience? In what ways do the ads reflect the culture and values of their presumed readers?

4. "The Anti-Drug" campaign follows a long line of similar White House initiatives that have sought to discourage drug use among young people. What assumptions do these particular ads make with regard to teenagers, drugs, and drug use?

@ Download or print this Starting a Conversation activity at **bedfordstmartins.com/ conversation**.

Opinion Columns

Opinion columns present focused arguments supported by analysis and evidence. They usually appear in magazines or newspapers, and to a lesser extent in journals and on the Web. The focus of the argument is often a recent event or controversy that has been covered elsewhere in the publication. It is common, for example, to find an opinion column in a newspaper advancing an argument about an event reported in a front-page story. The issues addressed in opinion columns generally reflect the interests of regular readers of the publication in which they appear. A column in the *New Yorker*, for instance, is far more likely to make an argument about literature or the arts than would a column in *Field & Stream*.

Opinion columns are typically brief, usually containing fewer than a thousand words. Compared to longer argumentative genres, such as essays and articles, they tend to rely more heavily on personal experience and reflection than on evidence from other sources, although it is not unusual for columnists to advance arguments about claims made in other publications. In general, opinion columns are designed simply, often as a single column of text without any illustrations or headings.

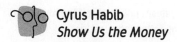

Cyrus Habib
Show Us the Money

Blind since the age of nine, Cyrus Habib is a Rhodes Scholar who is pursuing a career in law. In this opinion column written for the widely read and highly influential newspaper the *Washington Post*, he argues that the U.S. government should take steps to ensure that paper currency is recognizable to the blind. Habib focuses his argument on the Treasury Department's appeal of a federal court order to change U.S. currency so that the blind can use it. The appeal was later rejected.

Show Us the Money

America's Paper Currency Shortchanges the Blind

By Cyrus Habib, *The Washington Post*

Blind Americans may soon find themselves able to use money just like anyone else. That is unless the Treasury Department is successful this month in its appeal of a recent federal court order that paper currency be made recognizable to the blind, who are currently unable to distinguish one denomination from another.

I, for example, rely on the generosity of cab drivers, baristas, and store clerks each time I make a purchase with cash. That I have rarely been ripped off is a testament to their honesty or my charm, but I cannot help but protest the perpetual necessity for either. After all, there are 180 countries in which this is not the case, because their currency is designed to be distinguishable by all.

U.S. District Judge James Robertson asked the Treasury Department to determine the best means of making money distinguishable by the blind, citing the myriad solutions proposed by the organization that filed the lawsuit, the American Council of the Blind. These included using raised ink, modifying the size of certain bills, and producing a tactile mark to indicate a bill's denomination. The Treasury Department has objected to all such solutions, claiming that the $75 million price tag is simply too high.

Of course, Treasury's lawyers fail to mention that the cost would have been far lower had the department acted voluntarily when the $20 bill was redesigned in 1998 and the $10 bill was modified last year. Instead, it has decided to spend our tax money fighting the blind in court, appealing Judge Robertson's decision even before a final judgment on the nature of a solution could be reached.

Blind people in the United States suffer from a staggering 70 percent unemployment rate, and a disproportionately high percentage of those who are employed occupy jobs in the low end of the service sector. There is no question that the catastrophic poverty of America's blind requires a solution. Why not begin by giving us access to money at the most atomic level? How can blind Americans become truly independent, achieving the success we deserve and leaving behind the stigma of federal and state aid, without being able to differentiate between a dollar bill and a fifty?

The Treasury Department suggests using debit and credit cards, disregarding the fact that the lives of many blind Americans hinge upon financial exchanges for which plastic is often useless, such as catching a crosstown bus, purchasing a cup of coffee, or getting change for laundry.

These basic day-to-day experiences may not constitute reality for Treasury Secretary Henry Paulson and his team, but they certainly do for millions of blind and low-vision Americans.

Some have called the lawsuit frivolous, arguing that blind people have managed to survive for years by relying on others for help. Such reasoning does more than ignore the overwhelming poverty and hardship that plague the blind community; it dishonors the sacrifices millions of disabled Americans made to help bring about passage of the landmark Americans With Disabilities Act. Money is essential to a person's participation in society. Its accessibility to blind people should be considered as important as that of wheelchair ramps or Braille in elevators.

When it comes to accommodating disabilities such as blindness, let us continue to lead the world in practice as well as in principle. More important still, let us tell the world that we, too, believe that blindness should not be an obstacle to financial independence. In doing so, let us also take a significant step toward ameliorating the living conditions of blind Americans, now and for years to come.

The Treasury Department should obey Judge Robertson's order and show us the money.

The writer, a Rhodes Scholar and JD candidate at Yale Law School, is preparing an amicus brief on this case with Dean Harold Hongju Koh.

Starting a Conversation: Respond to "Show Us the Money"

In your writer's notebook, examine the strategies Habib uses to present his argument by responding to the following questions:

1. Habib introduces the issue by offering hope for the blind — the promise of currency that they can recognize — and then explaining that the Treasury Department is attempting to avoid making the change. What was your reaction, at an emotional level, to the first paragraph of the column? At what other points in the column does Habib try to elicit an emotional response from his readers?

2. What reasons does Habib offer to support his argument that U.S. currency should be changed? Which reason do you find most effective? Least effective? Why?

3. Habib refers to "180 countries" that make their currency distinguishable to blind people. How does this statistic further his argument? What other numbers or statistics does he use — and how do they support (or undermine) his overall claim?

4. Much of Habib's column is devoted to raising and countering objections to his position. Pick one of Habib's counterarguments, and explain why it either strengthens his argument or detracts from it.

 Download or print this Starting a Conversation activity at **bedfordstmartins.com/ conversation**.

5. "Show Us the Money" focuses primarily on problems faced by the blind. How does this column attempt to make the issue relevant for those who are not blind and therefore seem to have nothing directly at stake in this issue?

Letters to the Editor

Like opinion columns, letters to the editor offer an argument from a personal perspective. Sometimes the letter writers are well-known authors or local (or national) figures; sometimes they're representatives of an organization with a stake in an issue; sometimes they are average citizens who want to voice their opinion on an issue that affects them; and sometimes the writers are individuals who seem to have nothing better to do than tell neighbors — every week — how they should think and act.

Because editors decide which letters are published, the issues addressed in the letters tend to reflect the issues covered by the publication. In many cases, letters to the editor respond to previously published articles, editorials, opinion columns, and other letters to the editor. The design of the letters is generally quite simple, usually consisting of a salutation (*Dear Editor* or *To the Editor*), one or more paragraphs of plain text, and the name of the writer (in place of a signature).

Letters to the editor are usually brief, because of length limitations specified by the newspaper, magazine, journal, or Web site in which they appear, but many magazines and Web sites publish longer letters. Although brief letters typically provide little in the way of formal evidence to support an argument, longer letters might offer a thorough discussion that is carefully supported by evidence from personal experience and published sources.

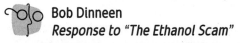 **Bob Dinneen**
Response to "The Ethanol Scam"

Bob Dinneen of the Renewable Fuels Association wrote the following letter in response to an August 2007 *Rolling Stone* feature article criticizing biofuels. In his letter, Dinneen observes that the editors and reporters at the magazine fail to understand "the complexities of world energy markets and the need for ethanol and other renewable fuels." In his point-by-point critique of Jeff Goodell's article, Dinneen draws on evidence from published studies and government reports to support his reasoning. You can read Goodell's *Rolling Stone* article on the Web at www .rollingstone.com/politics/story/15635751.

Letter to the Editor: Response to "The Ethanol Scam"

Posted Aug 23, 2007 11:13 AM

Rolling Stone received the following letter from Bob Dinneen of the Renewable Fuels Association, a corn lobby, in response to "The Ethanol Scam" [RS 1032].

An Urban Chic Straw Man

It doesn't come as a big surprise that a magazine best known for pop-rock reviews and social commentary fails to understand the complexities of world energy markets and the need for ethanol and other renewable fuels ("Ethanol Scam: Ethanol Hurts the Environment and Is One of America's Biggest Political Boondoggles," by Jeff Goodell). What is less surprising, but more disturbing, is the failure of the "journalist" to interview anyone with a working knowledge of the U.S. ethanol industry. Rather, he relies on oil industry reps and ethanol critics pushing personal agendas.

Nevertheless, since *Rolling Stone* felt the need to opine on America's ethanol industry, it is incumbent upon me to set the record straight.

First, let's address the classic straw man of the food versus fuel argument. Mr. Goodell, channeling the leading progressive minds of our time, Fidel Castro and Hugo Chavez, claims that a rush to ethanol production will starve poor, hungry populations around the world. What he fails to mention is that American farmers are on pace to produce more corn than any time in history. While it may be urban chic to chastise farmers for making a decent living, it doesn't detract from the fact that once again they have answered the call and will continue to feed the world and begin to help fuel a nation.

Stronger prices for commodities around the world encourage more agricultural production in developing nations, providing those farmers more income and an opportunity to improve their quality of life. And a better quality of life leads to less volatility and less likelihood these nations will foster the kind of authoritarians that pose a very real threat to world peace. Yes, people like Mr. Goodell's Hugo Chavez.

It is also disingenuous for Mr. Goodell to buy the spin of the nation's largest meat packers and food processors that corn prices alone are what is driving up the price of food. A study done by John Urbanchuk, an independent economist, found that oil and gasoline prices have twice the impact on consumer food prices that corn prices have. Given the current and recent prices of both petroleum products, it becomes pretty clear what the real factor behind rising food prices is. And conveniently left out of this argument is that corn prices are down over $1 since the beginning of the year. One should expect food prices to follow suit, if corn is indeed the culprit for higher prices.

Another popular argument from the status quo crowd is that ethanol makes no economic sense and is dependent upon government handouts to survive. While it is true that the incentives the federal government has put into place have fostered the development of a robust renewable fuels industry in this country, it is not as though that money disappears. In 2006 alone, the production and use of nearly 5 billion gallons of ethanol generated more than $2.7 billion in new tax revenue for the federal treasury, more than $2.3 billion for state and local government coffers, and reduced those pesky farm program payments publications like *Rolling Stone* loathe by more than $6 billion. All told, the $2.5 billion investment the federal government made in ethanol tax incentives was returned to taxpayers fourfold.

Again, Mr. Goodell omits an important

fact in this debate as well. There is no such thing as a free market when it comes to energy. For a century, America's petrochemical complex has been the beneficiary of generous subsidies and preferential tax treatment that have allowed them to become the massive, multinational corporations they are today. I am not arguing for or against these incentives, but merely noting that if we want to move away from fossil fuels, we must understand that it is not a level playing field.

Yet another common misconception offered by ethanol novices is that ethanol is at best energy neutral, meaning it takes as much energy to produce as it yields. As is to be expected, Mr. Goodell relied on the figures of an energy blogger for his facts. Inconveniently for his arguments, the federal government has different figures. According to the Argonne National Laboratories, ethanol yields nearly 70% more energy than it took to produce. Conversely, refined gasoline contains 20% LESS energy than it took to produce. Moreover, ethanol comes from a renewable resource while gasoline relies upon a finite feedstock whose availability continues to tighten.

And finally, only because my fingers are getting tired, Mr. Goodell dismisses out of hand the environmental benefits of ethanol production and use. According to Argonne National Laboratories, ethanol production and use today reduce greenhouse gas emissions by up to 29%. Future ethanol production from cellulosic feedstocks holds the potential to reduce greenhouse gas emissions by up to 90% compared to gasoline. While addressing greenhouse gas emissions and global climate change, ethanol use reduces tailpipe emissions that cause air pollution and has prompted the American Lung Association of Metropolitan Chicago to credit ethanol-blended gasoline with reducing smog formation by 25%.

It is entirely appropriate to have a debate about our energy policy in this country. But it is irresponsible to present one side of the argument without fully understanding the role renewable fuels like ethanol must play in our nation's energy future. Mr. Goodell and *Rolling Stone* would be doing right by their faithful readers if they would at least consider all the facts.

Bob Dinneen, President
Renewable Fuels Association
Washington, DC
www.EthanolRFA.org

Starting a Conversation: Respond to "Response to 'The Ethanol Scam'"

In your writer's notebook, reflect on how Dinneen responds to his writing situation by answering the following questions:

1. What is Dinneen's overall claim? Based on the content of this letter, what would you say was the main point presented by Jeff Goodell's article?

2. Given his job title and professional affiliation, what stake does Dinneen have in this issue? How might that affect a reader's willingness to trust his argument?

3. How would you characterize Dinneen's attitude toward *Rolling Stone* and its readers, generally? How would you characterize his overall tone? How do both affect the persuasiveness of his letter?

4. Dinneen responds to Goodell's argument, in part, by attacking Goodell's sources. On what grounds does he criticize them or question their authority?

5. Dinneen faults Goodell for weak reasoning, referring, for example, to a "classic straw man" fallacy in his argument (par. 3). Familiarize yourself with the logical fallacies outlined on pages 435–37, and then take another look at Dinneen's letter. What other errors in logic does he point out in his critique of Goodell's article? What logical errors, if any, does Dinneen himself make?

@ Download or print this Starting a Conversation activity at **bedfordstmartins.com/ conversation**.

Blogs

Blogs—short for Weblogs—are online forums that allow writers to present their opinions, observations, and reflections to a broad readership. They can consist of the contributions of a single writer, or they can draw on contributions from multiple writers. Blogs can be published and maintained by individuals, in a manner similar to putting material on a personal Web site. They can also be sponsored by news organizations, public interest groups, government agencies, corporations, and other organizations. When a blog is sponsored by an organization or a publication, the writer takes into account the purpose of the organization or publication and the interests, needs, and backgrounds of readers who visit the blog.

Blogs are frequently used to present arguments. Blog entries typically are brief and often present a personal perspective on an issue. However, because blogs have fewer length limitations than a piece in a newspaper, magazine, or journal might have, blog entries are more likely to rely on evidence from other sources than are opinion columns and letters to the editor. Because of their electronic format, they can also use multimedia illustrations, such as video and audio clips or interactive polls, and link to other sources. And because readers can reply publicly to a blog entry by posting responses and arguments of their own, conversations can be extended over time and can involve readers and writers more actively.

Barbara Ehrenreich
What America Owes Its "Illegals"

Barbara Ehrenreich, a writer and activist who often focuses on class issues, has written for *Time, Harper's, The Atlantic Monthly*, and many other magazines; her books include *Nickel and Dimed: On (Not) Getting By in America* (2001), *Bait and Switch: The (Futile) Pursuit of the American Dream* (2006), and *This Land Is Their Land: Reports from a Divided Nation* (2008). The following post first appeared on her blog

(www.barbaraehrenreich.com) and was subsequently reprinted in *The Nation* magazine. In it, Ehrenreich not only defends "illegals" but also reframes the issue in a way
that's both surprising and provocative. In changing the terms of the debate, she sheds
new light on our views of immigrants and immigration.

Barbara's Blog

print   share   discuss   RSS

What America Owes Its "Illegals"

June 05, 2007

Rush Limbaugh has been expecting liberals to start "whining" about the $5000 fine undocu-
mented immigrants will have to pay to gain citizenship under the new immigration bill,
but most liberals have been too busy chortling about the immigration-induced split in the
GOP to make their own case against the bill. So let a mighty whine rise over the land:
Undocumented workers shouldn't be fined; they should get a hefty bonus!

All right, they committed a "crime"—the international equivalent of breaking and entry.
But breaking and entry is usually a prelude to a much worse crime, like robbery or rape.
What have the immigrants been doing once they get into the US? Taking up time on the
elliptical trainers in our health clubs? Getting ahead of us on the wait-lists for elite private
nursery schools?

In case you don't know what immigrants do in this country, the Latinos have a word for
it—*trabajo*. They've been mowing the lawns, cleaning the offices, hammering the nails,
and picking the tomatoes, not to mention all that dish-washing, diaper-changing, meat-
packing, and poultry-plucking.

The punitive rage directed at illegal immigrants grows out of a larger blindness to the
manual labor that makes our lives possible: the touching belief, in the class occupied by
Rush Limbaugh among many others, that offices clean themselves at night and salad
greens spring straight from the soil onto one's plate.

Native-born workers share in this invisibility, but it's far worse in the case of immigrant workers, who are often, for all practical purposes, nameless. In the recent book *There's No José Here: Following the Lives of Mexican Immigrants*, Gabriel Thompson cites a construction company manager who says things like, "I've got to get myself a couple of Josés for this job if we're going to have that roof patched up by Saturday." Forget the Juans, Diegos, and Eduardos — they're all interchangeable "Josés."

Hence no doubt the ease with which some prominent immigrant-bashers forget their own personal reliance on immigrant labor, like Nevada's Governor Jim Gibbons, who, it turns out, once employed an undocumented nanny. And as the *Boston Globe* revealed late last year, Mitt Romney's lawn in suburban Boston was maintained by illegal immigrants from Guatemala.

The only question is how *much* we owe our undocumented immigrant workers. First, those who do not remain to enjoy the benefits of old age in America will have to be reimbursed for their contributions to Medicare and Social Security, and here I quote the website of the San Diego ACLU:

> Undocumented immigrants annually pay an estimated $7 billion more than they take out into Social Security, and $1.5 billion more into Medicare. . . . A study by the National Academy of Sciences also found that tax payments generated by immigrants outweighed any costs associated with services used by immigrants.

Second, someone is going to have to calculate what is owed to "illegals" for wages withheld by unscrupulous employers: the homeowner who tells his or her domestic worker that the wage is actually several hundred dollars a month less than she had been promised, and that the homeowner will be "holding" it for her. Or the landscaping service that stiffs its undocumented workers for their labor. Who's the "illegal" here?

Third, there's the massive compensation owed to undocumented immigrants for preventable injuries on the job. In her book *Suburban Sweatshops: The Fight for Immigrant Rights*, Jennifer Gordon reports such gruesome cases as a Honduran who died from inhaling paint while sanding yachts in Long Island and a Guatemalan worker whose boss intentionally burned him with hot pans of oil for not washing dishes fast enough. "Death rates for Latino workers," Gordon reports, "have risen over the past decade even as workplace fatality rates for non-Latinos have fallen."

When our debt to America's undocumented workers is eventually tallied, I'm confident that it will be well in excess of the $5000 fine the immigration bill proposes. There is still the issue of the original "crime." If someone breaks into my property for the purpose of trashing and looting, I would be hell-bent on restitution. But if they break in for the purpose of cleaning it — scrubbing the bathroom, mowing the lawn — then, in my way of thinking anyway, the debt goes in the other direction.

Starting a Conversation: Respond to "What America Owes Its 'Illegals'"

In your writer's notebook, respond to Ehrenreich's argument by answering the following questions:

1. What exactly is Ehrenreich advocating? In what ways is her position reasonable? In what ways is it not? How could she strengthen her argument?

2. The writer cites a Web site and two books. What specific points does she support with these sources? How are these points related to her overall claim?

3. Ehrenreich opens her essay by quoting conservative talk-show host Rush Limbaugh, but she also quotes the ACLU, an organization usually associated with liberal causes. Where on the political spectrum does she imagine her readers to be? Where does she place herself? How can you tell?

4. Although Ehrenreich seems to concede the point that illegal immigration is a crime, she qualifies her acceptance by putting the word *crime* in quotation marks and questioning its meaning (par. 2). What other strategies does she use to address counterarguments? What do these strategies, and Ehrenreich's general tone, indicate about her respect for opposing points of view?

@ Download or print this Starting a Conversation activity at **bedfordstmartins.com/ conversation**.

5. Ehrenreich refers to the "invisibility" of workers, a phenomenon that is "far worse" in the case of immigrant laborers. What does she mean by this? What larger issues does it suggest, outside of immigration?

Argumentative Essays

To some extent, argumentative essays resemble written debates. Writers typically advance a thoroughly considered and well-supported argument that addresses competing positions on the issue and explains why the writer's position is preferable to the others. Argumentative essays almost always draw on information from other sources (articles, books, Web sites, statistics, interviews, and so on) to provide evidence that supports the effort to convince readers of the merits of a particular stance on an issue or to persuade them to take action. Argumentative essays can also draw extensively on a writer's personal experience with an issue.

Writers of argumentative essays must carefully consider readers' needs, interests, backgrounds, and knowledge of an issue. A thorough understanding of readers' familiarity with the issue, their purposes for reading the essay, and the values, beliefs, and assumptions they bring to a reading of the essay can help a writer make thoughtful, strategic choices about how to present and support an argument. It can also help a writer determine how best to acknowledge and argue for the comparative inadequacy of competing positions on the issue.

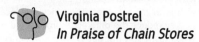

Virginia Postrel
In Praise of Chain Stores

Taking issue with conventional wisdom, Virginia Postrel argues in the following essay that chain retail stores are beneficial to their communities and to the country as a whole. Moreover, she suggests that those who oppose chains on principle are misguided—and may inadvertently be harming the very towns and cities they wish to protect. Postrel is the author of books such as *The Future and Its Enemies* (1998) and *The Substance of Style* (2003). She also writes a regular feature called "Commerce and Culture" for *The Atlantic Monthly*, where "In Praise of Chain Stores" originally appeared.

In Praise of Chain Stores
by Virginia Postrel

Every well-traveled cosmopolite knows that America is mind-numbingly monotonous—the most boring country to tour, because everywhere looks like everywhere else," as the columnist Thomas Friedman once told Charlie Rose. Boston has the same stores as Denver, which has the same stores as Charlotte or Seattle or Chicago. We live in a "Stepford world," says Rachel Dresbeck, the author of *Insiders' Guide to Portland, Oregon*. Even Boston's historic Faneuil Hall, she complains, is "dominated by the Gap, Anthropologie, Starbucks, and all the other usual suspects. Why go anywhere? Every place looks the same." This complaint is more than the old worry, dating back to the 1920s, that the big guys are putting Mom and Pop out of business. Today's critics focus less on what isn't there—Mom and Pop—than on what is. Faneuil Hall actually has plenty of locally owned businesses, from the Geoclassics store selling minerals and jewelry, to Pizzeria Regina ("since 1926"). But you do find the same chains everywhere.

The suburbs are the worst. Take Chandler, Arizona, just south of Phoenix. At Chandler Fashion Center, the area's big shopping mall, you'll find P. F. Chang's, California Pizza Kitchen, Chipotle Mexican Grill, and the Cheesecake Factory. Drive along Chandler's straight, flat boulevards, and you'll see Bed Bath & Beyond and Linens-n-Things; Barnes & Noble and Borders; PetSmart and Petco; Circuit City and Best Buy; Lowe's and Home Depot; CVS and Walgreens. Chandler has the Apple Store and Pottery Barn, the Gap and Ann Taylor, Banana Republic and DSW, and, of course, Target and Wal-Mart, Starbucks and McDonald's. For people allergic to brands, Chandler must be hell—even without the 110-degree days.

One of the fastest-growing cities in the country, Chandler is definitely the kind of place urbanists have in mind as they intone, "When every place looks the same, there is no such thing as place anymore." Like so many towns in America, it has lost much of its historic character as a farming community. The annual Ostrich Festival still honors one traditional product, but these days Chandler raises more subdivisions and strip malls than ostrich plumes or cotton, another former staple. Yet it still refutes the common assertion that national chains are a blight on the landscape, that they've turned American towns into an indistinguishable "geography of nowhere."

The first thing you notice in Chandler is that, as a broad empirical claim, the cliché that "everywhere looks like everywhere else" is obvious nonsense. Chandler's land and air and foliage are peculiar to the desert Southwest. The people dress differently. Even the cookie-cutter housing developments, with their xeriscaping and washed-out desert palette, remind you where you are. Forget New England clapboard, Carolina columns, or yellow Texas brick. In the intense sun of Chandler, the red-tile roofs common in California turn a pale, pale pink.

Stores don't give places their character. Terrain and weather and culture do. Familiar retailers may take some of the discovery out of travel — to the consternation of journalists looking for obvious local color — but by holding some of the commercial background constant, chains make it easier to discern the real differences that define a place: the way, for instance, that people in Chandler come out to enjoy the summer twilight, when the sky glows purple and the dry air cools.

Besides, the idea that America was once filled with wildly varied business establishments is largely a myth. Big cities could, and still can, support more retail niches than small towns. And in a less competitive national market, there was certainly more variation in business efficiency — in prices, service, and merchandise quality. But the range of retailing *ideas* in any given town was rarely that great. One deli or diner or lunch counter or cafeteria was pretty much like every other one. A hardware store was a hardware store, a pharmacy a pharmacy. Before it became a ubiquitous part of urban life, Starbucks was, in most American cities, a radically new idea.

Chains do more than bargain down prices from suppliers or divide fixed costs across a lot of units. They rapidly spread economic discovery — the scarce and costly knowledge of what retail concepts and operational innovations actually work. That knowledge can be gained only through the expensive and time-consuming process of trial and error. Expecting each town to independently invent every new business is a prescription for real monotony, at least for the locals. Chains make a large range of choices available in more places. They increase local variety, even as they reduce the differences from place to place. People who mostly stay put get to have experiences once available only to frequent travelers, and this loss of exclusivity is one reason why frequent travelers are the ones who complain. When Borders was a unique Ann Arbor institution, people in places like Chandler — or, for that matter, Philadelphia and Los Angeles — didn't have much in the way of bookstores. Back in 1986, when California Pizza Kitchen was an innovative local restaurant about to open its second location, food writers at the L.A. *Daily News* declared it "the kind of place every neighborhood should have." So what's wrong if the country has 158 neighborhood CPKs instead of one or two?

The process of multiplication is particularly important for fast-growing towns like Chandler, where rollouts of established stores allow retail variety to expand as fast as the growing population can support new businesses. I heard the same refrain in Chandler that I've heard in similar boomburgs elsewhere, and for similar reasons. "It's got all the advantages of a small town, in terms of being friendly, but it's got all the things of a big town," says Scott Stephens, who moved from Manhattan Beach, California, in 1998 to work for Motorola.

Chains let people in a city of 250,000 enjoy retail amenities once available only in a huge metropolitan center. At the same time, familiar establishments make it easier for people to make a home in a new place. When Nissan recently moved its headquarters from Southern California to Tennessee, an unusually high percentage of its Los Angeles–area employees accepted the transfer. "The fact that Starbucks are everywhere helps make moving a lot easier these days," a rueful Greg Whitney, vice president of business development for the Los Angeles County Economic Development Corporation, told the *Los Angeles Times* reporter John O'Dell. Orth Hedrick, a Nissan product manager, decided he could stay with the job he loved when he turned off the interstate near Nashville and realized, "You could really be Anywhere, U.S.A. There's a great big regional shopping mall, and most of the stores and restaurants are the same ones we see in California. Yet a few

> Stores don't give places their character. Terrain and weather and culture do.

miles away you're in downtown, and there's lots of local color, too."

Contrary to the rhetoric of bored cosmopolites, most cities don't exist primarily to please tourists. The children toddling through the Chandler mall hugging their soft Build-A-Bear animals are no less delighted because kids can also build a bear in Memphis or St. Louis. For them, this isn't tourism; it's life — the experiences that create the memories from which the meaning of a place arises over time. Among Chandler's most charming sights are the business-casual dads joining their wives and kids for lunch in the mall food court. The food isn't the point, let alone whether it's from Subway or Dairy Queen. The restaurants merely provide the props and setting for the family time. When those kids grow up, they'll remember the food court as happily as an older generation recalls the diners and motels of Route 66 — not because of the businesses' innate appeal but because of the memories they evoke.

The contempt for chains represents a brand-obsessed view of place, as if store names were all that mattered to a city's character. For many critics, the name on the store really *is* all that matters. The planning consultant Robert Gibbs works with cities that want to revive their downtowns, and he also helps developers find space for retailers. To his frustration, he finds that many cities actually turn away national chains, preferring a moribund downtown that seems authentically local. But, he says, the same local activists who oppose chains "want specialty retail that sells exactly what the chains sell — the same price, the same fit, the same qualities, the same sizes, the same brands, even." You can show people pictures of a Pottery Barn with nothing but the name changed, he says, and they'll love the store. So downtown stores stay empty, or sell low-value tourist items like candles and kites, while the chains open on the edge of town. In the name of urbanism, officials and activists in cities like Ann Arbor and Fort Collins, Colorado, are driving business to the suburbs. "If people like shopping at the Banana Republic or the Gap, if that's your market — or Payless Shoes — why not?" says an exasperated Gibbs. "Why not sell the goods and services people want?"

Starting a Conversation: Respond to "In Praise of Chain Stores"

In your writer's notebook, record your analysis of Postrel's essay by responding to the following questions:

1. Postrel's argument is more specific and thorough than her title might suggest. What is her thesis? What does she expect readers to believe or do after reading her essay?

2. Postrel's introductory paragraphs quote writers and pundits who dislike retail chains, without disputing them. What purposes do these paragraphs serve in her essay? Why is it essential for her argument to cite these views early on?

3. Who or what are "cosmopolites," and how are they related to readers of *The Atlantic Monthly*? According to Postrel, what do their assumptions

about small towns reveal about their social, economic, and geographic biases?

4. Postrel refers to "place" and "local color" at several points in her essay. What do these terms mean? In what ways are their definitions central to her argument?

@ Download or print this Starting a Conversation activity at **bedfordstmartins.com/ conversation**.

5. According to Postrel, how might a misplaced hostility to retail chains actually harm some communities? What specific advantages does she claim these stores provide, and who benefits from them? What kinds of evidence does she offer to prove her point?

How Can I Write an Argumentative Essay?

Many people believe that an argument is effective only if it's won, that unless they convince or persuade someone they've failed in their mission to change the world — or their community, or the minds of people they hang out with, or the people who read their Facebook pages. In fact, most written arguments aren't so much about winning or losing as about sharing the writer's perspective with others who share an interest in an issue. Think of it as exploring alternative ways of thinking, acting, and believing — as advancing a conversation about an issue. If you follow this line of thinking, you'll recognize that the effectiveness of your essay isn't based on whether you win the argument. It is based on your ability to affect the community of readers and writers to whom you direct your argument.

Then again, sometimes winning is all that matters. Application essays for medical or business school, no matter how well written, are seldom considered successful if the writer isn't accepted. The same is true of letters requesting scholarships. And if you're a teenage driver, either you get to borrow the car or you don't.

In this section, you'll learn about the processes and strategies involved in writing an argumentative essay. As you work on your essay, you'll follow the work of Donovan Mikrot, a first-year student who wrote an argumentative essay about controls on access to digital movies and television shows.

In Process

An Argumentative Essay about Digital Music

Donovan Mikrot wrote an argumentative essay for his introductory composition course. Donovan learned about his topic by reading articles and blogs about digital rights management for music and video. Follow his efforts to write his argumentative essay by visiting **bedfordstmartins.com/conversation**. You can read excerpts of interviews with Donovan and read drafts of his essay.

Find a Conversation and Listen In

Argumentative essays grow out of a belief that a choice must be made, a situation should be changed, or a mistake should be corrected. In general, people don't argue when they're happy with a situation, nor do they argue when they agree with one another. They argue because they believe that someone or something—a person, a group, a movement, a government—is wrong. As you consider possible subjects for your argumentative essay, take stock of the conversations taking place around you. Ask what bothers you. Ask what conflicts affect you, individually or as a member of a community. Look for an issue that matters not only to you but also to the people who might read your essay. Then take on the role of advocate and reflect on your writing situation—your purpose, your readers, and the contexts in which your writing will be read (see p. 13).

EXPLORE DISAGREEMENTS

Unless they're deeply conflicted, few people carry on extended arguments with themselves. The kinds of arguments that are worth addressing in academic essays revolve around issues that affect a larger community. To identify issues that might interest you and your readers, explore popular, professional, and academic conversations. In almost every case, you'll find points of disagreement and debate that bring people together in discussions—sometimes polite and sometimes anything but—about the challenges that confront us.

- **Popular conversations.** What's new in the media and the popular press? What's new on the Web? You can visit sites such as CNN.com's "Sound Off" pages and National Public Radio's opinion pages to learn about issues that have sparked discussion. On sites such as these, you can read commentary from other visitors to the site, read blogs and opinion columns, and view the latest news reports on issues that have spurred popular debate.

- **Professional conversations.** If you are involved or are planning to become involved in a particular profession, tune in to the conversations taking place in your field of interest. If you're working as an intern or at a part-time job, for example, listen to what your coworkers are talking about. Skim some trade and professional journals to find points of disagreement. Read some blogs that focus on your profession, and notice what people are arguing about.

- **Academic conversations.** Just as you will find disagreements in public and professional life, you will find them in academic disciplines. Look for disagreements in course readings, and pay attention to controversies addressed during class discussions and lectures. Ask professors and graduate students what's "hot" in their fields. Scan the tables of contents of recent issues of academic journals. Visit Web sites that focus on your discipline.

In Process

Generating Ideas about Conversations

Donovan Mikrot's interests in music and technology led him to explore conversations related to the general topic of digital rights management.

> Many devices that border on copyright infringement have been created for music and video recording. VCRs caused a major fight. The industry tried to make recording TV shows illegal, but they lost. Now TiVo and other DVRs are facing similar challenges, just like digital music. The CD player is becoming a thing of the past, and many companies are cashing in on new storage technologies to create new digital music players. The iPod is easy to use, and Apple is leading the market. The iPod has spawned an entire industry for peripherals. Can Apple's success with the iPod be duplicated by some company that distributes movies and TV shows? Could Apple do it? How about BlackBerry or Google? Is this how TiVo will reinvent itself? And how are the movie studios going to react? As foolishly as the music industry?

Donovan used the results of his freewriting to direct his attention to discussions about copyright protection on digital music and video. The discussions he found in blogs, in professional journals, and on Web sites led him to an interest in efforts to balance the rights of the artists and companies who own the copyright on movies and television shows, on the one hand, and the interests of consumers who feel they have a right to view digital content on any player they own, on the other hand.

Recognizing ongoing conversations can give you insights into debatable issues that might serve as the basis for your argumentative essay. Try listing issues from one or more of these areas—or from the writing project ideas at the end of this chapter—and then explore your thoughts about them (see pp. 33–37 for an overview of strategies for generating ideas). When you've finished, review what you've written to identify the areas that seem most promising, and then select one or two that interest you most. Jot down your thoughts about what you already know and what you would need to learn before you can develop your argument.

TRACK ONLINE CONVERSATIONS

Issues worth arguing about almost always become a topic of conversation. Increasingly, that conversation takes place online, through blogs, electronic mailing lists, newsgroups, and Web discussion forums. These resources are designed specifically to

Working Together: Try It Out Loud

Before you start developing your argument, hold an informal debate with your classmates about an issue that affects all of you. Form small groups, and choose an issue you're familiar with and that lends itself to argument, such as a disagreement affecting your hometown, school, or state. You might scan the school paper or a local publication for current issues worth discussing. Explain your perspective on the issue, and then state your position. Offer reasons and, if possible, evidence from personal experience or readings to support your argument. Ask the other members of your group to identify counterarguments, giving their own reasons and evidence. Take turns speaking while the other members of the group listen, respond, and ask questions.

When you are finished, take a few minutes to reflect on the exercise. What did you learn about presenting an argument? Did you have to adapt what you said based on your classmates' values, beliefs, and concerns? What kind of questions did they ask? What seemed to interest them the most about the issue? How did they react to your argument? What reasoning and evidence did they find most convincing? Least convincing?

@ Download or print this Working Together activity at **bedfordstmartins.com/conversation**.

support exchanges among writers and readers. By following these online conversations, you can not only learn more about your subject but also discover what other writers and readers think about it.

Blogs consist of chronologically ordered entries on a Web site and most closely resemble entries in a diary or journal. Blog entries usually include a title and a text message and can also incorporate images, audio, video, and other types of media. Many entries provide links to other pages on the Web. Blogs allow readers to post their responses to entries, so a single blog entry might be accompanied by several — sometimes hundreds — of responses.

You can find blogs that address your subject by turning to sites such as Ask.com Blogs (www.ask.com/?tool=bls) and Google Blogsearch (http://blogsearch.google.com). You can read more about blogs in Chapter 12.

Electronic mailing lists support and archive conversations among people who share an interest in an issue or belong to a particular community. You can read a message sent to a mailing list, sometimes referred to as a listserv, in the same way that you read other e-mail messages — and you can post your own messages. You can locate relevant mailing lists through sites such as Catalist (www.lsoft.com/lists/listref.html) and Tile.net (http://tile.net/lists).

Newsgroups and Web discussion forums allow users to post and respond to one another's messages using Web browsers. The messages are organized by topic and date, allowing you to view posts and responses by topic in the order in which they were written. Forum Zilla (www.forumzilla.com) and Google Groups (http://groups .google .com) are two good resources for locating these forums. You can also check the Web sites of magazines and newspapers that have published articles addressing your issue. Increasingly, they provide online forums to support discussion among readers.

Even though these resources can be helpful as you explore potential issues for your essay, take the time to learn more about the conversations you find online. You can locate print and electronic sources through your library's online catalog and through Web search sites and directories. If the sources you collect leave you with unanswered questions, you can conduct additional searches, talk to a librarian, or collect information through observations or interviews. Depending on your issue, you might also want to search for government documents.

Do you know how to locate online sources? See Chapter 12 for help.

ASK QUESTIONS ABOUT PROMISING ISSUES

Before you begin constructing an argument, determine which aspect of an issue interests you most. The best written arguments are usually focused and narrow. Be wary of writing about something as broadly defined as climate change or ethics in politics. Instead, try to find a subtopic that you can manage in the space and time available to you. For example, if you're interested in climate change, take a look at issues such as the carbon emissions that result from producing the batteries used in hybrid cars and trucks. Each of the following questions focuses your attention on a general issue in a different way, and each provides a useful starting point for an argumentative essay. Depending on the subject, you'll find that some questions are more relevant than others.

- **Values.** Why is this important to me? What about it will matter to readers? Can I make an argument without letting my emotions run away with me?

- **Definition.** Why do people disagree about this issue? What, exactly, is at stake?

- **Possibilities.** What could be accomplished if this issue is addressed? What might happen if it is not addressed?

- **Positions.** What positions have been taken on this issue? What intrigues me about those positions?

- **Strengths and weaknesses.** What are the strengths of other writers' arguments? What are the weaknesses?

In Process

Locating Sources

Donovan Mikrot was interested in the issue of copy protection for digital movies and television shows, a subject that would require him to learn about the most recent antipiracy technologies. He also wanted to find out what efforts were being made to ensure that digital video, once purchased, could be played on any digital video player. His Web searches led him to a blog entry that discussed the issue in depth and that had a series of replies from readers.

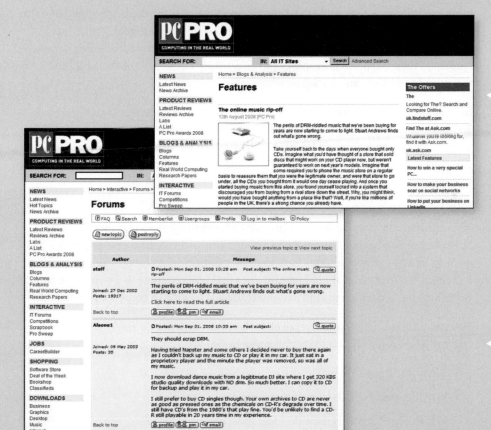

Donovan located a blog entry by Stuart Andrews on the PC Pro Web site.

Several readers had replied to the blog entry, in some cases extending and refining the argument.

Donovan saved a copy of Andrews's blog. Then he followed the links in the blog to related materials and saved those as well. Later, he printed a copy and highlighted key passages.

As you narrow your focus, ask yourself one last question: Is your goal to convince your readers to agree with you, or to persuade them to act? Be aware that getting people to act can be a far greater challenge than getting them to agree with you. For example, it's easy to convince someone that it's a good idea to spend more time studying. It can be far more difficult to persuade that person to set aside two more hours each day to do so. As you consider how you'll focus your argument, remember that it will take a strong argument to persuade your readers to act.

Build Your Argument

Putting together an effective argumentative essay starts with knowing what you want others to believe or how you want them to act. But that's just the beginning. To build your argument, you must develop a strategy for achieving your goal. Your strategy should reflect not only your overall goal but also a thorough understanding of your readers — their purposes in reading your essay, their knowledge of the issue, and their needs, interests, and backgrounds.

In short, you'll need to figure out how to get your readers to accept your argument. To do so, start by defining your overall claim, and then identify the reasons and supporting evidence that will be most convincing or persuasive to your readers. In addition, consider how opposing positions affect your argument, and make sure that your reasoning is sound.

DEFINE YOUR OVERALL CLAIM

It's important that you understand precisely what you want your readers to believe or do before you begin drafting. Your overall claim — the heart of the argument you want to make — will serve as a touchstone as you juggle the complexities of crafting an argument. Your claim should take into account your purpose as a writer, the conversation you've decided to join, and the readers you hope to convince or persuade.

You can begin to define your overall claim by brainstorming or freewriting (see pp. 33–34) in response to the following questions:

- What is my position on this issue?

- Which aspects of this issue interest me most?

- Which aspects of this issue do I feel most strongly about?

- What do I want my readers to believe or do as a result of reading my essay?

- What are my readers likely to think about this issue? What will it take to change their minds or get them to act?

- How does my position differ from those advanced by other writers? How is it similar?

Review what you've written. Then try to express, in one or two sentences, your overall claim. Later, your claim can serve as the basis for a thesis statement (see Chapter 15). For now, use it to direct your thinking about the argument you want to formulate.

DEVELOP REASONS TO ACCEPT YOUR OVERALL CLAIM

Few readers will accept "because I'm right" as a good reason to accept your position on an issue. They expect you to explain why you're right. Developing an explanation begins with identifying reasons that are consistent with your own perspective on the issue. At this stage of your writing process, don't worry about whether your readers will be convinced or persuaded by your reasoning. Instead, treat your efforts to develop reasons to accept your overall claim as you would any other form of brainstorming. As you generate a list of potential reasons, you can certainly begin to ask whether the reasons you've identified are well grounded, logical, and consistent with the values and beliefs held by you and your readers. And later, as you draft your essay, you can decide how to present your reasons to your readers. For now, though, your primary goal is to generate as many potential reasons as possible to support your overall claim.

Your understanding of an issue and the conversations surrounding it will provide a framework within which you can develop a set of reasons to support your overall claim. To guide your efforts, ask questions such as the following, and respond to them by brainstorming, freewriting, looping, clustering, or mapping:

- **Costs.** What costs are associated with not accepting and acting on your overall claim? Are there monetary costs? Will time and effort be lost or wasted? Will valuable resources be wasted? Will people be unable to lead fulfilling lives? Will human potential be wasted? Will lives be lost?

- **Benefits.** What will be gained by accepting and acting on your overall claim? Who or what will benefit if the claim is accepted and acted on? What form will these benefits take?

- **Alternatives, choices, and trade-offs.** What is gained by accepting and acting on your overall claim? What is lost by not doing so? In what ways are the potential costs or benefits associated with your overall claim preferable to those associated with rejecting it?

- **Parallels.** Can you find similarities between the overall claim you are making about this issue and claims made about other issues? Can you argue that, if your claim is accepted and acted on, the outcomes will be similar to those found for other issues? What consensus, if any, exists among experts on this issue about what similar situations have led to in the past?

- **Personal experience.** What does your personal experience tell you is likely to happen if your claim is accepted and acted on? What does it tell you might happen if it is rejected?

- **Historical context.** What does history tell you is likely to happen—or not happen—if your claim is accepted and acted on? What does it tell you might happen if it is rejected? What consensus, if any, exists among experts on this issue about what similar situations have led to in the past?

- **Values and beliefs.** In what ways is your overall claim consistent with your values and beliefs? With those of your readers? In what ways is it consistent with larger societal and cultural values and beliefs? How might it further those values and beliefs?

Examine the list of reasons you've generated to determine which ones fit best with your overall claim, your purpose, and what you know about your readers. Select the reasons that, individually and as a group, best support your overall claim.

CHOOSE EVIDENCE TO SUPPORT YOUR REASONS

Your argument will be effective only if you back up each of your reasons with evidence. Most readers will expect you to provide some sort of justification for accepting your reasons, and their assessment of your evidence will affect their willingness to accept your argument. The form your evidence takes will depend on your overall claim, the reasons themselves, and your readers' values and assumptions. In general, however, consider drawing on the following types of evidence to support your reasons:

- textual evidence, in the form of quotations, paraphrases, and summaries

- numerical and statistical data

- images, including photographs, drawings, animations, video, and sound

- tables, charts, and graphs

- information and ideas from interviews, observations, and surveys

- personal experience

- expert opinion

Take the following steps to identify evidence to support your reasons:

1. List the reasons you are using to support your overall claim.

2. For each reason, review your notes to identify relevant evidence.

3. List your evidence below each point.

4. Identify reasons that need more support, and locate additional evidence as necessary.

5. Consider dismissing or revising reasons for which you don't have sufficient evidence.

Effective arguments typically provide evidence that is both plentiful and varied in type. A writer arguing about the need to improve the U.S. health care system, for example, might draw on personal experience, interviews with friends and relatives, policy briefs from the American Medical Association, commentary by bloggers, reports issued by government agencies, and articles in popular and scholarly journals.

You can read more about how to use evidence to support your reasons in Chapter 17.

In Process

Choosing Evidence

Donovan Mikrot chose the evidence he would use in his essay by creating a list of reasons to support his overall claim that Hollywood should eliminate digital rights management on digital movies and TV shows. He reviewed his notes and sources, listing sources next to each reason, and decided whether he needed more or better evidence for each reason. He created a table in a word-processing file to keep track of his evidence.

Reason	Evidence/Source	Notes
DRM stifles innovation.	Electronic Frontier Foundation, Von Lohmann	The EFF report has a lot to choose from — maybe too much. Von Lohmann is an EFF lawyer.
Hollywood's insistence on DRM hurts consumers.	Breen, Andrews	Breen and Andrews both argue that people are inconvenienced when they can't back up movies or play them on different devices.
Lack of interoperability actually leads to piracy.	Breen, Manjoo	Frustration leads honest people to violate DRM restrictions.
DRM actually reduces profits.	Manjoo	If digital movies and television shows could be viewed on any player, people would buy more of them.

IDENTIFY AND CONSIDER OPPOSING CLAIMS

A critical part of developing and supporting your argument is identifying opposing claims, or counterarguments. You might assume that calling attention to competing positions in your essay will weaken your argument. Nothing is farther from the truth. Identifying opposing claims provides opportunities to test and strengthen your reasons and evidence by comparing them with those put forth by other writers. Considering counterarguments also allows you to anticipate questions and concerns your readers are likely to bring to your essay. And later, as you are writing your draft, your responses to these opposing claims provide a basis for clearly explaining to your readers why your argument is superior to others.

Remember that you're making an argument about your issue because people disagree about how to address it. If reasonable alternatives to your argument didn't exist, there would be no need for an argument in the first place. As a writer contributing to an ongoing conversation, you have a responsibility to indicate that you're aware of what has been said and who has said it. More important, you have a responsibility to consider carefully how your argument improves on the arguments made by other members of the conversation.

To identify opposing claims, review the sources you encountered as you learned about your issue. Identify the most compelling arguments you found, and ask how the reasons and evidence offered to support them compare to yours. Then ask whether you can think of reasonable alternative positions that haven't been addressed in the sources you've consulted. Finally, talk with others about your issue, and ask them what they think about it.

Working Together: Identify and Consider Opposing Claims

Working with a group of two or more classmates, carry out a "devil's advocate" exercise to identify and consider opposing claims. First, briefly describe your issue, overall claim, and reasons. Other members of the group should offer reasonable alternative arguments. One member of the group should serve as a recorder, taking careful notes on the exchange, listing opposing claims, reasons supporting those claims, and your response to the claims. Once the exchange (which might last between three and ten minutes) is completed, switch roles and repeat the activity for every other member of the group.

This activity can be carried out face-to-face or electronically. If you are working on the activity using a chat program or a threaded discussion forum, you can record your exchange for later review. Most chat programs allow you to create a transcript of a session, and threaded discussion forums will automatically record your exchange.

@ Download or print this Working Together activity at **bedfordstmartins.com/conversation.**

For each reason you expect to use in support of your overall claim, create a list of opposing points of view, briefly describing each one and noting where you found it. To determine whether you're making the best possible argument, consider each of these opposing claims in turn. Take notes on your response to each one, considering both its merits and its faults. Use what you've learned to reflect on and refine your overall claim and the reasons and evidence you've identified to support it. Later, you can use what you've learned to address counterarguments in your essay (see p. 442).

ENSURE THE INTEGRITY OF YOUR ARGUMENT

If you're familiar with the "buy this car, and get a date with this girl (or guy)" school of advertising, you know that arguments often lack integrity. Although weak arguments might be easier to develop, they usually backfire (notwithstanding the enduring success of automobile ads filled with attractive young men and women). Readers who recognize errors in reasoning or the use of inappropriate evidence are likely to reject an argument out of hand.

Acquainting yourself with common logical fallacies can help you not only ensure the integrity of your argument but also identify and address counterarguments based on fallacious reasoning and weak or inappropriate forms of evidence.

Some of the most common logical fallacies are described below.

Fallacies Based on Distraction

- **A red herring** is an irrelevant or distracting point. The term originated with the practice of sweeping a red herring (a particularly fragrant type of fish) across the trail being followed by a pack of hunting dogs to throw them off the scent of their prey. For example, the question *Why worry about the rising cost of tuition when the government is tapping our phones?* is a red herring (government surveillance has nothing to do with increases in college tuition).

- **Ad hominem attacks** attempt to discredit an idea or argument by suggesting that a person or group associated it with should not be trusted. These kinds of attacks might be subtle or vicious. If you hear someone say that a proposed wind farm should be rejected because its main supporter cheated on her taxes, or that school vouchers are bad because a principal who swindled a school district supports them, you're listening to an ad hominem attack.

- **Irrelevant history** is another form of distraction. For example, arguing that a proposal is bad because someone came up with the idea while they were using cocaine suggests that the state of mind of the person who originates an idea has something to do with its merits. It might well be the case that the idea is flawed, but you should base your assessment on an analysis of its strengths and weaknesses. Otherwise, you might as well say that an idea is undoubtedly sound because someone thought of it while he or she was sober.

Fallacies Based on Questionable Assumptions

- **Sweeping generalizations**, sometimes known as *hasty generalizations*, are based on stereotypes. Asserting that the rich are conservative voters, for example, assumes that everyone who is rich is just like everyone else who is rich. These kinds of arguments don't account for variation within a group, nor do they consider exceptions to the rule.

- **Straw-man attacks** oversimplify or distort another person's argument so it can be dismissed more easily. Just as a boxer can easily knock down a scarecrow, a writer who commits this fallacy might characterize an opposing position as more extreme than it actually is, or might refute obviously flawed counter-arguments while ignoring valid objections.

- **Citing inappropriate authorities** can take several forms: citing as an authority someone who is not an expert on a subject, citing a source with a strong bias on an issue, suggesting that an individual voice represents consensus when that person's ideas are far from the mainstream, or treating paid celebrity endorsements as expert opinion.

- **Jumping on a bandwagon**, also known as *argument from consensus*, implies that if enough people believe something, it must be true. This type of argument substitutes group thinking for careful analysis. The idea of jumping on a bandwagon refers to the practice, in early American politics, of parading a candidate through town on a bandwagon. To show support for the candidate, people would climb onto the wagon.

Fallacies Based on Misrepresentation

- **Stacking the deck** refers to the practice of presenting evidence for only one side of an argument. Most readers will assume that a writer has done this deliberately and will wonder what he or she is trying to hide.

- **Base-rate fallacies** are commonly found in arguments based on statistics. If you read that drinking coffee will triple your risk of developing cancer, you might be alarmed. However, if you knew that the risk rose from one in a billion to three in a billion, you might pour another cup.

- **Questionable analogies**, also known as *false analogies*, make inappropriate comparisons. They are based on the assumption that if two things are similar in one way, they must be similar in others. For example, a writer might argue that global warming is like a fever, and that just as a fever usually runs its course on its own, so too will the climate recover without intervention.

Fallacies Based on Careless Reasoning

- **Post hoc fallacies**, formally known as *post hoc, ergo propter hoc* fallacies ("after this, therefore because of this"), argue that because one event happened before a second event, the first event must have caused the second event. For example, a student might conclude that she received a low grade on an essay exam because she argued with an instructor during class. In fact, the real cause might be the poor quality of her exam responses.

- **Slippery-slope arguments** warn that a single step will inevitably lead to a bad situation. For instance, one of the most common arguments against decriminalizing marijuana is that it leads to the use of stronger narcotics. Indeed, some heroin or cocaine addicts might have first tried marijuana, but there is no evidence that *all* marijuana users inevitably move on to harder drugs.

- **Either/or arguments** present two choices, one of which is usually characterized as extremely undesirable. In fact, there might be a third choice, or a fourth, or a fifth.

- **Non sequiturs** are statements that do not follow logically from what has been said. For example, arguing that buying a particular type of car will lead to a successful love life is a non sequitur.

- **Circular reasoning**, also known as *begging the question*, restates a point that has just been made as evidence for itself. Arguing that a decline in voter turnout is a result of fewer people voting is an example of circular reasoning.

As you build your argument—and in particular, as you consider counterarguments and check your reasoning for fallacies—you might find that you need to refine your overall claim. In fact, most writers refine their argument as they learn more about an issue and consider how best to contribute to a conversation. As you prepare to write a first draft of your argumentative essay, take another look at your overall claim, reasons, and evidence. Do they still make sense? Do they stack up well against competing arguments? Do you have enough evidence to convince or persuade your intended readers? If you answer "no" to any of these questions, continue to develop and refine your argument.

Prepare a Draft

Building your argument prepares you to draft your essay. It allows you to decide how to frame your thesis statement, appeal to your readers, address counterarguments, take advantage of design opportunities, and organize your reasons and evidence.

MAKE AN ARGUMENTATIVE CLAIM

The overall claim you developed as you built your argument (p. 430) provides the foundation for your thesis statement—a brief statement that conveys the main point you want to make about your issue. In an argumentative essay, a thesis statement should be debatable, plausible, and clear.

- **A debatable thesis statement** is one with which readers can disagree. Saying that we should take good care of our children, for example, isn't particularly debatable. Saying that we need to invest more public funding in mandatory immunization programs, however, would almost certainly lead some readers to disagree. Even though your goal in writing an argumentative essay is to convince readers to accept or act on your argument, there's little to be gained in arguing for something with which everyone will agree. An argumentative essay is useful only if it makes people think and, ideally, change their attitudes, beliefs, or behaviors.

- **A plausible thesis statement** appears at the very least to be reasonable, and in fact the claim it makes might appear to be convincing or persuasive on its own. That is, although your claim should be debatable, don't make it so extreme that it comes across as ridiculous or absurd. For example, it's one thing to argue that the news media should pay more attention to political candidates' platforms and leadership qualities than to their personal failings; it's quite another to argue that a candidate's criminal record should be ignored.

- **A clear thesis statement** advances a claim that is easy to follow. It explains what readers should believe or how they should act. Typically, this involves using words such as *should*, *must*, or *ought*. It's important to remember that you are attempting to convince or persuade your readers. Unless you tell them what to believe or how to act, they won't be sure of your position.

An effective thesis statement will shape your readers' understanding of the issue, directing their attention to particular aspects of the issue and away from others. Consider, for example, the following thesis statements about athletes' use of performance-enhancing drugs.

Thesis statement 1: If for no other reason, athletes should avoid the use of performance-enhancing drugs to safeguard their personal health.

Thesis statement 2: To eliminate the use of performance-enhancing drugs, athletes themselves must take the lead in policing their sports.

Thesis statement 3: National and international governing bodies for sports should engage in a coordinated effort to educate aspiring athletes about ethics and sportsmanship.

These thesis statements would lead to significantly different argumentative essays. The first thesis statement directs readers' attention to the health consequences for athletes who use performance-enhancing drugs. The second suggests that athletes themselves should take charge of efforts to eradicate this form of cheating. The third thesis statement focuses attention on the contributions that might be made by what are essentially large corporate and government agencies. Each thesis statement is plausible and debatable, and each one tells readers what they should believe or act on. Yet each leads the reader to view the issue in a significantly different way.

Is your thesis statement focused enough? See Chapter 15 for help.

APPEAL TO YOUR READERS

As you work on your draft, consider the strategies you'll use to convince or persuade your readers to accept your argument. These strategies are essentially a means of appealing to — or asking — your readers to consider the reasons you are offering to support your overall claim and, if they accept them as appropriate and valid, to believe or act in a certain way.

Fortunately, you won't have to invent strategies on your own. For thousands of years, writers and speakers have used a wide range of appeals to ask readers to accept their reasons as appropriate and valid. Much of the work of ancient Greek and Roman thinkers such as Aristotle and Cicero revolved around strategies for presenting an argument to an audience. Their work still serves as a foundation for how we think about argumentation.

You can ask readers to accept your reasons by appealing to authority; emotion; principles, values, and beliefs; character; or logic. Most arguments are built on a combination of these appeals. The combination you choose will reflect your issue, purpose, readers, sources, and context.

Appeals to authority. When you present a reason by making an appeal to authority, you ask readers to accept it because someone in a position of authority endorses it. The evidence used to support this kind of appeal typically takes the form of quotations, paraphrases, or summaries of the ideas of experts in a given subject area, of political leaders, or of people who have been affected by an issue. As you consider whether this kind of appeal might be appropriate for your argumentative essay, reflect on the notes you've taken on your sources. Have you identified experts, leaders, or people who have been affected by an issue? If so, can you use them to convince your readers that your argument has merit?

Appeals to emotion attempt to elicit an emotional response to an issue. The famous "win one for the Gipper" speech delivered by Pat O'Brien, who portrayed Notre Dame coach Knute Rockne in the 1940 film *Knute Rockne: All American*, is an example of an appeal to emotion. At halftime during a game with Army, with Notre Dame trailing, he said:

Well, boys . . . I haven't a thing to say. Played a great game . . . all of you. Great game. I guess we just can't expect to win 'em all.

I'm going to tell you something I've kept to myself for years. None of you ever knew George Gipp. It was long before your time. But you know what a tradition he is at Notre Dame. . . . And the last thing he said to me — "Rock," he said, "sometime, when the team is up against it — and the breaks are beating the boys — tell them to go out there with all they got and win just one for the Gipper. . . . I don't know where I'll be then, Rock," he said — "but I'll know about it — and I'll be happy."

Using emotional appeals to frame an argument—that is, to help readers view an issue in a particular way—is a tried-and-true strategy. But use it carefully, if you use it at all. In some types of documents, such as scholarly articles and essays, emotional appeals are used infrequently, and readers of such documents are likely to ask why you would play on their emotions instead of making an appeal to logic (see below) or an appeal to authority.

Appeals to principles, values, and beliefs rely on the assumption that your readers value a given set of principles. Religious and ethical arguments are often based on appeals to principles, such as the need to respect God, to love one another, to trust in the innate goodness of people, to believe that all of us are created equal, or to believe that security should never be purchased at the price of individual liberty. If you make an appeal to principles, values, or beliefs, be sure your readers share the particular principle, value, or belief you are using. If they don't, you might need to state and justify your underlying assumptions at the outset—or you might want to try a different kind of appeal.

Appeals to character. Writers frequently use appeals to character. When politicians refer to their military experience, for example, they are saying, "Look at me. I'm a patriotic person who has served our country." When celebrities endorse a product, they are saying, "You know and like me, so please believe me when I say that this product is worth purchasing." Appeals to character can also reflect a person's professional accomplishment. When scientists or philosophers present an argument, for example, they sometimes refer to their background and experience, or perhaps to their previous publications. In doing so, they are implicitly telling their readers that they have been accurate and truthful in the past and that readers can continue to trust them. Essentially, you can think of an appeal to character as the "trust me" strategy. As you consider this kind of appeal, reflect on your character, accomplishments, and experiences, and ask how they might lead your readers to trust you.

Appeals to logic. A logical appeal refers to the concept of reasoning through a set of propositions to reach a considered conclusion. For example, you might argue that a suspect is guilty of murder because police found her fingerprints on the murder weapon, her blood under the murder victim's fingernails, scratches on the suspect's face, and video of the murder from a surveillance camera. Your argument would rely on the logical presentation of evidence to convince jurors that the suspect was the murderer and to persuade them to return a verdict of guilty. As you develop reasons to support your claim, consider using logical appeals such as deduction and induction.

- **Deduction** is a form of logical reasoning that moves from general principles to a conclusion. It usually involves two propositions and a conclusion.

  Proposition 1 (usually a general principle): Stealing is wrong.

  Proposition 2 (usually an observation): John stole a candy bar from the store.

  Conclusion (results of deductive analysis): John's theft of the candy bar was wrong.

  Deduction is often used to present arguments that have ethical and moral dimensions, such as birth control, welfare reform, and immigration policy.

- **Induction** is a form of logical reasoning that moves from specific observations to general conclusions, often drawing on numerical data to reveal patterns. Medical researchers, for example, typically collect a large number of observations about the effectiveness and side effects of new medications and then analyze their observations to draw conclusions about the effectiveness of the medications. Induction is based on probability — that is, whether something seems likely to occur in the future based on what has been observed. Three commonly used forms of induction are trend analysis (see p. 243), causal analysis (see p. 244), and data analysis (see p. 246).

You can use different types of appeals to support your claim. Emotional appeals can be mixed with appeals to character. A coach's address to a team before an important athletic competition often relies not only on appeals to emotion but also on appeals to character, asking the players' to trust what the coach has to say and to trust in themselves and their own abilities. Similarly, appeals to principle can be combined with appeals to emotion and logic.

To choose your appeals, reflect on your purpose, readers, sources, context, and overall claim. In your writer's notebook, record your responses to the following:

1. Put your overall claim in the form of a thesis statement.

2. Ask what sort of appeals are best suited to the claim

3. Sketch out promising appeals. Ask, for example, how you would appeal to authority, or how you would appeal to logic.

4. Ask how your readers are likely to respond to a given appeal.

5. Ask whether the kind of argument you are presenting lends itself to the use of particular appeals.

ADDRESS COUNTERARGUMENTS

Your readers will expect you to consider and address reasonable alternatives to your overall claim. They'll do so not only because it is appropriate to acknowledge the contributions of other authors who have written about an issue, but also because they want to understand why your argument is superior to the alternatives. If your readers are aware of opposing claims but notice that you haven't addressed them, they'll question your credibility. They might conclude that you haven't thought carefully about the issue, or they might wonder whether you haven't addressed opposing claims in your essay because you think the other claims are stronger than yours.

To address counterarguments, review the work you did to identify and consider opposing claims as you built your argument (see p. 434). Consider the strengths and weaknesses of each claim in relation to your argument and in relation to the other opposing claims you identified. Then decide whether to concede, refute, or ignore each claim.

Concede valid claims. Show your readers that you are being fair — and establish common ground with readers who might otherwise be inclined to disagree with you — by acknowledging opposing points of view and accepting reasonable aspects of counterarguments. For example, if you are arguing that your state government should spend more to repair roads and bridges, acknowledge that this will probably mean reducing funding for other state programs or increasing state taxes.

You can qualify your concession by explaining that although part of a counterargument is sound, readers should consider the argument's weaknesses. You might note, for example, that reducing funding for some state programs could be offset by instituting fees for those who use those programs most.

Refute widely held claims. A counterargument might be widely advocated or generally accepted yet still have significant weaknesses. If you identify widely held claims that have weaknesses such as cost, undesirable outcomes, or logical flaws, describe the counterargument, point out its flaws, and explain why your claim or reason is superior. For example, you might note that, although it is costly to maintain roads and bridges, allowing them to fall into disrepair will cost far more in the long run—in terms of both funding and loss of life.

Ignore competing claims. Don't assume that addressing counterarguments means giving every competing claim equal time. Some counterarguments will be much stronger than others, and some will be so closely related to one another that you can dismiss them as a group. Once you've addressed valid and widely held competing claims, you can safely ignore the rest. Even though your sense of fairness might suggest that you should address every counterargument, doing so will result in a less effective (and potentially much longer) essay.

As you present your discussion of counterarguments, maintain a reasonable and polite tone. You gain little, if anything, by insulting or belittling writers with whom you disagree, particularly when it's possible that some of your readers think a certain counterargument has merit. It is preferable—and generally more effective in terms of winning your argument—to carefully and politely point out the limitations of a particular counterargument.

CONSIDER GENRE AND DESIGN

A well-written argumentative essay uses design to help readers understand your argument more clearly, usually by simplifying the presentation of reasons and evidence or by setting a mood through the use of carefully selected illustrations. The design of your essay should reflect the formatting requirements of your assignment and the expectations of your readers, particularly your instructor.

In many cases, the appeals you choose to make to your readers will suggest design elements that can enhance your argument.

- **Photographs** can strengthen (or serve as) an emotional appeal. For instance, an argument in favor of tightening lending restrictions might show a family in front of the home they've lost to foreclosure.

- **Headings and subheadings** can help readers follow your reasoning about an issue.

- **Color** and **pull quotes** can underscore appeals to values, beliefs, and principles by calling a reader's attention to shared assumptions and important ideas.

- **Sidebars** can highlight an appeal to character by giving related information about a writer or a source without interfering with the flow of the argument.

- Appeals to authority often present statistical data in the form of **tables**, **charts**, and **graphs**.

Consider the placement of visual evidence carefully. In general, place illustrations as close as possible to the point where they are mentioned in the text, provide a title or caption that identifies or explains the illustration, and cite the source of the information.

You can find a detailed discussion of document design in Chapter 18.

FRAME YOUR ARGUMENT

Most written arguments rely on a well-established set of elements: a clearly expressed thesis statement, a thorough discussion of the reasons and evidence supporting the overall claim, careful consideration of counterarguments, and an introduction and a conclusion. The presentation of these elements, however, is as varied as the issues addressed in argumentative essays and the writers who tackle them.

Organization. As you organize your argumentative essay, give some thought to the sequence in which you present your reasons and evidence and discuss counterarguments. If you are drawing heavily on emotional appeals, for example, you might lead with a particularly striking appeal, one designed to outrage or excite your readers—or at least to get them to continue reading your essay. Similarly, you might end with a reason that would leave your readers feeling that they must do something about the issue you've raised. If you are crafting an argument that relies heavily on logical analysis, you should ask whether any of your appeals build on (or logically follow) other appeals. You should also ask whether some appeals are easier to understand and accept than others. If so, be sure to present them before you advance more complex or objectionable appeals. Counterarguments might all be addressed early on, discussed in turn, or withheld until you've established the reasons in support of your overall claim. Refer to Chapter 16 for additional guidelines on organizing and outlining an essay.

Introduction and conclusion. Pay particular attention to your introduction and conclusion. These important elements not only provide the framework within which your readers will understand the issue you are addressing but also influence their willingness to accept your argument. Once you've decided how to frame your introduction and conclusion, you can use a range of strategies to put them into words. In their introductions, writers of argumentative essays frequently rely on strategies such as asking a question, leading with a quotation, and telling a story. In their conclusions, they often use strategies such as speculating about the future, asking a question, and closing with a quotation. You can read more about strategies for introducing and concluding your essay in Chapter 16.

Review and Improve Your Draft

An effective argumentative essay makes its claim in such a manner that readers will understand an issue in a particular way, provides plausible and well-supported appeals to accept that claim, addresses likely counterarguments, and avoids the traps posed by logical fallacies and other forms of argument that lack integrity. Few writers can fully address all of these elements in a first draft, so don't expect to produce a finished essay in one sitting. Set aside enough time to review your draft and to revise it at least once. Allowing at least a day or two between completing your draft and reviewing it makes it easier to recognize opportunities for improvement and to clarify your thinking.

CONSIDER YOUR OVERALL CLAIM

Before you review any other part of your draft, spend some time reassessing your overall claim. Is it presented in such a manner that your readers will understand the issue in a specific way? Have you stated it clearly? Is it possible that your readers might reasonably misinterpret your claim, or might think of the issue differently than you do? Finally, is the claim stated in a way that is consistent with how you've framed your introduction and conclusion?

REVIEW YOUR REASONS, EVIDENCE, AND APPEALS

The presentation of your overall claim will set up expectations among your readers about how you're likely to support it. For example, if you've said that the city council needs to increase funding for a flood mitigation program, your readers are likely to expect that at least some of your reasons for making the claim will touch on the consequences of failing to fund the program at a reasonable level. As you review your draft, ask whether your reasons make sense individually, and then ask whether they work well together. Most important, ask how your readers are likely to react to each reason and whether you've provided enough evidence to support it.

In addition, ask whether your readers are likely to accept the kinds of appeals you've used to present your reasons and evidence. Always consider your readers' needs, interests, backgrounds, and knowledge of the issue. You might conclude, for instance, that an emotional appeal will backfire, or that your readers will expect more evidence from authorities, or that you could strengthen an appeal to values by explaining an underlying assumption.

EXAMINE YOUR TREATMENT OF COUNTERARGUMENTS

As you review how you've addressed counterarguments, put yourself in your readers' place. Doing so allows you to pose reasonable arguments that contradict your overall claim about the issue. If you believe a counterargument is plausible and likely to be raised by your readers, make sure you've responded to it. Your response need not be lengthy, but it should let readers know that you've considered the counterargument and found it less effective than the argument you're making.

Peer Review: Improve Your Argumentative Essay

One of the biggest challenges writers face is reading their own work as a reader rather than as the writer. Because you know what you're trying to say, you'll find it easy to understand your draft. To determine what you should do to revise your draft, ask a friend or classmate to read your essay and answer the following questions.

Purpose	1. How do you interpret my purpose for writing? Does my goal seem to be to convince or to persuade?
	2. Is my overall claim plausible and debatable? Do you agree with what I had to say? If not, what should I do to convince you?
	3. Do the reasons I've offered to support my claim seem sufficient and appropriate?
Readers	4. Did you find the issue significant? Why or why not?
	5. Does my reasoning seem sound? Did you catch any fallacies?
	6. Have I used argumentative appeals appropriately and effectively? Should I consider making any other kinds of appeals?
Sources	7. Does the evidence I've offered to support my appeals make sense? Can I add or clarify anything to help you understand the argument better? Do you think any of the evidence is unnecessary?
	8. Do my sources strike you as reliable and appropriate? Does any of the evidence I've used seem questionable? Have I relied on any sources too heavily?
	9. Is it clear which ideas and information are my own and which came from my sources?
Context	10. Have I clearly introduced and effectively handled counterarguments? Did I present them fairly?
	11. How familiar were you with this issue before reading my essay? Do I need to provide more (or less) background information or context? Did I fail to include any reasons or evidence that you expected?
	12. Could I strengthen any of my appeals by bringing in design elements, such as photographs or tables?

For each of the points listed above, ask your reviewers to provide concrete advice about what you should do to improve your draft. It can help if you ask them to adopt the role of an editor — someone who is working with you to improve your draft. You can read more about these and other collaborative activities in Chapter 4.

@ Download or print this Peer Review activity at bedfordstmartins.com/conversation.

ENSURE THE INTEGRITY OF YOUR ARGUMENT

Carefully review the reasons and evidence you've offered to support your overall claim. Then review the list of common logical fallacies starting on page 435. Make sure that your argument is free of these fallacies. Even an otherwise strong argument can fail to convince or persuade readers if it relies in part on questionable argumentative strategies.

✳ Student Essay

Donovan Mikrot, "Download This: Why Digital Rights Management is a Bad Idea for Hollywood"

The following argumentative essay was written by featured writer Donovan Mikrot. You can follow Donovan's efforts to write his essay by visiting **bedfordstmartins.com/conversation**. You can read excerpts of interviews in which he discusses his work on his essay, read the assignment, and read drafts of his essay.

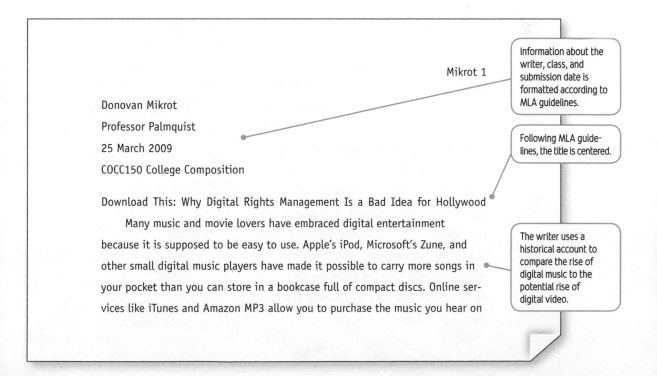

Mikrot 1

Donovan Mikrot

Professor Palmquist

25 March 2009

COCC150 College Composition

Download This: Why Digital Rights Management Is a Bad Idea for Hollywood

    Many music and movie lovers have embraced digital entertainment because it is supposed to be easy to use. Apple's iPod, Microsoft's Zune, and other small digital music players have made it possible to carry more songs in your pocket than you can store in a bookcase full of compact discs. Online services like iTunes and Amazon MP3 allow you to purchase the music you hear on

Information about the writer, class, and submission date is formatted according to MLA guidelines.

Following MLA guidelines, the title is centered.

The writer uses a historical account to compare the rise of digital music to the potential rise of digital video.

Mikrot 2

the radio or at a club in just a few seconds, or to find new artists that might interest you. Recently, these services have made digital music even more accessible by removing the digital rights management (DRM) software codes that restrict purchased files to a limited number of computers or MP3 players, allowing listeners to enjoy their music on a wide range of devices while still keeping it affordable—and ending a standoff between copyright holders and consumers that for years seemed impossible to resolve.

These developments in digital music have paved the way for a similar rise in digital video. Like MP3 players, portable video players make movies and TV shows easy to watch anywhere, anytime—but they are still under heavy DRM restrictions (Manjoo). Unlike CDs, DVDs cannot be "ripped" easily or legally to create digital files for personal use (Breen). If you own a DVD but want to watch the movie on your iPod, iPhone, or BlackBerry, you'll have to purchase another copy of the movie specifically for that device. Understandably, many movie lovers are upset about copy restrictions on digital video. Is it fair, they ask, to pay for new copies of movies they already own? It isn't fair, nor is it reasonable. Hollywood studios should follow the lead of the music industry and work to eliminate DRM on their digital movies and TV shows.

A sidebar provides a history of developments in digital rights management, allowing the writer to provide information that would not easily fit into the main text of the essay.

The writer contrasts the ease with which consumers can use digital music on different players with restrictions on digital video.

Following MLA guidelines, the author is identified in parentheses.

The writer makes his main point.

DRM Timeline

1984: The "Betamax defense" establishes that technology companies are not responsible for users' copyright infringements.

1998: Congress passes the Digital Millennium Copyright Act (DMCA).

1999: Napster is sued for violations of the DMCA.

2001: *Universal v. Reimerdes* permanently bans software that would unlock DVD content.

2003: A technology Web forum censors discussion about how to get around iTunes' DRM.

2004: Apple disables the Real-Network program Harmony, which tried to sell music compatible with iPods.

2005: Supreme Court rules that file-sharing software companies may be held liable for users' copyright infringement.

2005: Music companies seek to change the pricing on songs sold through iTunes; Apple refuses.

2006: The Motion Picture Association of America sues Load-'N'-Go, a company that loads DVDs onto iPods.

2008: Music companies allow Amazon's online MP3 store to sell albums without DRM.

2008: RealNetworks is forced to stop selling software that allows users to save DVDs on their computers.

2009: Apple agrees to institute flexible pricing on iTunes; in return, music studios allow Apple to sell DRM-free music.

Mikrot 3

The origins of the digital rights management issue go back to concerns about piracy in the earliest days of digital music. In 1998, Congress passed the Digital Millennium Copyright Act (DMCA), which had two components: it banned the act of removing DRM restrictions from digital files without permission, along with any software and hardware that could perform this action (Electronic Frontier Foundation 1). While this might seem like a reasonable measure to protect against illegal downloading, in reality the statute "reaches too far, chilling a wide variety of activities in ways Congress did not intend," according to the Electronic Frontier Foundation (EFF), a group that monitors the uses and abuses of digital rights policies (14). EFF attorney Fred Von Lohmann adds that before the DMCA, innovators were free to develop ground-breaking new technologies like the VCR without permission from Hollywood studios — even though VCRs allowed people to record and share TV shows. Because VCRs also had many other purposes, such as making and watching home videos, studios' charges of copyright infringement didn't hold up in court. At the time, this was known as the Betamax defense: "So long as your product is capable of substantial noninfringing uses, you will not be held responsible for infringements committed by end users you do not control" (Von Lohmann). This defense helped inventors stay on the right side of the law while they created a whole range of new technologies, and it still protected the copyrights of film and TV studios.

As digital music and video gained popularity, inventors assumed that the same rules would apply to the new hardware and software they developed for digital files. Instead, the DMCA lets music, computer, gaming, and other companies restrict technology and research that could potentially be used to get around their DRM — including research that would help address computer security issues (EFF). Inventors' hands are tied by the DMCA, and consumers are deprived of innovative new products that have plenty of legitimate uses, such as files that are already distributed without any DRM, simply because the tech-

> A partial quotation is used to support the writer's observation that DRM chills innovation.

> The writer identifies the source of the partial quotation and indicates why the group is viewed as an authority on the issue.

> A reason supports the writer's overall claim.

Mikrot 4

nology could be used in an illegal way. If companies want to protect their copyrighted content from piracy, they need to develop a solution that doesn't interfere with technological innovation.

> **A second reason supports the writer's overall claim.**

In addition to hurting inventors, Hollywood's insistence on DRM hurts consumers, who often find themselves out of luck when the videos they purchased for one device won't work on another. While most music CDs can be "ripped" to create digital files for personal use on a computer or an MP3 player, DVDs and Blu-Ray discs are protected by DRM, making it illegal to create a copy for personal use — something that would normally be allowed under the Fair Use guidelines of copyright law (Breen). In essence, as Stuart Andrews, a critic of DRM, notes, these DMCA-enforced restrictions end up dictating "what you're not allowed to do with your purchases and where you're not allowed to do it." Andrews asks, "Imagine what you'd have thought of a store that sold discs that work on your . . . player now, but weren't guaranteed to work on next year's models. . . . Why, you might think, would you have bought anything from a place like that?" If you purchase the right to listen to a song or watch a movie, it shouldn't matter which device you use to play it, part of the reason the music industry wisely decided to remove DRM from its digital files.

> **A third reason supports the writer's overall claim.**

The interoperability that CDs and DRM-free music files now allow isn't matched in digital video, which discourages people from buying digital movies and TV shows from online retailers. Although DRM was initially meant as an antipiracy measure, critics argue that restrictive DRM can actually drive otherwise law-abiding customers to pirate digital files out of frustration (Manjoo). Christopher Breen of Macworld.com notes,

> **Supporting evidence is provided in the form of a block quotation.**

> Pirates will be pirates and keel-hauling their youngest members does little except make their behavior more sympathetic. What seems to have worked, however, are measures of flexibility. . . . Make prices reasonable enough and digital rights management truly manageable, and the vast majority of people will choose to purchase media rather than steal it.

Mikrot 5

In other words, antipiracy measures that rely on restrictive DRM end up affecting average consumers more than they affect illegal downloaders, making DRM
both annoying for consumers and counterproductive for media companies.

In addition to inconveniencing customers and stifling innovation, DRM
can also hurt media companies by affecting how their products are priced and
distributed. The music industry learned this in a very clear way when Apple's
iTunes became the most popular online music source in the country, allowing
Apple to dictate universal 99-cent pricing for each DRM-locked song it sold,
even though the music industry wanted to charge more for more popular
songs. Inadvertently, DRM gave one company (Apple) a near monopoly that
allowed it to control the music industry's distribution channels and reduce
their profits for its own benefit — a situation that held until just recently,
when Amazon's DRM-free online music store emerged as a viable competitor
(Manjoo). If Hollywood studios aren't quicker to realize that they, too, need to
give consumers more freedom and a fairer system, they'll be heading into the
same sort of situation the music industry just resolved.

> A fourth reason supports the writer's overall claim.

To address consumer concerns and the growing market for digital video, a
collection of studios, technology companies, and retailers has formed the Digital Entertainment Content Ecosystem (DECE), to create a "new generation of
DRM" that would allow people to play movies and shows they've purchased on
any authorized DVD player, video player, phone, or computer they own
(Shiels). To date, however, Apple has refused to join the DECE, suggesting that
it sees little value in the DECE approach and setting the stage for continuing
consumer frustration (Manjoo). Although its goals are admirable, the DECE
must recognize that a new form of DRM is not the answer.

> The writer addresses a potential solution that, he suggests, is unlikely to succeed.

While retailers and copyright holders may think that DRM stops unrestricted files from falling into the hands of illegal downloaders, the opposite
also appears to be true: DRM actually encourages piracy by frustrating legitimate users with needless restrictions. Removing DRM — and the frustration felt

Mikrot 6

In his conclusion, the writer provides a summary of reasons supporting the removal of DRM from digital video.

by consumers — might actually help studios of all sizes turn a profit by giving films and TV shows a wider audience. There is simply too much opportunity — and potential for making money — for the entertainment industry to allow DRM to hobble the growth of digital video. If DRM restrictions are eased, innovation will flourish once again. Better players will be produced. Better video services will emerge. Better technologies will be developed for digital video formats. And consumers will enjoy lower prices. In the long run, film and TV lovers — and the companies that supply the media they love — will be far better off without DRM. If Hollywood studios and video retailers save their use of the DMCA for true cases of pirating, rather than using it to keep consumers from enjoying their videos and innovators from creating new technologies, they will regain the trust of consumers and will ultimately be more profitable.

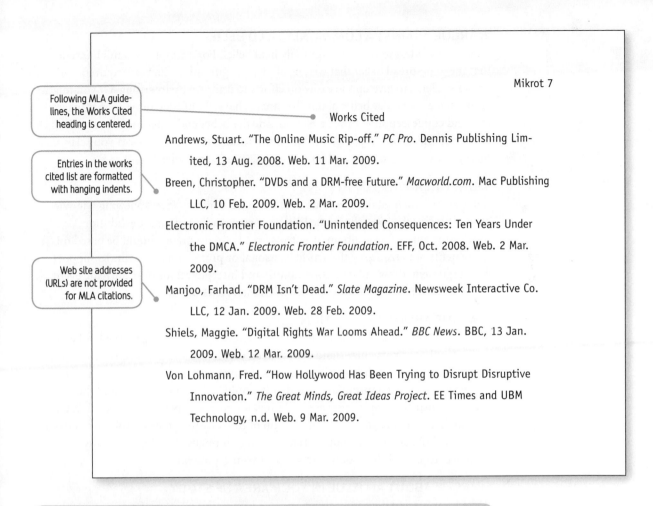

Mikrot 7

Following MLA guidelines, the Works Cited heading is centered.

Entries in the works cited list are formatted with hanging indents.

Web site addresses (URLs) are not provided for MLA citations.

Works Cited

Andrews, Stuart. "The Online Music Rip-off." *PC Pro*. Dennis Publishing Limited, 13 Aug. 2008. Web. 11 Mar. 2009.

Breen, Christopher. "DVDs and a DRM-free Future." *Macworld.com*. Mac Publishing LLC, 10 Feb. 2009. Web. 2 Mar. 2009.

Electronic Frontier Foundation. "Unintended Consequences: Ten Years Under the DMCA." *Electronic Frontier Foundation*. EFF, Oct. 2008. Web. 2 Mar. 2009.

Manjoo, Farhad. "DRM Isn't Dead." *Slate Magazine*. Newsweek Interactive Co. LLC, 12 Jan. 2009. Web. 28 Feb. 2009.

Shiels, Maggie. "Digital Rights War Looms Ahead." *BBC News*. BBC, 13 Jan. 2009. Web. 12 Mar. 2009.

Von Lohmann, Fred. "How Hollywood Has Been Trying to Disrupt Disruptive Innovation." *The Great Minds, Great Ideas Project*. EE Times and UBM Technology, n.d. Web. 9 Mar. 2009.

✳ Project Ideas

The following suggestions provide means of focusing your work on an argumentative essay or another type of argumentative document.

Suggestions for Essays

1. ARGUE ABOUT A SOCIAL TREND

Identify and discuss the relevance of a social trend, such as text-messaging, joining social-networking Web sites, or dressing in a particular manner. Then make an argument about (a) the advisability of following the trend, (b) the likely effects—short- or long-term—of the trend on society, or (c) the likelihood that the trend will have a lasting impact on society. Use evidence from online conversations and your personal observations to support your argument.

2. ARGUE AGAINST A COMMONLY HELD BELIEF

Urge your readers to reject a commonly held belief. For example, you might argue that the widespread belief that writing ability is a gift rather than an acquired skill causes students to give up too easily on efforts to improve their writing. Or you might argue that a particular belief about the innate character of men or women is inaccurate and condescending. In your essay, define the belief and make an overall claim about the effects of accepting it. Offer reasons and evidence to support your claim. Base your appeals on logic and on principles, values, and beliefs.

3. URGE READERS TO PATRONIZE THE ARTS

Make an argument about the value of attending a play or concert, viewing a movie or watching a television show, attending a poetry reading or an art exhibition, or purchasing a new music album or video game. Your argument should be based on the benefits of patronizing the arts for personal or professional growth. To support your argument, draw on your observations and interpretations of the artistic event or object. You might also use evidence from interviews or surveys.

4. ARGUE ABOUT A DEFINITION

Make an argument about a definition, such as how a problem or an issue has been defined or how a particular standard has been developed and applied. For example, you might argue that characterizations of state support for public education as a financial issue are inappropriate, and that it would be better to understand the issue as one of ensuring that citizens are well prepared to participate in a democracy. Or you might argue that your state's definition of intoxication (for example, .08 percent blood alcohol content) is inappropriate, and that it ought to be higher or lower. Use evidence from published sources to support your argument.

5. ARGUE ABOUT AN ISSUE IN YOUR AREA OF STUDY

Write an argumentative essay about an issue in a discipline or profession in which you have an interest. For example, if you are interested in human resources, you might argue about the implications of allowing employers to access employees' genetic profiles. The issue you choose should be under debate in the discipline or profession, so be sure to search professional or academic journals and online conversations among members of the discipline or profession for prevailing arguments.

Suggestions for Other Genres

6. WRITE AN OPINION COLUMN ABOUT A NEW LAW OR REGULATION

In an opinion column, identify a recently passed law or a new regulation (federal, state, or local), and discuss its potential impact. Offer a brief summary evaluation of its appropriateness or likely effects and make recommendations to your readers about how to respond to the law. For example, you might argue that a new law is so flawed that it should be repealed. Or you might argue that only by providing adequate funding to a local or state agency can a regulation be enforced effectively. Use evidence from government documents to support your argument.

7. WRITE A LETTER TO THE EDITOR ABOUT SUPPORTING A LOCAL INITIATIVE

In a brief letter to the editor (no longer than 300 words), argue that readers should support a local initiative, such as a food drive or a get-out-the-vote effort. Your letter should clearly state your overall claim and offer reasons to accept it. Because of the brevity of the letter, you should limit your use of evidence and rely primarily on reasoning.

8. WRITE A LETTER TO THE EDITOR ABOUT A PUBLISHED ARTICLE, EDITORIAL, OR OPINION COLUMN

Write a letter to the editor that responds to an article, editorial, or opinion column. In your letter, briefly summarize the argument made in the published piece and then offer a counterargument that is well supported by reasoning and evidence. Use evidence from the published piece as well as from other published sources and your personal experience.

9. WRITE A BLOG ENTRY ABOUT AN ISSUE RAISED IN ANOTHER BLOG

In a blog, argue about an issue addressed by the author of another blog. For example, you might take issue with an argument about the economic and political trade-offs of government rescues of failed financial institutions. Or you might argue about the advisability of joining social-networking Web sites such as Facebook or MySpace. Your blog entry should link to the blog entry that raised the issue, as well as to other relevant blogs. Use evidence from blogs and other published sources to support your argument. You should refer to your sources by using phrases such as "in an article published in *Newsweek* on July 23, 2007, Ann Smith argues" or by linking directly to the source.

10. CREATE A PUBLIC SERVICE ADVERTISEMENT

Create a full-page ad suitable for a magazine or Web site that urges readers to take action on a social issue, such as adoption or hunger. Your ad should use visual images and only enough text to clearly identify the issue and convey your argument to your readers. For inspiration, examine the ads shown on pages 407–410.

In Summary: Writing an Argumentative Essay

○ **Find a conversation and listen in.**

- Explore disagreements (p. 425).
- Track online conversations (p. 426).
- Ask questions about promising issues (p. 428).

○ **Build your argument.**

- Define your overall claim (p. 430).
- Develop reasons to accept your overall claim (p. 431).
- Choose evidence to support your reasons (p. 432).
- Identify and consider opposing claims (p. 434).
- Ensure the integrity of your argument (p. 435).

○ **Prepare a draft.**

- Make an argumentative claim (p. 438).
- Appeal to your readers (p. 439).
- Address counterarguments (p. 442).
- Consider genre and design (p. 443).
- Frame your argument (p. 444).

○ **Review and improve your draft.**

- Consider your overall claim (p. 445).
- Review your reasons, evidence, and appeals (p. 445).
- Examine your treatment of counterarguments (p. 445).
- Ensure the integrity of your argument (p. 447).

PART THREE

Working with Sources

11

Preparing to Use Sources in an Academic Essay

▶▶ With the growth of the Web and increasing amounts of information available through library databases, writers have become far less worried about finding enough sources than about finding the right sources. This chapter explores strategies for collecting information for a writing project and then looks at how you can keep track of that information.

How Should I Focus My Search for Sources?

As you prepare to search for sources, it's best to have an idea of what you're looking for. Focus your efforts to collect, read, evaluate, and take notes on sources by developing a research question—a brief question that asks about a specific aspect of your subject, reflects your writing situation, and is narrow enough to allow you to collect information in time to meet your deadlines.

Your research question will reflect the role you've adopted as a writer (see Part Two). To develop your research question, you'll generate ideas for potential research questions and assess each one in light of your interests, role, and writing situation.

Generate Potential Research Questions

Start to develop your research question by generating a list of questions about the conversation you've decided to join. Most research questions begin with the word *what, why, when, where, who,* or *how.* Some research questions use the word *would* or *could* to ask whether something is possible. Still others use the word *should* to analyze the appropriateness of a particular action, policy, procedure, or decision. Questions can focus on the following:

- **Information:** what is known—and not known—about a subject
- **History:** what has occurred in the past that is relevant to a subject
- **Assumptions:** what conclusions—merited or not—writers and readers have already made about a subject
- **Goals:** what the writers and readers involved in this conversation want to see happen (or not happen)
- **Outcomes:** what has happened so far, or what is likely to happen
- **Policies:** what the best procedures are for carrying out actions or for making decisions

Questions can also lead you to engage in the following kinds of thinking processes:

- **Reflecting:** considering the significance of a subject
- **Reporting:** seeking information; conveying what is known about a subject
- **Analyzing:** looking for similarities and differences among subjects or aspects of a subject; asking what leads to a specific result; asking about a series of events
- **Evaluating:** asking about strengths and weaknesses, advantages and disadvantages, or appropriateness

- **Problem solving:** defining problems, considering the outcomes of a problem, assessing potential solutions, and/or offering solutions

- **Advocating:** advancing arguments about a subject

By combining a specific focus, such as assumptions, with a specific type of thinking process, such as problem solving, you can create carefully tailored research questions, such as the ones that featured writer Jennie Tillson considered for her essay about the cost of college.

> What assumptions have shaped debates about rising tuitions?
>
> What assumptions have worked against a resolution of this problem?
>
> Why have college administrators been unable (or unwilling) to control tuition hikes?
>
> Why do so many families take out loans to pay for a college education?
>
> What can the government do to help reduce tuition costs?
>
> What can students do to manage tuition costs?

As you begin to generate potential research questions, ask yourself whether you are interested in focusing on such concerns as the current state of knowledge about your subject, its history, the assumptions informing the conversation about the subject, the goals of writers involved in the conversation, its likely outcomes, or policies associated with the subject. Then reflect on the range of options you have for thinking about these concerns. Are you interested, for example, in learning what others have done or are doing? Do you want to conduct analyses such as comparing alternatives, looking for cause-and-effect relationships, or tracing a sequence of events? Are you intrigued by the prospect of defining or solving problems?

Specific question words might also help you get started. If you are interested in conducting an analysis, for example, ask questions using the words *what, why, when, where, who,* and *how.* If you want to explore goals and outcomes, use the word *would* or *could.* If the conversation focuses on determining an appropriate course of action, generate questions using the word *should.* Consider the differences among these questions:

> **What** are the benefits of a college education?
>
> **Would** it be feasible to require colleges and universities to commit 5 percent of their endowments to financial aid?
>
> **Should** the U.S. Congress pass legislation to control tuition costs?

Each question would lead to differences in how to search for and select sources of information, what role to adopt as a writer, and how to organize and design the document.

Select and Refine Your Question

After reviewing your potential research questions, select a question that interests you, is consistent with the role you have adopted, and is appropriate for your writing situation. Then refine your question by referring to shared assumptions and existing conditions, narrowing its scope, and conducting preliminary searches.

REFLECT ON YOUR WRITING SITUATION

As you consider potential research questions, pay attention to your purpose and role. Your efforts to collect information should help you accomplish your purpose and address your readers' needs, interests, values, and beliefs. Keep in mind, however, that as you learn more about your subject, you might refine your purpose. In turn, that might lead to changes in your research question. If you think of your research question as a flexible guide—as a question subject to revision—you can increase the effectiveness of your document.

Sources help writers refine their purposes and create research questions that address their readers' needs, interests, values, and beliefs.

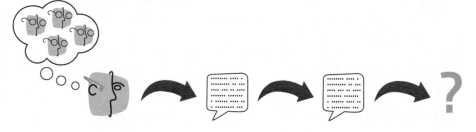

REFER TO SHARED ASSUMPTIONS AND EXISTING CONDITIONS

You can refine your research question by calling attention to assumptions that have been made by the community of writers and readers who are addressing your subject, or by referring to existing conditions relevant to your subject. Note the difference among these three versions of featured writer Ali Bizzul's research question about the health risks associated with weight gain among football players.

Original Question:
Why would football players risk their health — and even their lives — by putting on extra weight?

Alternative 1:
Given the widespread belief among coaches that extra bulk might reduce performance on the field, why would football players risk their health — and even their lives — by putting on extra weight?

Alternative 2:
In the face of recent high-profile deaths among college and professional football players, why would football players risk their health — and even their lives — by putting on extra weight?

As you refine your research question, experiment with using qualifying words and phrases such as the following:

Mix . . .	and Match
Although	we know that . . .
Because	it is uncertain . . .
Even though	it is clear that . . .
Given that	studies indicate . . .
If	recent events . . .
Now that	it has been shown . . .
Since	the lack of . . .
While	we cannot . . .

NARROW YOUR SCOPE

Early research questions typically lack focus. You can narrow the scope of your question by looking for vague words and phrases and replacing them with more specific words or phrases. The process of moving from a broad research question to one that might be addressed effectively in an academic essay might produce the following sequence:

Original Question:
What is behind the increased popularity of women's sports?

Refined:
What has led to the increased popularity of women's sports in colleges and universities?

Further Refined:
How has Title IX increased opportunities for women athletes in American colleges and universities?

In this example, the writer has narrowed the scope of the research question in two ways. First, the writer has shifted its focus from women's sports in general to women's sports in American colleges and universities. Second, the writer has moved from a general focus on the increased popularity of women's sports to a more specific focus on the opportunities brought about by Title IX, the federal legislation that mandated equal opportunities for women athletes.

CONDUCT PRELIMINARY SEARCHES

One of the best ways to test your research question is to conduct some preliminary searches in an online library catalog or database or on the Web. If you locate a vast amount of information in your searches, you might need to revise your question so that it focuses on a more manageable aspect of the subject. In contrast, if you find almost nothing, you might need to expand the scope of your question.

How Can I Develop a Search Plan?

Once you've created your research question, you'll need to make decisions about

- the types of sources you want to collect (such as books, articles, and opinion columns)

- the types of search tools (such as library catalogs, databases, and Web search sites) and research methods (such as browsing library shelves, consulting librarians, or conducting surveys) you will use

- the schedule you will follow as you conduct your search

Your decisions will become the heart of your search plan — a brief, informal plan that records your ideas about how to locate and collect information on a specific conversation about your subject. As you develop your plan, keep your research question in mind. Doing so will help you determine what types of sources, resources, and search strategies will be most productive.

Identify Relevant Types of Sources

Writers use information found in a variety of sources — electronic, print, and field — to support the points they make in their documents. To identify relevant sources for your writing project, consider the nature of the conversation you are joining, the scope and timeliness of your subject, the information you'll need to develop your ideas, and the evidence you'll need to support your points.

CONSIDER YOUR CONVERSATION

Ask yourself about the conversation you've decided to join. Does it focus on a highly specialized issue within a scholarly discipline, such as a discussion of gene splicing in biology? If so, the best sources usually are scholarly books and journal articles. Does it address a subject that has broad appeal, such as transportation problems in your state or region? If so, you can draw on a much wider range of sources, including newspaper and magazine articles, editorials and opinion columns, blogs, and Web sites.

CONSIDER THE SCOPE AND TIMELINESS OF YOUR SUBJECT

Is your subject broad, or is it highly focused? Is it of enduring interest? Some subjects, such as funding for higher education or reducing alcohol consumption by college students, tend to be discussed over an extended period of time in a wide range of sources. If your subject focuses on a recent event, however, it might be best to turn to magazine and newspaper articles, the Web, blogs, observation, surveys, or interviews.

CONSIDER WHAT YOU NEED TO LEARN

If your subject is unfamiliar to you, look for sources that offer general overviews or discuss important aspects of the subject. For example, the introductory chapters of scholarly books often provide general overviews of a subject, even when the rest of the book focuses on a narrow aspect of the subject. You can also look for overviews of a subject in magazine articles, in professional journal articles, and on the Web.

CONSIDER THE EVIDENCE YOU'LL NEED

As you consider what you want to say about your subject, think about the kind of evidence other writers have used to make their points. If most writers have used numerical data found in scholarly research reports, for example, be sure to search for those kinds of reports. Similarly, if you notice that writers tend to refer to expert opinion, search for documents written by recognized experts in the field.

Identify Appropriate Search Tools and Research Methods

Once you've identified the types of sources that seem most relevant, determine which search tools and research methods you might use to locate those sources. In general, you can use three sets of resources to locate information.

- **Electronic search tools,** such as online library catalogs, databases, and Web search sites, allow you to search and browse for sources using a computer. Electronic search tools provide access to publication information about—and in some cases to the complete text of—print and digital sources.

- **Print resources,** such as bibliographies, indexes, encyclopedias, dictionaries, handbooks, almanacs, and atlases, can be found in library reference and periodical rooms. Unlike electronic search tools, which typically cover recent publications, many print resources provide information about publications over several decades — and in some cases over more than a century.

- **Field research methods** allow you to collect information firsthand. These methods include conducting observations, interviews, and surveys; corresponding with experts; attending public events and performances; and viewing or listening to television and radio programs.

Featured writer Hannah Steiner, who wrote an informative essay about the use of hydrogen fuels (see p. 197), knew that her topic would require recent sources. As she put together her search plan, she decided to search databases for recent scholarly articles and to look for Web sites that reported recent research. To obtain the most up-to-date information, she also scheduled an interview with a professor of engineering at her university who had expertise in the area.

Review Your Plan

Your search plan might be an informal set of notes that will guide you as you gather information, or it might be a set of step-by-step instructions complete with details such as keywords to search, interview questions to ask, and observation forms to fill out. The choice is yours, but no matter how informal your plan, you should write it down. Doing so will help you remember the decisions you've made as you've prepared to collect your sources.

After developing your search plan, schedule time to search for and collect information. Next to each activity — such as searching databases, searching the Web, searching a library catalog, browsing library shelves, and conducting an interview — identify start dates and projected completion dates. Creating a schedule will help you budget and manage your time.

Share your plan with your instructor, your supervisor, your classmates, or a librarian. Each might suggest additional search tools, research methods, shortcuts, and alternative research strategies for your project. Take notes on the feedback you receive, and, if necessary, revise your plan.

How Can I Keep Track of My Sources?

If you've ever forgotten a phone number or misplaced tickets to a concert, you know how frustrating it can be to lose something. It can be just as frustrating to lose your interview notes or forget where you found a quotation or fact. Your writer's notebook is a good place to keep track of the information you collect during a writing project. You can also organize and save your sources, create a working bibliography, and create an annotated bibliography.

Manage Print Materials

Depending on the scope of your writing project, you might accumulate a great deal of print information, such as

- your written notes (in a notebook, on loose pieces of paper, on sticky notes, and so on)
- printouts from Web pages and databases
- articles sent through a library's fax-on-demand or interlibrary loan service
- printed word-processing documents, such as your outline and rough drafts
- books, magazines, newspapers, brochures, pamphlets, and government documents
- photocopies of articles, book chapters, and other documents
- letters, printed e-mail messages, and survey results

Rather than letting all this material build up in messy piles on your desk or stuffing it into folders in your backpack, create a filing system to keep track of your print documents. Filing systems can range from well-organized piles of paper labeled with sticky notes to three-ring binders to file cabinets filled with neatly labeled file folders.

Regardless of the approach you take, keep the following principles in mind:

- **Create an organizational scheme that allows you to locate your print materials.** Decide whether you want to group materials by topic, by date, by argument, by type of material (Web pages, photocopies, original documents, field sources, and so on), or by author.
- **Stick with your organizational scheme.** You'll find it difficult to locate materials if you use different approaches at different points in your writing project.
- **Make sure printed documents provide complete publication information.** If a source doesn't contain publication information, write it on the document. Publication information includes author, title, publisher, place and date of publication, and—for a Web source—sponsoring organization and URL.
- **Date your notes.** Indicating the date when you recorded information can help you reconstruct what you might have been doing while you took the note.

Dates are also essential for documenting Web sources and other online sources.

- **Write a brief note on each of your print materials.** Indicate how it might contribute to your project.

Manage Digital Materials

As you gather digital information, keep it organized. The simplest strategy is to store notes and copies in a single computer folder. Use descriptive file names to save your work. Rather than naming a file "Notes 1.doc," for instance, name it "Interview Notes from John Garcia, April 22.doc." However, the single-folder approach might not work well for larger projects. Scrolling through a long list of files in the folder will make it difficult to find a single document easily. As a result, you might find it more efficient to create multiple folders to hold related files.

⌞ Saving Work in a Single Folder

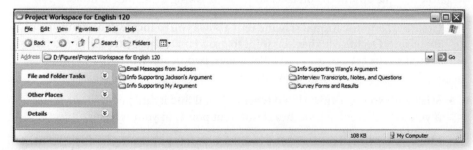

⌞ Saving Work in Multiple Folders

To save electronic sources, you can copy and paste; download; or use e-mail, bookmarking tools, or capture tools.

Copying and Pasting. You can use the Copy and Paste commands in your browser and word-processing program to save electronic documents and graphics. Be sure to copy and paste the URL and record the date when you accessed a Web page so that you can return to it if necessary and cite it appropriately.

Downloading. Downloading electronic sources to a hard drive, a flash drive, or a writable CD or DVD allows you to open them in a Web browser or word-processing program at a later point. This might save you time toward the end of your writing project, particularly when you are drafting your document.

The method for downloading copies of sources will vary according to the type of electronic source you're viewing.

- You can save Web pages using the File > Save As . . . or File > Save Page As . . . menu in your browser.

- You can save images and other media materials from the Web by right-clicking (in Windows) or command-clicking (on the Macintosh) on the item you want to save and selecting Save Image As . . . or Save Picture As . . . (or some similar command) from the pop-up menu.

- You can mark and save database records returned by a search.

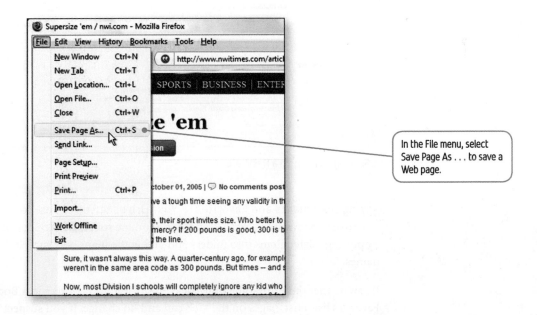

In the File menu, select Save Page As . . . to save a Web page.

Remember that saving a source does not automatically record the URL or the date on which you viewed the source for the first time. Be sure to record that information in your writing log, in your working bibliography (see p. 474), or in a document in the folder where you've saved your files.

Using E-mail. You can e-mail yourself messages containing electronic documents you've found in your research. Some databases, such as those from EBSCO and OCLC/FirstSearch, allow you to e-mail the text of selected records directly from the database.

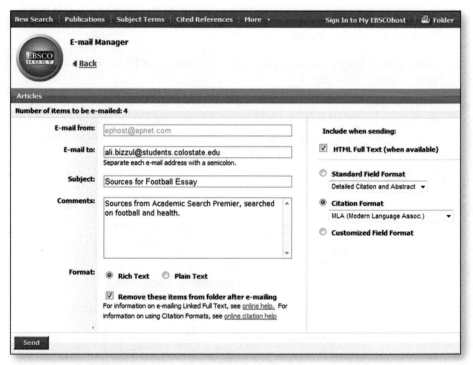

⌐ Sending E-mail from a Database

Saving Bookmarks and Favorites in Your Browser. You can use your Web browser's Bookmarks or Favorites list to keep track of online sources. Keep these lists organized by putting related items into folders and giving the items on your list descriptive names.

Be aware that there are some drawbacks to storing your sources in a Bookmarks or Favorites list. First, pages on the Web can and do change. If you suspect that the page you want to mark might change before you complete your writing project, download or print it so that you won't lose its content. Second, some Web pages are generated by database programs. In such cases, you might not be able to return to the page using a Bookmarks or Favorites list. A URL like the following usually indicates that a Web page is generated by a database program:

> http://firstsearch.oclc.org/FUNC/QUERY:%7Fnext=NEXTCMD%7F%22/FUNC/SRCH_RESULTS%22%7F
> entityListType=0%7Fentitycntr=1%7FentityItemCount=0%7F%3Asessionid=1265726%7F4%7F/fsres4.txt

Although the beginning portion of this long string of characters looks like a normal URL, the majority of the characters are used by the database program to determine which records to display on a page. In many cases, the URL works only while you are conducting your search. If you add such a URL to your Bookmarks or Favorites list, there's a good chance it won't work later.

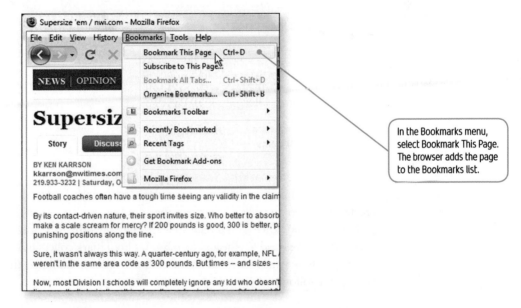

In the Bookmarks menu, select Bookmark This Page. The browser adds the page to the Bookmarks list.

Using Personal Bookmarking Sites. Personal bookmarking sites allow you to save your bookmarks to a Web site at no charge and view them from any computer connected to the Web. Some of these sites, such as Google Bookmarks, allow you to access your bookmarks through a toolbar. The Google toolbar (toolbar.google.com) provides access to your bookmarks as well as tools for organizing them, such as labels.

If you use more than one computer, you can benefit from the following sites:

Ask.com's MyStuff: mystuff.ask.com

Google Bookmarks: www.google.com/bookmarks/

Yahoo! Bookmarks: bookmarks.yahoo.com

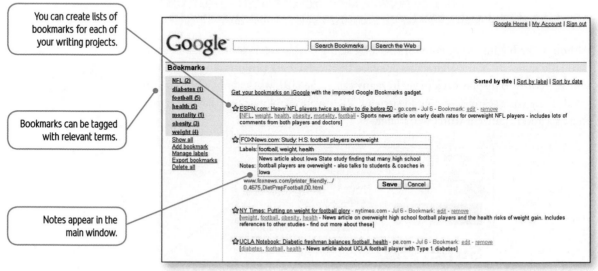

You can create lists of bookmarks for each of your writing projects.

Bookmarks can be tagged with relevant terms.

Notes appear in the main window.

⌐ **Google Bookmarks**

Using Social Bookmarking Sites. Social bookmarking sites allow you to create lists of bookmarks that other Web users can view. Most of these sites also allow you to create private bookmarks. For writers, the advantages of these sites include (1) the ability to save bookmarks and then view them at any time from any computer connected to the Web and (2) the ability to browse bookmark collections created by other users who share your interest in a subject. Leading social bookmarking Web sites include the following:

BlinkList: www.blinklist.com

ClipMarks: www.clipmarks.com

Delicious: delicious.com

StumbleUpon: www.stumbleupon.com

Using Web Capture Tools. A wide range of programs have been created to help writers keep track of the information they find online. Some of these programs work with your browser as toolbars or "add-ons" (a term used for programs that work within the Firefox browser). For example, most leading social bookmarking sites have created free tools that can be added to Internet Explorer and Firefox. By clicking on the ClipMark button, for instance, you can add a Web page—or portions of a page—to your collection of materials on ClipMarks. Some add-ons in Firefox offer powerful sets of tools for managing information. Both Zotero and ScrapBook allow you to save entire pages or parts of pages to your local computer. In addition, Zotero provides support for citing sources. Leading, no-fee Web capture tools include the following:

BlinkList Button: www.blinklist.com

ClipMarks Toolbar: clipmarks.com/install/

Delicious Tools: delicious.com/help/tools

ScrapBook Firefox Add-on: amb.vis.ne.jp/mozilla/scrapbook/

Zotero Firefox Add-on: www.zotero.org

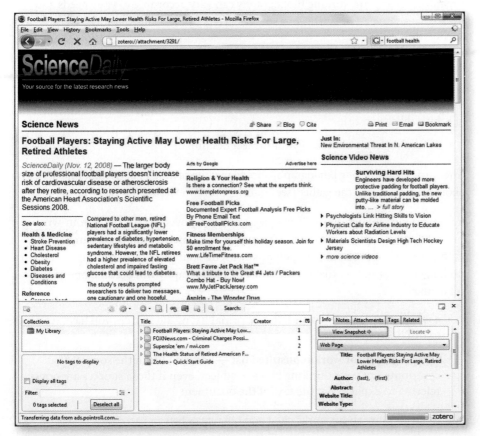

↳ **Zotero Firefox Add-on**

Backing Up Your Files. Whatever strategies you use to save and organize digital materials, replacing lost information takes time and effort. Avoid the risk of lost information by taking the time to make copies of your electronic files, saved Web pages, e-mail messages, and Bookmarks or Favorites lists.

Create a Working or an Annotated Bibliography

A bibliography is a list of sources with complete publication information, usually formatted according to the rules of a documentation system such as the Modern Language Association system (see Chapter 21) or the American Psychological Association system (see Chapter 22). As you start collecting information, create a working bibliography or an annotated bibliography to keep track of the sources you are using.

WORKING BIBLIOGRAPHIES

A working bibliography is a running list of the sources you've explored and plan to use in your writing project—with publication information for each source. The organization of your working bibliography can vary according to your needs and preferences. You can organize your sources in any of the following ways:

- in the order in which you collected your sources

- in categories

- by author

- by publication title

- according to an outline of your project document

The entries in a working bibliography should include as much publication information about a source as you can gather (see "Information You Should List in a Bibliography").

Your working bibliography will change significantly over the course of your writing project. As you explore and narrow your topic and, later, as you collect and work with your sources, you will add potentially useful sources and delete sources that are no longer relevant. Eventually, your working bibliography will become one of the following:

- **a works cited or references list**—a formal list of the sources you have referred to in a document

- **a bibliography or works consulted list**—a formal list of the sources that contributed to your thinking about a subject, even if those sources are not referred to explicitly in the text of the document

You can read more about works cited and references lists in Part Five.

TABLE 11.1
Information You Should List in a Bibliography

Type of Source	Information You Should List
All Sources	• Author(s) • Title • Publication year • Brief note — or annotation — describing or commenting on the source, indicating how you might use it in your document, or showing how it is related to other sources (for annotated bibliographies only)
Book	• Editor(s) of book (if applicable) • Publication city • Publisher • Series and series editor (if applicable) • Translator (if applicable) • Volume (if applicable) • Edition (if applicable)
Chapter in an Edited Book	• Chapter title • Publication city • Publisher • Editor(s) of book • Book title • Page numbers
Journal, Magazine, and Newspaper Article	• Journal title • Volume number or date • Issue number or date • Page numbers
Web Page, Blog Entry or Reply, Discussion Forum or Newsgroup Post, Email Message, and Chat Transcript	• URL • Access date (the date you read the source) • Sponsoring organization, if listed
Field Research	• Title (usually a description of the source, such as "Personal Interview with Ellen Page" or "Observation of Reid Vincent's Class at Dunn Elementary School") • Date (usually the date on which the field research was conducted)

@ The *Student Center for Joining the Conversation* Web site (**bedfordstmartins .com/conversation**) provides access to tools that allow you to save bibliographic information about each of your sources. With these tools, you can create a working bibliography formatted in either MLA or APA style.

Keeping your working bibliography up to date is a critical part of your writing process. It helps you keep track of your sources and increases the likelihood that you will cite all the sources you use in your document—an important contribution to your efforts to avoid plagiarism.

The first five sources from featured writer Ali Bizzul's working bibliography are shown in the following illustration.

Entries follow APA style
(see Chapter 22).

Bailes, J. E., Cantu, R. C., & Day, A. L. (2002). The neurosurgeon in sport: Awareness of the risks of heatstroke and dietary supplements. *Neurosurgery, 51*, 283–288. doi:10.1097/00006123-200208000-00002

Groeschen, T. (2008, October 17). Growing concern: Supersize me. *Cincinnati Enquirer*. Retrieved from http://news.cincinnati.com

Harp, J. B., & Hecht, L. (2005). Research letter: Obesity in the National Football League. *Journal of the American Medical Association, 293*, 1061–1062. doi:10.1001/jama.293.9.1061-b

Korth, J. (2006, January 29). A huge problem. *St. Petersburg Times*. Retrieved from http://tampabay.com/

Longman, J. (2007, November 30). Putting on weight for football glory. *New York Times*. Retrieved from http://www.nytimes.com

⌐ **Part of Ali Bizzul's Working Bibliography**

ANNOTATED BIBLIOGRAPHIES

An **annotated bibliography** provides a brief note about each of the sources you've listed, in addition to complete citation information. These notes, or annotations, are typically no longer than two or three sentences. The content, focus, and length of your annotations will reflect your purposes for creating an annotated bibliography.

- In some writing projects, you will submit an annotated bibliography to your instructor for review and comment. In this situation, your instructor will most likely expect a clear description of the content of each source and some indication of how you might use the source.

- In other writing projects, the annotated bibliography serves simply as a planning tool—a more detailed version of a working bibliography. As a result, your annotations might highlight key passages or information in a source, suggest how you can use information or ideas from the source, or emphasize relationships between sources.

- In still other projects, the annotated bibliography will be the final result of your efforts. In such cases, you would write your annotations for your readers, keeping their purposes, needs, interests, and backgrounds in mind.

An annotated bibliography is a useful tool even if you aren't required to submit it for a grade. By turning your working bibliography into an annotated bibliography, you can remind yourself of each source's information, ideas, and arguments and how the source might be used in your document.

The following annotated bibliography provides information that an instructor could use to assess a student's progress on a writing project.

Bailes, J. E., Cantu, R. C., & Day, A. L. (2002). The neurosurgeon in sport: Awareness of the risks of heatstroke and dietary supplements. *Neurosurgery, 51,* 283–288. doi:10.1097/00006123-200208000-00002

Bailes, Cantu, and Day discuss the rising numbers of heatstroke injuries and deaths among football players in the United States, and their study links some of these incidents to the use of dietary supplements. This source may help explain some of the extreme measures football players will take to gain or maintain weight, and the possibly fatal consequences of their decisions.

> Annotations provide brief summaries of the purpose and content of the sources.

Groeschen, T. (2008, October 17). Growing concern: Supersize me. *Cincinnati Enquirer.* Retrieved from http://news.cincinnati.com/

Groeschen interviews local experts in the Cincinnati area, including former NFL players, coaches, and team physicians, about the problem of weight gain among football players. He also cites alarming statistics from studies about obesity in young players. This article will help explain the perspectives of players and coaches themselves, showing that they regret focusing so much on their weight and that they're trying to help today's players stay healthy.

> Annotations are intended for the writer and the instructor. They indicate how and where the writer will use the source in the document.

Harp, J. B., & Hecht, L. (2005). Research letter: Obesity in the National Football League. *Journal of the American Medical Association, 293,* 1061-1062. doi:10.1001/jama.293.9.1061-b

Harp and Hecht studied obesity levels among NFL players during the 2003–2004 season. Their discussion includes the higher BMI (body mass index) of linemen and the potential health complications of excess weight for athletes. Their conclusions will help me demonstrate that weight gain is a problem even for professional players and poses serious risks to their health and safety.

⌐ Part of Ali Bizzul's Annotated Bibliography

In Summary: Preparing to Use Sources in an Academic Essay

○ Develop a research question (p. 460).

○ Plan your search for sources (p. 464).

○ Get feedback on your plan (p. 466).

○ Save and organize print and digital sources (p. 466).

○ Keep a working bibliography (p. 474).

○ Consider creating an annotated bibliography (p. 476).

12 Locating Sources

▶▶ Your search plan prepares you to begin collecting information. In this chapter, you'll explore strategies for locating information for a writing project. You'll find discussions of how to generate search terms; how to use online catalogs, databases, and the Web; how to take advantage of the print resources in a library; and how to use field research methods. As you consider the role these strategies might play in your writing project, keep in mind your writing situation and the conversation you've decided to join. Focusing on your purpose, readers, and context can help you make good decisions about whether and how to use the resources and search techniques discussed in this chapter.

How Can I Locate Sources Using Electronic Resources?

Writers can turn to four general sets of electronic resources to locate information about their subjects: library catalogs, databases, the Web, and media search sites. You can search these resources using techniques ranging from simple to advanced searches.

Generate Search Terms and Strategies

Regardless of your choice of electronic resource, the results of your searches will be only as good as your search terms. Even the best search tools can produce poor results—and all too often that's exactly what happens. To increase your chances of obtaining good results, spend time identifying search terms related to your subject and learning about the types of searches you might conduct.

IDENTIFY KEYWORDS AND PHRASES

You can identify useful search terms by building on your research question (see p. 40) or thesis statement (see Chapter 15) or by using a range of idea-generating techniques, such as brainstorming, freewriting, looping, and clustering (see p. 33). Dwight Haynes, for example, used freewriting to generate ideas for his searches. Then he highlighted promising keywords and phrases.

> I'm most interested in finding sources that can help me understand why some approaches to reducing college drinking —and binge drinking in particular, although it's not the only problem (date rape, drunk driving, and falling out of windows or trees, for example, are related to too much drinking)—work better than others. What's been done by schools with successful programs? How much do those programs cost? And why haven't schools made more progress on this problem? Is it just something that college students have to go through? But if that's the case, why do so many students swear off drinking all together —or maybe it's just a case of extremes all around, with some people drinking too much and some people swearing off it even though they wouldn't mind having a beer now and then?

You can also generate search terms by using your research question or thesis statement as a starting point. Hannah Steiner, for example, typed her research question in a word-processing program, formatted the most important words and phrases in color, and then brainstormed a list of related words and phrases.

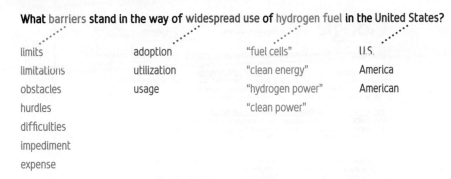

What barriers **stand in the way of** widespread use of hydrogen fuel **in the United States?**

limits	adoption	"fuel cells"	U.S.
limitations	utilization	"clean energy"	America
obstacles	usage	"hydrogen power"	American
hurdles		"clean power"	
difficulties			
impediment			
expense			

PLAN SIMPLE SEARCHES

Simple searches consist of entering one or more keywords or phrases in a search field and clicking on the search button. A simple search allows to you look for documents that contain a single word or phrase in the subject, title, text, or, in the case of databases, in other parts of a database record (see p. 488 for more information about databases). When you enter one or two words in the search field on Google or in your library catalog, for example, you are conducting a simple search.

Simple searches can return large sets of results. To increase the odds that your results will be relevant to your subject, consider adding keywords, using exact phrases, and using wildcards.

Adding Keywords. In most cases, using several keywords together will limit the number of results returned by your search. This strategy is especially helpful when searching the Web, which can produce thousands (sometimes millions) of hits for individual words or phrases. For example, adding *college* to a search for the keywords *binge* and *drinking* on Google will reduce the number of results by roughly 70 percent. Adding *students* to a search for *binge*, *drinking*, and *college* will reduce it even further. To find out how the search tool you are using treats multiple keywords, consult its help page — or conduct some test searches and review your results.

Searching for Exact Phrases. Sometimes the best way to locate information is to search for an exact phrase. To further refine your search, you might use *binge drinking* and *college students* as phrases. This would eliminate sources in which the words *binge* and *drinking* appear but are separated by other words. The simple search format in many catalogs, databases, and Web search sites permits you to specify phrases using quotation marks.

↳ A Simple Search with Keywords on Google

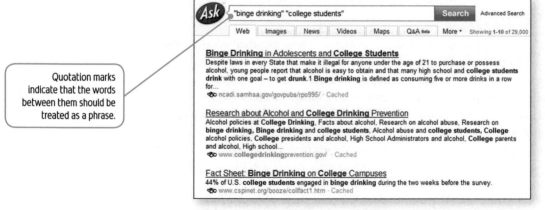

Quotation marks indicate that the words between them should be treated as a phrase.

↳ A Simple Search with Phrases on Ask.com

Using Wildcards. Sometimes you might not be sure what form of a word is most likely to occur. Rather than conducting several searches for *drink, drinking, drinkers, drunk,* and *drunken,* for example, you can combine keywords into a single wildcard search. Wildcards are symbols that take the place of letters or strings of letters. By standing in for multiple letters, they allow you to expand the scope of your search.

The following are the most commonly used wildcard symbols:

* usually takes the place of one or more characters, such as *drink**

? usually takes the place of a single character, such as *dr?nk*

Other wildcard symbols include !, +, #, and $. To find out whether wildcard symbols are supported, consult the help section in a catalog or database or the advanced search page of a Web search engine.

PLAN ADVANCED SEARCHES

In addition to simple searches, most library catalogs, databases, and Web search sites provide an advanced search page. These pages allow you to focus your searches in powerful ways using Boolean operators (which are used to search for all, some, or none of the words in a search box) and search limits (such as publication date and document characteristics).

Focusing Searches with Boolean Operators. Boolean operators let you focus a search by specifying whether keywords or phrases *can*, *must*, or *must not* appear in the results. Some Boolean operators also allow you to search for keywords or phrases that appear next to, before or after, or within a certain distance from one another in a document. Here is a list of commonly used Boolean operators and their functions.

Boolean Operator	Function	Example
AND/+ (plus)	Finds sources that include both search terms (either keywords or phrases)	hydrogen AND economy
OR	Finds sources that include either search term	energy OR power
NOT/− (minus)	Finds sources that include one search term but not the other	gasoline NOT oil
ADJ (adjacent)	Finds sources in which the search terms appear next to each other	fuel ADJ cells
NEAR	Finds sources in which the search terms appear within a certain number of words of each other (usually twenty-five; depending on the database or search engine, you might be able to change the default setting)	alternative NEAR energy
BEFORE	Finds sources in which search terms appear in a particular order	clean BEFORE power
Parentheses ( )	Although not strictly a Boolean operator, parentheses are used to group search terms and Boolean operators	hydrogen AND (fuel OR energy) AND (economy NOT economics)

Many databases, online catalogs, and Web search sites include the use of Boolean search terms—typically AND, OR, and NOT or plus (+) and minus (−) signs—in their advanced search forms or in expert search forms.

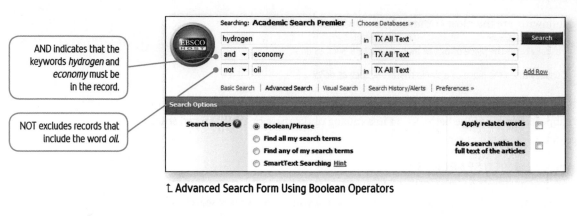

AND indicates that the keywords *hydrogen* and *economy* must be in the record.

NOT excludes records that include the word *oil*.

ꞁ Advanced Search Form Using Boolean Operators

AND requires both *fuel cells* and one of the parenthetical terms to be present.

NOT excludes records with the phrase *natural gas*.

Parentheses group two keywords; OR allows either of the terms to be present.

ꞁ Expert Search Form Using Boolean Operators

Limiting Searches. Search limits allow you to limit your searches to documents that have particular characteristics, such as publication date and document type. Although the specific limits that are available in an advanced search form vary across databases, library catalogs, and Web search sites, common limits include publication date (or, in the case of Web pages, the date on which a page was last updated), type of document, and the availability of full text (for databases).

Search Library Catalogs

Library catalogs provide information about the materials in a library's collection. Most libraries provide access to their catalogs through the Web, although some smaller libraries rely on traditional print catalogs. At a minimum, an online catalog will provide information about the author(s), title, publication date, subject heading, and call number for each source in the library's collection. Often it will also indicate the location of the source in the library and whether the source is available for checkout.

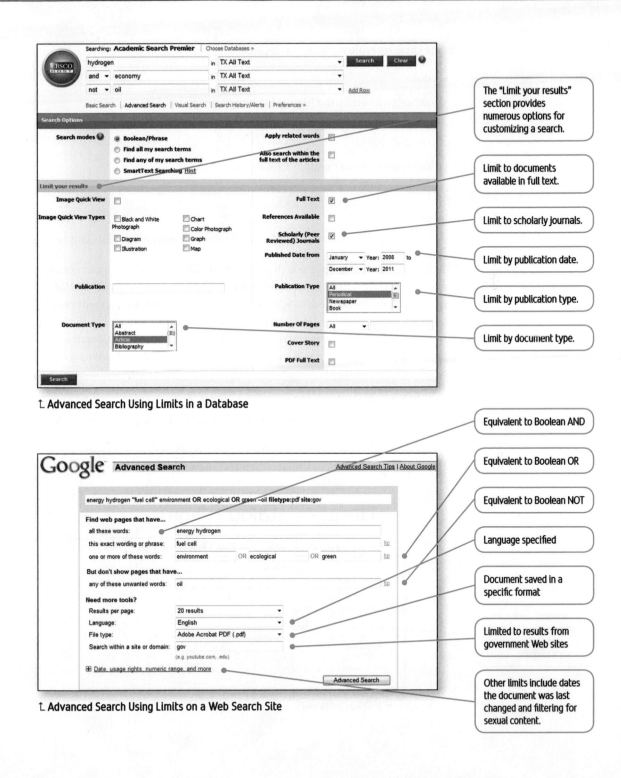

Ƚ Advanced Search Using Limits in a Database

Ƚ Advanced Search Using Limits on a Web Search Site

Online catalogs typically help you locate

- books

- journals owned by the library (although not individual articles)

- newspapers and magazines owned by the library (although not individual articles)

- documents stored on microfilm or microfiche

- videotapes, audiotapes, and other multimedia items owned by the library

- maps

- theses and dissertations completed by college or university graduate students

Although you can limit your search to the online library catalog at your college or university, you can benefit from searching other catalogs available on the Web. The Library of Congress online catalog (catalog.loc.gov), for example, presents a comprehensive list of publications on a particular subject or by a particular author. Some sites, such as WorldCat (www.worldcat.org), allow you to locate or search multiple online library catalogs. If your library doesn't have a listed publication in its collection, you can request it through interlibrary loan.

Most online library catalogs allow you to search or browse for sources by keywords and phrases, author(s), title, subject, and call number. The following examples illustrate common library catalog searches.

Search by Keyword. You can search for a specific keyword or phrase.

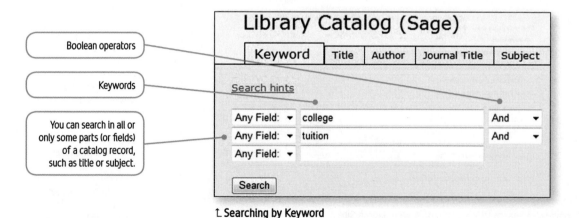

t. Searching by Keyword

Search by Author If you search by author, you can find sources written by a particular person or organization.

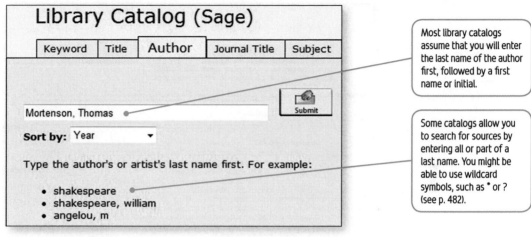

Most library catalogs assume that you will enter the last name of the author first, followed by a first name or initial.

Some catalogs allow you to search for sources by entering all or part of a last name. You might be able to use wildcard symbols, such as * or ? (see p. 482).

⌐ Searching by Author

Search by Title. If you know either the exact title of a source or some of the words in the title, you can search by title to find sources.

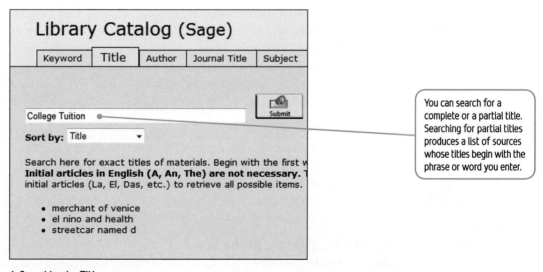

You can search for a complete or a partial title. Searching for partial titles produces a list of sources whose titles begin with the phrase or word you enter.

⌐ Searching by Title

Browse by Subject Heading. To locate sources related to a promising result, search by either call number or subject heading.

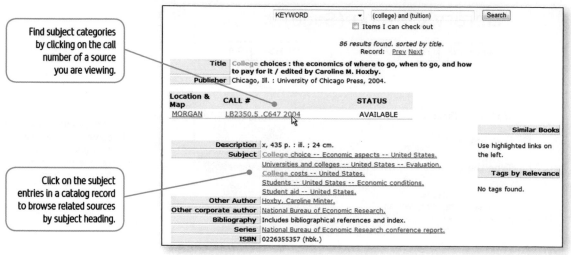

Find subject categories by clicking on the call number of a source you are viewing.

Click on the subject entries in a catalog record to browse related sources by subject heading.

ℒ **Searching by Call Number or Subject Heading**

Search Databases

Databases operate much like online library catalogs, although they focus on a different collection of sources. Whereas an online catalog allows you to search for publications owned by the library, a database allows you to search for sources that have been published on a particular topic or in a particular discipline regardless of whether the library owns the sources. Although some databases, such as ERIC (eric.ed.gov), can be accessed publicly through the Web, most are available only through library computers or a library Web site.

Databases supply publication information and brief descriptions of the information in a source; some — but not all — provide electronic copies of the source. Using the citation information provided by the database, you can check your library's online catalog for the title of the publication in which it appears. If your library does not own the publication, you can request it through interlibrary loan.

IDENTIFY RELEVANT DATABASES

Databases tend to specialize in particular subject areas and types of sources. To focus your search, try to identify the databases that will be most relevant to the subject you are addressing. Your decisions about which databases to search will be affected by your library's holdings, although some databases, such as ERIC, MedLine, and Science Direct, are available publicly via the Web (see p. 491). Large research libraries often subscribe to hundreds of databases, while smaller libraries might subscribe to only a handful. Most libraries provide a list of available databases. You can also consult a reference librarian about which databases might be appropriate for your search.

Databases generally fall into one of the following categories.

News and Information Databases. News and information databases focus on recently published articles in newspapers, such as the *New York Times*, and popular magazines, such as *Time* and *Newsweek*. Some databases of this type, such as LexisNexis Academic, also allow you to search articles distributed by news services, such as the Associated Press, and transcripts of radio and television programs. If your subject is likely to have been addressed in recent news coverage, consider searching one of these databases:

- Alternative Press Index
- Business News
- Ethnic NewsWatch
- LexisNexis Academic
- Newsbank
- Newspaper Source
- ProQuest Newspapers

Subject Databases. These databases provide information and abstracts (brief summaries) on sources about a broad subject area, such as education, business, or government. If your subject is related to a broad area of interest, consider searching databases that focus on general subjects, such as the following:

- Academic Search Premier
- ArticleFirst
- Business Search Premier
- Catalog of U.S. Government Publications
- Communication & Mass Media Complete
- Education Abstracts
- Health Source
- Humanities International Index

Bibliographies. Bibliographies provide information about publications in a specific discipline or profession, such as literary studies, computational linguistics, or the social sciences. The MLA Bibliography, for instance, provides information about sources dealing with English literature. On their database pages, many libraries provide guidance about the resources that are relevant to a particular profession or discipline. For example, if you are interested in a subject related to sociology, you might search the following databases:

- Family and Society Studies Worldwide

- Social Science Abstracts

- Sociological Abstracts

Citation Indexes. These indexes provide publication information and abstracts on sources that have referenced a specific publication. A list of these citations can lead you to other relevant sources on your subject, and they can expand your understanding of the conversation you are joining. If you have already located sources on your subject, you can search a citation database for articles that cite your sources. Depending on your topic, you might search the following databases:

- Arts & Humanities Citation Index

- Science Citation Index

- Social Sciences Citation Index

Full-Text Databases. A growing number of databases allow you to view or download the complete text of a source, either as exact replicas of the original or in a plain-text format. These files cut out the middle step of tracking down a physical copy of the periodical that published an article. If you don't know whether your library owns the sources returned by a search, or if you'd simply like to locate them more quickly, consider using full-text databases. Databases that offer some or all of their sources in full text include the following:

- Academic Search Premier

- ERIC

- IEEE Xplore

- JStor

- LexisNexis Academic

- ScienceDirect

Web-Based Databases. Libraries purchase access to most databases in a manner similar to subscribing to a journal or magazine, and they typically restrict access to the databases to library patrons, such as students, staff, and faculty. If your school library does not subscribe to databases that meet your needs, check whether another library in your area offers Web-based access to its databases (you might need to obtain a library card). Also consider using Deep Web search sites such as Academic Info (academicinfo.net) and Complete Planet (aip.completeplanet.com), which offer access to Web-based databases and specialized directories (see p. 494).

SEARCH WITHIN DATABASE FIELDS

To search for sources using a database, type keywords and phrases in the database's search fields. If you are conducting a basic search, the process will be similar to a search on a Web search site (see p. 481). The following illustrations show a simple search that featured writer Donovan Mikrot conducted on the basic search page of ArticleFirst and the results that were returned.

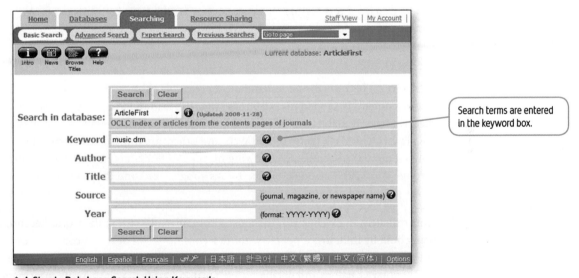

ᒑ **A Simple Database Search Using Keywords**

Just as you can in searches of online library catalogs, you can also focus a database search on specific fields, including

- Author
- Title
- Abstract
- Publication in which an article appears

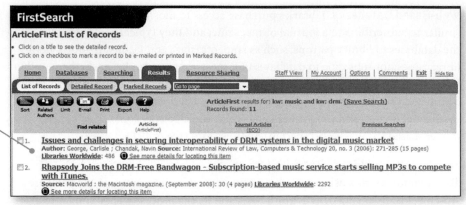

Results are displayed in a list. Each record can be added to a search folder for later viewing.

⌐ **Database Search Results**

Most databases also allow you to search all fields of a database record, much as you would search the Web (see the next section). EBSCO databases, for example, allow you to search "all text," while OCLC databases use the term *keyword* to refer to searches of all fields.

Search the Web

The Web has become the largest and most accessible "library" in the world. In addition to content developed for online use, the Web is home to a great deal of material that was once available only in print. For example, many magazines and journals are placing their back issues on the Web, and others are moving completely to online publication. Similarly, a growing number of books are now available online through sites such as Google Books (books.google.com) and Project Gutenberg (www.gutenberg.org).

Unfortunately, the Web is also the most disorganized library in the world because it's being built by millions of people without a common plan or much communication among them. Thus, to locate sources, you'll need to turn to Web search sites. Like online library catalogs and databases, Web search sites help you to locate information quickly and easily. However, while library catalogs and databases provide results that have been carefully selected by librarians and editors, the pages returned by Web searches can be uneven in quality, ranging from peer-reviewed articles in scholarly journals to home pages created by fifth graders.

As you search the Web, consider the types of search sites that are available and the types of searches you'll conduct on them.

IDENTIFY RELEVANT WEB SEARCH SITES

A surprisingly large number of Web search sites can help you locate sources about the conversation you've decided to join. Established sites, such as Ask, Google, Bing, and Yahoo!, constantly compete with newer sites, each hoping that you'll turn to them when you wish to conduct a search. To determine which ones might be best suited to the needs of your writing situation, learn about the types of Web search sites that are available.

@ Find a list of additional Web search engines, search sites, and other links at **bedfordstmartins.com/ conversation**.

Web Search Engines. When you use a Web search engine, you obtain information about Web pages and other forms of information on the Internet, including PDF files, PowerPoint files, Word files, blogs (see p. 497), and newsgroup posts (see p. 498). Web search engines typically allow you to search for Web pages, news, images, and video, among other options. They keep track of these sources by locating documents on Web sites and entering them in a searchable database.

Keep two cautions in mind as you use Web search engines. First, because most of them index only a portion of the Web—sometimes as much as 50 percent and sometimes as little as 5 percent—you should use more than one. Even if you don't find what you're looking for in your first choice, you might find it in another. Second, because Web pages can be moved, deleted, or revised, you might find that a search engine's results are inaccurate.

Leading Web search engines include the following:

- AllTheWeb: www.alltheweb.com
- AltaVista: www.altavista.com
- Ask: www.ask.com
- Excite: www.excite.com
- Gigablast: www.gigablast.com
- Google: www.google.com
- Bing: www.bing.com
- Yahoo! Search: search.yahoo.com

Web Directories. Unlike search engines, Web directories employ human editors to organize information about Web pages into categories and subcategories. Directories allow you to browse lists of Web sites by clicking on general topics, such as health or education, and then successively narrow your search by clicking on subtopics. Many directories also permit you to conduct keyword searches within specific categories.

This enables you to search within a collection of Web sites that the editors have judged to be relevant to your topic. The following are some leading Web directories:

- About.com: about.com
- Best of the Web: botw.org
- Google Directory: www.google.com/dirhp
- Internet Public Library: www.ipl.org
- Librarians' Index to the Internet: lii.org
- Open Directory Project: dmoz.org
- WWW Virtual Library: vlib.org
- Yahoo! Directory: dir.yahoo.com

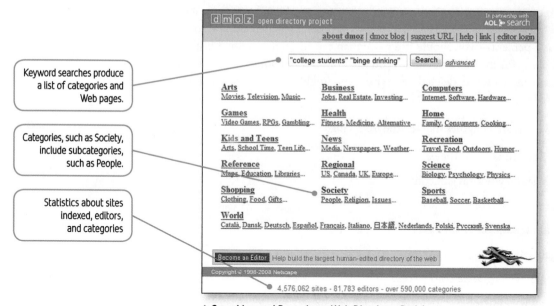

⌐ **Searching and Browsing a Web Directory, Part 1**

Deep Web Search Sites and Directories. Many specialized topics are addressed through databases or database-supported Web sites that, although accessible through the Web, are not indexed by conventional Web search sites such as Google or Yahoo!. These sites are referred to collectively as the Deep Web or the Invisible Web because they are not easily found by the search technologies used by leading search engines.

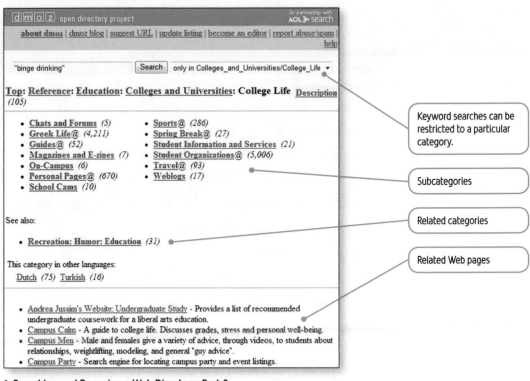

L Searching and Browsing a Web Directory, Part 2

To search the Deep Web, try sites such as Complete Planet, a directory of more than seventy thousand searchable databases and specialty search engines, and Scirus.com, a specialized search site focusing on the sciences. Leading Deep Web search sites and directories include the following:

- Academic Info: www.academicinfo.net

- Complete Planet: aip.completeplanet.com

- Deep Peep: www.deeppeep.org

- Internet Archive: www.archive.org

- Scirus: www.scirus.com

Meta Search Sites. On a meta search site, you can conduct a search on several Web search engines or Web directories at the same time. These sites typically search the major search engines and directories and then present a limited number of results on a single page.

Use a meta search site early in your search for information on the Web. You might use a meta search site to do a side-by-side comparison of various search sites and directories. When featured writer Donovan Mikrot searched for the phrase *digital rights management* on SRCHR.com, for example, he found that Google and Yahoo! produced more useful sets of results than did Live Search. Leading meta search sites include the following:

- Clusty: clusty.com
- Dogpile: www.dogpile.com
- ixquick: ixquick.com
- Mamma: www.mamma.com
- Metacrawler: www.metacrawler.com
- Search.com: www.search.com
- SurfWax: www.surfwax.com
- Zuula: www.zuula.com

Reference Search Sites. A reference search site allows you to search for information that has been collected in encyclopedias, almanacs, atlases, dictionaries, and other reference resources. Some reference sites, such as MSN Encarta and Encyclopedia Britannica Online, offer limited access to information from their encyclopedias at no charge and complete access for a fee. Other sites, such as Information Please and Bartleby.com, allow unrestricted access to recently published reference works, including the *Columbia Encyclopedia*, *The Encyclopedia of World History*, and *The World Factbook*.

One widely used reference site is Wikipedia, whose articles are collaboratively written by its readers. Because of its comprehensiveness, Wikipedia can serve as a useful starting point for research on a topic. However, because any reader can make changes to the site, it's best to double-check any information you find there.

Leading reference search sites include the following:

- Bartleby.com Reference: www.bartleby.com/reference
- Encyclopedia.com: www.encyclopedia.com
- Encyclopedia Britannica Online: www.britannica.com
- Google Knol: knol.google.com

- Information Please: www.infoplease.com

- MSN Encarta: encarta.msn.com

- Wikipedia: en.wikipedia.org

Government Documents Search Sites and Directories. Many government agencies and institutions have turned to the Web as the primary means of distributing their publications. USASearch.gov, sponsored by the U.S. government, allows you to search the federal government's network of online resources. Government Printing Office Access provides publication information about print documents and links to those publications that are available online. Sites such as FedStats and FedWorld give access to a wide range of government-related materials. In addition to these specialized sites, you can locate government publications through many Web directories, such as Yahoo!. Leading government documents sites include the following:

- About.com's U.S. Government Information Directory: usgovinfo.about.com

- FedStats: www.fedstats.org

- FedWorld: www.fedworld.gov

- Google U.S. Government Search: www.google.com/unclesam

- Government Printing Office Access: www.gpoaccess.gov

- GovSpot.com: www.govspot.com

- SearchGov.com: www.searchgov.com

- State and Local Government Directory: www.statelocalgov.net

- USASearch.gov: usasearch.gov

Blog Search Sites. Blogs — short for Weblogs — consist of chronologically ordered entries on a Web site and most closely resemble entries in a diary or journal. Blog entries usually include a title and a text message and can also incorporate images, audio, video, and other types of media. Many entries provide links to other pages on the Web.

The purposes of blogs vary.

- Some blogs report on events and issues. The bloggers who provided daily — sometimes hourly — reports on the 2008 political conventions offered valuable, firsthand insights into aspects of the conventions that were not addressed through the mainstream media. Similarly, the bloggers who reported on the Iraq War offered a perspective on events in Iraq and elsewhere that would not have been available otherwise.

- Some blogs alert readers to information elsewhere on the Web. These blogs cite recently published news reports and articles, the latest developments in a particular discipline, and new contributions to an ongoing debate—and provide commentary on that information.

- Some blogs serve as public relations spaces for institutions and organizations, such as corporations, government agencies, and colleges. These blogs typically focus on services or activities associated with the institution or organization.

- Some blogs serve largely as a space for personal reflection and expression. A blogger might share his or her thoughts about daily life, current events, or other issues with friends and family.

Writers can use blogs as sources of information and commentary on an issue and as sources of firsthand accounts by people affected by an issue. If you find blogs by experts in the field, you can begin a discussion with people involved in or knowledgeable about your topic. To locate blogs that are relevant to your research question, use the following blog search sites and directories:

- Ask.com Blogs: www.ask.com/?tool=bls

- Best of the Web Blogs: blogs.botw.org

- BlogCatalog: www.blogcatalog.com

- Blogdigger: www.blogdigger.com

- Google Blogsearch: blogsearch.google.com

- IceRocket: www.icerocket.com

- Technorati: technorati.com

Discussion Search Sites. Electronic mailing lists, newsgroups, and Web discussion forums support conversations among people who share an interest in a subject or belong to a particular community. You can read a message sent to a mailing list, sometimes referred to as a listserv, in the same way that you read other e-mail messages. Messages posted to newsgroups and Web discussion forums can be read using most Web browsers.

In addition to reading messages, you can post your own. Although there is no guarantee that you'll receive helpful responses, experts in a particular area often read and contribute to these forums. If you are fortunate enough to get into a discussion with one or more knowledgeable people, you might obtain useful information.

Mailing lists, newsgroups, and discussion forums can be located through the following search engines and directories:

- Catalist: www.lsoft.com/lists/listref.html
- CyberFiber: www.cyberfiber.com
- Google Groups: groups.google.com
- Tile.net: tile.net/lists

Search Media Sites

The Web is home not only to textual information, such as articles and books, but also to a growing collection of other types of media, such as photographs, podcasts, and streaming video. Image search sites have been available on the Web for a number of years. More recently, search sites have turned their attention to audio and video as well. You can locate useful information about your subject by searching for recordings of radio broadcasts, television shows, documentaries, podcasts, and other media.

@ Find a list of additional media search sites and directories at **bedfordstmartins .com/conversation.**

You can search for media using established search sites, such as Ask, Google, and Yahoo!, as well as a growing number of newer media search sites.

USE IMAGE SEARCH SITES AND DIRECTORIES

Image searches have long been among the search tools available to writers. Using Google's image search, for example, you can search for images using keywords and phrases, and you can conduct advanced searches by specifying the size and kind of image you desire. The following search sites and directories allow you to locate images:

- AltaVista Image Search: www.altavista.com/image/
- Ask Image Search: www.ask.com/?tool=img
- Bing Image Search: www.bing.com/images
- Ditto: ditto.com
- Google Image Search: images.google.com
- Picsearch: www.picsearch.com
- Yahoo! Image Search: images.search.yahoo.com

USE AUDIO SEARCH SITES

Thinking of the Web as the first place to visit for new music has become second nature for many of us. But the audio content available through the Web includes more than just music. You can also find radio broadcasts, recordings of speeches, recordings of natural phenomena, and other forms of sound. Sites such as FindSounds allow you to search for sounds and listen to them before downloading. Leading audio search sites include the following:

- FindSounds: www.findsounds.com
- Internet Archive: www.archive.org/details/audio

USE VIDEO SEARCH SITES

Through sites such as YouTube and Yahoo! Video, Web-based video has become one of the fastest-growing parts of the Web. You can view everything from news reports on CNN.com, to a video about the effects of a recent earthquake, to documentaries about the Iraq War. Of course, much of the material will be of little use in a writing project. With careful selection and evaluation, however, you might find video that will help you better understand and contribute to the discussion of your subject. The following are some leading video search sites:

- Ask Video Search: www.ask.com/?tool=vid
- Bing Video Search: www.bing.com/videos
- Blinkx: www.blinkx.com
- ClipBlast: www.clipblast.com
- Google Video: video.google.com
- Hulu: www.hulu.com
- Yahoo! Video Search: video.search.yahoo.com
- YouTube: www.youtube.com

Keep Track of Your Searches

One of the most important strategies you can use as you collect information is keeping track of your searches. Note the keywords or phrases and the search strategies you used with them (wildcards, Boolean search, author search, and so on), as well as how many sources the search turned up and whether those sources were relevant to your writing project. Keeping track of your searches will help you identify promising approaches; it will also ensure that you don't repeat your efforts.

In your writer's notebook, record the following information for each source you search:

> ✔ Resource that was searched
>
> ✔ Search terms used (keywords, phrases, names)
>
> ✔ Search strategies used (simple search, exact-phrase search, wildcard search, Boolean search)
>
> ✔ Date the search was conducted
>
> ✔ Number of results produced by the search
>
> ✔ Relevance of the results
>
> ✔ Notes about the search

Checklist for Recording Search Terms

How Can I Locate Sources Using Print Resources?

Contrary to recent claims, there is life (and information) beyond the World Wide Web. The print resources available in a library can help you locate a wealth of relevant material that you won't find online. If you are working on a writing project that has a historical component, for example, you'll find that bibliographies and indexes can point you toward sources that cannot be located using a database or a Web search engine. By relying on the careful selections librarians make when adding to a collection, you will be able to find useful, credible sources that reflect your purpose and address your subject.

To locate information using print resources, discuss your search plan with a librarian, visit the library stacks, browse periodicals, and check reference works.

Discuss Your Search Plan with a Librarian

As you begin collecting information about your subject, think about how your search plan can capitalize on your library's print resources. If you are uncertain about how you might use these resources, discuss your project with a reference librarian. Given the wide range of specialized print resources that are available, a few minutes of discussion with a knowledgeable librarian could save you a great deal of time or point you to key resources you might have overlooked.

Visit the Library Stacks

The library stacks—or shelves—house the library's collection of bound publications. By browsing the stacks and checking publications' works cited pages, you can locate related sources. Once you've decided that a source is relevant to your project, you can check it out or request it through interlibrary loan.

BROWSE THE STACKS

One of the advantages of the classification systems used by most libraries—typically the Library of Congress or Dewey decimal classification system—is that they are subject-based. Because books on similar subjects are shelved together, you can browse the stacks to look for sources on a topic. For example, if your research takes you to the stacks for books about alcohol abuse, you're likely to find books about drug abuse, treatment programs, and codependency nearby. When you find a publication that seems useful, check the works cited list for related works. The combination of browsing the stacks for sources and checking those sources' works-cited lists can lead you to publications relevant to your subject.

CHECK OUT RELEVANT ITEMS

You can usually take library books—and some periodicals and media items—home with you to read or view at your own pace. In some cases, a publication you want might not be available because it has been checked out, reserved for a course, or placed in off-site storage. If a publication has been checked out, you might be able to recall it— that is, ask that it be returned to the library and held for you. If it has been placed on reserve, ask whether you can photocopy or take notes on it. If it has been placed in off-site storage, you can usually request it at the circulation desk.

USE INTERLIBRARY LOAN

If you can't obtain a particular book, periodical, or media item from your library, use interlibrary loan to borrow it from another library. Most libraries allow you to request materials in person or on the Web. Some libraries let you check the status of your interlibrary loan request or renew interlibrary loan materials through the Web. To learn how to use interlibrary loan, consult your library's Web site or ask a librarian.

Browse Periodicals

Periodicals include newspapers, magazines, and academic and professional journals. A periodicals room—or journals room—contains recent issues that library visitors may browse. Many libraries also have a separate room for newspapers published in the last few weeks or months. To ensure everyone's access to recently published issues, most libraries don't allow you to check out periodicals published within the last year, and they usually don't allow newspapers to be checked out at all.

Older periodicals are sometimes placed in bound volumes in the stacks. Few libraries, however, keep back issues of newspapers in paper form. Instead, you can often find back issues of leading newspapers in full-text databases or in microform. *Microform* is a generic name for both microfilm, a strip of film containing greatly reduced images of printed pages, and microfiche, film roughly the size of an index card containing the same kinds of miniaturized images. You view these images using a microform reader, a projection unit that looks something like a large computer monitor. Many microform readers allow you to print full-size copies of the pages.

To help you locate articles in periodicals, most periodicals rooms provide access to electronic databases, which are more likely than print indexes and bibliographies to contain listings of recent publications. Once you've identified an article you want to review, you'll need to find the periodical in which it appears. Most online library catalogs allow you to conduct a title search for a periodical, in the same way you conduct a title search for a book. The online catalog will tell you the call number of the periodical and usually will give information about its location in the library. In addition, some libraries provide a printed list that identifies where periodicals are located. If you have difficulty finding a periodical or judging which publications are likely to contain articles relevant to your writing project, ask a librarian for assistance.

Check Reference Works

Reference rooms contain reliable print resources on a range of topics, from government to finance to philosophy to science. Although many of these reference books serve the same purposes as electronic databases, others offer information not available in databases. Using reference books to locate print resources has several advantages over using databases.

- **Most databases have short memories.** Databases typically index sources only as far back as the mid-1980s and seldom index anything published before 1970. Depending on your subject, a database might not allow you to locate important sources. If you use a reference book, however, you might be able locate print resources dating back a century or more.

- **Most databases focus on short works.** In contrast, many of the print resources in library reference rooms will refer you to books and longer publications as well as to articles in periodicals.

- **Many library reference resources are unavailable in electronic form.** For instance, the *Encyclopedia of Creativity*, which offers more than two hundred articles, is available only in print form.

- **Entries in print indexes are easier to browse.** Despite efforts to aid browsing, databases support searching far better than they do browsing.

Some of the most important print resources you can consult in a reference room include bibliographies, indexes, biographies, general and specialized encyclopedias, handbooks, almanacs, and atlases.

BIBLIOGRAPHIES

Bibliographies list books, articles, and other publications that have been judged relevant to a topic. Some bibliographies provide only citations, while others include abstracts—brief descriptions—of listed sources. Complete bibliographies attempt to list all of the sources published about a topic, while selective bibliographies attempt to list only the best sources on a topic. Some bibliographies limit their inclusion of sources by time period, often focusing on sources published during a given year.

You're likely to find several types of bibliographies in your library's reference room or stacks.

- **Trade bibliographies** allow you to locate books published about a particular topic. Leading trade bibliographies include *The Subject Guide to Books in Print*, *Books in Print*, and *Cumulative Book Index*.

- **General bibliographies** cover a wide range of topics, usually in selective lists. For sources on humanities topics, consult *The Humanities: A Selective Guide to Information Sources*. For sources on social science topics, see *Social Science Reference Sources: A Practical Guide*. For sources on science topics, go to bibliographies such as *Information Sources in Science and Technology*, *Guide to Information Sources in the Botanical Sciences*, and *Guide to Information Sources in the Physical Sciences*.

- **Specialized bibliographies** typically provide lists of sources—often annotated—about a topic. For example, *Bibliography of Modern American Philosophers* focuses on sources about important American philosophers.

Although most general and trade bibliographies can be found in the library reference room, specialized bibliographies are usually shelved in the library's stacks. To locate them, start by consulting a cumulative bibliography, such as *The Bibliographic Index: A Cumulative Bibliography of Bibliographies*, which identifies bibliographies on a wide range of topics and is updated annually. You might also search your library's online catalog using keywords related to your subject plus the keyword *bibliography*. If you need help finding bibliographies that are relevant to your subject, ask a reference librarian.

INDEXES

Indexes provide citation information for sources found in a particular set of publications. Many indexes also include abstracts—brief descriptions—that can help you determine whether a source is worth locating and reviewing. The following types of indexes can be found in libraries:

- **Periodical indexes** list sources published in magazines, trade journals, scholarly journals, and newspapers. Some periodical indexes, such as *The Reader's Guide to Periodical Literature*, cover a wide range of general-interest publications. Others, like *Art Index*, focus on periodicals that address a single subject. Still others focus on a small set or even an individual periodical; *The New York Times Index*, for example, lists articles published only in that newspaper and organizes entries by subject, geography, organization, and references to individuals.

- **Indexes of materials in books** can help you locate articles in edited books. Turn to resources such as the *Essay and General Literature Index*, which indexes nearly five thousand book-length collections of articles and essays in the arts, humanities, and social sciences. You might also find subject-specific indexes. *The Cumulative Bibliography of Asian Studies*, for example, covers articles in edited books.

- **Pamphlet indexes** list the pamphlets that libraries frequently collect. If your subject is likely to be addressed in pamphlets, ask a reference librarian whether your library has a pamphlet index. You can also consult the *Vertical File Index*, which lists roughly three thousand brief sources on ten to fifteen newsworthy topics each month.

- **Government documents indexes** list publications from federal, state, and local governments. The most useful indexes include *Monthly Catalog of United States Government Publications*, *CIS Index to Publications of the United States Congress*, *Congressional Record* (for daily proceedings of the House of Representatives and the Senate), *United States Reports* (for Supreme Court documents), and *Statistical Abstract of the United States* (for census data and other statistical records). These types of indexes might be found in either the reference room or a separate government documents collection in your library. Ask a reference librarian for help.

- **Citation indexes** allow you to determine which sources make reference to other publications, a useful strategy for finding sources that are engaged in the same conversation. For example, to learn which sources refer to an article published in a scientific journal, consult the *Science Citation Index*.

BIOGRAPHIES

Biographies cover key figures in a field, time period, or geographic region. *Who's Who in America*, for instance, provides brief biographies of important figures in the United States during a given year, while *Great Lives from History* takes a broader view, offering biographies of key figures in world history.

ENCYCLOPEDIAS

General encyclopedias attempt to provide a little knowledge about a lot of subjects. The purpose of a general encyclopedia, such as the *New Encyclopaedia Britannica*, is to present enough information about a subject to get you started on a more detailed search. Specialized encyclopedias, such as *The MIT Encyclopedia of the Cognitive Sciences*, take a narrower focus, usually covering a field of study or a historical period. Articles in specialized encyclopedias are typically longer than articles in general encyclopedias and offer more detailed coverage of subjects.

HANDBOOKS

Like encyclopedias, handbooks provide useful background information about a subject in a compact form. Unlike encyclopedias, most handbooks, such as *The Engineering Handbook* and the *International Handbook of Psychology*, cover a specific topic area. The entries in handbooks are also much shorter than the articles found in encyclopedias.

ALMANACS

Almanacs contain lists, charts, and tables of information of various types. You might be familiar with *The Old Farmer's Almanac*, which is known for its accuracy in predicting weather over the course of a year. Information in almanacs can range from the average rainfall in Australia to the batting averages of the 1927 Yankees to the average income of Germans and Poles before World War II.

ATLASES

Atlases provide maps and related information about a region or country. Some atlases take a historical perspective, while others take a topical perspective.

How Can I Gather Information Using Field Research?

Published documents aren't the only source of information for a writing project. Nor are they always the best. Publications—such as books, articles, Web sites, or television reports—offer someone else's interpretation of an event or an issue. By relying on such sources, you are looking through that person's eyes rather than through your own.

You don't have to use published reports to find out how an event or issue has affected people—you can ask them yourself. You don't have to watch television coverage of an event—you can go to the event yourself. You don't have to rely on someone else's survey of public opinion—you can conduct your own. And you don't have to do field research by yourself—you can form a team and share the work.

Choose Your Methods

Field research is research you conduct on your own, without consulting the Web or a library. Rather than relying on what someone has written, you can collect the information yourself. By conducting field research, you can draw your own conclusions.

Common forms of field research include interviews, observations, and surveys. You can also correspond with people who know about or have been affected by an issue or event, attend public events, and refer to informational radio and television programs.

INTERVIEWS

Interviews allow you to gather information about your subject from people who can provide firsthand accounts of events, authoritative interpretations of an issue, and reflections about their personal experiences. Interviews can be conducted in a face-to-face setting, on the telephone, or online, via e-mail, instant messaging, or Web cam. Interviews that are not conducted online are usually recorded and later transcribed for analysis. You can learn more about conducting an interview on page 186.

OBSERVATIONS

Observation allows you to learn about your subject by immersing yourself in it. For example, you might visit a mall to observe shopping habits in the last few days of the holiday season. Or you might study how activists approach students walking to the student center at midday. To keep track of your observations, you can take field notes, fill out an observation checklist, or record your observations in a voice recorder. Observing a subject firsthand allows you to understand it differently than you can through secondhand reports. Observation can also increase your credibility as a writer, in much the same way that a reporter on the scene has a degree of authority that a news anchor in a television studio cannot provide. You can read more about conducting an observation on page 129.

SURVEYS

Surveys allow you to obtain information from large groups of people. They can be conducted via paper forms, electronic forms, and even telephone calls. To learn about student and faculty attitudes and behaviors associated with academic integrity, for example, you might distribute a questionnaire at your college or university. The survey could help you answer *what, who,* or *how* questions such as the following: "What kinds of behaviors do you consider violations of academic integrity?" "Whom would you contact if you wanted to learn more about academic integrity issues?" "How likely are you to include sources you haven't actually read in a research essay's works cited list?" Surveys are less useful in obtaining the answers to *why* questions. In an interview, for instance, you can ask, "Why do you think students cheat or plagiarize?" and expect to get a reasonably well-thought-out response. In a survey, however, respondents seldom write lengthy responses to questions. You can learn more about surveys on page 372.

CORRESPONDENCE

Correspondence includes any textual communication—such as letters, faxes, and e-mail—as well as real-time communication using chat or instant messaging. If you use chat or instant messaging, be sure to save a transcript of the exchange. You can correspond with

- experts in a particular area
- people who have been affected by or involved with an issue or event
- staff at corporations, organizations, and government agencies

In general, it's helpful to explain who you are, what you are writing about, and why you want to correspond.

ATTENDING PUBLIC EVENTS

Public events, such as lectures, conferences, and public meetings and hearings, often provide writers with useful information. You can record public events by taking notes or bringing an audio or video recorder (if permitted). If you attend a public event in person or on the Web, find out whether a transcript of the proceedings will be available.

VIEWING OR LISTENING TO BROADCAST MEDIA

Writers frequently overlook radio and television as sources of information. News and information programs on television, such as *48 Hours*, might help you learn about the conversation you plan to join. To examine the programs in detail, you might want to record them. In addition, check the Web for radio programs and transcripts. National Public Radio's news information program *All Things Considered*, for instance, has audio archives going back to January 1996 that you can listen to online (visit www.npr.org and search the program's archives).

Enlist Help

Conducting field research can be time-intensive. If you and your classmates are working on an assignment that involves fieldwork, consider forming collaborative teams to collect information. You can use one or more of the following strategies:

- If you are conducting an observation or attending a public event, you'll find that a single perspective limits your ability to see what's happening. If another classmate is also conducting observations, you can help each other out. You might observe at the same time as your classmate so that together you can see more of what's happening. Or you and your classmate might observe the same setting at different times, effectively doubling the amount of information you can obtain. The additional information will help you better understand the contexts being observed. If you decide to work with a classmate, consider creating an observation checklist so that each observer will know what to look for.

- If you are conducting an interview, share your interview questions with a class-mate beforehand. Have your classmate role-play the interviewee. Then ask him or her how you might improve your questions .

- Similarly, if you are gathering information through correspondence, ask a classmate to review your letter or message before you send it and to offer suggestions for improving it.

- If you are conducting a survey, share drafts of your survey with a few class-mates. Ask them to note any questions that seem unclear, irrelevant, or ineffective. If they identify any questions that could be improved, ask them why they found the questions problematic and whether they have any suggestions for revision.

Assess Your Information

Field research methods don't always produce the results a writer needs. Before you use information collected through interviews, observation, or surveys, evaluate its accuracy and relevance by answering the following questions:

- Is the information you collected in an observation still relevant? Are your observation notes as complete as you had hoped they would be?

- Are the questions you asked in an interview or through correspondence still relevant to your writing project?

- Are the people you interviewed or corresponded with as qualified and knowledgeable as you expected?

- Were the questions you asked in an interview or through correspondence answered fully and honestly?

- Did survey respondents have adequate time to complete the survey? Did they appear to believe that their privacy would be respected?

In Summary: Locating Sources

○ Generate search terms and choose search strategies (p. 480).

○ Search your library's online catalog (p. 484).

○ Search relevant databases (p. 488).

○ Use appropriate Web search sites (p. 493) and media search sites (p. 499).

○ Browse the library stacks (p. 502).

○ Examine periodicals (p. 502).

○ Use the reference room (p. 503).

○ Conduct field research (p. 506).

13 Taking Notes

▶▶ Taking notes allows you to focus on what your sources tell you about your subject. By studying a source and noting the key points it makes, you'll gain a clearer understanding of the source as well as the conversation you've decided to join. Careful note taking also lays the foundation for drafting your document and helps you avoid plagiarism, making it one of the most important writing skills you can develop.

How Can I Record My Notes?

Some writers take notes by hand, on note cards, on photocopies of sources, in a notebook, on loose sheets of paper, on the transcript of an interview, or on correspondence. Other writers choose to take notes electronically, in a word-processing program, in a database program, in a bibliographic citation program such as EndNote or Reference Manager, in e-mail messages, or in a blog.

Your notes will be most useful if you take them systematically and consistently. For example, instead of writing some notes on sticky notes, some on note cards, and the rest in a word-processing file, take all your notes in one form. A consistent note-taking system will make it easier to find information later and will reduce the time and effort you'll need when you organize and draft your document.

What Methods Can I Use to Take Notes?

Notes — in the form of direct quotations, paraphrases, and summaries — provide you with a collection of important information, ideas, and arguments from your sources, as well as a record of your reactions to your sources. Notes can also include comparisons among sources and your thoughts about how to use them later in your document.

As you take notes, remember that they should reflect your purpose for working on a project and should provide direction for quoting, paraphrasing, and summarizing information, ideas, and arguments. If you keep your purpose as a writer in mind, you will avoid wasting time taking notes that won't be useful to you later.

Quote Directly

A direct quotation is an exact copy of words found in a source. When you quote directly in your notes, enclose the passage in quotation marks, identify the source, and list the page number (or paragraph number, if you are using a source that does not have page numbers) where the quotation can be found. Proofread what you have written to make sure it matches the original source exactly — including wording, punctuation, and spelling.

You should take direct-quotation notes when

- a passage in a source features an idea that you want to argue for or against
- a passage in a source provides a clear and concise statement that would enhance your document

- you want to use an authority's or expert's exact words
- you want to use the exact words of someone who has firsthand experience with an issue or event

When you are taking notes, be sure to place quotation marks around any quoted passage. If you don't, you might later think that the passage is a paraphrase or summary and unintentionally plagiarize it when you draft your document (see Chapter 14). The solution to this problem is simple: quote accurately when taking notes by using the checklist that appears on page 514. Later, when you integrate the quotations into your draft, you'll have a chance to modify or abbreviate them if necessary.

In some cases, however, it makes sense to modify a direct quotation while you're taking notes. You might want to quote only parts of a passage, add clarifying information to a quotation, or note an error in the original text.

MODIFY A DIRECT QUOTATION USING AN ELLIPSIS

When only part of a passage relates to your project, you might want to quote only that part in your notes. To indicate that you have changed a quotation by deleting words, use three spaced periods, called an ellipsis (. . .). If you don't, your readers will assume that the quotation you are presenting is identical to the text found in the source.

Original Passage

Under Congressional Republicans, however, funding to encourage community and national service through the Corporation has dropped in both nominal and real dollars. This year, the Republican FY 2007 Labor-Health and Human Services-Education appropriations ("LHHS") bill cuts these efforts $77 million (9 percent) below FY 2006 and $112.5 million (12 percent) below FY 2004, when the Corporation's funding was at its peak. In real terms, support for these volunteer programs will have been slashed 20 percent in the last four years. The result has been cuts in participation in all three national service programs.

Source: U.S. House of Representatives, Committee on Appropriations — Democratic Staff. House Republicans Slash National Service. September 12, 2006, p. 2.

> Three periods indicate material deleted from within a sentence.

Quotation Modified Correctly Using Ellipses

"Under Congressional Republicans . . . funding to encourage community and national service through the Corporation has dropped in both nominal and real dollars. . . . In real terms, support for these volunteer programs will have been slashed 20 percent

> Four periods indicate the deletion of one or more full sentences.

in the last four years. The result has been cuts in participation in all three national service programs" (U.S. House of Representatives, Committee on Appropriations—Democratic Staff 2).

MODIFY A DIRECT QUOTATION USING BRACKETS

To modify a direct quotation by changing or adding words, use brackets: [ ]. If you don't, readers will assume that the quotation you are presenting is identical to the text found in the source.

Quotation Modified Correctly Using Brackets

Bracketed information identifies the full name of the organization, which appeared as CNS in the passage.

"The [Corporation for National Service] is an independent agency with a 15-member board of directors that is appointed by the president and confirmed by the Senate" (Lenkowsky and Perry 299).

Even if you do use brackets and ellipses, you might substantially change the meaning of a text by adding, changing, or deleting words in a direct quotation. Check your notes against the original passages to be sure you aren't misrepresenting the source.

MODIFY QUOTATIONS USING "SIC"

If a passage you are quoting contains a misspelled word or an incorrect fact, use the word "sic" in brackets to indicate that the error occurred in the original passage. If you don't, your readers might think that the mistake is yours.

Quotation Modified Correctly Using "Sic"

"George W. Brush's [sic] interest in faith-based initiatives strongly shaped his national service agenda" (Vincent 221).

Checklist for Quoting

✔ Identify the author, the title, and the page or paragraph where the passage can be found.

✔ Surround all quoted material with quotation marks.

✔ Use ellipses, brackets, and "sic" as necessary.

✔ Check each note against its original passage to be sure you aren't introducing errors or misrepresenting the source.

Paraphrase

When you restate a passage from a source in your own words, you are paraphrasing. Typically, a paraphrase is roughly as long as the original passage. You can use paraphrases to illustrate or support points you make in your document or to refer to ideas with which you disagree. Even though you are using your own words when you paraphrase, you must still cite the source because the paraphrase presents ideas and information that are not your own.

One of the most common problems with paraphrasing is mirroring the source material too closely—that is, making such minor changes to the words and sentence structure of a source that your paraphrase remains nearly identical to the original passage. Another common problem is distorting the meaning of the source.

Consider the differences among the original passage below and the appropriate and inappropriate paraphrases that follow it.

Original Passage

"Skiing, for years a popular if somewhat expensive hobby, has ceded space on the mountains to snowboarding, which many find easier to master and cheaper to gear up for."

Source: Mark Clothier, "Snowboarding: The Latest Thing Going Down," CNN.com.

Appropriate Paraphrase

Snowboarding has made rapid gains on its more expensive—and more difficult to learn—cousin, alpine skiing, observes Mark Clothier.

> Preserves the meaning of the original passage without replicating the sentence structure and wording.

Inappropriate Paraphrase

Skiing, which has long been a popular if somewhat costly hobby, has yielded space on the hills to snowboarding, which most people find easier to learn and less expensive, observes Mark Clothier.

> Does not differ sufficiently from the original; uses the same sentence structure and changes only some key words.

Inappropriate Paraphrase

Snowboarding has replaced skiing as the leading way of heading downhill in the middle of winter, largely because it is easier to learn and less expensive, observes Mark Clothier.

> Distorts the meaning of the original passage.

When paraphrasing, focus on understanding the key ideas in the passage, and then restate them in your own words. Begin a paraphrase with the phrase "In other words." This strategy reminds you that it's important to do more than simply change a few words in the passage. In addition, you might want to set the original source aside while you paraphrase so that you won't be tempted to copy sentences directly from it. After you've completed your paraphrase, check it for accuracy.

Checklist for Paraphrasing

✔ Be sure that you understand the passage by reading it and the surrounding text carefully.

✔ Restate the passage in your own words. Make sure that you do more than simply change a few key words.

✔ Compare the original passage with your paraphrase. Make sure that you have conveyed the meaning of the passage but that the wording and sentence structure differ from those in the original passage.

✔ Note the author, the title, and the page or paragraph where the original passage can be found.

Summarize

A summary is a concise statement of the information, ideas, and arguments in a source. Writers often summarize an entire source, but they can also summarize lengthy passages. You can write summaries to capture the overall argument and information in a source or to record a writer's main idea so that you can later respond to it. Keep in mind that summaries must include a citation of the source.

Here is an original passage from a source you might consult while researching social-networking Web sites. A note containing a summary of the passage follows the original.

Original Passage

On a fateful day in November, only 400 out of 3,000 students showed up for classes at San Antonio's Warren High School, after threats against the school were posted on the popular free online social network site MySpace. The warnings said two boys were planning to use guns to shoot up the school, and most of the students stayed home out of fear for their lives. Teachers and administrators were in a "high state of anxiety," says Pascual Gonzales, executive director of communications for the district, and extra police were called to the school. Although it was a prank that got out of hand, and the involved students were arrested, the incident demonstrates the power of online social networks to link people in communities and across the world.

Source: Odvard Egil Dyrli, "The Online Edge," *District Administration*, March (2006): 99.

Appropriate Summary

Commentator Odvard Egil Dyrli underscores the power of social-networking sites like MySpace by recounting a recent prank—the posting of threats against a San Antonio high school—that led 2,600 of the school's 3,000 students to stay home for fear of an attack (99).

Problems can arise when a writer fails to summarize ideas and instead either creates a close paraphrase or writes a patchwork paraphrase that is little more than a series of passages copied from the source.

Original Passages from a Source's Introduction

A primary tenet of American society revolves around access to positions of influence and equality of opportunity. Educational attainment provides the central vehicle through which upward mobility can occur. . . . This study examines patterns of attendance at four-year and selective four-year colleges across students from single- and two-parent families. In particular, we examine whether these students differ in their choice of colleges to which they apply, are admitted, and which they attend. . . . Differences in access might arise from two possible sources. First, disrupted and intact families may differ in the resources they can bring to bear to prepare their children for college. Second, the impact of these resources on college choices of children from disrupted and intact families may differ. Our results suggest that although both influences are present, differences in the levels of resources account for the largest proportion of the difference in the college choices between children from disrupted and intact families.

Source: Dean Lillard and Jennifer Gerner, "Getting to the Ivy League: How Family Composition Affects College Choice." *Journal of Higher Education* 70.6 (1999): 709.

Inappropriate Summary

Lillard and Gerner argue that higher education provides the primary means through which upward mobility occurs in the United States. They studied patterns of attendance at four-year and selective four-year colleges across college applicants from single- and two-parent families, focusing in particular on differences in decisions about which college to apply to, admissions decision, and colleges attended. They found that differences in the financial and educational resources accounted for the primary difference in college choices between children from single- and two-parent families.

> The highlighted passages are paraphrased too closely.

Appropriate Summary

In the article "Getting to the Ivy League: How Family Composition Affects College Choice," Dean Lillard and Jennifer Gerner stress that a student's ability to obtain loans, his or her likelihood of getting financial aid, and family support all affect college admissions choices. Students who grow up in poor families or weak school districts are at a disadvantage compared to students from affluent families and schools, and they may not be given the resources they need to help them with the college application process.

> The summary gives a broad overview of the article's argument and avoids close paraphrases of key points.

To avoid mirroring the language and sentence structure of the source, begin your summary with "The author argues that" or "The author found that." You might want to set aside the original source while you write your summary so that you won't be tempted to copy sentences directly from it. After you've completed your summary, check it for accuracy.

Checklist for Summarizing

✔ Be sure that you understand the source by reading it carefully.

✔ Summarize the main and supporting points in your own words. Make sure that you do not merely string together a series of close paraphrases of key passages.

✔ Check for unintentional plagiarism by comparing the original source with your summary.

✔ Note the author, the title, and, if you are summarizing only part of a source, the pages or paragraphs where the information can be found.

Compare Sources and Start Planning Your Document

Paying attention to your sources as a group—not just to individual sources—helps you to see connections among them and allows you to gain a more complete understanding of your subject. It can also be useful when you begin planning and organizing your document, since those connections can help you frame your ideas. Review your notes to identify aspects of arguments that seem to build on points raised in other sources as well as differences in how sources address a subject.

Featured writer Ali Bizzul, for example, noticed that several of her sources brought up similar examples. She made a note of one such instance and wrote a reminder to herself.

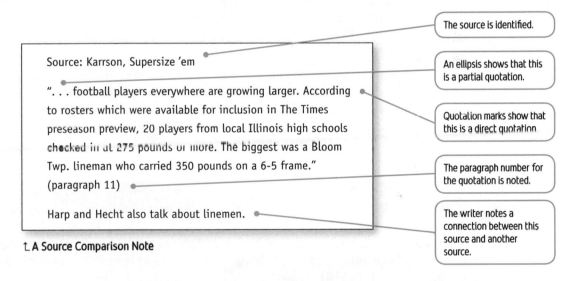

Source: Karrson, Supersize 'em

> The source is identified.

". . . football players everywhere are growing larger. According to rosters which were available for inclusion in The Times preseason preview, 20 players from local Illinois high schools checked in at 275 pounds or more. The biggest was a Bloom Twp. lineman who carried 350 pounds on a 6-5 frame." (paragraph 11)

> An ellipsis shows that this is a partial quotation.

> Quotation marks show that this is a direct quotation

> The paragraph number for the quotation is noted.

Harp and Hecht also talk about linemen.

> The writer notes a connection between this source and another source.

↟ A Source Comparison Note

In addition to comparing how your sources address a common subject, start planning how to use those sources. Planning notes are directions to yourself about how you might use a source in your project document; how you might organize information; or how you might use the information, ideas, and arguments you've encountered.

Ali Bizzul wrote planning notes—such as "How will this tie in? Use in introduction?"—in the margins of her source notes as she prepared to write her essay.

As you plan your document, pay attention to how the authors of your sources might respond to one another. If you have an idea of the overall point you'd like to make,

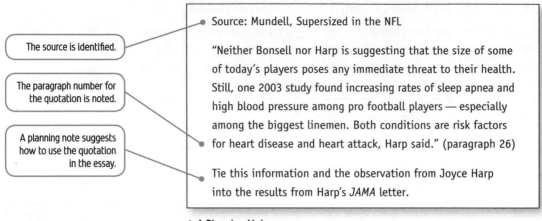

The source is identified.

The paragraph number for the quotation is noted.

A planning note suggests how to use the quotation in the essay.

Source: Mundell, Supersized in the NFL

"Neither Bonsell nor Harp is suggesting that the size of some of today's players poses any immediate threat to their health. Still, one 2003 study found increasing rates of sleep apnea and high blood pressure among pro football players — especially among the biggest linemen. Both conditions are risk factors for heart disease and heart attack, Harp said." (paragraph 26)

Tie this information and the observation from Joyce Harp into the results from Harp's *JAMA* letter.

↳ A Planning Note

you should also consider how they might respond to you. Once you've finished taking notes, review them to identify patterns in the authors' points. In particular, look for disagreements. As you learn more about a conversation, you'll begin to understand how writers align themselves. As a result, you'll be prepared to decide which ones might provide support for your ideas.

In Summary: Taking Notes

○ Decide how you will record your notes; then take notes systematically and consistently (p. 512).

○ Take notes to quote passages directly (p. 512).

○ Take notes to paraphrase key ideas (p. 515).

○ Take notes to summarize whole sources or lengthy passages (p. 516).

○ Compare the arguments, ideas, and information in sources, and write notes that help you plan your document (p. 519).

14 Avoiding Plagiarism

▶▶ Few writers intentionally try to pass off the work of others as their own. However, deadlines and other pressures can lead writers to take notes poorly and to cite sources improperly. In addition, access to documents through the Web and full-text databases has made it all too easy to copy and paste work from other writers without acknowledging its source.

Failing to cite your sources can lead to serious problems. Your readers will not be able to determine which ideas and information in your text are your own and which are drawn from your sources. If they suspect you are failing to acknowledge your sources, they are likely to doubt your credibility and suspect your competence, and they might even stop reading your document. More seriously, submitting academic work that does not properly identify sources might result in a failing grade or some other disciplinary action.

What Is Plagiarism?

Plagiarism is a form of intellectual dishonesty. It involves either unintentionally using someone else's work without properly acknowledging where the ideas or information came from (the most common form of plagiarism) or intentionally passing off someone else's work as your own (the most serious form of plagiarism).

Plagiarism is based on the notion of copyright, or ownership of a document or an idea. Like a patent, which protects an invention, a copyright protects an author's investment of time and energy in the creation of a document. Essentially, it assures authors that someone else won't be able to steal ideas from their work and profit from that theft without penalty.

Unintentional Plagiarism

In most cases, plagiarism is unintentional, and most cases of unintentional plagiarism result from taking poor notes or failing to use notes properly. You are plagiarizing if you

- quote a passage in a note but neglect to include quotation marks and then later insert the quotation into your document without remembering that it is a direct quotation

- include a paraphrase that differs so slightly from the original passage that it might as well be a direct quotation

- don't clearly distinguish between your ideas and those that come from your sources

- neglect to list the source of a paraphrase, quotation, or summary in your text or in your works cited list

Although unintentional plagiarism is, by definition, something that the writer hasn't planned to do, it is nonetheless a serious issue and, when detected, is likely to have consequences. Some instructors might require that an assignment be rewritten; others might impose a penalty, such as a lowered or failing grade.

Intentional Plagiarism

Intentional plagiarism, though less common than unintentional plagiarism, can lead to serious academic penalties, ranging from a reduced grade on an assignment to failure of a course to expulsion. Intentional plagiarism includes

- engaging in "patchwork writing," or piecing together passages from multiple sources without acknowledging the sources of the passages and without properly quoting or paraphrasing

- creating fake citations to mislead a reader about the sources of information used in a document

- copying or closely paraphrasing extended passages from another document and passing them off as the writer's original work

- copying an entire document and passing it off as the writer's original work

- purchasing a document and passing it off as the writer's original work

Plagiarism in Group Projects

Peer review and other collaborative activities raise important, and potentially confusing, questions.

- If another writer suggests changes to your document and you subsequently incorporate them into your document, are you plagiarizing?

- What if those suggestions significantly change your document?

- If you work with a group of writers on a project, do you need to identify which parts each of you wrote?

- Is it acceptable to list yourself as a coauthor if another writer does most of the work on a collaborative writing project?

The answers to these questions will vary from situation to situation. In general, it's appropriate to use comments from reviewers in your document without citing them. If a reviewer's comments are particularly helpful, you might acknowledge his or her contributions in your document; writers often thank reviewers in a footnote or endnote or in an acknowledgments section. It is usually appropriate to list coauthors on a collaboratively written document without identifying the text that each coauthor wrote, although some instructors ask that individual contributions be noted in the document or on a cover page. If you are uncertain about what is appropriate, ask your instructor.

What Are Research Ethics?

Research ethics are based on the notion that writing is an honest exchange of information, ideas, and arguments among writers and readers who share an interest in a subject. As a writer, you'll want to behave honestly and ethically. In general, you should do the following:

- Acknowledge the sources of the information, ideas, and arguments you use in your document. By doing so, you show respect for the work that others have done before you.

- Accurately and fairly represent the information, ideas, and arguments from your sources to ensure that you do not misrepresent other writers' work to your readers.

- Provide citation information for your sources. These citations help your readers understand how you have drawn your conclusions and where they can locate those sources should they want to consult them.

These three rules are the essence of research ethics. Ultimately, failing to act ethically—even when the failure is unintentional—can reflect poorly on you and your document. If your readers suspect that you have acted unethically, they will question the accuracy and credibility of the information, ideas, and arguments in your document. If they suspect that you have sacrificed research ethics altogether, they'll probably stop reading your document.

By adhering to research ethics—acknowledging your sources, representing them fairly, and citing them accurately—you can earn the trust of your readers and increase the chances that they'll pay attention to your argument. The following illustration, from Jennie Tillson's essay about the high costs of college tuition, demonstrates a writer's adherence to research ethics.

Although crediting other authors for their work is important, you don't need to document every fact and idea used in your document because some of that information falls under the category of common knowledge. Common knowledge is information that is widely known, such as the fact that the Declaration of Independence was signed in 1776. Or it might be the kind of knowledge that people working in a particular field, such as petroleum engineering, use on a regular basis.

If you're relatively new to your topic, it can be difficult to determine whether information in a source is common knowledge. As you explore your topic, however, you will begin to identify what is generally known. For instance, if three or more sources use the same information without citing its source, you can assume that the information is common knowledge. However, if those sources cite the source of that information, make sure you cite it as well.

Asking Permission to Use a Source

The concept of fair use deals with how much of a source you can borrow or quote. According to Section 107 of the Copyright Act of 1976—the fair use provision (available at www.copyright.gov/title17/)—writers can use copyrighted materials for purposes of "criticism, comment, news reporting, teaching (including multiple

One way colleges should use tuition money to benefit students is by redesigning their financial aid systems. Although colleges have reportedly increased their need-based financial aid, most of these precious funds go to boost tuition aid for middle-class students. Tamar Lewin from the *New York Times* wrote, "student borrowing has more than doubled in the last decade, and students from lower-income families, on average, get smaller grants from the colleges they attend than students from more affluent families." Basing more award decisions on financial need instead of merit would allow more students from lower-income families to attend college. As hard economic times continue to affect family finances, some colleges are even offering emergency aid and loans, particularly in cases where parents have lost jobs (Young). More colleges must take similar steps to ensure that students from all economic backgrounds have a fighting chance at affording an education.

> An attribution identifies the source of a quotation.

> Quotation marks indicate a partial quotation. Since this Web source has no page or paragraph number, no parenthetical citation is included.

> A parenthetical source citation indicates a paraphrase.

Lewin, Tamar. "College May Become Unaffordable for Most in US" *New York Times*. New York Times Co., 8 Dec. 2008. Web. 19 Jan. 2009.

Nyhan, Paul. "College Divide Threatens to Keep the Poor in Poverty." *Seattle Post-Intelligencer*. Seattle Post-Intelligencer, 27 Sept. 2005. Web. 17 Jan. 2009.

Quinn, Jane Bryant. "Colleges' New Tuition Crisis." *Newsweek*. Newsweek, 2 Feb. 2006. Web. 18 Jan. 2009.

Tillson, Jennifer. "Survey on College Choices." Colorado State U. Feb. 2009. E-mail Survey.

Young, Lauren. "College Costs: Coping with the Meltdown." *Business Week Online* 8 Oct. 2008. *Gale General OneFile*. Web. 21 Jan. 2009.

> Complete source information is included in the works cited list.

> Sources are cited in MLA style.

Adhering to Research Ethics

copies for classroom use), scholarship, or research." In other words, writers generally don't need to seek permission to make brief quotations from a source or to summarize or paraphrase a source.

If you are working on an assignment for a course—and do not plan to publish the assignment on the Web or in print—you generally can use material from another source without seeking permission. Remember, however, that in all cases you must still cite the source of the material you use.

Dear Ms. Jackson:

I am a student and am writing an essay for my writing class, English Composition 200, at Colorado State University. The essay will be used only for educational purposes and will be distributed on our class Web site, which is available only to my instructor and members of my class, for a period of three weeks during April and May of this year.

Or "... on the Web at www.myschool.edu"

I would like to include in my essay the following image, which is displayed on your site at www.westernliving.org/images/2302a.jpg, and would greatly appreciate your permission to do so:

Insert or describe the passage or image. For example: "paragraphs 3 to 5 of the article," a thumbnail of the image, or the URL of a document or an image on the Web.

If you are able to grant me the requested permission, please respond to this e-mail message. My deadline for completing my project is April 22. I appreciate your quick response.

Or "... sign the enclosed copy of this letter and return it to me."

If you are not the copyright holder or do not have authority to grant this request, I would appreciate any information you can provide concerning the current copyright holder.

Thank you for considering this request.

Sincerely,

Sara Petrovich
Sara.Petrovich@students.colostate.edu
(970) 555-1515

Provide contact information, such as name, address, e-mail address, phone number, fax number.

ᒐ **Sample Permission Request**

Writers who plan to publish their work should seek permission to use material from a source if they want to quote a lengthy passage or, in the case of shorter works such as poems and song lyrics, if they want to quote a significant percentage of the source. Writers who wish to use multimedia sources, such as images, audio, or video, should consider either seeking permission to use the source or linking directly to it. Be cautious, however, about linking directly to multimedia sources, since some Web sites specifically ask that you not link to content on their site (typically because doing so increases the demand on Web servers).

If you seek permission to use a source, explain why and how you want to use it. Many authors and publishers allow academic use of their work but frown on commercial uses. When you contact an author or a publisher, include your name and contact information, the source you wish to use, the purpose for which you will use the source, and the time during which it will be used.

If you contact an author or a publisher by mail, include a self-addressed, stamped envelope. It will save the recipient the cost of responding by mail, indicates that you are serious, and, perhaps most important, shows good manners.

How Can I Avoid Plagiarism?

In most cases, writers who plagiarize do so unintentionally. You can avoid unintentional plagiarism by learning the following writing skills:

- **Conducting a knowledge inventory** will help you determine what you know—and need to learn—about your subject.

- **Taking notes accurately** (see Chapter 13) will allow you to differentiate between a direct quotation from a source and a paraphrase or summary written in your own words.

- **Integrating quotations, paraphrases, and summaries** into a document (see Chapter 17) will ensure that the information and ideas from your sources aren't mistaken for your own work.

- **Citing sources** in the text and in a works cited or references list (see Chapters 21 and 22) will let your readers know that you are giving credit to the sources from which you have drawn information, ideas, and arguments.

- **Recognizing the most common excuses for intentional plagiarism** will help you resist the kinds of shortcuts that get writers into trouble.

Conduct a Knowledge Inventory

You can avoid unintentional plagiarism by having a clear understanding of your subject. When you are just beginning to learn about a conversation, you might find it difficult not only to express your own ideas clearly but also to restate or reframe the information, ideas, and arguments you've encountered in your sources. The result might be a document composed of passages that have been copied without attribution or paraphrased too closely. To prevent these difficulties, conduct a knowledge inventory by answering three questions:

1. What do you already know about the subject?

2. What don't you know?

3. What do you want to know?

Your answers can serve as a starting point for brainstorming, collecting and working with sources, and planning. They can also serve as a guide for discussing the subject with others. Once you've completed your knowledge inventory, meet with your instructor, consult a librarian, or talk with people who are knowledgeable about the subject. Ideally, these discussions will help you determine the most productive way to learn more about your subject. For example, you might identify key concepts that you need to understand more fully to write about your subject more effectively.

Take Notes Carefully

Unintentional plagiarism often results from sloppy note taking. Notes might contain direct quotations that are not surrounded with quotation marks, paraphrases that differ in only minor ways from the original passage, and summaries that contain original passages from a source. Quoting, paraphrasing, and summarizing accurately and appropriately as you take notes is the first—and arguably the most important—step in avoiding unintentional plagiarism.

For guidance on quoting, paraphrasing, and summarizing, see Chapter 13. To learn more about integrating quotations, paraphrases, summaries, numerical information, and illustrations into your document, see Chapter 17.

Attribute Ideas Appropriately

To distinguish between your ideas and those obtained from your sources, use attributions—words and phrases that alert your readers to the source of the ideas or information you are using. As you draft your document, use the author's name or the title of the source whenever you introduce ideas from that source. Phrases such as "According to Tom Siller . . ." or "As Ellen Vincent indicates . . ." let your readers know that information from a source will follow.

You can learn more about using attributions to identify the origin of quotations, paraphrases, and summaries in Chapter 17.

Identify Your Sources

Include a complete citation for each source you refer to in your document. The citation should appear both in the text of the document and in a works cited or references list.

In the following examples, the writer includes MLA-style parenthetical citations that refer readers to a works cited list at the end of the document. Both MLA style and APA style use a combination of attributions and parenthetical information to refer to sources.

> Jessica Richards argues, "We need to develop an efficient, cost-effective means of distributing hydrogen fuels before we can move to a hydrogen economy. If we don't, we'll be operating in crisis mode when the next serious oil shortage arrives" (322).

> "We need to develop an efficient, cost-effective means of distributing hydrogen fuels before we can move to a hydrogen economy" (Richards 322).

Be sure to cite the page or paragraph numbers for paraphrased and summarized information as well as for direct quotations. The following paraphrase of Jessica Richards's comments about energy needs includes the page number of the original passage in parentheses.

> Jessica Richards argues that we need to create an "efficient, cost-effective" system for delivering hydrogen fuels now, instead of while we are facing a critical oil shortage (322).

To learn how to document sources using the MLA and APA documentation systems, see Chapters 21 and 22.

Understand Why Writers Plagiarize

Although most plagiarism is unintentional, some students do plagiarize deliberately. The causes of intentional plagiarism range from running out of time to seeing little value in a course. The most common reasons offered to explain intentional plagiarism—

and the steps you can take to avoid falling victim to the temptation to engage in it—are listed below.

- **"It's easier to plagiarize."** Some people believe that it takes less work to cheat than to create an original document. That's probably true—but only in the short term. If you are pursuing a college degree, you will probably work in a profession that requires writing ability and an understanding of how to work with information. When you're assigned to write a report or a proposal down the road, you might regret not taking the time to hone your writing and research skills.

- **"I ran out of time."** Most writers occasionally find themselves wondering where all the time has gone and how they can possibly complete an assignment on schedule. If you find yourself in this situation, contact your instructor about a revised deadline. You might face a penalty for turning in work late, but it will almost certainly be less severe than the penalty for intentional plagiarism.

- **"I couldn't care less about this assignment."** It's not unusual to put off assignments that don't interest you. Rather than avoiding the work, try to approach the assignment in a way that interests you (see p. 33). If that fails, ask your instructor if you can customize the assignment so that it better aligns with your interests.

- **"I'm no good at writing."** A lot of people have doubts about their ability to earn a good grade in a writing course. Occasionally, however, some students convince themselves that plagiarizing is a reasonable alternative to writing their own document. If you lack confidence, seek assistance from your instructor, a campus writing center, a tutoring center, one of the many writing centers on the Web (such as the Writing@CSU Web site at writing.colostate.edu), or a friend or family member. Even with only modest support, you'll probably do much better than you think you can.

- **"I didn't think I'd get caught."** Some students believe—and might even have experiences to support their belief—that they won't get caught plagiarizing. Most writing instructors, however, become familiar with their students' writing styles. If they notice a sudden change in style, or encounter varying styles in the same document, they might become suspicious. The availability of plagiarism detection software also increases the likelihood that plagiarism will be detected.

- **"Everybody cheats."** Some students plagiarize because they believe that many of their classmates are doing so. They fear that, if they don't plagiarize, they'll be at a competitive disadvantage. In fact, however, the number of students who plagiarize is quite low. Don't be persuaded by dramatic statistics showing that cheating is the norm. The reality is that few students plagiarize intentionally, and those who do still tend to earn lower grades than their peers.

- **"This course is a waste of my time."** If you view a course as little more than a box that needs to be checked, you might be tempted to put in as little effort as possible. However, turning in work that isn't your own can backfire. If you are caught plagiarizing, you'll probably receive a reduced—or failing—grade for the assignment or the course. Instead of plagiarizing, talk with your instructor or an academic adviser about your lack of interest. You might find that the course actually has some relevance to your interests and career plans.

What Should I Do If I'm Accused of Plagiarism?

If your instructor expresses concerns about the originality of your work or the manner in which you've documented information, ideas, and arguments from sources, ask for a meeting to discuss the situation. To prepare for the meeting, do the following:

- Review your document to identify passages that might have raised suspicions.

- Collect the materials you used in your writing project, such as copies of your sources, responses to surveys, interview transcripts, and so on.

- Collect materials you wrote during the project, such as the results of brainstorming and freewriting sessions; organizational materials you created, such as clusters, maps, and outlines; and the rough and final drafts of your document.

- Reflect on your writing process.

During the meeting, listen to your instructor's concerns before responding. It's natural to feel defensive, but you'll probably be more comfortable if you take notes and try to understand why your instructor has questions about your document. Once your instructor is finished expressing his or her concerns, think carefully about what has been said and respond as clearly as possible. Your instructor might ask follow-up questions, most likely about the sources you've used, your writing process, and the document you've written.

If you find that you have engaged in unintentional plagiarism, ask your instructor for guidance about how to avoid it in the future and ask what sort of penalty you will face. If your instructor determines that you have plagiarized intentionally, ask what consequences you will face.

If you and your instructor are unable to resolve the situation, you might face a disciplinary process. To prepare for that process, learn as much as you can about the academic integrity policies at your institution.

In Summary: Avoiding Plagiarism

○ Understand the definition of plagiarism and the concept of copyright (p. 522).

○ Understand and follow research ethics (p. 523).

○ Seek permission to use sources when necessary (p. 524).

○ Conduct a knowledge inventory (p. 528).

○ Cite and document your sources (p. 529).

○ Resist temptations to plagiarize intentionally (p. 529).

○ Know what to do if you are accused of plagiarism (p. 531).

PART FOUR

Crafting and Polishing Your Contribution

15

Developing a Thesis Statement

As you shift your attention toward crafting your own contribution to a conversation, you'll start to plan your document. That process begins with choosing a main point and drafting a thesis statement. It also includes deciding what points and evidence you will use to support your thesis statement.

How Can I Choose a Main Point?

Your main point is the most important idea or argument you want to convey to your readers. Your choice of a main point will be influenced by what you've learned about your subject and by your writing situation.

Review Your Notes

Begin choosing your main point by reading quickly through your notes. As you review your notes, do the following:

- List important information, ideas, and arguments that you've come across in your reading.

- Identify your interest—personal, academic, professional—in those ideas and arguments.

- List ideas that you've come up with as a result of your own thinking about the subject.

When you complete your review, identify the ideas you would most like to address in your document.

Consider Your Writing Situation

Reviewing your notes will help you deepen your understanding of your subject. That understanding, in turn, will affect how you view your purpose and role as a writer and, by extension, the main point you want to make in your document. Use the following questions to help choose your main point:

- How have the sources you've consulted changed your thinking about the subject?

- Have your purposes—the reasons you are working on this project—changed since you started the project? If so, how do you view your purpose now?

- Has your role as a writer—for example, to inform or to solve a problem—changed since you started your project? If so, how do you view your role now?

- Will focusing on a particular idea help you address your readers' purposes, needs, interests, and backgrounds?

- Can you address this idea given the requirements and limitations of your writing project?

After you've answered these questions, choose a main point that is both interesting to you and consistent with the demands of your writing situation. Jot it down in a sentence or two.

Information from sources can change writers' purposes as they develop a main point.

How Can I Draft My Thesis Statement?

Your thesis statement provides a clear, focused expression of the main point you want to make. To develop your thesis statement, reflect on your main point and how it might be affected by the type of document you will write and the information, ideas, and arguments you've encountered in your reading.

Consider the Type of Document You Will Write

An effective thesis statement will reflect the type of document—or genre—you plan to write. Depending on the genre, your readers will have different expectations about how you present your thesis statement. Readers of an academic essay will expect a calm, clearly written statement of what you want them to learn, believe, or do. Readers of an informative newspaper article will expect you to identify, in a balanced and seemingly unbiased manner, what you want them to learn. Readers of an opinion column will expect you to be more assertive, and perhaps even more entertaining, about your main point. Consider how the following thesis statements, all addressing problems with the recruitment of athletes at a university, reflect the type of document the writer plans to draft.

Argumentative Academic Essay

The university should ensure that its recruiting practices are in full compliance with NCAA regulations.

Informative Newspaper Article

The university is taking steps to bring its recruiting practices in line with NCAA regulations.

Opinion Column

The university's coaches need to get their act together before the NCAA slaps them with sanctions.

Identify Important Information, Ideas, and Arguments Related to Your Main Point

Begin developing your thesis statement by identifying important information, ideas, and arguments related to your main point. When you first explored a conversation (see Chapter 2), you asked questions to learn about your subject. Review those questions and examine them for key words and phrases. Then look through your notes to see how your sources address those questions or use those key words and phrases. Consider the following example, which shows a list of initial questions and important information, ideas, and arguments found in sources that address the dangers of revealing personal information online.

> Megan circled key words and phrases in her initial questions about her subject, then identified which sources address those key words and phrases.

Questions about social networking & privacy:

Is (privacy) a right? Does that right exist (online) too?

How does (social networking) relate to the right to privacy?

Is social networking more vulnerable to invasions of privacy than other forms of communication?

Which (Web users) in particular are most at risk — (teenagers, children)?

What are the consequences or (dangers) of privacy being invaded online?

What my sources say:

(Teenagers) often underestimate the (dangers) of revealing personal information online (Jacobi 235).

Preserving (privacy) is often at odds with joining (social-networking Web sites) (Cardenas 132).

People need to take (responsibility) for preserving sensitive, private information (Safety Online para. 22).

Even experienced (Web users) reveal personal, sensitive information by mistake (Jackson 5).

Draft Alternatives

An effective thesis statement can invite your readers to learn something new, suggest that they change their attitudes or beliefs, or argue that they should take action of some kind. Consider how the following thesis statements reflect these three ways of focusing a main point.

Main Point

Preserving privacy on social-networking Web sites is an individual responsibility.

Thesis Statement: Asking Readers to Learn Something New

Social-networking Web sites don't reveal personal information; people reveal personal information.

Thesis Statement: Asking Readers to Change Their Attitudes or Beliefs

We should view the use of social-networking sites in educational settings with a great deal of caution.

Thesis Statement: Asking Readers to Take Action

People who use social-networking Web sites should learn how to safeguard sensitive, personal information.

Experiment with different approaches to determine which one works best for your writing situation. The thesis statement you choose should convey your main point in a way that addresses your purpose and your readers' needs, interests, backgrounds, and knowledge of a subject. For example, if you're focusing on the causes of a problem, your thesis statement should identify those causes. If you're advocating a particular solution to a problem, your thesis statement should identify that solution.

Focus Your Thesis Statement

A broad thesis statement does not encourage your readers to learn anything new, change their attitudes or beliefs, or take action. The following thesis statement is too broad.

Broad Thesis Statement

Educating users of social-networking sites about the dangers of these sites would be a good idea.

There's no conversation to be had about this topic because few people would argue with such a statement. A more focused thesis statement would define what should be done and who should do it.

Focused Thesis Statement

The publishers of social-networking Web sites should design their communication tools and Web page templates to highlight the dangers of publishing sensitive, personal information online.

To focus your thesis statement, ask what your readers would want to know about your subject, what attitudes should be changed, or what action should be taken. Consider their likely responses to your thesis statement and attempt to head off potential counterarguments or questions.

How Can I Support My Thesis Statement?

Presenting your thesis statement effectively involves far more than knowing what you want others to understand or believe or how you want them to act. You must develop a strategy to accomplish your goal. That strategy will reflect not only your purposes as a writer but also your readers' needs, interests, backgrounds, and knowledge of a subject. It will also take into account your understanding of the conventions typically used in the type of document you plan to write.

Choose Supporting Points

In longer documents, such as essays, reports, and Web sites, writers usually present several points to support their thesis statement. The kinds of supporting points they choose vary according to the type of document they are writing. In informative documents, for example, writers might focus on the three or four most important aspects of the subject they want readers to understand. In analytical documents, they might choose points that help readers understand the results of the analysis. In argumentative documents, writers usually offer a series of claims that will lead readers to accept the argument they are advancing.

To choose your supporting points, consider brainstorming, freewriting, looping, or clustering. As you generate ideas, reflect on your purpose, your role as a writer, the type of document you intend to write, and your readers.

- **Writing to reflect.** Which of your observations are most significant? What kind of impression do you want to create? (See Chapter 5.)

- **Writing to inform.** What do you want to convey to your readers? What are they most likely to want to know about the subject? (See Chapter 6.)

- **Writing to analyze.** How will you present the results of your analysis? What questions might your readers have about each part of your analysis? (See Chapter 7.)

- **Writing to evaluate.** What is the best way to present your criteria and the results of your evaluation? (See Chapter 8.)

- **Writing to solve problems.** How will you define the problem, and how will you present your solution? What questions do you think your readers will have about your problem definition, proposed solution, and alternative solutions? (See Chapter 9.)

- **Writing to convince or persuade.** How can you convince your readers to accept your thesis statement? How do you think they might respond to your argument? What sort of counterarguments might they propose? (See Chapter 10.)

Select Evidence

For each point you make in your document, you'll need evidence — such as details, facts, personal observations, and expert opinions — to back up your assertions and help your readers understand your ideas.

You can draw evidence from your sources in the form of quotations, paraphrases, summaries, numerical data, and visual images. You can also gather evidence firsthand by conducting interviews, observations, and surveys, or by reflecting on your personal experience. Chapters 5 through 10 contain detailed suggestions for locating and choosing evidence for specific purposes.

Use the following prompts to help identify evidence to support your thesis statement:

1. List the points you are using to support your thesis statement.

2. Identify relevant evidence from your sources, personal experience, or your own field research, and then list that evidence below each point. You might need to review your sources to locate additional evidence, or even obtain additional sources.

3. Determine whether you are relying too heavily on information from a single source, or on one type of evidence.

As you select supporting evidence, consider the genre (type of document) you plan to write. The type of evidence used in various genres can differ in important ways. Articles in magazines, newspapers, and Web sites, for example, are more likely to rely on interviews, observation, and illustrations as primary sources of evidence than are academic essays, whose writers tend to draw information from published sources found in a library or database. Multimodal essays, in contrast, are likely to use not only textual information and images but also audio, video, and animation.

Review and Arrange Your Supporting Points and Evidence

Once you have chosen your evidence, strategies such as labeling, grouping, clustering, and mapping can help you determine how to present that evidence to support your points. These strategies will also help you later as you decide how to organize your ideas.

LABELING EVIDENCE

Labeling can help you understand at a glance how and where you will use your evidence. For example, you might label notes or sources containing the evidence you want to use in your introduction with "Introduction," those that you plan to use to define a concept with the name of that concept, and so on. If you have taken electronic notes or have saved electronic sources, as featured writer Jennie Tillson did, you have a number of options. Once you've labeled your notes and sources, you can organize them into groups and put them in order.

Label at the top of a note in a word-processing file

Although MLA does not recommend including URLs in works cited lists, it can be helpful to keep track of them in your notes.

MLA recommends using paragraph numbers only when paragraphs are numbered in the source. However, you can include them in your notes to help identify key passages.

Economic Issues

Bryant Quinn, Jane. "Colleges' New Tuition Crisis." *Newsweek* 2 Feb. 2006. Web. 18 Apr. 2006. <http://www.msnbc.msn.com/id/4050965/site/newsweek/>.

Provides insights into the impact of higher tuition on students and their families, with some excellent information about the impact on students from poor and working-class families.

Key quotes:

"For lower-income people, that's easier said than done. The cost crisis is resegregating higher education, not by color but by class. Students of modest means are finding it harder to afford a bachelor's degree. Increasingly, they're shifting out of four-year colleges and universities and into two-year community colleges." (par. 3).

↑ **Labeling Electronic Notes and Sources**

GROUPING EVIDENCE

Grouping involves categorizing the evidence you've selected to support your points. Paper-based notes and copies of sources can be placed in related piles or file folders; sources and notes in word-processing files or a personal digital assistant can be saved into larger files or placed in electronic folders; items in Bookmarks or Favorites lists can be sorted by category. You can learn more about organizing evidence from sources on page 550.

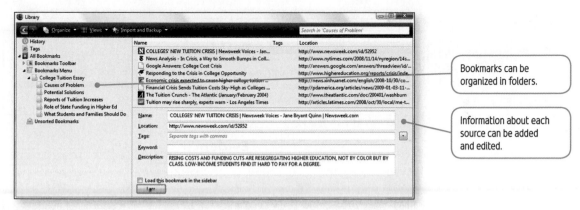

Bookmarks can be organized in folders.

Information about each source can be added and edited.

ʟ **Grouping Electronic Notes and Sources**

CLUSTERING

You can use clustering to explore the relationships among your thesis statement, supporting points, and evidence. Clustering involves arranging these elements visually on a sheet of paper or on a computer screen. By putting your thesis statement at the center of the cluster and your supporting points around it, you can explore how evidence relates to a supporting point, and how the supporting points relate to one another and to the thesis statement.

You can use clustering at several points in a writing project: as you begin to explore your topic, as you brainstorm to come up with ideas, as you explore relationships among the material you've collected, and now as you begin to arrange your own ideas.

Follow these steps to arrange supporting points and evidence in a cluster:

1. In the middle of a sheet of paper, or in the center of an electronic document (word-processing file or graphics file), write your thesis statement.

2. Place your supporting points around the thesis statement.

3. Next to each point, list the evidence you'll present to support it.

4. Think about the relationships among your supporting points and evidence, and draw lines and circles to show those relationships.

5. Annotate your cluster to indicate the nature of the relationships you've identified.

MAPPING

Mapping allows you to explore sequences of supporting points and evidence. For example, you might use mapping to create a timeline or to show how an argument

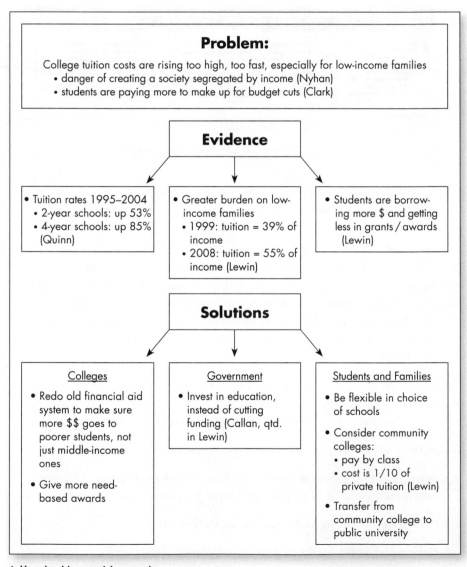

ㄴ **Mapping Ideas and Arguments**

builds on one supporting point after another. Mapping can be particularly effective as you begin to think about organizing your document, and it often relies on the organizing patterns discussed in Chapter 16, such as chronology, cause/effect, comparison/contrast, cost/benefit, and problem/solution.

In Summary: Developing a Thesis Statement

- Review your notes and sources (p. 536).

- Choose a main point (p. 536).

- Draft your thesis statement (p. 537).

- Identify supporting points for your thesis statement (p. 540).

- Select your evidence (p. 541).

- Review and arrange your supporting points and evidence (p. 542).

16

Organizing and Drafting

⏩ As you've learned about and considered your subject, you've encountered new information, ideas, and arguments. In response, you've considered how to craft your own contribution to the conversation you've decided to join. How you frame your contribution—that is, how you organize your points, construct your paragraphs, and introduce and conclude your document—can have a profound effect on readers' understanding of your subject and on their willingness to accept your main idea. This chapter offers guidance on how to use what you've learned to create an effective, readable document.

How Can I Organize My Document?

A well-organized document allows a reader to anticipate — or predict — what will come next. Choose an appropriate organizing pattern by reflecting on your writing situation, thesis statement, supporting points, reasons, and evidence. Then start organizing your document by creating a formal or informal outline to guide you as you write.

Choose an Appropriate Organizational Pattern

Common organizational patterns for documents include the following.

Chronology. The document's organization reflects the order in which events occur over time. For example, you might focus on a sequence of events in a recent election or during the course of a certain time span. Biographies and memoirs are generally organized chronologically. They portray the earliest events first and move forward in time.

Description. The document provides a point-by-point description of the physical attributes of a subject. For example, you might focus on the typical architectural features of a suburb or use a spatial arrangement that mimics the movement of the human eye as it takes in an image (left to right, top to bottom, near to far, and so on). Description is best for documents that address physical spaces, objects, or people — things that we can see and observe — rather than theories or processes that are not visible.

Definition. The document lays out the distinguishing characteristics of a subject and then provides examples and reasoning to explain what differentiates it from similar subjects. For instance, an essay defining "pride" might begin by stating that it is an emotion and then move on to explain why that particular emotion is not as harmful as many people believe.

Cause/effect. The document is organized according to factors that lead to (cause) an outcome (effect). For example, you might identify the reasons behind a recent strike by grocery store employees or the health risks that contribute to heart disease.

Process explanation. The document outlines the steps involved in doing something or explains how something happens. For example, you might help readers understand the stages of nuclear fission or teach them what steps to take in the event of a meltdown in a nearby power plant.

Pro/con. Ideas and information are organized according to the arguments made for (pro) and against (con) a particular position. For example, you might consider the arguments for and against increased reliance on wind power.

Multiple perspectives. The document arranges information, ideas, and arguments according to a range of perspectives about a subject. Documents using this organizational pattern frequently provide an analysis supporting one perspective. For example, a document addressing the use of tidal power as an alternative energy source might present the perspectives of utility companies, environmentalists, oceanographers, legislators, and waterfront residents and ultimately favor one group over the others.

Comparison/contrast. The document identifies similarities and differences among the information, ideas, and arguments relevant to a subject. Documents that compare and contrast can be constructed in one of two ways. The writer might present each relevant point individually and then compare each item point-by-point. Or the writer might present one item first, considering all of the points relevant to that item, and then move on to the second item. For example, a document analyzing a policy initiative to decriminalize marijuana possession might compare current drug laws to alcohol prohibition or attempt to contrast medical and recreational uses of marijuana.

Strengths/weaknesses. The document examines positive and negative aspects of a subject, such as increasing federal funding for health care by instituting a national lottery, or the overall quality of life in your city. Documents using this organizing principle typically work toward a conclusion that one or two considerations outweigh the others.

Costs/benefits. The trade-offs associated with a subject, usually a choice or proposal of some sort, are considered in turn. For example, an evaluative essay might discuss why the expenses associated with implementing a particular educational initiative are justified (or not) by the potential for higher test scores.

Problem/solution. Documents define a problem and discuss the appropriateness of one or more solutions. If multiple solutions are proposed, the writer usually argues for the superiority of one over the others. For instance, an informative article might explain the problem of "brain drain," in which highly educated and skilled workers move out of state, and then argue in support of a proposal to retain and attract more skilled workers.

Your choice of organizing pattern will reflect your purpose and the role or roles you adopt as a writer (see Chapters 5–10). It should also reflect the points you are making in your document and the reasons and evidence you use to support those points. Keep in mind that a writer may use more than one organizational pattern in a document. For instance, a process explanation often works in tandem with chronology, since both present steps in a sequence. Similarly, a document presenting multiple perspectives might also adopt a strengths/weaknesses pattern to evaluate the merits of each perspective.

Create an Outline

Not all documents require an outline, but creating one will usually help you put your thoughts in order. As you develop an outline, you'll make decisions about the sequence in which you'll present your supporting points and the evidence you'll use to back them up.

CREATE AN INFORMAL OUTLINE

Informal outlines can take many forms: a brief list of words, a series of short phrases, or even a series of sentences. You can use informal outlines to remind yourself of key points to address in your document or of notes you should refer to as you draft. Featured writer Dwight Haynes, who wrote an evaluative essay about anti-drinking campaigns on college campuses, created the following informal outline. Each item in his outline represents a section he planned to include in his essay.

> Dwight identified sources he could use in each subsection.

1. Introduction
2. Establish two approaches to addressing binge drinking on campus
3. Evaluate each approach
   - Social norms (Turner, Wechsler, DeJong)
   - Environmental (Weitzman, Jaschik)
4. Conclusion

⌐ **Dwight Haynes's Informal Outline**

You can also create a "thumbnail outline," a type of informal outline that helps you group your ideas into major sections. Featured writer Donovan Mikrot wrote the following thumbnail outline as he worked on his argumentative essay about the music industry. Donovan identified the major sections he wanted to include in his essay and noted which sources he could use to provide background information and to support his argument.

Introduction

The music industry has made digital music more accessible and affordable by removing digital rights management (DRM) software codes. Digital movies, however, remain under heavy restrictions that are frustrating to consumers.

Thesis Statement

The current state of digital rights management isn't fair. Hollywood studios should follow the lead of the music industry and work to eliminate DRM on digital video.

How did we get here?

Historical overview from the DMCA to DRM-less music files. Use EFF and Von Lohmann.

How does DRM affect entertainment companies and consumers?

The DMCA keeps new companies from marketing innovative technology if it could be used to pirate DRM files. Locked-down files actually encourage piracy because consumers don't want to buy the same movie three times to get different formats. DRM can end up costing companies money. Use Andrews, Breen, and Manjoo.

What should be done?

Movie studios should eliminate DRM to encourage innovation, satisfy consumers, and increase profits.

↳ Donovan Mikrot's Informal Outline

CREATE A FORMAL OUTLINE

A formal outline provides a complete and accurate list of the points you want to address in your document. Formal outlines use Roman numerals, letters, and Arabic numerals to indicate the hierarchy of information. An alternative approach, common in business and the sciences, uses numbering with decimal points.

Thesis Statement: Three barriers stand in the way of widespread hydrogen usage: as a fuel, it is expensive to produce, difficult to store, and complicated to distribute.

I. Introduction
    a. Shift from powerful cars to fuel-efficient, environmentally friendly vehicles
    b. Promise of hydrogen fuel (Crabtree, Dresselhause, & Buchanan)
    c. Barriers to hydrogen economy

II. How fuel cells work
    a. Diverting electrons to create electricity (DOE, "Hydrogen Fuel")
    b. Potential uses (DOE, "Hydrogen Fuel")

III. Barrier 1: Costs and inefficiency of producing hydrogen gas
    a. Abundance of hydrogen versus availability as gas
    b. Expense associated with current technologies (DOE, "Hydrogen Production")
    c. Environmental concerns

IV. Barrier 2: Difficulty of storing hydrogen gas
    a. Heavy tanks for compressed gas (DOE, "Hydrogen Storage")
    b. Complicated production and storage of liquid (DOE, "Hydrogen Storage")
    c. Metal hydrides (Crabtree et al.)
    d. Possibility of materials-based storage (Crabtree et al.)

V. Barrier 3: Complications of distributing hydrogen gas
    a. Small network of pipelines (DOE, "Hydrogen Distribution")
    b. Trucking not energy-efficient (DOE, "Hydrogen Distribution")
    c. Time and money needed to build infrastructure

VI. Conclusion
    a. Slow transition to hydrogen economy (Troxel interview)
    b. New technological developments (Crabtree et al.)

ᒧ Hannah Steiner's Topical Outline

Writers use formal outlines to identify the hierarchy of arguments, ideas, and information. You can create a formal outline to identify

@ View a guide for using your word-processing program's outlining tool at **bedfordstmartins.com/ conversation**.

- your thesis statement
- the supporting points you want to make
- the sequence in which those points should be presented
- evidence to support your points
- the notes and sources you should refer to as you work on your draft

The most common types of formal outlines are topical outlines and sentence outlines.

Topical outlines present the topics and subtopics you plan to include in your document as a series of words and phrases. Items at the same level of importance should be phrased in parallel grammatical form. In her topical outline for her informative essay about the potential use of hydrogen fuels, featured writer Hannah Steiner identified her main point, suggested the supporting points she wants to make, mapped out the support for her points, and used a conventional system of Roman numerals and letters.

Sentence outlines use complete sentences to identify the points you want to cover. Sentence outlines begin the process of converting an outline into a draft of your document. They can also help you assess the structure of a document that you have already written.

Using her topical outline as a starting point, Hannah Steiner wrote a sentence outline to test her ideas. Part of her sentence outline is shown here.

Thesis Statement: Three barriers stand in the way of widespread hydrogen usage: as a fuel, it is expensive to produce, difficult to store, and complicated to distribute.

III. Refining pure hydrogen gas is currently too costly and environmentally inefficient to be effective.

   a. Although hydrogen is the most abundant element in the universe, it is usually bonded to other elements.

   b. The separation process requires a lot of energy — and a lot of money.

   c. Research done by scientists at the U.S. Department of the Environment found that one of the most cost-effective means of obtaining hydrogen is to separate it from natural gas.

⌐ **Part of Hannah Steiner's Sentence Outline**

Use Your Outline to Begin Drafting

Creating an effective outline can greatly reduce the time needed to write your first draft. Use your outline to evaluate your work in progress by asking the following questions:

- Have I provided an effective organization for my essay?
- Have I covered all of my supporting points?
- Have I addressed my supporting points in sufficient detail?
- Have I provided sufficient evidence for my points?
- Have I relied too heavily on any particular sources?
- Do any sections seem out of order?

As you review your purpose and your outline, check that you have organized your points in a way that will allow you to achieve your purpose and address the needs and interests of your readers.

You can use your outline as the basis for a rough draft of your document. If you created an informal outline, you can begin to flesh it out by translating key points in your outline into sentences or paragraphs. If you created a formal outline, you can turn major headings in the outline into headings or subheadings in your draft and then use the points under each heading as the basis for topic sentences for paragraphs. If your outline is highly detailed, you can use minor points as the basis for supporting sentences within each paragraph.

If your outline contains references to specific notes or sources, make sure that you use those notes or sources in your draft. Take advantage of the time you spent thinking about which sources are most appropriate for a particular section of your document.

As you work on your document, you might find it necessary to reorganize your ideas. Think of your outline as a flexible guide rather than a rigid blueprint.

How Can I Draft Effective Paragraphs?

Writers use paragraphs to present and develop a central idea. Depending on the complexity of your thesis statement and the type of document you are writing, a single paragraph might be all you need to present a supporting point and its associated reasoning and evidence, or it might play only a small role in conveying your thinking about your subject. You can enhance the effectiveness of your document by creating paragraphs that are focused, organized, and well developed and by using transitions that clearly convey the relationships between paragraphs.

Focus on a Central Idea

Each of your paragraphs should focus on a single idea. Paragraphs often have a topic sentence in which the writer makes an assertion, offers an observation, or asks a question. The rest of the sentences in the paragraph elaborate on the topic. Consider the following paragraph, drawn from Hannah Steiner's informative essay.

> Another major challenge is the need to build an infrastructure for distributing hydrogen fuel to consumers. Unlike the oil and gas pipelines already in place, hydrogen has no dedicated delivery system. Current hydrogen pipelines cover only a fraction of the area that natural gas pipelines serve, and hydrogen's small molecule size and its ability to damage pipe metals almost guarantee higher costs and more potential problems (DOE, "Hydrogen Distribution"). Putting liquefied hydrogen in tanker trucks is currently the most cost-effective way to carry the fuel long distances, but the energy required to make hydrogen gas into a liquid offsets a lot of the savings (DOE, "Hydrogen Distribution"). Plus, this method requires fossil fuels to power the trucks that carry the hydrogen. The process of building local hydrogen production plants and creating the equivalent of our current gas stations is likely to be long, tedious, and costly.

The central idea of the paragraph is provided in the first sentence, following the transitional phrase "Another major challenge."

The second sentence explains the lack of a delivery system for hydrogen fuel.

The third and fourth sentences use evidence from a source to convey the problems with distribution.

The final sentences offer Hannah's interpretation of the evidence.

Follow an Organizational Pattern

Effective paragraphs follow an organizational pattern, often the same one that the document as a whole follows, such as chronology, description, or costs/benefits (see p. 548). These common patterns help readers anticipate what you'll say. Readers who recognize a pattern, such as process explanation, will find it easier to focus on your ideas and argument if they understand how you are organizing your paragraph. Note how the following paragraph uses the problem/solution organizing pattern.

> What can we do to help adolescent female athletes avoid illicit drug use? How can we help them avoid the pitfalls of competitive athletics? Parents, coaches, and the athletes themselves all play a crucial role in averting bad choices. First, parents and

The paragraph uses a problem/solution organizing pattern.

The central idea of the paragraph is provided in the third sentence.

One part of the solution to the larger problem is provided.

The fifth sentence provides evidence from a source to illustrate the nature of the problem.

coaches need to be aware that performance-enhancing drugs are a problem. Some adults believe that steroid use is either minimal or nonexistent among teenagers, but one study concluded that "over half the teens who use steroids start before age 16, sometimes with the encouragement of their parents. . . . Seven percent said they first took 'juice' by age ten" (Dudley, 1994, p. 235).

Use Details to Capture Your Readers' Attention

An effective paragraph does more than simply convey information—it provides details that bring a subject to life. Consider the differences between the following paragraphs from featured writer Caitlin Guariglia's essay on her family trip to Italy.

Example 1: Minimal Details

The next morning we met our tour guide. He was full of life. He took us to the main historical sites that day. They were spectacular, but I enjoyed listening to Marco more than anything we saw.

Example 2: Extensive, Concrete Details

The next morning we met our tour guide Marco. A large, sturdy man who looked like my grandmother cooked for him, he was confident and full of life. He took us to the main historical sites that day: the Vatican, the Colosseum, the Pantheon, the Roman Forum. While all of that was spectacular, I enjoyed listening to Marco more than anything we saw. He was a true Roman, big, proud, and loud. The Italian accent made it seem like he was singing everything he said, making it all seem that much more beautiful.

Both examples convey the same main idea. The first example, however, does little more than state the facts. The second example, by providing details about the tour guide's physical appearance, personality, and voice, gives readers a more concrete and more intimate understanding of the subject. (For advice about integrating details from your sources effectively, see Chapter 17.)

Create Transitions within and between Paragraphs

Transitions are words and phrases, such as *however* and *on the other hand*, that show how one sentence builds on another and how a new paragraph is related to the one that came before it. By signaling these relationships, transitions help readers anticipate how the information and ideas they are about to read are related to the information and ideas they've just read. Common transitions and their functions are presented below.

To Help Readers Follow a Sequence
furthermore
in addition
moreover
next
first/second/third

To Elaborate or Provide Examples
for example
for instance
such as
in fact
indeed
to illustrate

To Compare
similarly
in the same manner
like
as in

To Contrast
however
on the other hand
nevertheless
nonetheless
despite
although/though

To Signal a Concession
I admit that
of course
granted

To Introduce a Conclusion
as a result
as a consequence
because of
therefore
thus
for this reason

As you create transitions, pay attention to the order in which you introduce new information and ideas in your paragraphs. In general, it is best to begin a sentence with a reference to information and ideas that have already been presented and to introduce new information and ideas at the end of the sentence. Consider the following examples, which begin a new paragraph.

Introducing New Information First

Hydrogen fuels are far more difficult and expensive to store than are fossil fuels, in addition to being expensive to produce.

Building on Information That Has Already Been Presented

In addition to being expensive to produce, hydrogen fuels are also far more difficult and expensive to store than are fossil fuels.

The second example, by referring immediately to information that has been presented in the previous paragraph, provides an effective transition to a new paragraph, even as it introduces new information about hydrogen fuels. In contrast, readers of the first example would not have the benefit of seeing how the new information fits into what they've already read until they reached the end of the sentence.

How Can I Draft My Introduction?

All readers expect documents to include some sort of introduction. Whether they are reading a home page on a Web site or an opening paragraph in a research report, readers want to learn quickly what a document is about. As you begin to draft, consider strategies you might use to frame and introduce your main point. Keep track of those strategies so that you can revise your introduction later on. Many writers find that crafting an effective introduction is the most challenging part of drafting. If you run into difficulties, put your introduction aside and come back to it after you've made more progress on the rest of the document. There's no law that says you have to write the introduction first.

Frame Your Introduction

Your introduction provides a framework within which your readers can understand and interpret your main point. By calling attention to a specific situation, by asking a particular question, or by conveying a carefully chosen set of details, you can help your readers view your subject in a particular way. Consider, for example, the differences between two introductions to an essay about the recent downturn in spending among young people.

Introduction 1

In the face of a downturn in the economy, frugality is undergoing a revival in America. Young people are cutting up their credit cards, clipping coupons, and sticking to detailed budgets. In effect, they are adopting the very habits they mocked during the heady days of easy credit and weekend shopping sprees. Secondhand stores and thrift stores like Goodwill and the Salvation Army are drawing record numbers of customers, while once stable retail giants like Circuit City and Sharper Image have gone out of business (*Wall Street Journal*). In fact, retail sales during the Christmas season were down 2.8% last year, the lowest since 1995 (CNNMoney.com). The causes of this sea change in the spending habits of young Americans are complex and varied: high rates of unemployment, fewer jobs for recent graduates, difficulty securing credit, and that elusive factor economists call "consumer confidence."

Introduction 2

The new frugal spending habits of American consumers between the ages of 18 and 34 are endangering the very people who are trying to save money. Plagued with rising unemployment, widespread hiring freezes, and difficulty securing credit, young Americans are naturally turning to their spending habits as one area they can control. They are cutting down on how much money they spend in restaurants, bars, retail stores, and entertainment. As a result, usually robust Christmas sales were down an alarming 2.8% last year, the lowest since 1995 (CNNMoney.com). Even once stable retail giants like Circuit City and Sharper Image have gone out of business (*Wall Street Journal*). Although the desire to hold onto their money is logical, all this coupon clipping, budgeting, and thrift-store shopping threatens the key to economic recovery, what economists call "consumer confidence." If we don't loosen our grip on our wallets and inject some much-needed cash into the system, we will face far more dire economic consequences in the years to come.

The first introduction frames the subject as an explanation of the causes of changing habits of consumption. The second introduction frames the subject as a warning that these changing habits might be causing more harm than good. Even though each introduction draws on the same basic information about current rates of spending, and even though both do a good job of introducing the essay, they ask readers to focus their attention on different aspects of the subject.

You can frame your discussion by calling attention to specific aspects of a topic, including the following:

- The agent: a person, an organization, or a thing that is acting in a particular way
- The action: what is being done by the actor
- The goal: what the actor wants to achieve by carrying out the action
- The result: the outcome of the action

Introduction 2

The new frugal spending habits of American consumers between the ages of 18 and 34 are endangering the very people who are trying to save money. Plagued with rising unemployment, widespread hiring freezes, and difficulty securing credit, young Americans are naturally turning to their spending habits as one area they can control. They are cutting down on how much money they spend in restaurants, bars, retail stores, and entertainment. As a result, usually robust Christmas sales were down an alarming 2.8% last year, the lowest since 1995 (CNNMoney.com). Even once stable retail giants

Agent

Action

Goal

Result

like Circuit City and Sharper Image have gone out of business (*Wall Street Journal*). Although the desire to hold onto their money is logical, all this coupon clipping, budgeting, and thrift-store shopping threatens the key to economic recovery, what economists call "consumer confidence." If we don't loosen our grip on our wallets and inject some much-needed cash into the system, we will face far more dire economic consequences in the years to come.

Select an Introductory Strategy

The ability to frame your readers' understanding of a subject is a powerful tool. By directing their attention to one aspect of a subject, rather than to others, you can influence their beliefs and, potentially, their willingness to take action.

Your introduction offers probably the best opportunity to grab your readers' attention and shape their response to your ideas. You can introduce your document using one of several strategies.

STATE THE TOPIC

Tell your readers what your subject is, what conversation you are focusing on, and what your document will tell them about it. In the following example, George Chauncey begins by announcing his topic in a straightforward manner (see p. 172).

> The place of lesbians and gay men in American society has dramatically changed in the last half century. The change has been so profound that the harsh discrimination once faced by gay people has virtually disappeared from popular memory. That history bears repeating, since its legacy shapes today's debate over marriage.

ESTABLISH THE CONTEXT

In some cases, you'll want to give your readers background information about your subject or an overview of the conversation that has been taking place about it. Notice, for example, how Bob Dinneen sets up his letter to the editor of *Rolling Stone* magazine in response to an article about ethanol (see p. 414).

> It doesn't come as a big surprise that a magazine best known for pop-rock reviews and social commentary fails to understand the complexities of world energy markets and the need for ethanol and other renewable fuels ("Ethanol Scam: Ethanol Hurts the Environment and Is One of America's Biggest Political Boondoggles," by Jeff Goodell). What is less surprising, but more disturbing, is the failure of the "journalist" to inter-

view anyone with a working knowledge of the U.S. ethanol industry. Rather, he relies on oil industry reps and ethanol critics pushing personal agendas.

Nevertheless, since *Rolling Stone* felt the need to opine on America's ethanol industry, it is incumbent upon me to set the record straight.

STATE YOUR THESIS

If your essay urges readers to accept an argument, evaluation, solution, or interpretation, use your introduction to get right to your main point. In her analytical essay, featured writer Ali Bizzul describes the situation many younger football players find themselves in (see p. 261).

> Bigger is better — or so says the adage that seems to drive much of American culture. From fast food to television sets to the "average" house, everything seems to be getting bigger. This is especially true for the athletes who play America's favorite fall sport — football. Twelve- and thirteen-year-olds are bulking up so they can make their junior-high football teams. High school players are adding weight to earn college scholarships. And the best college players are pulling out all the stops in hopes of making an NFL team. All of this is occurring despite the belief of many football coaches that extra weight does little to enhance a football player's performance — and might even derail it. Even worse, the drive to put on the pounds carries significant health risks for football players, both now and later in life. Despite what they believe, overweight players are less effective than their lighter peers — and at far greater risk of devastating harm.

DEFINE A PROBLEM

If your purpose is to propose a solution to a problem, you might begin your document by defining the problem. Senator John Kerry uses this strategy to introduce his letter to Stephen C. Preston about unauthorized e-mail monitoring by Small Business Administration (SBA) managers (see p. 340).

> The purpose of this correspondence is to address the troubling findings set forth in a recent report issued by the SBA's Office of Inspector General (OIG). The OIG report indicates that SBA managers in the Office of Disaster Assistance (ODA) accessed the emails of an SBA employee who served as a confidential source to the Senate Committee on Small Business and Entrepreneurship. According to the

OIG's report, the monitoring took place after the ODA employee submitted hearing testimony to the committee on an anonymous basis. I am extremely concerned that this practice discourages potential whistleblowers from reporting misconduct to Congress.

MAKE A SURPRISING STATEMENT

Grab your readers' attention by telling them something they don't already know. It's even better if the information is shocking, unusual, or strange. Consider, for example, how Tayari Jones opens her literacy narrative (see p. 122).

> In elementary school, I spent a great deal of energy trying to explain the difference between atheism and devil worship. Until second grade I answered the commonplace query: "Where do you go to church?" with this: "My father says that we don't believe in God."

ASK A QUESTION

Asking a question invites your readers to become participants in the conversation. At the end of his introduction, featured writer Dwight Haynes asks a question and invites his readers to take an interest in his evaluation of programs that aim to prevent binge drinking (see p. 325).

> Over the past few decades, alcohol consumption among college students has received a great deal of attention. Despite humorous portrayals of college parties and the drunken antics depicted in movies and on television, serious concerns have been raised about health, safety, and academic issues associated with heavy drinking on campus. Most alarming, excessive levels of drinking are thought to cause between 1,400 and 1,700 student deaths each year (Jaschik, para. 4). Also significant are the physical harm and violent behavior that tend to arise from heavy drinking: 500,000 students each year sustain injuries as a result of alcohol use, and another 600,000 per year report being victims of alcohol-fueled assaults, including rape (Wechsler, Nelson, Lee, Seibring, Lewis, & Keeling, 2003, para. 1). Heavy drinking has been blamed for a host of other problems as well, including vandalism, alcohol poisoning, and academic failure. Rather than waiting until after students suffer the consequences of alcohol abuse to intervene, colleges have found that preventative programs can teach better habits and help students avoid the problems caused by

underage or irresponsible drinking. What kinds of approaches are colleges using to reduce student drinking, and how well do they work?

TELL A STORY

Everyone loves a story, assuming that it's told well and has a point. You can use a story to introduce a subject to your readers, as featured writer Caitlin Guariglia does for her reflective essay about a trip to Italy (see p. 144).

> Crash! The sound of metal hitting a concrete wall is my first vivid memory of Rome. Our tour bus could not get any farther down the tiny road because cars were parked along both sides. This, our bus driver told us, was illegal. He did not tell us, exactly; he grumbled it as he stepped out of the bus. He stood there with his hands on his hips, pondering the situation. Soon, people in the cars behind us started wandering up to stand next to the bus driver and ponder along with him. That, or they honked a great deal.

PROVIDE A HISTORICAL ACCOUNT

Historical accounts can help your readers understand the origins of a situation and how the situation has changed over time. Featured writer Hannah Steiner compares the days of Henry Ford with the drivers of today to introduce her informative essay about moving toward a hydrogen economy (see p. 197).

> In the early twentieth century, the products of Henry Ford's assembly lines introduced Americans to the joys of the open road. Large, powerful automobiles quickly became a symbol of wealth and success. With gas prices sky-high, Americans today are being forced to take a good, long look at their choices. The SUVs, trucks, and minivans popular until recently are largely viewed as symbols of excess and environmental irresponsibility, and many consumers now prefer fuel-efficient or hybrid vehicles, like the successful Toyota Prius. In fact, some drivers have become so determined to escape their pricey dependence on fossil fuels that they've begun to seek out alternative energy sources.

LEAD WITH A QUOTATION

A quotation allows your readers to learn about the subject from someone who knows it well or has been affected by it. Featured writer Jennie Tillson prefaces her problem-solving essay with a quotation from Benjamin Franklin (see p. 390).

> "In this world nothing can be said to be certain, except death and taxes."
> — Benjamin Franklin, in a letter to Jean-Baptiste Leroy,
> November 13, 1789

> Please add one more item to that list, Mr. Franklin: higher college tuition. Each year, college tuition increases as surely as winter follows fall and spring follows winter.

DRAW A CONTRAST

Drawing a contrast asks your readers to make a comparison. Cyrus Habib, for example, begins his opinion column, "America's Paper Currency Shortchanges the Blind," by contrasting the everyday experiences of the blind with those of sighted Americans (see p. 412).

> Blind Americans may soon find themselves able to use money just like anyone else. That is unless the Treasury Department is successful this month in its appeal of a recent federal court order that paper currency be made recognizable to the blind, who are currently unable to distinguish one denomination from another.

PROVIDE A MAP

The most direct way of signaling the organization of your document is to provide a map, or preview, of your supporting points in your introduction.

> This report will cover three approaches to treating cancer of the bladder: chemotherapy, a combination of chemotherapy and radiation, and surgical removal of the organ.

How Can I Draft My Conclusion?

Your conclusion provides an opportunity to reinforce your message. It offers one last chance to achieve your purposes as a writer and to share your final thoughts about the subject with your readers.

Reinforce Your Points

At a minimum, your conclusion should sum up the major points you've used to support your thesis statement. You might also want to restate your thesis statement (in different words) to reinforce your main point. If you didn't include a thesis statement in your introduction, consider stating your main point in your conclusion. Ending with a clear indication of what you want someone to think, believe, understand, or do as a result of reading your document gives you one final opportunity to influence your readers.

In her problem-solving essay, Jennie Tillson summarizes her problem definition and argues for the need to address it (see p. 395).

> The rising price of higher education affects not only students and their families, but the larger American society and economy as well. If we do not address the lack of access to higher education for the least affluent members of our society, we run the risk of creating a permanent gap between the poor and the wealthy, where even the best and brightest from poor and working-class families can't pursue the American dream. Our colleges, our students, and our government all must commit themselves to solving the problem of college tuition, so that we protect the opportunities of all students to earn a college degree and a more financially secure life. Our future depends on it.

Select a Concluding Strategy

Conclusions that simply summarize a document, like Jennie's, are common — and sometimes effective, especially when the writer has presented complex concepts. But a conclusion can do much more than simply restate your points. It can also give your readers an incentive to continue thinking about what they've read, to take action about the subject, or to read more about it.

As you draft, think about what you want to accomplish. You can choose from a range of strategies to write an effective conclusion.

OFFER ADDITIONAL ANALYSIS

Extend your discussion of a subject by supplying additional insights. In his evaluative essay, featured writer Dwight Haynes summarizes and reflects on the results of his evaluation of programs to reduce binge drinking (see p. 329).

> While social norms marketing appears to offer a strong combination of positive outcomes and ease of implementation, the environmental approach is more effective overall. Despite being more complicated and demanding more school and community resources, it delivers stronger results by involving students' entire college community. The environmental approach has a much greater scope than that of the social norms marketing approach and is suitable for schools of all sizes and types.

Therefore, it has the potential to affect not only students who drink heavily because they think that's the normal thing to do, but also students who are either unaware of the dangers of using alcohol or who will moderate their drinking only in the face of severe consequences for not doing so. Given appropriate resources, a program based on the environmental approach to curb heavy drinking is likely to be the best choice.

SPECULATE ABOUT THE FUTURE

Reflect on what might happen next. Featured writer Hannah Steiner speculates about the future in her informative essay (see p. 201).

It is certain, though, that at some point, the fossil fuels that have sustained our society's electricity and run our motor vehicles for over a century will run out — or become so expensive that they'll no longer provide an economically viable source of energy. Whether that day comes in five years or fifty, we need to shift to a new energy source — one that is practical, economical, and environmentally friendly. Hydrogen has demonstrated great promise as a new candidate for fuel. To realize that promise, however, we must work to remove the barriers that currently prevent hydrogen's emergence as a mainstay of our future economy.

CLOSE WITH A QUOTATION

Select a quotation that does one of the following:

- offers deeper insight into the points you've made in your document

- points to the future of the subject

- suggests a solution to a problem

- illustrates what you would like to see happen

- makes a further observation about the subject

- presents a personalized viewpoint from someone who has experienced the subject you are portraying

Virginia Postrel concludes her argumentative essay about the value of chain stores (see p. 423) with a quotation about the predicament facing American cities.

The contempt for chains represents a brand-obsessed view of place, as if store names were all that mattered to a city's character. For many critics, the name on the store really *is* all that matters. The planning consultant Robert Gibbs works with cities that want to revive their downtowns, and he also helps developers find space for retailers. To his frustration, he finds that many cities actually turn away national chains, preferring a moribund downtown that seems authentically local. But, he says, the same local activists who oppose chains "want specialty retail that sells exactly what the chains sell — the same price, the same fit, the same qualities, the same sizes, the same brands, even." You can show people pictures of a Pottery Barn with nothing but the name changed, he says, and they'll love the store. So downtown stores stay empty, or sell low-value tourist items like candles and kites, while the chains open on the edge of town. In the name of urbanism, officials and activists in cities like Ann Arbor and Fort Collins, Colorado, are driving business to the suburbs. "If people like shopping at the Banana Republic or the Gap, if that's your market — or Payless Shoes — why not?" says an exasperated Gibbs. "Why not sell the goods and services people want?"

CLOSE WITH A STORY

Tell a story about the subject you've discussed in your document. The story might suggest a potential solution to the problem, offer hope about a desired outcome, or illustrate what might happen if a desired outcome isn't realized. For instance, Wangari Maathai concludes her Nobel Peace Prize acceptance speech with a cautionary story about the stream near her childhood home (see p. 349).

> I would drink water straight from the stream. Playing among the arrowroot leaves I tried in vain to pick up the strands of frogs' eggs, believing they were beads. But every time I put my little fingers under them they would break. Later, I saw thousands of tadpoles: black, energetic, and wriggling through the clear water against the background of the brown earth. This is the world I inherited from my parents.
>
> Today, over 50 years later, the stream has dried up, women walk long distances for water, which is not always clean, and children will never know what they have lost. The challenge is to restore the home of the tadpoles and give back to our children a world of beauty and wonder.

CLOSE WITH A QUESTION

Questions provide an effective means of inviting readers to consider the implications of the ideas explored in an essay. After summarizing the information she provided in her analytical essay, featured writer Ali Bizzul closes with a compelling question (see p. 265).

Given the potential dangers to their health and the fact that being large does little to make them effective players, why do athletes work so hard to get bigger? Perhaps they think the statistics won't apply to them personally—that adding pounds will improve their individual performance. Athletes also know that gaining weight is much easier than gaining muscle, and if weight gives players the slightest advantage, they may think the risks are worth it. Do these players love their sport so much that they will continue to sacrifice their health—or even their lives—for it? They may, if they remain unaware of the consequences, and if they push themselves to their limits without fully understanding the risks.

CALL YOUR READERS TO ACTION

Make a recommendation or urge your readers to do something specific. For example, you might ask them to participate in solving a problem by donating time, money, or effort to a project. Or you might ask them to write to someone, such as a politician or corporate executive, about an issue. Calls to action ask readers not just to accept what you've written but to do something about it, as Cyrus Habib does in his opinion column "Show Us the Money" (see p. 413).

When it comes to accommodating disabilities such as blindness, let us continue to lead the world in practice as well as in principle. More important still, let us tell the world that we, too, believe that blindness should not be an obstacle to financial independence. In doing so, let us also take a significant step toward ameliorating the living conditions of blind Americans, now and for years to come.

The Treasury Department should obey Judge Robertson's order and show us the money.

LINK TO YOUR INTRODUCTION

This technique is sometimes called a "bookends" approach because it positions your introduction and conclusion as related ends of your document. The basic idea is to turn your conclusion into an extension of your introduction.

- If your introduction uses a quotation, end with a related quotation or respond to the quotation.

- If your introduction uses a story, extend that story or retell it with a different ending.

- If your introduction asks a question, answer the question, restate the question, or ask a new question.

- If your introduction defines a problem, provide a solution to the problem, restate the problem, or suggest that readers need to move on to a new problem.

In Summary: Organizing and Drafting

○ Choose an appropriate organizational pattern (p. 548).

○ Use your outline to begin drafting your document (p. 554).

○ Develop effective paragraphs (p. 554).

○ Draft your introduction (p. 558).

○ Draft your conclusion (p. 564).

17

Using Sources Effectively

▶▶ As you draft your document, your own ideas should take center stage. Don't lose track, however, of the contributions that your sources can make. Using evidence from sources can strengthen your document and show how knowledgeable you've become about the conversation you're entering. In this chapter, you'll learn how to integrate sources into your document and how to work with numerical information, images, audio, and video.

Much of the information in this chapter is based on MLA style, which is commonly used in the humanities. See Chapter 22 for guidelines on APA style, which is used in many social sciences.

How Can I Use Sources to Accomplish My Purposes as a Writer?

Your sources can help you introduce ideas, contrast the ideas of other authors with your own, provide evidence for your points, define concepts, illustrate processes, clarify statements, set a mood, provide examples, and qualify or amplify a point. You can present information from sources in several ways:

- as a quotation, paraphrase, or summary

- as numerical information

- as illustrations such as images, audio, video, and animations

Depending on the point you want to make, some types of evidence might be more effective than others. Be sure to consider how your readers will react to the information you provide. In some cases, for example, numerical evidence might lend better support for a point than a quotation would.

As you draft your document, identify what you want the information from your sources to accomplish. Consider how quotations, paraphrases, summaries, numerical information, and various types of illustrations from your sources might lead your readers to see the subject you are addressing in terms that are most favorable to your purposes. By selecting source information carefully, you can present ideas that are more pointed than you might want to make on your own. Calling opponents of a proposal "inflexible" and "pig-headed," for example, might signal your biases too strongly. Quoting someone who uses those terms, however, allows you to get the point across without undermining an otherwise even and balanced tone.

The following are some of the most effective ways to use information, ideas, and arguments from sources as you contribute to a written conversation about a subject.

Introduce a Point

You can use a quotation, paraphrase, or summary to introduce a point to your readers.

Quotation Used to Introduce a Point

"When I came around the corner, a black bear was standing in the middle of the trail," said Joan Gibson, an avid hiker. "We stared at each other for a moment, wondering who would make the first move. Then the bear looked off to the right and shambled up the mountain. I guess I wasn't worth the trouble." Joan Gibson's story, like those of most hikers who encounter bears in the woods, ends happily. But the growing encroachment of humans on rural areas once left largely to wildlife is causing difficulties not only for people who enjoy spending time in the wide-open spaces but also for the animals that make those spaces their home.

Paraphrase Used to Introduce a Point

A *New York Times* article recently reported that human-bear encounters in Yosemite National Park, which had been on the decline during most of the last decade, has more than doubled in the past year (Spiegel A4). Although no humans have been injured and only one incident resulted in a decision to destroy a bear, park officials point to the uptick in encounters as a warning sign that . . .

Your choice of a quotation or paraphrase will frame the point you want to make, calling your readers' attention to a specific aspect of an idea or argument and laying the groundwork for a response. Think about how the following quotation leads readers to view a public debate about education reform as a battle between reformers and an entrenched teachers union.

> "The teachers union has balked at even the most reasonable proposals for school reform," said Mary Sweeney, press secretary for Save Our Schools, which has sponsored a referendum on the November ballot calling for funding for their voucher plan. "We believe the November election will send a wake-up call about the need to rethink their obstructionist behaviors."

Phrases such as "balked at even the most reasonable proposals" and "their obstructionist behaviors" place the blame for the problem on the teachers union.

> If Sweeney and supporters of Referendum D are successful, the educational landscape in . . .

In contrast, note how the following quotation frames the debate as a question of how best to spend scarce education funds.

> "In the past decade, state and local funding of public education in real dollars has declined by 7.2 percent," said Jeffrey Allister, state chair of the governor's Special Commission on Education Reform. "Referendum D, if passed, would further erode that funding by shifting state dollars to private schools." As the state considers the merits of Referendum D, which would institute the first statewide voucher program in the United States, opponents of the measure have . . .

Phrases such as "funding of public education in real dollars has declined" and "further erode that funding" call attention to the financial challenges faced by schools.

Contrast Ideas

When you want to indicate that disagreement exists on a subject, you can use source information to illustrate the nature and intensity of the disagreement. The following example uses partial quotations (see p. 581) to highlight differences in proposed solutions to a problem.

> Solutions to the state's higher education funding shortfall range from traditional approaches, such as raising taxes, to more radical solutions, among them privatizing state colleges and universities. Advocates of increased taxes, such as Page Richards of the Higher Education Coalition, argue that declines in state funding of higher education "must be reversed immediately or we will find ourselves in a situation where we are closing rural community colleges and only the wealthiest among us will have access to the best education" (A4). Those in favor of privatizing higher education suggest, however, that free-market approaches will ultimately bring about "a fairer situation in which the poor, many of whom have no interest in higher education, are no longer asked to subsidize higher and higher faculty salaries and larger football stadiums" (Pieters 23).

Base your choices about how to contrast ideas on the clarity and length of your sources and on the effects you hope to achieve. If you want to express complex ideas as concisely as possible, you might use paraphrase and summary. If you want to convey the emotional qualities of an author's position on a subject, use quotations.

Provide Evidence

Documents that consist of a series of unsupported assertions amount to little more than a request for the reader's trust. Even when the writer is eminently trustworthy, most readers find such documents easy to dismiss. In contrast, providing evidence to support your assertions increases the likelihood that your readers will accept your main point. Note the differences between the following passages.

Unsupported Assertion

No evidence is provided to support the writer's assertion.

Given a choice between two products of comparable quality, reputation, and cost, American consumers are far more likely to purchase goods that use environmentally friendly packaging. Encouraging the use of such packaging is a good idea for America.

Supported Assertion

Given a choice between two products of comparable quality, reputation, and cost, American consumers are far more likely to purchase goods that use environmentally friendly packaging. A recent study by the High Plains Research Institute found that the shelf life of several biodegradable plastics not only exceeded the shelf life of the products they were used to package but also cost less to produce (Chen and Lohann 33). In addition, a study by the Consumer Products Institute found that, when made aware that products were packaged in environmentally friendly materials, consumers were more likely to buy those products.

> Summaries of the results of two studies provide evidence for the assertion made in the first sentence.

Similarly, visual sources can lend support to an assertion. An assertion about the unintended consequences of military action, for example, might be accompanied by a photograph of a war-torn street or a wounded child.

Align Yourself with an Authority

Aligning yourself with an authority shows your readers that your points are supported by a leader in that area—such as a subject-matter expert, a scientist, a politician, or a religious figure—and that you are not alone in your convictions. Essentially, this technique allows you to borrow the credibility and status of someone who has compiled a strong record of accomplishment. Start by making an assertion, and follow it with supporting information from a source, such as a quotation, paraphrase, or summary.

Although voice recognition appears to be a promising technology, challenges associated with vocabulary, homonyms, and accents have slowed its widespread implementation. "The computer right now can do a very good job of voice recognition," said Bill Gates, co-founder and chairman of Microsoft Corporation (59). "Demonstrations are good but whenever you get it out and start working with it, it has a hard time, particularly if you are working with a very large vocabulary. It certainly will re-define the way we think of the machines when we have that voice input" (Gates 59).

Define a Concept, Illustrate a Process, or Clarify a Statement

Writers commonly turn to information from sources to define concepts, illustrate processes, or clarify statements when the information is clearer and more concise than what they might write themselves. For example, to define a concept, you might quote or paraphrase a dictionary or an encyclopedia. To help readers understand a complex process, such as the steps involved in cellular respiration, you might use an illustration.

Writers also use information from sources to clarify their statements. A writer might explain a point by providing examples from sources or by using quotations or paraphrases to back up an assertion.

> Studies have found connections between weight loss and coffee intake. This doesn't mean that drinking a couple of cups of coffee each day leads to weight loss. However, three recent studies reported that individuals who increased their coffee intake from fewer than three cups to more than eight cups of coffee per day experienced weight losses of up to 7% over a two-month period (Chang; Johnson and Salazar; Neiman). "It may be that increased caffeine intake led to a higher metabolic level, which in turn led to weight loss," noted John Chang, a senior researcher at the Centers for Disease Control. "Or it might be that drinking so much coffee depressed participants' appetites" (232).

Set a Mood

You can also choose quotations and illustrations with an eye toward establishing an overall mood for your readers. The emotional impact of images of a celebration at a sporting event, an expression of grief at a funeral, or a calming mountain vista can lead your readers to react in specific ways to your document. Similarly, a striking quote, such as "The screams of pain coming out of that room will stay with me as long as I live," can evoke a particular mood in your readers.

Provide an Example

It's often better to *show* with an example than to *tell* with a general description. Examples provide concrete evidence in your document. Featured writer Caitlin Guariglia uses an example from a well-known film to illustrate a point in her essay about her family's relationship with food.

> And the obsession with eating! My grandmother feeds us constantly. My dad and I always laugh at that scene in *Goodfellas* where the mobsters show up at two in the morning after killing someone, and one mobster's mother whips up a full pasta meal for them. We know that my grandmother would do the same thing: "Are you hungry?

Here, sit, eat!" Grandma holds interventions over pasta. If she is unhappy with something someone in the family is doing, she invites everyone over for pasta, and we hash it out together. Was this something all Italians do? Or was my idea of a typical Italian person all wrong? Our time in Rome clarified some of these questions for me.

Amplify or Qualify a Point

You can use amplification to expand the scope of a point. In her analytical essay, featured writer Ali Bizzul uses information from a source to broaden her discussion of the dangers football players face when they add bulk.

> NFL offensive linemen who weigh less than 300 pounds are often described as "undersized," so it's no surprise that young football players are getting the message that bigger is better—and bulking up. A recent study of high school linemen in Iowa showed that 45% were overweight and 9% were severely obese, while only 18% of other young males were overweight; even more troubling, a study in Michigan revealed that among football players from ages 9 to 14, 45% could be considered overweight or obese (as cited in Longman, 2007).

Qualifications, in contrast, allow you to narrow the scope of a statement. You can use qualifications to present a point more precisely, reducing the possibility that your readers might misunderstand your meaning. Ali Bizzul makes it clear that deaths related to weight gain are a rare occurrence in football.

> Although such fatalities are unusual, a growing number of doctors believe that use of dietary supplements increases the risk of heatstroke among football players.

How Can I Integrate Sources into My Draft?

Source material can be used to introduce important concepts, establish a main idea, and support or elaborate on a point. Writers use a range of strategies, such as quoting, paraphrasing, and summarizing, to integrate information, ideas, and arguments from sources into their documents. In the following example, the evidence takes the form of a quotation and a paraphrase, both of which support a point introduced in the first sentence of the paragraph.

One way colleges should use tuition money to benefit students is by redesigning their financial aid systems. Although colleges have reportedly increased their need-based financial aid, most of these precious funds go to boost tuition aid for middle-class students. Tamar Lewin from the *New York Times* writes, "Student borrowing has more than doubled in the last decade, and students from lower-income families, on average, get smaller grants from the colleges they attend than students from more affluent families." Basing more award decisions on financial need instead of merit would allow more students from lower-income families to attend college. As hard economic times continue to affect family finances, some colleges are even offering emergency aid and loans, particularly in cases where parents have lost jobs (Young). More colleges must take similar steps to ensure that students from all economic backgrounds have a fighting chance at affording an education.

By quoting a recent *New York Times* article on the issue, featured writer Jennie Tillson strengthens her argument about the burden of student loans on lower-income families. The quotation, along with a subsequent paraphrase of a passage from another source, provides evidence to support her point that colleges should rethink how they award financial aid. Finally, she follows the quotation and paraphrase with a sentence that restates the main point of the paragraph — and an important supporting point for her argument.

You can integrate sources by quoting, paraphrasing, summarizing, presenting numerical information, and using illustrations. When you do so, be sure to distinguish your ideas and information from those found in your sources.

Identify Your Sources

You should identify the sources of information in your document for several reasons. First, doing so fulfills your obligation to document your sources. Second, it allows you (and your readers) to recognize the boundaries between your ideas and those borrowed from sources. Third, it can help you strengthen your document by calling attention to the qualifications or experiences of the person whose ideas you are incorporating.

USE ATTRIBUTIONS AND IN-TEXT CITATIONS

Whenever you quote, paraphrase, or summarize, distinguish between your ideas and the information you obtained from your sources by using attributions — brief comments such as "according to" or "as the author points out" — to alert your readers that the point is not your own.

Writers who use the MLA or APA documentation system also provide citations—
or acknowledgments of source information—within the text of their document to
indicate where borrowed material ends. These citations, in turn, refer readers to a list
of works cited or a list of references at the end of the document.

Note the following examples, which use attributions and in-text citations.

MLA Style

Pamela Coke argues, "Education reform is the best solution for fixing our public
schools" (22).

"Education reform is the best solution for fixing our public schools" (Coke 22).

APA Style

Pamela Coke (2008) has argued, "Education reform is the best solution for fixing our
public schools" (p. 22).

"Education reform is the best solution for fixing our public schools" (Coke, 2008, p. 22).

> Attributions identify the author of the quotations.

> MLA-style in-text citations include the author's name and exact page reference.

> APA-style in-text citations include the author's name, publication date, and exact page reference.

When you acknowledge material you've borrowed from sources, try to vary the
wording of your attributions. Be aware, however, that the verbs in attributions can
convey important shades of meaning. For example, saying that someone "alleged"
something is quite different from saying that someone "confirmed" something. The
form your attributions take will depend on your use of citation style. MLA recommends present tense ("the author points out"), while APA recommends past tense
("the author pointed out").

Some Common Attributions

according to	claims	expresses	reports
acknowledges	comments	inquires	says
affirms	confirms	interprets	states
alleges	declares	muses	suggests
asserts	denies	notes	thinks
assumes	describes	observes	wonders
asks	disputes	points out	writes
believes	emphasizes	remarks	

You can learn more about text citations in Chapter 21 (MLA style) and Chapter 22 (APA style).

PROVIDE A CONTEXT

Skilled writers know the importance of providing a context for the source information they include in their documents. It's not enough to simply put text within two quotation marks and move on. Such "orphan quotations"—quotations dropped into a paragraph without any introduction—are confusing. Worse, paraphrases and summaries inserted without context can easily be mistaken for plagiarism.

To provide a clear context for your source information, establish why the quotation, paraphrase, or summary is reliable by identifying the source's credentials. In addition, indicate how it relates to your main idea and what it contributes to the point you are making. If you don't, readers will wonder why it's there.

> Description of the findings

> Attribution identifies the source as experts.

> The writer follows APA style; parenthetical citation identifies the page number where the quotation was found.

However, Wechsler et al. (2003) analyzed trends at schools using social norms marketing and revealed that the campaigns did not necessarily decrease student drinking; in some cases, schools even reported higher alcohol consumption, according to seven criteria that measured whether students drank, how much, and how often. The team, from the Harvard School of Public Health's College Alcohol Study, suggested that because social norms marketing was first developed at a small school that wasn't very diverse, it might not be as suitable for schools with many different kinds of people. As the researchers explained, "Individual students' drinking behaviors align more closely to the drinking behaviors of their immediate social group rather than to the overall student population at a given school" (p. 492).

Quote Strategically

A well-chosen quotation can have a powerful impact on your readers' perception of your main point and on the overall quality of your document. Quotations can also add a sense of immediacy by bringing in the voice of someone who has been affected by a subject or lend a sense of authority to your document by conveying the words of an expert. Quotations can range in form from brief partial quotations to extended block quotations. As you integrate quotations, you might need to modify them to suit your purpose and to fit the flow of your sentences. When you do, be careful to punctuate them properly.

USE PARTIAL, COMPLETE, OR BLOCK QUOTATIONS

Quotations can be parts of sentences (partial), whole sentences (complete), or long passages (block). When you choose one type of quotation over another, consider the length and complexity of the passage as well as the obligation to convey ideas and information fairly.

Partial quotations can be a single word, a phrase, or most of a sentence. They are often used to convey a well-turned phrase or to complete a sentence using important words from a source, as in the following example.

> Weitzman (2004) notes that by changing the "contextual forces," such as the availability of alcohol, that encourage students to drink, this approach more strongly emphasizes policies that directly put a stop to excessive drinking—unlike the social norms marketing approach, which relies on influencing individual behavior (p. 187).

Quotation marks indicate the borrowed phrase.

Source information, including the page number containing the quotation, is clearly identified.

Complete quotations are typically one or more full sentences and are most often used when the meaning of the passage cannot be conveyed adequately by a few well-chosen words, as in the following example.

> I smiled when I read Elizabeth Gilbert's memoir *Eat, Pray, Love*. Gilbert writes, "The Neapolitan women in particular are such a gang of tough-voiced, loud-mouthed, generous, nosy dames, all bossy and annoyed and right up in your face just trying to friggin' *help* you for chrissake, you dope—*why they gotta do everything around here?*" (78).

Block quotations are extended quotations (usually more than four typed lines) that are set off in a block from the rest of the text. In general, use a colon to introduce the quotation, indent the entire quotation one inch from the left margin, and include source information according to the documentation system you are using (such as MLA or APA). Since the blocked text indicates that you are quoting directly, you do not need to include quotation marks.

> Instead of cutting education funding, states should provide more money for schools, especially now when jobs are scarce and even trained workers are eager to return to school. Patrick Callan, president of the National Center for Public Policy and Higher Education, observes:

> Parenthetical citation indicates that this material was quoted in another source. In block quotations, the citation information is placed after the period.

When the economy is good, and state universities are somewhat better funded, we raise tuition as little as possible. When the economy is bad, we raise tuition and sock it to families, when people can least afford it. That's exactly the opposite of what we need. (qtd. in Lewin)

MODIFY QUOTATIONS AS APPROPRIATE

You can modify quotations to fit your draft. It is acceptable, for example, to delete unnecessary words or to change the tense of a word in a partial quotation so that it fits your sentence. Keep in mind, however, that writers have an obligation to quote sources accurately and fairly. You should indicate when you have added or deleted words, and you should not modify quotations in a way that distorts their meaning.

The most useful strategies for modifying quotations include using ellipses (. . .) to indicate deleted words, using brackets ([ ]) to clarify meaning, and using "sic" to note errors in a source.

The following example shows the use of brackets to change the tense of a verb in a partial quotation.

Original Quotation

"They treated us like family and refused to accept a tip."

Modified Quotation

> Brackets indicate that the tense of a word has been changed.

It's a place where the staff treats you "like family and refuse[s] to accept a tip," said travel writer Melissa Ancomi.

You can learn more about strategies for modifying quotations on pages 513–514.

PUNCTUATE QUOTATIONS CORRECTLY

Use the following rules for punctuating quotations:

- Use double quotation marks (" ") around partial or complete quotations. Do not use quotation marks for block quotations.

- Use single quotation marks (' ') to indicate quoted material within a quotation.

  "The hotel manager told the guests to 'make yourselves at home.'"

- Place commas and periods inside quotation marks.

- Place question marks and exclamation points outside quotation marks if the punctuation pertains to the entire sentence rather than the quotation. In the following example, the original quotation is not a question, so the question mark should be placed after the quotation mark.

> But what can be gained from following the committee's recommendation that the state should "avoid, without exceptions, any proposed tax hike"?

- Place question marks and exclamation points inside quotation marks if the punctuation pertains to the quotation itself.

> Dawn Smith asked an important question: "Do college students understand the importance of avoiding running up the debt on their credit cards?"

- Place colons and semicolons outside quotation marks.

> Many college students consider themselves "free at last"; all too often, however, they find that freedom has its costs.

- When citation information is provided after a partial or complete quotation, place the punctuation mark (comma, period, semicolon, colon, or question mark) after the parenthetical citation.

> "Preliminary reports have been consistent," Yates notes. "Without immediate changes to current practices, we will deplete known oil supplies by mid-century" (335).

- At the end of a block quotation, place the final punctuation before the parenthetical citation.

- Use three spaced periods (ellipsis) to indicate an omission within a sentence.

> According to critic Joe Robinson, Americans are overworked: "Ask Americans how things are really going and you'll hear stories of . . . fifty- and sixty-hour weeks with no letup in sight" (467).

- Place a period after the ellipsis to indicate an omission at the end of a sentence.

> The most recent information indicates, says Chen, that "we can expect a significant increase in costs by the end of the decade. . . . Those costs, however, should ramp up slowly" (35).

Paraphrase Information, Ideas, and Arguments

A paraphrase is a restatement, in your own words, of a passage from a source. Paraphrases can be used to illustrate or support a point you make in your document or to illustrate another author's argument about a subject.

Your notes are likely to include a number of paraphrases of information, ideas, and arguments from your sources. (See pp. 515–516 for more on paraphrasing.) Before you integrate a paraphrase into your document, make sure that it is an accurate and fair representation of the source. Reread the source, and double-check your paraphrase against it. Then revise the paraphrase as necessary so that it fits the context and tone of your document. Use attributions and citations to ensure a smooth transition between your ideas and ideas from the source.

In the following example, note how featured writer Donovan Mikrot lets readers know where his statement ends and where the support for his statement, in the form of a paraphrase, begins.

The writer's idea —

As digital music and video gained popularity, inventors assumed that the same rules would apply to the new hardware and software they developed for digital files. Instead, the DMCA lets music, computer, gaming, and other companies restrict technology and research that could potentially be used to get around their DRM — including research that would help address computer security issues (EFF).

Source of paraphrase (in this case, a Web document) is cited per MLA style.

Summarize Sources

A summary is a concise statement, written in your own words, of the information, ideas, and arguments found in a source (see pp. 516–518 for more on summarizing). When you integrate a summary into your draft, review the source to make sure your summary is an accurate and fair representation. In addition, be sure to identify the source and include a citation.

You can summarize an entire source, parts of a particular source, or a group of sources to support your ideas.

SUMMARIZE AN ENTIRE SOURCE

Writers frequently summarize an entire work. In some cases, the summary might occupy one or more paragraphs or be integrated into a discussion contained in one or more paragraphs. In other cases, the summary might be as brief as a single sentence.

In her analytical essay about the health risks faced by overweight athletes, featured writer Ali Bizzul provides a detailed summary of a scholarly article published in the *Journal of the American Medical Association*.

> According to Harp and Hecht (2005), two researchers at the University of North Carolina who conducted a study of 2,168 professional football players competing in the 2003–2004 season, 97% of NFL players would be considered "overweight" and 56% "obese" under the Body Mass Index (BMI) guidelines published by the National Institutes of Health for men in their twenties (see Fig. 1). The researchers noted that the group of football players with the highest rates of obesity — the linemen — also had higher blood pressure readings and higher incidences of sleep-disordered breathing than any other group of football players.

According to APA style, the authors are identified in an attribution and the publication year is provided parenthetically.

The main point of the article

Additional information from the article

In contrast, Ali offers a much briefer, "nutshell" summary of another source.

> In an editorial in the medical journal *Neurosurgery*, three sports-medicine specialists noted that after a 1994 federal law exempted dietary supplements from regulation by the Food and Drug Administration, heat-related injuries among football players began to rise (Bailes, Cantu, & Day, 2002).

The entire source is summarized; because it is a summary, not a direct quotation, page numbers are not necessary.

SUMMARIZE SPECIFIC INFORMATION AND IDEAS FROM A SOURCE

You can also use summaries to convey key information or ideas from a source. In the following example, the writer of an essay summarizes a section of a book about college admissions. His summary is highlighted in yellow.

> Bill Paul, author of *Getting In: Inside the College Admissions Process*, a book that tells the stories of several students applying to an elite Ivy League institution, shares three suggestions for students who want to get into a college. Paul bases these suggestions on his discussions with Fred Hargadon, who in 1995 was dean of admissions at Princeton. Hargadon suggested that the best way students can enhance their chances for acceptance into the college of their choice is to read widely, learn to speak a second language, and engage in activities that interest and excite them and that also help them develop their confidence and creativity (235–49).

Summary is introduced with the author of the book, title, and specific source of the ideas.

Per MLA style, exact pages are cited.

SUMMARIZE A GROUP OF SOURCES

In addition to summarizing a single source, writers often summarize groups of sources. Such collective summaries (often introduced by phrases such as "Numerous authors argue . . ." or "The research in this area seems to indicate that . . .") allow you to establish a point briefly and with authority. They are particularly effective at the beginning of a document, when you are establishing the nature of the conversation you are joining, and can serve as a transitional device when you move from one major section of the document to another.

When you summarize a group of sources, separate the citations with a semicolon. MLA guidelines require including author and page information, as in the following example.

> Several critics argue that the Hemingway code hero is not always male (Graulich 217; Sherman 78; Watters 33).

In APA style, the author and the date of publication must be included.

> The benefits of early detection of breast cancer have been well documented (Page, 2007; Richards, 2007; Vincent, 2008).

Present Numerical Information

If it suits your subject, you might use numerical information, such as statistics, in your document. You can present this information within sentences, or you might use tables, charts, or graphs, as featured writer Jennie Tillson did in her problem-solving essay about college tuition costs.

If you use tables, charts, or graphs, you still need to accurately and fairly present the numerical information in your document and clearly identify the source of the data, just as you would for textual information. For more information about using tables, charts, and graphs, see page 604.

Use Images, Audio, and Video

Including images in your print document or adding images, audio, or video files to your electronic document can enhance its effectiveness. Use caution, however, when taking images and audio or video files from other sources. Simply copying a photograph or an audio or video file into your document might be a form of plagiarism.

Featured writer Hannah Steiner carefully documented the source of the image she used in her informative essay. Because she was writing an academic essay—rather than a document intended for publication and wide distribution—she did not seek permission to use it. (In contrast, the publisher of this book sought and received permission to publish that image.)

Only by investing in educating their citizens during hard economic times will states see the benefits of having educated workers and business owners — and higher-earning taxpayers — in the state during better times. For this reason, higher education should be a top priority in even trimmed-down state budgets so that students and their families won't face drastic increases in tuition.

At the same time, students still ultimately bear the responsibility for finding the best path to an affordable college education. Students and their families are a necessary part of the solution. They should be willing to apply to a variety of schools, including those they can afford more easily without financial aid. Many students and their families are now considering less expensive routes to a college degree, such as enrolling in public universities or community colleges in their home states (Young). Out of eighty-seven college freshmen surveyed at Colorado State University, 80% were likely to recommend community college to a sibling or friend concerned about tuition costs (Tillson). When asked about the benefits of attending community college, students responded that they saw it as "easier to afford" and appreciated that it "makes it easier to work and attend school at the same time" (see fig. 1). The survey shows that students today are giving community colleges serious thought as an alternative to a four-year university.

> A parenthetical reference to the figure is provided.

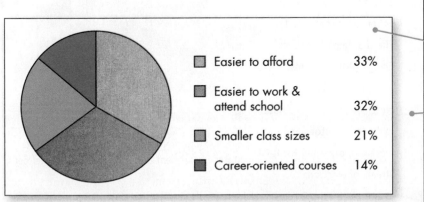

> The figure is located immediately below where it is mentioned in the text.

> The figure summarizes key findings from a survey.

Fig. 1: The perceived benefits of choosing a community college. Based on survey data from Tillson

> A caption provides information about the source of the data.

↑ A Chart Presenting Information in an Essay

the most promising alternatives in development is hydrogen—an abundant fuel that is environmentally safe, is far more versatile than gasoline or diesel, can be used to create electricity and fuel internal combustion engines, and produces no waste. Because of these attributes, some experts have argued that a hydrogen economy—an energy system that uses only a hydrogen-oxygen reaction to create energy and electricity—could solve many fuel-related problems, from global warming to America's dependence on foreign oil (Crabtree, Dresselhause, and Buchanan 39). At first glance, hydrogen appears to be the perfect choice. However, three barriers stand in the way of widespread hydrogen usage: as a fuel, it is expensive to produce, difficult to store, and complicated to distribute.

The key to a hydrogen economy is the fuel cell, which uses hydrogen gas and oxygen to produce electricity. In a way, a fuel cell is like a battery, but it never requires charging and it produces only electricity, heat, and water vapor (see Fig. 1). The U.S. Department of Energy (DOE) explains that hydrogen fuel cells use electrode plates to separate hydrogen's protons and electrons, diverting the stream of electrons to create electricity. A "stack" of fuel cells is scalable, so the same basic structure has many different uses ("Hydrogen Fuel"). In theory, stacks of hydrogen fuel

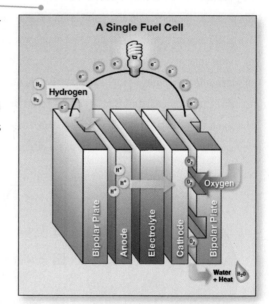

Fig. 1: Simplified model of a fuel cell. United States Department of Energy, "Hydrogen Fuel Cells."

The figure is located next to where it is referred to in the text.

A parenthetical reference to the figure is provided.

Text is "wrapped" around the figure and caption (see chapter 18).

The figure illustrates a complex process that would be too difficult to describe using text alone.

A caption provides information about the source of the figure.

ⵑ An Image Providing an Overview of a Complex Process

If you are creating an electronic document, such as a Web page or a multimedia presentation, use the following guidelines to integrating digital illustrations:

- Make a link between your document and a document that contains an image, a sound clip, or a video clip—rather than copying the image and placing it in your document.

- If it isn't possible or appropriate to create a link to another document, contact the owner of the image, sound clip, or video clip for permission to use it.

- If you cannot contact the owner, review the fair-use guidelines discussed on pages 524–525 for guidance about using the material.

As you would for any sources you cite in your document, make sure you fairly present images, audio, or video and identify the author or creator.

How Can I Ensure I've Avoided Plagiarism?

Because plagiarized material will often differ in style, tone, and word choice from the rest of your document, your readers are likely to notice these differences and wonder whether you've plagiarized the material—or, if not, why you've written a document that has so many stylistic inconsistencies. If your readers react negatively, it's unlikely that your document will be successful.

You can avoid plagiarism by quoting, paraphrasing, and summarizing accurately and appropriately; distinguishing between your ideas and ideas in your sources; and identifying sources in your document.

Quote, Paraphrase, and Summarize Accurately and Appropriately

Unintentional plagiarism usually occurs when a writer takes poor notes and then uses the information from those notes in a document. As you draft, do the following:

- Look for notes that differ from your usual style of writing. More often than not, if a note doesn't sound like your own writing, it isn't.

- Place quotation marks around any direct quotations, use ellipses and brackets appropriately (see pp. 513–514), and identify the source and the page or paragraph number of the quotation.

- Make sure that paraphrases differ significantly in word choice and sentence structure from the passage being paraphrased, and identify the source and page or paragraph number from which you took the paraphrase.

- Make sure that summaries are not just a series of passages or close paraphrases copied from the source.

Distinguish between Your Ideas and Ideas in Your Sources

Failing to distinguish between your ideas and ideas drawn from your sources can lead readers to think other writers' ideas are yours. Examine how the following writer might have failed to distinguish his ideas from those of Joel Levine and Lawrence May, authors of a source he used in his essay.

Failing to Credit Ideas to a Source

According to Joel Levine and Lawrence May, authors of *Getting In*, entrance exams are an extremely important part of a student's college application and carry a great deal of weight. In fact, a college entrance examination is one of the two most significant factors in getting into college. The other, unsurprisingly, is high school grades.

Because the second and third sentences fail to identify Levine and May as the source of the information about the second important factor affecting admissions decisions — high school grades — the passage implies that the writer is the source of that information.

As it turns out, the writer actually included the necessary attribution in his essay.

The attribution "they claim" credits the source of the information to Levine and May.

Quotation marks are used to indicate a partial quotation.

Giving Credit to the Source

According to Joel Levine and Lawrence May, authors of *Getting In*, entrance exams are an extremely important part of a student's college application and carry a great deal of weight. In fact, they claim that a college entrance examination is "one of the two most significant factors" in getting into college (the other, unsurprisingly, is high school grades).

You can use attributions to distinguish between your ideas and those obtained from your sources. As you draft your document, use the name of an author or the title of the source you're drawing from each time you introduce ideas from a source.

Examples of Attribution

According to Scott McPherson . . .

Jill Bedard writes . . .

Tom Huckin reports . . .

Kate Kiefer observes . . .

Bob Phelps suggests . . .

In the words of Pamela Coke . . .

As Ellen Page tells it . . .

Reid Vincent indicates . . .

Jessica Richards calls our attention to . . .

Check for Unattributed Sources in Your Document

Writers sometimes neglect to identify the sources from which they have drawn their information. You should include a complete citation for each source you refer to in your document. The citation should appear in the text of the document (as an in-text citation, footnote, or endnote) or in a works cited list, references list, or bibliography.

The following examples use MLA style for citing sources; more detailed information about the sources appears in a list of works cited at the end of the document. In the first example, the writer uses a combination of attribution and parenthetical information; in the second example, the writer provides only a parenthetical citation.

> Reid Vincent argues, "We must explore emerging energy technologies before we reach a peak oil crisis" (322).

> "We must explore emerging energy technologies before we reach a peak oil crisis" (Vincent 322).

MLA-style in-text citations include the author's name and exact page reference.

If you are using MLA format, be sure to cite page or paragraph numbers not only for direct quotations but also for paraphrased and summarized information. (If no page or paragraph numbers are provided, such as in a Web source, cite the author only.) The following paraphrase of Reid Vincent's comments about energy needs includes the page number of the original passage in parentheses.

> Reid Vincent argues that we need to investigate new energy technologies now, instead of while we are facing a critical oil shortage (322).

To learn more about identifying sources in your document, see page 578. For more information on the MLA and APA documentation systems, see Chapters 21 and 22.

How Should I Document My Sources?

In addition to citing your sources within the text of your document, you should provide complete publication information for each source you've used. Fully documenting your sources helps you avoid plagiarism, gives credit to others who have written about a subject, and creates a record of their work that your readers can follow and build on. By documenting your sources, you show that you are aware that other writers have contributed to the conversation about your subject and that you respect them enough to acknowledge their contributions.

Documenting your sources can help you achieve your purposes as a writer, such as establishing your authority and persuading your readers. If your readers find that you haven't documented your sources, either they'll suspect that you're careless or they'll decide that you're dishonest. In either case, they won't trust what you have to say.

Choose a Documentation System

Many professional organizations and publications have developed their own rules for formatting documents and citing sources. As a result, writers in various disciplines know how to cite their sources clearly and consistently, and their readers know what to expect. For example, a psychologist writing an article for the *Journal of Counseling Psychology* knows that submissions to the journal go through a rigorous review for substance and style before being accepted for publication. The journal requires that writers use the documentation system created by the American Psychological Association (APA). Given the high level of competition for space in the journal, the writer knows that even if the article is substantive and compelling, it will not be accepted for publication if it does not use APA style appropriately. After ensuring that the article is clearly written and well argued, the writer will double-check the article to be certain it follows the APA's formatting and source citation guidelines.

The documentation systems most commonly used in academic disciplines are the following:

- **MLA.** This style, developed by the Modern Language Association, is used primarily in the humanities—English, philosophy, linguistics, world languages, and so on. See Chapter 21.

- **APA.** Developed by the American Psychological Association, this style is used mainly in the social sciences—psychology, sociology, anthropology, political science, economics, education, and so on. See Chapter 22.

- *Chicago.* Developed by the University of Chicago Press, this style is used primarily in history, journalism, and the humanities.

- **CSE.** This style, developed by the Council of Science Editors (formerly the Council of Biology Editors), is used mainly in the physical and life sciences—chemistry, geology, biology, botany, and so on—and in mathematics.

Your choice of documentation system will be guided by the discipline or field within which you are writing and by any documentation requirements associated with your writing project. If your project has been assigned to you, ask the person who assigned it or someone who has written a similar document which documentation system you should use. If you are working on a project for a writing class, your instructor will usually tell you which documentation system to follow.

You should also consider the genre you have chosen for your document. The manner in which sources are cited can vary widely from one type of document to another. For example, while academic essays and articles appearing in scholarly journals typically use a documentation system such as MLA or APA, newspaper and magazine articles often do not; instead they identify sources in the main text of the document rather than in a works cited or references list. If you write an electronic document that cites other online sources, you might simply link to those sources.

Provide In-Text References and Publication Information

How you document sources will depend on your writing situation. Most often, you will (1) provide a reference to your source within the text and (2) provide a complete set of citations for your sources in a works cited or references list.

The specific format of your in-text citations will depend on the documentation system you are following. If you use MLA or APA style, you will refer to sources in the text of your document using a combination of attributions and parenthetical information and include a list of sources at the end of your document. The works cited list (MLA) or references list (APA) includes the following key publication information about each source:

- author(s) and/or editor(s)

- title

- publication date

- publisher and city of publication (for books)

- periodical name, volume, issue, and page numbers (for articles)

- URL and access date (for online publications)

Each documentation system creates an association between in-text citations and the works cited or references list. See Chapters 21 and 22 for documentation models.

In Summary: Using Sources Effectively

○ Use sources to support your points (p. 572).

○ Indicate the boundaries between source material and your own ideas (p. 577).

○ Modify direct quotations carefully (p. 582).

○ Revise paraphrases to fit your style (p. 584).

○ Summarize entire sources, parts of sources, or groups of sources (p. 584).

○ Integrate numerical information appropriately (p. 586).

○ Integrate images, audio, and video responsibly (p. 586).

○ Check for unintentional plagiarism (p. 589).

○ Document your sources (p. 592).

18 Designing Your Document

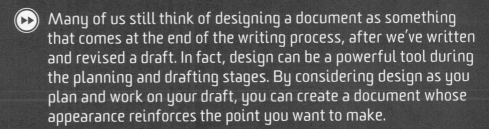

Many of us still think of designing a document as something that comes at the end of the writing process, after we've written and revised a draft. In fact, design can be a powerful tool during the planning and drafting stages. By considering design as you plan and work on your draft, you can create a document whose appearance reinforces the point you want to make.

Your design decisions—such as selecting appropriate fonts, including compelling illustrations, and presenting information in charts and tables—can have powerful effects on how you shape and present your ideas. They will also play a critical role in how your readers understand and react to your document. Understanding design principles and elements, as well as the design conventions of documents typically assigned in college courses, can help you craft a unique and substantial contribution to a conversation.

How Can I Use Design Effectively?

Although the most important factor in the success of your writing project is the ability to express your ideas and arguments clearly, you should also think about how the design of your document can help you achieve your purpose, affect your readers, and meet their expectations.

Understand Design Principles

Before you begin formatting text or inserting illustrations, consider how the design principles of balance, emphasis, placement, repetition, and consistency can help you accomplish your goals as a writer.

Balance is the vertical and horizontal alignment of elements on your pages (see the example on page 597). Symmetrical designs create a sense of rest and stability and lead readers' eyes to focus on a particular part of a document. In contrast, asymmetrical — or unbalanced — designs suggest movement and guide readers' eyes across the page.

Emphasis is the placement and formatting of elements, such as headings and sub-headings, so that they catch your readers' attention. You can emphasize an element in a document by using a color or font that distinguishes it from other elements; by placing a border around it and adding a shaded background; or by using an illustration, such as a photograph, drawing, or graph.

Placement is the location of elements on your pages. Placing elements next to or near each other suggests that they are related. An illustration, for example, is usually placed near the passage in which it is mentioned.

Repetition is the use of elements, such as headers and footers, navigation menus, and page numbers, throughout the pages in your document. As readers move from page to page, they tend to expect certain elements, such as page numbers, to appear in the same place. In addition, repeated elements, such as a logo or Web navigation menu, help establish a sense of identity across the pages in your document.

Consistency is the extent to which you format and place elements such as text, headings, footnotes, and illustrations in the same way throughout your document. Treating each design element consistently will help readers recognize the role it plays in your document and, by extension, will help them locate the information they seek. A consistent design can also convey a sense of competence and professionalism to your readers, increasing their confidence in the quality and credibility of your document.

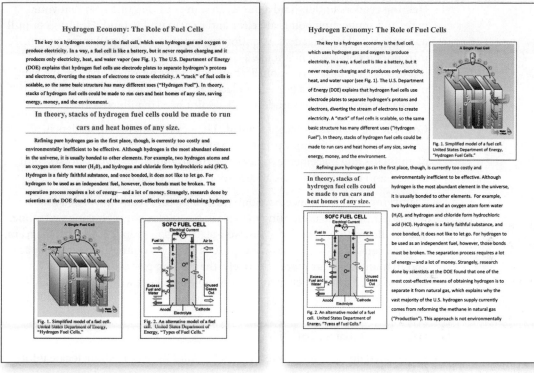

⌐ Symmetrical (left) and Asymmetrical (right) Layouts

You should also keep two other principles in mind: simplicity and moderation. An overly complex design can obscure important ideas and information. Using design elements moderately to create a simple yet effective design is the best approach.

Design for a Purpose

A well-designed document presents your information, ideas, and arguments in a manner that helps you accomplish your purposes.

You might use design to achieve any of the following goals:

- **Setting a tone.** One of the most powerful tools writers have for accomplishing their purpose is establishing an emotional context for their readers. You can set a tone by using a particular color scheme, such as bright, cheerful hues, or by selecting photographs or drawings with a strong emotional impact.

- **Helping readers understand a point.** Design your document so that your main and supporting points are clear and easy to understand. Headings or pull quotes can call your readers' attention to important ideas and information. To introduce a point, you might use a contrasting font or color to signal the importance of the information. To highlight a definition or an example, you might enclose it inside a border or place the passage in a pull quote (p. 602). You can also help readers understand a point by using illustrations.

- **Convincing readers to accept a point.** The key to convincing readers is providing them with appropriate, relevant evidence. Drawing on the principles of emphasis and placement, you can use illustrations, marginal glosses, pull quotes, and bulleted lists to call attention to that evidence.

- **Clarifying complex concepts.** Sometimes a picture really is worth a thousand words. Rather than attempting to explain a complex concept using text alone, add an illustration. A well-chosen, well-placed photograph, flowchart, diagram, or table can define a complex concept such as photosynthesis in far less space, and in many cases far more effectively, than a long passage of text can. You can also clarify the key elements of a complex concept with bulleted and numbered lists.

Design for Your Readers

A well-designed document helps readers understand its organization, locate information and ideas, and recognize the function of its different parts. It is also easy on their eyes: readers working with a well-designed document will not have to strain to read the text or discern illustrations. Use document design to do the following.

Help readers understand the organization of a document. You can use headings and subheadings to signal the content of each part of the document. If you do, keep in mind the design principles of emphasis and consistency: format your headings in a consistent manner that helps them stand out from other parts of the document.

Help readers locate information and ideas. Many longer print documents use tables of contents and indexes to help readers locate information and ideas. Web sites typically provide a mix of menus and navigation headers and footers to help readers move around the site. You can distinguish these navigation aids from the surrounding text by using bordered or shaded boxes or contrasting fonts.

Help readers recognize the function of parts of a document. You might want to include passages that differ from the main text of your document, such as sidebars and "For More Information" sections. If so, help readers understand their function by making them stand out visually. You might design a sidebar with a

Jenna Albetter
Professor Garcia
AR414
27 April 2009

Images of Women in Seventeenth-Century Dutch Art and Literature

Artists and their artwork do not exist in a vacuum. The images artists create help shape and in turn are shaped by the society and culture in which they are created. The artists and artworks in the Dutch Baroque period are no exception. In this seventeenth-century society of merchants and workers, people of all classes purchased art to display in their homes. As a result, artists in the period catered to the wishes of the people, producing art that depicted the everyday world (Kleiner and Tansey 864). It is too simplistic, however, to assume that this relationship was unidirectional. Dutch Baroque genre paintings did not simply reflect the reality surrounding them; they also helped to shape that reality. For instance, members of seventeenth-century Dutch society had very specific ideas regarding the roles of women. These ideas, which permeated every level of society, are represented in the literature and visual art of the period (Franits, Paragons 17).

The Concept of Domesticity

During the seventeenth century, the concept of domesticity appears to have been very important in all levels of Dutch society; literally hundreds of surviving paintings reflect this theme. Such paintings depict members of every class and occupation, and according to Wayne Franits, a specialist in seventeenth-century Dutch art, they served the dual purpose of both entertaining and instructing the viewer. They invite the viewer to inspect and enjoy their vivid details, but also to contemplate the values and ideals they represent (Franits, "Domesticity" 13).

Images of domesticity in the visual arts grew immensely in popularity around the middle of the seventeenth century. Although there is no definitive explanation for this rise in popularity, there is a long history in Dutch art and literature of focusing on domestic themes. In the early sixteenth century, Protestant reformers and humanists wrote books and treatises on domestic issues. Their main focus was the roles and responsibilities of members of the family, especially the women.

Albetter 2

This type of literature continued to be produced, and flourished, in the first half of the seventeenth century (Franits, "Domesticity" 13). Perhaps the most well-known and influential work of literature of this type is Jacob Cats's book Houwelyck, or Marriage. Published in 1625, this was a comprehensive reference book for women of all ages, but especially young women, regarding matters of marriage and family. Although many other similar books were being published in the Netherlands and England during this period, Cats's work was perhaps the most extensive; it even contained an alphabetical index for quick reference (Franits, Paragons 5).

Cat's How to Guide: Houwelyck

Houwelyck, which by mid-century had sold over 50,000 copies, making it a best-seller for its time, contained instruction for women on the proper behavior for the six stages of life: Maiden, Sweetheart, Bride, Housewife, Mother, and Widow. It is particularly telling that these stages of life were defined in reference to the roles of men. Although Cats's book specifically addressed women, it had implications for men as well (Westermann 119). According to Cats, by laying out the roles and duties of the woman, his book "encompasses also the masculine counter-duties" (qtd. in Westermann 119).

The illustration on the title page of the first edition of Cats's work shows what was considered the ideal role for a woman at this time. Created by Adriaen van de Venne, Stages of Life (Fig. 1) depicts several figural groups arranged on a hill. It shows life as a large hill, with marriage as its pinnacle, and then heading down toward widowhood and death (Westermann 120). This depiction seems to reflect the expectations society held for its women—that a woman's goal in life should be to provide a man with a good, proper wife and, once that duty has been fulfilled, to wait dutifully for death.

Images of young women are numerous in the visual art of this period. Gerard Dou's Portrait of a Young Woman (Fig. 2) exemplifies this type of work. This painting demonstrates that portraiture was highly influenced by contemporary ideals of feminine virtue. The young woman's pose is passive, self-contained, and somewhat rigid, communicating her dignity, humility, and modesty, which were all considered very important in a young girl. She holds a songbook in her lap, which not only indicated her skill in the arts but was also considered a symbol of docility. Near her rest

> Use of a contrasting font and color helps readers understand the document's organization.

⌐ **Headings and Subheadings in an Essay**

shaded or colored box or format a list of related readings or Web links in a contrasting font or color.

What Design Elements Can I Use?

Understanding the range of design elements at your disposal will enable you to decide which ones to use in your document. These elements include fonts, line spacing, and alignment; page layout strategies; color, shading, borders, and rules; and illustrations.

Use Fonts, Line Spacing, and Alignment

Font, line-spacing, and alignment choices are the most common design decisions that writers make. They are also among the most important, since poor choices can make a document difficult to read. The examples on pages 600–601 provide an overview of the key features of fonts as well as the uses of fonts, line spacing, and alignment.

@ View guides for using your word-processing program to design documents at **bedfordstmartins.com/ conversation**.

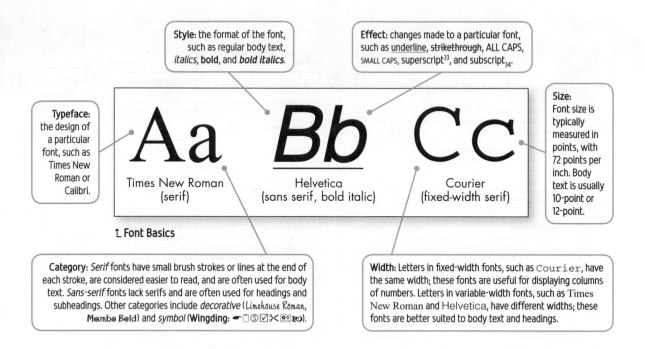

Style: the format of the font, such as regular body text, *italics*, **bold**, and ***bold italics***.

Effect: changes made to a particular font, such as <u>underline</u>, ~~strikethrough~~, ALL CAPS, SMALL CAPS, superscript[33], and subscript[34].

Typeface: the design of a particular font, such as Times New Roman or Calibri.

Times New Roman (serif)

Helvetica (sans serif, bold italic)

Courier (fixed-width serif)

Size: Font size is typically measured in points, with 72 points per inch. Body text is usually 10-point or 12-point.

⌐ **Font Basics**

Category: *Serif* fonts have small brush strokes or lines at the end of each stroke, are considered easier to read, and are often used for body text. *Sans-serif* fonts lack serifs and are often used for headings and subheadings. Other categories include *decorative* (*Limehouse Roman*, *Mambo Bold*) and *symbol* (**Wingding:** ☞▯☺☑✂☀☜).

Width: Letters in fixed-width fonts, such as `Courier`, have the same width; these fonts are useful for displaying columns of numbers. Letters in variable-width fonts, such as Times New Roman and Helvetica, have different widths; these fonts are better suited to body text and headings.

Use Page Layout Elements

Page layout is the placement of text, illustrations, and other objects on a page or screen. Successful page layout draws on a number of design elements, including white space, margins, columns, headers and footers, page numbers, headings, lists, captions, marginal glosses and pull quotes, and sidebars. The example on page 602 illustrates these design elements.

Use Color, Shading, Borders, and Rules

Color, shading, borders, and rules (lines running horizontally or vertically on a page) can increase the overall attractiveness of your document, call attention to important information, help readers understand the organization of your document, help readers recognize the function of specific passages of text, and signal transitions between sections. As you use these design elements, exercise restraint. Avoid using more than three colors on a page, unless you are using a photograph or work of art. Be cautious, as well, about using multiple styles of rules or borders in a document.

Line spacing refers to the amount of space between lines of text. Larger line spacing appears easier to read, so you'll often find increased line spacing in introductory paragraphs, executive summaries (which provide an overview of a longer document), and sidebars (see p. 602).

When text is crammed together vertically, it is difficult to read and to add comments. Keep this in mind if you are creating a document such as an essay on which someone else might write comments.

GLOBAL WARMING

"Just give up that car"

DROPPING KNOWLEDGE IS A CITIZENS GROUP that hosts a compelling website enabling you to exchange ideas on contemporary global issues by posting questions, answering others' inquiries and contemplating responses given by leading voices of our time. To the question "What can I do, and tell others to do, to stop global warming?" German-born director Wim Wenders (photo) responds, "Sell your car, ride your bike and use public transportation." So does he follow his own advice?

Says Wenders: "I don't have a car anymore. I tell you, it's a big relief. I ride my bike in Berlin, I take the S-Bahn, the subway, the trains. My life is so much better. I don't get tickets anymore. I don't have the hassle. I can read more. Just give up that car!"—FRAUKE GODAT

FIND OUT MORE: DROPPINGKNOWLEDGE.ORG

WEALTH

Africa: Richer than you think?

AFRICA IS PORTRAYED BY THE MEDIA AS A BELEAGUERED, poverty-stricken continent, while India and China are cast as economic superpowers. Statistics paint a more nuanced picture. While it's true that some of the world's poorest countries are in Africa, the continent as a whole is wealthier than India, which must divide its gross domestic product among a larger population. Africa's average per capita GDP in 2005 was $954, more than $200 higher than India's. Per capita GDP is higher than India's in a surprising 20 out of 53 countries in Africa. Twelve African nations have a higher per capita GDP than China.

Imagine the investments and business activities lost as a consequence of this biased image, says Vijay Mahajan, a professor with the McCombs School of Business at the University of Texas at Austin. To combat that image problem, Mahajan is writing a book about Africa's potentially powerful consumer market, to be released next summer by Wharton School Publishing.—MARCO VISSCHER

DECEMBER 2007 **ODE 25**

PHOTOGRAPH BY DONATA WENDERS/2005

↳ Using Fonts, Line Spacing, and Alignment

Alignment refers to the horizontal arrangement of text and illustrations (such as photos and drawings). You can select four types of alignment.

- **Left alignment** has a straight left margin and a "ragged" right margin; it is typically the easiest to read.
- **Right alignment** has a straight right margin and a ragged left margin.
- **Centered alignment** is seldom used for body text but can make headings stand out.
- **Justified alignment** has straight alignment on both the left and right margins. It adds a polished look and can be effective in documents that use columns — but it also produces irregular word spacing and hyphenation, which can slow the reading process.

Fonts are a complete set of type of a particular size and typeface. As you choose fonts, consider the following:

- **Select fonts that are easy to read.** For body text, avoid decorative fonts and italics.
- **Select fonts that complement each other.** A serif body font, such as Times New Roman or Garamond, works well with a sans-serif heading font, such as Arial, Helvetica, or Calibri.
- **Exercise restraint.** Generally, use no more than four different fonts in a document.

Pull quotes highlight a passage of text — frequently a quotation — through the use of borders, white space, distinctive fonts, and contrasting colors.

Headings and subheadings identify sections and subsections, serve as transitions, and allow readers to locate information more easily.

White space — literally, empty space — frames and separates elements on a page.

Numbered and bulleted lists (not shown) display brief passages of related information using numbers or symbols (usually round "bullets"). The surrounding white space draws the eye to the list, highlighting the information for your readers, while the brief content in each entry can make concepts or processes easier to understand.

Margins are the white space between the edge of the page or screen (top, bottom, right, and left) and the text or graphics in your document.

Marginal glosses are brief notes in a margin that explain or expand on text in the body of the document.

Captions describe or explain an illustration, such as a photograph or chart.

Sidebars are brief discussions of information related to, but not a central part of, your document. Sidebars simplify the task of integrating related or supporting information into the body of the article by setting that information off in a clearly defined area.

Columns generally appear in newspaper and magazine articles — and, to a growing extent, in articles published on the Web. Essays, on the other hand, are typically formatted in a single column. Columns can improve the readability of a document by limiting the eyes' physical movement across the page and by framing other elements.

Headers, footers, and page numbers appear at the top or bottom of the page, set apart from the main text. They help readers find their way through a document; they provide information, such as the title of the document, its publication date, and its author; and they frame a page visually.

⌐ **Using Page Layout Elements**

EDITORIAL

Our DNA needs protection from 'genome hackers'

In the excited rush to develop personal genomics, issues of privacy have been left behind

A DOCUMENT shredder is a good investment for anyone worried about identity theft. Why make it easy for someone to grab your credit card and bank account numbers from discarded statements?

The information contained in the DNA that we all leave lying around on items such as coffee cups and discarded tissues is just as sensitive, but there is no equivalent of a document shredder for genetic detritus. This is what makes the relative ease with which we hijacked commercial services to obtain genome scans from a reporter's "abandoned" DNA so disturbing (see page 6).

What should be done to shield our genes from prying eyes? Procedures used by some companies can be abused by a determined person and extra steps could prevent this, either by putting the submitted samples under greater scrutiny, or using more checks to verify who the companies are dealing with. Ultimately, though, preserving genetic privacy will require new laws, and the political resolve to push them through.

Many countries have been slow to respond to the challenges posed by technological advances in genetics. Last year, for instance,

the US Congress passed the Genetic Information Nondiscrimination Act to great fanfare. Conveniently forgotten was the fact that concerned members of Congress had been trying to pass such a law for 13 years.

Indeed, GINA reads like a law fashioned for a previous decade. When its provisions come into effect in the coming months, the law will prevent employers and health insurers from discriminating on the basis of DNA tests that suggest future health problems. Its drafting reflected a situation in which individual tests for particular genetic mutations were ordered by doctors. Against this background, controlling the use of test results by

"Lawmakers did not envision genome scans being available over the internet for a few hundred dollars"

organisations with the most obvious power to discriminate was a good move.

Those who drafted GINA did not envision a world in which genome scans can be ordered over the internet for a few hundred dollars. In deciding how to protect our privacy, lawmakers should assume that complete sequencing of our "abandoned" DNA will soon be cheap. They must identify key points at which the law can be tightened without putting a brake on legitimate genetic research and valuable clinical testing.

As a start, we suggest looking at the legality of extracting and analysing DNA left on everyday items such as coffee cups. This option needs to be available to the police and to defence lawyers. The rest of us do not need to behave as if we're living in an episode of CSI. ■

Beware the climate crunch

ONE of the factors behind the credit crunch was a failure to see the big picture: a riskier deal is a lot riskier when everyone is making similar gambles. Once things start going wrong, there can be a domino effect.

Our planet's climate is also precariously balanced. Push it too far and we could trigger a series of positive feedbacks that cause catastrophic change. For example, if rapid warming in the Arctic releases yet more greenhouse gases, runaway warming could happen (see page 32). It is impossible to say how likely such scary scenarios are, which is why official reports barely mention them. But an unquantifiable risk is not the same as no risk. As the financial collapse shows, sometimes the doomsayers get it right. ■

Grizzly crossing

IF YOU ever find yourself on the Trans-Canada Highway in Banff National Park, keep an eye open for odd-looking bridges. They are covered in bushes and trees as if they have fallen into disuse. Anything but: these are grizzly bridges and they are a vital artery allowing bears and other wild animals to cross. They have been so successful that more will now be built to help North America's wildlife roam free (see page 40). It's a small step, but a timely reminder that it is still in our power to make good some of the damage we do to the natural world. ■

➜ What's hot on NewScientist.com

GREEN TECHNOLOGY Social approach needed for green-tech success There's no shortage of research into green transportation technology, but engineers may need help from sociologists to find the best way to get it on the road

ROBOTS Eye-rolling robots give humans a clue Humans could get along with robots more easily if the machines were to "leak" subtle non-verbal clues – such as quick glances at a particular object –

as they speak, just as people do. Watch a video demonstration of robot body language

NEUROSCIENCE Why are some people driven to amputate their own limb? Apotemnophilia is a rare condition in which otherwise mentally normal people desire to amputate a healthy limb. Brain imaging in these individuals is now shedding light on how the brain combines different sensory inputs into a unified body image

NEUROECONOMICS Brain quirk could explain credit crunch With hindsight, the causes of the current global financial meltdown seem obvious, even predictable. Now brain imaging offers one explanation for why so few investors challenged foolhardy financial advice

EXPLORING MARS Up close and personal on the surface of the Red Planet High-resolution 3D images from the surface of Mars are providing evidence of ancient

climate cycles. See our gallery of Martian images

ENVIRONMENT City dwellers harm the climate less Our large urban centres are often assumed to have a disproportionately large impact on the environment, but a new study shows there are climate advantages to city living

For breaking news, slide-shows, video and online debate, visit www.NewScientist.com

↳ Using Color, Shading, Borders, and Rules

Signal the organization of a document. In a longer print document, headers, footers, headings, and subheadings might be formatted with a particular color to help readers recognize which section they are reading. On a Web site, pages in each section could share the same background or heading color.

Be consistent. Use the same colors for top-level headings throughout your document, another color for lower-level headings, and so on. Use the same borders and shading for sidebars. Use rules consistently in pull quotes, headers, and footers. Don't mix and match.

Signal the function of text. A colored or shaded background, as well as colored type, can be used to differentiate captions and pull quotes from body text. Rules can also separate columns of text on a page or screen.

Call attention to important information. Color, borders, and shading can subtly yet clearly emphasize an illustration, such as a table or chart, or an important passage of text, by distinguishing it from the surrounding body text.

Use Illustrations

Illustrations—charts, graphs, tables, photographs and other images, animations, audio clips, and video clips—can expand on or demonstrate points made in the text of your document. They can also reduce the amount of text needed to make a point, help readers better understand your points, and increase the visual appeal of your document.

Photographs and other images. Photographs and other images, such as drawings, paintings, and sketches, are frequently used to set a mood, emphasize a point, or demonstrate a point more fully than is possible with text alone.

Charts and graphs. Charts and graphs represent information visually. They are used to make a point more succinctly than is possible with text alone or to present complex information in a compact and more accessible form. They frequently rely on numerical information.

Tables. Like charts and graphs, tables can present complex information, both textual and numerical, in a compact form.

Other digital illustrations. Digital publications allow you to include a wider range of illustrations, including audio, video, and animations, which bring sound and movement to your document.

As you work with illustrations, keep the following guidelines in mind:

- **Use an illustration for a purpose.** Illustrations are best used when they serve a clear function in your document. Avoid including illustrations simply because you think they might make your document "look better."

- **Place illustrations near the text they illustrate.** In general, place illustrations as close as possible to the point where they are mentioned in the text. If they are not explicitly mentioned (as is often the case with photographs), place them at a point in the document where they are most relevant to the information and ideas being discussed.

- **Include a title or caption that identifies or explains the illustration.** The documentation system you are using, such as MLA or APA, will usually offer advice on the placement and format of titles and captions. In general, documentation systems suggest that you distinguish between tables and figures (which are all other illustrations), number tables and figures in the order in which they appear in the document, and use compound numbering of tables and figures in longer documents (for example, the second table in Chapter 5 would be labeled "Table 5.2"). Consult the documentation system you are using for specific guidelines on illustrations.

What Design Conventions Should I Follow?

Understanding the design conventions of the type of document you plan to write will help you create a document that meets your readers' expectations. Genres are characterized not only by distinctive writing styles, types of evidence, and organizational patterns but also by distinctive types of design. An article in a newsmagazine such as *Time* or *Newsweek*, for example, is characterized by the use of columns, headings and subheadings, pull quotes, and illustrations, while an academic essay is characterized by wide margins, double-spaced lines, and comparatively restrained use of color and illustrations. Your readers will expect your document to be similar in design to other examples of that genre. This doesn't mean that you can't depart from those conventions should the need arise, but be sure to take your readers' expectations into account as you do so.

As you design your document, consider the typical design conventions associated with the genre you've chosen. Doing so will allow you to meet your readers' expectations and will also convey an impression of competence and professionalism. The following sections describe the design conventions of the most common types of documents assigned in writing classes.

Academic Essays

The design of academic essays is neither flashy nor complex. Their most obvious design features — wide margins, readable fonts, and double-spaced lines — are intended to help their intended audience, typically instructors and classmates, read and comment on them.

Because the writing assignments given by most college instructors focus on the written expression of ideas and arguments, academic essays in the past have tended to use images sparingly, if at all, and to make limited use of design elements such as color, shading, borders, and rules. However, with changes in word-processing technology, writers of academic essays have begun to take advantage of these design options. Keep in mind that some instructors prefer that design elements be kept to a minimum in essays. If you are uncertain about your instructor's preferences, ask for guidance.

The following pages are taken from an essay written for a composition class. They reflect the writer's awareness of his instructor's expectations about line spacing, margins, documentation system, page numbers, and a title page.

For other sample essays formatted in MLA style, see pages 144, 197, 390, and 447. For sample essays formatted in APA style, see pages 259 and 323.

Checklist for Designing Academic Essays	
	✔ Cover page with title, name, and course information
	✔ Readable body font (for example, 12-point Times New Roman)
	✔ Double-spaced lines
	✔ Wide margins, one inch or larger
	✔ Consistent use of the assigned documentation system
	✔ Headers and footers in a readable font that is distinct from the body font
	✔ If used, headings and subheadings formatted in fonts and colors that distinguish them from the body text and show the relative importance of heading levels
	✔ If used, illustrations labeled and placed either within the text near relevant passages or in an appendix, according to the instructor's preferences

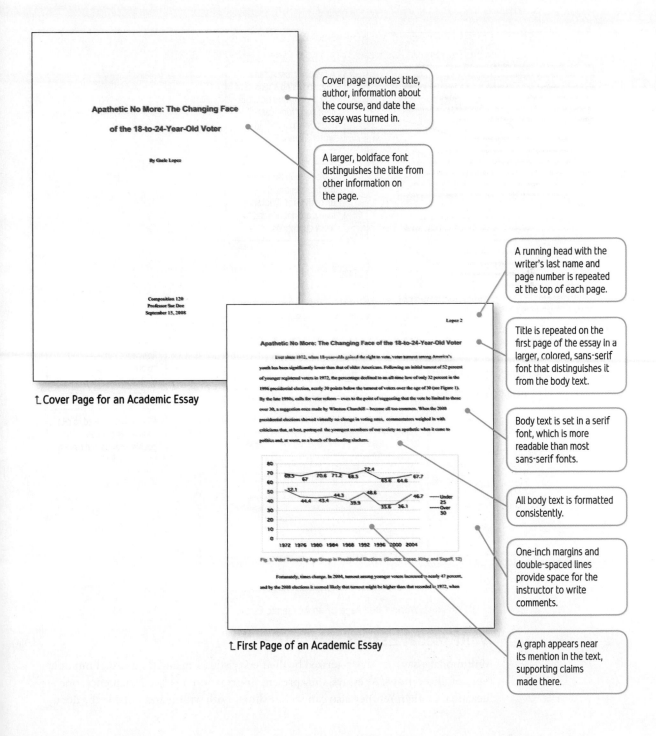

Apathetic No More: The Changing Face

of the 18-to-24-Year-Old Voter

By Gisele Lopez

Composition 120
Professor Sue Doe
September 15, 2008

⌐ **Cover Page for an Academic Essay**

Cover page provides title, author, information about the course, and date the essay was turned in.

A larger, boldface font distinguishes the title from other information on the page.

Lopez 2

Apathetic No More: The Changing Face of the 18-to-24-Year-Old Voter

Ever since 1972, when 18-year-olds gained the right to vote, voter turnout among America's youth has been significantly lower than that of older Americans. Following an initial turnout of 52 percent of younger registered voters in 1972, the percentage declined to an all-time low of only 32 percent in the 1996 presidential election, nearly 30 points below the turnout of voters over the age of 30 (see Figure 1). By the late 1980s, calls for voter reform – even to the point of suggesting that the vote be limited to those over 30, a suggestion once made by Winston Churchill – became all too common. When the 2000 presidential elections showed virtually no change in voting rates, commentators weighed in with criticisms that, at best, portrayed the youngest members of our society as apathetic when it came to politics and, at worst, as a bunch of freeloading slackers.

Fig. 1. Voter Turnout by Age Group in Presidential Elections. (Source: Lopez, Kirby, and Sagoff, 12)

Fortunately, times change. In 2004, turnout among younger voters increased to nearly 47 percent, and by the 2008 elections it seemed likely that turnout might be higher than that recorded in 1972, when

⌐ **First Page of an Academic Essay**

A running head with the writer's last name and page number is repeated at the top of each page.

Title is repeated on the first page of the essay in a larger, colored, sans-serif font that distinguishes it from the body text.

Body text is set in a serif font, which is more readable than most sans-serif fonts.

All body text is formatted consistently.

One-inch margins and double-spaced lines provide space for the instructor to write comments.

A graph appears near its mention in the text, supporting claims made there.

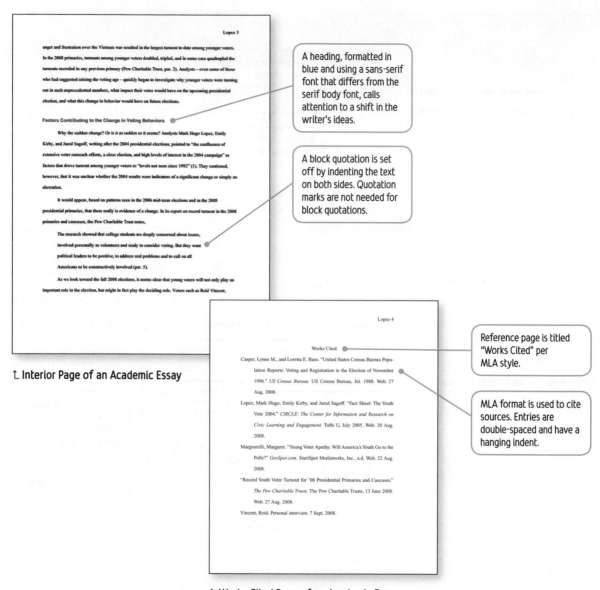

A heading, formatted in blue and using a sans-serif font that differs from the serif body font, calls attention to a shift in the writer's ideas.

A block quotation is set off by indenting the text on both sides. Quotation marks are not needed for block quotations.

⌐ Interior Page of an Academic Essay

Reference page is titled "Works Cited" per MLA style.

MLA format is used to cite sources. Entries are double-spaced and have a hanging indent.

⌐ Works Cited Page of an Academic Essay

Multimodal Essays

Multimodal essays are characterized by their essayistic form and their use of multiple types of illustrations. As essays, they present information in a linear sequence, one idea after another. Yet they also can include links, both within and outside the document, allowing readers to use them in a manner similar to a Web site. As multimodal documents, they combine text with images, animation, sound, and video. Multimodal essays can vary widely not only in form but also in the software used to create them. For example, one writer might use a word-processing program to create a document that contains text, photographs, illustrations, and charts; another might use a multimedia presentation program (such as PowerPoint) to present an essay as a series of slides with text and illustrations; and yet another might use a Web-development program, such as Dreamweaver, to create an essay as a Web site. Because multimodal essays rely heavily on digital illustrations, they are usually best viewed on a computer or projected onto a screen.

The following example shows a selection of pages from a multimodal essay created for a first-year composition course. As you review the pages, consider how they combine text, illustrations, color, headings and subheadings, sidebars, lists, and links to clearly convey the writer's ideas about the resurgence in the popularity of metal music.

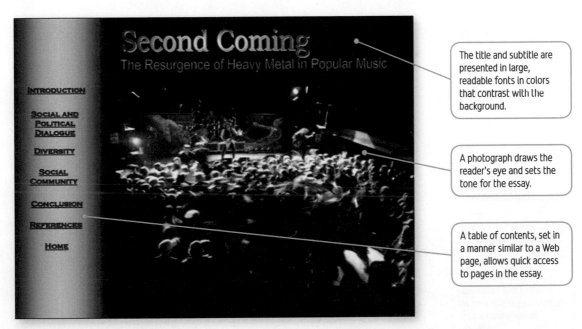

The title and subtitle are presented in large, readable fonts in colors that contrast with the background.

A photograph draws the reader's eye and sets the tone for the essay.

A table of contents, set in a manner similar to a Web page, allows quick access to pages in the essay.

ㄴ Cover Page of a Multimodal Essay

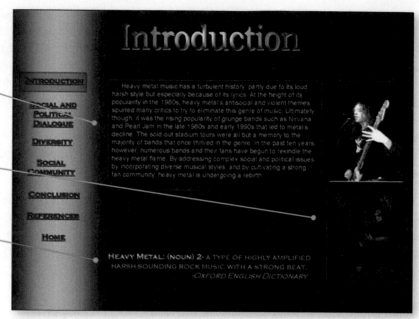

Body text is presented in a readable sans-serif font that contrasts with the background.

Photographs illustrate key ideas in the text.

Source information and credits are provided for photographs.

ꜛ **Introductory Page of a Multimodal Essay**

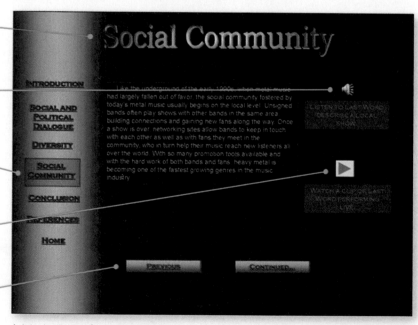

Page headings are formatted consistently throughout the essay.

Readers can listen to an interview by following the link.

A shaded box appears over the active section as viewers click through the presentation.

Readers can view a performance by following the link.

Previous and Continued buttons help readers move through sections of the essay.

ꜛ **Interior Page of a Multimodal Essay**

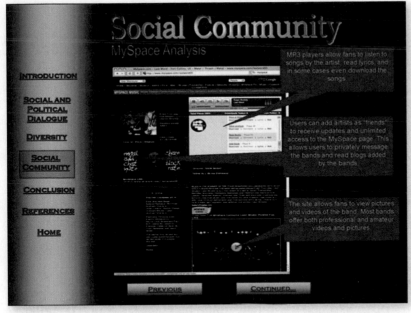

L Interior Page of a Multimodal Essay

Checklist for Designing Multimodal Essays

✔ Consistent overall design throughout the document (placement of titles and text; use of fonts, colors, rules, and illustrations)

✔ Readable heading and subheading fonts (for example, 16-point Times New Roman or Verdana)

✔ Readable body font designed for on-screen reading (for example, 11-point Calibri or Georgia)

✔ Appropriate and consistent color scheme

✔ Text presented in brief, readable chunks, using bulleted and numbered lists when appropriate

✔ Illustrations labeled and placed near relevant text passages

✔ If used, transitions between pages (dissolves, page flips) are quick and not distracting

✔ If used, background sound is clear but not distracting

Articles

Articles appear in a wide range of publications, including newspapers, magazines, scholarly and professional journals, and Web sites, among others. Depending on the publication in which they appear, articles might use headings and subheadings, columns, sidebars, pull quotes, and a wide array of illustrations. Writers of articles need to consider several factors that affect design: the overall design of the publication to which they submit their article, the audience the publication addresses, the subjects typically addressed in the publication, and the style and tone used by other articles in the publication.

Large headline in color contrasts with the text and subheading. Subheading summarizes the key points of the article, allowing the reader to quickly decide whether to read it.

Byline is set in a bold, sans-serif font to differentiate it from the main body text.

Pull quotes in large, sans-serif font highlight key ideas and information in the article.

Newspaper article is formatted in columns.

Captioned photos add visual interest and information.

⌐ Front Page of a Student Newspaper

The article on the previous page was written for Indiana University's student newspaper, the *Indiana Daily Student*. It draws heavily on visual elements to set a mood, call attention to key points, and convey information. (For a sample magazine article, see p. 602.)

(For a sample magazine article, see p. 602.)

Checklist for Designing Articles

✔ Column layout appropriate for the target publication and target audience

✔ Typically use single-spacing for text

✔ Readable body font (for example, 10- or 11-point Century Schoolbook)

✔ Color, borders, shading, and rules used appropriately

✔ Heading and subheadings formatted in font and colors that distinguish them from body text and show the relative importance of heading levels

✔ Illustrations labeled and placed near relevant passages

Web Sites

Web sites consist of linked pages, typically organized through a home page and navigational devices such as menus, tables of contents, indexes, and site maps. The main pages of Web sites usually provide broad overviews of the topic, and related pages add detailed information. The designs used for Web sites are growing more similar to those found in magazines, with a heavy use of images and other illustrations. Information is highlighted though fonts, colors, borders, shading, rules, tables, and an expanded range of digital illustrations.

Web sites pose intriguing design challenges. In addition to many of the design elements that are used in print documents, you also must choose from the expanded range of design options for publishing online, such as selecting an organizational structure for the site, selecting navigation tools, and using digital illustrations. Most important, you must have some familiarity with the range of Web sites you can create, such as informative Web sites; articles for Web-based journals, magazines, and newspapers; corporate Web sites; personal home pages; and blogs, to name only a few of the types of sites that can now be found on the Web.

@ View a guide for creating and designing Web sites at **bedfordstmartins .com/conversation**.

The following example shows pages from the Globalization101.org Web site, which focuses on issues related to the effects of international trade, investment, cultural exchange, and communication.

A banner, containing text and images, identifies the site and its publisher.

A menu provides links to major sections and contact information.

A search tool

An illustration draws the reader's eye to a key page.

A navigation footer provides links to major sections and site information.

⌐ Web Site Home Page

A link to the home page is found on every page.

A large heading in a contrasting color identifies the issue.

Links to related issue briefs

Links to related information are provided in a side menu.

A photograph illustrates a key point raised in the body text.

Body text is formatted in a readable sans-serif font.

Extra space after each paragraph helps differentiate one from another.

Headings help readers scan for important information.

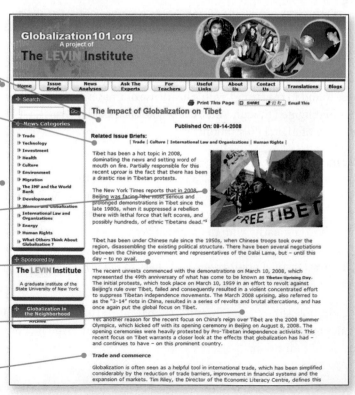

⌐ Web Site Content Page

Checklist for
Designing
Web Sites

✔ Organizational structure consistent with the purpose of the site and the needs and expectations of readers

✔ Home page provides links to main pages on the site

✔ Home page and main pages offer navigation tools appropriate for readers of the site

✔ Overall design consistent across the site (placement of titles, text, and navigation tools; use of fonts, colors, rules, and illustrations)

✔ Information presented in brief, readable chunks, using bulleted and numbered lists whenever possible

✔ Readable body font in a font family designed for on-screen reading (for example, 11-point Verdana or Georgia)

✔ Headings and subheadings formatted in fonts and colors that distinguish them from body text and show the relative importance of heading levels

✔ Informational flags used to help readers understand links and images

✔ Appropriate use of color

✔ Illustrations placed near the passages to which they refer

✔ Images kept as small as possible (in kilobytes), while being clear and easy to see

✔ Contact information and other relevant information included and easy to locate

In Summary: Designing Your Document

○ Understand and apply the principles of balance, emphasis, placement, repetition, and consistency (p. 596).

○ Design to achieve your purposes (p. 597).

○ Design to address your readers' needs, interests, values, and beliefs (p. 598).

○ Use design elements to increase the readability and effectiveness of your document (p. 599).

○ Follow the design conventions of the type of document you are creating (p. 605).

19 Writing with Style

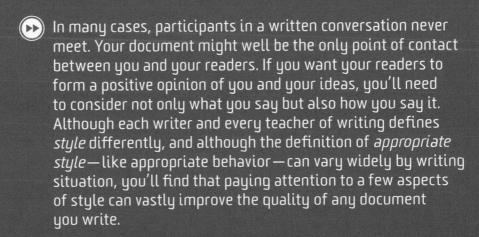

In many cases, participants in a written conversation never meet. Your document might well be the only point of contact between you and your readers. If you want your readers to form a positive opinion of you and your ideas, you'll need to consider not only what you say but also how you say it. Although each writer and every teacher of writing defines *style* differently, and although the definition of *appropriate style*—like appropriate behavior—can vary widely by writing situation, you'll find that paying attention to a few aspects of style can vastly improve the quality of any document you write.

How Can I Begin to Write with Style?

Good style begins with an understanding of your writing situation. By reading the work of other writers addressing your subject, you can gain insights into the style that appears to be appropriate for the conversation you've decided to join. For example, if you are involved in a subject that is being addressed by scholars working in the social sciences, you might find that documents written about your subject use long and fairly complex sentences, do not use *I* or other first-person pronouns, and cite sources using the American Psychological Association's documentation system. You might also find that the authors of the documents you have read are cautious about making strong assertions — that they hedge their claims through the use of phrases such as "these results appear to suggest" or "it appears that." In contrast, if you are involved in a subject that is being written about in the popular media, such the *Wall Street Journal*, *Time*, or CNN.com, you might find that the sentences are comparatively brief and occasionally refer to the author in the first person. You might also find that the authors cite sources in a general way in the body of their documents and are more likely to make strong claims.

In addition to understanding your writing situation, you can draw on a number of general principles to develop an appropriate style. Regardless of the subject you are addressing, your readers will appreciate it if you write concisely, use active voice and passive voice effectively, adopt a consistent point of view, and choose your words carefully.

Write Concisely

Readers don't want to work any harder than necessary to understand and engage with the information, ideas, and arguments in a document. They get unhappy if they have to put in extra effort to read a document — so unhappy, in fact, that they'll often give up.

One of the keys to writing clearly is keeping your words to a minimum. Consider the following examples.

> Please join me, Dr. Watson. I have concluded that I am in a situation in which I require your assistance.

> Come here, Dr. Watson. I need you.

> Help!

The second example, reputed to be the first words ever spoken on a telephone, was spoken by Alexander Graham Bell after he'd spilled acid on his pants. Had he spoken the first sentence instead, he might have wasted crucial time while he waited a few extra seconds for his assistant to figure out what he was being asked to do. The simple exclamation of "Help!" might have been even more effective and would certainly have taken less time to utter. Then again, it might have been too vague for his assistant to figure out just how he needed to act and what sort of help was required.

In general, if two sentences provide the same information, the briefer sentence is usually easier to understand. In some cases, however, writing too little will leave your readers wondering what you are trying to get across.

The following three techniques can help you write more concisely:

- **Remove unnecessary modifiers.** Unnecessary modifiers are words that provide little or no additional information to a reader, such as *fine*, *many*, *somewhat*, *great*, *quite*, *sort of*, *lots*, *really*, and *very*.

    Example Sentence with Unnecessary Modifiers

    The Volvo S80 serves as a really excellent example of a very fine performance sedan.

    Revised Example

    The Volvo S80 serves as an excellent example of a performance sedan.

- **Remove unnecessary introductory phrases.** Avoid phrases such as *there are*, *there is*, *these have*, *these are*, *here are*, *here is*, *it has been reported that*, *it has been said that*, *it is evident that*, *it is obvious that*, and so on. Sentences beginning with *It goes without saying*, for example, allow you to emphasize a point, but you can often recast such sentences more concisely by simply stating the point.

    Example Sentence with Unnecessary Introductory Phrase

    It goes without saying that drinking water should be clean.

    Revised Example

    Drinking water should be clean.

- **Eliminate stock phrases.** Search your document for phrases that you can replace with fewer words, such as the following.

Stock Phrase	Alternative
as a matter of fact	in fact
at all times	always
at that point in time	then
at this point in time	now, currently
at the present time	now, currently
because of the fact that	because
by means of	by
due to the fact that	because
in order to	to
in spite of the fact that	although, though
in the event that	if

Example Sentence with Stock Phrase

Call the security desk in the event that the alarm sounds.

Revised Example

Call the security desk if the alarm sounds.

Use Active and Passive Voice Effectively

Active voice and *passive voice* describe two distinctly different types of sentences. A sentence written in active voice specifies an actor—a person or thing—who carries out an action.

Active Voice

Juan took an exam.

The tornado leveled the town.

Carmelo Anthony scored the game-winning basket with .2 seconds remaining in overtime.

In contrast, a sentence written in passive voice indicates that something was done, but it does not necessarily specify who or what did it.

Passive Voice

The exam was taken by Juan.

The town was leveled.

The game-winning basket was scored with .2 seconds remaining in overtime.

In general, you'll want to emphasize the actor, because sentences written in active voice are easier to understand and provide more information.

Passive voice, however, can be effective when active voice would require the inclusion of unnecessary information. For example, many scientific experiments are conducted by large teams of researchers. Few readers would want to know which members of the team carried out every task discussed in an article about the experiment. Rather than using active voice (for example, "Janelle Knott, assisted by Jen Lee and Victor Garza, anesthetized the mice, and then Jen Lee and Richard Simpson examined their eyes for lesions"), you can use passive voice ("The mice were anesthetized, and their eyes were examined for lesions"). In this case, the sentence written in passive voice is clearer, easier to understand, and free of unnecessary information.

Passive voice is also useful if you wish to emphasize the recipient of the action, rather than the person or thing carrying out the action. Police reports, for example, often use passive voice ("The suspect was apprehended at the corner of Oak and Main Streets").

Adopt a Consistent Point of View

Writers usually adopt a particular point of view:

- First person: *I, we*

- Second person: *you*

- Third person: *she, he, it, one, they,* or nouns that describe a particular group or person, such as *doctors, teachers, engineer, lawyer, Mr. Smith,* or *Lee Chen.*

When writers shift their point of view within a sentence, readers notice—and sometimes have to stop and ask themselves what just happened. Consider the following example.

Shift in Point of View

After the climbers reached the summit in record time, we burst into song.

The sentence begins with a third-person point of view (*the climbers*) and then shifts to the first person (*we*). The sentence would be easier to understand if it were written in either first-person or third-person point of view.

Consistent Point of View

After the climbers reached the summit in record time, they burst into song.

After we reached the summit in record time, we burst into song.

Choose Your Words Carefully

Pay attention to level of formality and the extent to which specialized terms are used in the conversation about your subject. Pay attention as well to the variety and specificity of your choice of words.

Formality. Reading other documents that contribute to the conversation about your subject will give you insights into the level of formality you should strive for when you draft, revise, and edit your document. Some written conversations, such as those conducted on blogs and Web discussion forums, are relatively informal and can even show lack of respect for the opinions of other participants in the discussion. Others, such as those conducted through scholarly journals or magazines such as the *Nation* or *Atlantic Monthly*, adopt a formal, restrained tone. Still others, such as those conducted through many popular media outlets, are casual but respectful. As you read about your subject, note the level of formality and the manner in which writers refer to ideas and arguments in other sources.

Informal Writing

It was awesome to see how great the U.S. soccer team did in the last World Cup.

Formal Writing

The performance of the U.S. soccer team in the most recent World Cup was gratifying.

Specialized language. Specialized language, sometimes called jargon, can allow writers and readers to communicate effectively and efficiently—but only if everyone involved is familiar with the terms. If you are contributing to a conversation in which specialized language is used heavily, familiarize yourself with the terms your readers will expect you to use. For example, if you plan to write an article for a Web site that focuses on motorcycle touring, you can write more concisely and with greater accuracy if you use the proper terminology.

Ineffective Use of General Language

Braking that involves a mechanism that coordinates proportionally the amount of pressure applied to your front and rear brakes during turns that get progressively tighter can be hazardous if you fail to initiate the turn properly.

Effective Use of Specialized Language

Linked braking during decreasing-radius turns can be hazardous if you fail to initiate the turn properly.

In contrast, readers who are unfamiliar with specialized language will find it more difficult to understand your point. For example, although most Americans have at least a passing familiarity with basketball, many would find it difficult to understand the following statement.

Ineffective Use of Specialized Language for a General Audience

Box-and-one defenses are largely ineffective against well-executed pick-and-roll plays that result not in shots, but in skip passes, particularly if the pick-and-rolls are initiated on the baseline.

Variety. Variety is the spice of life. It's also the key ingredient in an effective document. Even a well-conceptualized and thoroughly supported argument can fail to impress if it's presented in dull, monotonous language. Consider the differences between the following examples.

Lack of Varied Word Choice

The U.S. space program has benefited the U.S. in more ways than most U.S. government programs, largely because of the important technologies that have found their way into the U.S. economy.

Varied Word Choice

NASA has benefited the nation in more ways than most federal programs, largely because of the important technologies that have found their way into the U.S. economy.

How Can I Polish My Style?

You can improve the overall quality of your document by varying your sentence patterns, creating effective transitions, varying your source attributions, avoiding sexist language, consulting a handbook, and reading widely.

Vary Your Sentence Structure

Each sentence falls into one of four general categories.

Statements: Dick runs fast.

Questions: How fast did Dick run?

Commands: Run, Dick, run.

Exclamations: Way to go, Dick!

There are also four basic sentence structures, distinguished by the types and numbers of *clauses* they contain. A clause — a group of words containing a subject and a verb — can be either *independent* or *dependent*. (Sometimes these types of clauses are referred to as *main* and *subordinate*.) The primary difference between these types of clauses is that independent clauses can function on their own as a complete sentence, while dependent clauses cannot.

Simple Sentence (a single independent clause)
Jane runs fast.

Compound Sentence (two or more independent clauses)
Jane runs fast, but she doesn't run as fast as Dick.

Complex Sentence (an independent clause and a dependent clause)
Although Jane runs fast, Dick is faster.

Compound-Complex Sentence (two or more independent clauses and at least one dependent clause)
The Dick and Jane readers, which your grandparents might have read as children, were wildly successful, but they have faded into the comfortable oblivion of history.

Mixing sentence types and structures creates an appealing rhythm in your writing. However, if you neglect to vary your sentences, readers are likely to find your document monotonous and boring. To keep your readers' interest, write sentences with varying types, structures, and lengths. Consider the following examples.

Similar Sentence Structure and Length

We decided to spend the morning at El Rastro. El Rastro is a Sunday-morning flea market extraordinaire. We decided to take the subway to get there. A man stood quite close as we got on. I found this strange in an uncrowded subway station. Then I felt his hand in my left pocket. I also felt his hand on my back. It's a good thing that I'm ticklish. I instinctively shrugged away from his hands. Then I swore loudly and imaginatively at him. (It's inappropriate to swear on a Sunday in Spain. I wouldn't have done it under normal circumstances.) He had almost gotten away with my sunglasses. This would almost certainly have disappointed him. I know it would have inconvenienced me.

> Each sentence uses the same sentence type (statements) and the same simple sentence structure. Sentence length ranges from seven to nine words.

Varied Sentence Structure and Length

We decided to spend the morning at El Rastro, a Sunday-morning flea market extraordinaire. As we got on the subway to get to El Rastro, I noticed that a man was standing quite close to me — strange, since the subway wasn't crowded. Then I felt one of his hands in my left pocket and the other hand on my back. (Fortunately, I'm ticklish.) "What's going on?" I thought, instinctively shrugging away and swearing at him (an inappropriate thing to do on a Sunday morning in Spain, but I was caught off guard). He had almost gotten away with my sunglasses, which would have disappointed him and inconvenienced me.

> Sentence types include statements and a question. Sentence structures include simple, compound, and complex. Sentence length ranges from three to twenty-nine words.

Create Effective Transitions

Transitions help readers understand the relationships among sentences, paragraphs, and even sections of a document. Essentially, they smooth the way for readers, helping them understand how information, ideas, and arguments are related to one another. Transitions are most effective when they don't call attention to themselves, but instead move the reader's eye along to the next sentence, paragraph, or section. Consider the following examples of the steps involved in preparing fish.

No Transitions

Catch the fish. Clean the fish. Filet the fish. Cook the fish. Eat the fish. Catch another fish.

Inconsistent Transitions

First, catch the fish. Secondly, clean the fish. When you've done that, filet the fish. Next, cook the fish. Fifth, eat the fish. After all is said and done, catch another fish.

Consistent Transitions

First, catch the fish. Second, clean the fish. Third, filet the fish. Fourth, cook the fish. Fifth, eat the fish. Finally, catch another fish.

Transitions frequently appear as words and phrases, such as those used in the previous example. They can also take the form of sentences and paragraphs. Transitional sentences often appear at the end or beginning of paragraphs and serve to link two paragraphs. Transitional paragraphs call attention to a major shift in focus within a document. Several examples of transitions appear below.

Transitional Words

first, second, third, . . . finally

however

nonetheless

Transitional Phrases

on the one hand . . . on the other hand

as a result

in turn

Transitional Sentences

The results of the tests revealed a surprising trend.

Incredibly, the outcome was far better than we could have hoped.

Transitional Paragraphs

In the next section, we explore the reasons behind this surprising development. We focus first on the event itself. Then we consider the reasons underlying the event. Our goal is to call attention to the unique set of relationships that made this development possible.

Headings and subheadings can also act as transitions. Section headings serve as transitions by signaling to the reader, through formatting that differs from body text, that a new section is beginning. You can read more about formatting headings and subheadings in Chapter 18.

Introduce the Work of Other Authors Effectively

Readers appreciate clear indications of the source of a quotation, paraphrase, or summary. (For more information about these methods of integrating the work of other authors, see Chapter 17.) Far too many writers show little imagination in how they introduce that work.

Common Attributions

The author wrote . . .

The author said . . .

The author stated . . .

Somewhat More Imaginative Attributions

The author expressed the opinion that . . .

The author denied this, noting . . .

In response, the author observed that . . .

To make your writing stand out, vary the words and phrases that identify the sources of the information, ideas, and arguments you use in your document. As you do so, remember to present information, ideas, and arguments from your sources as fairly and accurately as possible. You might enhance the stylistic impact of a passage by writing that someone "ridiculed" a particular idea. However, if he or she were only raising questions about the idea, doing so would be unfair both to your source and to the idea itself.

Avoid Sexist Language

It is still technically correct to use male pronouns, such as *he*, *him*, and *his*, when the gender of a noun, such as *doctor* or *nurse*, is unspecified. Most readers, however, object to this assumption—or at least they are sensitive to it. Readers are even more likely to object if you make the mistake of referring to representatives of particular professions using gender-specific pronouns.

> When describing your symptoms to a doctor, be sure to tell him everything that's relevant. Similarly, when a nurse is taking your blood pressure, feel free to let her know how you feel.

By implying that all doctors are men and all nurses are women, the writer of this passage plays into common stereotypes. The result is that many readers will form a negative opinion of the writer.

To avoid sexist language, recast your sentences so that generic references (for example, *the doctor*) are plural (*doctors*).

Sexist Language

A doctor who pursues an advanced specialization might need to spend as many as fifteen years of study before he can go into practice on his own.

Nonsexist Language

Doctors who pursue advanced specializations might need to spend as many as fifteen years of study before they can go into practice on their own.

Consult a Good Handbook

The strategies discussed in this chapter provide a good starting point for improving your style. Your decisions about style, however, are likely to touch on a far wider range of concerns than are covered here. As you work to improve your writing, consult a good handbook covering the finer points of writing. In it, you'll find detailed discussions and numerous examples of ways to polish your style.

Read Widely

The most effective means of improving your style might be the most enjoyable: read as widely and as frequently as you can. Reading widely exposes you to the styles used by published authors—and helps you realize that effective style comes in almost as many varieties as there are authors. Reading frequently keeps you engaged with words so that you can draw on them more easily as you work on your own writing.

In Summary: Writing with Style

○ Write concisely (p. 618).

○ Use active and passive voice to accomplish your purpose (p. 620).

○ Adopt a consistent point of view (p. 621).

○ Pay attention to word choice (p. 622).

○ Vary your sentence structure (p. 624).

○ Use transitions (p. 625).

○ Introduce the work of other authors effectively (p. 627).

○ Avoid sexist language (p. 628).

○ Consult a writing handbook (p. 628).

○ Read widely and frequently (p. 628).

20 Revising and Editing

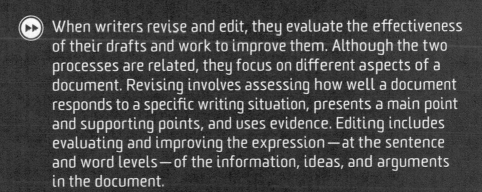

When writers revise and edit, they evaluate the effectiveness of their drafts and work to improve them. Although the two processes are related, they focus on different aspects of a document. Revising involves assessing how well a document responds to a specific writing situation, presents a main point and supporting points, and uses evidence. Editing includes evaluating and improving the expression—at the sentence and word levels—of the information, ideas, and arguments in the document.

What Should I Focus on When I Revise?

Revising involves rethinking and re-envisioning what you've written. It focuses on such big-picture issues as whether the document you've drafted is appropriate for your writing situation; whether your thesis statement is sound and well supported; whether you've properly integrated sources into your document; whether you've organized and presented your information, ideas, and arguments clearly and effectively; and whether you've made appropriate decisions about genre and design.

Consider Your Writing Situation

As you revise, ask whether your document helps you achieve your purposes. If your assignment directed you to inform readers about a particular subject, for instance, consider whether you've provided appropriate information, whether you've offered enough information, and whether that information is presented clearly. If your purpose is to convince or persuade your readers, ask whether you have chosen appropriate reasons and evidence and presented your argument as effectively as you can. You'll find revision suggestions for specific types of assignments in Chapters 5 to 10.

In addition, review your readers' needs, interests, backgrounds, and knowledge of the subject. During revision, imagine how your readers will react to your document by asking questions such as these:

- Will my readers trust what I have to say? How can I establish my credibility?

- Will my readers have other ideas about how to address this subject? How can I convince them that they should believe what I say?

- Will my readers find my evidence appropriate and accurate? Is my selection of evidence consistent with their values, beliefs, and experiences?

As writers begin to revise, they think about how readers will react to the documents they have written.

Finally, identify your requirements, limitations, and opportunities (see pp. 31–32). Ask yourself whether you've met the specific requirements of the assignment, such as length and number of sources. Evaluate your efforts to work around limitations, such as lack of access to information. Think about whether you've taken full advantage of your opportunities and any new ones that have come your way.

Consider Your Presentation of Ideas

As you revise, ask how well you are conveying your ideas to your readers. First, check the clarity of your thesis statement. Is it phrased in a way that is compatible with the needs and interests of your readers? Second, ask whether the supporting points in your document help your readers understand and accept your thesis statement. As you make this assessment, keep in mind your primary role as a writer — such as advocate, reporter, or interpreter.

- **Writing to reflect.** Have you created a dominant impression of your subject or indicated the significance of your observations for readers? (See Chapter 5.)

- **Writing to inform.** Is the level of detail you've provided consistent with your readers' knowledge of the subject? Have you clearly defined any key concepts and ideas? (See Chapter 6.)

- **Writing to interpret or analyze.** Are your analyses clear and accurate? Have you provided appropriate and sufficient background information to help your readers follow your reasoning? (See Chapter 7.)

- **Writing to evaluate.** Have you clearly described the subject, defined your evaluative criteria, and provided a clear rationale for your judgments? (See Chapter 8.)

- **Writing to solve problems.** Have you clearly defined the problem, considered alternative solutions, and discussed your proposed solution? (See Chapter 9.)

- **Writing to persuade.** Have you made a clear overall point, provided supporting points, and presented evidence for your points? (See Chapter 10.)

Consider Your Use and Integration of Sources

Think about how you've used source information in your document. Review the amount of evidence you've provided for your points and the appropriateness of that evidence for your purpose and readers. If you are arguing about an issue, determine whether you've identified and addressed reasonable opposing viewpoints.

It's also important that you integrate your sources effectively into your document and acknowledge them according to the documentation system you are following. Ensure that you have cited all your sources and that you've clearly distinguished between your ideas and those of other writers. Review your works cited or references list for completeness and accuracy. Remember that lack of proper documentation can reduce your document's effectiveness and diminish your credibility. You can learn more about integrating sources in Chapter 17. For guidelines on documenting your sources, see Chapters 21 and 22.

Consider the Structure and Organization of Your Document

Your readers should be able to locate information and ideas easily. As you read your introduction, ask whether it clearly and concisely conveys your main point and whether it helps your readers anticipate the structure and organization of your document. Reflect on the appropriateness of your organizing pattern (see p. 548) for your purpose and readers. If you've used headings and subheadings, evaluate their effectiveness.

Make sure your document is easy to read. Check for effective paragraphing and paragraph structure (see p. 554). If you have several small paragraphs, you might combine paragraphs with similar ideas. If you have a number of long paragraphs, break them up and add transitions. Finally, ask whether your conclusion leaves your readers with something to think about. The most effective conclusions typically provide more than just a summary.

Consider Genre and Design

Consider both the genre — or type — of document that you are writing and your use of design principles and elements (see Chapter 18). If your assignment gave you a choice of genres, ask whether the genre you've selected is appropriate, given your purpose and readers. For example, would it be more effective to reach your readers via an informative Web site, an opinion column, or a brochure? Would it be more effective to publish your document as a blog entry or as a letter to the editor of a magazine or newspaper? Regardless of the type of document you're writing, make sure that you've followed the conventions associated with it, such as level of formality, accepted sources of evidence, and organization.

Take a careful look, as well, at how you've designed your document. Does it resemble what your readers will expect? For example, if you're writing an academic essay, have you double-spaced your lines, used a readable font, and set wide margins? If you're creating a Web site, have you made it easy for your readers to find their way around? Have you consistently formatted your headings and subheadings? Have you used design principles and elements to achieve your purpose and consider your readers?

What Strategies Can I Use to Revise?

You can draw on several strategies for reviewing and improving your document. As you use them, keep track of your ideas for revision by writing comments on sticky notes or in the margins of print documents, by using the Comment tool in word-processing documents, or by creating a to-do list in your writer's notebook.

@ View a guide for using your word-processing program's Comment tool at **bedfordstmartins.com/ conversation**.

Save Multiple Drafts

You might not be happy with every revision you make. To avoid wishing that you hadn't made extensive revisions to a draft of your document, save a new copy of your draft before every major revising session. You can either add a number to your drafts' file names, such as Draft1.doc, Draft2.doc, and so on; add the date, such as Draft-April6.doc and Draft-April10.doc; or use some other naming system that works for you. What's important is that you save multiple versions of your drafts in case you don't like the changes you've made.

Highlight Your Main Point, Supporting Points, and Evidence

As you revise, make sure that your main point (usually expressed as a thesis state-ment), supporting points, and evidence are fully developed. An effective way to do this is to identify and examine each element in your draft, both individually and as a group of related points. If you are working with a printed document, use a highlighter, colored pens or pencils, or sticky notes. If you are working in a word-processing pro-gram, use the highlighting tool to mark the text. You might use different colors to highlight your main point, supporting points, and evidence. If you are focusing solely on the evidence in your document, use different colors to highlight evidence from different sources (to help you check whether you are relying too heavily on a single source) or to differentiate the types of evidence you are using (such as quotations, paraphrases, summaries, and numerical data).

Challenge Your Assumptions

It's easy to accept ideas and arguments that you've worked so hard to develop. But what would a reader with fresh eyes think? Challenge your main point, supporting points, and evidence by using one of the following strategies. Keep track of your challenges by using the Comment tool in your word-processing program.

PUT YOURSELF IN THE PLACE OF YOUR READERS

As you read, pretend that you are one of your readers. Try to imagine a single reader — or, if you're ambitious, a group of readers. Ask questions they might ask. Imagine concerns they might bring to their reading of your document. A reader interested in solving a problem might ask, for example, whether a proposed solution is cost-effective, is more appropriate than alternative solutions, or has unacceptable side effects. As you revise, take these questions and concerns into account.

PLAY DEVIL'S ADVOCATE

A devil's advocate raises reasonable objections to ideas and arguments. As you review your document, identify your key claims, and then pose reasonable objections to them. Make note of these potential objections, and take them into account as you revise.

PLAY THE "SO WHAT?" GAME

As you read your document, ask why readers would care about what you are saying. By asking "so what?" questions, you can gain a better understanding of what your readers are likely to care about and how they might respond to your arguments and ideas. Make note of your responses to these questions, and consider them as you revise.

Scan, Outline, and Map Your Document

Use the following strategies to review the structure, organization, and design of your document:

- **Scan headings and subheadings.** If you have used headings and subheadings, they can help you track the overall flow of your ideas. Ask whether the organization they reveal is appropriate for your writing situation and your role as a writer.

- **Scan the first sentence of each paragraph.** A quick reading of the first sentence of each paragraph can reveal points at which your ideas shift. As you note these shifts, think about whether they are appropriate and effective.

- **Outline your document.** Create a topical or sentence outline of your document (see p. 550) to assess its structure and organization. This strategy, sometimes called a reverse outline, helps you identify the sequence of your points and the amount of space you've devoted to each aspect of your document. If you are viewing your document in a word-processing program, use the Styles tool to assign levels to headings in your document; then view it in Outline view.

- **Map your document.** On paper or in a graphics program, draw a map of your document. Like an outline, a map can help you identify the organization of your points and the amount of evidence you've used to support them. As you review

@ View a guide for using your word-processing program's Styles tool at **bedfordstmartins.com/ conversation**.

the organization and structure of your document, reflect on whether it is appropriate given your purpose, readers, argument, and available information.

Ask for Feedback

After spending long hours on a project, you might find it difficult to identify problems that your readers might have with your draft. You might read the same paragraph eight times and still fail to notice that the evidence you are using to support a point actually contradicts it. Or you might not notice that your document's organization could confuse your readers. You can ask for feedback on your draft from a friend, relative, colleague, or writing center tutor. It's generally a good idea to ask for help from someone who will be frank as well as supportive and to be specific about the kinds of comments you're looking for. Hearing "it's just fine" from a reviewer will not help you to revise. You can learn more about engaging in a peer review in Chapter 4.

Checklist for Revision

✔ Review your writing situation. Does your document help you achieve your purposes? Does it address your readers' needs, interests, values, and beliefs? Does it meet the writing assignment's requirements? Does it effectively work around limitations and take advantage of opportunities?

✔ Evaluate the presentation of your ideas. Does your document provide a clear and appropriate thesis statement? Do your supporting points and evidence support your thesis statement, and are they consistent with your primary role as a writer?

✔ Assess your use and integration of sources. Have you offered adequate support for your points, considered reasonable opposing viewpoints, integrated and acknowledged your sources, and distinguished between your work and that of other writers?

✔ Examine the structure and organization of your document. Is the introduction clear and concise, does it convey your main point, and does it help your readers anticipate the structure of your document? Is the organizational structure easy to follow? Are paragraphs easy to read? Are transitions effective? Does the conclusion provide more than just a summary of the document?

✔ Evaluate genre and design. Does the genre you've created help you accomplish your purpose? Have you followed the style and design conventions associated with the type of document you've created?

What Should I Focus on When I Edit?

Editing involves assessing the effectiveness, accuracy, and appropriateness of the words and sentences in a document. Before you begin to edit, remember that editing focuses on your document's words and sentences, not on its overall structure or ideas. If you're uncertain about whether you've organized your document as effectively as possible or whether you've provided enough support for your argument, deal with those issues first. In the same way that you wouldn't start painting a house until you've finished building the walls, hold off on editing until you're confident that you're finished revising.

Focus on Accuracy

You risk damaging your credibility if you provide inaccurate information in your document. To reduce this risk, do the following:

- **Check your facts and figures.** Your readers might think that you're deliberately misleading them if you fail to provide accurate information. As you edit, return to your original sources or your notes to check any facts and figures.

- **Check every quotation.** Return to your original sources or consult your notes to ensure that you have quoted each source exactly. Make sure that you have noted any changes to a quotation with ellipses or brackets and that those changes haven't altered the original meaning of the passage (see pp. 513–514). Be sure to cite each source both in the text and in a works cited or references list (see Chapters 21 and 22).

- **Check the spelling of every name.** Don't rely on electronic spelling checkers, which provide the correct spelling for only the most common or prominent names.

Focus on Economy

Editing for economy involves reducing the number of words needed to express an idea or convey information. Often you can achieve greater economy in your writing by removing unnecessary modifiers, removing unnecessary introductory phrases such as *there are* and *it is*, and eliminating stock phrases (see pp. 619–620). Editing for economy generally makes it easier for your readers to understand your meaning, but you should use care; your readers still need to understand the point you are trying to make.

Focus on Consistency

Editing your document for consistency helps you present information and ideas in a uniform way. Use the following techniques to edit for consistency:

- **Treat concepts consistently.** Review your document for consistent treatment of concepts, information, ideas, definitions, and anecdotes.

- **Use numbers consistently.** Check the documentation system you are using for its guidelines on the treatment of numbers. You might find, for instance, that you should spell out the numbers zero through ten and use Arabic numerals for numbers larger than ten.

- **Treat your sources consistently.** Avoid referring to some sources using first names and to others using honorifics, such as *Dr.*, *Mr.*, or *Ms.* Also check that you have cited your sources appropriately for the documentation style you are using, such as MLA or APA (see Chapters 21 and 22). Review each reference for consistent presentation of names, page numbers, and publication dates.

- **Format your document consistently.** Avoid any inconsistencies in your use of fonts, headings, and subheadings and in your placement and captioning of images, tables, charts, and other illustrations (see Chapter 18).

Focus on Style

Your readers will judge you—and what you have to say—not only on what you say but also on how you say it. Edit for matters of style by choosing the right words, using the active and passive voice appropriately, adopting a consistent point of view, rewriting complex sentences, varying your sentence length and structure, providing transitions, and avoiding sexist language (see Chapter 19).

Focus on Spelling, Grammar, and Punctuation

As you put the finishing touches on your document, keep a dictionary and a good grammar handbook close by. Poor spelling doesn't necessarily affect your ability to get your point across—in most cases, readers will understand even the most atrociously spelled document—but it does affect what your readers think of you. If you ignore spelling errors in your document, you'll erode their confidence in your ability to present ideas or make an argument. The same goes for grammar and punctuation. If your sentences have subject-verb agreement problems or don't use the appropriate punctuation, readers might not trust that you have presented your facts correctly.

What Strategies Can I Use to Edit?

Thorough editing involves making several passes through your document to ensure that you've addressed accuracy, economy, consistency, style, spelling, grammar, and punctuation. The following tips can make that process both easier and more productive.

Read Carefully

As you've worked on your document, you've become quite familiar with it. As a result, it can be easy to read what you *meant* to write instead of what you actually wrote. The following strategies can help you read with fresh eyes:

- **Set your document aside before you edit.** If time permits, allow a day or two to pass before you begin editing your document. Taking time off between revising and editing can help you see your document more clearly.

- **Pause between sentences for a quick check.** Sometimes writers let meaning take precedence over the structure and expression of their sentences. Avoid getting caught up in the flow of your document by stopping after each sentence. Slowing down can help you identify problems with your text.

- **Read aloud.** Reading your document aloud can help you find problems that might not be apparent when it's read silently.

- **Read in reverse order.** To check for problems with individual sentences, start at the end of your document and read the last sentence first, and then work backward through the document. To check for problems at the word level, read each word starting with the last one in the document. Disrupting the normal flow of your document can alert you to problems that might not stand out when you read it normally.

Mark and Search Your Document

Use the following marking and searching strategies to edit for accuracy, economy, consistency, and style:

- **Mark your document.** As you read, use a highlighter pen or the highlighting tool in your word-processing program to mark errors or information that should be double-checked. Consider using different colors to highlight specific types of problems, such as sexist language or inconsistent use of formal titles.

- **Use the Find and Replace tools.** Use your word-processing program to edit concepts, names, numbers, and titles for consistency and accuracy. Once you've identified a word or phrase that you'd like to check or change, you can search for it throughout your document. If you are referring to sources using a parenthetical citation style, such as MLA or APA, use the Find tool to search for an opening parenthesis. If you discover that you've consistently misspelled a word or name, use the Replace tool to correct it throughout your document.

- **Use the Split Window tool.** Some word-processing programs allow you to split your window so that you can view different parts of your document at the

@ View a guide for using your word-processing program's Highlighting, Find and Replace, and Split Window tools at **bedfordstmartins.com/ conversation**.

same time. Use this tool to ensure that you are referring to a concept in the same way throughout your document or to check for consistent use of fonts, headings, subheadings, illustrations, and tables.

Use Spelling, Grammar, and Style Tools with Caution

Most word-processing programs provide tools to check spelling, grammar, punctuation, and style. Used with an awareness of their limitations, these tools can significantly reduce the effort required to edit a document.

Spelling checkers have two primary limitations. First, they can't identify words that are spelled correctly but misused — such as *to/two/too*, *their/they're/there*, and *advice/advise*. Second, spelling checkers are ineffective when they run into a word they don't recognize, such as proper names, technical and scientific terms, and unusual words. To compound this problem, spelling checkers often suggest replacement words. If you accept suggestions uncritically, you might end up with a paper full of incorrect words and misspelled names.

The main limitation of grammar, punctuation, and style checkers is inaccurate advice. Although much of the advice they offer is sound, a significant proportion is not. If you are confident about your knowledge of grammar, punctuation, and style, you can use the grammar- and style-checking tools in your word-processing program to identify potential problem areas in your document. These tools can point out problems you might have overlooked, such as a subject-verb agreement problem that occurred when you revised a sentence. However, if you don't have a strong knowledge of grammar, punctuation, and style, you can easily be misled by inaccurate advice.

@ View a guide for using your word-processing program's Spelling, Grammar, and Style tools at **bedfordstmartins.com/ conversation**.

If you have any doubts about advice from your word-processing program's spelling checker, consult an up-to-date dictionary. If you have concerns about the suggestions you receive from the grammar-, punctuation-, and style-checking tools, consult a good grammar handbook.

Ask for Feedback

One of the biggest challenges writers face is reading a draft of their own work as a reader rather than as the writer. Because you know what you're trying to say, you'll find it easy to understand your draft. And because you've read your document so many times, you're likely to overlook errors in spelling, punctuation, and grammar. After you've edited your document, ask a friend, relative, or classmate to proofread it and to make note of any problems.

Checklist for Editing

✔ Ensure that your document is accurate. Check facts and figures, quotations, and the spelling of names.

✔ Edit for economy. Strive to express your ideas and argument concisely yet clearly.

✔ Ensure that your document is consistent. Use concepts, numbers, and source information consistently. Check your document for consistent use of formatting and design.

✔ Improve your style. Strive for economy, use appropriate words, check your verbs, rewrite overly complex sentences, vary sentence length and structure, and remove sexist language.

✔ Check for correct spelling, grammar, and punctuation. Use your word-processing program's spelling, grammar, punctuation, and style tools; consult a grammar handbook and a dictionary (p. 628); and ask someone to proofread your draft.

In Summary: Revising and Editing

○ Focus on the big picture when you revise by keeping your writing situation in mind (p. 632).

○ Revise more effectively by saving multiple drafts; highlighting; challenging your assumptions; scanning, outlining, and mapping your document; and asking for feedback (p. 635).

○ Focus on accuracy, economy, consistency, style, spelling, grammar, and punctuation when you edit (p. 638).

○ Take advantage of editing strategies (p. 639).

PART FIVE

Documenting Sources

21 Using MLA Style

Modern Language Association (MLA) style, used primarily in
the humanities, emphasizes the authors of a source and the
pages on which information is located in the source. Writers
who use the MLA documentation system cite, or formally
acknowledge, source information within their text using
parentheses, and they provide a list of sources in a works
cited list at the end of their document. The works cited list
also indicates the medium of the source (print, Web, film,
manuscript, and so on).

To see student essays formatted and documented in MLA
style, turn to any of the following examples in Part Two:

> Caitlin Guariglia, *Mi Famiglia*, page 144

> Hannah Steiner, *Barriers on the Road to a Hydrogen
> Economy*, page 197

> Jennie Tillson, *Death, Taxes, and College Tuition*,
> page 390

> Donovan Mikrot, *Download This: Why Digital Rights
> Management Is a Bad Idea for Hollywood*, page 447

For more information about MLA style, consult the *MLA
Handbook for Writers of Research Papers*, Seventh Edition.
Information about the *MLA Handbook* can also be found at
www.mla.org.

CITATIONS WITHIN YOUR TEXT

ENTRIES IN YOUR WORKS CITED LIST

Books

Sources in Journals, Magazines, and Newspapers

Print Reference Works

Field Sources

Media Sources

Electronic Sources

How Do I Cite Sources within the Text of My Document?

MLA style uses parentheses for in-text citations to acknowledge the use of another author's words, facts, and ideas. When you refer to a source within your text, provide the author's last name and specific page number(s) — if the source is paginated. Your reader can then go to the works cited list at the end of your document to find a full citation.

1. Basic format for a source named in your text Most often, you will want to name the author of a source within your sentence rather than in a parenthetical citation. By doing so, you create a context for the material (words, facts, or ideas) that you are including, and you indicate where the information from the author begins. When you are using a direct quotation, paraphrase, or summary from a source and have named the author in your sentence, place only the page number in parentheses after the borrowed material. The period follows the parentheses.

> Vargas points out that drowning doesn't happen in the manner you might expect; children slip underwater quietly, making very little noise to alert unsuspecting parents or guardians (14).

When you are using a block (or extended) quotation, the parenthetical citation comes after the final punctuation and a single space (see p. 581).

If you continue to refer to a single source for several sentences in a row within one paragraph — and without intervening references to another source — you may place your reference at the end of the paragraph. However, be sure to include all of the relevant page numbers.

2. Basic format for a source not named in your text When you have not mentioned the author in your sentence, you must place the author's name and the page number in parentheses after the quotation, paraphrase, or summary. Again, the period follows the parentheses.

> After car accidents, "drowning is the second-leading cause of unintentional deaths" among toddlers (Vargas 14).

3. Entire source If you are referring to an entire source rather than to a specific page or pages, you do not need a parenthetical citation.

The explorations of race in ZZ Packer's *Drinking Coffee Elsewhere* can be linked thematically to the treatment of immigrants in Lahiri's work.

4. Corporate, group, or government author Cite the corporation, group, or government agency as you would an individual author. You may use abbreviations for the source in subsequent references if you add the abbreviation in parentheses at the first mention of the name.

The Brown University Office of Financial Aid (BUOFA) has adopted a policy that first-year students will not be expected to work as part of their financial aid package (12). BUOFA will award these students a one-time grant to help compensate for the income lost by not working (14).

5. Unknown author If you are citing a source that has no known author, such as the book *Through Palestine with the 20th Machine Gun Squadron*, use a brief version of the title in the parenthetical citation.

The members of the squadron rode horses while the cooks were issued bicycles, requiring the cooks to exert quite a lot of effort pedaling through the desert sand (*Through Palestine* 17).

6. Two or more works by the same author For references to authors with more than one work in your works cited list, insert a short version of the title between the author and the page number, separating the author and the title with a comma.

(Ishiguro, *Unconsoled* 146)

(Ishiguro, *Remains* 77)

7. Two or more authors with the same last name Include the first initial and last name in the parenthetical citation.

(G. Martin 354)

(F. Martin 169)

8. Two or three authors Include the last name of each author in your citation.

Casting physically attractive actors wins points with film audiences: "Primitive as the association between outward strength and moral force may be, it has its undeniable appeal" (Clarke, Johnson, and Evans 228).

9. Four or more authors Use only the last name of the first author and the abbreviation "et al." (Latin for "and others"). There is no comma between the author's name and "et al."

(Barnes et al. 44)

10. Literary work Along with the page number(s), give other identifying information, such as a chapter, scene, or line number, that will help readers find the passage.

The sense of social claustrophobia is never as palpable in *The Age of Innocence* as when Newland realizes that all of New York society has conspired to cover up what it believes to be an affair between him and Madame Olenska (Wharton 339; ch. 33).

11. Work in an edited collection or anthology Cite the author of the work, not the editor of the collection or anthology. (See also item 28 on p. 654.)

In "Beneath the Deep, Slow Motion," Leo says, "The Chinese call anger a weary bird with no place to roost" (Barkley 163).

12. Sacred text Give the name of the edition you are using, along with the chapter and verse (or their equivalent).

He should consider that "where no counsel is, the people fall: but in the multitude of counselors there is safety" (*King James Bible*, Prov. 11.14).

In the Qur'an, sinners are said to be blind to their sins ("The Cow" 2.7).

13. Two or more works cited together Use a semicolon to separate entries.

Forethought is key in survival, whether it involves remembering extra water on a safari trail or gathering food for a long winter in ancient times (Wither and Hosking 4; Estes and Otte 2).

14. Source quoted in another source Ideally, you should track down the original source of the quotation. If you must use a quotation cited by another author, use the abbreviation "qtd. in" (for "quoted in") when you cite the source.

> President Leonid Kuchma insisted that "we cannot in any instance allow the disintegration or division of Ukraine" (qtd. in Lisova A1).

15. Source without page numbers Give a section, paragraph, or screen number, if numbered, in the parenthetical citation.

> Teters believes that the mascots dehumanize Native Americans, allowing spectators to dismiss the Native Americans' true culture as well as their hardships (Saraceno, par. 20).

If no numbers are available, list only the author's name.

> Although his work has been influenced by many graphic artists, it remains essentially text-based (Fitzgerald).

How Do I Prepare the List of Works Cited?

MLA-style research documents include a reference list titled "Works Cited," which begins on a new page at the end of the document. If you wish to acknowledge sources that you read but did not cite in your text, you may include a second list titled "Works Consulted" and include them in that list.

The list is alphabetized by author. If the author's name is unknown, alphabetize the entry using the title of the source. If you cite more than one work by the same author, alphabetize the group under the author's last name, with each entry listed alphabetically by title (see item 21 on p. 651).

All entries in the list are double-spaced, with no extra space between entries. Entries are formatted with a hanging indent: the first line of an entry is flush with the left margin, and subsequent lines are indented one-half inch.

In longer documents, a list of works cited may be given at the end of each chapter or section. In electronic documents that use links, such as a Web site, the list of works cited is often a separate page to which other pages are linked. To see works cited lists in MLA style, see pages 149, 202, 396, and 453.

Books

16. One author List the author's last name first, followed by a comma and the first name. Italicize the book title and subtitle, if any. List the city of publication and the publisher, separated by a colon, then insert a comma and the publication year. End with the medium "Print" and a period.

Pollan, Michael. *In Defense of Food: An Eater's Manifesto*. New York: Penguin, 2008. Print.

17. Two or three authors List all the authors in the same order as on the title page, last name first for only the first author listed. Use commas to separate authors' names.

Singh, Simon, and Edzard Ernst. *Trick or Treatment: The Undeniable Facts about Alternative Medicine*. New York: Norton, 2008. Print.

18. Four or more authors Provide the first author's name (last name first) followed by a comma, and then the abbreviation "et al." (Latin for "and others").

Christensen, Hans, et al. *Images of Culture: Art History as Cultural History*. Copenhagen: Museum Tusculanum, 2009. Print.

19. Corporate or group author Write out the full name of the corporation or group, and cite the name as you would an author. This name is often also the name of the publisher.

National Geographic. *Essential Visual History of World Mythology*. Washington: Natl. Geographic, 2008. Print.

20. Unknown author When no author is listed on the title or copyright page, begin the entry with the title of the work. Alphabetize the entry by the first word of the title other than *A*, *An*, or *The*.

The Haunted Man and the Ghost's Bargain. MacLean: IndyPublish, 2009. Print.

21. Two or more books by the same author Use the author's name in the first entry. Thereafter, use three hyphens followed by a period in place of the author's name. List the entries alphabetically by title.

Chopra, Deepak. *Life after Death: The Burden of Proof*. New York: Three Rivers, 2008. Print.

How do I cite books using MLA style?

When citing a book, use the information from the title page and the copyright page (on the reverse side of the title page), not from the book's cover or a library catalog. Consult pages 651–655 for additional models for citing books.

A Tatar, Maria. **B** *Enchanted Hunters: The Power of Stories in Childhood.* **C** New York:

D Norton, **E** 2009. **F** Print.

A **The author.** Give the last name first, followed by a comma, the first name, and the middle initial (if given). Omit titles such as *MD*, *PhD*, or *Sir*; include suffixes after the name and a comma (O'Driscoll, Gerald P., Jr.). End with a period.

B **The title.** Give the full title; include the subtitle (if any), preceded by a colon. Italicize the title and subtitle; capitalize all major words. End with a period.

C **The city of publication.** If more than one city is given, use the first one listed. Insert a colon.

D **The publisher.** Give a shortened version of the publisher's name (*Harper* for HarperCollins Publishers; *Harcourt* for Harcourt Brace; *Oxford UP* for Oxford University Press). Do not include the words *Publisher* or *Inc.* Follow with a comma.

E **The year of publication.** If more than one copyright date is given, use the most recent one. Use "n.d." if no date is given. End with a period.

F **The medium consulted.** For a book, insert "Print" and end with a period.

---. *Reinventing the Body, Resurrecting the Soul: How to Create a New Self*. New York: Random House, 2009. Print.

---. *Why Is God Laughing? The Path to Joy and Spiritual Optimism*. New York: Harmony, 2008. Print.

22. Editor(s) Use the abbreviation "ed." or "eds."

Burkhardt, Frederick, ed. *Charles Darwin: The* Beagle *Letters*. Cambridge: Cambridge UP, 2008. Print.

23. Author with an editor Include the name of the editor (first name first) after the title. Use the abbreviation "Ed." (meaning "Edited by").

Gunn, Thom. *Selected Poems*. Ed. August Kleinzahler. New York: Farrar, 2009. Print.

24. Translated book List the author first and then the title, followed by the name of the translator and publication information. Use the abbreviation "Trans."

Robuchon, Joel. *The Complete Robuchon*. Trans. Robin H. R. Bellinger. New York: Knopf, 2008. Print.

25. Edition other than the first Include the number of the edition and the abbreviation "ed." (meaning "edition") after the title.

El Saadawi, Nawal. *The Circling Song*. 2nd ed. London: Zed, 2009. Print.

26. Republished book Indicate the original date of publication after the title.

Steinbeck, John. *The Winter of Our Discontent*. 1961. New York: Penguin, 2008. Print.

27. Multivolume work Include the total number of volumes and the abbreviation "vols." after the title.

Ciment, James. *Encyclopedia of the Jazz Age: From the End of World War I to the Great Crash*. 2 vols. Armonk: Sharpe, 2008. Print.

If you have used only one of the volumes in your document, include the volume number after the title. List the total number of volumes after the publication information.

Misiroglu, Gina. *American Countercultures: An Encyclopedia of Nonconformists, Alternative Lifestyles, and Radical Ideas in US History*. Vol. 1. Armonk: Sharpe, 2008. Print. 3 vols.

28. Work in an edited collection or anthology Begin your citation with the author. Surround the title of the selection with quotation marks. Follow this with the title of the anthology or collection in italics, the abbreviation "Ed." (meaning "Edited by"), and the names of the editor(s) (first name first) as well as publication information. Then give the inclusive page numbers for the selection or chapter. End with the medium.

Kotey, Phyllis. "Judging under Disaster: The Effect of Hurricane Katrina on the Criminal Justice System." *Hurricane Katrina: America's Unnatural Disaster*. Ed. Jeremy Levitt and Matthew Whitaker. Lincoln: U of Nebraska P, 2009. 105-31. Print.

If you are using multiple works from the same anthology, you may include the anthology itself in your list of works cited and cross-reference it in the citations for individual works. Do not include the medium in the cross-referenced entries.

Conselice, Christopher J. "The Universe's Invisible Hand." Groopman 39-47.

Dyson, Freeman. "Our Biotech Future." Groopman 64-74.

Groopman, Jerome, ed. *The Best American Science and Nature Writing 2008*. Boston: Houghton, 2008. Print.

29. Foreword, introduction, preface, or afterword Begin with the author of the part you are citing and the name of that part. Add the title of the work; "By" or "Ed." and the work's author or editor (first name first); and publication information. Then give the inclusive page numbers for the part. End with the medium.

Navratilova, Martina. Foreword. *Crisis: 40 Stories Revealing the Personal, Social, and Religious Pain and Trauma of Growing Up Gay in America*. Ed. Mitchell Gold (with Mindy Drucker). Austin: Greenleaf, 2008. ix-xi. Print.

If the foreword or other part has a title, include the title in quotation marks between the author and the name of the part.

Nordhaus, Ted. "From the Nightmare to the Dream." Introduction. *Break Through: From the Death of Environmentalism to the Politics of Possibility*. By Michael Shellenberger. New York: Houghton, 2007. 1-19. Print.

30. Sacred text Include the title of the version as it appears on the title page. If the title does not identify the version, place that information directly after the title.

Holy Bible: New International Version. Grand Rapids: Zondervan, 2008. Print.

31. Dissertation or thesis Cite as you would a book, but include an appropriate label such as "Diss." or "MA thesis" after the title. Add the school and the year before any publication information.

Ramos, Lisa Y. *A Class Apart: Mexican Americans, Race, and Civil Rights in Texas*. Diss. Columbia U, 2008. Ann Arbor: UMI, 2009. Print.

Sources in Journals, Magazines, and Newspapers

32. Article in a journal Enclose the article title in quotation marks. After the journal title, list the volume number, add a period, and insert the issue number, with no space. Then insert the year of publication in parentheses, a colon, and inclusive page numbers. Include the issue number regardless of whether the journal restarts its pagination for each issue or each volume. End with the medium.

Van Riper, Frank, and Judith Goodman. "Life in Venice." *American Scholar* 78.2 (2009): 12-13. Print.

33. Article in a monthly or bimonthly magazine After the author's name and title of the article, list the title of the magazine, the date (use abbreviations for all months except May, June, and July), and inclusive page numbers. End with the medium.

Moreno, Patti. "Setting Your Sites." *Organic Gardening* Apr. 2009: 18. Print.

34. Article in a weekly or biweekly magazine Give the exact date of publication, inverted.

Gessen, Keith. "The Accused: The Political Fallout of a Murder Trial." *New Yorker* 23 Mar. 2009: 42-53. Print.

How do I cite articles from periodicals using MLA style?

Periodicals include journals, magazines, and newspapers. This page gives an example of a citation for a print journal article. Models for citing articles from magazines and newspapers are on pages 655–658.

If you need to cite a periodical article you accessed electronically, follow the guidelines below and see also item 56 on page 661 and item 65 on page 665.

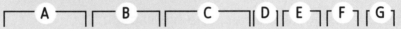

Kushner, Aviya. "McCulture." *Wilson Quarterly* 33.1 (2009): 50-66. Print.

A   **The author.** Give the last name first, followed by a comma, the first name, and the middle initial (if given). Omit titles such as *MD*, *PhD*, or *Sir*; include suffixes after the name and a comma (O'Driscoll, Gerald P., Jr.). End with a period.

B   **The article title.** Give the full title; include the subtitle (if any), preceded by a colon. Enclose the title and subtitle in quotation marks, and capitalize all major words. Place a period inside the closing quotation mark.

C   **The periodical title.** Italicize the periodical title; exclude any initial *A*, *An*, or *The*; capitalize all major words.

D   **The volume number and issue number.** For journals, include the volume number, followed by a period (no space) and the issue number.

E   **The date of publication.** For journals, give the year in parentheses, followed by a colon. For monthly magazines, don't use parentheses; give the month and year. For weekly magazines and newspapers, don't use parentheses; give the day, month, and year, in that order. Abbreviate the names of all months except May, June, and July.

F   **Inclusive page number(s).** For numbers 100 and above, give only the last two digits and any other preceding digits if different from the first number (22-28, 402-10, 1437-45, 592-603). Include section letters for newspapers, if relevant. End with a period.

G   **The medium consulted.** For print journals, magazines, and newspapers, insert "Print" and end with a period.

35. Article in a newspaper If the name of the newspaper begins with *The,* omit the word. If the newspaper is not a national newspaper (such as the *Wall Street Journal, Christian Science Monitor,* or *Chronicle of Higher Education*) or if the city of publication is not part of its name, add the city in square brackets after the name of the newspaper: [Salem]. List the date in inverted order, and if the masthead indicates that the paper has more than one edition, give this information after the date ("natl. ed.," "late ed."). Follow with a colon and a space, and then list the page numbers (use the section letter before the page number if the newspaper uses letters to designate sections). If the article does not appear on consecutive pages, write only the first page number and a plus sign (+), with no space between. End with the medium.

Pfanner, Eric. "A Fix for Music Piracy: Tack a Fee on Broadband." *New York Times* 26 Jan.
    2009: B4. Print.

36. Unsigned article Begin with the title of the article. Alphabetize by the first word other than *A, An,* or *The.*

"Bailed-out Carmakers Must Detail Spending." *Virginian-Pilot* [Norfolk] 23 Mar. 2009: B8.
    Print.

37. Editorial Include the word "Editorial" after the title.

"Science Prevails." Editorial. *San Francisco Chronicle* 10 Mar. 2009: A10. Print.

38. Letter to the editor Include the word "Letter" after the title.

Millstein, Ira A. "Boards Often Failed in Their Duty." Letter. *Wall Street Journal* 25 Feb.
    2009: A14. Print.

39. Review After the author and title of the review, include the words "Rev. of" followed by the title of the work under review; a comma; the word "by" (for a book) or "dir." (for a play or film); and the name of the author or director. Continue with publication information for the review.

Thomson, Desson. "'Youth': Coppola's Dizzying Spin on Fleeting Time." Rev. of *Youth*
    without Youth, dir. Francis Ford Coppola. *Washington Post* 11 Jan. 2008: C01.
    Print.

40. Published interview Begin with the person interviewed. If the published interview has a title, give it in quotation marks. If not, write the word "Interview." If an interviewer is identified and relevant to your project, give that name next. Then supply the publication data.

Morrison, Van. "The Grouchy Transcendentalist." Interview by David Fricke. *Rolling Stone*
2 Apr. 2009: 28-29. Print.

Print Reference Works

41. Entry in an encyclopedia, dictionary, thesaurus, handbook, or almanac
Unless the entry is signed, begin your citation with the title of the entry in quotation marks, followed by a period. Give the title of the reference work, italicized, and the edition (if available) and year of publication. If the work is arranged alphabetically, you may omit the volume and page numbers.

"Blog." *Encyclopaedia Britannica*. 2010. Print.

If a reference work is not well known, provide all of the bibliographic information.

Hischak, Thomas S. "South Pacific." *Oxford Companion to the American Musical: Theatre, Film, and Television*. Oxford: Oxford UP, 2008. Print.

42. Map or chart Generally, treat a map or chart as you would a book without authors. Give its title, the word "Map" or "Chart," and publication information. For a map in an atlas, give the map title (in quotation marks), followed by publication information for the atlas and page numbers for the map. If the creator of the map or chart is listed, use his or her name as you would an author's name.

Thomas Guide: San Diego County. Map. Chicago: Rand, 2009. Print.

"Africa: Political." Map. *Oxford Atlas of the World*. 11th ed. London: Oxford UP, 2007. 105. Print.

43. Government publication In most cases, cite the government agency as the author. If there is a named author, editor, or compiler, provide that name after the title. Use the abbreviations "Dept." for department, "Cong." for Congress, "S." for Senate, "H." or "HR" for House of Representatives, "Res." for resolution, "Rept." for report, "Doc." for document, and "GPO" for Government Printing Office.

United States. Dept. of Defense. *Photographic History of Walter Reed Army Medical Center (WRAMC)*. Washington: GPO, 2009. Print.

If you are citing from the *Congressional Record*, the entry is simply *Cong. Rec.* followed by the date, a colon, the page numbers, and the medium.

44. Brochure or pamphlet Format the entry as you would for a book (see p. 651).

UNESCO. *The Right to Education*. Paris: UNESCO, 2008. Print.

Field Sources

45. Personal interview Place the name of the person interviewed first, words to indicate how the interview was conducted ("Personal interview," "Telephone interview," or "E-mail interview"), and the date.

Templeton, Santo. Personal interview. 26 Feb. 2009.

46. Personal survey Place the title of the survey first, followed by the location of the survey if it was conducted in a particular city or state, the date the survey was first distributed, and an indication of how the interview was conducted ("Telephone survey," "E-mail survey," "Web survey," "Mail survey," or "Face-to-face survey").

"Survey of Student Attitudes to Proposed College Budget Cuts." St. Olaf College. 15 Feb. 2010. E-mail survey.

47. Unpublished letter If the letter was written to you, give the writer's name, the words "Letter to the author" (no quotation marks), and the date letter was written. End with the form of the material: use "MS" (meaning "manuscript") for a handwritten letter and "TS" (meaning "typescript") for a typed letter.

Wilden, Raquel. Letter to the author. 11 May 2010. TS.

If the letter was written to someone else, give that name rather than "the author."

48. Lecture or public address Give the speaker's name and the title of the lecture (if there is one). If the lecture was part of a meeting or convention, identify that event. Conclude with the event data, including venue, city, and date. End with the appropriate label ("Lecture," "Panel discussion," "Reading").

Anam, Tahmima. Harvard Book Store, Cambridge. 10 Jan. 2008. Reading.

Media Sources

49. Film or video recording Generally begin with the title of the film or recording. Always supply the name of the director (following the abbreviation "Dir."), the distributor, and the year of original release. You may also insert other relevant information, such as the names of the performers or screenplay writers, before the distributor. End with the medium ("Film," "DVD," "Videocassette"). For DVDs and videocassettes, include the original release date.

Slumdog Millionaire. Dir. Danny Boyle. Perf. Dev Patel and Freida Pinto. Fox Searchlight,
    2008. Film.

Before the Rain. Dir. Milcho Manchevski. 1994. Criterion Collection, 2008. DVD.

50. Television or radio program Include the title of the program, the network or station, the call letters and city (if any), the date on which the program aired, and the medium ("Radio," "Television"). If there are relevant persons to name (such as the author, director, host, narrator, or actor), include that information after the title. If the program has named episodes or segments, list those in quotation marks. If the material you're citing is an interview, include the word "Interview" and, if relevant, the name of the interviewer.

"Terry Moran's Moment of Truth." *Nightline*. Host Terry Moran. ABC. WCVB, Boston, 25 Mar.
    2009. Television.

Fresh Air. Host Terry Gross. Natl. Public Radio. WHYY, Philadelphia, 12 Jan. 2009.
    Radio.

Holder, Eric. Interview by Katie Couric. *CBS Evening News*. CBS. KCTV, Kansas City, 8 Apr.
    2009. Television.

51. Sound recording Begin with the name of the person whose work you want to highlight: the composer, the conductor, or the performer. Next list the title, followed by the names of other artists (composer, conductor, performers), with abbreviations indicating their roles. The recording information includes the manufacturer and the date. End with the medium of the recording ("CD," "LP," "Audiocassette," "Audiotape," "MP3 file").

Von Otter, Anne-Sofie. *Bach: Cantatas*. Concerto Copenhagen. Cond. Lars Ulrik Mortensen.
    Deutsche Grammaphon, 2009. CD.

If you wish to cite a particular track on the recording, give its performer and title (in quotation marks), and then proceed with the information about the recording. For live recordings, include the date of the performance between the title and the recording data.

Cash, Johnny. "Folsom Prison Blues." *The Great Lost Performance*. Rec. 27 July 1990.
    Island, 2007. MP3 file.

52. Live performance Generally, begin with the title of the performance. Then give the author and director; the major performers; and the theater, city, and date. End with "Performance."

The Importance of Being Earnest. By Oscar Wilde. Dir. Spiro Veloudos. Perf. Hannah Barth
    and Robert Bonnatto. Lyric Stage, Boston. 9 May 2008. Performance.

53. Work of art Give the name of the artist; the title of the work (italicized); the date of composition; the medium of composition; the name of the collection, museum, or owner; and the city. If you are citing artwork published in a book, add the publication information for the book and the medium of publication ("Print") at the end.

Perret, Mai-Thu. *Bikini (White Cake)*. 2008. Acrylic plaster. Aspen Art Museum, Aspen.

54. Advertisement Provide the name of the product, service, or organization being advertised, followed by the word "Advertisement." Then provide the usual publication information.

Celebrex. Advertisement. *Smithsonian* Feb. 2009: 10-12. Print.

55. Cartoon Treat a cartoon like an article in a newspaper or magazine. Give the cartoonist's name, the title of the cartoon if there is one (in quotation marks), the word "Cartoon," and the publication data for the source.

Ziegler, Jack. "Three-Martini Science." Cartoon. *New Yorker* 2 Mar. 2009: 51. Print.

Electronic Sources

56. Article from an online database or subscription service Cite it as you would a print article, and then give the name of the database in italics, the medium consulted ("Web"), and the date you accessed the article. (See also item 32 on p. 655.)

How do I cite articles from databases using MLA style?

Libraries subscribe to services such as LexisNexis, ProQuest, InfoTrac, and EBSCOhost that provide access to databases of digital texts. The databases provide publication information, abstracts, and the complete text of documents in a specific subject area, discipline, or profession. (See also Chapter 12.)

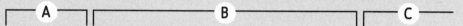

Taylor, Corey M. "Blue Order: Wallace Stevens's Jazz Experiments." *Journal of Modern*

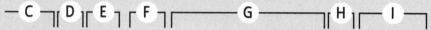

Literature 32.2 (2009): 100-17. *General Reference Center Gold*. Web. 21 Feb. 2009.

A **The author.** Give the last name first, followed by a comma, the first name, and the middle initial (if given). Omit titles such as *MD*, *PhD*, or *Sir*; include suffixes after the name and a comma (O'Driscoll, Gerald P., Jr.). End with a period.

B **The article title.** Give the title and subtitle (if any), preceded by a colon. Enclose the full title in quotation marks, and capitalize all major words. Place a period inside the closing quotation mark.

C **The periodical title.** Italicize the periodical title; exclude any initial *A*, *An*, or *The*; capitalize all major words.

D **The volume number and issue number if appropriate.** For journals, give the volume number, and then insert a period (no space) and the issue number.

E **The date of publication.** For journals, give the year in parentheses, followed by a colon. For monthly magazines, don't use parentheses; give the month and year. For weekly magazines and newspapers, give the day, month, and year.

F **Inclusive page number(s).** Include section letters for newspapers, if relevant. If no pagination is given, use "n. pag."

G **The name of the database.** Italicize the name of the database, followed by a period.

H **The medium consulted.** Use "Web" followed by a period.

I **The date of access.** Use the day-month-year format; abbreviate all months except May, June, and July. End with a period.

Levin, Harry. "Form and Formality in *Romeo and Juliet.*" *Shakespeare Quarterly* 11.1 (1960):
  3-11. *JSTOR.* Web. 29 Mar. 2009.

57. Short work from a Web site Include the author (if available), the title of the
document in quotation marks, and the title of the Web site in italics. Then give the
sponsor or publisher followed by a comma, the date of publication or last update
followed by a period, the medium ("Web"), and the access date. (See also p. 664.)
Do not include URLs in works cited entries.

Thompson, Michael. "Helping America's Boys." *PBS Parents.* PBS, 2008. Web. 8 Feb.
  2009.

58. Academic course or department Web site For a course page, give the name of
the instructor, the course title in italics, a description such as "Course home page,"
the course dates, the department, the institution, the medium, and your date of
access. For a department page, give the department name, a description such as
"Home page," the institution, the date of the last update, the medium, and the date
of access.

Agatucci, Cora. *WR 123: English Composition III (Research-Based Academic Writing).* Course
  home page. Winter 2009. Humanities Dept., Central Oregon Community Coll. Web.
  20 Jan. 2009.

Dept. of English and Technical Communication. Home page. Missouri U of Science and
  Technology, 2008. Web. 22 Mar. 2009.

59. Personal Web site If the site has no title, give a description such as "Home page."

Gaiman, Neil. Home page. Harper, 2009. Web. 5 Jan. 2009.

**60. Message posted to a newsgroup, electronic mailing list, or online discussion
forum** Cite the name of the person who posted the message and the title (from the
subject line, in quotation marks); if the posting has no title, add the phrase "Online
posting". Then add the name of the Web site (italicized), the sponsor or publisher,
the date of the message, the medium ("Web"), and the date you accessed the posting.

Sandman-Hurley, Kelli. "Dyslexia — What Is It?" *Learning Disabilities Discussion List.* Natl.
  Inst. for Literacy, 3 Oct. 2008. Web. 29 May 2009.

How do I cite works from Web sites using MLA style?

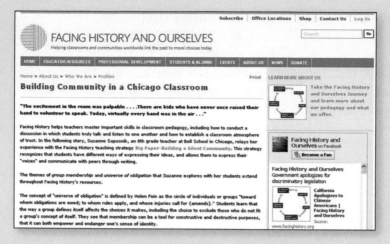

You will likely need to search the site to find some of the citation information you need. For some sites, all of the details may not be available; find as many as you can. Remember that the citation information you provide should allow readers to retrace your steps electronically to locate the sources. Consult pages 661–666 for additional models for citing Web sources.

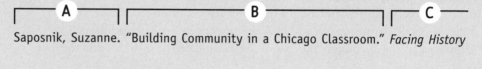

Saposnik, Suzanne. "Building Community in a Chicago Classroom." *Facing History*

and Ourselves. Facing History and Ourselves, n.d. Web. 12 Apr. 2009.

A **The author of the work.** Give the last name first, followed by a comma, the first name, and the middle initial (if given). Omit titles such as *MD*, *PhD*, or *Sir*; include suffixes after the name and a comma (O'Driscoll, Gerald P., Jr.). Insert a period. If no author is given, begin with the title.

B **The title of the work.** Give the full title; include the subtitle (if any), preceded by a colon. Enclose the title and subtitle in quotation marks, and capitalize all major words. Place a period inside the closing quotation mark.

C **The title of the Web site.** Give the title of the entire site, italicized. If there is no clear title and it is a personal home page, use "Home page" without italicizing it. End with a period.

D **The name of the sponsoring organization.** Look for the sponsor's name at the bottom of the site's home page. If no publisher or sponsor is available, use "N. p." Follow with a comma.

E **The date of publication or most recent update.** Use the day-month-year format; abbreviate all months except May, June, and July. If no date is given, use "n.d." End with a period.

F **The medium consulted.** For works found online, use "Web" followed by a period.

G **The date you accessed it.** Give the most recent date you accessed the site. End with a period.

61. Article or page on a wiki Because the material on a wiki is likely to change, include your date of access.

"Surrealism." *Wikipedia*. Wikimedia Foundation, 12 Dec. 2009. Web. 3 Jan. 2009.

62. Blog To cite an entry or a comment on a Weblog, give the author of the entry or comment (if available), the title of the entry or comment in quotation marks, the title of the blog (italicized), the sponsor or publisher, the date the material was posted, the medium, and the access date.

Reddy, Sudeep. "Warren Buffett on the Economy." *WSJ Blogs: Real Time Economics*. Dow
     Jones, 28 Feb. 2009. Web. 2 Apr. 2009.

63. E-mail message Cite the sender of the message; the title (from the subject line); a phrase indicating the recipient of the message ("Message to"); the date of the message; and the medium ("E-mail"). (Note that MLA's style is to hyphenate the word *e-mail*.)

Willford, Latrisha. "Critique of 'Anna's Ordinary Blues.'" Message to the author. 19 Aug. 2009.
     E-mail.

Pabon, Xavier. "Brainstorming for Essay." Message to Brayden Perry. 24 Apr. 2009. E-mail.

64. Online book Cite an online book as you would a print book; then give title of the database or Web site (italicized), the medium ("Web"), and the access date (see also item 16 on p. 651).

Lambert, Joshua N. *American Jewish Fiction*. New York: Jewish Publication Society, 2009.
     Google Book Search. Web. 27 Mar. 2009.

65. Online periodical article Provide the author, the title of the article (in quotation marks), and the name of the Web site (in italics). Then add the publisher or sponsor, the date of publication, the medium ("Web"), and your date of access (see also items 32–40 on pp. 655–658).

Crawford, Kinon. "Food for Thought." Letter. *LA Times.com*. Los Angeles Times, 26 Mar. 2009.
     Web. 15 Apr. 2009.

Flanagan, Caitlin. "What Girls Want." *The Atlantic.com*. Atlantic Monthly Group, Dec. 2008.
     Web. 4 May 2009.

66. Online film or video clip (See also item 49 on p. 660.)

"Making Biodiesel." *Make Magazine*. YouTube, 14 Aug. 2008. Web. 1 May 2009.

67. Online image Treat maps, charts, advertisements, and other visual documents you find online as you would the print versions, but include the Web site (italicized), sponsor or publisher of the site, the medium ("Web"), and your date of access. For a work of art found online, omit the medium of composition, and after the location, add the title of the Web site or database (italicized), the medium consulted ("Web"), and your date of access. (See also item 42 on p. 658 and items 53–55 on p. 661.)

"Central Park, New York." Map. *Google Maps*. Google, 26 June 2009. Web. 26 June 2009.

Johns, Jasper. *Perilous Night*. 1982. Natl. Gallery of Art, Washington. *National Gallery of Art*. Web. 10 Oct. 2009.

Minisode Network. Advertisement. *MySpace*. MySpace.com, 2008. Web. 12 Dec. 2009.

68. DVD or CD-ROM Treat a work published on DVD or CD-ROM as you would a book, noting "DVD" or "CD-ROM" as the medium.

Orman, Suze. *Stop Identity Theft Now Kit*. Salt Lake City: TrustID, 2008. CD-ROM.

69. Computer software or video game Cite computer software as you would a book. Provide additional information about the medium on which it is distributed ("CD-ROM," "Xbox 360," and so on) and the version.

Unchartered: Drake's Fortune. Foster City: Sony Computer Entertainment, 2007. CD-ROM.

70. Other online sources For other online sources, adapt the guidelines to the medium. Include as much information as necessary for your readers to easily find your source. The example below is for a radio program available in an online archive.

"This I Used to Believe." *This American Life*. Host Ira Glass. Chicago Public Radio. WBEZ, Chicago. 17 Apr. 2009. Web. 7 May 2009.

22

Using APA Style

American Psychological Association (APA) style, used primarily in the social sciences and in some of the natural sciences, emphasizes the author(s) and publication date of a source. Writers who use the APA documentation system cite, or formally acknowledge, information within their text using parentheses and provide a list of sources, called a reference list, at the end of their document.

To see student essays formatted and documented in APA style, turn to either of the following examples in Part Two:

> Ali Bizzul, *Living (and Dying) Large*, page 259
>
> Dwight Haynes, *Making Better Choices: Two Approaches to Reducing College Drinking*, page 323

For more information about APA style, consult the *Publication Manual of the American Psychological Association*, Sixth Edition. Information about these publications can be found on the APA Web site at www.apa.org.

CITATIONS WITHIN YOUR TEXT

ENTRIES IN YOUR REFERENCE LIST

Books

Sources in Journals, Magazines, and Newspapers

Print Reference Works

Field Sources

Media Sources

Electronic Sources

Other Sources

How Do I Cite Sources within the Text of My Document?

APA uses an author-date form of in-text citation to acknowledge the use of another writer's words, facts, or ideas. When you are summarizing or paraphrasing, provide the author's last name and the year of publication either in the sentence or in parentheses at the end of the sentence. You may include a page or chapter reference if it would help readers find the original material in a longer work. When you are quoting, the citation in parentheses must include the page(s) or paragraph(s) (for sources that do not have pages) in which the quotation can be found.

Although APA requires page numbers only for direct quotations, your instructor might prefer that you include a page or paragraph number with every source you cite in your document. If you're not certain of the requirements for your project, ask your instructor for guidance.

1. Basic format for a source named in your text Place the publication year in parentheses directly after the author's last name. Include the page number (with "p." for page) in parentheses after a direct quotation.

> Singer (2009) noted that "the most apt historical parallel to the current period in the development of robotics may well turn out to be World War I" (p. 32).

> According to Singer (2009), today's advances in robotics are most like the era of World War I.

Note that APA style requires using the past tense or present perfect tense to introduce the material you are citing: *Renfrew argued* or *Renfrew has argued*.

2. Basic format for a source not named in your text Insert a parenthetical note that gives the author's last name and the year of the publication, separated by a comma. For a quotation, include the page or paragraph number of the source.

> Across a range of services and offices, "from drivers' licenses and home improvement permits to voter registration, government was slow moving, unresponsive, and maddeningly hard to navigate" (Galston, 2009, p. 52).

> Across a range of services and offices, government processes became slower and less accessible to citizens (Galston, 2009).

3. Two authors List the last names of both authors in every mention in the text. If you mention the authors' names in a sentence, use the word "and" to separate the last names, as shown in the first example. If you place the authors' names in the parenthetical citation, use an ampersand (&) to separate the last names, as shown in the second example.

> Rosenthal and Barry (2009) observed that "the world's largest corporations, such as Wal-Mart and Microsoft, are themselves some of the world's largest economies" (p. xi).

> Multinational corporations are becoming an increasingly important area of study for scholars of international relations and economics (Rosenthal & Barry, 2009).

4. Three, four, or five authors In parentheses, name all the authors the first time you cite the source, using an ampersand (&) before the last author's name. In subsequent references to the source, use the last name of the first author followed by the abbreviation "et al." (Latin for "and others").

> A broader understanding of what constitutes student learning, including learning time spent outside the classroom, is necessary for improving the quality of education (Weiss, Little, Bouffard, Deschenes, & Malone, 2009). Disadvantaged students would benefit the most from such an expanded definition of learning (Weiss et al., 2009).

5. Six or more authors In all references to the source, give the first author's last name followed by "et al."

> Knop et al. (2009) acknowledged that the relationship between attention-deficit/ hyperactivity disorder (ADHD) and alcoholism in high-risk males of alcoholic fathers needs further study.

6. Corporate, group, or government author In general, cite the full name of the corporation, group, or government agency the first time it is mentioned in your text. If you add an abbreviation for the name in square brackets the first time you cite the source, you can use the abbreviation in subsequent citations.

> Prekindergarten programs that receive state funding are governed by different standards than licensed day-care centers, creating unequal opportunities for many chil-

dren (National Association of Child Care Resource and Referral Agencies [NACCRRA], 2009). State-funded programs were more likely to adhere to early education benchmarks than private centers were (NACCRRA, 2009).

7. Unknown author Sources with unknown authors are listed by title in the list of references (see item 18 on p. 673). In your in-text citation, shorten the title as much as possible without introducing confusion. Add quotation marks to article titles, and italicize book titles.

> The debate over evolution and creationism continues in the wake of recent scientific discoveries ("Fossil," 2008).

8. Two or more works by the same author in the same year After organizing the works alphabetically by title, insert a lowercase letter after the publication year ("2009a" or "2009b").

> Sokol (2009a) has argued that funding for technical assistance programs must keep pace with local needs.

9. Two or more authors with the same last name Use the authors' initials in each citation.

> While C. W. Mills (2006) has advocated viewing these issues as societal ones, not just a personal problem of a particular man or woman, D. Mills (2007) has suggested that issues such as homelessness and hunger can become impersonal and overlooked as a result.

10. Two or more works cited together List the sources in alphabetical order, and separate them with semicolons. If you are referring to two or more sources by the same author, order those sources chronologically and give the author's last name only once (Gharib, 2007, 2009).

> Lack of effective communication while trying to exert control makes it difficult to set boundaries and accept the subject's ambitions and exertions (Castillo & Nugent, 2007; Timothy & Igler, 2008).

11. Source cited in another source Ideally, you should track down the original source of the information. If you cannot find the original, mention its author and indicate where it was cited.

> McLeod (2009) acknowledged that some hoaxers believe in their causes so deeply that they even rationalize their deception of others (as cited in Ayoub, 2009).

12. Source with no page numbers Many visual documents, such as brochures, and electronic sources, such as Web sites and full-text articles from databases, lack page numbers. If the source has numbered paragraphs, indicate the paragraph number. If the paragraphs are not numbered, include the section heading and indicate which paragraph in that section contains the cited material.

> Lazar (2009) reported on recent data suggesting that "people who own or interact regularly with animals may be healthier than people who don't" (para. 2).

13. E-mail, letters, and other personal communication Give the first initial(s) and last name of the person with whom you corresponded, the words "personal communication," and the date. Don't include personal communication in your reference list.

> (A. L. Chan, personal communication, October 9, 2009)

14. Web site For an entire Web site, give the URL in parentheses in your text, and don't include it in your reference list. To cite a quotation from a Web site, give the paragraph number and include the source in your reference list.

> The WAC Clearinghouse (http://wac.colostate.edu) provides a collection of books developed for distribution on the Web.

> O'Loughlin (2008) has shown that many students need "direct instruction rather than just unfettered exploration in order to learn" (para. 5).

How Do I Prepare the Reference List?

The reference list contains publication information for all sources that you have cited within your document, with two exceptions. Entire Web sites and personal communication, such as e-mail messages, letters, and interviews, are cited only in the text of the document.

Begin the list on a new page at the end of the document, and center the title "References" at the top. Organize the list alphabetically by author (if the source is an organization, alphabetize it by the name of the organization; if the source has no known author, alphabetize it by title). All of the entries should be double-spaced with no extra space between entries. Entries are formatted with a hanging indent: the first line is flush with the left margin, and subsequent lines are indented one-half inch. Only the initial word and proper nouns (names of people, organizations, cities, states, and so on) in a source title and subtitle are capitalized.

In longer documents, a reference list may be given at the end of each chapter or section. In electronic documents that use links, such as Web sites, the reference list is often a separate page to which other pages are linked.

For examples of reference lists in APA style, see pages 266 and 331.

Books

15. One author List the author's last name followed by a comma and the first initial. Insert the date in parentheses and italicize the title. Follow with the place of publication and the publisher, separated by a colon.

Zimmer, C. (2008). *Microcosm:* E. coli *and the new science of life*. New York, NY: Pantheon Books.

16. Two or more authors List the authors in the same order as the title page does, each with last name first. Use commas to separate authors and use an ampersand (&) before the final author's name. List every author up to and including seven; for a work with eight or more authors, give the first six names followed by three ellipses dots and the last author's name. (Do not use an ampersand in such cases.)

Holldobler, B., & Wilson, E. O. (2009). *The superorganism: The beauty, elegance, and strangeness of insect societies*. New York, NY: W. W. Norton.

17. Corporate or group author Write out the full name of a corporate or group author. If the corporation is also the publisher, use "Author" for the publisher's name.

National Geographic. (2008). *Abraham Lincoln's extraordinary era*. Washington, DC: Author.

18. Unknown author When no author is listed on the title or copyright page, begin the entry with the title of the work. Alphabetize the entry by the first significant word of the title (not including *A, An,* or *The*).

On the road of life. (2007). Naperville, IL: Sourcebooks.

How do I cite books using APA style?

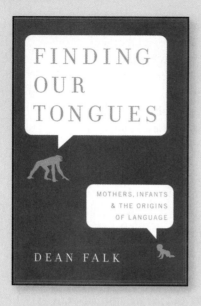

When citing a book, use the information from the title page and the copyright page (on the reverse side of the title page), not from the book's cover or a library catalog. Consult pages 673–676 for additional models for citing books.

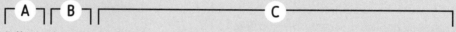

A **B** **C**

Falk, D. (2009). *Finding our tongues: Mothers, infants and the origin of language.*

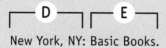

D **E**

New York, NY: Basic Books.

A The author. Give the last name first, followed by a comma and initials for first name and, if any, middle name. Separate initials with a space (Leakey, R. E.). Separate the names of multiple authors with commas; use an ampersand (&) before the final author's name.

B The year of publication. Put the most recent copyright year in parentheses, and end with a period (outside the parentheses).

C The title and, if any, the subtitle. Give the full title; include the subtitle (if any), preceded by a colon. Italicize the title and subtitle, capitalizing only the first word of the title, the first word of the subtitle, and any proper nouns or proper adjectives. End with a period.

D The place of publication. If more than one city is given, use the first one listed. Use an abbreviation for U.S. states and territories; spell out city and country names for locations outside the U.S. (Cambridge, England). For Canadian cities, also include the province. Insert a colon.

E The publisher. Give the publisher's name. Omit words such as *Inc.* and *Co.* Include and do not abbreviate such terms as *University*, *Books*, and *Press*. End with a period.

19. Two or more books by the same author(s) Give the author's name in each entry and list the titles in chronological order.

Lehrer, J. (2007). *Proust was a neuroscientist*. Boston, MA: Houghton Mifflin.

Lehrer, J. (2009). *How we decide*. Boston, MA: Houghton Mifflin.

20. Translated book List the author first followed by the year of publication, the title, and the translator (in parentheses, identified by the abbreviation "Trans."). Place the original date of the work's publication at the end of the entry.

Weil, P. (2008). *How to be French: Nationality in the making since 1789* (C. Porter, Trans.). Durham, NC: Duke University Press. (Original work published 2002)

21. Edition other than the first Note the edition ("2nd ed.," "Rev. ed.") after the title.

Cialdini, R. B. (2009). *Influence: Science and practice* (5th ed.). Boston, MA: Pearson Education.

22. Author with an editor Include the editor's name and the abbreviation "Ed." in parentheses after the title.

Weyl, H. (2009). *Mind and nature: Selected writings on philosophy, mathematics, and physics* (P. Pesic, Ed.). Princeton, NJ: Princeton University Press.

23. Work in an edited collection or anthology, including a foreword, introduction, preface, or afterword Begin the entry with the author, the publication date, and the title of the chapter or selection (not italicized). Follow this with the word "In," the names of the editors (initials first), the abbreviation "Ed." or "Eds." in parentheses, the title of the anthology or collection (italicized), inclusive page numbers for the chapter or selection (in parentheses, with the abbreviation "pp."), and the place and publisher.

Harless, N. L. (2008). Please help my son not die. In T. Ratner (Ed.), *Reflections on doctors: Nurses' stories about physicians and surgeons* (pp. 9-20). New York, NY: Kaplan Publishing.

Bellamy, D. (2008). Introduction. In T. Rice (Ed.), *Voyages of discovery: A visual celebration of ten of the greatest natural history expeditions* (pp. 8-9). Buffalo, NY: Firefly Books.

24. Sacred text Treat as you would a book (see items 15–18 on p. 673).

The Bible: Authorized King James version. (2008). New York, NY: Oxford University Press.

25. Dissertation or thesis Give the author, date, and title before identifying the type of work (doctoral dissertation or master's thesis). End with the name of the database and the identifying number, or the URL.

Grogan, J. L. (2009). *A cultural history of the humanistic psychology movement in America* (Doctoral dissertation). Available from ProQuest Dissertations and Theses database. (UMI No. 3311487)

26. Two or more sources by the same author in the same year List the works alphabetically, and include lowercase letters (*a*, *b*, and so on) after the dates.

Stover, D. (2009a). NASA's escape pod. *Popular Science, 274*(4), 47.

Stover, D. (2009b). Stealth reborn. *Popular Science, 274*(1), 42-45.

Sources in Journals, Magazines, and Newspapers

27. Article in a journal paginated by volume Most journals continue page numbers throughout an entire annual volume, beginning again at page 1 only in the first volume of the next year. After the author and publication year, provide the article title, the journal title, the volume number (italicized), and the inclusive page numbers.

Carlsson, F., & Brown, E. J. (2009). The art of making an exit. *Science, 323*, 1677-1679.

28. Article in a journal paginated by issue Some journals begin at page 1 for every issue. Include the issue number (in parentheses, not italicized) after the volume number.

Gravener, J. A., Heedt, A. A., Heatherton, T. F., & Keel, P. K. (2008). Gender and age differences in associations between peer dieting and drive for thinness. *International Journal of Eating Disorders, 41*(1), 57-63.

29. Article in a magazine The author's name and the publication date (year and month for monthly magazines; year, month, and date for weekly or biweekly magazines) are followed by the title of the article, the magazine title (italicized), and the

volume number (also italicized) and the issue number, if any. Include all page numbers.

Strong, D. (2008, November). What great leaders know. *Men's Health, 23*(9), 108-114.

Sherman, G. (2008, April 7). Testing Horace Mann. *New York*, 22-27, 107-108.

30. Article in a newspaper List the author's name and the complete date (year first). Next give the article title followed by the name of the newspaper (italicized). Include all page numbers, preceded by "p." or "pp."

Diller, L. (2009, March 27). Powerful proponent of psychiatric drugs for children primed for a fall. *San Francisco Chronicle*, p. A13.

31. Unsigned article Begin with the article title, and alphabetize in the reference list by the first word in the title other than *A*, *An*, or *The*. Use "p." or "pp." before page numbers.

The path less traveled. (2009, April 21). *The Boston Globe*, p. A10.

32. Editorial Include the word "Editorial" in square brackets after the title.

Loaded guns should stay banned in national parks [Editorial]. (2008, December 12). *The Denver Post*, p. B10.

33. Letter to the editor Include the words "Letter to the editor" in square brackets after the title of the letter, if any.

Whitney, R. A. (2009, February 18). Heed discrimination laws in medical care of disabled [Letter to the editor]. *The Boston Globe*, p. A14.

34. Review After the title of the review, include the words "Review of the book . . ." or "Review of the film . . ." and so on in square brackets, followed by the title of the work reviewed. If the reviewed work is a book, include the author's name after a comma; if it's a film or other media, include the year of release.

Benfey, C. (2009, April 5). Hard-knock lives [Review of the book *Dear husband*, by J. C. Oates]. *The New York Times Book Review*, p. 6.

How do I cite articles from print periodicals using APA style?

Periodicals include journals, magazines, and newspapers. This page gives an example of a citation for an article in a magazine. Models for citing articles from journals and newspapers are on pages 676–679. If you need to cite a periodical article you accessed electronically, follow the guidelines below and see pages 681–685.

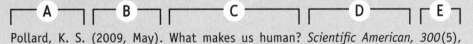

Pollard, K. S. (2009, May). What makes us human? *Scientific American, 300*(5),

44-49.

A **The author.** Give the last name first, followed by a comma and initials for first and middle names. Separate the names of multiple authors with commas; use an ampersand (&) before the final author's name.

B **The year of publication.** Put the year in parentheses and end with a period (outside the parentheses). For magazines and newspapers, include the month and, if relevant, the day (2008, April 13).

C **The article title.** Give the full title; include the subtitle (if any), preceded by a colon. Do not underline, italicize, or put the title in quotation marks. Capitalize only the first word of the title, the first word of the subtitle, and any proper nouns or proper adjectives. End with a period (unless the article title ends with a question mark).

D **The periodical title.** Italicize the periodical title, and capitalize all major words. Insert a comma.

E **The volume and issue number, if relevant.** For magazines and journals with volume numbers, include the volume number, italicized. For magazines and for journals that start each issue with page 1, include the issue number in parentheses, not italicized. Insert a comma.

F **Inclusive page number(s).** Give all of the numbers in full (248-254, not 248-54). For newspapers, include the abbreviation "p." or "pp." for page and section letters, if relevant (p. B12). End with a period.

Corliss, R. (2009, April 27). Zac to the future [Review of the motion picture *17 Again*, 2009]. *Time, 173*(16), 49.

When the review is untitled, follow the date of the review with the bracketed information.

Sealy, S. (2009, April). [Review of the motion picture *Crossing Over*, 2009]. *Film Journal International, 104*(4), 139-140.

Print Reference Works

35. Entry in an encyclopedia, dictionary, thesaurus, handbook, or almanac
Begin your citation with the name of the author or, if the entry is unsigned, the title of the entry. Proceed with the date, the entry title (if not already given), the title of the reference work, the edition number, and the pages. If the contents of the reference work are arranged alphabetically, omit the volume and page numbers.

Roth, G., and Deci, E. L. (2009). Autonomy. In S. J. Lopez (Ed.), *Encyclopedia of positive psychology*. Hoboken, NJ: Wiley.

36. Government publication
Give the name of the department, office, agency, or committee that issued the report as the author. If the document has a report or special file number, place that in parentheses after the title.

Executive Office of the President, Office of Management and Budget. (2009). *A new era of responsibility: Renewing America's promise*. Washington, DC: Government Printing Office.

37. Brochure or pamphlet
Format the entry as you would a book (see items 15–18 on p. 673); insert "n.d." if there is no publication date.

AARP. (n.d.). *How the Fair Housing Act helps persons with disabilities*. Washington, DC: Author.

Field Sources

38. Personal interview
Treat unpublished interviews as personal communications, and include them in your text only (see item 13 on p. 672). Do not cite personal interviews in your reference list.

39. Unpublished survey data Give the title of the survey first, followed by the date the survey was distributed, and the words "Unpublished raw data."

Survey of student attitudes to proposed college budget cuts. (2010, February 10). Unpublished raw data.

40. Unpublished letter Treat unpublished letters as personal communications, and include them in your text only (see item 13 on p. 672). Do not cite unpublished letters in your reference list.

41. Lecture or public address Provide the name of the speaker, followed by the full date of the presentation and the title of the speech if there is one. End the entry with a brief description of the event and its location.

Angell, M. (2008, September 17). *Reforming our health system: Why neither candidate has the answer.* Louis Clark Vanuxem Lecture presented at Princeton University, Princeton, NJ.

Media Sources

42. Film or video recording List the director and producer (if available), the date of release, the title, the medium in square brackets ("Motion picture" or "DVD"), the country where the film was made, and the studio or distributor.

Macdonald, K. (Director). (2009). *State of play* [Motion picture]. United States: Universal Pictures.

43. Television or radio program List the director, writer, producer, host, or reporter (if available); the broadcast date; the title, followed by "Television" or "Radio" and "broadcast" or "series episode" in square brackets; the name of the series; and the city and name of the broadcaster.

Gaviria, M. (Writer/producer), & Cohen, W. (Producer). (2008, January 8). The medicated child [Television series episode]. In *Frontline*. Boston, MA: WGBH.

Ryssdal, K. (Host), & Rose, J. (Reporter). (2009, April 23). Drug prices based on effectiveness. *Marketplace* [Radio broadcast]. Boston, MA: WBUR.

44. Sound recording List the author of the song; the date; the song title, followed by "On" and the recording title in italics; the medium in square brackets; and the production data. If the song was recorded by an artist other than the author, add "Recorded by" plus the artist's name in square brackets after the song title and the recording year in parentheses after the production data.

Young, N. (2009). Fuel line. On *Fork in the road* [CD]. Burbank, CA: Reprise Records.

Electronic Sources

45. Article with a DOI A DOI (Digital Object Identifier) is a unique number assigned to specific content, such as a journal article. If a DOI is available, include it; you do not need to provide a database name or URL.

Griffith, L. C. (2008). Neuroscience: Love hangover. *Nature, 451*(7174), 24-25. doi: 10.1038/451024a

46. Article without a DOI If no DOI is available, give the URL for the journal's home page.

Parekh, N. (2008). Dietary fats and age-related macular degeneration. *Topics in Clinical Nutrition, 23*(4), 347-356. Retrieved from http://www.topicsinclinicalnutrition.com/

47. Online periodical article An article published online is unlikely to have page numbers. Include the URL for the site from which the article was retrieved.

Schwenk, T. L. (2009, April 30). Physician continuity from inpatient to outpatient care is declining. *Journal Watch General Medicine*. Retrieved from http://general-medicine .jwatch.org/cgi/content/full/2009/430/1?q=featured_jw

48. Web document For a stand-alone Web source such as a report, or a section within a larger Web site, cite as much of the following information as possible: author, publication date, document title, and URL. If the content is likely to be changed or updated, include your retrieval date.

Zamora, D. (2009, February 7). *Women's health: Preventing top 10 threats*. Retrieved from http://www.mayoclinic.com/health/womens-health/WO000014

How do I cite online articles using APA style?

Many periodical articles can be accessed online, either through a journal or magazine's Web site or through a database. (See also Chapter 12.)

A   B   C

Carver, C. S., & Harmon-Jones, E. (2009). Anger is an approach-related affect:

C   D   E   F

Evidence and implications. *Psychological Bulletin, 135*(2), 183-204.

G

doi:10.1037/a0013965

A   **The author.** Give the last name first, followed by a comma and initials. Separate the names of multiple authors with commas; use an ampersand (&) before the final author's name.

B   **The date of publication.** Put the year in parentheses and end with a period (outside the parentheses). For magazines and newspapers, include the month and, if relevant, the day (2008, April 13).

C   **The article title.** Give the full title; include the subtitle (if any), preceded by a colon. Do not underline, italicize, or put the title or subtitle in quotes. Capitalize only the first word of the title, the first word of the subtitle, and any proper nouns or proper adjectives. End with a period.

D   **The periodical title.** Italicize the periodical title, and capitalize all major words. Insert a comma.

E   **The volume number and issue number.** For magazines and journals, include the volume number, italicized. For magazines and for journals that start each issue with page 1, include the issue number in parentheses, not italicized. Insert a comma.

F   **Inclusive page number(s).** Give all of the numbers in full (317-327, not 317-27). For newspapers, include the abbreviation "p." or "pp." for page numbers and, if relevant, section letters (p. B12).

G   **The DOI.** Give the unique Digital Object Identifier (DOI), if available; you do not need to provide a retrieval date, database name, or URL. If there is no DOI, include the words "Retrieved from" and the URL of the journal or magazine home page.

World Bank Institute. (2008). *Business case for collective action against corruption.* Retrieved from http://info.worldbank.org/etools/antic/businessCases.asp

49. Online book Cite the electronic version only if a print version is not available or is hard to find.

Tyler, G. W. (n.d.). *Evolution in the systems age.* Retrieved from http://onlineoriginals.com/ showitem.asp?itemID=142

50. E-mail message or real-time communication Because e-mail messages and real-time communication, such as text messages, are difficult or impossible for your readers to retrieve, APA does not recommend including them in your reference list. You should treat them as personal communication and cite them parenthetically in your text (see item 13 on p. 672).

51. Message posted to a newsgroup, electronic mailing list, or online discussion forum List the author, posting date, and the title of the post or message subject line. Include a description or the message or post in square brackets. End with the URL where the archived message can be retrieved. Include the name of the group, list, or forum if it's not part of the URL.

Bradely, R. (2009, April 1). Re: Inquiry on constitution exam [Online discussion list comment]. Retrieved from http://h-net.msu.edu/cgi-bin/logbrowse.pl?trx=vx&list =PSRT-L&month=0904&week=a&msg=ej%2bfGloZzR8Nv7%2bpyNmB3Q&user=&pw=

52. Article or page on a wiki Because the material on a wiki is likely to change, include a retrieval date.

Bullying. (n.d.). *The Psychology Wiki.* Retrieved January 7, 2009, from http://psychology .wikia.com/wiki

53. Blog To cite an entry on a blog, give the author (or screen name, if available), the date the material was posted, and the title of the entry. Include the description "Web log post" in square brackets and the URL. To cite a comment on a blog, use the description "Web log comment".

Farrell, P. (2008, November 17). SAD: The demon beast of winter [Web log post]. Retrieved from http://blogs.webmd.com/anxiety-and-stress-management

How do I cite works from Web sites using APA style?

You will likely need to search the Web site to find some of the citation information you need. For some sites, all of the details may not be available; find as many as you can. Remember that the citation you provide should allow readers to retrace your steps electronically to locate the sources. Consult pages 681–685 for additional models for citing Web sources.

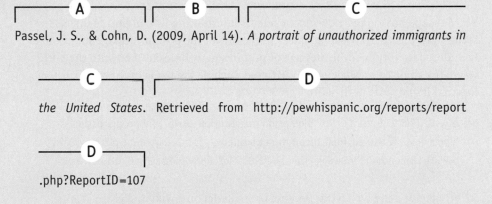

Passel, J. S., & Cohn, D. (2009, April 14). *A portrait of unauthorized immigrants in*

A   B   C

the United States. Retrieved from http://pewhispanic.org/reports/report

C   D

.php?ReportID=107

D

A   **The author of the work.** Give the last name first, followed by a comma and initials. Separate the names of multiple authors with commas; use an ampersand (&) before the final author's name. If the source has no author, list the title first and follow it with the date.

B   **The date of publication.** Put the year in parentheses and include the month and day, if available. If there is no date, use "n.d." in parentheses. End with a period (outside the parentheses).

C   **The title of the work.** Give the full title, italicized; include the subtitle (if any), preceded by a colon. Capitalize only the first word of the title, the first word of the subtitle, and any proper nouns or proper adjectives.

D   **Retrieval information.** Include a retrieval date if the material is likely to be changed or updated, or if it lacks a set publication date. (Because this report has a set publication date, the retrieval date is not necessary.) End with the URL.

54. Podcast Give the name of the producer, the date of the podcast, and the title. Include a description in square brackets and the URL.

Willer, R. (Producer). (2009, March 19). Lecture 18: The Southern culture of honor [Audio podcast]. Retrieved from http://webcast.berkeley.edu/courses

55. Online video post Give the name of the creator, the date it was posted, and the title. Include a description in square brackets and the URL.

Izzard, E. (2007, June 20). Supermarket psychology [Video file]. Retrieved from http://www.youtube.com/watch?v=b4iYigkyVeQ

56. Computer software or game Sometimes a person is named as having rights to the software or game: in that case, list that person as the author. Otherwise, begin the entry with the name of the program or game, and identify the source in square brackets after the name as "Computer software" or "Computer game." Treat the organization that produces the software or game as the publisher. If you're referring to a specific version that isn't included in the name, put this information last.

Norton Internet Security 2009 [Computer software]. Cupertino, CA: Symantec.

Other Sources

57. General advice about other sources For citing other types of sources, APA suggests that you use as a guide a source type listed in its manual that most closely resembles the type of source you want to cite.

Acknowledgments

© George Chauncey. Reprinted by permission of Basic Books, a member of Perseus Books Group.

Page 180: Courtesy of the Colorado State University Libraries. Reproduced by permission.

Page 185: U.S. Department of Energy.

Page 198: U.S. Department of Energy.

Page 208: Copyright © 2009 Digital Trends. Reproduced by permission.

Page 209: (Top) Courtesy of International Federation of the Phonographic Industry (IFPI). Reproduced by permission. (Bottom) J. Stephen Downie, "The Scientific Evaluation of Music Information Retrieval Systems: Foundations and Future," *Computer Music Journal*, Volume 28, Number 2 (Summer 2004), pp. 12–23. Copyright © 2004 by the Massachusetts Institute of Technology.

Page 213: Rahul K. Parikh, MD. "Race and the White Coat." This article first appeared in Salon.com, at http://www.salon.com. An online version remains in the Salon archives. Reprinted with permission.

Page 218: Aida Akl. "U.S. Population Hits 300 Million." First broadcast on the English news program *VOA News Now*, August 22, 2006. www.voanews.com. Photo credit Rick Maiman/AP Images.

Page 226: Stephen King. "J. K. Rowling's Ministry of Magic." From *Entertainment Weekly*, August 9, 2007. Copyright © 2007 Time, Inc. All rights reserved. Reprinted by permission.

Page 230: Tamara Draut. "Generation Debt." From *Strapped: Why America's 20- and 30- Somethings Can't Get Ahead* by Tamara Draut. Copyright © 2005 by Tamara Draut. Used by permission of Doubleday, a division of Random House, Inc.

Pages 238–239: Courtesy of Wolters Kluwer Health Medical Research. Reproduced by permission.

Page 272: Courtesy of San Francisco Health Plan. Reprinted by permission.

Page 273: (Top) Copyright © 2009 President and Fellows of Harvard College. Reprinted with permission from Harvard Family Research Project. www.hfrp.org. (Bottom) Zenong Yin, John Hanes Jr., Justin B. Moore, Patricia Humbles, Paule Barbeau, and Bernard Gutin, *Evaluation and the Health Professions*, Volume 28, Issue 1, pp. 67–89. Copyright © 2005 by Sage Publications. Reprinted by permission of Sage Publications.

Page 277: Sam Eifling. "Booster Shot: How Well Do These Energy Drinks Work?" Posted Tuesday, September 20, 2005 54am ET. Copyright © 2005 Sam Eifling. Reprinted by permission of the author. Illustration copyright © 2005 Mark Alan Stamaty. Reprinted with permission of the artist.

Page 283: Erica Lies. "Mary Tyler more: Why Tina Fey Is the Best Thing to Happen to Women in TV Comedy." From *Bitch Magazine*, Summer 2008, Issue 40, pp. 27–30. Special thanks to Andi Zeisler, whose editorial insight made this piece what it is and Tara Bracco for all the advice.

Page 286: Nicole Revilli/NBCU Photo Bank/AP Images.

Page 288: Paul Goldberger. "Bowery Dreams: A New Home for the New Museum of Contemporary Art." From *The New Yorker*, November 19, 2007. Copyright © by Paul Goldberger. Reprinted by special permission of the author. paul@paulgoldberger.com.

Page 289: New York Times/Redux.

Page 292: UNESCO. "Education for All Global Monitoring Report, UNESCO." From Chapter 2, "The Six Goals: How Far Have We Come," in *Education for All Global Monitoring Report 2008, Summary*. © UNESCO 2007. Reprinted by permission of the Bureau of Public Information, UNESCO Publishing. Photo credit Ami Vitale/Panos Pictures.

Page 295: Photo credit Giacomo Pirozzi/Panos Pictures.

Page 301: Christina Hoff Somers and Sally Satel. "Emotional Correctness." From *One Nation Under Therapy* by Christina Hoff Somers and Sally Satel. Copyright © 2005 by the author and reprinted by permission of St. Martin's Press, LLC.

Page 310: Courtesy of Harvard School of Public Health. Reproduced by permission.

Page 336: Copyright © PC Magazine/Ziff Davis Media. Reproduced by permission.

Page 337: (Top) Courtesy of Visa, Inc. Photo copyright © Doug Rosa. Reproduced by permission. (Bottom) Federal Trade Commission/FTC.gov.

Page 346: Jami Jones. "Drug Testing Needs Improvement, Not Clearinghouse." From *Landline Magazine*, November 2, 2007. Copyright © 2007 Jami Jones. Reprinted with the permission of the author.

Page 350: Wangari Maathai. "Trees for Democracy." Speech delivered by Wangari Maathai after receiving the 2004 Nobel Peace Prize in the Oslo City Hall, Oslo, Norway. Copyright © 2004 The Nobel Foundation 2004. The Nobel Foundation, Pressens Bild AB 2004, SE 112 88 Stockholm, Sweden. Reprinted with permission.

Page 359: Courtesy of Dan Hughes. www.northwestskater.com.

Page 365: Richard H. Thaler and Cass R. Sunstein. "Easy Does It: How to Make Lazy People Do the Right Thing." First published in *The New Republic*, April 9, 2008. Reprinted with the permission of the authors.

Page 402: Ruth Sternberg. "Arts at the Core: How Six School Districts Integrate Arts Education into the Curriculum."

Index